The Tragedy of Andersonville

TRIAL OF CAPTAIN HENRY WIRZ
THE PRISON KEEPER

BY

GENERAL N. P. CHIPMAN
Judge Advocate of the Military Court

Lt. Co. H, and Major 2d Iowa Inf'y; Col. and Adj't A. D. C. U. S. Vol.
Brevet Brig. Gen'l

SECOND EDITION
Revised and Enlarged

Distributing Agency:
Captain E. L. Hawk, 18th and 114th Ohio Inf'y.
Geo. W. Ficks, 50th Pa. Vols.
Sacramento, California

Address:
Geo. W. Ficks,
Manager

Published by the Author
1911

COPYRIGHT AUGUST, 1911
BY N. P. CHIPMAN
SACRAMENTO, CALIFORNIA.

THE BLAIR-MURDOCK COMPANY
SAN FRANCISCO, CALIFORNIA.

THE TRAGEDY AT ANDERSONVILLE

By General N. P. Chipman
Originally Published in 1911

©2000 DSI digital reproduction
First DSI Printing: November 2000

Published by **DIGITAL SCANNING, INC.**
Scituate, MA 02066
www.digitalscanning.com

All rights reserved, which includes the right to reproduce this book or portions thereof in any form whatsoever except as provided by the U.S. Copyright Law. For information address Digital Scanning, Inc.

Trade Paperback ISBN: 1-58218-168-3
Hardcover ISBN: 1-58218-169-1
eBook ISBN: 1-58218-170-5

Digital Scanning and Publishing is a leader in the electronic republication of historical books and documents. We publish our titles as eBooks, as well as traditional hardcover and trade paper editions. DSI is committed to bringing many traditional and little known books back to life, retaining the look and feel of the original work.

CONTENTS

CHAPTER I.

Motive Shown for the Publication of the Evidence Taken at the Trial of Wirz—Charges Made by Jefferson Davis in 1890—The Revival of these Accusations by the United Daughters of the Confederacy, in 1905, that Wirz Was "Judicially Murdered" and Died a Martyr after Conviction upon Charges of Which He was Innocent—Erection of Monument to Wirz in 1909 at Andersonville—False and Misleading Inscriptions on the Monument—Protest of the Grand Army of the Republic—Proceedings at National Encampment in 1906 at Minneapolis—Important Feature of Trial—Exposure of Confederate Policy and Its Guilty Participation in Crime—More Union Soldiers Died at Andersonville Than Killed in Action in Combined Battles of Second Bull Run, Antietam, Chancellorville, Gettysburg, and the Wilderness. Pages 11-18.

CHAPTER II.

Jefferson Davis and Andersonville—His Published Article Briefly Outlined and Its Specific Charges Noted and Examined—Some Gross Misstatements Corrected—His Accusations Revived and Reasserted by the United Daughters of the Confederacy by Inscriptions on the Wirz Monument—Issues of Wirz's Defenders and Confederacy Clearly Defined—Charge Refuted That Federal Government Responsible for Deaths. Pages 19-26.

CHAPTER III.

Some Hitherto Unpublished Facts—Organization of the Court—The Charges and Specifications—Special Pleas Interposed—Jurisdiction of the Court—Once in Jeopardy—Right of Parole Claimed—Argument—Pleas Overruled—Facts as to Wirz's Arrest—Wirz Pleads Not Guilty—Rules of Procedure—Circumstances of Wirz's Arrest—Wirz's Military Status—His Place of Burial—The True Significance of the Trial. Pages 27-50.

CHAPTER IV.

Location of Andersonville Prison—Description of the Prison Pen—Wirz Assigned to Its Command—Early Condition of the Prisoners Deplorable—Official Reports of Rebel Officers—Injunction to Abate Prison as a Nuisance Because of Noxious Odors—Upon Whom Rested Responsibility of—Origin of Dead Line—Rebel Authorities at Richmond Informed—Mortality Increased—In One Month 2,993 Died. Pages 51-64.

CHAPTER V.

Condition of the Prison Continued—Sufferings of Prisoners Depicted—Report of Colonel D. T. Chandler—Report of Dr. Joseph Jones—Causes of Sickness and Death Shown—Responsibility Fixed—Confederate Authorities at Richmond Had Full Knowledge—Colonel Chandler's Testimony—Testimony of Dr. Jones—Six Square Feet to the Man—Barely Room to Comfortably Lie Down—Inadequate Police Control—Prisoners Try, Condemn, and Hang Six of Their Number—Prisoners Murdered by Their Fellow-Prisoners for Their Clothing and Food—The Bodies of the Dead Mutilated—Reports by Surgeon Stevenson, Surgeon White, and Surgeon Thornburg—Dr. Jones's Report Graphic Description of Prison and Hospital—Causes of Death and Unparalleled Suffering. Pages 65-110.

CHAPTER VI.

Conditions at the Prison (continued)—Reports and Testimony of Surgeons on Duty at the Prison, Namely: Dr. Amos Thornburg: Dr. F. T. Castlen: Dr. G. S. Hopkins; Dr: G. LeB. Rice; Dr. John C. Bates; Dr. R. G. Roy; Dr. B. J. Head—Testimony of Dr. William Balser, Who Had Occasion to Treat a Large Number of Prisoners from Andersonville on Their Way to Freedom from Prison Life—They were Living Skeletons—Seventy-five Per Cent of Dead Might Have Been Saved by Proper Care—Actual Square Feet to Man 27, or 3 by 9 Feet. Pages 111-142.

CHAPTER VII.

Conditions at Andersonville Continued—Testimony of Rev. Father Hamilton—No Shelter from Sun or Storms—Father Hamilton Crawled into Burrows to Administer Last Sacrament to Dying—Prisoners Covered with Vermin—Testimony of Citizens Living in the South—Publicity of the Suffering of Prisoners—Supplies Were Obtainable and Sufficient to Have Sustained the Prisoners—Prisoners Might Have Been Sheltered—The Prison Might Have Been Enlarged—Means of Transportation Available—Supplies Sent by Sanitary Commission. Page 143-162.

CHAPTER VIII.

Testimony of Union Soldiers, Prisoners at Andersonville—Their Descriptions of the Horrors of That Prison Pen—Personal Experiences—Men Fight for Room to Lie Down—Private Property Taken from Them—Testimony of Major-General J. H. Wilson and Colonel George Welling of the U. S. Army on Condition of Prison at Close of the War—Simple Remedies Pointed Out—General Wilson Concludes that There was Sinister Design in the Location and Its Restricted Area—Goldwin Smith's Opinion of Treatment of Prisoners on Both Sides—General Sherman Found Supplies Abundant in Georgia in 1864. Pages 163-191.

CHAPTER IX.

Conditions at Prison (continued)—Testimony of Father Hamilton and Other Witnesses Called for the Defense—Horrors of the Prison Pen Confirmed—Witnesses for Defense Corroborate Testimony of the Prosecution in Many Essential Particulars—Diary of Rev. Father Clavereul—Father Clavereul's Account a Most Pathetic Picture of Human Suffering. Pages 192-239.

CHAPTER X.

Treatment of Prisoners (continued)—Cruel and Inhuman Punishments Inflicted—Balls and Chains Used as Means of Punishment—Prisoners Confined in the Stocks and Left Exposed to the Weather—The "Dead-Line" and Its Attendant Perils—Ferocious Dogs Used to Hunt Down Escaping Prisoners—Prisoners Torn and Mutilated by These Dogs—Prisoners Die from Effects—Impure and Deadly Vaccine Matter Used for Vaccination of the Prisoners, Causing Many Horrible Deaths—Wirz Boasts of His Service to the Rebellion in Slaying Prisoners—Revolting Manner of Handling and Burying the Dead—Testimony of Rebel Witnesses Confirms Testimony of Wirz's Cruelty to Prisoners—Report on Prisons by United States Sanitary Commission and Committee of House of Representatives. Pages 240-300.

CHAPTER XI.

Testimony of Witnesses for Defense upon the Specifications of Acts of Cruelty and of Murder in Violation of the Laws of War—Man Shot on Dead Line—Hunted Down by Dogs—Put in Stocks and Chain Gang—Wirz Kicked and Abused Prisoners—Very Profane—High Temper—Carried Pistol—Threatened to Use It—Some Acts of Kindness Shown—Witnesses Never Heard of His Killing or Treating a Prisoner Cruelly—Negative Testimony. Pages 301-332.

CHAPTER XII.

Testimony of Witnesses to the Charge of Murder—Prisoners Shot by Wirz—Prisoners Shot by His Order—Prisoners Killed by the Dogs—Many Instances of Wirz's Brutality—Men Killed by Being Shot in Stocks and Chain Gang. Pages 333-353.

CHAPTER XIII.

Résumé of the Foregoing Chapters—Some Comment upon and Deductions from the Evidence—Mortuary Statistics—Johnson's Island and Andersonville Compared—Table of Deaths by Months—Number of Dead at Andersonville, 13,171—Deaths in Twenty-five Federal Prisons in 1864 Compared with Andersonville—Stockade and Its Terrors Described—Condition of Prisoners Known at Richmond—Hospital and Prison Co-ordinated to Destroy Life—The Conspiracy—Charge of Murder—Photograph of Johnson's Island Prison—Statement of Soldiers on Duty There and at Fort Delaware Prison. Pages 354-385.

CHAPTER XIV.

Some Interesting Facts as to the Preparation of the Case for Trial—Personnel of the Court—Proceedings at Close of the Trial—Jurisdiction of the Court Discussed—The Law and Facts as to Conspiracy Stated—Review of the Record by the Judge Advocate-General—Approval of the Sentence by the President—Execution of the Sentence—Law of Nations Systematically Violated—Conditions Surrounding Prisoners Who Were Witnesses—Burial of Wirz's Body. Pages 386-437.

CHAPTER XV.

The Cartel Suspended—Exchanging of Prisoners Interrupted—Causes Therefor—Violation of Cartel by Rebels—Right to Exchange Denied to Negro Soldiers and Their Officers—When Captured Treated as Felons—Sufferings of Prisoners Due to Treatment They Received, not Because Cartel Was Suspended—Rebel Commissioner Robert Ould, Maneuvering to Get Excess of Prisoners Held by Federals and Use Them at Critical Period of War—Action of Our Government Fully Vindicated—Report of General Hitchcock, Federal Commissioner of Exchange, Covering Entire Subject—Letter of General Grant, Part of Which is Inscribed on the Wirz Monument—Interview with Colonel John McElroy, a Prisoner at Andersonville—The Evolution of Slaves to the Status of United States Soldiers—Some Interesting Facts About the Negro as a Soldier. Pages 438-473.

CHAPTER XVI.

Andersonville Cemetery Made Beautiful—Expedition in Spring of 1865 to Provide for Its Permanent Care—Report of Captain Jas. M. Moore, U. S. A.—Important and Interesting Report of Clara Barton, Founder of the Red Cross Society, to the American People—Report of Dorence Atwater, Who Kept the Death Register, to the Relatives of the Martyred Dead—Interesting Letter of Superintendent of Cemetery—Inscriptions on State Monuments—Patriotic Work Done by Woman's Relief Corps at Prison Park—A Parting Word with the Reader by the Author—Bill Pending in Congress to Appropriate Money by Government to Erect Monument to Confederate Navy—Discussion in United States Senate—Views Expressed in Public Press—Dangerous Step for Government to Thus Give Official Sanction to Rebellion and Treason. Pages 474-521.

ILLUSTRATIONS

	PAGE.
Frontispiece—The Author	
Members of the Court	29
Judge Advocates	36
Group—Wirz Monument, Captain Wirz, Jefferson Davis	43
Plan of Stockade	56
Prison Grounds	57
Map of Georgia	71
Plan of Bakery	71
Prison Grounds and Stockade	113
Scene at the North Gate—Issuing Rations	142
View of South Gate from Outside	167
Dividing Squad Rations by Numbers.	167
Prison Relics Gathered by Clara Barton	203
Burying the Dead in Trenches	215
Prison and Surroundings, and Scenes Enacted. Sketched by Thomas O'Dea, a Prisoner	245
A Typical Soldier—Figure Surmounting the Connecticut Monument	269
Monument Erected by Massachusetts	303
Group of Views of Cemetery	317
Monument Erected by Michigan	329
Indiana	337
Wisconsin	345
Rhode Island	357
New Jersey	367
Iowa	373
Ohio	394
Pennsylvania	418
Illinois	437
Connecticut	450
Maine	466
Monument to Lizabeth Turner	476
Tablet of Woman's Relief Corps	482
Providence Spring	484
Group—Entrance to Prison Grounds and to Cemetery; Views within Cemetery and Photograph of Jas. M. Bryant, Superintendent	494
Johnson's Island, Photograph of Buildings	377
Group—Members of Woman's Relief Corps; Committee on Transfer of Prison Grounds to the Government	500
Group—Members of Woman's Relief Corps; Board of Managers of Prison Grounds	506
The Empty Sleeve	511

LOSING OUR STANDARDS.

ONE is tempted to ask of what use are standards of any kind. Why seek to have any, either private or public. if in a few years they will dissolve in a flux of good feeling? If there ever was a war fought on behalf of democracy, of individual liberty, of substantial Christianity, it was the American Civil War. Both sides cannot have been right; nor is it true that both were ready to spill blood merely because of a Constitutional question. To insist now that there was no difference in the ideals and purposes of the two forces of 1861 is to reduce history to the plane of the moving-picture shows, to make light of the greatest sacrifices ever offered in this or any country for principle or patriotism. It is to decry the men that saved the Union if we declare that there was only a chance difference between their views and those of their opponents, or to assert that time has wiped out all the principles for which Lincoln and his followers stood. To take such a position is to say that there is nothing steady in our political firmament, that there are no fixed stars of morality by which human beings must steer.

—The Nation, New York.

PREFACE

RECENT events, to which I shall call attention in the opening chapter of this volume, imperatively demand the publication of the evidence taken at the trial of Captain Henry Wirz, the keeper of the rebel prison at Andersonville, Georgia, to place before the world the facts upon which his conviction and sentence to death were founded.

A monument has been erected to his memory, close by the scenes of the crimes with which he was charged, avowedly intended to proclaim his innocence; to condemn those who participated in his trial; to discredit the proceedings themselves as illegal; to denounce the witnesses as having given false testimony; and to declare that the Federal government was responsible for the terrible sufferings of the Union prisoners at Andersonville.

The erection of this monument has opened a chapter in the history of the Rebellion upon which the public now demands that the light of truth be thrown. Happily for the realization of this demand, the history of this one of the many rebel prisons was laid bare by judicial investigation, in the trial of Captain Wirz, and that inquest was so full, and the character of the proof so indisputable, that the faithful historian need never hesitate in portraying the sufferings of Union soldiers, or of fixing the responsibility where it rightfully belongs.

Ever since the inauguration of the Wirz monument movement, I have been urged to publish a fuller report of the evidence adduced at the trial than has heretofore reached the public, especially as the inscriptions engraven upon the monument renew the misleading and unsupported charges made by Jefferson Davis in his lifetime, as will hereinafter appear.

Finally, at the National Encampment of the Grand Army of the Republic, at Atlantic City, having received the following letter, I resolved, in obedience to it, to undertake the task; and I offer this volume in vindication of the verdict rendered in this remarkable case, and as the record of sufferings such as no prisoners of war in any civilized country, at any modern period, were ever called upon to endure:

FORTY-FOURTH NATIONAL ENCAMPMENT,
GRAND ARMY OF THE REPUBLIC,
ATLANTIC CITY, NEW JERSEY,
September 19, 1910.

GEN. N. P. CHIPMAN,
  Sacramento, California.

Comrade: In the passing years since the close of the Civil War an endeavor has been made to create the belief in the public mind that Captain Henry Wirz, C. S. A., commander of the Andersonville Rebel Prison, who was tried and convicted by a military commission of which you were Judge Advocate, for cruel and inhuman treatment of Union prisoners, in violation of the laws of war, was innocent of the charges laid against him, and suffered an ignominious death through false and exaggerated testimony, sacrificing his life rather than make a defense which would fix the guilt upon officers of the Confederacy higher in authority; that in fact there were no preventable cruelties or suffering at that prison, and that the thirteen thousand Union dead who lie in the Andersonville Cemetery perished of disease and climatic causes wholly unavoidable.

Recently, in line with this studied effort to falsify what we believe to be the truth of history, the organization known as the "Georgia Division of the United Daughters of the Confederacy" has challenged the facts as they were recorded in the trial of Wirz; has proclaimed him a martyr, and, in sight of the cemetery where repose the bodies of our noble dead, has erected a lasting monument to his memory.

We deem it just and right that the world should know the truth disclosed at this important trial, for the evidence, as we understand the findings of the court, not only justified the verdict against Wirz, but implicated and held responsible some of the Confederate officers high in authority, in the execution of a policy which made a charnel-house of the Andersonville Prison.

In justice to the memory of the brave and unhappy Union soldiers who perished miserably through the enforcement of that inhuman policy, we call upon you to place within the reach of the public the facts relating to this trial; and we trust that, in the volume that you may publish, you will make it so complete in its presentation of the evidence that the truth may be vindicated and the falsity of the inscriptions placed upon the Wirz monument be made clearly to appear.

Yours in F. C. & L.,

HARRY WHITE,
Commander of the National Association of Union Prisoners of War.

JOSEPH C. KILLGORE, President,

ROBERT B. MCCULLY, Secretary,
National Society of Andersonville Prisoners.

J. H. STIBBS,
12th Iowa Infantry, Brevet Brigadier-General; Member of Wirz Military Commission.

The necessity at the present time for an honest statement regarding the Wirz trial seems to be paramount, and we believe no one more fitted to perform this duty than yourself.

LOUIS WAGNER, Past Commander-in-Chief.
THOS. J. STEWART, Past Commander-in-Chief.
S. S. BURDETT, Past Commander-in-Chief.
ROBT. B. BEATH, Past Commander-in-Chief.
LEO. RASSIEURS, Past Commander-in-Chief.
S. R. VAN SANT, Commander-in-Chief.
C. MASON KINNE, Past Senior Vice-Commander-in-Chief.
JOHN MCELROY, Past Senior Vice-Commander-in-Chief.
WM. JAMES, Junior Vice-Commander-in-Chief Elect.
CHAS. C. ROYCE, Past Vice-Commander-in-Chief.
E. L. HAWK, Department Commander, Department of California and Nevada.

CHAPTER I.

MOTIVE SHOWN FOR THE PUBLICATION OF THE EVIDENCE TAKEN AT THE TRIAL OF WIRZ—CHARGES MADE BY JEFFERSON DAVIS IN 1890—THE REVIVAL OF THESE ACCUSATIONS BY THE UNITED DAUGHTERS OF THE CONFEDERACY, IN 1905, THAT WIRZ WAS "JUDICIALLY MURDERED" AND DIED A MARTYR AFTER CONVICTION UPON CHARGES OF WHICH HE WAS INNOCENT— ERECTION OF MONUMENT TO WIRZ IN 1909 AT ANDERSONVILLE—FALSE AND MISLEADING INSCRIPTIONS ON THE MONUMENT—PROTEST OF THE GRAND ARMY OF THE REPUBLIC—PROCEEDINGS AT NATIONAL ENCAMPMENT IN 1906 AT MINNEAPOLIS— IMPORTANT FEATURE OF TRIAL—EXPOSURE OF CONFEDERATE POLICY AND ITS GUILTY PARTICIPATION IN CRIME—MORE UNION SOLDIERS DIED AT ANDERSONVILLE THAN KILLED IN ACTION IN COMBINED BATTLES OF SECOND BULL RUN, ANTIETAM, CHANCELLORVILLE , GETTYSBURG, AND THE WILDERNESS .

TWENTY years ago I was urged to write the story of the Andersonville Rebel Prison, as disclosed by the evidence at the trial of Captain Henry Wirz, its keeper. It had seemed to me that this was one of the chapters of the Rebellion better kept closed. As an illustration of the horrors of war it will always stand unparalleled. As furnishing a study of human suffering upon a stupendous scale, and as showing that modern civilization has not mitigated the cruelties to which a professedly Christian people may resort, the past century has exhibited nothing like it. But even this seemed not to justify the portrayal at a time when the healing processes after national disruption might, presumably, be doing their perfect work.

It was left for Jefferson Davis to furnish the motive for recalling the true story of Andersonville and to induce me to publish at that time a small volume in reply to his statements, to which wide publicity had been given. Whatever of responsibility there then was for opening this ghastly wound to bleed afresh, rested upon the head of the late Confederacy, for he not only invited reply, but he imperatively challenged it. And now after twenty years the whole grim and gruesome story of the Andersonville Rebel Prison is revived and a fresh challenge thrown down, carrying with it the reiteration of the charges made by Mr. Davis as published in 1890, and demanding their refutation.

Upon leaving the cars at Andersonville, Georgia, the visitor who goes to pay a tribute of love or respect to the memory of the Union dead who lie in the National Cemetery nearby must first pass by an enduring monument erected near the station, to the memory of Captain Wirz, by the "Georgia Division of the United Daughters of the Confederacy." Some facts which should be given touching the erection of this monument will confirm the opinion, widely expressed, that the time is opportune for the publication of the evidence adduced at the Wirz trial.

In the *Confederate Veteran* for October, 1906, published at Nashville, Tennessee, is an article from which I quote as follows:

Initial movement for Wirz monument. Mrs. A. B. Hall, of Savannah, Ga., on Dec. 5th, 1905, sent a greeting to the Chapters of the Georgia Division, U. D. C., and published the following proceedings: the resolutions of Mrs. L. G. Young, of Savannah, read at the convention of the Georgia Division, U. D. C., held in Macon, Oct. 25, 1905, were as follows:

"Whereas, Captain Henry Wirz, commandant of the stockade prison at Andersonville, Ga., was judicially murdered under false charges of cruelty to prisoners; and whereas, after an interval of forty years, these false charges are reiterated on signboards in public places, from the pulpit, and on monuments; therefore, be it resolved: That the United Daughters of the Confederacy in Georgia use their influence to obtain the necessary funds to place a suitable memorial to Captain Wirz in Andersonville, Ga., upon which a statement of facts shall be engraved in enduring brass or marble, showing that the Federal government was solely responsible for the condition of affairs at Andersonville."

"Committees to carry out the resolutions were appointed,—on selection of site, on inscription, on designs,-and an advisory board and a treasurer were appointed."

When this movement came to be generally known, a universal protest was evoked in all parts of the North, and in many parts of the South it was strongly condemned. The surviving Union veterans of the Civil War, of whom there still remain more than half a million, were vehement in their expressions of indignant disapproval, and, in their organized capacity as members of the Grand Army of the Republic, they voiced their feelings with burning emphasis.

Commander-in-Chief Tanner, at the National Encampment at Minneapolis, in August, 1906, made it one of the subjects of his annual address.[1] He said:

In the course of the last few months I have received quite a number of communications concerning the proposition to erect at or near Andersonville a monument in honor of Captain Wirz, who was in charge of Andersonville Prison. Most of these communications were appeals addressed to me as Commander-in-Chief, imploring me to take steps to prevent the erection of such a monument, urging me, if necessary to that end, to lay the matter before Congress, or to bring it to the attention of the President.

[1] Proceedings at Minneapolis, 1906, p, 109.

After pointing out that he had no power to comply with the request, he continued:

Since the manuscript was placed in the hands of the printer I have been reliably informed that the plot of ground upon which to place the Wirz monument has been purchased. The veterans of the Confederate army are not to any appreciable degree interested. I first learned of the monument early in the year and quietly and earnestly canvassed the matter with quite a number of prominent ex-Confederates, for I recognized on the first meeting thereof that such a matter carried out would do more to interrupt the flow of good feeling between the North and the South, and would roll back more effectively the waves of reconciliation, than any other one matter of which the mind of man can conceive.

A good many of them [ex-Confederates] had no hesitation in privately telling me that they agreed with me that the erection of the memorial to such a character could have no practical result except to smirch to a greater or less degree every memorial erected throughout the South to the real representatives of valor in the Confederate army.

The subject is one which I deprecate extremely the necessity of calling, to public attention. It is a matter I would have preferred that the hallowing effects of time might wipe from the memory of man; but under the circumstances, standing as I do, I have felt it would be cowardly not to make mention of this matter as I have.

The committee on resolutions, to which this and other subjects dealt upon by the Commander-in-Chief were referred, recommended that the matter be passed over to the incoming Council of Administration. General Ketcham, of Indiana, presented a minority report, as follows:[1]

COMMANDER AND COMRADES: The Wirz monument movement is in the air. It cannot be overlooked or ignored. Prisoners of War Associations have passed resolutions on the subject, Department Encampments have discussed and acted on it, and the Commander-in-Chief has called the attention of this encampment to it. Under these circumstances we cannot close our eyes nor hide our heads in the sand and say we know naught of it. To pass it by silently is to leave it open for the suggestion that the Grand Army of the Republic is either tacitly acquiescing in the movement or fears to take a stand in regard to it.

On behalf, thereof, of the minority of your committee, and in obedience to the wishes of the Department of Indiana and its delegates in this encampment, I beg leave to submit the following memorial and resolution:

"We learn with deep regret and profound sorrow of the intention of the United Daughters of the Confederacy to build a monument to the memory of Captain Wirz in the vicinity of, Andersonville National Cemetery and Andersonville Prison, now the property of the Woman's Relief Corps. We are told that this action is taken by the ladies in a spirit of equity; believing he was unjustly hanged, and feeling it just that the world should know the Confederacy's treatment of prisoners of war was conducted on humane principles.

[1] Proceedings at Minneapolis, 1906, p. 182.

"We are wholly at loss to perceive how a supposed spirit of equity could be subserved by seeking to keep alive the darkest blot in the history of the Rebellion.

"Captain Wirz was tried by a commission of just men, of high character and lofty patriotism; competent and capable to hear and weigh the evidence and determine the law and the facts. It had jurisdiction beyond question; its personnel was of the highest character; the trial covered a period of nearly two months, and the testimony of the witnesses, some one hundred and forty in number, including the witnesses called on his behalf, covered some five thousand pages of written matter, and a synopsis of it covers some six hundred printed pages.

"It is now too late to attempt to revise, reverse, or discredit the findings and judgment of that commission. Its conclusion will stand through the ages as the verdict of history.

"We had hoped in this, the dawning of the new century, when the bitterness and animosities of the century that is dead and gone ought to be buried in oblivion, that a newer, brighter, loftier spirit of patriotism would have grown in that section of the country that over forty years ago found itself in armed rebellion against the power and authority of the nation. Time has softened if not effaced the physical effects of the bitter strife; the moral effects, we regret to see, largely remain.

"The intelligent lover of his country—the whole country—can only view the proposed monument as symbolizing the old spirit of the Rebellion, and as commemorating the prowess of a convicted and executed felon, whose title to fame rests upon his success in destroying the armies of his country by cruel and barbarous atrocities inflicted upon helpless prisoners committed to his custody, by which thirteen thousand of the country's defenders were sent untimely to their long homes, and other thousands suffered beyond the pen of man to describe or the thoughts of men to conceive.

"A monument to him will represent not honor but infamy; will belittle the meed of praise bestowed by monuments to the real soldiers who accomplished great deeds in a great way, although in a misguided cause; will detract from their just fame and glory, and constitute not only an affront to the conscience and patriotism of the land we love, but a reproach to the quickened and enlightened spirit of the age.

"We wish to go on record in solemn and deliberate protest against such a cruel and wanton affront to the ideals represented by this Grand Army of the Republic, and by the patriotic citizens of the nation throughout its entire length and breadth.

"Resolved, That the Commander-in-Chief communicate with General Stephen E. Lee, Commander-in-Chief of the Confederate Veterans' Association, and express to him the hope and wish of the Grand Army of the Republic that the association of which he is commander would in such manner as may to it seem proper express its disapproval of the proposed action." Respectfully submitted,

WILLIAM A. KETCHAM,
Of the minority of the Committee on Resolutions.

A comrade asked General Ketcham what evidence he had that these women intended erecting the monument or could build it. Comrade Ketcham said:

"I wrote to Miss Alice Baxter, Secretary of the United Daughters of the Confederacy, to know what the fact was and I have her letter here as follows:

Replying to your letter, I take pleasure in sending you the enclosed articles. These articles with reference to the building of the monument, the steps that are being taken, the subscriptions that are being made, and the papers that are being written in the public schools telling how atrocious was the conduct of the Union officials, and how humane and just was the conduct of the Confederate officials. Please return when you are through. We propose erecting the monument to Captain Wirz in a spirit of equity, believing that the world should know that the Confederacy's treatment of prisoners of, war was conducted on humane principles. I note you are a lawyer. Perhaps if you study both sides of this question you will come to see there are two sides to the question. We were much pleased with Corporal Tanner when he was South. We do not desire to stir up bitterness, but we are unwilling for the South to remain under false charges.

Sincerely yours,
ALICE BAXTER.

Past Department Commander Ketcham supported the minority report in a vigorous and eloquent speech. Past Commander-in-Chief Torrance followed in advocacy of the majority report. He said:

Do not let us open up Pandora's box of evils. Let us quietly suffer the indignity, if it is an indignity. And what will the monument be when erected? When you present yourself before a monument the question arises, What is it, and in whose honor is it erected? When you come in front of the Wirz monument it will not be to a soldier, not to a man who gained distinction on the battlefield, but one whose only claim to recognition is that he was hanged as a murderer, just as a thousand of other criminals have been hanged in this country. And I will tell you, my comrades, that neither the Daughters of the Confederacy nor the men of the Confederacy, nor the men nor the women of the North and South, nor all combined, can erect a monument in memory of any one that will live an hour unless the monument rests upon a noble life and represents a living truth and principle.

Commander-in-Chief Tanner then took the floor and, among other things, said:

My good friend Torrance has just said that the best thing to do is to keep silence. If we keep silent we will be with the comrades who were murdered in Andersonville. They are silent; they have been silent all these years. Before my mind's eye to-day there comes a picture of the horrors of that awful time, when they stripped the dead and chucked their corpses in wagons and dragged them out and chucked them in a ditch, and there comes to me an hour when I walked the wards at Annapolis going up and down looking for comrades of my own regiment, and behind me came my name in a faint voice. I looked about me and none of the emaciated faces could I recognize. I turned back to the third bed and said, My poor fellow did I ever know you? With a sob in the throat he answered. Don't you know Billy Moore? He was one of the stalwart men of my own company. The mother of the boy would not have recognized him. You can all recall such instances as that.

To get down to the concrete matter here, I did know last January that this thing was being talked of. When I went South in March to attend Joe Wheeler's funeral at Atlanta every moment that I could spare I was conferring with Confederates of high and low degree. Not one had a word in favor of the monument. It is the women—and we cannot get into a warfare with women; but we can stand up for conscience and right, if we are men, without getting into a warfare with women. Finally, last night, or this morning at one o'clock, it came to this, that those who feel as I do would voice this matter in a dignified appeal from the Grand Army of the Republic, that appeal to be prepared by your incoming Commander-in-Chief and such as he may see fit to call to his aid, that appeal to be addressed to that splendid gentleman Stephen D. Lee, one of the few surviving lieutenant-generals of the Confederate army, the present chief of the Confederate Veterans, and with that an appeal to him to use his influence to prevent this outrage from being perpetrated. I came into this encampment to-day caring not what was done so that it might be done dignifiedly and be true to the truth of history, but if you take no action then I tell you that your silence will be seized upon, and in every chapter of the Daughters of the Confederacy it will be said that you felt that you could not consistently protest and that you were afraid to meet the issue that they raised. I say that my friend the distinguished attorney-general of Indiana never put more strength and conservatism in any document in all his brilliant career than when he appeared before you with that memorial culminating as it did in a plain, simple, dignified resolution asking of the Commander-in-Chief of the Confederate Veterans, on the part of the Grand Army of the Republic, that he use his influence to prevent the erection of the monument. It is no time to keep silent. It is time to speak out man-fashion in a dignified way, and let the country know that the Grand Army of the Republic makes its dignified protest against the exaltation of the man who sent to horrible death so many of our comrades and who caused such inexpressible anguish in the hearts of the people of the North. With all my heart and soul I second the resolution offered by Comrade Ketcham.

On motion the previous question was ordered, and, the main question being put, the minority report and resolution were adopted.

Whatever may have been the opinion of individual ex-confederate soldiers or individual citizens of the South, it is quite certain that no serious effort was made to prevent the erection of this monument with all that was proclaimed in its justification and with all its false implications.

In reviewing the matter in an extended article, the *Confederate Veteran* concludes:

The purpose of this article is not to antagonize our friends, the enemy. Indeed, it is not to condemn them, as from their point of view many of them honestly think such a monument should not be erected; but the opportunity by these issues is improved to make fresh record of the deeds of that ill-fated Confederate officer. As Americans honor the French officer Lafayette, the Southern people should ever specifically honor the name of Captain Henry Wirz. Our Grand Army friends are not so bad as many believe them to be. Men here actually opposed the Wire monument movement through a misconception of the facts. . . . I am attempting the delicate and difficult task of rescuing a wronged man's memory. They never fail who die in a great cause. Let the monument be built."

On the title page of this magazine is printed the following: "Officially represents: United Confederate Veterans; United Daughters of the Confederacy; Sons of Veterans and other organizations; Confederate Brethren Memorial Association. The *Veteran* is approved and indorsed by a larger and more elevated patronage than any other publication in existence."

If it be true, as Miss Baxter wrote as late as in 1905, that papers were being written in the public schools telling "how atrocious was the conduct of the Union officials, and how humane and just was the conduct of the Confederate officials," and if the *Confederate Veteran*, with its large and "elevated patronage," in advocating the erection of this monument, expressed a widespread sentiment, can there be any doubt that behind the movement was the purpose to revive and reassert the charges which Mr. Davis, among the last acts of his life, defiantly published to the world? Can it be wondered at that there is a fresh demand for the means of obtaining the evidence upon which he was found guilty of conspiracy with Wirz in the commission of the awful crime for which Wirz suffered?

Is the revered name of Lafayette to have no higher place in the hearts of the Southern people than the name of Wirz? Are the portraits of the noble Marquis and Captain Wirz to hang side by side equally honored in Southern homes?

Past Commander-in-Chief Torrance gave expression to a commendable sentiment, when he said that the men and women of the North and South combined can never "erect a monument in memory of any one that will live an hour unless the monument rests upon a noble life and represents a living truth and principle."

It has never been claimed, and never will be claimed, by the authors of the Wirz monument that it "rests upon a noble life" or that it "represents a living truth or principle." Captain Wirz was not a citizen of Georgia; he had no military record of consequence; his residence in Andersonville was that of a soldier in camp for the time only; he did not fall in honorable battle.

18   THE TRAGEDY OF ANDERSONVILLE.

Witnesses at his trial testified that he boasted that he was destroying more "Yankee soldiers than General Lee was killing in the Wilderness"; and it is true that under his ministration more prisoners were killed, through causes into which we are now to inquire, than were killed in action in the Union ranks in the combined battles of the Second Bull Run, Antietam, Chancellorsville, Gettysburg, the Wilderness, and Appomattox. What, then, was the motive, what the true significance, of this shaft erected at that particular place?

The services which the monument was meant to signalize, and for which Wirz was to be immortalized, were performed at Andersonville, but their commemoration at that place has a deeper meaning. The Wirz shaft was to be a perpetual interrogation—"Why this awful slaughter?" To which the inscriptions give answer: That the Federal government was alone responsible; that Wirz was falsely accused, illegally tried, and condemned upon charges of which he and the Confederate government were alike innocent and that—"To rescue his name from the stigma attached to it by embittered prejudice this shaft is erected by the Georgia Division of the Daughters of the Confederacy."

The most important feature of the record of this trial, however, is its exposure of the policy of the Confederate government and its guilty participation in the crime of Andersonville. And it is this fact that will always attach historic value to the evidence taken at this remarkable trial, which it is now proposed to lay before the world.

INSCRIPTIONS ON WIRZ MONUMENT.

The Daughters of the Confederacy originally formulated inscriptions to go on the Wirz monument in somewhat different and more offensive form than finally adopted, as will appear from their proceedings already quoted. The terms "judicially murdered" were eliminated and one or two other changes made, but the true purpose and meaning of the challenge are in no substantial sense modified.

NORTH SIDE.

"When time shall have softened passion and prejudice, when Reason shall have stripped the mask from misrepresentation, then Justice, holding evenly her scales, will require much of past censure and praise to change places.—Jefferson Davis, December, 1888."

SOUTH SIDE.

"Discharging his duty with such humanity as the harsh circumstances of the times, and the policy of the foe admitted, Captain Wirz became at last the victim of a misdirected popular clamor. He was arrested in time of peace while under the protection of parole, tried by a military commission of a service to which he did not belong, and condemned to ignominious death on charges of excessive cruelty to federal prisoners. He indignantly spurned a pardon proffered on condition that he would incriminate President Davis and thus exonerate himself from charges of which both were innocent."

EAST SIDE.

"In memory of Captain Henry Wirz, C. S. A. Born Zurich, Switzerland, 1822. Sentenced to death and executed at Washington, D. C., November 10, 1865. To rescue his name from the stigma attached to it by embittered prejudice this shaft is erected by the Georgia Division, United Daughters of the Confederacy."

WEST SIDE.

"It is hard on our men held in Southern prisons not to exchange them, but it is humanity to those left in the ranks to fight our battles. At this particular time to release all rebel prisoners would insure Sherman's defeat and would compromise our safety here.—Ulysses S. Grant, August 18, 1864."

CHAPTER II.

JEFFERSON DAVIS AND ANDERSONVILLE —HIS PUBLISHED ARTICLE BRIEFLY OUTLINED AND ITS SPECIFIC CHARGES NOTED AND EXAMINED—SOME GROSS MISSTATEMENTS CORRECTED—HIS ACCUSATIONS REVIVED AND REASSERTED BY THE UNITED DAUGHTERS OF THE CONFEDERACY BY INSCRIPTIONS ON THE WIRZ MONUMENT—ISSUES OF WIRZ'S DEFENDERS AND CONFEDERACY CLEARLY DEFINED—CHARGE REFUTED THAT FEDERAL GOVERNMENT RESPONSIBLE FOR DEATHS.

IN *Belford's Magazine* for January and February, 1890, are two articles contributed by Mr. Jefferson Davis, entitled "Andersonville and Other War Prisons." In the opening article Mr. Davis says: "Some eminent citizens of the North, who are furthest removed from the class known as Southern sympathizers during the war between the States, but who desire to know the whole truth, have requested me to write an article, to appear in some periodical published in the North, on the subject of the prison at Andersonville, Ga. The invitation is accepted, both as to the subject and place of publication, from the wish to vindicate the conduct of the Confederacy, and because the proposed channel is that which will most assuredly reach those who have generally seen but one side of the discussion."[1]

The history of Mr. Davis's article is not without interest. It was originally prepared for the *North American Review*, through the urgent request of Mr. Charles Redpath, who, as the managing editor of that periodical, visited Mr. Davis. Mr. Allen Thorndike Rice, the editor, whose death occurred soon thereafter, from political motives postponed the publication. Meanwhile the *Review* had published an article by Lord Wolseley reflecting somewhat upon Mr. Davis, and the latter was asked by Mr. Rice's successor to reply. This he did, but his contribution was severely pruned by the editor, which so incensed Mr. Davis that he withdrew his article on Andersonville, and among one of the last acts of his life, turned it over to *Belford's* for publication. The article must therefore be considered as premeditated; it had been under examination for over a year, and finally went before the public, by Mr. Davis's request, without alteration or abridgment, and as a last message in defense of his beloved Confederacy.

[1] *Belford's Magazine*, January, 1890.

Mr. Davis's long public service, his high position in the Confederacy, his intimate knowledge of all its movements as the head of the Rebellion, his generally conceded character for honesty and integrity gain for his statements of fact *prima facie* acceptance in the minds of many. I think, however, that before the unprejudiced reader has reached the final chapter of this book he will have concluded that neither Mr. Davis's statements nor his method of dealing with this grave matter can be received as at all satisfactory or reliable.

He first charges that Andersonville became necessary as a prison because of the Federal violation of the cartel for the exchange and parole of prisoners. But the admitted failure or refusal of the Federal authorities to observe the cartel furnishes no justification for cruel and unusual treatment and starvation of prisoners in his power. If, as he claims, the prisons at Richmond had become so overcrowded as to make the stockade at Andersonville a necessity, or if after its establishment the number greatly exceeded any possibility of adequate or humane care, still its enlargement was but the obvious demand of humanity, and should have been made. Mr. Davis characterizes it as "offensive" to make inquiry why this overcrowding was not provided against and he scorns to make answer.

We shall see, as we progress with the evidence, how simple a matter this expedient would have been; how ready and willing hands besought and were refused the privilege of enlarging the boundaries of their prison pen and relieving its congestion.

The alleged violation of the cartel is wholly irrelevant as a defense for violating the usages of civilized warfare. It was so decided by the military court which tried Wirz, and all writers on civil or military law support that decision. There is, however, a full and satisfactory defense of the Federal action in this matter which will be made the subject of a chapter of this volume, but in no event can it be allowed that the fact that Mr. Davis had more prisoners than he wished to feed relieved him from the duty of feeding them.

He informs us that Andersonville, Ga., was selected after careful investigation for the following reasons: "It was in the high pine wood region; in a productive farming country, and had never been devastated by the enemy; was well watered, was near Americus, a central depot for collecting the tax in kind and purchasing provisions for the armies."[1] Much evidence was adduced at the trial of Wirz, as we shall see, confirming the very important fact here admitted, for it bore

---

[1] *Belford Magazine,* January, 1890.

directly upon the issue whether short rations resulted from any scarcity or physical inability to supply sufficient food. Mr. Davis seems to have assumed that because an abundance of food was available it must logically follow that it was furnished to the prisoners, properly prepared for consumption and in proper quantities. But here was the very issue being tried. In this high pine wooded region prisoners perished for lack of shelter and fuel; in this productive farming country they wasted away to skeletons and died of starvation; in this well watered region was enacted the tragedy of the Ancient Mariner:

> "Water, water, everywhere,
> Nor any drop to drink."

Having satisfied his conscience with the statement that food, fuel, water, and pure air abounded, he adds: "It was not starvation, as has been alleged, but acclimation, unsuitable diet and despondency which were the potent agents of disease and death. These it was not in our power to remove. The remedy demanded alike of humanity and good faith was the honest execution of the cartel."

Mr. Davis seems to have been obsessed with the idea that the cartel was the cause of all this suffering. Is it true that these potent agencies of disease and death were beyond his power to remove? Let me not anticipate too much the proofs that are to be marshalled in proper sequence, from the lips of eye-witnesses, many of them having been in the rebel service. We shall see as we advance whether the cartel or starvation was the more potent agent of disease and death at that fateful place; whether it is conceivable that the failure to exchange prisoners, in the face of the terms demanded by the rebel government, can acquit that government of its culpability in the treatment of prisoners; and whether it was not in the power of the Confederacy to have properly fed and cared for these brave men. These were all matters of legitimate inquiry at the trial, and it is my purpose to make known the evidence, that the world may judge between unsupported statements and conclusions and the sworn testimony of the witnesses of the harrowing scenes in this tragic chapter of the Civil War.

If human testimony, subjected to all the tests of its credibility known to the law, can be believed, there will be laid before the reader such an array of proofs as to place beyond the realm of reasonable doubt that not less than seventy-five per cent of the thirteen thousand who perished at Andersonville and the two thousand who died on their way to their homes or shortly after reaching them, died from the effects of starvation and other preventable causes—chiefly, however, from simple undoubted starvation, or causes directly induced thereby.

To show the nature and character of the alleged facts assumed to have come to the surface since the trial, and upon which rest the conclusions to which Mr. Davis would lead his reader, something should be said. As an example, he quotes from an anonymous letter published in the New York *News* of August 5, 1865, and to give it weight he attributes the authorship to an officer on General Sheridan's staff. This writer was one Martin S. Harris, private of the 5th New York Artillery, and never had any relations with Sheridan. He was a witness for the defense at the trial and testified at great length. His testimony will be noticed in its proper place.

Mr. Davis speaks of Wirz as the unhappy victim of a misdirected popular clamor, and says he was denied the favorable testimony of those who came as witnesses in his behalf, and "died a martyr to a cause through adherence to truth." He cites as an instance of the unfairness of the trial the case of the Rev. Father Peter Whelan, who was a witness for the prisoner. He quotes this gentleman as saying that, upon reporting at Washington, the Judge Advocate of the court found out what he knew and dismissed him without allowing the prisoner to call him as a witness. So glaring a perversion of fact as Mr. Davis is here guilty of should excite grave doubt as to his veracity in other particulars, and shows with what reckless abandon Mr. Davis came to the defense of Andersonville. The fact is that Father Whelan was called by the defense and testified at great length.[1] His testimony will not be overlooked in subsequent pages.

Mr. Davis quotes from General Imboden, as showing "that after the bulk of the prisoners were removed, leaving in the fall of 1864 about five thousand, who could not bear transportation, by renovation of the post the premises were much improved; that at one time it was thought by the medical officer nearly all the sick would die, but by the use of vegetables in such quantities as could be procured and an acid beer made from corn meal and sorghum molasses, the death rate fell from about three thousand in August to one hundred and sixty for the month of December." The inquirer after the truth in reading this paragraph could not fail to conclude that the physical condition

---

[1] Record, p. 426.

of these five thousand unfortunates must have been low indeed if they could not stand the fatigue of being moved in cars, and that the condition of the sick was such as to indicate their speedy death. Apparently some were sick unto death and the remainder were too sick to bear transportation—i.e. all were grievously sick, but impending death did not threaten all. But mark how adroitly this report of General Imboden is woven into the defense—"the death rate fell from three thousand in August to one hundred and sixty in December." Why? Because resort was had to a very simple expedient. But in August there were over thirty-two thousand prisoners in that same enclosure, while in December there were about five thousand. In August the country abounded in vegetables of all kinds; corn meal and sorghum molasses were equally available from which to make acid beer. We shall see how insistent was the demand for resort to the simple means used by General Imboden to preserve these precious lives. Mr. Davis nowhere suggests that acid beer and vegetables could not be had in August. The evidence is full and conclusive on the point. It may not be doubted that to this humane officer many of the hapless prisoners owe their lives. But what shall be said of the policy pursued previous to December and of those responsible for its execution?

Colonel Robert Ould, Confederate Commissioner of Exchange, is quoted by Mr. Davis as having said that he was subpoenaed for the defense, but that the prisoner was denied the privilege of calling him. Here is told but a half truth, manifestly as a reflection on the fairness of the trial. Colonel Ould was subpoenaed by the defense to testify to matters relating to the exchange of prisoners. After discussion, upon the objection of the Judge Advocate, the court held the testimony to be irrelevant, and Colonel Ould was discharged by request of counsel for the prisoner.

Perhaps the most glaring departure from the truth to be found in Mr. Davis's article is the statement, based upon what Mr. Davis understood Colonel R. H. Chilton to have written, that Colonel D. H. Chandler, assistant adjutant-general and inspector-general of the Confederate army, testified to the single fact that his report was never seen by Mr. Davis, and that this officer was asked no other question. Colonel Chandler's report, made August 5, 1864, will be laid before the reader. His oral testimony will also be given, showing a condition at the prison which he reported to the secretary of war, Mr. Seddon, to be a "disgrace to the Confederacy." Evidence will be given from which the court was fully justified in finding that this report was traced to Mr. Davis, and from which the inference was plainly deducible that the rebel authorities at Richmond supinely ignored Colonel Chandler's recommendations and permitted the shocking slaughter of innocent men to proceed—at that time dying at the rate of over one hundred per day.

Mr. Davis closes his first article by the remarkable charge, based upon a letter received by him from a fellow-prisoner of Wirz, that a night or two before his execution three men came to Wirz's cell and had some conversation with him; that Wirz told his fellow-prisoner, after the visitors had departed, that they offered him his liberty if he would testify against Mr. Davis. This instance has no especial bearing upon the justness of the verdict of the Wirz trial. The story has grown into historical proportions by its iteration and reiteration, and was finally adopted by the Daughters of the Confederacy as one of the inscriptions to be placed on the Wirz monument. If it found credence sufficient to warrant its so bold use, it must mean that Wirz preferred death to committing a breach of fidelity to his chief, and thus showed himself a brave and worthy subordinate if not an innocent man. This story, coming from an unnamed and unknown fellow-prisoner of Wirz, itself based upon a statement of Wirz, the United Daughters of the Confederacy have engraved upon the Wirz monument in the following form:

"He indignantly spurned a pardon proffered him on condition that he would incriminate President Davis and thus exonerate himself from charges of which both were innocent."

But history is not made of such unsubstantial figments of the imagination as came secondhand to Mr. Davis in this unconfirmed and anonymous manner. In truth, the government needed the support of no such witness as Wirz would have been. No human being, under the circumstances surrounding him, would have believed Wirz's testimony. Besides no such confession was necessary. Wirz had claimed at his trial that he was obeying the orders of his superiors, and that the Richmond authorities were responsible and not he, as will appear in the course of this volume. It is unbelievable that so dastardly a proposition came from Federal authority, and it finds place in this publication only because it apparently has some believers and because Mr. Davis had the audacity to give it currency by his public indorsement. Mr. Davis was himself a prisoner at Fortress Monroe at that time. He was not being held as a murderer or common malefactor. The crime with which he was to have been tried was high treason, as defined by the Constitution, and not for specific incidents occurring during the war, however much he might be responsible for them. And he was finally so indicted but never tried.

Not to overlook the single remaining item to which Mr. Davis devoted his attention in his first *Belford* article,[1] he makes passing mention of the charges that bloodhounds were used to capture prisoners, but dismissed the subject with a mere statement that "he had been informed that some fox and deer hounds were used to track prisoners, and that no bloodhounds were used." The evidence will be given upon this point, and it will show that ferocious dogs were employed and were the means of several deaths. This pack of dogs was part of the force under Wirz's direction, and was in charge of an enlisted man by the name of Wesley W. Turner. We shall hear much of these dogs and the part they played in the Andersonville horror.

I have thus sketched the points made by Mr. Davis on the general subject of the treatment of prisoners; also, the data on which he would have the public rely in reaching its conclusions. The true facts are to follow as narrated by witnesses subject to the pains and penalties of perjury, and in part from unimpeachable official reports of rebel officers and agents, recounted under circumstances and at a time when, if there was a motive to color the record, it was a motive to minimize rather than exaggerate what they saw and wrote down.

Mr. Davis's second article[2] is exclusively devoted to the cartel of which I have already spoken and will be given consideration in a chapter on that subject, although it formed no part of the case for or against Wirz. So great stress, however, has been laid on its alleged violation by the Federal authorities, as the chief cause of the suffering of our soldiers, that it must not, be ignored. One of the inscriptions on the Wirz monument reads:

"It is hard on our men held in Southern prisons not to exchange them, but it is humanity to those left in the ranks to fight our battles. At this particular time to release all rebel prisoners would insure Sherman's defeat and would compromise our safety here.—Ulysses S. Grant, Aug. 18, 1864."

This unexplained statement confronts every visitor at Andersonville, and the plain implication is that when he enters the National Cemetery his eyes are to behold the resting place of thirteen thousand

[1] *Belford's Magazine,* January, 1890.
[2] *Belford's Magazine,* January, 1890.

Union soldiers who perished through the neglect of their government; and who could have been saved only, as Mr. Davis charged, by "an honest execution of the cartel."

Can we marvel at the indignation aroused among the victorious men who followed Grant from Belmont and Fort Donelson to Appomattox, when they see emblazoned on the Wirz shaft this atrocious perversion of history—this impeachment of the honor of a great name and the wisdom, justice, and humanity of a great nation?

With the issues thus clearly defined by the defenders of Wirz and the Confederacy, we now approach the blackest page anywhere to be found in the annals of war among civilized nations in recent times— a page, too, written amid internecine strife, on the one side to preserve the Union of states believed to be the most beneficent in existence; on the other avowedly, by its constitution, founded on the righteousness and rightfulness of human slavery. The one was fundamentally right and the other was fundamentally and eternally wrong. It was in this struggle that the tragedy of Andersonville became possible.

CHAPTER III.

SOME HITHERTO UNPUBLISHED FACTS—ORGANIZATION OF THE COURT—THE CHARGES AND SPECIFICATIONS —SPECIAL PLEAS INTERPOSED —JURISDICTION OF THE COURT—ONCE IN JEOPARDY—RIGHT OF PAROLE CLAIMED—ARGUMENT —PLEAS OVERRULED—FACTS AS TO WIRZ'S ARREST—WIRZ PLEADS NOT GUILTY—RULES OF PROCEDURE—CIRCUMSTANCES OF WIRZ'S ARREST—WIRZ'S MILITARY STATUS—HIS PLACE OF BURIAL—THE TRUE SIGNIFICANCE OF THE TRIAL.

THE trial of Henry Wirz in many respects brought to light the most startling page in the history of the Rebellion. Some interesting facts relating to that trial were not known to the public at the time; other facts of the greatest significance were brought out by the record, such as, for example, those implicating the rebel government. These were buried out of sight by the universal demand that the prisoner, who was regarded as immediately responsible, should not escape punishment; and, with his execution, the secondary, but really the most important, result of the trial was overshadowed by the rapidly recurring political movements of that eventful period. It is now proposed to give the true history and exact results of that trial.

I was at the time on duty at the War Department at Washington, and at times had been assigned to try cases as Judge Advocate of courts-martial and military commissions. The Andersonville horror had made so deep an impression upon the nation that when it was known that Wirz, the keeper of that prison, was under arrest, his trial became imperative. He was lodged in the old Capitol Prison, in Washington, and I was directed by Secretary of War Stanton, upon the recommendation of Judge Advocate-General Holt, to prepare the case for trial. It was known that the mortality had been great, yet few persons at the North, not even the prisoners themselves, were aware that over 13,000 had died miserably at that horrible place, and few had any conception that a great crime had been committed.

While Secretary of War Stanton and Judge Advocate-General Halt, and probably some other high officials, as well as President Johnson, suspected that the heads of the rebel government were largely responsible for the awful suffering, it was not until I had spent some months in searching out proofs, and arranging the facts, that this suspicion deepened into conviction.

By August, 1865, the evidence had been marshalled, charges and specifications were prepared and served upon the prisoner, and the military commission constituted to try him. The arraignment of Wirz upon these charges and specifications, then for the first time published to the world, sent a thrill of horror throughout the United States.

Mr. Davis was a prisoner confined in Fortress Monroe. The question as to what proceedings should be taken against him as the leader of the Rebellion was before the cabinet and was a serious problem. His complicity and that of some of his cabinet officers in the crime of Andersonville was for the first time charged. It was thought undesirable for many reasons to furnish any pretext for bringing the ex-president to the capital. But to proceed against Wirz with Davis named as a co-conspirator presented a question of some moment.

The nature of the charges was known to Secretary Stanton, and I had reason to believe that he was familiar with the form and substance of the specifications, although it is quite probable that neither the president nor other members of the cabinet had such knowledge. Wirz had pleaded not guilty and the court had adjourned until the next day.

Upon reassembling a package was placed in my hands from the War Department which proved to be an order dissolving the court. Wirz was remanded to prison, and I was ordered to report immediately to the War Department, while the members of the court went their way in the greatest perplexity, and in utter ignorance of the meaning of so abrupt a termination of the trial. This proceeding, as we shall see later on, formed the basis of a special plea interposed by Wirz.

I have never been informed of the reason that impelled this extraordinary and precipitate action by the secretary of war, for of his knowledge of every step taken in the case, I had every assurance, and yet he appeared to be unusually disturbed at the coupling of Davis's name and other high rebel functionaries with that of Wirz. The result of it all was that I was directed to prepare new charges and specifications, leaving out the names of Davis, Seddon, and others of Davis's cabinet, and proceed against Wirz.

General Holt alone knew, for I had talked much with him, of the extent and character of the evidence I had gathered in support of the

THE MILITARY COMMISSION THAT TRIED CAPTAIN WIRZ, KEEPER OF THE ANDERSONVILLE PRISON.

conspiracy charge. He was in full sympathy with my view, that the trial should be made the means of bringing to light and giving the history and the whole truth as to this prison, and not simply to submit evidence to convict Wirz, which was of comparatively small consequence and the work of only a few days. It was finally concluded to retain the charges and specifications in their then form, omitting the names mentioned, and substituting certain persons of less note who had been connected with the prison, adding the words "and others unknown," and in that form of pleading submit all the evidence touching upon the alleged conspiracy. To this course the secretary of war consented, and the court was again constituted as before. Wirz was again arraigned and pleaded not guilty, after interposing certain pleas in bar which were overruled, as will later appear, and the trial began. It opened August 23, 1865, and closed October 24, 1865, lasting sixty-three days. The court was composed of officers who had seen much service, and some of them were men of national reputation. In its personnel the court was unimpeachable, and its findings must challenge, respect and confidence.

The facts appearing in the following pages, except as otherwise indicated, are taken from the record of the Wirz trial, published in Executive Document No. 23, 40th Congress, 2nd Session. The introductory page explains when and by what authority it was published and how the evidence was prepared. It comprises a volume of 850 closely printed pages, including a very complete index. Where reference is made to this publication it will be designated "Record." In quoting from the testimony and official reports such portions will be used as will present the substance of the evidence, omitting immaterial details.

ORGANIZATION OF THE COURT.

Letter from the Secretary of War Ad Interim,[1] in answer to a resolution of the House of April 16, 1866, transmitting a summary of the trial of Henry Wirz.

December 7, 1867.—Referred to the Committee on the Judiciary and ordered to be printed.

[1] Record, p. 1.

FACTS AND RESULTS OF TRIAL.

WAR DEPARTMENT,
Washington City, December 5, 1867.

SIR: In compliance with a resolution of the House of Representatives, dated April 16, 1866, I have the honor to send herewith a summary of the proceedings, &c., of the trial of Henry Wirz.

Very respectfully, your obedient servant, U. S. GRANT,
Secretary of War ad interim.

Hon. S. COLFAX, *Speaker of the House of Representatives.*

THE TRIAL OF HENRY WIRZ.

[Prepared in the office of the Adjutant General United States army, in accordance with the following resolution of Congress]:

THIRTY-NINTH CONGRESS-FIRST SESSION.

CONGRESS OF THE UNITED STATES,
In the House of Representatives, April 16, 1866.

On motion of MR. GARFIELD,[1]

Resolved, That the Secretary of War be requested to have prepared for publication the proceedings of the trial of Henry Wirz,- in which shall be embraced, as nearly as practicable in the language of the witnesses, a summary of the testimony given, and the decisions, findings, and sentence of the court, together with the address of the judge advocate, and that made in defence of the prisoner.

Attest: EDWARD MCPHERSON, *Clerk.*

The order convening the court and the charges and specifications were as follows:[2]

WAR DEPARTMENT, ADJUTANT GENERAL'S OFFICE,
Washington, August 23, 1865.

[Special Orders No. 453.]
[Extract.]

. . . .

3. A special military commission is hereby appointed to meet in this city at 11 o'clock a. m. on the 23d day of August, 1865, or as soon thereafter as practicable, for the trial of Henry Wirz, and such other prisoners as may be brought before it.

DETAIL FOR THE COMMISSION.

Major General L. Wallace, United States volunteers.
Brevet Major General G. Mott, United States volunteers.
Brevet Major General J. W. Geary, United States volunteers.
Brevet Major General L. Thomas, Adjutant General United States army.
Brigadier General Francis Fesseden, United States volunteers.
Brigadier General E. S. Bragg, United States volunteers.[3]
Brevet Brigadier General John F. Ballier, colonel ninety-eighth Pennsylvania volunteers.
Brevet Colonel T. Allcock, lieutenant colonel fourth New York heavy artillery.
Lieutenant Colonel J. H. Stibbs, twelfth Iowa volunteers.
Colonel N.P. Chipman, additional aide-de-camp, judge advocate of the commission, with such assistants as he may select, with the approval of the Judge Advocate-General.

The commission will sit without regard to hours.

By order of the President of the United States: E. D. TOWNSEND,
Assistant Adjutant General.

[1] Afterwards President of the United States.
[2] Record, p. 2.
[3] General Bragg was relieved on account of illness and did not participate in the findings. Record, p. 511.

On August 23, 1865, in Washington, D. C., all the members named in the foregoing order and the judge advocate being present, the commission proceeded to the trial of Henry Wirz, who, having been brought before the commission, and having heard the order convening it read, was asked whether he had any objection to any member named therein, to which he replied in the negative.

The judge advocate then laid before the commission the correspondence requesting the services of Major A. A. Hosmer as assistant judge advocate, and the approval of the Judge Advocate-General of such selection.

The members of the commission were then duly sworn by the judge advocate, and the judge advocate and assistant judge advocate were duly sworn by the president of the commission respectively in the presence of the accused.

Henry G. Hayes, D. Wolfe Brown, and William Hinks were duly sworn by the judge advocate as reporters to the commission.

The accused was then duly arraigned on the following

CHARGES AND SPECIFICATIONS.

CHARGE I. Maliciously, wilfully, and traitorously, and in aid of the then existing armed rebellion against the United States of America, on or about the first day of March, A. D. 1864, and on divers other days between that day and the tenth day of April, 1865, combining, confederating, and conspiring together with John H. Winder, Richard B. Winder, Joseph White, W. S. Winder, R. R. Stevenson, and others unknown, to injure the health and destroy the lives of soldiers in the military service of the United States, then held and being prisoners of war within the lines of the so-called Confederate States and in the military prisons thereof, to the end that the armies of the United States might be weakened and impaired; in violation of the laws and customs of war.

Specification.—In this: that he, the said Henry Wirz, did combine, confederate, and conspire with them, the said John H. Winder, Richard B. Winder, Joseph White, W. S. Winder, R. R. Stevenson, and others whose names are unknown, citizens of the United States aforesaid, and who were then engaged in armed rebellion against the United States, maliciously, traitorously, and in violation of the laws of war, to impair and injure the health and to destroy the lives, by subjecting to torture and great suffering, by confining in unhealthy and unwholesome quarters, by exposing to the inclemency of winter and to the dews and burning sun of summer, by compelling the use of impure water and by furnishing insufficient and unwholesome food, of large numbers of federal prisoners, to-wit, the number of thirty thousand, soldiers in the military service of the United States of America, held as prisoners of war at Andersonville, in the State of Georgia, within the lines of the so-called Confederate States, on or before the first day of March A. D. 1864, and at divers times between that day and the tenth day of April, A. D. 1865, to the end that the

FACTS AND RESULTS OF TRIAL.

armies of the United States might be weakened and impaired, and the insurgents engaged in armed rebellion against the United States might be aided and comforted: and he, the said Henry Wirz, an officer in the military service of the so-called Confederate States, being then and there commandant of a military prison at Andersonville, in the State of Georgia, located by authority of the so-called Confederate States, for the confinement of prisoners of war, and as such commandant, fully clothed with authority, and in duty bound to treat, care, and provide for such prisoners held as aforesaid, as were or might be placed in his custody, according to the laws of war, did, in furtherance of such combination, confederation, and conspiracy, and incited thereunto by them, the said John H. Winder, Richard B. Winder, Joseph White, W. S. Winder, R. R. Stevenson, and others whose names are unknown, maliciously, wickedly, and traitorously confine a large number of such prisoners of war, soldiers in the military service of the United States, to the amount of thirty thousand men, in unhealthy and unwholesome quarters, in a close and small area of ground, wholly inadequate to their wants and destructive to their health, which he well knew and intended; and while there so confined, during the time aforesaid, did, in furtherance of his evil design, and in aid of the said conspiracy, wilfully and maliciously neglect to furnish tents, barracks, or other shelter sufficient for their protection from the inclemency of winter and the dews and burning sun of summer; and with such evil intent did take and cause to be taken from them their clothing, blankets, camp equipage, and other property of which they were possessed at the time of being placed in his custody; and with like malice and evil intent, did refuse to furnish or cause to be furnished food, either of a quality or quantity sufficient to preserve health and sustain life; and did refuse and neglect to furnish wood sufficient for cooking in summer, and to keep the said prisoners warm in winter, and did compel the said prisoners to subsist upon unwholesome food, and that in limited quantities entirely inadequate to sustain health, which he well knew; and did compel the said prisoners to use unwholesome water, reeking with the filth and garbage of the prison and prison guard, and the offal and drainage of the cook-house of said prison, whereby the prisoners became greatly reduced in their bodily strength, and emaciated and injured in their bodily health; their minds impaired and their intellects broken; and many of them, to-wit, the number of ten thousand, whose names are unknown, sickened and died by reason thereof, which he, the said Henry Wirz, then and there well knew and intended; and so knowing and evilly intending, did refuse and neglect to provide proper lodgings, food or nourishment for the sick, and necessary medicine and medical attendance for the restoration of their health, and did knowingly, wilfully, and maliciously, in furtherance of his evil designs, permit them to languish and die from want of care and proper treatment; and the said Henry Wirz, still pursuing his evil purposes, did permit to remain in the said prison, among the emaciated sick and languishing living, the bodies of the dead, until they became corrupt and loathsome, and filled the air with foetid and noxious exhalations, and thereby greatly increased the unwholesomeness of the prison, insomuch that great numbers of said prisoners, to-wit, the number of one thousand, whose names are unknown, sickened and died by reason thereof; and the said Henry Wirz, still pursuing his wicked and cruel purpose, wholly disregarding the usages of civilized warfare, did at the time and place aforesaid maliciously and wilfully subject the prisoners aforesaid to cruel, unusual and infamous punishment upon slight, trivial, and fictitious pretences, by fastening large balls of iron to their feet, and binding large numbers of the prisoners aforesaid closely together with large chains around their necks and feet, so that they walked with the greatest difficulty; and being so confined were subjected to the burning rays of the sun, often without food or drink for hours and even days; from which said cruel treatment large numbers, to-wit, the number of one hundred, whose names are unknown, sickened, fainted, and died: and he, the said Wirz, did further cruelly treat and injure said prisoners, by maliciously confining them within an instrument of torture called "the stocks," thus depriving them of the use of their limbs, and forcing them to lie, sit, and stand for many hours without the power of changing position, and being without food or drink, in consequence of which many, to-wit, the number of thirty, whose names are unknown, sickened and died: and he, the said Wirz, still wickedly pursuing his evil purpose, did establish and cause to be designated within the prison enclosure containing said prisoners, a "dead-line," being a line around the inner face of the stockade or wall enclosing said prison, and about twenty feet distant from and within said stockade; and having so established said dead-line, which was in many places an imaginary line, and in many other places marked by insecure and shifting strips of boards nailed upon the tops of small and insecure stakes or posts, he, the said Wirz, instructed the prison-guard stationed around the top of said stockade to fire upon and kill any of the prisoners aforesaid who might touch, fall upon, pass over, or under, or across the said "dead-line"; pursuant to which said orders and instructions, maliciously and needlessly given by said Wirz, the said prison-guard did fire upon and kill a large number of said prisoners, to-wit, the number of about three hundred; and the said Wirz, still pursuing his evil purpose, did keep and use ferocious and bloodthirsty beasts, dangerous to human life, called bloodhounds, to hunt down prisoners of war aforesaid, who made their escape from his custody, and did then and there wilfully and maliciously suffer, incite, and encourage the said beasts to seize, tear, mangle, and maim the bodies and limbs of said fugitive prisoners of war, which the said beasts, incited as aforesaid, then and there did, whereby a large number of said prisoners of war, who during the time aforesaid made their escape and were recaptured, and were by the said beasts then and there cruelly and inhumanly injured, insomuch that many of said prisoners, to-wit, the number of about fifty, died: and the said Wirz, still pursuing his wicked purpose, and still aiding in carrying out said conspiracy, did use and cause to be used for the pretended purposes of vaccination, impure and poisonous vaccine matter, which said impure and poisonous matter was then and there, by the direction and order of said Wirz, maliciously, cruelly, and wickedly deposited in the arms of many of said prisoners, by reason of which large numbers of them, to-wit, one hundred, lost the use of their arms, and many of them, to-wit, about the number of two hundred, were so injured that they soon thereafter died: all of which he, the said Henry Wirz, well knew and maliciously intended, and in aid of the then existing rebellion against the United States, with a view to assist in weakening and impairing the armies of the United States, and in furtherance of the said conspiracy and with the full knowledge, consent, and connivance of his co-conspirators aforesaid, he the said Wirz then and there did.

CHARGE II.—Murder, in violation of the laws and customs of war.

Specification 1.—In this: that the said Henry Wirz, an officer in the military service of the so-called Confederate States of America, at Andersonville, in the State of Georgia, on or about the eighth day of July, A. D. 1864, then and there being commandant of a prison there located by the authority of the said so-called Confederate States, for the confinement of prisoners of war, taken and held as such from the armies of the United States of America, while acting as said commandant, feloniously, wilfully, and of his malice aforethought, did make an assault, and he, the said Henry Wirz, a certain pistol, called a revolver, then and there loaded and charged with gunpowder and bullets, which said pistol the said Henry Wirz, in his hand there and then had and held, to, against, and upon a soldier belonging to the army of the United States, in his the said Henry Wirz's custody as a prisoner of war, whose name is unknown, then and there feloniously, and of his malice aforethought, did shoot and discharge, inflicting upon the body of the soldier aforesaid a mortal wound with the pistol aforesaid, in consequence of which said mortal wound, murderously inflicted by the said Henry Wirz, the said soldier thereafter, to-wit, on the ninth day of July, A. D. 1864, died.

[Then follow twelve other specifications charging murder of prisoners in his keeping, namely; second, by jumping upon and stamping to death; third, by shooting with a revolver; fourth, by shooting with a revolver; fifth, by confinement in the stocks; sixth, by confining in the stocks; seventh, by binding the necks and feet with iron balls and chains; eighth, by ordering a sentinel to shoot a prisoner; ninth, by ordering a sentinel to fire upon and killing a prisoner; tenth, by the same means; eleventh, by ferocious dogs in the pursuit of prisoners; twelfth, by ordering a sentinel to shoot a prisoner; thirteenth, by beating a prisoner upon the head with a revolver.]

(Signed): By order of the President of the United States.

N. P. CHIPMAN, *Colonel and A. D. C. Judge Advocate.*

After full argument and deliberation, the court found Wirz guilty of the first charge and its specifications, striking out the word "bloodhounds" and inserting "dogs" in lieu thereof, and restoring the names of Jefferson Davis and all others originally named as co-conspirators, except General Lee. Upon the second charge the court found the prisoner guilty of eleven distinct murders out of the thirteen charged, and of three murders by use of the dogs, not charged but shown by the evidence.[1]

[1] Record, p. 305.
In military trials the court may amend the charges or specifications to accord with the evidence.

While the verdict was not a conviction of the conspirators other than Wirz, it was the equivalent of an indictment found against them for the wholesale and needless mortality charged.

Colonel N. P. Chipman, Judge Advocate, 1863.   General N. P. Chipman, 1906.   Colonel A. A. Hosmer, Ass't Judge Advocate, 1863.

The evidence was of a most convincing character, for the findings rested largely upon the official reports of rebel officers, made alone for the eye of their superiors at Richmond. Much of the testimony was given by rebel officers who had been on duty at the prison, and there were called as witnesses nearly one hundred of the surviving prisoners.

Messrs. Hughes, Denver, and Peck, a prominent law firm of Washington, represented the prisoner to this point of his arraignment, but withdrew from the case, and Messrs. Louis Schadd and O. S. Baker entered their appearance for the prisoner, who, being called upon to plead, interposed the following pleas:

PLEAS INTERPOSED

That he was protected from punishment because he was included in the convention entered into, on April 26, 1865, between Major-General William T. Sherman and General Joseph E. Johnston, on the surrender of the latter. Also, because he was at Andersonville,

Georgia, when arrested, in the full enjoyment of his liberty, and that he was promised, upon giving such information as might be required of him concerning said prison, that "he should have safe conduct going and returning to his home, and should not be arrested as a prisoner." Also, that the military commission was without jurisdiction to try him. Also, that he was once in jeopardy and pleaded not guilty, and the commission was without authority to again arraign and put him upon his trial. Also, that the charges and specifications do not charge any offence punishable under the laws of war.

These pleas presented questions going to the legality of the proceedings and to the jurisdiction of the court, and as they have been put forward at this late day as showing that Wirz was "judicially murdered," i.e. that he paid the penalty of his life by reason of a trial unknown to the laws of war, and in violation of all law, it becomes important to set forth the argument which was addressed to the court after which the pleas were overruled.

ARGUMENT ON SPECIAL PLEAS.

The JUDGE ADVOCATE said that he did not consider it necessary to discuss the motion to quash the charges and specifications, on the ground of insufficiency and indefiniteness. That question had already been decided by the court, at one stage of its proceedings. The court would, no doubt, be able to determine, by an examination of the charges and specifications, whether they were sufficiently definite to meet the requirements of the law.

The next question was that raised by the plea setting out the fact that a court, consisting of the same members as this, has already taken cognizance of this case, had had the prisoner arraigned before them upon charges similar to those now preferred, and that the prisoner had pleaded "not guilty." It is alleged by the counsel that, by that proceeding, the prisoner has once, according to the contemplation of the Constitution, been put in jeopardy for the offences charged, and that, therefore, this court cannot proceed to try the prisoner.

In answer to this objection, the judge advocate said he did not deem it necessary to do more than read the following official opinion, given by the chief of the Bureau of Military Justice, the expounder, so far as the army is concerned, of all questions relating to military law:

JUDGE ADVOCATE GENERAL'S OFFICE,
October 23, 1864.

MAJOR: Your letter of the 17th instant has been received. In reply, I have to state that a party who has been arraigned before a court-martial on charges and specifications to which he has pleaded, should not, in the sense of the eighty-seventh article of war, be regarded as having been tried upon them, unless the government had pursued the case to a formal acquittal or conviction. Under the constitutional provision which declares that no person "shall be subject for the same offence to be twice put in jeopardy of life or limb," it has been held that "the jeopardy spoken of can be interpreted to mean nothing short of the acquittal or conviction of the prisoner, and the judgment of the court thereon." (4 Wash. C. C. R., 409.) To the same effect are the opinions of McLean, J., in United States vs. Shoemaker, 2 McLean R., 114, and of Story, J., in United States vs. Perez, 9 Wheaton, 579. The courts of Massachusetts, New York, Illinois, Kentucky and Mississippi fully sustain this view. If anything less than a formal acquittal or conviction cannot be treated as having even put the party "in jeopardy," *a fortiori*, it cannot be held as amounting, within the meaning of the eighty-seventh article of war, to a "trial."

A withdrawal of any charge may be made by the judge advocate, with the assent of the court; and upon such charge, if the interests of public justice require it, the party may be again arraigned.

Very respectfully, your obedient servant,   J. HOLT,
Major J. M. WILLETT,   *Judge Advocate General.*
Judge Advocate.

The JUDGE ADVOCATE remarked that under this decision the question raised might be considered as *res adjudicata*. He then continued his argument as follows:

Laying aside for the present the discussion of the plea to the jurisdiction,[1] which may be properly taken up at any time during the trial, there seem to be but two questions seriously urged by counsel for the present consideration of the court. These are:

First. Shall this court dismiss the case at bar because Captain Noyes, a staff officer of Brevet Major-General Wilson, violated, as is alleged, a promise made to this prisoner to grant him safe conduct to General Wilson's headquarters and back again to his home? And second, admitting that the prisoner complied with the terms exacted of rebel soldiers and officers by the Sherman and Johnston convention, does the agreement made by those generals absolve this prisoner from responsibility for offences and crimes committed in violation of the laws of war?

Supposing the promise and the circumstances under which it was given to be such as alleged by counsel, of which we as yet have no proof, the first point raised by the counsel seems to me to present simply a violation of compact or contract entered into between the prisoner and a staff officer of General Wilson, with which this court can have nothing to do. If a promise made by that officer to grant the prisoner a safe conduct to and from any point has been violated, his remedy is upon General Wilson; and the circumstance ought not to be pleaded before this court in excuse of crimes previously committed by him. If General Wilson sent for the prisoner for any purpose whatever, promising him a safe return, and afterwards discovered that he was guilty of having committed most atrocious crimes, he was fully justified in revoking the safeguard by himself given, and taking immediate steps to bring the criminal to justice. A general always has the right to rescind his own order; and I think General Wilson would have found it difficult to answer to his superior officers if he had released from arrest, and allowed to return to his home, so great a criminal as the prisoner at the bar stands charged with being, rather

---

[1] The question of jurisdiction will be found fully argued, Record, p. 723; in this book, chap. XIV; also the law and facts discussed under the conspiracy charge.

than violate the promise set out in the plea. General Wilson had no power (and it is not alleged that he had) to absolve the prisoner from the responsibility attaching to his crime.

The books tell us of four special pleas in bar, which are good, if proved. These are former acquittal, former conviction, attainder, and pardon. Attainder, however, is, I believe, not known to the practice in this country. But I nowhere find that a special plea in bar is good when it simply alleges the violation of a promise by one who is not pretended to have possessed power to do more than offer a safeguard, and which he was at any time at liberty to revoke. I suppose the gentlemen will not insist that a promise of safe conduct works a general pardon or condonement of all past crimes. It sometimes happens that criminals turning "State's evidence," as it is called, are, by a sort of implied pledge made to them by the government, allowed to go unpunished, though, even in a case of this character, the government may, at its discretion, violate its pledge. But the plea involving the point now under discussion has not for its basis even an implied pledge of the government. It simply presents a case analogous to one where a police officer, arresting a criminal, says to him, "Come with me to the magistrate's office, and I will see that you are not injured"; the magistrate, upon an investigation, discovers the crime, and, as in duty bound, pays no regard whatever to the promise of the police officer, but at once takes steps for the proper trial and punishment of the offender. In such a case, would any court entertain seriously a plea that the prisoner should be discharged without trial because of the promise made to him by the officer who, in the first instance, made the arrest? It is not alleged that Captain Noyes acted upon instructions given him by the President of the United States, nor is it shown that he acted upon instructions even of General Wilson; but assuming the latter to be true, the case is similar to the illustration just given. I insist, therefore, that the plea is not good and should be overruled.

The second point and objection made by the counsel seems to present a question of more difficulty, yet, so far as the rights of this prisoner are concerned, it is quite as easily disposed of. The court must bear in mind that this plea, which is in the nature of a plea in bar, must contain one of the three elements already referred to. Former acquittal is not assumed, nor former conviction. There remains, then, only the plea based upon pardon, and I suppose it is under this head that the counsel hope, if at all, to secure a lodgment for their plea. If members will turn to Archibold's Criminal Pleading, page 87, they will discover that a plea in bar of this class must set out in terms the pardon granted, which the plea here filed does not pretend to do; and on page 357, Wharton's Criminal Law, it will be found that the pardon must correctly recite the offence, and a misrecital will render it inoperative. The plea, therefore, is bad.

But I suppose counsel will insist that the agreement entered into between General Sherman and General Johnston may be construed to be in the nature of a general amnesty or pardon. It is not necessary for this court to determine the precise legal interpretation of the agreement cited. It will be quite enough if the court satisfy itself that that agreement does not affect its right to hold the prisoner at bar to answer for the crimes alleged. It is very certain from the action of the government contemporary with that agreement, and from the subsequent action of the chief executive, and the opinion of the attorney-general, officially expressed, that neither a treaty of peace, nor a general amnesty or pardon, nor a universal absolution of crimes committed by rebels during war, entered into the terms of the capitulation required by General Grant of General Lee, and later, by General Sherman of General Johnston. It will be remembered that in the first convention between Generals Sherman and Johnston, a certain plan of settlement was agreed upon by them and forwarded to the president for his approval, and upon this plan General Sherman proposed to declare peace from the Potomac to the Rio Grande. It will be remembered, too, with what promptness the government disapproved the plan; and one of the chief objections was that the terms worked a general amnesty or pardon, and made the punishment of treason and treasonable offences impossible. One of the reasons assigned for the disapproval of that convention was in these words: "It practically abolishes the confiscation laws and *relieves rebels of every degree, who have slaughtered our people, from all pains and penalties for their crimes.*"

No language could more clearly show that the government had no intention to grant an implied pardon for such offences as those charged against this prisoner.

It will be remembered, too, that later, and since the war in the field practically ended, the chief executive has issued his amnesty proclamation, every paragraph of which demonstrates that he does not regard the agreement made by Generals Grant and Lee and by Generals Sherman and Johnston, as working the pardon of any person coming within the terms of the agreement; and as the result of the president's interpretation, we know that the executive mansion is daily beseiged from morning till night with applicants for pardon, embracing all ranks and grades of society, the enlisted soldier and the major-general of the late rebel army, as well as the private citizen. It will be recollected, also, that a United States judge for the district of Virginia has, since the date of the agreement set out in the plea, charged the grand jury that it was their right and duty, notwithstanding that agreement, to inquire into the offence of treason committed by any person who had been engaged in rebellion against the United States government. It may be mentioned, also, that in a recent proceeding before the criminal court of this district, the attorney-general of the United States pronounced his official opinion that the Rebellion is still existing. With these very clear indications of the view taken by the government, I submit that this court time to be included in the terms of surrender; is it to be supposed that the terms of that capitulation would exempt the assassin from apprehension and trial for his atrocious crime? With just as little reason does the prisoner now before this court claim exemption from trial on the charges here preferred. He is charged with having engaged in wholesale murder, by starvation and other inhuman treatment, such as will shock the moral sensibilities of the civilized world—crimes of which neither General Sherman nor the President, at the time of the agreement cited, could have had any knowledge, and which could not therefore have been condoned by that agreement. And is it now to be said, when these atrocities have been fully brought to light since the date of the agreement, that the perpetrator of them is to be discharged from custody, and allowed to take his place again in society, with the right to demand the protection of the laws of the country? The proposition is too monstrous for serious consideration.

The most that could, with any plausibility, be claimed is that all acts of war committed by this prisoner as a belligerent and coming within the usages of civilized warfare may be considered as pardoned, but it cannot be admitted for one moment that anything short of a special pardon by the president of the United States, setting forth precisely the offences pardoned, can give exemption from trial for acts in violation of the laws and customs of civilized warfare, especially when they involve crimes so enormous and atrocious as those charged upon the prisoner here arraigned.

Mr. BAKER said, that, in the first place, the court must consider the fact that the prisoner was until recently an humble servant of the so-called "southern confederacy"; and it was in that capacity that he had charge of the Union prisoners.

It must be considered also that the prisoner is before the court not as a convicted criminal, but simply as a person charged with crime. It is not to be assumed that he is guilty of the atrocious acts cited by the judge advocate— acts which may never be proved, and which, in the opinion of counsel, would never be proved.

The prisoner had been simply one of the instruments of an atrocious rebellion; and would any member of the court maintain that any lieutenant, or colonel, or major-general in the United States service should be held accountable for every murder in violation of the laws of war, committed in his command (unknown perhaps to him), during the last four years? Counsel was ready to admit that if the prisoner were guilty of one-half the crimes charged upon him, he should suffer at the hands of a proper tribunal the penalty of the law.

The prisoner, if counsel had been correctly informed, had been invited to come within the Union lines, under a promise that he should have a safe conduct going and returning. His arrest, under such circumstances, was a violation of good faith and of the laws and usages of civilized war. The judge advocate had said that a commanding general had the right to revoke or set aside his own orders at any time; but would this court consider that a major-general in the service of the United States would be deserving of his stars, if he should entice within his lines an humble servant of the so-called "confederacy," under a promise that he should be allowed to return safely, and should then, in violation of that promise, hold him as a prisoner and try him for murder? Surely the position of the judge advocate could not be sustained by any authorities which would be recognized by this court; therefore this prisoner is now held wrongfully.

As to the judge advocate's illustration of a criminal committed by a magistrate, in violation of a promise, the case was not analogous to the one here presented, because, in the first place, a magistrate would have no authority to make such a promise, and, in the second place, he would have no right to discharge a criminal brought before him. But a commanding general, under the circumstances cited in the plea, would have the right to make a promise of the kind described, and when made, it would be his right and his duty to keep it.

As to the plea alleging the unconstitutionality of the present proceeding, on the ground that the prisoner has already been once arraigned and has pleaded, counsel did not deem it necessary to consume time in discussion of that question. Nor would he prolong the argument on the motion to quash the charges and specifications, as he had had no time to examine them critically. He would leave the decision of the question to the discretion of the court.

The court was cleared for deliberation; and when the doors were reopened, the decision of the court was announced, sustaining the motion of the judge advocate.

The prisoner then pleaded not guilty to each of the several charges and specifications.

The following rules, adopted by the commission for the government of its proceedings, were read:

I. The commission will hold its sessions in the following hours: Convene at 10 a. m., sit till 1 p. m., and then take a recess of one hour. Resume business at 2 p. m.

II. The prisoner will be allowed counsel, who shall file evidence of having taken the oath prescribed by act of Congress, or shall take said oath before being admitted to appear in the case.

III. The examination of witnesses shall be conducted, on the part of the government, by one judge advocate, and by one counsel on the part of the prisoner.

IV. The testimony shall be taken in shorthand by reporters, who shall first take an oath to record the evidence faithfully and truly, and not to communicate the same, or any part thereof, or any proceedings on the trial, except by authority of the presiding officer.

V. The argument of any motion will, unless otherwise ordered by the court, be limited to five minutes, by one judge advocate, and one counsel on behalf of the prisoner. Objections to the testimony will be noted on the record and decided upon argument, limited as above, on motion. When the testimony is closed, the case will be summed up by one counsel for the defence, and the argument shall be closed by the judge advocate.

THE PICTURE OF THE WIRZ MONUMENT, THE TWO PICTURES OF CAPTAIN WIRZ AND THE PICTURE OF JEFFERSON DAVIS AT THE BOTTOM OF THE GROUP WERE TAKEN FROM THE "CONFEDERATE VETERAN," PUBLISHED AT NASHVILLE, TENN.

VI. The lieutenant in charge of the guard will have the prisoner in attendance during the trial, and be responsible for his security. Counsel may have access to him in the presence but not in the hearing of the guard.

VII. The counsel for the prisoner will immediately furnish the judge advocate with a list of the witnesses required for the defence, whose attendance will be procured in the usual manner.

As we have seen, it was claimed at the trial that Wirz was arrested and tried in violation of his parole, and this alleged fact, too, is made the subject of one of the tablets on the Wirz monument. His counsel submitted no evidence in support of his plea. The Judge Advocate, unwilling to allow so grave a matter to pass without a record of the facts being made, submitted the proofs which here follow:

TESTIMONY OF MARK D. ROBINSON.

Am employed as a clerk to this commission. The first time I met Captain Wirz was last Sunday, at the Old Capitol Prison.

[A letter, dated Andersonville, Georgia, May 7, 1865, signed "Hy. Wirz, captain C. S. A.," was here handed to witness.]

I have seen that document. I showed it to him at that interview and asked him if that was the letter which he had written to General Wilson, or a copy. He said that it was the letter which he had sent; and he went on to explain that he wrote a letter and had it copied; that that was the copy, and that he sent it instead of sending the original. He said that was the letter that was sent at his direction. The prisoner did not read all of the letter; he sketched over it pretty carefully. I requested him three times to read it, so as to be sure.

[The judge advocate offered the letter in evidence. Counsel for the accused objected to its reception, on the ground that the original document must be produced or its absence satisfactorily accounted for, and that the evidence showed this letter to be a copy. The court overruled the objection. The following letter was then read and put in evidence:][1]

ANDERSONVILLE, GA., May 7, 1865.

GENERAL: It is with great reluctance that I address you these lines, being fully aware how little time is left you to attend to such matters as I now have the honor to lay before you, and if I could see any other way to accomplish my object I would not intrude upon you. I am a native of Switzerland, and was before the war a citizen of Louisiana, and by profession a physician. Like hundreds and thousands of others, I was carried away by the maelstrom of excitement and joined the southern army. I was very seriously wounded at the battle of "Seven Pines," near Richmond, Virginia, and have nearly lost the use of my right arm. Unfit for field duty, I was ordered to report to Brevet Major-General John H. Winder, in charge of federal prisoners of war, who ordered me to take charge of a prison in Tuscaloosa, Alabama. My health failing me, I applied for a furlough and went to Europe, from whence I returned in February, 1864. I was then ordered to report to the commandant of the military prison at Andersonville, Georgia, who assigned me to the com-

---

[1] Record, p. 17 et seq.

FACTS AND RESULTS OF TRIAL.

mand of the interior of the prison. The duties I had to perform were arduous and unpleasant, and I am satisfied that no man can or will justly blame me for things that happened here, and which were beyond my power to control. I do not think that I ought to be held responsible for the shortness of rations, for the overcrowded state of the prison, (which was of itself a prolific source of fearful mortality,) for the inadequate supplies of clothing, want of shelter, &c., &c. Still I now bear the odium, and men who were prisoners have seemed disposed to wreak their vengeance upon me for what they have suffered—I, who was only the medium, or, I may better say, the tool in the hands of my superiors. This is my condition. I am a man with a family. I lost all my property when the Federal army besieged Vicksburg. I have no money at present to go to any place, and, even if I had, I know of no place where I can go. My life is in danger, and I most respectfully ask of you help and relief. If you will be so generous as to give me some sort of a safe conduct, or, what I should greatly prefer, a guard to protect myself and family against violence, I should be thankful to you; and you may rest assured that your protection will not be given to one who is unworthy of it. My intention is to return with my family to Europe, as soon as I can make the arrangements. In the mean time I have the honor, general, to remain, very respectfully, your obedient servant,   HY. WIRZ, Captain. C. S. A.
Major-General J. H. WILSON, U. S. A.,
        Commanding Macon, Georgia.

Cross-examined by counsel:

The prisoner was in the Old Capitol Prison when I had this conversation with him. I was sent there to serve on him a copy of the charges and specifications last Sunday afternoon. I took the letter there to ascertain if it was a copy of the original. The judge advocate gave it to me. The prisoner did not read all of the letter; he just sketched over it very carefully. By that I mean he would read a few lines, and then skip a few lines. I supposed he was reading it; he looked at it, but did not read it aloud. I cannot swear positively that he did anything more than simply look at it; but to the best of my knowledge I think he read parts of it.

TESTIMONY OF CAPTAIN HENRY E. NOYES.

Am captain, United States cavalry, aide-de-camp to Major-General Wilson, [The letter of Wirz to General Wilson was here handed to the witness.]

I have seen it before at the headquarters of General Wilson. It did not come to those headquarters in regular course of mail. An officer was sent from headquarters to Andersonville, and he brought back this paper, which was found among the papers of Captain Wirz's office. This is the signature of General Wilson on the indorsement.

The JUDGE ADVOCATE stated that he had recalled the witness for the purpose of examining him as to a matter set out in a plea filed by the counsel who first appeared for the defence, and reiterated by the counsel who now represented the accused: that was the allegation that the government had pledged its faith to the prisoner that he should not be prosecuted nor injured if he would go to Macon, to General Wilson's headquarters. He (the judge advocate) wished to explode that idea now, and that was his only purpose in calling the witness.

The WITNESS. I was on duty at Macon from the 20th of April, 1865, till about the 20th of May, when I came to Washington with Captain Wirz and the records of the Andersonville Prison. I returned to Macon, arriving there in July, and I have come back here in answer to a subpœna.

About the first or second of May, 1865, I was ordered by General Wilson to Alabama to take the news of the repudiation of the Sherman armistice to our forces in Alabama, the nearest command being that of General Grierson, at Eufaula.[1] On my way there I passed through Andersonville, where the train, a special one, stopped to wood and water. I got out of the train there and walked around. I noticed a crowd collected, and saw a number of our men who had been prisoners there, very sick. They were evidently preparing to go to Macon, where General Wilson had ordered all the sick to be brought. I saw a number of officers and soldiers in confederate uniform, some of them appearing to have authority. Two or three of them had pieces of paper which they were presenting to the sick men to sign. That first attracted my attention casually. Finally I got upon the train, and, as it was about to start, I heard a remark that attracted my attention. It was to this effect: "Hurry up and sign these paroles, or you'll die here anyhow." I looked out of the window and saw Captain Wirz. I could not swear that he made the remark which I heard, but I have heard his voice since, and I think it was his voice. As neither Captain Wirz nor anybody at Andersonville could have known that the armistice was repudiated, and as it was evident that they were paroling our sick men, I was on the point of getting out of the cars to remonstrate on the subject, when the whistle blew and the train started off. The sick men there were mostly so sick that they had to have men supporting them on each side. Very few of them, if any, could write their names, but simply touched the pen as the paper was presented to them.

When I got back to Macon, I reported to General Wilson what I had seen, who told me I must go there again and arrest Captain Wirz. I left that day or the next, about the 6th of May, and took a party of men with me. As I had to stay over night, and as there were no accommodations at Andersonville, I went on to Americus, about ten miles beyond, where I remained over night, coming back to Andersonville on a freight train next morning. There I accomplished my mission, that is, I arrested Captain Wirz, and gathered together all the records which I thought important, excepting the hospital records. These I did not take because Dr. Roy said they were not yet complete, and that if I would send him down some clerks he would see that they were completed. This I agreed to do.

The immediate circumstances of Captain Wirz's arrest were these: I went to his house and saw him there; the family were about him, that is, his wife and two daughters. It is a very hard thing to take a man from his family, and particularly so in that case, as Mrs. Wirz and one of the daughters at least were crying and having considerable trouble. To pacify them and to do the thing as quietly as I could, I told Mrs. Wirz, and also told the captain, that they need not distress themselves at all; that on his arrival at Macon, if General Wilson was satisfied that he had done no more than his duty, and

---

[1] This is the Sherman-Johnston convention referred to in the prisoner's plea.

FACTS AND RESULTS OF TRIAL.   47

had simply acted in accordance with his orders, he would probably be released. That was the sum and substance of the conversation. General Wilson did not direct me to make any promise to the prisoner, or to give him any safe conduct, and I do not consider that I did.

He was conveyed to Macon under guard, and remained there under guard; he was not on parole at all. I have no doubt that my conversation might have been construed, by those who were very anxious that it should be so, into a promise that he would be returned, but I had no doubt in my mind that General Wilson would hold him as a prisoner. I intended to convey to him no promise of safe return, but merely intended to pacify his family and himself; he was very much excited. These are all the circumstances which I remember, particularly connected with the arrest.

He remained under our headquarter guard until about the 20th of May, when I was ordered to convey him to Washington, with all the Andersonville records, including the hospital records, which General Wilson had sent an officer for, and the flags which General Wilson had captured in his campaign through Alabama and Georgia. I had trouble all the way till we came north of the Ohio River, on account of our men who had been at Andersonville recognizing the prisoner. I have read in the newspapers that I endangered my life to protect him. There is a misconception on that point, but I do not think the prisoner could have got here alive if there had not been an officer in charge of the party. At Chattanooga, where I was stopping temporarily, I sent him to the post prison to be taken care of, as I knew that outside of that he would collect a great crowd. He had on good, fair-looking confederate clothes, and a hat, and was pretty decently dressed generally. When I saw him again I hardly knew him; all his clothes were stripped off him, he had only a part of his hat, no coat, a very dirty shirt, a portion of a pair of pants pretty badly torn, and shoes. Whenever I got him where there were any of our soldiers I had to hurry him off and get him under a strong guard in order to save him. I had trouble in getting him on board the boat at Nashville. I think that but for the guard I had, and my personal presence, they would have taken hold of him there, and if they had got hold of him I do not suppose he would ever have reached Washington. He was afterwards disguised.

At Louisville he still had his extremely dilapidated appearance, which, if there was nothing else, would have attracted attention. He said that he had some friends there. Between those friends and myself we succeeded in getting a complete suit of black and a beaver hat. He also had his face shaved clean, which entirely altered his appearance, so much so that we were not troubled at all after that. I do not think he was recognized after that, although a good many soldiers must have seen him, particularly at Cincinnati.

TESTIMONY OF MAJOR GENERAL J. H. WILSON.[1]

The circumstances connected with the arrest of the prisoner were simply these: On arriving at Macon, as a matter of course, inquiry was at once

---
[1] Record, p. 269 et seq.

made as to the condition of the Andersonville Prison, and who were responsible for its condition. I sent officers down there to investigate the matter, and among others Lieutenant Rendelbrook, Fourth United States Cavalry, and one of my staff officers, Captain Noyes, now Major Noyes. They made a trip there and returned, reporting to me that the man Wirz who had been in charge of the prison was still there. I immediately ordered Noyes to return to the prison, arrest him, and bring him to Macon. He brought him to Macon, and I do not know how long he was kept there; several days, however. The first party who went to Andersonville brought back the paper—whether sent by Wirz or not I do not know—which has been produced in court; a letter addressed to me asking protection, among other things, on which I made an indorsement recommending the trial of Wirz. Afterwards when he was brought forward himself I simply remanded him to prison and wrote a letter to the secretary of war, requesting that he might be brought to trial, in order that the matter might be thoroughly investigated. No protection was ever guaranteed to him by me. I ordered his arrest for the purpose of bringing him to trial, and for no other purpose, and with the special intention that he should not have the benefit of the amnesty or armistice between Sherman and Johnston, so far as I could prevent it. [A paper was here handed to witness.] That is the letter to which I refer. That is my signature to the indorsement. The statement of the escaped prisoner referred to in the indorsement is the statement of, I think, three or four men whom I requested to make statements to accompany this paper, with the expectation that an investigation would be made.

Before sending for Captain Wirz I had no information that he wanted my protection, except that document which came up with the first party. I had received it before I sent for him; that is my impression; I cannot positively say in reference to it, however. I sent Captain Noyes, now Major Noyes, and Lieutenant Rendelbrook for him. Captain Noyes reported to me his presence at Andersonville, and the fact that he was generally believed to be responsible for what had been done there. When I sent those parties I had no thought or knowledge that Captain Wirz was there. I had not supposed that any man who was responsible for so much would have stayed. I may have heard there was such a man as Wirz and that he had command of the prison, but I did not think of it then. My object in sending the first time was to investigate matters connected with the Andersonville Prison, and the atrocities alleged to have been perpetrated there. As a matter of course if Captain Wirz, or anybody else, was there, they were one of the principal objects aimed at, though not specified in my orders to the officers or in my own mind. I cannot remember what they reported to me about Captain Wirz when they returned, more than that he was there, and that sick and wounded soldiers, of whom there were some two hundred, and some of whom had been brought up, had sworn that he was the author of their condition and their misery. He was living there; I do not know if it was in a house. There were Union prisoners there. There were some two hundred and fifty shadows of soldiers, men who could not possibly have been moved without endangering their lives. A great many of those men died after they were brought to my hospitals. My impression is that the letter was brought by Lieutenant Rendelbrook; it was brought by the party who went down. The letter, together with the representations of the officers that he was there, and that they believed he was the responsible party, first called my attention to Captain Wirz. I think the officers went back very soon afterwards. I know that I issued orders immediately for his arrest—verbal instructions to Captain Noyes.

Captain Noyes when he returned to me made no report more than that he had brought the man and had him confined under guard. Captain Noyes spoke of the family crying and expressing great fear that he was going to be hanged or made away with. He brought the books and papers upon the first trip; that is my impression. Those books and papers were sent by Captain Noyes, at the time the prisoner was transmitted, to the Adjutant General of the United States army at Washington. He brought me, I think, a receipt for the books and papers.

I did not give, or cause to be given, to the prisoner any assurances as an inducement for him to deliver himself up. Nor was any such assurance authorized. The officer whom I sent being an officer of discretion and prompt obedience, I don't think he ever intended to give the prisoner any assurances of any kind; except that he should not be hurt just upon the ground at the time. He probably gave him some assurance of that kind, that he should not be killed or handled roughly, so as to quiet his family. That is my interpretation of the whole matter. I know that Captain Noyes had no jurisdiction to give any other sort of assurance of protection. His simple object in going there was to arrest Wirz, and we had special instructions to parole no person in Georgia, and to give no protection to any one except from the military authority. There were no prisoners paroled in Georgia except upon that condition. When I had Captain Wirz brought to my headquarters I did not offer him any safe conduct of any kind in returning, except that the guard were instructed to protect him and deliver him safely into such hands as the secretary of war might direct. My officers reported to me that they risked their own lives in protecting him. At Chattanooga he was attacked by the troops, and but for the personal interposition of Captain Noyes he would have been disposed of. Captain Noyes disguised him in some way or another and managed to get him through.

Congress, on March 9, 1906 (Stat. L, 56), passed a law authorizing the secretary of war to ascertain the location and condition of all the graves of soldiers of the Confederate army and navy, who died in Federal prisons and military hospitals in the North and were buried near their place of confinement, with power to acquire and control the ground.

The judge advocate-general of the army, on January 29, 1910, made a report on the status of Captain Wirz: That he did not form a part of any of the Confederate armies that surrendered at different times between April 9 and 26, 1865, as his command was exercised under the direct control and supervision of a bureau of the Confederate war department at Richmond. For that reason he was not included in the armistice agreed upon between the commanding generals of the Union and Confederate forces at Greensboro, North Carolina, on April 26, 1865. As the prison at Andersonville was not an integral part of General Johnston's command, it was the opinion of the judge advocate-general, that Captain Wirz was not included within the operation of the clause of that agreement requiring each officer and man to give his individual obligation in writing not to take up arms against the government. As Captain Wirz did not die in a prison camp or hospital and never occupied the status of a prisoner of war, but was executed in pursuance of the approved sentence of a military commission, upon conviction of offenses in violation of the laws of war, and as his remains were given decent burial, the opinion held that his case is not within the operation of the statute of March 9, 1906.

It further appears, that his body was interred by the side of Atzerodt[1] in the arsenal grounds of Washington City; that his remains were subsequently removed, under cimcumstances not known to the department, to the Olivet Cemetery,[2] where they now rest, the grave being marked by a small marble block inscribed with the name Wirz on the upper face.

[1] One of President Lincoln's assassins.
[2] Near Washington City.

CHAPTER IV.

LOCATION OF ANDERSONVILLE PRISON—DESCRIPTION OF THE PRISON PEN—WIRZ ASSIGNED TO ITS COMMAND—EARLY CONDITION OF THE PRISONERS DEPLORABLE OFFICIAL REPORTS OF REBEL OFFICERS—INJUNCTION TO ABATE PRISON AS A NUISANCE BECAUSE OF NOXIOUS ODORS—UPON WHOM RESTED RESPONSIBILITY OF—ORIGIN OF DEAD LINE—REBEL AUTHORITIES AT RICHMOND INFORMED—MORTALITY INCREASED—IN ONE MONTH 2,993 DIED.

TO give an adequate description of the prison pen and the sufferings of the unhappy inmates during the fatal summer of 1864 would be impossible. The evidence to which the reader's attention will first be directed will, in large degree, be taken from the reports and testimony of those least likely to exaggerate,—namely, those in the service of the Confederacy. The issues were clearly drawn by Mr. Davis, and have been reopened and reasserted by the inscriptions placed on the Wirz monument, that the sufferings of Union prisoners at Andersonville were not unusual, nor, such as they were, were they preventable, and that no criminal liability attached to any one for the management of the prison. It may be confidently asserted that the case of the prosecution will find ample support of the general charges of conspiracy, in the evidence solely furnished by those who were in the rebel service. The testimony of the surviving prisoners in their description of the horrors through which they passed will be found to be confirmed and corroborated by those who either purposely or unavoidably were compelled by the fate of war to become witnesses to, or were participators in, the crime unfolded at the trial.

The stockade at Andersonville was originally built in the winter of 1863-4, and was first occupied by prisoners in the latter part of February, 1864. It was intended to have a capacity for 10,000 prisoners and contained about eighteen acres. It continued without enlargement until June 18, 1864, when it contained 22,000 prisoners. It was then increased about one-third, its actual inner area being about twenty-four acres. The following description of the prison pen is given by Dr. Joseph Jones, an ex-surgeon of the rebel army, and to whom Mr. Davis refers in his *Belford* articles as eminent in his profession and of great learning and probity. He made an official report to Surgeon-General Moore, which was produced in evidence and identified by Dr. Jones himself, who was a witness. This report will follow in a subsequent chapter, as furnishing indubitable proof of conditions at Andersonville. He thus described the enclosure:

The stockade was in the form of a parallelogram 20 feet high, formed of strong pine logs firmly planted in the ground, with two small stockades surrounding the prison—one sixteen, the other twelve, feet high, these latter being intended for offense and defense. If the inner stockade should at any time be forced by the prisoners, the second proved another line of defense, while in case of an attempt to deliver the prisoners by a force operating upon the exterior, the outer line forms an admirable protection to the Confederate troops, and a most formidable obstacle to cavalry or infantry. Earthworks on eminences surmounted by cannon swept the entire enclosure.[1]

Colonel D. T. Chandler, to whom reference has already been made, in his report, which will also be given, further described the interior:[2]

A railing around the inside of the stockade about twenty feet from it constitutes the dead-line, beyond which prisoners are not allowed to pass. A small stream passes from west to east through the enclosure and furnishes the only water for washing accessible to the prisoners. Bordering this stream, about three and one-quarter acres near the center of the enclosure are so marshy as to be at present [August, 1864] unfit for occupation, reducing the available area to about twenty-three and one-half acres, which gives somewhat less than six square feet to each prisoner, there being scarcely room enough for all the prisoners to lie down at the same time.

The interior was entirely denuded of trees or other shelter, and no barracks or buildings of any kind placed inside. It was simply a large human corral into which prisoners were turned like so many cattle, and, as we shall see, without the care or attention ordinarily given to domestic animals.

Lieutenant-Colonel Alexander W. Persons, 55th Georgia Volunteers, was assigned to command the troops at Andersonville Prison some time in February, 1864, and remained until some time in May. His testimony relates to the inception of the prison, bears upon its origin and early conditions, and approximates the date of Wirz's command there.

TESTIMONY OF LT.-COL. ALEXANDER W. PERSONS.[3]

I have been employed for the last four or five years in the Confederate States army. I was lieutenant-colonel of the 55th Georgia Volunteers. I was on duty at Andersonville from some time in February, 1864, till about the last of May, 1864. I was sent there to command the troops. Subsequently I was advanced

[1] Record, p. 620.
[2] Record, p. 224.
[3] Record, p. 99 et seq.

THE PRISON PEN AND ITS COMMANDER.   53

to the command of the post and remained in the character of post commander until I was relieved-which was some time in May or June. Directly after my command was captured at Cumberland Gap, I went to Richmond and reported directly to the secretary of war for duty. He gave me instructions to report to General Winder. General Winder instructed me to report at Andersonville. He stated that at that post there were three separate and distinct departments; one was known as the officer commanding the troops, another as the officer commanding the prison, the other as the officer commanding the post. He assigned me to duty as the officer commanding the troops, I think there was no prison officer there when I first went there. The first prison commander proper was Captain Wirz. He assumed control of the prison the latter part of February or some time in March, 1864. He came direct from Richmond, my understanding was, by order of General Winder. I saw an official order to that effect. I received a communication about the time Captain Wirz reached there; whether he brought the communication or not, I do not know; I received it by hand about the time he came. That communication was from General Winder.

The letter merely stated that Captain Wirz was an old prison officer, a very reliable man and capable of governing prisons, (that is about the substance of it,) and it wound up saying that I could give him command of the prison proper. I don't recollect the date; it was the last of February, I think, or about the 1st of March—not later than the middle of March. I don't remember who was the ranking officer in charge of the guards and sentinels on duty at that time; he was perhaps a captain of my regiment. The control of the prison and prison-guards was assumed by Captain Wirz pretty soon after he reported. Captain Wirz had control of the sentinels after they were put on duty—after guard-mounting. Under the instructions I had, a requisition was made upon me for troops to guard the prison. I was under instructions to make an order or requisition upon the officer commanding the troops for the number required by the officer commanding the prison. They were then immediately detailed; guard-mounting was gone through with and they were ordered to the prison, where Captain Wirz, commanding the prison, had jurisdiction and control, of them. He had control of the prison, and of the guards after they passed into his hands. That continued to be the rule while I was there.

The prison was laid out by Captain W. Sidney Winder, by order of General Winder. The original capacity of the prison was for ten thousand; so he told me. I reached there just before they completed the work on the prison; they had one-half of a side to finish when I reached there. I suppose they had some fifteen or twenty negroes at work there. I know the stream that passes through the stockade, above and below the stockade. About one to three miles from there there is a stream five or six times the size of the stream upon which the prison is located. It occurred to me that that would have been a preferable place to the one where the prison was located. I suggested that to W. S. Winder—I believe I recollect distinctly that it was one of the Winders—about the time I went there—about the time the prison was built. W. S. Winder told me that he had absolute discretion in the location of the prison; that he examined a great many places in southwestern Georgia.

I knew General Winder; he relieved me, I think, some time about the last of May or 1st of June. He was, as I understand, in command of all the prisoners; had control over everything. W. S. Winder was a son of General John H. Winder. I knew Richard B. Winder; he was a quartermaster at that prison. He had the duty of quartermaster, such as furnishing transportation. I think the bakehouse was under him; also the furnishing of fuel; all the duties devolving upon a quartermaster fell to him. The Winders seemed to act in concert; they worked together.

While there I took steps to erect shelter for the prisoners inside the stockade. When I was there, the railroad upon which the prison was located was worked to its greatest possible capacity in feeding Lee's and Johnston's armies, and it was with the greatest difficulty that I could get transportation on that road. Perhaps in ten or twenty days they would give me one train. I held constant communication with the superintendent of the road, and every time I could get a train I would have that train loaded with lumber and brought through. During my stay, I had concentrated there, I suppose, about five or six train-loads of lumber. I suppose there were six, eight, or ten cars in a train. There were altogether about fifty carloads. I was in the act of erecting shelter, was just carrying the lumber, when I was relieved by General Winder. He arrived there about the same day I was relieved. I went into the stockade several times after I was relieved from duty, and I saw no shelter there. I saw forty or fifty houses springing up outside of the grounds. The lumber disappeared in that way. I suppose there were between fifteen and twenty thousand prisoners in the stockade at the time I was relieved.

INJUNCTION TO RESTRAIN THE REBEL AUTHORITIES FROM CONTINUING THE PRISON.

Some time in the latter part of that summer, after he was relieved from duty at Andersonville, Colonel Persons was employed to bring a bill for an injunction to abate the nuisance caused by the prison. He prepared the case for trial and was on the point of appearing before the judge of the district court, when he received a communication from General Howell Cobb, as to which he testified:[1]

I was interested in a proceeding to enjoin the rebel authorities from further continuing the prison at Andersonville. In the character of counsel, I drew a bill for an injunction to abate the nuisance. The graveyard made it a nuisance, and the military works, fortifications, etc., made it highly objectionable to the property-holders there, and the prison generally was a nuisance, from the intolerable stench, the effluvia, the malaria that it gave up, and things of that sort. After I drew the bill, I went to see the judge of the district court; I read the bill to him, and asked him for the injunction. He simply said that he would appoint a day on which he would hear the argument in chambers. He appointed a day; I made preparations for trial, went down, or was in the act of going, when

[1] Record, p. 101.

I received an official communication from General Howell Cobb, of Georgia, in which he asked me if I was going to appear.

[Mr. BAKER objected to witness stating the contents of the communication.]

I expect I destroyed that official correspondence; I have no recollection whether I destroyed it or put it away. I have not thought of it since. General Cobb asked me if that bill was to be charged to me, the bill against my government, as he termed it. In reply to his communication, I wrote him that I drew the bill, and that it could be charged to me. He replied, through his adjutant-general, Major Harrit, that he deemed it inconsistent with my duty as a Confederate officer to appear in a case like that, of a bill against the government; and he therefore ordered me out of the case, and I obeyed the order. General Cobb at that time commanded the department of Georgia and the reserve force of Georgia. I said that he ordered me out of the case. Let me be more explicit on that point. He wanted to know if I drew the bill; I said that I did; I discovered by the tenor of his communication that I would be treated by court-martial, or something of that sort, and, to stave the matter off, I said to him that if he deemed what I had done in the matter unofficerlike, I would retire from the case. He said he did deem it that way, and would be glad if I would retire without being driven from it.

UPON WHOM THE RESPONSIBILITY FOR OVERCROWDING THE PRISON RESTS.

Of the conditions which led to the attempt to abate the nuisance, Colonel Persons testified:

That camp was a nuisance to all intents and purposes. The first reason was that the dead were buried so near the surface of the ground that it gave out an intolerable stench. A swarm of green flies spread like locusts over that section of the country. Then the filth of the camp, arising from different causes, necessarily concentrated there. That, with divers other causes, made it a terrible nuisance. I could not have had it otherwise if I had been in command there. If I had ordered it otherwise, I do not think the order could have been carried out, for this reason: when that prison was in its very infancy, in its very inception, and when the officers were instructed not to build accommodations for more than 10,000, there were 40,000 prisoners sent there. Captain Wirz was not to be blamed for that.

The authorities were responsible for that; I cannot say who. The great blunder on the part of the government was the concentration of so many men at one place without preparations being made to receive them. The authorities were notified of the fact, but to no advantage. I think that some of the higher officials were responsible, but who they were I cannot say. I sent notifications through General Winder that the prison was worked beyond its capacity, that it was a vast, unwieldy thing, and to send no more prisoners; but they kept coming. After I left there, there came over 40,000; no man on earth could have abated the rigors of that prison except the man who wielded the power over them. I do not know that man. General Winder was in advance of me, and several others were in advance of him. Who was responsible I cannot say. About that time an order was issued from the office of the adjutant and inspector-general putting General Winder in command of all the prisoners east of the Mississippi, giving him absolute control

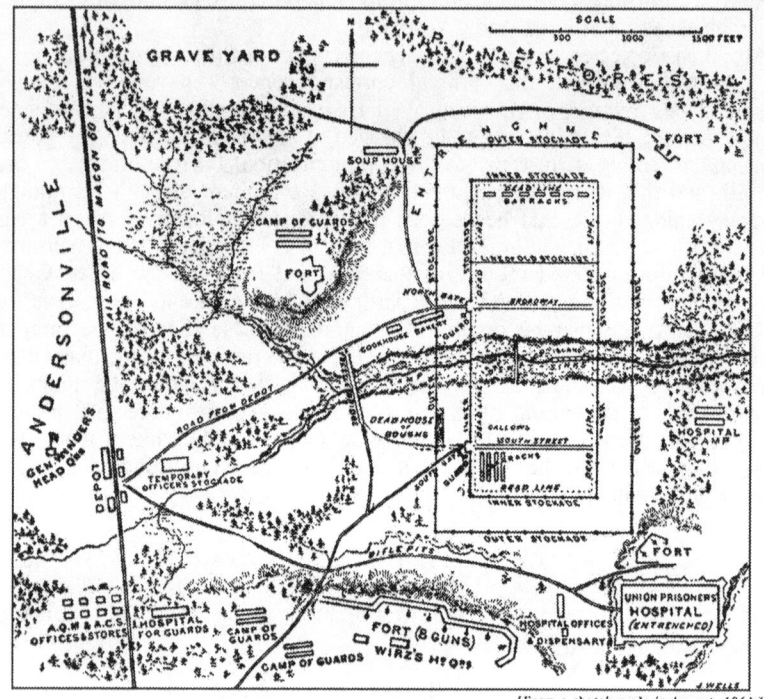

[From a sketch made in August, 1864.]
PLAN OF STOCKADE AND SURROUNDINGS AT ANDERSONVILLE

The outlines of the forts represented in the above out differ from those on the opposite page, which are correct, owing to the fact that the person who made the sketch was not allowed to approach the forts.

and dominion over them. That order came from General S. Cooper, adjutant and inspector-general. I saw that order; I read it closely. The substance of it was about this: They were reorganizing the different prison departments. Some man was put in command the other side of the Mississippi, and General Winder was put in supreme command on this side.

No officer had any right to interfere with him in any shape, form, or fashion; and it was made the duty of all officers at adjacent posts or anywhere else, on requisition made by General Winder or any of his subordinates for troops, to furnish them forthwith. The order gave him absolute supreme dominion and control over that thing. All officers in command of prisoners were to report to him, and to take orders from him. I do not recollect the date of that order; it was about the last of summer. I saw the name of General S. Cooper, adjutant and inspector-general, to that order. I studied it particularly because I commanded an adjacent post, and I wanted to understand my duty. I do not know whether it said it was by order of the president or not. I simply know that General Cooper's name was to it.

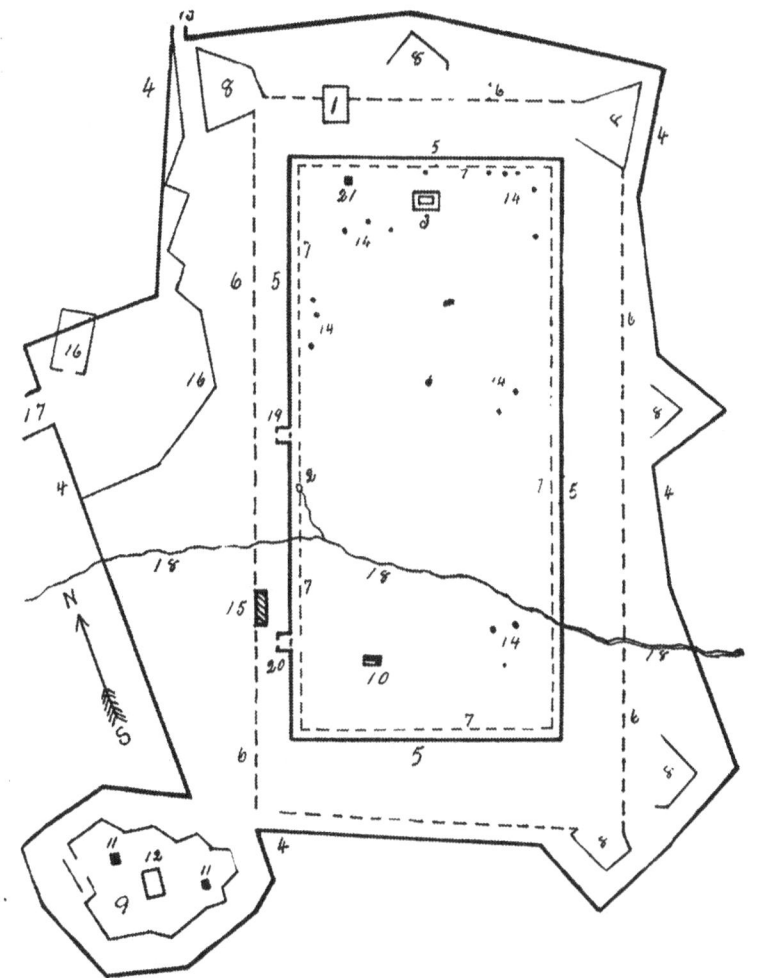

[Made from actual survey.]

PLAT OF ANDERSONVILLE PRISON GROUNDS

DESCRIPTION: 1 Care-taker's House, erected by National W. R. C. 2. "Providence Spring." 3 Site of proposed National Monument. 4 outline of purchased Property. 5 Outline of Stockade enclosing prisoners. 6 Outline of Outer Stockade (only Partially completed). 7 "Dead Line." 8 Confederate Forts and Batteries. 9 Main Fort, or "Star Fort," southwest corner. 10 Site of Gallows, where marauder were hung. 11 Powder Magazines in "star Fort." 12 Site of capt. Wirtz Headquarters. 13 Gate to Roadway leading to the Cemetery. 14 Wells and Tunnels dug by prisoners. 15 Site of Dead House. 16 Entrenched Camp for Guards. 17 Roadway, 100 feet wide leadlne to railroad station 18 "Stockade Creek," a branch of Sweetwater. 19 North Gate of Stockade. 20 South Gate of Stockade. 21 Flag Staff.

Of the origin of the dead-line he testified:

I do not know who originated the dead-line. It originated some time after Captain Wirz reported there, while I was in command of the post. I did not originate it. It was the duty of the commanding officer to originate it.

It will not be found practicable to follow the history of the prison in chronological order. Most of the records pertaining to the prison were destroyed or scattered to the four winds when the Rebellion collapsed, and it was possible only to obtain fugitive and fragmentary documents throwing light on the subject. The following extracts from the record will show that the condition at Andersonville was not unknown at Richmond.[1]

TESTIMONY OF C. M. SELPH.

I have been in the Confederate army for the last four years as captain in the adjutant-general's department—assistant adjutant-general,—and also in the inspector-general's department. Those departments were combined—they were separated about the beginning of 1864; I was assistant inspector-general, on duty in the office.

I am acquainted with the handwriting of Major-General Howell Cobb.

[A letter was here handed to the witness.]

I am pretty sure that is a letter from Howell Cobb. It was received in the adjutant-general's office, May 21, 1864, and was sent to the inspector-general's office May 26th.

[The JUDGE ADVOCATE read to the court and put in evidence—stating that he did so to show that the rebel war department at Richmond was cognizant of the condition of Andersonville Prison—a letter of which the following is a copy:]

HEADQUARTERS GEORGIA RESERVES,
MACON, GEORGIA, May 5, 1864.

GENERAL: Under your orders to inform myself of the condition of the prison at Andersonville, with a view of furnishing from the reserve corps the necessary guard for its protection and safety, I made a visit there and have just returned, and now submit the result of my examination.

There are now in the prison about twelve thousand prisoners, in an area of less than eighteen acres, with a stockade around it about fifteen feet high. I presume the character of the prison is well understood at Richmond, and therefore give no description of it. The danger of the prisoners escaping is not so great as I had supposed. With a guard of twelve hundred men, four pieces of artillery, and a cavalry company, all apprehension of escape would be quieted. . . .

I took the liberty of making several suggestions for rendering the prison more secure; and if the tools could be had, I would recommend that the entire prison grounds should be surrounded by fortifications, which could be put up by the troops, whose health would be promoted by the employment.

The most important change is the one suggested in the accompanying report of my chief surgeon, Dr. Eldridge, that is, erection of hospital buildings outside of the prison. Upon that point there cannot be two opinions among intelligent men. It ought to be done at once, and such is the opinion of every sensible man that has examined the prison.

The prison is already too much crowded, and no additional prisoners should be sent there until it can be enlarged. The effect of increasing the number within the present area must be a terrific increase of sickness and death during the summer months. I understand that an order has been given for enlarging the prison. If it was possible to make another prison it would be much better, for I doubt very much whether the water will be sufficient for the accommodation of the

---

[1] Record, p. 219 et seq.

increased number of prisoners. The general management of the prison under Colonel Persons is good, and he manifests a laudable desire to discharge his duties in the most efficient manner. The duties of the inside command are admirably performed by Captain Wirz, whose place it would be difficult to fill.

I take the liberty of enclosing a copy of Dr. Eldridge's report.

I am, general, very respectfully, yours, &c.,

HOWELL COBB,
Major-General, Commanding.

GENERAL S. COOPER,
Adjutant-General, Richmond, Va.

[Indorsed:]

Howell Cobb, Major-General, Headquarters Georgia Reserves, Macon, May 5, 1864. Report on the prison at Andersonville, Georgia. One enclosure. A. & I. G. O. received May 26, 1864. Received A. & I. G. O. May 21, 1864.

WITNESS. Howell Cobb was brigadier-general of the Georgia Reserves at that time.

[Another paper was here handed to the witness.]

This paper bears official marks of the department; it is the enclosure which accompanied General Cobb's letter.

[The Judge Advocate read to the court and put in evidence the paper, of which the following is a copy:]

HEADQUARTERS GEORGIA RESERVES,
MACON, GEORGIA, May 6, 1864.

MAJOR: In obedience to instructions from Major-General Howell Cobb, I have the honor to make the following report of my visit in company with the general to the prison camp at Andersonville. I found the prisoners, in my opinion, too much crowded for the promotion or even continuance of their present health, particularly during the approaching summer months. The construction of properly arranged barracks would of course allow the same number of men to occupy the enclosures, with material advantage to their comfort and health. At present their shelters consist of such as they can make of the boughs of trees, poles, &c., covered with dirt. The few tents they have are occupied as a hospital. I found the police of the camp, though not very good, as well arranged as their crowded condition and the limited number of shovels would allow. Since necessary tools have been received for ditching, &c., (which has been very recently,) it is proposed to arrange the sinks so that the fecal matter may be at once carried away by the stream running through the enclosure, which will at once materially improve the condition of the camp. I found the condition of a large number of the Belle Island prisoners on their arrival to be such as to require more attention to their diet and cleanliness, than to the actual administration of medicines, very many of them suffering from chronic diarrhœa combined with the scorbutic disposition, with extreme emaciation as the consequence. The hospital being within the enclosure, it has been found impracticable to administer such diet and give them such attention as they require, as unless constantly watched, such diet as is prepared for them is stolen and eaten by the other prisoners. There is a fine stream within a few hundred yards of the present enclosure, across which, in my opinion, there should be made another enclosure, with sufficient hospital buildings, two stories high, to accommodate from eight hundred to one thousand patients. Such an enclosure as I should suggest (a plank fence ten feet high) would require but very few additional guards, which guard appears to be the objection urged at Richmond to a separate enclosure.

The patients upon their admission into the hospital should be well washed, and a pool arranged on the side of the stream, and furnished only with a clean shirt, with which dress they would hardly attempt to escape. The nurses could be detailed with such discretion that but few would attempt to escape, and with frequent roll-calls, they would be absent but a few hours before detected, and would be readily caught by the dogs always at hand for that purpose. I consider the establishment of a hospital outside of the present enclosure as essential to the proper treatment to the sick, and most urgently recommended its immediate construction. I would also recommend the construction of as many bathing-pools within the prison as the stream would warrant, feeling assured from the appearance of the prisoners that their use would contribute materially to the health of the bathers. Other improvement would be suggested but for the difficulty of obtaining labor, tools, and materials; but with those above mentioned, the urgent necessities of the prison would be supplied.

The bakery just being completed will be the means of furnishing better-prepared food, particurly bread, the half-cooked condition of which has doubtless contributed to the continuance of the bowel affections. I will add that as far as I have been able to judge from my short visit the management of the medical department of the prison, under the direction of Chief Surgeon J. F. White, reflects credit upon that officer, who seems well qualified for the position he occupies. I have the honor to be, very respectfully, your obedient servant,

E. J. ELDRIDGE
MAJOR LAMAR COBB, *Chief Surgeon Georgia Reserves.*
A.A. and I. General, Georgia Reserves, Macon, Georgia.

[Indorsed:]

E.J. Eldridge, Chief Surgeon, Headquaters Georgia Reserves, Macon, May 6, 1864. Report of the prison at Andersonville, Georgia.

[A letter from Captain Wirz, the prisoner, was here handed to the witness.]

I do not know whether that letter bears the marks of the department; it may be the mark of General Winder's office. He was commandant of the post in the city of Richmond; Major Turner was commandant of Libby Prison, Richmond. I do not know whether these reports were made through him.

[The handwriting of the prisoner, and of General John H. Winder, to the letter, was proved by Captain J. H. Wright, previously sworn as witness for the prosecution; and the JUDGE ADVOCATE offered the letter in evidence. Counsel for the accused objected, on the ground that there was no proof of the official character of the paper. The objection was overruled and the paper was received in evidence. The following is a copy:[1]

CAMP SUMTER, ANDERSONVILLE, GEORGIA, May 8, 1864.

MAJOR: I have the honor to make the following report in regard to the Confederate States military prison at this post.

I was assigned to the command of the prison by Colonel A. W. Persons, the commandant of the post, on the 27th of March, 1864, having reported to him for duty by order of General J. H. Winder, commanding Confederate States military prison. I found the prison in a bad condition owing to the want of tools, such as axes, spades, and lumber to erect proper buildings; Captain W. S. Winder, and his successor, Colonel A. W. Persons, had left nothing untried to supply th [ese] so important articles. Only two weeks ago I received axes, spades, &c., from Columbus, Georgia, and went to work cutting ditches, &c., and I hope to have everything in the interior of the prison completed in two weeks. The bakery, which could not be completed for want of lumber, is now in operation. The necessity of enlarging the stockade is unavoidable, and I shall commence as soon as I can gather a sufficient number of negroes. I would most respectfully ask you to present to the authorities at Richmond the impediment thrown in my way by having the hospitals inside the prison.

---

[1] Record. p. 221.

The number of prisoners on the 1st day of April was	7,160
I received up to to-day, from various sources	5,787
I received to-day, recaptured	7
Total	12,954
The number of dead from the 1st of April to 8th of May is	728
The number of escaped from the 1st of April to the 8th of May is	13 741
Leaving on hand	12,213

I would also call your attention to the danger of having our present guard force withdrawn and their places supplied by the reserve forces of Governor Brown.

In conclusion allow me to make a few remarks concerning myself. I am here in a very unpleasant position, growing out of the rank which I now hold, and suggest the propriety of being promoted. Having the full control of the prison, and consequently of the daily prison guard, the orders which I have to give are very often not obeyed with the promptness the occasion requires, and I am of opinion that it emanates from the reluctance of obeying an officer who holds the same rank as they do. My duties are manifold, and require all my time in daytime, and very often part of the night, and I would most respectfully ask that two commissioned officers (lieutenants) would be assigned to me for duty.

I am, major, most respectfully, your obedient servant,

H. WIRZ,
MAJOR THOS. TURNER, C. S. A. *Captain Commanding Prison*

[Indorsed:]

Andersonville, Georgia, Camp Sumter, May 8, 1864. Captain Henry Wirz, commanding prison, reports in reference to the general condition of the prison, and suggests the propriety of increased rank being given him. Richmond, Virginia, May 25, 1864. Respectfully forwarded, recommended. THOS. P. TURNER, Major Commanding.

Approved and respectfully forwarded. Captain Wirz has proved himself to be a very diligent and efficient officer, whose superior in commanding prisoners and incident duties I know not. JNO. H. WINDER, Brigadier-General.

I have had opportunities of noticing the signatures of J. A. Seddon, rebel secretary of war, and of Colonel H. L. Clay, assistant adjutant-general.

[A paper was here handed to the witness.]

I recognize here the signature of Colonel H. L. Clay, assistant adjutant-general, and the initials of Mr. Seddon, secretary of war. Mr. Seddon was in the habit of signing papers and referring them by his initials.

[The signature of Brigadier-General Jno. H. Winder was identified by Captain J. H. Wright, heretofore sworn as a witness for the prosecution. The Judge Advocate then read and put in evidence the letter from John H. Winder, brigadier-general, to General S. Cooper, of which the following is a copy:]

CAMP SUMTER, ANDERSONVILLE, GEORGIA, July 21, 1864.

GENERAL: Your indorsement on the letter of S. B. Davis, relating to the strength of the guard of this post, contains a very severe censure, which I am sure would not have been made if you had had a clear comprehension of this post, of its wants and its difficulties. Reflect for a moment; 29,201 prisoners of war, many of them most desperate characters, a post a mile long by half a mile wide, the stockade for prisoners within 160 yards of a mile in circumference, numerous avenues leading to the post to be guarded, public property to be cared for, guards for working parties, and the ordinary camp guards for the troops, and you can form some estimate of the number it would require for these purposes...

You speak in your indorsement of placing the prisoners properly. I do not exactly comprehend what is intended by it. I know of but one way to place them, and that is to put them into the stockade, where they have between four and five square yards to the man. This includes streets and two (2) acres of ground about the stream. Respectfully, your obedient servant,

JNO. H. WINDER,[1]
Brigadier-General.

GENERAL S. COOPER,
    Adjutant and Inspector-General.

[Indorsed:]

Camp Sumter, Andersonville, Georgia, July 21, 1864. Brigadier-General J. H. Winder reporting condition of this post, its wants and difficulties. Respectfully submitted to the secretary of war. H. L. CLAY, Assistant Adjutant-General.

Adjutant and Inspector-General's Office, August 3, 1864. Noted. Filed. J. A. S.

[Counsel for the accused asked the Judge Advocate to indicate for what purpose these papers were put in evidence.]

THE JUDGE ADVOCATE. In the introduction of these documents, I do not hesitate to state generally that while the government considers the prisoner an atrocious criminal, there are others above and higher than him, whom the government will seek to hold responsible for these great crimes; and it is for the purpose of proving on those who had the power to alleviate the sufferings of Union prisoners a knowledge of their condition, that these documents were introduced.

MR. BAKER. That will be satisfactory, if you state in that general way what is introduced for such and such general purposes.

THE JUDGE ADVOCATE. I state that generally with reference to the papers I am now introducing.

It will be observed that early in May, 1864, the prison was reported as too much crowded, and General Cobb recommended that no more prisoners should be sent until it was enlarged; that the result of increasing the number within the present area must be "a terrific increase of sickness and death during the summer months." He also suggested that another prison would be better, for he doubted that there would be sufficient water if the present enclosure were enlarged. Notwithstanding these recommendations, prisoners continued to arrive until it contained, at the time of its enlargement, over twenty-two thousand.

It was some time before Surgeon Eldridge's recommendation to erect a hospital outside the stockade, and remove the sick for treatment under more favorable conditions, was attempted to be carried out. And when the attempt was made, instead of being a building two stories high, it offered little better facilities for treating the sick than were given them inside the enclosure, and, as we shall see, the sick prisoners in the hospital died about as fast as the sick in the stockade for whom there was no room in the hospital. The lumber which

---

[1] Winder gives the swamp area as two acres. Deduct this and the streets and dead-line area, and note the small space to each prisoner.

Colonel Persons had assembled in large quantities was used neither for barracks, for the well, nor at the hospital for the sick. And the temporary shelter constructed outside the enclosure was inadequate to receive more than half the number requiring treatment. We learn from Dr. Jones's report that the mean strength of the prison in March was 7,500, and the total deaths 283; in April, mean strength 10,000, and deaths 576; in May, mean strength 15,000, and deaths 708; in June, mean strength 22,291, and deaths 1,201. In March they died at the rate of 37 per 1,000, and in June at the rate of 53 per 1,000.

From a table found in Dr. Jones's report, which covered the months of March, April, May, June, July, and August, the following appears: "Per cent of deaths to mean strength, sick and well: March, 3.77; April, 5.76; May, 4.72; June, 5.38; July, 6.64; August, 9.09." This report shows that the ratio of mortality was progressive, and the forecast made by General Cobb proved all too true. And in August it reached the frightful proportions of nearly one in ten of all the sick and well per month.

In General Winder's report of July 21, 1864, he says he knows of no way to place the prisoners, except to put them in the stockade, "where they have between four and five square yards to the man. This includes streets and two acres of ground about the swamp." Upon its reference to the secretary of war it received scant attention, as is shown by the indorsement: "Noted. File. J. A. S." (James A. Seddon.)

TESTIMONY OF CAPTAIN J. H. WRIGHT.[1]

I have been in the Confederate service. I was captain and quartermaster for the Confederate troops at Andersonville. I know the signature of J. H. Winder. [A paper was here handed the witness.] That is his signature. It resembles his son's signature very much, but I am confident it is his from the fact that he signed his "Jno. H. Winder," and his son signs his "J. H. Winder." I know the handwriting of the prisoner. I find the prisoner's handwriting on that paper.

[The following paper was put in evidence:]

Consolidated Return for Confederate States Military Prison, Camp Sumter, Andersonville, Georgia, for the Month of August, 1864.

Prisoners on hand 1st of August, 1864:		
In camp	29,985	
In hospital	1,693	31,678
Received from various places during August	3,078	
Recaptured	4	3,082
Total		34,760

[1] Record, P. 147.

Died during the month of August	2,993	
Sent to other parts	23	
Exchanged	21	
Escaped	30	3,067
Remaining on hand		31,693
Of which there are on the 31st of August—		
In camp	29,473	
In hospital	2,220	
		31,693

The same complaint has been made again against the carelessness and insufficiency of the guard of the thirty prisoners. Eleven escaped while on parole of honor not to escape as long as they would be employed to work outside.

The balance of nineteen escaped, some on bribing the sentinel with greenbacks, some simply walking off from the guard while returning from the place where the tools are deposited at night that are used in the stockade in daytime. Perhaps twenty-five more escaped during the month, but were taken up by the dogs before the daily return was made out, and for that reason they are not on the list of escaped nor recaptured.

That only four were recaptured is owing to the fact that [neither] the guard nor the officers of the guard reported a man escaped. The roll-call in the morning showed the man missing, but he was too far gone to be tracked. As we have no general court-martial here, all such offenses go unpunished, or nearly so.

The worthlessness of the guard forces is on the increase day by day.

H. WIRZ,
Captain Commanding Prison.

[Indorsed:]

Consolidated return for Confederate States military prison for the month of August, 1864. Respectfully forwarded to General S. Cooper, adjutant and inspector-general, September 5, 1864. JNO. H. WINDER, Brigadier-General.

It thus appears that in August, there were 34,760 prisoners in confinement, of whom 2,993 died. It will be remembered that Surgeon Eldridge spoke in his report, as does Captain Wirz, of dogs being used to "take up" escaped prisoners. We shall see that these animals were not used alone to track escaped prisoners, but that they were permitted and encouraged to attack and rend them.

CHAPTER V.

CONDITION OF THE PRISON CONTINUED — SUFFERINGS OF PRISONERS DEPICTED — REPORT OF COLONEL D. T. CHANDLER—REPORT OF DR. JOSEPH JONES—CAUSES OF SICKNESS AND DEATH SHOWN — RESPONSIBILITY FIXED — CONFEDERATE AUTHORITIES AT RICHMOND HAD FULL KNOWLEDGE — COLONEL CHANDLER'S TESTIMONY—TESTIMONY OF DR. JONES — SIX SQUARE FEET TO THE MAN— BARELY ROOM TO COMFORTABLY LIE DOWN—INADEQUATE POLICE CONTROL— PRISONERS TRY, CONDEMN, AND HANG SIX OF THEIR NUMBER—PRISONERS MURDERED BY THEIR FELLOW-PRISONERS FOR THEIR CLOTHING AND FOOD—THE BODIES OF THE DEAD MUTILATED—REPORTS BY SURGEON STEVENSON, SURGEON WHITE, AND SURGEON THORNBURG—DR. JONES'S REPORT GRAPHIC DESCRIPTION OF PRISON AND HOSPITAL—CAUSES OF DEATH AND UNPARALLELED SUFFERING.

WHILE Captain C. M. Selph was on the witness-stand, he was called upon to identify the report of Colonel D. T. Chandler and other documents, which will now be laid before the reader.

It must be conceded by any one who will read the report of Colonel D. T. Chandler that it was of supreme importance in the inquiry. Colonel Chandler was assigned to the duty of inspecting this prison and of reporting thereon. He was an officer of high standing in his department and was a graduate of West Point. It was of first importance also to show that this report and its enclosures reached Richmond, and had the attention of the proper officers of the rebel government. And it was of no less importance to ascertain what action, if any, was taken upon the report. Upon these points the testimony found in the record makes it clear that the Richmond authorities had full knowledge of the facts. That such is beyond dispute, and that nothing was done to carry out the recommendations of Colonel Chandler or to ameliorate the sufferings at the prison by those who had ample power to act, when so strongly urged, appears indisputably throughout the record. The significance of this report from every standpoint justifies its publication with but little abbreviation. I quote from the record:[1]

[Another paper, being a report from Lieutenant-Colonel Chandler to R. H. Chilton, was here handed to witness.]

This document bears the signature of Lieutenant-Colonel Chandler, assistant adjutant and inspector-general in the same department as mine. It is marked as being received August 17, 1864.

[The paper was read and put in evidence. The following is a copy.]

---
[1] Record, p. 224 et seq.

ANDERSON, July 5, 1864.[1]

COLONEL: Having, in obedience to instructions of the 25th ultimo, carefully inspected the prison for Federal prisoners of war and post at this place, I respectfully submit the following report:

The Federal prisoners of war are confined within a stockade 15 feet high, of roughly hewn pine logs, about 8 inches in diameter, inserted 5 feet into the ground, enclosing, including the recent extension, an area of 540 by 260 yards. A railing around the inside of the stockade, and about 20 feet from it, constitutes the "dead-line," beyond which the prisoners are not allowed to pass, and about 31¼ acres near the center of the enclosure are so marshy as to be at present unfit for occupation—reducing the available present area to about 23½ acres, which gives somewhat less than 6 square feet[2] to each prisoner. Even this being constantly reduced by the additions to their number. A small stream passing from west to east through the enclosure, at about 150 yards from its southern limit, furnishes the only water for washing accessible to the prisoners. Some regiments of the guard, the bakery and cook-house, being placed on the rising grounds bordering the stream before it enters the prison, render the water nearly unfit for use before it reaches the prisoners. This is now being remedied in part by the removal of the cook-house. Under the pressure of their necessities the prisoners have dug numerous wells within the enclosure, from which they obtain an ample supply of water to drink, of good quality. Excepting the edges of this stream, the soil is sandy and easily drained, but from 30 to 50 yards on each side of it the ground is a muddy marsh, totally unfit for occupation, and having been constantly used as a sink since the prison was first established, it is now in a shocking condition and cannot fail to breed pestilence. An effort is being made by Captain Wirz, commanding the prison, to fill up the marsh and construct a sluice—the upper end to be used for bathing, etc., and the lower end as a sink, but the difficulty of procuring lumber and tools very much retards the work, and threatens soon to stop it. No shelter whatever nor material for constructing any has been provided by the prison authorities, and the ground being entirely bare of trees, none is within reach of the prisoners. nor has it been possible, from the overcrowded state of the enclosure, to arrange the camp with any system. Each man has been permitted to protect himself as best he can, stretching his blanket, or whatever he may have, above him on such sticks as he can procure, thatches of pine or whatever his ingenuity may suggest and his cleverness supply. Of other shelter there is and has been none.

The whole number of prisoners is divided into messes of 270, and subdivisions of 90 men, each under a sergeant of their own number and selection, and but one Confederate States officer, Captain Wirz, is assigned to the supervision and control of the whole. In consequence of this fact, and the absence of all regularity in the prison grounds, and there being no barracks or tents, there are and can be no regulations established for the police consideration of the health, comfort, and sanitary condition of those within the enclosure, and none are practicable under existing circumstances. In evidence of their condition, I would cite the facts that numbers have been found murdered by their comrades, and that recently, in their desperate efforts to provide for their own safety, a court organized among themselves by authority of General Winder, commanding the post, granted on their own application, has tried a large number of their fellow-prisoners, and sentenced six to be hung, which sentence was duly executed by themselves within the stockade, with the sanction of the post commander. His order in the case has been forworded by him to the war department.

There is no medical attendance provided within the stockade. Small quantities of medicines are placed in the hands of certain prisoners of each squad or division, and the sick are directed to be brought out by sergeants of squads daily, at "sick call," to the medical officers who attend at the gate. The crowd at these times is

---

[1] The true date was August 5th, as appears further along.
[2] The original report reads 6 square feet, and not 6 feet square, and probably excluded the swamp.

so great that only the strongest can get access to the doctors, the weaker ones being unable to force their way through the press; and the hospital accommodations are so limited that though the beds (so-called) have all or nearly all two occupants each, large numbers who would otherwise be received are necessarily sent back to the stockade. Many—twenty yesterday—are carted out daily, who have died from unknown causes and whom the medical officers have never seen. The dead are hauled out daily by the wagonload, and buried without coffins, their hands in many instances being first mutilated with an axe in the removal of any finger rings they may have. The sanitary condition of the prisoners is as wretched as can be, the principal causes of mortality being scurvy and chronic diarrhœa, the percentage of the former being disproportionately large among those brought from Belle Island. Nothing seems to have been done, and but little if any effort made to arrest it by procuring proper food. The ration is 1/3 pound of bacon and 1¼ pound unbolted corn meal, with fresh beef at rare intervals, and occasionally rice. When to be obtained—very seldom—a small quantity of molasses is substituted for the meat ration. A little weak vinegar unfit for use has sometimes been issued. The arrangements for cooking and baking have been wholly inadequate, and though additions are now being completed it will still be impossible to cook for the whole number of prisoners. Raw rations have to be issued to a very large proportion who are entirely unprovided with proper utensils and furnished so limited a supply of fuel they are compelled to dig with their hands in the filthy marsh before mentioned for roots, etc. No soap or clothing has ever been issued.

After inquiring, I am confident that by slight exertions, green corn and other anti-scorbutics could readily be obtained. I herewith hand two reports of Chief Surgeon White, to which I would respectfully call your attention. The present hospital arrangements were only intended for the accommodation of the sick of 10,000 men, and are totally insufficient, both in character and extent, for the present needs; the number of prisoners being now more than three times as great, the number of cases requiring medical treatment is in an increased ratio. It is impossible to state the number of sick, many dying within the stockade, whom the medical officers never see or hear of until their remains are brought out for interment. The rate of death has been steadily increased from 37 4-10 per mil. during the month of March last to 62 7-10 per mil. in July. Of the medical officers, but ten hold commissions; nearly all of the others are detailed from the militia, and have accepted the position to avoid serving in the ranks, and will relinquish their contracts as soon as the present emergency is passed and the militia is disbanded. But little injury would result from this, however, as they are generally very inefficient. Not residing at the post, only visiting it once a day at sick call, they bestow but little attention to those under their care. The small-pox hospital is under the charge of Dr. E. Sheppard, P. A. C. S. More than half the cases in it have terminated fatally. The management and police of the general hospital grounds seem to be as good as the limited means will allow, but there is pressing necessity for at least three times the number of tents and amount of bedding now on hand. The supply of medicines is wholly inadequate, and frequently there is none, owing to the great delays experienced in filling the requisitions.

It is believed no other point in the State offers the same advantages of healthy location and facilities for safe-keeping of the prisoners, that is not more accessible to raids. Nor can I learn that any advantage can be gained by removal to any other part of the State. I am decidedly of opinion that not over 15,000 prisoners should be kept at this point, the running water not being sufficient for more than that number; and because it is impossible for one man to exercise a proper supervision over them, and that all over that number should be sent elsewhere. At my request a survey of the grounds has been made by Colonel Harkie, Fifty-fifth Georgia Regiment, and civil engineer, with a view to drainage. His report is herewith submitted, with a recommendation that his plan be carried out by the engineer department, that being the only one authorized to impress the necessary labor. The necessity for it is urgent. I also recommend that a supply of clothing be furnished for issue to the prisoners, and that soap and anti-scorbutics be regularly issued to them. Attention is specially invited to the report of Chief Surgeon

White, relative to the construction of barracks, and the supply of additional tents for hospital use, and I would respectfully suggest that commissioned officers of the medical staff be sent to replace the contract physicians and doctors detailed from the militia, and that they be required to reside at the post. The transportation of the post is entirely insufficient, and authority is needed by the quartermaster to impress wagons and teams and saw-mills, when not employed by the government or railroads and *kept diligently occupied,* and instructions given to the quartermaster in charge of transportation to afford every facility practicable for transporting lumber and supplies necessary for prisoners. Bake-pans, or sheet-iron for making them, should at once be furnished. The telegraph line should be continued from Fort Valley to Andersonville, thirty-one miles. Attention is respectfully called to the accompanying copy of an order issued by Brigadier-General Gardner, to convert all moneys belonging to prisoners, in the hands of the quartermaster at Richmond, into Confederate currency, and at the prices established by government, without consulting the wishes of the prisoners on the subject. It will be seen by the account book forwarded with this, that some of these claim considerable amounts. The injustice of compelling them to receive our currency against their consent is apparent.

In conclusion I beg leave to recommend that no more prisoners be sent to this already overcrowded prison, and that at the two additional localities selected by General Winder under instructions from General Bragg-the one near Milan, Georgia, the other some point in Alabama south of Cahawba—arrangements be at once made for the excess over 15,000 at this post, and such others as may be captured. Since my inspection was made, over 1,300 prisoners have been added to the number specified in the reports herewith. With a view of relieving to some extent this point as soon as possible, I respectfully suggest that 2,000 of those who most need the change, especially the Belle Isle prisoners, be at once sent to Macon, to occupy the quarters vacated by the Federal officers, that being the greatest number that can be properly accommodated with shelter at that point.

It is absolutely necessary that the regulations for the government of the prisoners be legibly painted on boards and exposed in conspicuous places, say by nailing on the sutler's shop and on the inner face of the stockade at various points. Those established by Captain Wirz, herewith submitted, are approved, with the exception of paragraph 4th, which it is recommended shall be stricken out.

I am, colonel, your obedient servant,

D. T. Chandler,
Assistant Adjutant and Inspector-General.

Colonel R. H. Chilton,
Assistant Adjutant and Inspector-General.

Colonel Chandler made a supplemental report on August 5, 1864, which went forward with the principal report. In it he commends Captain Wirz as an efficient officer, and closes with the following recommendation as to General Winder:

My duty requires me respectfully to recommend a change in the officer in command of the post, Brigadier-General J. H. Winder, and the substitution in his place of some one who unites both energy and good judgment with some feeling of humanity and consideration for the welfare and comfort (so far as is consistent with their safe-keeping) of the vast number of unfortunates placed under his control; some one who at least will not advocate deliberately and in cold blood the propriety of leaving them in their present condition until their number has been sufficiently reduced by death to make the present arrangement suffice for their accommodation; who will not consider it a matter of self-laudation and boasting that he has never been inside of the stockade, a place the horrors of which it is difficult to describe, and which is a disgrace to civilization; the condition of which he might, by the exercise of a little energy and judgment, even with the limited means at his command, have considerably improved.

CONDITIONS AS DESCRIBED BY CONFEDERATES. 69

In obedience to instructions, I shall next proceed to the headquarters of the army of Tennessee, and request that any communications for me be forwarded there to the care of the chief of staff.

I am, colonel, very respectfully, your obedient servant,

D. T. CHANDLER,[1]
Assistant Adjutant and Inspector-General.

COL. R. H. CHILTON,
Assistant Adjutant and Inspector-General,
C. S. A., Richmond, Va.

[Another paper being exhibited to witness, he identified it as another enclosure of the report previously read. It was offered in evidence. The following is a copy:]

Consolidated Return for Confederate States Military Prison at Camp Sumter, Andersonville, Georgia, for the Month of July, 1864.

Prisoners on hand on 1st of July, 1864, in camp	25,005	
in hospital	1,362	26,367
Prisoners received during the month from various places	7,064	
recaptured	12	7,076
Total		33,443
Died during the month	1,742	
Escaped	20	
Sent to other posts	3	1,765
Total on hand		31,678
Of which there are in camp		29,998
Of which there are in hospital		1,680

The number escaped from stockade and not recaptured, from the 1st of April up to date, is 27 men.

Average number of prisoners each day	29,030
Average number of dead each day	56 1/5

H. WIRZ,
Captain Commanding Prison.

There was a consolidated report submitted by Wirz for the week ending July 31, 1864, which shows that 529 died in that week, 96 having died on July 31st. On that day 1,776 were reported in hospital and the deaths daily were 5.4 per cent. At this rate, in 18½ days the entire 1,776 would be in their graves.

I think the reader should learn from the witness and the official papers just what became of this damning record of the tragedy being enacted at Andersonville, and what action, if any, it evoked:[2]

[1]Record, p. 227.
[2]Record, p. 230 et seq.

WITNESS. When these papers were submitted to the department they were forwarded to the secretary of war with indorsement, immediately on their receipt by Colonel Chilton, inspector-general.

[A paper was here shown to the witness.]

That is Colonel Chilton's signature; that is his indorsement made at the time.

[The paper was then offered in evidence. The following is a copy:]

ADJUTANT AND INSPECTOR-GENERAL'S OFFICE, August 18, 1864.

Respectfully submitted to the secretary of war. The condition of the prison at Andersonville is a reproach to us as a nation.

The engineer and ordinance departments were applied to for implements, authorized their issue, and I so telegraphed General Winder.

Colonel Chandler's recommendations are concurred in.

By order of General S. Cooper: R. W. CHILTON, *A. A. & I. G.*

Q. This reads, "respectfully submitted to the secretary of war, etc." Was the report so submitted?

A. Yes, sir.

Q. In whose handwriting is the name "Mr. Wellford" on this paper (Exhibit 23)?

A. It is in the handwriting of Judge Campbell, assistant secretary of war.

Q. Who is Mr. Wellford?

A. He was the attorney for the war department.

Q. [Another paper being shown to witness.] Whose indorsement is that?

A. That is the indorsement of Judge Campbell to the secretary of war.

Q. [The attention of witness being directed to another part of the same paper.] Whose writing is that?

A. Mr. Wellford's writing.

Q. What was Mr. Wellford's duty?

A. To examine the papers, to make an analysis of them, and submit them to the secretary of war with his opinion.

[The paper was then offered in evidence. The following is a copy:]

SECRETARY OF WAR:

These reports show a condition of things at Andersonville which calls very loudly for interposition of the department in order that a change may be made.

J. A. CAMPBELL,
Assistant Secretary of War.

Report of Inspection of military prison at Andersonville, Georgia—(18 enclosures.)[1]

D. T. CHANDLER, *Lieutenant-Colonel, etc.*

This report discloses a condition of things imperatively demanding prompt and decisive measures of relief. The discomforts and sufferings of the prisoners seem almost incredible; and the frightful percentum of mortality, steadily increasing until in the month of July it had attained the extent of 62 and 7-10 per thousand, appears to be only a necessary consequence of the criminal indifference of the authorities charged with their care and custody. No effectual remedy for all the evils seems available so long as the numbers are in such large excess over that for which the prison was designed; but some things can be . . . at once to ameliorate the con . . . Colonel Chandler, whose recommend . . . are approved by Colonel Chilton, suggests the relief of General Winder and substitute . . . some other commander. The state . . . things disclosed in the reports cannot—

[1] This indorsement is given as fully as its mutilated condition made possible.

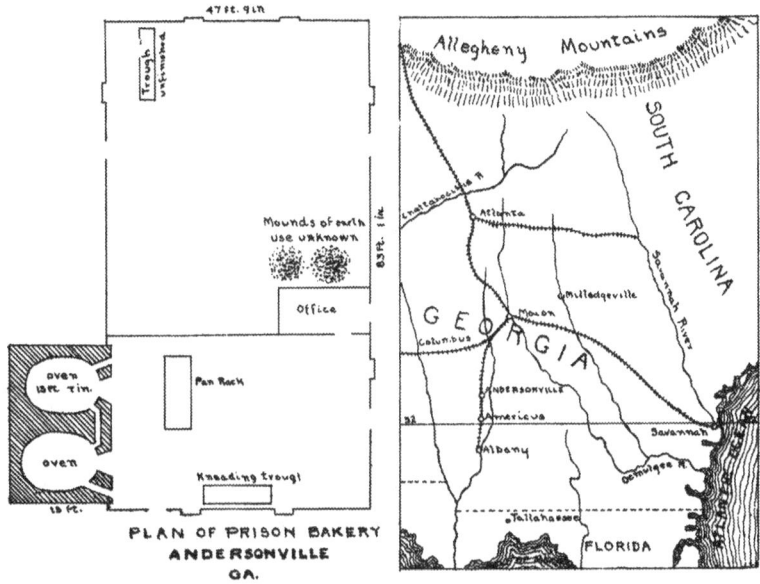

MAP OF GEORGIA.

WITNESS. These indorsements show the report was laid before the secretary of war. I do not know of any action taken on the report by the secretary of war. General Winder was assigned to the command of all the prisoners about two weeks afterwards, I think. He was assigned as commissary-general of prisoners. An analysis of the report was made and extracts were sent to the surgeon-general, the quartermaster-general, the commissary-general; in fact all the bureaus of the war department. I have no evidence that this report went before Jefferson Davis. I have no positive evidence at all that it ever went to Mr. Davis.

Q. Did you learn from a staff officer of Jefferson Davis that this report was laid before him; and if so, in what way did you receive the intelligence?

[Mr. Baker objected to the question on the ground that the charges and specifications embraced no charge against Jefferson Davis. The Court, after deliberation, overruled the objection.]

A. I cannot say that I did. It is mere inference that it was so laid before him, and I would hardly be authorized in stating that inference.

Q. Can you recollect the language made use of by the officer referred to?

MR. BAKER. We object.

THE PRESIDENT. Cannot the witness state the facts on which the inference is founded?

WITNESS. I have a very indistinct recollection of the conversation with the aide of Jefferson Davis.

[Mr. Baker objected to the witness stating the facts on which his inference is founded. The Court, after deliberation, overruled the objection.]

WITNESS. As I said before, I will not hazard a statement of the conversation that I had. My recollection is so indistinct that I am not willing to hazard my own inference. The question of the judge-advocate was doubtless suggested by a remark which I made to him yesterday, though I stated at the time that I would not hazard it as testimony. Consequently cannot state any facts on which I base the inference.

By the COURT:
The conversation was between Colonel Woods and myself in regard to the Andersonville Prison, and during that conversation I obtained the impression that President Davis had some knowledge of it; but I am not willing to hazard that as testimony, for I have a very indistinct recollection. The inference to which I allude was formed at the time of this conversation. I recollect that that was my inference.

By the JUDGE ADVOCATE:
It was subsequent to these reports. I don't recollect how long after; it must have been very shortly afterwards. Colonel Woods was John Taylor Woods, a lieutenant in the navy, and aide to President Davis. I think a paper of this kind, on a subject of this magnitude, would find its way to the president of the so-called Confederate States, in the ordinary course of proceedings. Extracts were made and sent to the quartermaster and commissary departments about the time the report was handed in.

[Exhibit 19 was here shown to witness.]
These words, "Extract made for C. S. General," are in my handwriting.
[Exhibit 18 was here shown to witness.]
These words, "Extracts from within report have been sent to the different bureaus, and directions to General Winder for correction and remedy of the evils, etc.," are in my handwriting.
[A paper was here exhibited to witness.]
The endorsement upon that paper is by the surgeon-general. The paper was an enclosure of Colonel Chandler's report. S. D. Moore was the surgeon-general of the Confederate army.
[The paper was then offered in evidence. The following is a copy:]

CHIEF SURGEON'S OFFICE, August 2, 1864.

COLONEL: I have the honor to submit the following report of the sanitary condition of the Confederate States military prison:

The number of sick on morning report is one thousand three hundred and five (1,305) in hospital, and five thousand and ten (5,010) in quarters.

The total number of deaths from the organization of the prison, (February 24, 1864,) up to date, is 4,585.

The following table exhibits the ratio per one thousand (1,000) of mean strength during the different months:

Month.	Mean strength.	Deaths.	Ratio per 1,000 of mean strength.
March	7,500	283	37.4
April	10,000	576	57.6
May	15,000	708	47.2
June	22,291	1,201	53.87
July	29,030	1,817	62.7

There is nothing in the topography of the country that can be said to influence the health of the prison.

The land is high and well drained, the soil light and sandy, with no marshes or other source of malaria in the vicinity, except the small stream within the stockade. The densely crowded condition of the prisoners, with the innumerable little shelters irregularly arranged, precludes the enforcement of proper police, and prevents free circulation of air.

The lack of barrack accommodation exposes the men to the heat of the sun during the day and to the dew at night, and is a prolific source of disease.

The margins of the stream passing through the stockade are low and boggy, and having been recently drained, have exposed a large surface covered with vegetable mould to the rays of the sun, a condition favorable to the development of malarious diseases. It is the design of the commandant of the prison to cover the surface with dry sand, but the work has been unavoidably retarded.

The absence of proper sinks (and the filthy habits of the men) have caused a deposit of fecal matter over almost the entire surface of this bottom land.

The point of exit of the stream through the walls of the stockade is not sufficiently bold to permit a free passage of ordure.

When the stream is swollen by rains the lower portion of this bottom land is overflowed by a solution of excrement, which, subsiding and the surface exposed to the sun, produces a horrible stench.

Captain Wirz, the commandant of the prison, has doubtless explained to you the difficulties which have prevented these, with other projected improvements, in the way of bathing and other arrangements for cleanliness.

Respectfully submitted:

ISAIAH H. WHITE,
COLONEL CHANDLER. *Chief Surgeon Post.*

[Indorsed:]

Andersonville, Ga., August 4, 1864. Respectfully submitted with inspection report. D. T. CHANDLER, A. A. & I. G.

[Remarks in pencil:] Surgeon Cooney has been ordered to inspect and report on hospital accommodations for prisoners.

Surgeon White was authorized some time since to send his requisitions for supplies direct to the medical purveyors. Not having supplies is his own fault; he should have anticipated the wants of the sick by timely requisitions. All requisitions are approved by the medical directors.

It is impossible to order medical officers in place of the contract physicians. They are not to be had at present. S. D. MOORE, Surgeon-General.

Colonel Chandler testified as a witness at great length and explained in much detail the character of his inspection and from what data his report was made. As we have the result of his investigations in his report, it is not necessary to set out his testimony at length. Among other things, he said:

I have no retraction to make in regard to the condition of the prison at Andersonville, as represented in my report. . . . I noticed that General Winder seemed indifferent to the welfare of the prisoners, indisposed to do anything, or to do as much as I thought he ought to do, to alleviate their sufferings. I remonstrated with him as well as I could, and he used that language which I reported to the department. When I spoke of the great mortality existing among the prisoners, and pointed out to him that the sickly season was coming on and that it must necessarily increase unless something was done for their relief,—the swamp, for instance, drained; proper food furnished them, and in better quantity; and other sanitary suggestions which I made to him—he replied to me that he thought it was better to let half of them die than to take care of the men. I would like to state to the court that before he used this language to me, my assistant, who was with me, Major Hall, had reported to me that he had used similar language to him, made use of similar expressions. I mention this to show the court that I am not mistaken; that my recollection is clear. I told him (Major Hall) I thought it incredible; that he must be mistaken. He told me no; that he had not only said it once, but twice, and, as I have stated, he subsequently made use of the same expression to me.

Colonel Chandler points out some things that might easily have been done: that the prison pen might, with little labor, have been drained to a stream a few hundred yards off on lower ground; that more wood might have been furnished; that the cook-house should have been moved from the stream above the stockade, as also should the garrison camps; that green corn should have been purchased, of which he saw plenty, also cabbages and other vegetables; that a large number of the prisoners should be sent elsewhere, or the stockade much enlarged; that in its crowded condition, six feet square, as he estimated, being available to the man, it was not possible to erect shelter or barracks. Of Wirz he said: "Facts have come to my knowledge in relation to Captain Wirz of which I had no suspicion at the time I recommended him as an efficient officer." Of the prison rules he said:

I cannot speak positively as to my recollection of paragraph 4 of the rules submitted by Captain Wirz, which I did not approve. My impression now is that it had reference to punishing men who attempted to escape. I remember having a conversation with General Winder on this subject and calling his attention to the fact that it was the duty of a soldier to his country to escape if he could, and that it was his duty to keep him, to prevent escape, but not to punish him for doing his duty, and he concurred in that.

We shall see how inhumanly and recklessly Wirz enforced his rule in disregard of this plain injunction.

Speaking of his report, Colonel Chandler testified:

On my return to Richmond in October, I spoke to Colonel Chilton, chief of the bureau, with reference to my report, and he told me that it had not been acted upon. The former secretary of war had been relieved and General Breckinridge appointed secretary. At my instance Colonel Chilton urged the department to take the matter up, for the reason that General Winder had rather decried the correctness of some statements that I had made, and I made a counter report, furnishing evidence of the accuracy of my report. I went myself to Judge Campbell and asked him to take it up, and he promised that he would do so. I do not believe it was ever taken up; that is to say, I do not think it was ever decided. Judge Campbell might have been considering it at the time of the evacuation.

If it seemed incredible to Colonel Chandler that General Winder should recommend so atrocious a policy as that of starving the prisoners to death or killing them off by exposure, in order to relieve the congestion, what must we think of the Richmond authorities who, knowing what was transpiring at Andersonville, not only lifted not a hand to stay the slaughter, but promoted Winder to larger powers in his command over the prisons?

Incredible as it may seem, we yet have the proof that with knowledge of the fact that General Winder proposed to relieve the crowded condition of the prison by a process which meant death to thousands, the Richmond authorities promoted him and increased the scope of his opportunities for further enforcing his diabolical policy.

Further evidence was introduced to show what was done with this report.

TESTIMONY OF R. T. H. KEAN.[1]

I was employed as a private soldier for some eight or ten months in 1861, in the army of Northern Virginia, then commanded by General Johnston. From February, 1862, till April, 1862, I was assistant adjutant-general of the brigade commanded by Brigadier-General George W. Randolph. In April, 1862, when Mr. Randolph became secretary of war, I was appointed chief of the bureau of war at Richmond, and remained so until April of the present year. I know Mr. Seddon's handwriting. The words "Noted, filed, J. A. S," on General Winder's report, are, I believe, his handwriting. I am familiar with the handwriting of the assistant secretary, Judge Campbell. The indorsement signed "J. A. Campbell, A. S. W.," on Colonel Chandler's report, is in his handwriting. The brief is in the handwriting of R. B. Welford, who was a clerk in the war office. He was an intelligent lawyer, and his duties were chiefly of a legal character. When legal questions were to be investigated they were referred to him for evisceration, and bulky documents were frequently referred to him and he digested and briefed them; he would sometimes at the same time express an opinion on the contents. I remember that a report was made by Colonel Chandler with regard to the Andersonville prison. I was on duty there as chief of bureau of war. . . . It was laid before the secretary of war, Mr. Seddon, I think, by the assistant secretary, Judge Campbell. Judge Campbell and myself had some conversation about it. I am not quite certain whether it was before or after it was submitted to the secretary, but I think it was on the day the report was received in the war office from the adjutant-general's office. After I had got through with the press of my own duties I glanced over it hastily, not having time to read it very deliberately, and it was the subject of some conversation between Judge Campbell and myself, the conversation being some comments on matters stated in the report. The conversation on the part of Judge Campbell is very well indexed by this indorsement. I do not remember to have had any conversation with him about the report after it was submitted to the secretary. . . . I do not know that the report was acted upon by the secretary of war. I think I should have known it if it had been. I do not mean to say that I knew all the action the secretary of war took by a great deal, but it would probably have been in my way

[1] Record, P. 399 et seq.

to know it if action had been taken upon it. I am unable to say how long it lay upon his table.... The matter was subsequently called to his attention. About the 1st of February, I think, a day or two before his resignation, after his resignation was sent in and before it was accepted, Lieutenant-Colonel Chandler, the officer who made the report, was in Richmond for the purpose of desiring some action upon it. A controversy had grown up between him and General Winder in reference to the subject-matter of the report, which had resulted in an issue of veracity between them. That, as Colonel Chandler stated to me, and as Colonel Chilton, the inspector-general, adjutant-general's office, stated to me, rendered it very desirable to Colonel Chandler that some disposition should be made of the paper. I do not know that any action was ever taken upon it. None was taken at that time. As I stated, the resignation was pending at the time, and he went out of office on the 7th of February. General Breckinridge came into office on the 8th, and gave very little attention to the papers from that time. The indorsement on this paper was made by me and that is my signature. I was at that time acting chief of the bureau of war. This indorsement was in relation to the same report, and was the same matter in controversy between Colonel Chandler and General Winder. I was in the habit sometimes of presenting such matters to the secretary with a verbal statement; at other times when it was difficult to speak to him, I would put the paper on his table, with a memorandum of this kind, not intended as an official document, but as a memorandum, merely to accompany the paper into his hands and draw attention to it, and then it was of no further use. This is a paper of that character.

[The paper, of which the following is a copy, was submitted in evidence by the judge advocate and is appended to this record:]

Honorable Secretary of War:

These papers involve a painful personal issue between the inspecting officer and General Winder. Colonel Chilton, acting inspector-general, has requested, for this reason, that action be taken on them, so as to relieve one or the other of the parties.   Respectfully,

R. T. H. KEAN,
February 6, 1865.   *Chief of Bureau of War.*

From the way in which Judge Campbell spoke of this report at the time referred to just now, I think it excited special interest on his part. That was the first and only conversation I distinctly remember.

Throughout the history of Andersonville, it will be found that General Winder was the moving spirit of evil. It was he who suggested to Colonel Chandler that it was better to let the prison relieve its congestion by death than by enlargement,—a sentiment in harmony with the policy pursued by his faithful subordinate Wirz. The removal of Winder was urged by Colonel Chandler, but he was not only not removed but was promoted. The testimony of J. B. Jones and Philip Cashmyer will explain Winder's hold at the source of all power in the Confederacy: They testified:

CONDITIONS AS DESCRIBED BY CONFEDERATES.   77

TESTIMONY OF J. B. JONES.[1]

I was a clerk in the rebel war department during the past four years. I received from the mails all the letters addressed to the secretary of war; they were brought to me from the post-office by messengers. It was my duty to open them and read them. I made a brief synopsis of the contents and sent them to the secretary. The report of Colonel Chandler in relation to the Andersonville Prison was a report that should have gone to the adjutant-general, but that document was sent to my office by mistake. I turned it over and looked at it; I did not pretend to read it. I read a few heads of paragraphs, and it was either sent by me immediately to the secretary, or possibly, probably it was sent for by the secretary, because he may have expected it. I did not read lengthy reports; indeed they did not come there. I was in the office after Mr. Seddon took charge of the war department. I remained there till the evacuation, this spring. I cannot be positively certain about his custom with regard to laying business before the president, but he had frequent conferences with the president, almost daily when they were both well. I have seen him going there, taking his papers himself.

TESTIMONY OF PHILIP CASHMYER.[2]

For the last four years I was detective officer under General Winder. I was with General Winder from the time he commenced his duties as provost marshal until he died. I was his special confidential detective. Well, my duties were, any important matters such as detectives have to attend to I attended to for him, such as examining prisoners and making reports upon them and matters of that sort. I was admitted into his family also. The relations existing between him and Mr. Jefferson Davis were very friendly indeed, very confidential. I often heard General Winder say so. I often saw him go there and come from there. I remember when an effort was made by Generals Bragg and Ransom to have him removed, Mr. Davis—President Davis—was his special friend then. When the order relieving General Winder came from the war department he took it and went up to Mr. Davis. The order was relieving him from duty in Richmond. He took it and went over and saw President Davis, and he indorsed on it, as well as I can recollect, "that it was entirely unnecessary and uncalled for." After that General Winder was sent to Goldsboro, North Carolina, to take the field; he was there a week or two, and an order then came for him to go to Andersonville and take command there. His powers were not extended for some months after that. They were then. They made him commissioner-general, commissary-general of prisoners. They called him commissioner-general. I still continued with him till he died in my tent at Florence, South Carolina. As well as I can recollect, the order sending W. S. Winder to Andersonville to lay out the prison came from the war department. General Winder desired to send him, and the war department sanctioned it. I saw the son go with the general down to the war department and come from there.

There are certain indisputable facts established by the Chandler report and its history which can never be explained away nor changed

[1] Record, p. 419.
[2] Record, p. 421.

nor affected by inscriptions upon monuments to Wirz or to any or all others implicated in the crime of Andersonville.

Early in May, as we have seen, the situation was brought home to heads of departments at Richmond; they were warned that the very fate which later befell the unhappy prisoners would surely overtake them unless remedial measures were promptly taken; they were not only not taken, but every movement at Richmond aggravated the existing conditions and made more certain the deadly result. And when Chandler arrived upon the scene his quickened sense of justice and humanity revolted at the picture spread out before him. Soldier-like and manlike, he laid the facts in their true light before his superiors at Richmond. A hundred Union veterans were dying daily in a pen not fit for occupancy by dumb animals. Half-fed with indigestible food, without shelter, many of the sick without medical attendance, and none of the sick with adequate care or attention, this mass of human beings was crowded into an open space, with but six feet square to the man,—a picture of human wretchedness and neglect unparalleled!

The record traces this picture, faithfully drawn, through the hands of high officials, bearing indorsements which left no doubt of the importance of the document. On its face it pointed out the inhuman sentiment uttered by the man Winder, who was the guiding spirit at Andersonville, recommending his removal and the appointment of some one who would not deliberately say that it was better to let the men die and thus relieve the survivors.

On this document as it passed along to the secretary of war and to the President, Adjutant-General Cooper, by his assistant, Colonel Chilton, indorsed his opinion as follows:

The condition of the prison at Andersonville is a reproach to us as a nation. Colonel Chandler's recommendations are concurred in.

Assistant Secretary of War Campbell made this indorsement:

These reports show a condition at Andersonville which calls loudly for interposition of the department in order that a change may be made.

The evidence was that the secretary of war took no step to better conditions at Andersonville. General Winder was promoted to a sphere of enlarged authority over prisons. The papers bear the mark: "Noted. File. J. A. S.," which were known to be the indorsement of Secretary of War Seddon. As late as February 6, 1865, the chief of the bureau of war makes the following indorsement:

Honorable Secretary of War:
These papers involve a painful personal issue between the inspecting officer and General Winder. Colonel Chilton, acting inspector-general, has requested, for this reason, that action be taken on them, so as to relieve one or other of the parties.
February 6, 1865.
R. T. H. KEAN,
Chief of the Bureau of War.

By this time the policy of Winder had been fully executed, and nearly thirteen thousand hapless, helpless defenders of the Union had perished miserably.

In the volumes of the War of the Rebellion some light is thrown upon the action of the rebel war department. The following letter written by Major Hall will be read with interest:

WYTHEVILLE, November 22, 1864.[1]

COLONEL R. H. CHILTON,
 Assistant Adjutant and Inspector-General, Richmond.
 COLONEL: I am surprised to see that Captain Wirz, commanding prison at Andersonville, Ga., in his report of 27th of September, makes me responsible for the following: "Major Hall remarked that it, the prison at Andersonville, was about on par with the Federal prison on Johnson's Island." I did not express any such opinion, nor did I ever use any language, which the utmost ingenuity could pervert into such a misrepresentation of my conviction.
 The report of inspection of the post and prison at Andersonville forwarded by Colonel Chandler, assistant adjutant and inspector-general, 5th of August ultimo, was made by notes taken by both of us on the spot. He consulted with me while preparing it, and as you will perceive, the fair copy is in my handwriting. I fully concur in it. Colonel Chandler's communication to you of this date is also in accordance with my observation of the facts and the statements in which reference is made to me and with my full knowledge and consent. My recollection of General Winder's language, quoted by Colonel Chandler and Captain Wirz, relative to the issue of peas, rice, fuel, etc., is clear and distinct. No vestige remained of the 1,000 posts to which Captain Wirz refers and no allusion to them was made. The only hut or other building in the stockade was a small frame house used exclusively as a sutler's shop. On each of my visits of inspection to the interior of the stockade, I noticed a large number of men digging in the marsh for roots and learning their purpose, called Colonel Chandler's attention to the fact. At my request, Captain Wirz went with me to the stockade on one occasion specially to attend "sick call," as I desired to obtain accurate information in regard to the manner of conducting it.
 I am, colonel, very respectfully, your obedient servant,
W. CARVEL HALL,
Major and Assistant Adjutant-General.

This letter was sent to the war department at Richmond, at its request, for an explanation of the damaging report made by Colonel Chandler in August. It seems that the war department was busying itself to discredit Colonel Chandler's report and him personally, when it ought to have been putting forth every possible effort to relieve the conditions at Andersonville which were pronounced a "disgrace to the Confederacy" by official reports. The carnival of death was allowed

[1] War of Rebellion, vol. VII, series 2, p. 1156.

to proceed unchecked, in pursuance of the policy announced by General Winder to Colonel Chandler, that it was better to let the condition of congestion in the prison be relieved by death than by any of the means recommended.

Major Hall reiterates the fact that he saw many men digging in the swamp for roots for fuel. Remembering what a disgusting and offensive place this swamp had become, saturated as it was with human excrement, we may understand the meaning of the lack of fuel to cook the raw rations issued to the prisoners, when men would resort to such a place for what existed in abundance within sight of the prison and the prisoners begging for the privilege to go after it.

By far the most comprehensive report made of the prison conditions at Andersonville was made by Dr. Joseph Jones, who tells us that while on a visit to Richmond, in August, 1864, "hearing of the unusual mortality among the Federal prisoners at Andersonville, he expressed to the surgeon-general, S. P. Moore, C. S. A., a desire to visit Camp Sumter, with the design of instituting a series of inquiries upon the nature and causes of the prevailing diseases."

It will be seen that he was sent by the surgeon-general, not to devise methods to alleviate any suffering which he might find to exist among the prisoners, but "in order that this great field for pathological investigation may be explored *for the benefit of the medical department of the Confederate army.*" Surgeon-General Moore confessedly knew at that time the conditions there existing and his letter of introduction is dated August 6, 1864. It is true, as will appear, that Dr. Jones's report never reached Surgeon-General Moore, as explained by Dr. Jones, but the facts recorded by him are none the less important or significant in the inquiry we are making, and were known at Richmond through other sources.[1] This report is valuable to the medical profession, but for our present purpose it furnishes indubitable proof that the horrors of Andersonville have not been overdrawn, and it corroborates in many particulars the report of Colonel Chandler; in fact, for graphic and soul-harrowing description of human suffering, it excels anything spoken by witnesses who were themselves victims.

Surgeon Jones testified that he went to Andersonville about September 16, 1864, and that after examining the prison hospital he entered the prison pen. His permit is dated September 17, 1864, and he says that he spent three weeks in his examination of the sick in the hospital

---

[1] But see preliminary report by Dr. Jones, *infra*.

CONDITIONS AS DESCRIBED BY CONFEDERATES. 81

and in the stockade, going so far in his investigations, as he testified, to make "some score of post-mortem examinations." With this introduction to this important evidence, let the record speak.[1]

TESTIMONY OF DR. JOSEPH JONES.

By the JUDGE ADVOCATE:
Q. Where do you reside?
A. In Augusta, Georgia.
Q. Are you a graduate of any medical college?
A. Of the University of Pennsylvania.
Q. How long have you been engaged in the practice of medicine?
A. Eight years.
Q. Has your experience been as a practitioner, or rather as an investigator of medicine as a science?
A. Both.
Q. What position do you hold now?
A. That of medical chemist in the Medical College of Georgia, at Augusta.
Q. How long have you held your position in that college?
A. Since 1858.
Q. How were you employed during the Rebellion?
A. I served six months in the early part of it as a private in the ranks, and the rest of the time in the medical department.
Q. Under the direction of whom?
A. Under the direction of Dr. Moore, surgeon-general.
Q. Did you, while acting under his direction, visit Andersonville, professionally?
A. Yes, sir.
Q. For the purpose of making investigations there?
A. For the purpose of prosecuting investigations ordered by the surgeon-general.
Q. You went there in obedience to a letter of instructions?
A. In obedience to orders which I received.
Q. Did you reduce the results of your investigations to the shape of a report?
A. I was engaged at that work when General Johnston surrendered his army.
[A document being handed to witness.]
Q. Have you examined this extract from your report and compared it with the original?
A. Yes, sir; I have.
Q. Is it accurate?
A. So far as my examination extended, it is accurate. [The document just examined by witness was offered in evidence, and is as follows:]

Observations upon the diseases of the Federal prisoners, confined in Camp Sumter, Andersonville, in Sumter County, Georgia, instituted with a view to illustrate chiefly the origin and causes of hospital gangrene, the relations of continued and malarial fevers and the pathology of camp diarrhœa and dysentery, by Joseph Jones, surgeon P. A. C. S., professor of medical chemistry in the Medical College of Georgia, at Augusta, Georgia.

[1] Record, p. 618 et seq.

THE TRAGEDY OF ANDERSONVILLE.

Hearing of the unusual mortality among the Federal prisoners confined at Andersonville, Georgia, in the month of August, 1864, during a visit to Richmond, Virginia, I expressed to the surgeon-general, S. P. Moore, Confederate States of America, a desire to visit Camp Sumter, with the design of instituting a series of inquiries upon the nature and causes of the prevailing diseases. Smallpox had appeared among the prisoners, and I believed that this would prove an admirable field for the establishment of its characteristic lesions. The condition of Peyer's glands in this disease was considered as worthy of minute investigation. It was believed that a large body of men from the northern portion of the United States, suddenly transported to a warm southern climate, and confined upon a small portion of land, would furnish an excellent field for the investigation of the relations of typhus, typhoid, and malarial fevers.

The surgeon-general Confederate States of America furnished me with the following letter of introduction to the surgeon in charge of the Confederate States military prison at Andersonville, Georgia:

CONFEDERATE STATES OF AMERICA, SURGEON-GENERAL'S OFFICE,
RICHMOND, VIRGINIA, August 6, 1864.

SIR: The field of pathological investigations afforded by the large collection of Federal prisoners in Georgia, is of great extent and importance, and it is believed that results of value to the profession may be obtained by a careful investigation of the effects of disease upon the large body of men subjected to a decided change of climate and the circumstances peculiar to prison life. The surgeon in charge of the hospital for Federal prisoners, together with his assistants, will afford every facility to Surgeon Joseph Jones, in the prosecution of the labors ordered by the surgeon-general. Efficient assistance must be rendered Surgeon Jones by the medical officers, not only in his examinations into the causes and symptoms of the various diseases, but especially in the arduous labors of post mortem examinations. The medical officers will assist in the performance of such post mortems as Surgeon Jones may indicate, in order that this great field for pathological investigation may be explored for the benefit of the medical department of the Confederate army.   S. P. MOORE, *Surgeon-General.*

Surgeon ISAIAH H. WHITE,
In charge of hospital for Federal prisoners, Andersonville, Georgia.

In compliance with this letter of the surgeon-general, Isaiah H. White, chief surgeon of the post, and R. R. Stevenson, surgeon in charge of the prison hospital, afforded the necessary facilities for the prosecution of my investigations among the sick outside of the stockade. After the completion of my labors in the military prison hospital, the following communication was addressed to Brigadier-General John H. Winder, in consequence of the refusal on the part of the commandant of the interior of the Confederate States military prison to admit me within the stockade upon the order of the surgeon-general:

CAMP SUMTER,
ANDERSONVILLE, GEORGIA, September 16, 1864.

GENERAL: I respectfully request the commandant of the post of Andersonville to grant me permission and to furnish the necessary pass to visit the sick and medical officers within the stockade of the Confederate States prison. I desire to institute certain inquiries ordered by the surgeon-general. Surgeon Isaiah H.

White, chief surgeon of the post, and Surgeon R. R. Stevenson in charge of the prison hospital, have afforded me every facility for the prosecution of my labors among the sick outside of the stockade.

Very respectfully, your obedient servant,
JOSEPH JONES, *Surgeon P. S. C. S.*

Brigadier-General JOHN H. WINDER,
  Commandant, Post Andersonville.

In the absence of General Winder from the post, Captain Winder furnished the following order:

CAMP SUMTER,
ANDERSONVILLE, September 17, 1864.

CAPTAIN: You will permit Surgeon Joseph Jones, who has orders from the surgeon-general, to visit the sick within the stockade that are under medical treatment. Surgeon Jones is ordered to make certain investigations which may prove useful to his profession.

By direction of General Winder:

Very respectfully,
W. S. WINDER, *A. A. G.*

Captain H. WIRZ, *Commanding Prison.*

Description of the Confederate States Military Prison Hospital at Andersonville. Number of Prisoners, Physical Condition, Food, Clothing, Habits, Moral Condition, Diseases.

The Confederate military prison at Andersonville, Georgia, consists of a strong stockade, 20 feet in height, enclosing 27 acres. The stockade is formed of strong pine logs, firmly planted in the ground. The main stockade is surrounded by two other similar rows of pine logs, the middle stockade being 16 feet high, and the outer 12 feet. These are intended for offence and defence. If the inner stockade should at any time be forced by the prisoners, the second forms another line of defence; while in case of an attempt to deliver the prisoners by a force operating upon the exterior, the outer line forms an admirable protection to the Confederate troops, and a most formidable obstacle to cavalry or infantry. The four angles of the outer line are strengthened by earthworks upon commanding eminences, from which the cannon, in case of an outbreak among the prisoners, may sweep the entire enclosure; and it was designed to connect these works by a line of rifle-pits, running zig-zag, around the outer stockade; these rifle-pits have never been completed. The ground enclosed by the innermost stockade lies in the form of a parallelogram, the larger diameter running almost due north and south. This space includes the northern and southern opposing sides of two hills, between which a stream of water runs from west to east. The surface soil of these hills is composed chiefly of sand, with varying admixtures of clay and oxide of iron. The clay is sufficiently tenacious to give a considerable degree of consistency to the soil. The internal structure of the hills, as revealed by the deep wells, is similar to that already described. The alternate layers of clay and sand, as well as the oxide of iron, which forms in its various combinations a cement to the sand, allow of extensive tunneling. The prisoners not only constructed numerous dirt huts with balls of clay and sand, taken from the wells which they have excavated all over those hills, but they have also, in some cases, tunneled extensively from these wells. The lower portions of these hills, bordering on the stream, are wet and boggy from the constant oozing of water. The stockade was built originally to accommodate only 10,000 prisoners, and included at first 17 acres. Near the close of the month of June, the area was enlarged by the addition of 10 acres.[1] The ground added was situated on the northern slope of the largest hill.

The following table presents a view of the density of the population of the prison, at different periods:

Table illustrating the mean number of prisoners in the Confederate States military prison at Andersonville, Georgia, from its organization, February 24, 1864, to September, 1864, and the average number of square feet of ground to each prisoner.

	Mean strength of Federal prisoners.	Area of stockade in square feet.	Average number of square feet allowed to each prisoner.
March, 1864	7,500	740,520	98.7
April, 1864	10,000	740,520	74
May, 1864	15,000	740,520	49.3
June, 1864	22,291	740,520	33.2
July, 1864	29,030	1,176,120	40.5
August, 1864	32,899	1,176,120	35.7

Within the circumscribed area of the stockade the Federal prisoners were compelled to perform all the offices of life—cooking, washing, urinating, defecation, exercise, and sleeping. During the month of March the prison was less crowded than at any subsequent time, and then the average space of ground to each prisoner was only 98.7 feet, or less than seven square yards. The Federal prisoners were gathered from all parts of the Confederate States east of the Mississippi, and crowded into the confined space, until in the month of June the average number of square feet of ground to each prisoner was only 33.2, or less than four square yards. *These figures represent the condition of the stockade in a better light even than it really was; for a considerable breadth of land along the stream, flowing from west to east, between the hills, was low and boggy, and was covered with the excrement of the men, and thus rendered wholly uninhabitable, and in fact useless for every purpose except that of defecation.* The pines and other small trees and shrubs, which originally were scattered sparsely over these hills, were in a short time cut down and consumed by the prisoners for firewood, and no shade tree was left in the entire enclosure of the stockade. With their characteristic industry and ingenuity, the Federals constructed for themselves small huts and caves, and attempted to shield themselves from the rain and sun and night damps and dew. But few tents were distributed to the prisoners, and those were in most cases torn and rotten. In the location and arrangement of these tents and huts no order appears to have been followed; in fact, regular streets appeared to be out of the question in so crowded an area; especially, too, as large bodies of prisoners were from time to time added suddenly without any previous preparations. The irregular arrangement of the huts and imperfect shelters was very unfavorable for the maintenance of a proper system of police.

The police and internal economy of the prison was left almost entirely in the hands of the prisoners themselves; the duties of the Confederate soldiers acting as guards being limited to the occupation of the boxes or lookouts ranged around the stockade at regular intervals, and to the manning of the batteries at the angles of the prison. Even judicial matters pertaining to themselves, as the detection

---

[1] Other reports and most of the authorities say the stockade was enlarged about one-third.

CONDITIONS AS DESCRIBED BY CONFEDERATES.

and punishment of such crimes as theft and murder, appear to have been in a great measure abandoned to the prisoners. A striking instance of this occurred in the month of July, when the Federal prisoners within the stockade tried, condemned, and hanged six (6) of their own number, who had been convicted of stealing and of robbing and murdering their fellow-prisoners. They were all hung upon the same day, and thousands of the prisoners gathered around to witness the execution. The Confederate authorities are said not to have interfered with these proceedings. In this collection of men from all parts of the world, every phase of human character was represented; the stronger preyed upon the weaker, and even the sick who were unable to defend themselves were robbed of their scanty supplies of food and clothing. Dark stories were afloat, of men, both sick and well, who were murdered at night, strangled to death by their comrades for scant supplies of clothing or money. I heard a sick and wounded Federal prisoner accuse his nurse, a fellow-prisoner of the United States army, of having stealthily, during his sleep, inoculated his wounded arm with gangrene, that he might destroy his life and fall heir to his clothing.

. . . .

The large number of men confined within the stockade soon, under a defective system of police, and with imperfect arrangements, covered the surface of the low grounds with excrements. The sinks over the lower portions of the stream were imperfect in their plan and structure, and the excrements were in large measure deposited so near the borders of the stream as not to be washed away, or else accumulated upon the low boggy ground. The volume of water was not sufficient to wash away the feces, and they accumulated in such quantities in the lower portion of the stream as to form a mass of liquid excrement. Heavy rains caused the water of the stream to rise, and as the arrangements for the passage of the increased amounts of water out of the stockade were insufficient, the liquid feces overflowed the low grounds and covered them several inches, after the subsidence of the waters. The action of the sun upon this putrefying mass of excrements and fragments of bread and meat and bones excited most rapid fermentation and developed a horrible stench. Improvements were projected for the removal of the filth and for the prevention of its accumulation, but they were only partially and imperfectly carried out. As the forces of the prisoners were reduced by confinement, want of exercise, improper diet, and by scurvy, diarrhœa, and dysentery, they were unable to evacuate their bowels within the stream or along its banks, and the excrements were deposited at the very doors of their tents. The vast majority appeared to lose all repulsion to filth, and both sick and well disregarded all the laws of hygiene and personal cleanliness. The accommodations for the sick were imperfect and insufficient. From the organization of the prison, February 24, 1864, to May 22nd, the sick were treated within the stockade. In the crowded condition of the stockade, and with the tents and huts clustered thickly around the hospital, it was impossible to secure proper ventilation or to maintain the necessary police. The Federal prisoners also made frequent forays upon the hospital stores and carried off the food and clothing of the sick. The hospital was, on the 22nd of May, removed to its present site without the stockade, and five acres of ground covered with oaks and pines appropriated to the use of the sick.

The supply of medical officers has been insufficient from the foundation of the prison.

The nurses and attendants upon the sick have been most generally Federal prisoners, who in too many cases appear to have been devoid of moral principle, and who not only neglected their duties, but were also engaged in extensive robbing of the sick.

From the want of proper police and hygienic regulations alone it is not wonderful that from February 24 to September 21, 1864, 9,479 deaths, nearly one-third the entire number of prisoners, should have been recorded. I found the stockade and hospital in the following condition during my pathological investigations, instituted in the month of September, 1864:

At the time of my visit to Andersonville a large number of Federal prisoners had been removed to Millen, Savannah, Charleston, and other parts of the Confederacy, in anticipation of an advance of General Sherman's forces from Atlanta, with the design of liberating their captive brethren; however, about 15,000 prisoners remained confined within the limits of the stockade and Confederate States military prison hospital.

In the stockade, with the exception of the damp lowlands bordering the small stream, the surface was covered with huts, and small ragged tents and parts of blankets and fragments of oilcloth, coats, and blankets stretched upon sticks. The tents and huts were not arranged according to any order, and there was in most parts of the enclosure scarcely room for two men to walk abreast between the tents and huts. I observed men urinating and evacuating their bowels at the very tent doors and around the little vessels in which they were cooking their food. Small pits, not more than a foot or two deep, nearly filled with soft offensive feces, were everywhere seen, and emitted under the hot sun a strong and disgusting odor. Masses of corn-bread, bones, old rags, and filth of every description were scattered around or accumulated in large piles.

If one might judge from the large pieces of corn-bread scattered about in every direction on the ground, the prisoners were either very lavishly supplied with this article of diet, or else this kind of food was not relished by them.

Each day the dead from the stockade were carried out by their fellow-prisoners and deposited upon the ground under a bush arbor, just outside the southwestern gate. From thence they were carried in carts to the burying ground, one-quarter of a mile northwest of the prison. The dead were buried without coffins, side by side, in trenches four feet deep.

The low grounds bordering the stream were covered with human excrements and filth of all kinds, which in many places appeared to be alive with working maggots. An indescribable sickening stench arose from these fermenting masses of human dung and filth.

There were nearly 5,000 seriously ill Federals in the stockade and Confederate States military prison hospital, and the deaths exceeded one hundred per day, and large numbers of the prisoners who were walking about, and who had not been entered upon the sick reports, were suffering from severe and incurable diarrhœa, dysentery, and scurvy. The sick were attended almost entirely by their fellow-prisoners, appointed as nurses, and as they received but little attention, they were compelled to exert themselves at all times to attend to the calls of nature, and hence they retained the power of moving about to within a comparatively short period of the close of life. Owing to the slow progress of the diseases most prevalent, diarrhœa, and chronic dysentery, the corpses were as a general rule emaciated.

I visited two thousand sick within the stockade, lying under some long sheds which had been built at the northern portion for themselves. At this time only one medical officer was in attendance, whereas at least 20 medical officers should have been employed.

I found no record of the sick in the stockade previous to September 14, 1864. It appears that previous to this date no record was preserved of the diseases treated within the stockade; and the following includes all the medical statistics which I was able to collect within the prison walls proper:

Morning reports of Acting Assistant Surgeon F. J. Wells, in charge of Federal sick and wounded in stockade.

Date.	Remaining last report.	Taken sick.	Total sick.	Returned to duty.	Discharged.	Sent to general hospital.	Died.	Remaining.
1864.								
September 14......	936	64	1,000	....	....	76	36	888
September 15......	888	515	1,403	....	....	114	58	1,231
September 16......	1,231	13	1,244	....	....	16	70	1,159
September 17......	1,159	88	1,247	....	....	109	36	1,102
September 18......	1,102	906	2,008	....	....	3	50	1,955
September 19......	1,955	....	1,955	....	....	32	42	1,881
September 20......	1,881	....	1,881	....	....	63	44	1,774

If this table be compared with the following one, from the Confederate States military prison hospital, during the same period, we will see that the number of deaths was as great in the stockade as in the hospital; notwithstanding the disparity in the number of medical officers of attendance upon the sick in both instances, being 346 in the former and 344 in the latter.

Consolidated morning reports of Surgeon R. R. Stevenson, in charge of Confederate States military prison hospital, Andersonville, September 14-20, 1864.

Date.	Remaining in hospital at last report.	Received from stockade.	Received from attendants.	Total in hospital.	Returned to stockade.	Deserted.	Detailed from hospital.	Died.	Remaining in hospital.	Medical officers on duty in hospital—surgeons.	Medical officers—assistant surgeons.	Act'g assistant surgeons.	Total medical officers on duty in hospital.
1864.													
Sept. 14...	1,609	76	...	1,685	1	...	49	37	1,598	3	11	8	22
Sept. 15...	1,598	114	...	1,712	14	...	...	47	1,651	3	11	8	22
Sept. 16...	1,651	16	...	1,667	1	...	...	49	1,617	3	11	8	22
Sept. 17...	1,617	109	4	1,730	...	...	...	40	1,690	3	11	8	22
Sept. 18...	1,690	3	...	1,693	...	...	...	58	1,635	3	11	9	23
Sept. 19...	1,635	32	1	1,668	...	2	...	55	1,611	3	11	9	23
Sept. 20...	1,611	63	2	1,676	...	...	...	48	1,628	3	11	9	23

Died in stockade, from its organization, February 24, 1864, to September 21, 3,254
Died in hospital during same time 6,225

Total deaths in hospital and stockade 9,479

Scurvy, diarrhœa, dysentery, and hospital gangrene were the prevailing diseases. I was surprised to find but few cases of malarial fever, and no well-marked cases either of typhus or typhoid fever. The absence of the different forms of malarial fever may be accounted for in the supposition that the artificial atmosphere of the stockade, crowded densely with human beings and loaded with animal exhalations, was unfavorable to the existence and action of the malarial poison. The absence of typhoid and typhus fevers amongst all the causes which are supposed to generate these diseases, appeared to be due to the fact that the great majority of these prisoners had been in captivity in Virginia, at Belle Island, and in other parts of the Confederacy for months, and even as long as two years, and during this time they had been subjected to the same bad influences, and those who had not had these fevers before either had them during their confinement in Confederate prisons or else their systems, from long exposure, were proof against their action.

The effects of scurvy were manifested on every hand, and in all its various stages, from the muddy, pale complexion, pale gums, feeble, languid muscular motions, lowness of spirits, and fœtid breath, to the dusky, dirty, leaden complexion, swollen features, spongy, purple, livid, fungoid, bleeding gums, loose teeth, œdematous limbs covered with livid vibices, and petechiæ, spasmodically flexed, painful and hardened extremities, spontaneous hemorrhages from mucous canals, and large ill-conditioned spreading ulcers covered with a dark purplish fungus growth. I observed that in some of the cases of scurvy the parotid glands were greatly swollen, and in some instances to such an extent as to preclude entirely the power to articulate. In several cases of dropsy of the abdomen and lower extremities, supervening upon scurvy, the patients affirmed that previously to the appearance of the dropsy they had suffered with profuse and obstinate diarrhœa, and that when this was checked by a change of diet, from Indian corn bread baked with the husk, to boiled rice, the dropsy appeared. The severe pains and livid patches were frequently associated with swellings in various parts, and especially in the lower extremities, accompanied with stiffness and contractions of the knee joints and ankles, and often with a brawny feel of the parts, as if lymph had been effused between the integuments and aponeurosis, preventing the motion of the skin over the swollen parts. Many of the prisoners believed that the scurvy was contagious, and I saw men guarding their wells and springs, fearing lest some man suffering with the scurvy might use the water and thus poison them. I observed also numerous cases of hospital gangrene and of spreading scorbutic ulcers, which had supervened upon slight injuries. The scorbutic ulcers presented a dark, purple fungoid, elevated surface, with livid swollen edges, and exuded a thin, fœtid, sanious fluid instead of pus. Many ulcers which originated from the scorbutic condition of the system appeared to become truly gangrenous, assuming all the characteristics of hospital gangrene. From the crowded condition, filthy habits, bad diet, and dejected, depressed condition of the prisoners, their systems had become so disordered that the smallest abrasion of the skin from the rubbing of a shoe, or from the effects of the sun, or from the prick of a splinter, or from scratching, or a mosquito bite, in some cases, took on rapid and frightful ulceration and gangrene. The long use of salt meat, ofttimes imperfectly cured, as well as the almost total deprivation of vegetables and fruit, appeared to be the chief causes of the scurvy. I carefully examined the bakery and the bread furnished the prisoners, and found that they were supplied almost entirely with corn bread from which the husk had not been separated. This husk acted as an irritant to the alimentary canal, without adding any nutriment to the bread. As far as my examination extended, no fault could be found with the mode in which the bread was baked; the difficulty lay in the failure to separate the husk from the cornmeal. I strongly urged the preparation of large quantities of soup made from the cow and calves heads with the brains and tongues, to which a liberal supply of sweet potatoes and vegetables might have been advantageously added. The materials existed in abundance for the preparation of such soup in large quantities with but little additional expense. Such aliment would have been not only highly nutritious, but it would also have acted as an efficient remedial agent for the removal of the scorbutic condition. The sick within the stockade lay under several long sheds which were originally built for barracks. These sheds covered two floors, which were open on all sides. The sick lay upon the bare boards, or upon such ragged blankets as they possessed, without, as far as I observed, any bedding or even straw. Pits for the reception of feces were dug within a few feet of the lower floor, and they were almost never unoccupied by those suffering with diarrhœa. The haggard, distressed countenances of these miserable, complaining, dejected, living skeletons, crying for medical aid and food, and cursing their government for its refusal to exchange prisoners, and the ghastly corpses, with their glazed eyeballs staring up into vacant space, with the flies swarming down their open and grinning mouths, and over their ragged clothes, infested with numerous lice, as they lay amongst the sick and dying, formed a picture of helpless, hopeless misery which it would be impossible to portray by words or by the brush.

CONDITIONS AT THE HOSPITAL.

Some hundred or more of the prisoners had been released from confinement in the stockade on parole, and filled various offices as clerks, druggists, and carpenters, etc., in the various departments. These men were well clothed, and presented a stout and healthy appearance, and as a general rule they presented a much more robust and healthy appearance than the Confederate troops guarding the prisoners.

The entire grounds are surrounded by a frail board fence, and are strictly guarded by Confederate soldiers, and no prisoner except the paroled attendants is allowed to leave the grounds except by a special permit from the commandant of the interior of the prison.

The patients and attendants, near two thousand in number, are crowded into this confined space and are but poorly supplied with old and ragged tents. Large numbers of them are without any bunks in the tents, and lie upon the ground, ofttimes without even a blanket. No beds or straw appeared to have been furnished. The tents extend to within a few yards of the small stream, the eastern portion of which, as we have before said, is used as a privy and is loaded with excrements; and I observed a large pile of corn bread, bones, and filth of all kinds, thirty feet in diameter and several feet in height, swarming with myriads of flies, in a vacant space near the pots used for cooking. Millions of flies swarmed over everything and covered the faces of the sleeping patients, and crawled down their open mouths, and deposited their maggots in the gangrenous wounds of the living, and in the mouths of the dead. Mosquitoes in great numbers also infested the tents, and many of the patients were so stung by these pestiferous insects, that they resembled those suffering with a slight attack of measles.

The police and hygiene of the hospital was defective in the extreme; the attendants, who appeared in almost every instance to have been selected from the prisoners, seemed to have in many cases but little interest in the welfare of their fellow-captives. The accusation was made that the nurses in many cases robbed the sick of their clothing, money, and rations, and carried on a clandestine trade with the paroled prisoners and Confederate guards without the hospital enclosure, in the clothing and effects of the sick, dying, and dead Federals. They certainly appeared to neglect the comfort and cleanliness of the sick entrusted to their care in a most shameful manner, even after making due allowances for the difficulties of the situation. Many of the sick were literally encrusted with dirt and filth and covered with vermin. When a gangrenous wound needed washing, the limb was thrust out a little from the blanket, or board, or rags upon which the patient was lying, and water poured over it, and all the putrescent matter allowed to soak into the ground floor of the tent. The supply of rags for dressing wounds was said to be very scant, and I saw the most filthy rags which had been applied several times, and imperfectly washed, used in dressing recent wounds. Where hospital gangrene was prevailing, it was impossible for any wound to escape contagion under these circumstances. The results of the treatment of wounds in the hospital were of the most unsatisfactory character, from this neglect of cleanliness, in the dressings and wounds themselves, as well as from various other causes which will be more fully considered. I saw several gangrenous wounds filled with maggots. I have frequently seen neglected wounds amongst the Confederate soldiers similarly affected; and as far as my experience extends, these worms destroy only the dead tissues and do not injure specially the well parts. I have even heard surgeons affirm that a gangrenous wound which had been thoroughly cleansed by maggots, healed more rapidly than if it had been left to itself. This want of cleanliness on the part of the nurses appeared to be the result of carelessness and inattention, rather than of malignant design, and the whole trouble can be traced to the want of proper police and sanitary regulations, and to the absence of intelligent organization and division of labor. The abuses were in a large measure due to the almost total absence of system, government, and rigid but wholesome sanitary regulations. In extenuation of these abuses it was alleged by the medical officers that the Confederate troops were barely sufficient to guard the prisoners, and that it was impossible to obtain any number of experienced nurses from the Confederate forces. In fact the guard appeared to be too small, even for the regulation of the internal hygiene and police of the hospital.

The manner of disposing of the dead was also calculated to depress the already desponding spirits of these men, many of whom have been confined for months, and even for nearly two years, in Richmond and other places, and whose strength has been wasted by bad air, bad food, and neglect of personal cleanliness. The dead-house is merely a frame covered with old tent-cloth and a few bushes, situated in the southwestern corner of the hospital grounds. When a patient dies, he is simply laid in the narrow street in front of his tent, until he is removed by Federal negroes detailed to carry off the dead; if a patient dies during the night, he lies there until the morning, and during the day even the dead were frequently allowed to remain for hours in these walks. In the dead-house the corpses lie upon the bare ground, and were in most cases covered with filth and vermin.

At short intervals in the lanes between the tents, wooden boxes are arranged for the reception of the excrements of those patients who are unable to walk to the sinks along the banks of the stream; as a general rule these are not emptied until they are filled with excrements. At all times the emaciated men, worn down to skeletons by diarrhœa and dysentery, are seen evacuating their bowels into these filthy receptacles, which from their wooden structure can never be kept properly cleansed. Notwithstanding the objectionable arrangements, these surgeons, from the limited resources of the purveying department of the Confederate States, appear to be unable to devise any better mode of collecting and removing the excrements of the sick. Metallic or earthenware vessels would be far preferable, but it is said that they cannot be obtained at the present time.

Time and again I saw patients, who apparently had ample strength to walk to the sinks, evacuate their bladders within the tent doors. The whole soil appeared to be saturated with urine and filth of all kinds and emitted a most disgusting odor.

The cooking arrangements are of the most defective character. Five large iron pots similar to those used for boiling sugar-cane, appeared to be the only cooking utensils furnished by the hospital for the cooking of near two thousand men; and the patients were dependent in great measure upon their own miserable utensils. They were allowed to cook in the tent doors and in the lanes, and this was another source of filth, and another favorable condition for the generation and multiplication of flies and other vermin.

The air of the tents was foul and disagreeable in the extreme, and in fact the entire grounds emitted a most nauseous and disgusting smell. I entered nearly all the tents and carefully examined the cases of interest, and especially the cases of gangrene, upon numerous occasions, during the prosecution of my pathological inquiries at Andersonville, and therefore enjoyed every opportunity to judge correctly of the hygiene and police of the hospital.

There appeared to be almost absolute indifference and neglect on the part of the patients of personal cleanliness; their persons and clothing in most instances, and especially of those suffering with gangrene and scorbutic ulcers, were filthy in the extreme and covered with vermin. It was too often the case that patients were received from the stockade in a most deplorable condition. I have seen men brought in from the stockade in a dying condition, begrimed from head to foot with their own excrements, and so black from smoke and filth that they resembled negroes rather than white men. That this description of the stockade and hospital has not been overdrawn, will appear from the reports of the surgeons in charge, appended to this report.

I have drawn up for the consideration of the surgeon-general and the use of the medical department of the Confederate States the following tables, giving a consolidated view of the diseases of the Federal prisoners confined at Andersonville and also of the Confederate forces acting as a guard around the stockade and hospital.

[These tables are more especially of interest to medical men and are omitted.]

The following table covers the period from March, 1864, to August, inclusive:

CONDITIONS AS DESCRIBED BY CONFEDERATES.

GENERAL SUMMARY.

1864.	Remaining last report.			Taken sick during month.	Aggregate.	Returned to duty, (stockade).	Died.	Remaining.			Mean strength.		Number treated.	Deaths.	Ratio per 1,000 men.	
	Sick.	Convalescent.	Total.					Sick.	Convalescent.	Total.	Enlisted men.	Total.			Cases.	Deaths.
March	....	....	....	1,530	....	353	283	500	136	636	7,500	7,560	1,530	283	204	37
April	500	136	636	2,425	3,061	1,463	576	468	554	1,022	10,000	10,000	3,061	576	306	57
May	468	554	1,022	8,583	9,605	6,276	708	1,150	1,471	2,621	15,000	15,000	9,605	708	640	47
June	1,150	1,471	2,621	7,969	10,590	5,311	1,201	....	....	4,078	22,291	22,291	10,590	1,201	475	53

1864.	Remaining last report.		Taken sick or wounded during the month.	Supervening disease.	Aggregate.	Returned to duty.	Died.	Remaining.			Mean strength.		Average number on sick report daily.		
	Sick.	Total.						Sick.	Wounded.	Total.	Enlisted men.	Total.	In hospital.	In quarters.	Total.
July	4,078	4,078	10,624	210	14,912	6,548	1,742	6,386	26	6,412	29,030	29,030	1,237	4,574	5,311
August	6,386	6,412	10,915	431	17,758	9,443	2,992	4,836	56	4,892	32,899	32,899	1,934	3,933	5,868

We will examine first the consolidated report of the sick and wounded Federal prisoners. During six months, from the 1st of March to the 31st of August, 42,686 cases of diseases and wounds were reported. No classified record of the sick in the stockade was kept after the establishment of the hospital without the prison. This fact, in conjunction with those already presented relating to the insufficiency of medical officers and the extreme illness and even death of many prisoners in the tents in the stockade, without any medical attention or record beyond the bare number of the dead, demonstrates that these figures, large as they appear to be, are far below the truth.

During this period of six months no less than 565 deaths are recorded under the head of *morbi vanie*. In other words, those men died without having received sufficient medical attention for the determination of even the name of the disease causing death.

During the month of August, 53 cases and 53 deaths are recorded as due to marasmus. Surely this large number of deaths must have been due to some other morbid state than slow wasting. If they were due to improper and insufficient food, they should have been classed accordingly, and if to diarrhœa or dysentery or scurvy, the classification should in like manner have been explicit.

We observe a progressive increase of the rate of mortality, from 3.11 per cent in March to 9.09 per cent of mean strength, sick and well, in August. The ratio of mortality continued to increase during September, for notwithstanding the removal of one-half of the entire number of prisoners during the early portion of the month, one thousand seven hundred and sixty-seven (1,767) deaths are registered from September 1st to 21st, and the largest number of deaths upon any one day occurred during this month, on the 16th, viz: 119.

The entire number of Federal prisoners confined at Andersonville was about 40,611; and during the period of near seven months, from February 24th to September 21st, nine thousand four hundred and seventy-nine (9,479) deaths were recorded; that is, during this period near one-fourth, or, more exactly, one in 4.2, or 23.3 per cent, terminated fatally. This increase of mortality was due in great measure to the accumulation of the sources of disease, as the increase of excrements and filth of all kinds, and the concentration of noxious effluvia, and also to the progressive effects of salt diet, crowding, and the hot climate.

CONCLUSIONS.

1st. The great mortality among the Federal prisoners confined in the military prison at Andersonville was not referable to climatic causes, or to the nature of the soil and waters.

2nd. The chief causes of death were scurvy and its results, and bowel affections—chronic and acute diarrhœa and dysentery. The bowel affections appear to have been due to the diet, the habits of the patients, the depressed, dejected state of the nervous system and moral and intellectual powers, and to the effluvia arising from the decomposing animal and vegetable filth. The effects of salt meat, and an unvarying diet of corn-meal, with but few vegetables, and imperfect supplies of vinegar and syrup, were manifested in the great prevalence of scurvy. This disease, without doubt, was also influenced to an important extent in its origin and course by the foul animal emanations.

3rd. From the sameness of the food and form, the action of the poisonous gases in the densely crowded and filthy stockade and hospital, the blood was altered in its constitution, even before the manifestation of actual disease. In both the well and the sick the red corpuscles were diminished; and in all diseases uncomplicated with inflammation, the fibrous element was deficient. In cases of ulceration of the mucous membrane of the intestinal canal, the fibrous element of the blood was increased; while in simple diarrhœa, uncomplicated with ulceration, it was either diminished or else remained stationary. Heart clots were very common if not universally present in the cases of ulceration of the intestinal mucous membrane, while in the uncomplicated cases of diarrhœa and scurvy, the blood was fluid and did not coagulate readily, and the heart clots and fibrous concretions were almost universally absent. From the watery condition of the blood, there resulted various serous effusions into the pericardium, ventricles of the brain, and into the abdomen. In almost all the cases which I examined after death, even the most emaciated, there was more or less serous effusion into the abdominal cavity. In cases of hospital gangrene of the extremities, and in cases of gangrene of the intestines, heart clots and fibrous coagula were universally present. The presence of those clots in the cases of hospital gangrene, while they were absent in the cases in which there were no inflammatory symptoms, sustains the conclusion that hospital gangrene is a species of inflammation, imperfect and irregular though it may be in its progress, in which the fibrous element and coagulation of the blood are increased, even in those who are suffering from such condition of the blood, and from such diseases as are naturally accompanied with a decrease in the fibrous constituent.

4th. The fact that hospital gangrene appeared in the stockade first and originated spontaneously without any previous contagion, and occurred sporadically all over the stockade and prison hospital, was proof positive that this disease will arise whenever the conditions of crowding, filth, foul air, and bad diet are present. The exhalations from the hospital and stockade appeared to exert their effects to a considerable distance outside of these localities. The origin of hospital gangrene among these prisoners appeared clearly to depend in great measure upon the state of the general system induced by diet, and various external noxious influences. The rapidity of the appearance and action of the gangrene depended upon the powers and state of the constitution, as well as upon the intensity of the poison in the atmosphere, or upon the direct application of poisonous matter to the wounded surface. This was further illustrated by the important fact that hospital gangrene, or a disease resembling it in all essential respects, attacked the intestinal canal of patients laboring under ulceration of the bowels, although there were no local manifestations of gangrene upon the surface of the body. This mode of termination in cases of dysentery was quite common in the foul atmosphere of the Confederate States military hospital, in the depressed, depraved condition of the system of these Federal prisoners.

5th. A scorbutic condition of the system appeared to favor the origin of foul ulcers, which frequently took on true hospital gangrene. Scurvy and hospital gangrene frequently existed in the same individual. In such cases, vegetable diet, with vegetable acids, would remove the scorbutic condition without curing the hospital gangrene. From the results of the existing war for the establishment of the independence of the Confederate States, as well as from the published observations of Dr. Trotter, Sir Gilbert Blane, and others of the English navy and army, it is evident that the scorbutic condition of the system, especially in crowded ships and camps, is most favorable to the origin and spread of foul ulcers and hospital gangrene. As in the present case of Andersonville, so also in past times when medical hygiene was almost entirely neglected, those two diseases were almost universally associated in crowded ships. In many cases it was very difficult to decide at first whether the ulcer was a simple result of scurvy or of the action of the prison or hospital gangrene, for there was great similarity in the appearance of the ulcers in the two diseases. So commonly have those two diseases been combined in their origin and action, that the description of scorbutic ulcers, by many authors, evidently includes also many of the prominent characteristics of hospital gangrene. This will be rendered evident by an examination of the observations of Dr. Lind and Sir Gilbert Blane upon scorbutic ulcers.

6th. Gangrenous spots followed by rapid destruction of tissue appeared in some cases where there had been no known wound. Without such well-established facts, it might be assumed that the disease was propagated from one patient to another. In such a filthy and crowded hospital as that of the Confederate States military prison at Andersonville, it was impossible to isolate the wounded from the sources of actual contact of the gangrenous matter. The flies swarming over the wounds and over the filth of every kind, the filthy, imperfectly washed and scanty supplies of rags, and the limited supply of washing utensils, the same wash-bowl serving for scores of patients, were sources of such constant circulation of the gangrenous matter that the disease might rapidly spread from a single gangrenous wound. The fact already stated, that a form of moist gangrene, resembling hospital gangrene, was quite common in this foul atmosphere, in cases of dysentery, both with and without the existence of the disease upon the entire surface, not only demonstrates the dependence of the disease upon the state of the constitution, but proves in the clearest manner that neither the contact of the poisonous matter of gangrene, nor the direct action of the poisonous atmosphere upon the ulcerated surface, is necessary to the development of the disease.

7th. In this foul atmosphere amputation did not arrest hospital gangrene; the disease almost invariably returned. Almost every amputation was followed finally by death, either from the effects of gangrene or from the prevailing diarrhœa and dysentery. Nitric acid and escharotics, generally, in this crowded atmosphere, loaded with noxious effluvia, exerted only temporary effects; after their application to the diseased surfaces, the gangrene would frequently return with redoubled energy; and even after the gangrene had been completely removed by local and constitutional treatment, it would frequently return and destroy the patient. As far as my observation extended, very few of the cases of amputation for gangrene recovered. The progress of these cases was frequently very deceptive. I have observed after death the most extensive disorganization of the structures of the stump, when during life there was but little swelling of the part, and the patient was apparently doing well. I endeavored to impress upon the medical officers the view that in this disease treatment was almost useless, without an abundant supply of pure fresh air, nutritious food, and tonics and stimulants.

CONDITIONS AS DESCRIBED BY CONFEDERATES. 97

Such changes, however, as would allow of the isolation of the cases of hospital gangrene appeared to be out of the power of the medical officers.

8th. The gangrenous mass was without true pus, and consisted chiefly of broken-down, disorganized structures. The reaction of the gangrenous matter in certain stages was alkaline.

9th. The best, and in truth the only, means of protecting the large armies and navies, as well as prisoners, from the ravages of hospital gangrene, is to furnish liberal supplies of well-cured meat, together with fresh beef and vegetables, and to enforce a rigid system of hygiene.

10th. Finally, this gigantic mass of human misery calls loudly for relief, not only for the sake of suffering humanity, but also on account of our own brave soldiers now captives in the hands of the Federal government. Strict justice to the gallant men of the Confederate armies, who have been or who may be so unfortunate as to be compelled to surrender in battle, demands that the Confederate government should adopt that course which will best secure their health and comfort in captivity; or at least leave their enemies without a shadow of an excuse for any violation of the rules of civilized warfare in the treatment of prisoners.

Q. You have made some estimates based upon what you term the "mean strength"; will you explain to the court what you mean by that?
A. The mean strength for a month in an army is generally taken by choosing three points in the month, the first, the middle, and the latter part of it, adding them together and dividing the total number.
Q. The total of the three added?
A. Yes, sir. I do not know exactly how it was done at Andersonville. This was taken from the records there entitled "mean strength."
Q. Continue your explanation of how the estimate was made, and then you can make any qualifications with regard to it. You say you divided the number of prisoners at the first of the month, the middle of the month, and the last of the month by three; then what did you do?
A. That would give you the mean strength, the average number present during the month—that is in armies.
Q. That cannot always be accurate, can it?
A. No, sir; it is not accurate in armies. I do not know exactly what course they adopted with the prisoners, but presume it was done in the same way. Two or three thousand might have been received and two or three thousand sent away, and in that way the whole number during the month would be pretty much unchanged. In the Confederate service it was not a truly accurate number.
Q. You used the term "Confederate States military hospital"; does that refer always to the Federal prisoners' hospital?
A. There was a Confederate States military hospital there, that went by the name of Sumter hospital.
Q. In the returns you include only hospitals containing Federal prisoners?
A. Yes; I think I always used the term "Confederate States military prison hospitals."
Q. When did you forward your report or complete it?

A. I will state to the court that I was engaged in the preparation of that report in the month of September, 1864. I went from Andersonville to the hospitals connected with the Army of Tennessee, and labored there until November; I then returned to Augusta, just about the time that General Sherman commenced his march from Atlanta. I was then cut off from the reception of answers to numerous inquiries I had made of officers at Andersonville and with the Army of Tennessee, and set about preparing the report for the surgeon-general. I had just completed the report which I placed in the hands of the judge advocate under orders from the government when the Confederacy went to pieces. That report never was delivered to the surgeon-general, and I was unaware that any one knew of its existence at all until I received orders from the United States government to bring it and deliver it to this court in testimony. I make this statement to relieve myself of the charge of turning state's evidence, as it were, against those with whom I was formerly associated; it was done in obedience to an order from the government.

Q. Have your sympathies been with the Rebellion during the war?

A. Entirely so.

Q. Then your report was made out in the interest of the Confederate government.

A. In the interest of the Confederate government; for the use of the medical department; *in the view that no eye would ever see it but that of the surgeon-general.* I beg leave to make a statement to the court. That portion of my report which has been read is only a small part of the report. The original report contains the excuses which were given by the officers present at Andersonville, which I thought it right to embody with my labors; it also contains documents forwarded to Richmond by Dr. White and Dr. Stevenson and others in charge of the hospitals. Those documents contained important facts as to the labors of the medical department and their efforts to better the condition of things.

Q. Are your conclusions correctly stated in this extract?

A. Part of my conclusions are stated; not the whole. A portion of my conclusions and also my recommendations are not stated.

Q. Touching the subject of exchange?

A. Yes, sir; the general difficulties environing the prisoners and their officers.

Q. But the condition of things at Andersonville you have correctly described in the report of which this is an extract?

A. I endeavored to do so in that report so far as my means of investigation would allow. I would also state that the results of my examination of gangrene, scurvy, and other diseases have been omitted from the report. They were very extended. I was there for three weeks and *made some score of post-mortem examinations.* I endeavored, in this report to the surgeon-general, to condense the results of all those labors; in fact that was the end and aim of the investigation.

The following preliminary report made by Dr. Jones, found in the records of the War of the Rebellion, is important as showing that he had added his testimony to that of Colonel Chandler as to existing conditions at Andersonville. This report follows:

MACON, GA., October 19, 1864.[1]

Surgeon-General S. P. MOORE, Confederate States Army,
    War Department, Richmond, Va.

Sir: I have the honor to give the following brief outline of my labors, conducted in accordance with the orders of the surgeon-general:

Immediately after the brief report upon hospital gangrene, forwarded to the surgeon-general, I repaired to Camp Sumter, Andersonville, Ga., and instituted a series of investigations upon the diseases of the Federal prisoners.

The field was of great extent and extraordinary interest. There were more than 5,000 seriously sick in the hospital and stockade, and the deaths ranged from 90 to 130 each day.

Since the establishment of this prison on 24th of February, 1864, to the present time, over 10,000 Federal prisoners have died; that is—near one-third of the entire number have perished in less than seven months.

I instituted careful investigations into the condition of the sick and well and performed numerous post-mortem examinations. The medical topography of Andersonville and the surrounding country was examined, and the waters of the streams, springs, and wells around and within the stockade and hospital carefully analyzed.

Diarrhœa, dysentery, scurvy, and hospital gangrene were the diseases which have been the main cause of this extraordinary mortality. The origin and character of the hospital gangrene which prevailed to so remarkable a degree and with such fatal effects amongst the Federal prisoners, engaged my most serious and earnest consideration. More than 30,000 men, crowded upon twenty-seven acres of land, with little or no shelter from the intense heat of a Southern summer, or from the rain and from the dew of night, with coarse corn bread from which the husk had not been removed, with but scant supplies of fresh meat and vegetables, with little or no attention to hygiene, with festering masses of filth at the very doors of their rude dens and tents, with the greater portion of the banks of the stream flowing through the stockade a filthy quagmire of human excrements alive with working maggots, generated by their own filthy exhalations and excretions, an atmosphere that so deteriorated and contaminated their solids and fluids that the slightest scratch and even the bites of small insects were in some cases followed by such rapid and extensive gangrene as to destroy extremities and even life itself.

A large number of operations have been performed in the hospital on account of gangrene following slight injuries and mere abrasion of the surface. In almost every case of amputation for gangrene the disease returned, and a large proportion of the cases have terminated fatally.

I recorded careful observations upon the origin and progress of these cases of gangrene, and examined the bodies after death and noted the pathological changes of the organs and tissues. The results of these observations will be forwarded to the surgeon-general at the earliest practicable moment.

After concluding my labors among the Federal prisoners, I moved to Macon and instituted a series of inquiries and investigations upon the hospital gangrene which

[1] War of Rebellion, vol. VII, series 2, p. 1012

has prevailed to so great an extent in the Army of the Tennessee during the recent disastrous campaign, and especially since the evacuation of Atlanta.

. . . .

These active labors in the field will engage my attention for one or two months longer, and immediately after the close of the investigation (if Providence permit) I will prepare my full report upon hospital gangrene, which will embody the results of my investigations upon this disease in various parts of the Confederacy, in the general hospitals in Virginia, South Carolina, and Georgia, and will embrace also the more recent investigations at Andersonville, Macon, and Columbus, Ga. I will spare no effort and no expenditure of time and labor in the preparation of this report, with the hope that it may prove of value to the medical department of the Confederate Army and worthy of the consideration of the surgeon-general.

If favored, I hope to be able to place this report in the hands of the surgeon-general about the 1st of next May or June.

JOSEPH JONES,
Surgeon, Provisional Army, C. S.

Surgeon Jones was mentioned by Jefferson Davis, in his *Belford* articles, as a man of "great learning and undoubted probity." He was sent, as Dr. Jones and Mr. Davis both tell us, purely in the interest of science and not to devise methods of better treatment. Mr. Davis says that Dr. Jones's report was made for the eye of the surgeon-general alone, and he intimates that it was perfidious to use it against the rebel government for that reason.

It will be remembered that when Dr. Jones was on the witness stand he testified that the report had been finished but had not been sent forward when the war closed. Much was made of this fact as relieving the rebel authorities at Richmond from the responsibility which this report would, if *received,* have imposed.

The knowledge of the Richmond authorities abundantly appears through other means. But we now see that Dr. Jones by this preliminary report gave those authorities information about Andersonville Prison shortly after his investigation. It will be observed here as in other evidence that the bodies of our dead were frequently used "in the interest of science." How many were thus violated and their identity destroyed we do not know. Nor can we wonder that where so little regard was given for human life, less regard was shown for the bodies of the dead.

Dr. Jones points out that the prisoners died as rapidly in the stockade as in the hospital. He gives the total deaths in the stockade, to September 21st, as 3,254, and in the hospital, for the same period, as 6,225; a total of 9,479.

He further says:[1]

During the period of six months no less than 565 deaths are recorded under the head of *morbi canie*. In other words, the men died without having received sufficient medical attention for the determination of even the names of the disease causing death.

During the month of August, 53 cases and 53 deaths are recorded as due to marasmus.[2] Surely this large number of deaths must have been due to some other morbid state than slow wasting. If they were due to improper and insufficient food, they should have been classed accordingly.

We observe a progressive increase of the rate of mortality, from 3.11 per cent in March, to 9.09 per cent of mean strength, sick and well, in August.

Dr. Jones then points out that the ratio of mortality continued to increase during September. He continued:

The entire number of Federal prisoners at Andersonville was about 40,611; and during the period of near seven months, from February 24 to September 21, nine thousand four hundred and seventy-nine (9,479) deaths were recorded; that is, during this period one-fourth, or, more exactly, one in 4.2 or 23.3 per cent, terminated fatally.

He then sums up the causes, which he had already elaborately pointed out, as follows:

This increase of mortality was due in great measure to the accumulation of the sources of disease; as the increase of excrements and filth of all kinds, and the concentration of noxious effluvia, and also to the progressive effects of salt diet, crowding and hot climate.

A glance at the "sources of disease" which he enumerates will show how easily most of them could have been avoided by remedial agencies within reach.

Captain Wirz made a report of date November 1, 1864, which was forwarded through proper channels to Adjutant-General Cooper on November 8th.[3]

This report shows that on October 1st, the number remaining in prison was reduced to 8,662. Of these, at that date 2,071, and at the end of the month 2,479, were reported in hospital. There died in hospital during the month 1,560, or 34.2 per cent of all the sick. There were sent away 2,866. The mean strength for the month was about 6,100. It thus appears that as late as November 1st, over 25 per cent of the mean strength died and over 34 per cent of those reported in hospital.

[1] Record, p. 637.
[2] A wasting of flesh without fever or apparent disease.—*Webster*.
[3] War of Rebellion, vol. VII, series 2, p. 1082.

Surgeon White made the following report in November, 1864:

OFFICE CHIEF SURGEON, CONFEDERATE STATES MILITARY PRISONS,
GEORGIA AND ALABAMA.
CAMP LAWTON, GA., November 9, 1864.

Surgeon R. R. STEVENSON, In charge Post, Andersonville, Ga.[1]

Sir: . . . We have been quite busy for the last two days in selecting the sick to be exchanged. After getting them all ready at the depot, we were notified by telegraph not to send them and had to take them back to the stockade. Many of these poor fellows already broken down in health, will succumb through despair.

I. H. WHITE,
Chief Surgeon.

CONFEDERATE STATES OF AMERICA.[2]
SURGEON-GENERAL'S OFFICE.
RICHMOND, VA.,—, 186—.

Report of the Sanitary Condition. of the Confederate States Military Prisons at Camps Sumter and Lauton, Georgia, by Surgeon Isaiah H. White.

The law of Congress creating a hospital fund to provide for the comfort of the sick and wounded is completely abrogated by the commissary department failing to fill requisitions for funds.

The authority granted in your telegram of September 22, to divide the excess of funds at Andersonville among the new prisons, has been thwarted by the commissary at that post failing to supply funds. A large excess of funds at Andersonville will be turned over to the treasury because the commissary at that post has failed to supply himself with funds to meet requisitions while thousands of sick, both at this post and Andersonville, are in a state of suffering that would touch the heart of even the most callous. Will not the commissary-general supply the funds even after the monthly statement of hospital fund has been forwarded?

ISAIAH H. WHITE,
Surgeon, Provisional Army, C. S.

This report bears an indorsement of Surgeon-General Moore, November 15, 1864, referring it to the commissary-general. Surgeon White had pointed out that thousands of the sick prisoners were "in a state of suffering that would touch the heart of even the most callous."

The commissary-general on November 18th made an indorsement complaining that his bureau had not been supplied with money. "When the indebtedness of this bureau is relieved," he said, "and funds furnished in addition, to procure supplies for the armies in the field, it is hoped that enough will be found to meet the regular demands of the hospital. This bureau scarcely expects to realize such a healthful condition of the country, and can take no action in conflict with the law, which is conclusive on the subject."

On November 20th, Surgeon-General Moore indorsed the document: "Respectfully submitted to the secretary of war to know what can be done under the circumstances."

[1] War of Rebellion, vol. VII. series 2, p. 1114.
[2] War of Rebellion, vol. VII, series 2, p. 1130.

As was the case with most of the reports that went forward to the Richmond authorities, suggesting needed relief at Andersonville, this one slumbered in pigeonholes and nothing was done.

ANDERSONVILLE, GA., September 16, 1864.
Office of the Surgeon in Charge[1]
C. S. Military Prison Hospital,

Surgeon-General S. P. MOORE, C. S. Army, Richmond, Va.:

Sir: I have the honor to report to you that I have been assigned to duty by Surgeon I. H. White, chief surgeon post, in charge of C. S. military prison hospital. In assuming the responsibilities of so important a position and before entering upon my duties I deem it necessary to make the following statement of the sanitary condition of the hospital and appliances for the comfort of the sick and wounded. The topography, climate, and prevalent diseases of the country have been given you in former reports by my predecessor. I shall confine myself principally to the following:

1. *Nature of Barrack Accommodations.*—The stockade (in the shape of a parallelogram) includes twenty-seven acres of ground. A considerable stream of water passes through it, running east and west. In this space of ground from 30,000 to 40,000 prisoners have been crowded; no protection whatever from the burning rays of the sun, except such as could be made from blankets or dirt hovels. Along the banks of the stream the ground is quite boggy, and water is continually oozing from the low banks. Recently four sheds have been built inside the stockade. These were the beginning of a series of barracks capable of accomodating 270 men each. A temporary structure is erected on the banks of the stream and is used as a privy. All the inmates of the prison use this humid cesspool of excrementitious matter as a privy except the sick, and they are compelled to dig small holes near their hovels and use them for the deposit of feces. The stream that flows through the stockade overflowed its low swampy banks in the early part of the season, and the amount of fecal matter deposited a short distance from the outside of the stockade is enormous. At all times of the day and night a most noisome stench arises from the decomposing excrementitious matter deposited in the prison and hospital grounds. From 3,000 to 4,000 sick and wounded men are inside the stockade. The number of medical men is entirely inadequate for the demands of the sick. At present writing only four medical officers are on duty, whereas to take the proper care of the sick and wounded there should be not less than twenty-five efficient medical officers constantly on duty in the stockade, in order to meet the wants of the sick and keep the proper register and reports. Under the present regime hundreds die in the stockade and are buried whose names and diseases are unknown. This can be remedied by no other means than by a sufficient corps of medical officers. All the medical officers who have been on duty here are detailed men from the militia and contract physicians, and as a matter of course are very inefficient.

2. *Nature of Hospital Accommodations.*—The hospital is situated near the southwest corner of the stockade, covering about five acres of ground, enclosed by a frail board fence. A sluggish stream of water flows through the southern part of this lot. The ground is sloping and facing the southeast. On the south-

---

[1] War of Rebellion, vol. VII, series 2, p. 830.

west side of the enclosure is a swamp about 300 yards in width and on the northwest side the stream which flows through the stockade, the banks being very low and subject to overflow. From these swamps arise putrid exhalations at times almost insupportable. It will be seen by the accompanying drawing *"A,"* that the hospital is but a short distance from the confluence of the branch and the creek, and although on rolling tableland it is much lower than the surrounding country, and very near where the branch disembogues from the stockade, occupying a position that all the surrounding depressing agencies would seem to center in the hospital, as well as the stockade. The number of medical officers is deficient, with a few exceptions being composed of men who are either detailed or under contract. On examining the roster I find that twenty-four medical officers are charged to the hospital, and yet but twelve are on duty. The rest either by order of General Brown (at their own request) are off on sick leave or leave of indulgence. In order to attend to the wants of the sick and wounded not less than thirty efficient medical officers should be on duty in the hospital. Confusion will necessarily occur without this number. From 1,800 to 2,500 patients are crowded into this space. Tents of a very inferior quality are the only means of protection, a majority of them being the small A tents. Temporary bunks are erected in most of them by driving forks into the ground and placing small poles or boards to lie on. A great number of patients are compelled to lie on the ground in consequence of the smallness of the tents. The cooking arrangements are very deficient; two large kettles erected on a furnace are nearly all the vessels that are used. The bread is baked outside of the hospital in the stockade enclosure. The bread is of the most unhealthy character, being made of coarse, unbolted cornmeal. This, of itself, under the most favorable circumstances, must prove a source of great irritation to the bowels. Scurvy, gangrene, and bowel affections are prevailing at present to an alarming extent. Frequent issues of green corn, peas, molasses, vinegar, rice, flour, and sweet potatoes are being made, and under suitable hospital accommodations the condition of the sick could be greatly ameliorated. The purveyor's department has been able to supply nearly all the necessary medicines. The indigenous remedies are being extensively used with much good effect. The medical officers in charge of the different wards and divisions are all diligent and seem willing to discharge their duties, although laboring under many and great disadvantages. Great efforts have been made to make the stockade secure and prevent the escape of prisoners, and but little attention paid to the hygienic and sanitary condition of the sick. Surgeon I. H. White, chief surgeon post, informed me that timely requisitions have been made on the quartermaster's department for the necessary materials to make the sick and wounded comfortable, but thus far he has been unable to procure scarcely anything. The means of transportation being very limited, both by railroad and teams, has proved a source of great annoyance. I would respectfully suggest that the necessary steps be taken to secure transportation for hospital material over all other stores except ammunition. This would at once remedy a great evil.

The greatest amount of confusion seems to have prevailed in consequence of soliciting attachés for the hospital from Federal prisoners in place of disabled Confederate soldiers. Great waste in property, medicines, and provisions has been the result. This I shall endeavor to correct as speedily as possible.

I would respectfully request that an efficient quartermaster and commissary be ordered to report to me for special hospital duty, with full power from the war department to provide for the comfort of the sick and wounded Federal prisoners. Without an arrangement of this kind I very much fear the hospital department in C. S. military prison will continue to be neglected.

Hoping that this communication may meet with favorable consideration, I have the honor to be, very respectfully, your obedient servant,

R. R. STEVENSON,
Surgeon in Charge.

This report was sent to the surgeon-general late in September, while Dr. Jones was pursuing his investigations. Over a month had elapsed since Colonel Chandler's report had reached the surgeon-general and other officers at Richmond. Surgeon Stevenson is the person who has published a book in defense of the administration of the Andersonville prison, entitled "The Southern Side," and yet he himself reported a condition almost paralyzing in its shocking details. What can be said in palliation of a situation which warranted the statement—"Under the present regime hundreds die in the stockade and are buried, whose names and diseases are unknown." Into this stockade, he tells his chief, "30,000 to 40,000 prisoners have been crowded; no protection whatever from the burning rays of the sun, except such as could be made from blankets or dirt hovels." Such was that stockade.

Of the hospital he speaks but little more favorably; so situated "that all the surrounding depressing agencies would seem to center in the hospital, as well as in the stockade."

He says further: "Great efforts have been made to make the stockade secure and prevent the escape of prisoners, and but little attention paid to the hygienic and sanitary condition of the sick."

He adds: "Surgeon I. H. White, chief post surgeon, informs me that timely requisitions have been made on the quartermaster's department for the necessary materials to make the sick and wounded comfortable, but thus far he has been unable to procure scarcely anything."

On October 31, 1864, Surgeon Stevenson made a report, through Surgeon White, to General Winder,[1] in which he reports:

Remaining in hospital, October 1	1970
Admitted for treatment during month	1943
Total under treatment during month	3913
Died	1595

[1] War of Rebellion, vol. VII, series 2, p. 1075.

This report shows that nearly 41 per cent of those under treatment died in the month of October. Is it not remarkable that no steps were taken, such as had been "frequently suggested" as necessary, to reform the death-dealing policy and methods? What must have been the condition previously if Surgeon Stevenson could truthfully say there had been "a marked improvement in the health of the prisoners" in October, when 41 out of every 100 in hospital died?[1]

FIRST DIVISION C. S. MILITARY PRISON HOSPITAL,[2]
Surgeon E. D. EILAND, September 5, 1864.
In Charge First Division C. S. Military Prison Hospital:

Sir: As officer of the day for the past twenty-four hours I have inspected the hospital and found it in as good a condition as the nature of the circumstances will allow. A majority of the bunks are still unsupplied with bedding, while in a portion of the division, the tents are entirely destitute of either bunks, bedding, or straw, the patients being compelled to lie upon the bare ground. I would earnestly call your attention to the article of diet. The corn bread received from the bakery, being made up without sifting, is wholly unfit for the use of the sick, and often, as in the last twenty-four hours, upon examination, the inner portion is found to be perfectly raw. The meat (beef) received by the patients does not amount to over two ounces per day, and for the last three or four days no flour has been issued. The corn bread cannot be eaten by many, for to do so would be to increase the diseases of the bowels, from which a large majority are suffering, and it is therefore thrown away. All then that is received by way of subsistence is two ounces of boiled beef and a half pint of rice soup per day, and under these circumstances all the skill that can be brought to bear upon their cases by the medical officers will avail nothing. Another point to which I feel it my duty to call your attention is the deficiency of medicines. We have little more than indigenous barks and roots with which to treat the numerous forms of disease to which our attention is daily called. For the treatment of wounds, ulcers, etc., we have literally nothing except water. The wards, some of them, are filled with gangrene, and we are compelled to fold our arms and look quietly upon its ravages, not even having stimulants to support the system under its depressing influences, this article being so limited in supply that it can only be issued for cases under the knife. I would respectfully call your earnest attention to the above facts, in the hope that something may be done to alleviate the sufferings of the sick.

Very respectfully, your obedient servant,

J. CREWS PELOT,
Assistant Surgeon, Provisional Army C. S., Officer of the Day.

These medical officers were on duty at Andersonville Prison when Colonel Chandler made his inspection and report. The document

---

[1] I do not find this report in Dr. Stevenson's book. It would illy support this volume entitled "Southern Side."

[2] War of Rebellion, vol. VII, series 2, p. 773.

above given was a report a month later and shows that no improvement followed Colonel Chandler's inspection and recommendations.

Eliminating the impossible corn bread, "wholly unfit for the use of the sick," we have here the evidence that *"two ounces of boiled beef and a half pint of rice soup"* constituted the daily ration. Let us contrast this dietary with the dietaries furnished by the British in the war of 1812 to their prisoners, and ours furnished to the rebel prisoners. In the Dartmoor Prison in England, our men taken prisoners were allowed for the first five days in the week 24 ounces of coarse brown bread, 8 ounces of beef, 4 ounces of barley, one-third ounce of onions, one-third ounce of salt, and 16 ounces of turnips daily (or more than 50 ounces of solid food); and for the remaining two days the usual allowance of bread was given with 16 ounces of pickled fish. At the Melville Island Prison, at Halifax, the prisoners were given 16 ounces of bread, 16 ounces of beef, and one gill of peas; the American agent furnishing coffee, sugar, potatoes, and tobacco. The United States allowed to the rebel prisoners held by us 38 ounces of solid food at first; but afterwards, in June, 1864, the ration was reduced to 34½ ounces per day.[1]

CONFEDERATE STATES OF AMERICA,
SURGEON-GENERAL'S OFFICE.
RICHMOND, VA., —, 186—.

Report of the Sanitary Condition of the Confederate States Military Prisons at Camps Sumter and Lawton, Georgia, by Surgeon Isaiah H. White.[2]

. . . .

Having been ordered to this post, I am lending my aid to the surgeon in charge in the construction of hospital accommodations. Temporary sheds are being constructed sufficient in number and capacity to accommodate 2,000 sick.

Great difficulty is experienced in procuring from the quartermaster's department the necessary tools for the advancement of the work. Any number of laborers can be obtained among the prisoners, and with the necessary tools the work could soon be completed. The law of Congress creating a hospital fund to provide for the comfort of sick and wounded is completely abrogated by the commissary department failing to fill requisitions for funds.

The authority granted in your telegram of September 22, to divide the excess of funds at Andersonville among the new prisons, has been thwarted by the commissary at that post in failing to supply funds. Thus we are crippled and embarrassed by the quartermaster's and commissary departments, the one failing to furnish on requisition those things which should be furnished by the quartermaster's department, and the other to furnish funds with which to purchase them in the market.

[1] Martyria A. C. Hamlin, Dakin and Metcalf, Cambridge Press, 19, 1866, p. 81.
[2] War of Rebellion, vol. VII, series 2, p. 1137.

A large excess of funds at Andersonville will be turned over to the treasury, because the commissary at that post has failed to supply himself with funds to meet requisitions, while thousands of sick both at this post and Andersonville are in a state of suffering that would touch the heart of even the most callous.

Will not the commissary-general supply the funds, even after the monthly statement of hospital fund has been forwarded?

Humanity and the fame of the government demand that the extreme suffering among the prisoners should be alleviated.

. . . .

ISAIAH H. WHITE,
Surgeon, Provisional Army, C. S.

[First indorsement:] Surgeon-General's Office, November 17, 1864. Respectfully referred to the secretary of war for information as to the relative responsibility of the several departments for the actual condition of the sick and wounded prisoners of war at this camp. S. P. MOORE, Surgeon-General, C. S. Army.

[Second indorsement:] November 20, 1864. Commissary-general and quartermaster-general for prompt attention and report. J. A. S., Secretary of War.

This cry of humanity had been going up to Richmond for seven or eight months with the uniform result—no action. Even now, in November, when 41 per cent per month of the sick were dying, the Richmond authorities were satisfied with indorsements on the appeals which finally ended in pigeonholes and nothing done. The appeal to "humanity" and to the "fame" of the government was futile.

SURGEON THORNBURG'S REPORT.

Dr. Amos Thornburg, surgeon at Andersonville, testified fully. His testimony will be found in subsequent pages. He made a report to Dr. Joseph Jones from which I make some excerpts as further illustrating the frightful conditions against which our soldiers had to contend.[1]

In order to show you the kind of material we have to work on it will be necessary to first give you a list of the most prevalent diseases among the prisoners, consequent on great mental and nervous depression, from long confinement in over-crowded and badly arranged prisons, seclusion from society, long-deferred hope, a lack of cleanliness, insufficient supply of nourishing food, a want of proper exercise, of both body and mind, and from breathing an atmosphere so much vitiated by *idio miasma* as to be insufficient to produce the proper degree of oxygenation of the blood, a condition so necessary to both mental and bodily soundness. This depraved blood then affords an imperfect stimulus to the brain and nervous system, and as a result we have languor and inactivity of the mental and nervous functions, with a tendency to headache, syncope, hypochondriasis, and hemeralopia. The diseases most commonly met with are diarrhœa, dysentery,

---

[1] War of Rebellion, series 2, vol. VIII, p. 625.

intermittent and remittent fever, with continued, or camp, fever, as many term it. We also have catarrhal affections, with occasional pneumonia, and plueritis, and, above all, scorbutus.

As it so rarely happens in the course of a long experience of the medical practitioner or surgeon that he has an opportunity of witnessing this most formidable and loathsome disease in all its aggravated forms, it might not be amiss to introduce in this place a detailed account of that fearful disease, as it has prevailed and is still prevailing in this prison. But as that would be a work of supererogation and lead us too far from our subject, we will not attempt the task. Out of 30,000 prisoners who have been confined at this place during the past spring and summer, perhaps not less than one-half have suffered from this disease in some of its various forms.

As a sequel to the above-named diseases we have edema, anasarca, ascites, hydrothorax, ansemia, and ulcers of nearly every variety and form. These ulcers are produced from the slightest causes imaginable. A pin scratch, a prick of a splinter, a pustula, an abrasion, or even a mosquito bite are sufficient causes for their production. The phagedenic ulcer is the most common variety met with among the prisoners, and usually commences from some of the causes enumerated above, or from wounds or injuries of a more serious nature. When from any of these causes an ulcer forms, it speedily assumes a phagedenic appearance and extends over a large extent of surface, and presents irritable, jagged, and everted edges, and slowly destroys the dead tissues down to the bone. The surface presents a large ash-colored or greenish yellow slough and emits a very offensive odor. After the slough is removed by appropriate treatment, the parts beneath show but little tendency to granulate. Occasionally, however, apparently healthy granulations spring up and progress finely for a time, and again fall into sloughing, and thus, by an alternate process of sloughing and phagedenic ulceration, large portions of the affected member or large masses of the body are destroyed. In this condition gangrene usually sets in, and if not speedily arrested soon puts an end to the poor sufferer's existence.

. . . .

Early in the spring smallpox made its appearance in the prison, and as a prophylactic measure we were ordered to vaccinate "all who could not show a healthy scar." Consequently we went to work, and in a week or ten days 2,000 or 3,000 were vaccinated. Out of these nearly every man who happened to be affected with scurvy was attacked with ulceration of the pustule. These small ulcers soon began to slough and extend over a large extent of surface. These sloughs would become detached, the parts beneath suppurate, as in the case of other ulcers in a sloughy condition, until at last the ulcer would become phagedenic and destroy every structure in its track for a considerable extent. In this condition gangrene would set in, and if the disease be not speedily arrested by powerful escharotics, emollient poultices, and the proper vegetable diet, amputation became necessary, or the poor wretch would sink under the irritation; diarrhœa or dysentery would supervene and speedily destroy the patient. The next and most common form of ulcers with us are what we call the scorbutic ulcer.

In severe cases of scurvy we have the upper and lower extremities covered with blue or livid spots, varying from the size of a millet seed to three or four inches in diameter, or the whole leg may be of a dark livid or copper color. These blotches become painful, open and ulcerate. This condition continues for a time, and finally slough, destroying whole toes, feet, and even arms and legs, apparently without there being sufficient energy or vitality in the system to set up inflammatory action.

He submits a table of cases treated in ward five, second division of the hospital, for July, August, September, and to October 5, 1864. He expresses regret that he cannot give the statistics of other wards. He says: "It will be seen by the above statement that we have treated, in a little over three months, 325 patients, and out of that number 208 have died."

I quote further:

We will close this paper, lest we weary you with dry and uninteresting matter, by giving a short description of our so-called hospital. We have from 1,600 to 2,000 patients, besides nurses and attendants, crowded together in small and almost useless tents erected on less than three acres of ground. The hospital is erected on a narrow tongue of land between two small creeks, on each side of which are swamps forty and fifty yards in width; on the west and up these creeks from the hospital are the camps and stockade. Now, all the debris from over 30,000 human beings has to pass along the small brook on the north of the hospital grounds and within a stone's throw of patients' tents.

A large portion of this filth is deposited on the marsh and produces a most sickening stench. Our patients are carried from the stockade and placed in the tents by the attendants. We put in the common small A tent four patients, in the large wall tent eight, and in the common fly from six to eight. About one-third have bunks or scaffolds and the remainder have to lie on the ground without straw or anything else to protect them from its dampness.

Those who are not fortunate enough to have a blanket are compelled to lie on the damp ground with no covering but their clothing, which in many instances they have worn for six months without washing.

The diet is of the coarsest kind, consisting of boiled beef, rice, molasses, and coarse corn bread baked without sifting, and from one to two ordinary-sized biscuits. To this we sometimes have added a small allowance of vegetables, such as peas, potatoes, and collards. These vegetables are generally issued raw and the patients are compelled to hire their comrades to cook them in some sort of style and pay them out of their scanty allowance.

With these facts before you, you will not wonder at the fearful mortality presented in our report and in the tabular statement from our ward, presented above.

Feeling we have done our whole duty, both in the eyes of God and man, we leave the matter to rest with those whose duty it was to furnish supplies and build up a hospital that might have reflected credit on the government *and saved the lives of thousands of our race.*

Who were the persons to whom Dr. Thornburg refers? The answer stands out in all these pages. They could by means at hand have "saved the lives of thousands of our race." Why did they not do it?

CHAPTER VI.

CONDITIONS AT THE PRISON (continued)—REPORTS AND TESTIMONY OF SURGEONS ON DUTY AT THE PRISON, NAMELY: DR. AMOS THORNBURG; DR. F. T. CASTLEN; DR. G. S. HOPKINS; DR. G. LEB. RICE; DR. JOHN C. BATES; DR. R. G. ROY; DR. B. J. HEAD—TESTIMONY OF DR. WILLIAM BALSER, WHO HAD OCCASION TO TREAT A LARGE NUMBER OF PRISONERS FROM ANDERSONVILLE ON THEIR WAY TO FREEDOM FROM PRISON LIFE— THEY WERE LIVING SKELETONS—SEVENTY-FIVE PER CENT OF DEAD MIGHT HAVE BEEN SAVED BY PROPER CARE—ACTUAL SQUARE FEET TO MAN 27, OR 3 BY 9 FEET.

IT may be said that Colonel Chandler and Dr. Jones had not the means of fully informing themselves, and that they based their conclusions upon a superficial examination of existing conditions. Colonel Chandler's high official rank repels all suggestion of wilful misrepresentation. He must be presumed to have reported only what he saw or learned from reliable sources. Dr. Jones's personal character and professional standing have, as we have seen, the indorsement of Mr. Davis, and Dr. Jones tells us that his record was made for the eyes of the Confederate authorities alone. He, therefore, wrote with entire freedom. It seemed not to have occurred to him that he was furnishing important evidence which some day would most convincingly show that a great crime had been committed at Andersonville, and that he was forging the links in the chain of proofs which would tend to fix the guilt on the officials who sent him on his mission.

But the evidence does not depend alone on the two important reports found in the preceding chapter, corroborated as they are by the other reports quoted. There were several surgeons called as witnesses who were on duty at Andersonville at different times during the entire period of the prison's existence. It is to this evidence I shall now turn.

TESTIMONY OF DR. AMOS THORNBURG.[1]

Dr. Amos Thornburg, whose report appears in the preceding chapter, was assigned to duty there on April 14, 1864, and remained until the prison was closed. He testified:

My commission bears date October 29, 1862. I served a little over two years in the field, except what time I was a prisoner. On the 10th of March, 1864,

[1] Record, p. 332.

I was relieved from field duty on account of my health and sent back to a hospital at Oxford, Georgia. I stayed there two or three weeks, and was then ordered to Andersonville to report to the commander of the prison there. I reported there on the 14th of April, 1864. I reported to Colonel Persons, who was in command of the post. He sent me to Dr. White, the surgeon of the post, and Dr. White assigned me to duty in the stockade. I prescribed in quarters there for two or three months, and was then assigned to duty at the hospital outside the stockade by Surgeon White. He was the surgeon in charge of the prison as well as the hospital. I then remained in the hospital until the post was broken up, about the 5th of May, 1865, as well as I recollect. I think the hospital was removed outside the stockade in June or in the latter part of May. I remained prescribing in quarters part of the time inside the stockade, and the remainder of the time at the gate, I suppose till the latter part of June. I have no data to fix the time when I was sent to the hospital for duty. From the time I went there until I left, Captain Wirz was in command of the prison.

While I was on duty in the hospital I frequently made reports to Surgeon White in regard to the condition of the hospital, when I was officer of the day, which would happen generally about once or twice a week.

[A paper was here handed to the witness.]

That is a copy of one of my reports. I think it is a true copy. I also made reports to Dr. Stevenson; this report was made to Dr. Stevenson. I found Dr. White in charge when I went there on the 15th of April, and he remained till about the time the prisoners were removed to Camp Lawton. I think he went with General Winder. That was in the beginning of September. Surgeon R. R. Stevenson succeeded him, and continued chief surgeon until the latter part of the month of September, 1864; I think about the 25th. Surgeon H. H. Clayton succeeded Dr. Stevenson, and continued in charge until the place was captured by General Wilson or the post was abandoned.

[The paper shown to witness, and of which the following is a copy, was then placed in evidence:]

C. S. M. P. HOSPITAL,
ANDERSONVILLE, GEORGIA, September 26, 1864.

SIR: I would most respectfully call your attention to the very bad sanitary condition of the second division, as well as the whole hospital to the immense quantity of filth accumulating in the streets, and to the filthiness of the tents and patients, and to the fact that it cannot be otherwise until we are furnished with the means with which to work; patients lying on the cold ground without bed or blanket; and also that we have a very scanty supply of medicines, and that the rations are not of the proper kind and not issued in proper quantity. Hoping that the proper steps may be taken to remedy these defects.

I am, sir, your obedient servant. A. THORNBURG.
Assistant Surgeon, P. A. C. S.

R. R. STEVENSON,
    Surgeon in Charge.

When Dr. White was in charge I made similar reports to him. This was not the only report I ever made to Dr. Stevenson on the subject; not by a great many. There was a quantity of hospital clothing, bed sacks, sheets, &c., sent there, I think a short time before Dr. White left the post. I do not know the number, but

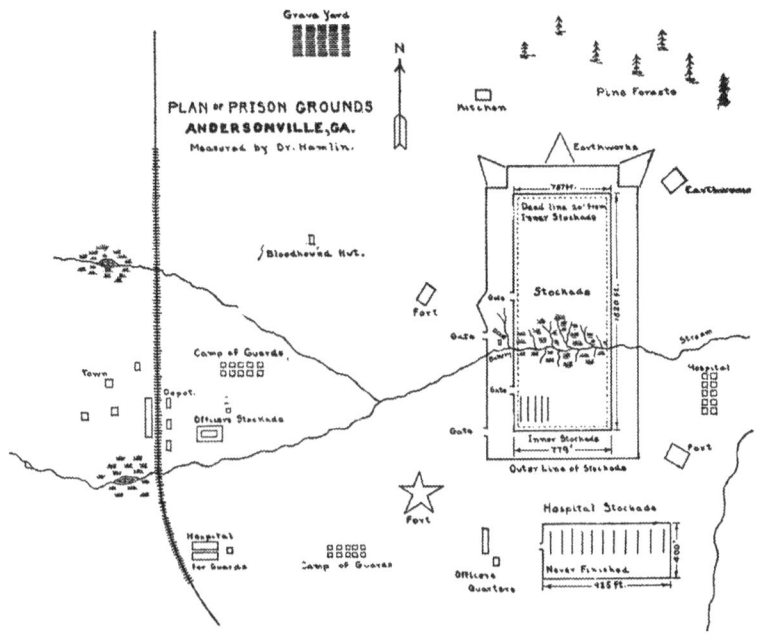

there were several bales. When Dr. Stevenson was in charge I was in charge of the surgical ward in the second division, generally known as the gangrene ward. I had for that ward some scaffoldings fixed up for bunks, and I frequently made application for bed sacks, sheets, &c. I got a few bed sacks, but they would soon become dirty and I would send them off to be washed, and perhaps not see them any more. The next thing I would see would be some prisoner with a pair of pantaloons on made out of a bed sack, and I would make application for more. I knew that the prisoners needed the things, being destitute of clothing, and I made no complaints about their taking them. I very seldom got anything that I made requisition for. Dr. Stevenson never offered me any excuse. Sometimes, when I would talk to him in person, he would tell me that he aimed to have a hospital constructed, when he could use these things and have them better cared for, but that if they were issued in there they would be made way with, and it would be a clear loss to the government. That time did not come while I was in charge. The only hospital we had at that time was a tent. After Dr. Clayton took charge, about the first of January, 1865, he began for the first time to construct a hospital, and he had it pretty well on towards completion at the time the post was broken up. It was not entirely completed. It was used. We got all the sick out of the tents into those sheds that were built for the purpose of making a hospital. The food that was issued was such as the other prisoners and the soldiers outside could get from the commissary, mostly bacon, beef, or pickled pork. The bacon was generally very good; the beef sometimes was rather poor. The pickled pork that came in was very frequently partly spoilt; it smelt badly, was hardly fit for use, and we had at times condemned it and sent it back. The meal that was issued was very coarse, and at first was not sifted even for the hospital. That was under Dr. White. There were very few vegetables issued during his administration. Sometimes we would get a few collards, and tomatoes, and sweet potatoes, &c., but in very small quantities. That was under Dr. White. It was a little better under Dr. Stevenson; but very little was issued—not enough to supply the demands of the sick. The cooking department was also very bad; we had to cook in large kettles, such as is used in boiling sorghum, and the things could not be cooked as they should have been. The vegetables were sometimes issued raw and divided out among the prisoners, and the quantity was very small. They had sometimes to get their comrades to cook them, and they generally charged a portion of the articles for cooking them. They complained to me that what few vegetables they did get did them no good, which I knew to be a fact, and so reported in some of my reports.

The supply of medicines was generally insufficient. The surgeon in charge would generally make a requisition for medicine to have it on the first of the month, but it was usually the 10th before we got the supply, and when we did get it, such articles as opium, quinine, and other valuable medicines, which were very scarce in the Confederacy, would be exhausted in the course of ten or twelve days, and we would have to rely on such indigenous remedies as were furnished by the medical purveyor. We had large quantities of them, but we had no laboratory to prepare them properly. They were generally put up in decoctions and infusions by the hospital steward. The prevailing diseases were scorbutus, gangrene, diarrhœa, dysentery, intermittent and remittent fever, typhoid and typhus fever. Proper provisions were the remedy that was needed for scorbutus, gangrene, and kindred diseases; it was a waste of medicine. What medicine we gave I considered thrown away, because we did not have proper diet for the patients, and consequently the medicine did no good; yet they were very anxious to get medicine to relieve them, and we would prescribe what we had and have it administered to them, but I looked upon it as a waste of medicine, because we did not have proper diet. I regard diet as the main thing in the treatment of most of the diseases we had to contend with. We had a great deal of hospital gangrene at one time.

I never knew much about the hospital fund. I only knew that there were orders from the war department, the assistant inspector-general's office, that the prison hospital should be on an equal footing with the Confederate hospitals, and that the surgeon in charge should be allowed to draw the same fund. A portion of the time the fund was a dollar a day for each patient, and after a while it got to be two dollars and two and a half dollars a day. I think it amounted to that towards the last, but I did not see the order. I know of no reason why it could not have been drawn at Andersonville. It was generally drawn at other hospitals. The fund was sufficient to buy vegetables for the Confederate hospitals, and sometimes large amounts of the fund were turned over to other and more needy hospitals. My understanding was—and I had a little knowledge of it, too—that if they did not use all the hospital fund for that purpose, they were allowed to use it for other purposes, such as fitting up the hospitals. There

TESTIMONY OF CONFEDERATE SURGEONS. 115

was an order issued from Richmond directing that the surplus fund be turned over to the quartermaster at the end of each month. I do not remember the date of the order. I saw the weekly account current one time in the hands of the hospital steward, Mr. Kerr. I had made complaints to him about the condition of the patients and the condition and the amount of the rations that came in and the amount of vegetables and other nourishing diet that was to be bought with the hospital fund. Mr. Kerr, to convince me that these things were sent in, showed me the weekly statement for that week. In looking at it I remarked that those things never came into the hospital—at least, that no considerable part of them had come in, and I made some little complaint about it to the other surgeons, and we began to talk about having an investigation of the matter. We called on Mr. Kerr after that for the book, but he remarked that Dr. Stevenson had it in his charge, and we were not allowed to see it. I never saw it after that until Dr. Stevenson left and Dr. Clayton took charge. At that time, myself and three or four other surgeons went up and asked Dr. Clayton to let us see the account current. He showed it to us, and on examination we found that large quantities of things which appeared by the book to have been bought had never come into the hospital. We made a statement of the facts to the surgeon-general and forwarded it by mail. A few days afterwards Dr. Eiland was ordered to Montgomery. He had taken an active part in this investigation, and we requested him as he went through to Montgomery to stop at Columbus, Georgia, and make a statement to the medical director. He did so. At the time he made that statement, Dr. Gilliard, one of the surgeon-general's assistants, happened to be at Columbus, in the office of the medical director. He and Dr. Flewellen came down immediately and investigated the case, and found that there had been some errors in regard to the hospital fund. Dr. Stevenson went to Columbia, South Carolina, and was there the last news I had from him.

The mortality was generally great while I was at Andersonville. I attribute it to the want of proper diet and the crowding together of too many men in the prison and in the hospital. There was too small a space of ground for the number of prisoners we had there. There was a great lack of shelter and a lack of fuel. I think that was also a cause of mortality. I believe that is all the causes I can recollect just now.

The worst cases that were in the stockade were brought generally to the hospitals for treatment. While I prescribed there, for the first few months the hospitals outside were very much crowded, and they could not make room for all the patients that ought to have been sent out. I would sometimes prescribe while at the stockade gate for five hundred patients in a day. In order to do that we had to prescribe by formulas; to make out formulas for different diseases and number them, and then just examine a man and set down the number of the prescription that he was to take opposite his name, with directions. Frequently there would be no vacancies in the hospital at all. Some days we could not send any to the hospital. At other times perhaps fifty, sixty, or a hundred men would have died during the day previous and there would be that many vacancies, and we would be allowed to send in a *pro rata* number to fill those vacancies. There were generally some ten or twelve surgeons and assistant surgeons prescribing at the stockade gate, and each one would be allowed to send in a certain number to fill the vacancies. Some days we would send in one, two, three apiece, sometimes ten apiece, and some days, when the hospital would be enlarged, as high as thirty or forty apiece. One day we sent three or four hundred among us out of the stockade to the hospital. I presume there were a good many in the stockade that could not come out, and if they did not have friends to carry them out in their blankets or upon their backs, they would perhaps not get prescriptions. Sometimes the sergeants who drew the rations and had charge of the squads would represent to the surgeons the cases of men who were not able to come out, and had requested them to get certain medicines; and if the diseases were such as we could prescribe for, we would very frequently set the name of such a man down and the number of the prescription that he should have, and that medicine was then issued to the sergeant, and he delivered it to the man, I suppose. Deaths occurred in the stockade frequently. I suppose some died that never had got prescriptions. Sometimes there would be a very sick man brought from the stockade, and he would be marked in the surgeon's book for admittance to the hospital; he would have to remain at the gate until all the surgeons got through prescribing, so that the men who carried them to the hospital could discriminate and take the proper ones. It generally took us from eight o'clock in the morning till twelve o'clock noon before we would get through prescribing, and sometimes very bad cases would die while waiting there to be carried to the hospital. I had charge of so many divisions in the stockade, and frequently when a man from one of my divisions would die in that way, the clerk who kept the death register would ask me the man's rank and regiment and name, and the squad to which he belonged. Several men might have died at my post when I was prescribing and I could not recollect anything about any particular one. There would be two or three dead, and we could not identify them. After that I adopted the plan of writing the name, rank, regiment, and disease of each man on a piece of paper and pinning it to the breast of his coat or some part of his clothing. It worked very well, and I recommended Dr. White to issue an order requesting all the surgeons who prescribed at the stockade gate to adopt the same plan. He did issue such an order, and the system was adopted June, 1864. Up to that time there were more or less of these imperfect records. Very frequently men died in the stockade who could not be identified by any person in there, because men suffering from scurvy would frequently fall dead in the streets. It was also not unfrequently the case that a man was murdered in there, and murdered perhaps away from his friends, and he would be carried out of the stockade gate and nobody could identify him.

So far as the names of the men and the diseases that they had, the hospital register was kept with great accuracy. If a man came to me I would diagnose his case, and send him to the hospital with a statement of the disease which I considered that he had. That was generally entered upon the register, but, perhaps, he would have half a dozen supervening diseases after he went into the hospital. The supervening diseases were hardly ever entered on the register, but generally only the disease with which he went from the stockade. I do not know what entry was made on the register when a man was shot in the stockade. I suppose the cause of death would be called *"vulnus sclopeticum"*; that is the technical name for gunshot wound, and I suppose that would be the entry. Such an entry might be in the case of a man who had received wounds on the field of battle somewhere.

Q. If a man in the stockade had been shot in the stockade, and the hospital register showed that he died of scorbutus, what would be the fact in that case?

A. I do not suppose the register would show that, unless the man so shot was a patient, and under treatment for scorbutus at the time.

Q. Examine the register now handed you, and examine it with some care, and state whether you recognize it, and whether it has any appearance of having been tampered with or changed since you saw it at the hospital.

[Objected to by Mr. Baker until the book was proved, and objection overruled.]

A. I recognize the book as being the hospital book kept at Andersonville. I see no marks that would indicate that it had been tampered with, except some pencil marks on the margin, which I suppose are check marks.

[The witness pointed out the marks referred to.]

[The hospital register was offered in evidence and accompanies the record.]

F. M. TRYON, clerk to the commission, a witness on the part of the prosecution, being duly sworn, was examined as follows:

Q. Examine the register and state what the pencil marks are.

A. This book was given to me by Colonel Chipman to prepare an exhibit of the number of deaths, &c., which I did; and, in taking off the number of deaths I made the check marks referred to by the witness.

[The examination of Dr. AMOS THORNBURG was then resumed.]

Q. Examine the three indexes of the hospital register handed to you and see if you recognize them?

A. I do; and, so far as I can see, they are all correct.

[The books were put in evidence by the Judge Advocate, and accompany this record.]

Q. I notice in this register very many entire columns representing that a patient was admitted, for instance, August 8, and died August 8, and in the column of remarks, "died in quarters," and again admitted August 9, died August 9, "died in quarters," and so on all through the book; what does the remark "died in quarters" mean?

A. I think Dr. Stevenson, perhaps, would have to make a report of those cases, and they would have to be reported as having died of something, and as having died in hospital. I think, perhaps, there was an order that caused him to report them on the death register in hospital, and yet in the remarks they are put down "died in quarters"; that means in the stockade. I never knew how he fixed up that difficulty. There were a great many things in reference to the hospital that I never could understand, and this was one of them. I suppose "unknown" would be the entry in cases where the surgeon could not make out a proper diagnosis of the case. Those six men that were hung were marked as having died of "asphyxia." I do not recollect the date those men were hung, but I know they were all marked as having died of asphyxia. I asked the clerk in the hospital how he had entered those cases, and he referred me to the book, and showed me that he had marked them "asphyxia."

THE JUDGE ADVOCATE. On page 110 of the hospital record there are given the names of six men who died of asphyxia, and in the column of remarks, "Tried by court-martial, and executed inside the prison;" that is the record.

WITNESS. Those are no doubt the men who were hung.

Q. I notice on examining this register that a large proportion of the patients recorded as having been admitted died in hospital, many of them the day they were admitted, or immediately after, and that a few seem to be recorded as "returned to the stockade." Will you state to the court what your observation was with regard to the proportion that were returned to the stockade after being treated in the hospital?

A. Well, I have no data from which I can state how many were returned to the stockade. The proportion, however, was small. Sometimes a man would come to the hospital and be treated there and relieved of his disease, but in the meantime some of the surgeons would become acquainted with him, and, perhaps, would have him detailed as a nurse, or, perhaps he would be detailed outside the stockade for some other business, and hence he was not returned to quarters. The proportion actually returned to quarters was very small. I never met among my own patients—those I had treated myself—any cases where I was unable to give a diagnosis of the cause of death, and where I had to report the disease as "unknown." I have met with patients after they were dead where I could not tell the cause of death. I have frequently seen men brought out of the stockade dead, and I did not know what they died of.

My idea is that a large proportion could have been saved by proper diet and proper quarters, perhaps one-half. I will say that one-half might have been saved if we had had proper nourishing diet and the proper kind of hospital accommodations.

Q. Remembering the condition of these prisoners, and the scanty supply of fuel they had, was there weather there that would have killed them—frozen them to death?

A. Yes, sir; I suppose there was, in their emaciated condition. I do not know of any cases of that kind. I cannot give the temperature in summer in that climate. I think I have not seen a thermometer since I have been in that country. Last summer, I suppose, the hottest day we had would not have gone over 96 degrees or 98 degrees in the shade. In the summer of 1865 I should think it went up to 108 degrees in the shade. It was pretty hot in the sun. I could not tell how many degrees in the sun.

THE JUDGE ADVOCATE. I call the attention of the court to page 337 of the hospital register, where I find this record: "T. Gerrity, 106 Penna., frozen to death; admitted January 3; died January 3; died in the stockade."

WITNESS. I cannot give the temperature under the rays of the sun in summer. It would be mere guess-work. A man who had to ride in it, as I have had to do, would think it was almost up to boiling-point. I suppose it would run up to 150 degrees in the sun. I never saw it tried, but I would think so. In that remark I refer to the summer of 1865. It was not so high at any time during the summer of 1864, because that was a wet summer.

Q. Would the heat be somewhere in that neighborhood?

A. I think that would be a fair proportion. When the thermometer was over one hundred in the shade, I think it would stand a great many degrees higher in the sun.

TESTIMONY OF DR. F. G. CASTLEN.

Dr. F. G. Castlen was on duty as regimental surgeon of the Third Georgia Reserves. He testified as to some matters not properly bearing upon the question to which the evidence is now more particularly being directed. The testimony will be given here, but should be considered in connection with subsequent chapters. He testified:[1]

I have been in the Confederate army during the last two years. From May until September, 1864, at Andersonville; the remaining portion of the time in South Carolina. I was surgeon of the Third Georgia Reserves while at Andersonville. I occasionally had opportunities of observing the prisoners in the stockade at Andersonville. Their condition was deplorable; language could not express the condition in which I saw them at that time. The stench was intolerable. It sometimes came up to my camp, a half a mile distant. It was only during an east wind that I was troubled with the stench arising from the stockade. I saw negroes at work there at one time. I do not know in what numbers; twenty or thirty, I suppose.

It was a pine country about there. Farms were carried on there. I have seen cucumbers, squashes, cabbages, potatoes, collards, and melons in market. I was at market frequently. I saw different kinds of vegetables there at different times—not all I have mentioned at the same time. I don't suppose my regiment procured their vegetables from the market; they generally got them from their homes. I have seen vegetables in the camp at different times. I do not know that they purchased them at market.

At one time my regiment was very unhealthy. That was in June, I think. They were in a very healthy condition afterwards. I had no difficulty in getting medicines that I wanted.

I have seen the prisoner, Captain Wirz. I do not know what his duties were officially at Andersonville. I saw acts of cruelty committed by Captain Wirz on one or two occasions. At one time the prisoners were being removed, I think to Savannah. One prisoner was out of the ranks; Captain Wirz jerked and struck him, I think, once or twice; don't remember how many times, but I think once or twice.

I saw one man who had been bitten by the dogs. I saw the dogs bite him. I saw the dogs running down the swamp below my camp. I went down, and when I reached the brow of the hill, I heard the dogs baying; going down, I saw this man up the tree. I heard some one order him down. I don't know who it was. He came down, and I saw the dogs seize him. Captain Wirz was there with the hounds.

TESTIMONY OF DR G. S. HOPKINS.

Dr. G. S. Hopkins was sent by General Winder to make a report on the prison, and remained there from some time in July, 1864, until September of that year. His report of August 1, 1864, to General

---

[1] Record, p. 108 et seq.

Winder, is embodied in his testimony. It shows in concrete form the causes of disease and mortality; the preventive measures suggested for relieving the stockade and the hospital. It reaches beyond mere corroboration of Colonel Chandler's report and more than confirms Dr. Jones's statements. He testified:[1]

TESTIMONY OF DR. G. S. HOPKINS.

I reside in Thomasville, Georgia, about one hundred or one hundred and ten miles from Andersonville. I have resided in the South during the Rebellion. I was at Andersonville during the summer of 1864. In July, 1864, an order was issued by the governor of the State of Georgia putting the physicians into the militia service. He claimed that they were liable to the militia service, though exempt by Confederate law. I went to Macon then and had my choice either to go into the medical department or to go into the trenches. I did not feel able to shoulder the musket. I was assigned to duty at Andersonville, and ordered to report to Chief Surgeon White on the 22d of July, 1864. I remained there until September 8, when I was ordered to report to the commanding officer at Camp Lawton, the new prison at Millen. I graduated as a physician in March, 1845.

I there received orders to make a thorough inspection of the Federal prison and hospital at that place, and report, if I possibly could, the causes of disease and mortality among the Federal prisoners, and to make such suggestions as I deemed necessary to prevent further sickness and mortality. Chief Surgeon White and Acting Assistant Surgeon Watkins were on the committee with me under this order. On the 29th of July we made a thorough inspection of the prison and hospital in obedience to that order. I have my report here.

[The paper which was exhibited to witness, of which the following is a copy, was offered in evidence, and is attached to this record:]

ANDERSONVILLE, GEORGIA, August 1, 1864.

GENERAL: In obedience to your order of July 28th requiring us to make a careful examination of the Federal prison and hospital at this place, and to ascertain and report to you the cause of disease and mortality among the prisoners, and the means necessary to prevent the same, this has been complied with, and we respectfully submit the following:

Causes of Disease and Mortality.

1. The large number of prisoners crowded together.
2. The entire absence of all vegetables as diet, so necessary as a preventive of scurvy.
3. The want of barracks to shelter the prisoners from sun and rain.
4. The inadequate supply of wood and good water.
5. Badly cooked food.
6. The filthy condition of prisoners and prison generally.
7. The morbific emanations from the branch or ravine passing through the prison, the condition of which cannot be better explained than by naming it a morass of human excrement and mud.

Preventive Measures.

1. The removal immediately from the prison of not less than 15,000 prisoners.
2. Detail on parole a sufficient number of prisoners to cultivate the necessary

---
[1] Record, p. 376.

supply of vegetables, and until this can be carried into practical operation, the appointment of agents along the different lines of railroad to purchase and forward a supply.

3. The immediate erection of barracks to shelter the prisoners.

4. To furnish the necessary quantity of wood, and have wells dug to supply the deficiency of water.

5. Divide the prisoners into squads, place each squad under the charge of a sergeant, furnish the necessary quantity of soap, and hold these sergeants responsible for the personal cleanliness of his squad; furnish the prisoners with clothing at the expense of the Confederate government, and if the government be unable to do so, candidly admit our inability and call upon the Federal government to furnish them.

6. By a daily inspection of bake-house and baking.

7. Cover over with sand from the hillsides the entire "morass" not less than six inches deep, board the stream or water-course and confine the men to the use of the sinks, and make the penalty for disobedience of such orders severe.

For the Hospital.

We recommend—

1st. The tents be floored with planks; if planks cannot be had, with puncheons; and if this be impossible, then with fine straw, to be frequently changed.

2d. We find an inadequate supply of stool-boxes, and recommend that the number be increased, and that the nurses be required to remove them as soon as used, and before returning them see that they are well washed and limed.

3d. The diet for the sick is not such as they should have, and we recommend that they be supplied with the necessary quantity of beef soup with vegetables.

4th. We also recommend that the surgeons be required to visit the hospitals not less than twice a day.

We cannot too strongly recommend the necessity for the appointment of an efficient medical officer to the exclusive duty of inspecting daily the prison hospital and bakery, requiring of him daily reports of their condition to headquarters.

We have the honor to remain, general, very respectfully,

T. S. HOPKINS,

Brigadier-General JOHN H. WINDER. *Acting Assistant Surgeon.*

[Indorsed:] Inspection report of Andersonville Prison, July, 1864.

The name of H. E. Watkins, acting assistant surgeon, is also attached to this report. I submitted the report to Chief Surgeon White. I waited two days, supposing that he would hand in his report. As that did not make its appearance, I called on him at his headquarters. He asked me "if I had written out my report." I told him that I was waiting for him, but that I had written out some suggestions. I read them. He approved them, saying I had written the truth. He told me to take my report to the Sumter Hospital, have it copied, getting Dr. Watkins to sign it with me, and then send it to his headquarters, and he would send it to General Winder. I did so. Several days elapsed. I heard nothing of the report until the field-officer, Colonel Harkey, of the Fifty-fifth Georgia, who was messing with me, told a gentleman in my presence that two medical reports had been submitted to him and other officers for inspection to report upon them. I asked him if he had mine. He said he had. They were to decide, I think, which report was to be received. The chief surgeon did not sign our report, but made another one. His report was rather different; he did not make altogether the same recommendations that I did. When I read him my report he approved it, and told me that he would sign it if I had it copied and sent to him. I did have it copied, and sent it up immediately. I know that he did not sign it, because I saw the report afterward, and I saw his report, which was different. I was assigned to the engineer department. The engineer officer in charge told me that he had from 1,000 to 1,200 negro men on the works. I was the surgeon assigned to that department. None of my cases died, except one man, who went away and died after he got home. Those men were under my charge from July 22, 1864, till, I think, the 8th of September, when I left, having been ordered to Millen. I went down with a portion of them.

Q. Did you find, by your examination, that Captain Wirz was in any degree the cause of the ills complained of—the overcrowding of the prisoners, etc.?

A. I do not know at whose door the fault lay; but the facts were evident. Captain Wirz's sign at his office designated him as the "commandant of the interior of the prison." I could not see any great difficulty in carrying out those suggestions I made. I think I could have had it done without much trouble. I cannot say if Captain Wirz was responsible for the overcrowded condition of the prison; I don't know who was responsible for it.

Q. In your opinion was Captain Wirz responsible for the evils existing when you made your report? Did you discover anything which led you to believe that he was in any degree guilty in that respect?

A. If I am compelled to answer that question, I must state, unhesitatingly, that it was the implicit confidence which General Winder had in Captain Wirz that caused that state of things to exist; otherwise, the general would certainly have visited the prison, and seen for himself its condition. General Winder did not visit the prison while I was there, that I ever knew of. I never heard of his going to the prison. He might have gone there without my knowledge; I cannot say that he did not visit the prison.

This report was made a few days before Colonel Chandler came upon the scene. Let me ask the reader to examine the seven causes, here set down by Dr. Hopkins, of the great mortality at the prison, and ask himself whether there is a single one of these causes which might not have been removed. Look at the preventive measures suggested. Were they not practical? Do we not know from the evidence already given that it was within the power of the prison management to have carried out every one of the seven preventive measures recommended? Here were thirty-odd thousand human beings for whose health and comfort and lives the rebel government had assumed the responsibility. They were starving for want of food; suffering for so simple and abundant a thing as water; exposed in their nakedness to the burning sun by day and the chill and dews and storm of the night; breathing foul air from the morass and dying at the rate of a hundred a day, and the sick with grossly inadequate medical attendance!

TESTIMONY OF DR. G. L. B. RICE.

Dr. Jones came along in September, and from him we learn that there had been no abatement of the horrible conditions which Dr.

TESTIMONY OF CONFEDERATE SURGEONS. 123

Hopkins had pointed out and which might easily have been remedied. And we shall see that these conditions were not improved until near the time when the prison was closed and comparatively few remained.

Dr. G. L. B. Rice was on duty at the prison from August 1, 1864, until about the middle of March, 1865. He testified to some facts which are given here, relating more particularly to Wirz, but should be remembered when the conduct of Wirz is being shown. He testified:[1]

I was on duty at Andersonville from about August 1, 1864, until March 10, 1865, I think. I was ordered to report to Dr. White, and he assigned me to duty at the stockade to attend the sick prisoners. We prescribed outside the stockade; I have forgotten the length of time; it was three or four weeks, more or less; after that I was sent to the hospital; a few days after I got there I was ordered to go into the stockade and report as officer of the day. I did so, and I found the stockade in a deplorable condition. I saw a great deal of suffering, filth, and everything that was bad and unpleasant. We prescribed by formulas or numbers. I commenced prescribing as I had been in the habit of doing at home; but I was informed that I would not be allowed to do that, that they had not the medicines. I was handed a list of the medicines that we had to use; they were in formulas and numbers from one up to a certain point—I have forgotten what; we had to use those; it was a new thing to me; I was not accustomed to it, and my opinion was that we could do very little good with that kind of prescription; I regarded that as a very unsafe method of practice. On some of those formulas which I had, the ingredients, I think, were put down; I know that they were toward the last; I did not analyze any of those potions to ascertain whether the report made on the label was true; I had to take their word for it. I complained of that method of practice among the surgeons. I asked them if there was no chance to do better. They said there was not; that some of them had gone to the chief surgeon and complained, and they said there was no other chance, and I concluded that if they could not do any better, I could do no better, and I did not make the attempt. . . .

I knew a great many to die there who I believe died from hunger and starvation and from cold and exposure. I think it was the 10th of March, 1865, when I left the prison. The rigors of the prison did not cease or lighten during the winter; the prisoners were exposed more or less all that time. If all the surgeons had been sent away, and if the prisoners had got the vegetables which they should have had, and more room, a great many more men could have been saved. They needed the right kind of diet more than medicine. They needed also additional room, I made verbal suggestions to Dr. Stevenson in relation to the wood of the stockade —that it was entirely inadequate—and the great necessity for having a larger supply of vegetables for the stockade and hospital. I mentioned to him one day that I had a good many vegetables at home-more than we needed—that they were rotting, and that if he would allow me to go home for a few days, I would bring those vegetables down for the prisoners without any charge; or if he could

[1] Record, p. 381 et seq.

not do that he could send some man to get them; that they were all going to waste and doing nobody any good, and that, if they were brought to the prison and used properly, they might save some men's lives. He observed that he would like to have them, and turned off and said no more about it. They were not sent for.

Q. Do you know anything about the investigation of the conduct of Dr. Stevenson?

A. I was there when a couple of surgeons came on. He was tried for making away with the money that was sent there for the use of the hospital, so I heard. That was the understanding. There was an investigation had. I think he was found guilty. I was called into the room where they were carrying on the investigation, and was asked a few questions by the committee. I do not know the amount of money Dr. Stevenson embezzled. I heard it was from $100,000 to $150,000. I don't know whether it was so or not.

I saw the hounds at Andersonville almost every day. I know that at one time when I was living in a little tent I lost my pocket-book; the hounds were brought and put on the track; that was a few days after I got there. I saw them there nearly every day after that. I one day saw a man who was torn by them; I forget the date; I have no idea of the time. He was knocked up very badly. His skin was not torn, but you could see the blue marks of the prints of the dogs' teeth. I happened to be passing Captain Wirz's headquarters about the time they brought the man up, and I asked some one what was the matter with him. He could hardly walk, and seemed to be bent over from the effects of scurvy, I presumed. I soon found that he had made his escape the night previous, and had been brought in by this man who had the dogs—had been caught by them. I saw the marks of teeth on the man's flesh. I have no idea what month that was. The man was nearly naked; he had nothing on but a shirt, I think. They told me that his clothes had been torn off by the dogs; that he attempted to climb a tree and that the dogs pulled him down.

I saw two dead bodies there during the time I was there on duty—one in the stockade and one in the hospital. The one in the hospital was shot through the breast. I walked in there one morning to attend to my duties, and I heard that a man had been shot that night by the sentry. I walked around to where he was and inquired of some prisoners how it happened, and they told me that he was a poor crippled man, (I think he had crutches lying by him,) who had walked up near the paling and the sentry had shot him. That case was in the hospital. I saw the other in the stockade near the south gate. I do not know how the entry was made in those cases in the hospital register.

The bad condition of the hospital and stockade continued all the time until I left, which was, I think, the 10th of March, 1865. I saw a great many die in the hospital from starvation, as well as in the stockade. I don't know whether Captain Wirz had anything to do with the rations in the hospital. I know that the chief surgeon had something to do with the rations. I did not speak with Dr. Stevenson again after I had told him once about the vegetables at my house. I never spoke of that matter to him any more. I frequently spoke to him. I several times told him about other things that they needed—straw, bunks, etc., to keep them from lying on the ground.

Dr. John C. Bates went to Andersonville on duty in September, 1864, and remained on duty until the latter part of March, 1865. One cannot read the descriptions given by this witness without feelings of infinite pity for the unhappy creatures whose sufferings he portrays. His testimony shows conclusively that nothing was done to improve the conditions, notwithstanding all the reports that had gone forward to the Richmond authorities. The witnesses whom I am now quoting speak first hand, and their testimony comes to us with all the more force since they make us see the prison in all its horror.

Be it remembered, too, that these witnesses were in the rebel service, and that nothing but the sacredness of their oaths to "testify to the truth and nothing but the truth" would ever have impelled them to make these damning disclosures.

TESTIMONY OF DR. JOHN C. BATES.[1]

I have been residing for the past four or five years in the State of Georgia. I am a practitioner of medicine, and have been engaged in that profession since 1850. I have been on duty at the Andersonville Prison as acting assistant surgeon. I was assigned there on the 19th of September, 1864; reported for duty on the 22d, and left there on the 26th of March, 1865. [A paper was here handed to witness.] I think I have seen that before. It is a pass given me by Captain Wirz to enter the stockade. [The pass was then put in evidence.] I was ordered by Medical Director Stout to report to I. H. or J. H. White, surgeon in charge. He having been hurt by some railroad accident, I reported to Dr. R. R. Stevenson.

I reported to Dr. Stevenson, who assigned me to the third division of the military prison hospital, under Dr. Sheppard; I was assigned to the fifteenth ward, as then designated.

Upon going to the hospital I went immediately to the ward to which I was assigned, and, although I am not an over-sensitive man, I must confess I was rather shocked at the appearance of things. The men were lying partially nude and dying and lousy, a portion of them in the sand and others upon boards which had been stuck up on little props, pretty well crowded together, a majority of them in small tents, looking to be tents that were not very serviceable at best. I went around and examined all that were placed in my charge. That was the condition of the men. By and by, as I became familiarized with the condition of affairs, the impressions which were at first produced upon me wore off, more or less. I became familiar with scenes of misery and they did not affect me so much. I inquired into the rations of the men; I felt disposed to do my duty; and after the men found that I was inclined to aid them so far as I could in my sphere of action, they frequently asked me for a teaspoonful of salt, or an order for a little siftings that came out of the meal. I would ask them what they wanted the siftings for; some of them wished them to make some bread. I would inquire

[1] Record, p. 27 et seq.

into the state of their disease, and if what they asked for would injure them, I would not allow them to have it. I would give them an order for sifted meal where I found that the condition of the patient required something better than siftings. They would come at times in considerable numbers to get these little orders for an extra ration, or if not a ration, whatever portion they could get. I spent a considerable portion of my time in writing orders, and I did it very laconically. I had three words that constituted a *bona fide* order, which should be respected by the head cook or baker. We commonly called him Bob—his name was Allen; he was from Illinois. The order would read in this way: "Bob—meal—Bates." If any more words were attached to it, it was not a genuine order. I used that discrimination in order to favor the sickest of them, so that they might get what they could, at the expense, perhaps, of those who could get along better without it. These orders were constantly applied for, and I would sign them till my patience was almost worn out. The meat ration was cooked at a different part of the hospital; and when I would go up there, especially when I was medical officer of the day, the men would gather around me and ask me for a bone. I would grant their requests so far as I saw bones. I would give them whatever I could find at my disposition without robbing others. I well knew that an appropriation of one ration took it from the general issue; that when I appropriated an extra ration to one man, some one else would fall minus upon that ration. I then fell back upon the distribution of bones. They did not presume to ask me for meat at all. So far as rations are concerned, that is about the way matters went along for some time after I went there.

Clothing we had none; they could not be furnished with any clothing, except that the clothing of the dead was generally appropriated to the living. We thus helped the living along as well as we could.

Of vermin or lice there was a very prolific crop there. I got to understand practically the meaning of the term "lousy"; I would generally find some upon myself after retiring to my quarters; they were so numerous that it was impossible for a surgeon to enter the hospital without having some upon him when he came out, if he touched anybody or anything save the ground, and very often if he merely stood still any considerable length of time he would get them upon him.

When I went to the hospital I found the men destitute of clothing and bedding; there was a partial supply of fuel, but not sufficient to keep the men warm and prolong their existence. Shortly after I arrived there I was appointed officer of the day. I learned that the officer of the day was in supreme command of all pertaining to the hospital, and that it was my duty as such to go into the various wards and divisions of the hospital and rectify anything that needed to be cared for. In visiting the hospital I made a pretty thorough examination. As a general thing, the patients were destitute; they were filthy and partly naked. There seemed to be a disposition only to get something to eat. The clamor all the while was for something to eat. They asked me for orders for this, that, and the other—peas or rice, or salt, or beef tea, or a potato, or a biscuit, or a piece of corn bread, or siftings, or meal.

Medicines were scarce; we could not get what we wished. We drew upon the indigenous remedies; they did not seem to answer. We gathered up large quantities of them, but very few served for medicines as we wished. We wanted the best and most powerful anti-scorbutics, as well as something that was soothing and healing, especially to the lining membrane of the alimentary canal, and such things as were calculated to counteract a dropsical disposition and a gangrenous infection. Those were prominent things in the hospital. We had not at all times the proper remedies to administer, and the indigenous remedies did not serve us, and could not serve us in those complaints. We were obliged to do the best we could.

There was in my ward a boy of fifteen or sixteen years, in whom I felt a particular interest. My attention was more immediately called to him from his youth, and he appealed to me in such a way that I could not well avoid heeding him. He would often ask me to bring him a potato, a piece of bread, a biscuit, or something of that kind, which I did; I would put them in my pocket and give them to him. I would sometimes give him a raw potato, and as he had the scurvy, and also gangrene, I would advise him not to cook the potato at all, but to eat it raw, as an anti-scorbutic. I supplied him in that way for some time, but I could not give him a sufficiency. He became bed-ridden upon the hips and back, lying upon the ground; we afterwards got him some straw. Those bed-ridden sores had become gangrenous. He became more and more emaciated, until he died. The lice, the want of bed and bedding, of fuel and food, were the cause of his death.

I was a little shy. I did not know that I was allowed to take such things to the patients; and I had been so often arrested that I thought it necessary to be a little shy in what I did, and keep it to myself. I would put a potato in my pocket and would turn around and let it drop to this man or others. I did not wish to be observed by anybody. When I first went there, I understood that it was positively against the orders to take anything in.

I can speak of other cases among the patients; two or three others in my ward were in the same condition; and there were others who came to their death from the bad condition of things and the lack of necessary supplies. That is my professional opinion.

I had occasion to visit the entire hospital occasionally, and so far as I saw its condition was generally the same as I have been describing. At the time I went there, I think, from the best observations I could make, there were, perhaps, 2,000 or 2,500 sick in that hospital.

We had cases of chilblains or frost-bitten feet. Most generally, in addition to what was said to be frost-bite, there was gangrene. I did not see the sores in the original chilblains. I do not think I can say if there were any amputations or any deaths resulting from sufferings of that character, not having charged my mind as to whether the amputations were in consequence of chilblains, or because, from accidental abrading of the surface, gangrene set in. But for a while amputations were practiced in the hospital almost daily, arising from a gangrenous and scorbutic condition, which, in many cases, threatened the saturation of the whole system with this gangrenous or offensive matter, unless the limb was amputated. In cases of amputation of that sort, it would sometimes became necessary to reamputate, from gangrene taking hold of the stump again. Some few successful amputations were made. I recollect two or three which were successful. I kept no statistics; those were kept by the prescription clerks and forwarded to headquarters. I did not think at the time that the surgeon-in-chief did all in his power to relieve the condition of those men, and I made my report accordingly.

In visiting the wards in the morning I would find persons lying dead; sometimes I would find them lying among the living. I recollect on one occasion telling my steward to go and wake up a certain one, and when I went myself to wake him up he was taking his everlasting sleep. That occurred in another man's ward, when I was officer of the day. Upon several occasions, on going into my own wards, I found men whom we did not expect to die, dead from the sensation of chilblains produced during the night. This was in the hospital. I was not so well acquainted with how it was in the stockade. I judge, though, from what I saw, that, numbers suffered in the same way there.

The effect of scurvy upon the systems of the men as it developed itself there was the next thing to rottenness. Their limbs would become drawn up. It would manifest itself constitutionally. It would draw them up. They would go on crutches sideways, or crawl upon their hands and knees or on their haunches and feet as well as they could. Some could not eat unless it was something that needed no mastication. Sometimes they would be furnished beef tea or boiled rice, or such things as that would be given them, but not to the extent which I would like to see. In some cases they could not eat corn bread; their teeth would be loose and their gums all bleeding. I have known cases of that kind. I do not speak of it as a general thing. They would ask me to interest myself and get them something which they could swallow without subjecting them to so much pain in mastication. It seemed to me I did express my professional opinion that men died because they could not eat the rations they got.

I cannot state what proportion of the men in whose cases it became necessary to amputate from gangrenous wounds, and also to reamputate from the same cause, recovered. Never having charged my mind on the subject, and not expecting to be called upon in such a capacity, I cannot give an approximate opinion which I would deem reliable. In 1864, amputations from that cause occurred very frequently indeed; during the short time in 1865 that I was there, amputations were not frequent.

I cannot state with any certainty the proportion of prisoners treated in the hospital who recovered and were sent back to the stockade. There were clerks appointed to keep all those accounts, and I tried to confine myself strictly to my own duty, and did not interest myself in any statistical enumeration of facts or data.

The prisoners in the stockade and the hospital were not very well protected from the rain; only by their own meager means, their blankets, holes in the earth, and such things. In the spring of 1865, when I was in the stockade, I saw a shed thirty feet wide and sixty feet long-the sick principally were in that. They were in about the same condition as those in the hospital. As to the prisoners generally, their only means of shelter from the sun and rain were their blankets, if they carried any along with them. I regarded that lack of shelter as a source of disease.

Rice, peas, and potatoes were the common issue from the Confederate government; but as to turnips, carrots, tomatoes, and cabbage, of that class of vegetables, I never saw any. There was no green corn issued. Western Georgia is generally considered a pretty good corn-growing country.

[Mr. Baker objected to the line. of examination that was being pursued by the judge-advocate, on the ground that it was taking too wide a range, and that the evidence elicited was not connected in any way with the defendant. The court, after deliberation, overruled the objection. The witness resumed.]

Green corn could have been used as an anti-scorbutic and as an antidote. A vegetable diet, so far as it contains any alterative or medical qualities, serves as an anti-scorbutic.

The ration issued to the patients in the hospital was corn meal, beef, bacon—pork occasionally but not much of it; at times, green corn, peas, rice, salt, sugar, and potatoes. I enumerate those as the varieties served out. Potatoes were not a constant ration; at times they were sent in, perhaps a week or two weeks at a time, and then they would drop off. The daily ration was less from the time I went there in September, through October, November, and December, than it was from January till March 26th, the time I left. I never made a calculation as to the number of rations intended for each man; I was never called to do that. So far as I saw, I believe I would feel safe in saying that, while there might have been less, the amount was not over twenty ounces for twenty-four hours.

From January to March the rations were better than they had been before. The surgeon of the post had been changed. Dr. Stevenson was superseded by Dr. Clayton, who, I thought, interested himself very much to relieve the sufferings of the prisoners there. While Dr. Stevenson was director of the hospital, I never saw much interest manifested on his part to relieve the necessities of the prisoners.

Q. What number of ounces of healthy nutritious food is necessary to support life and health ?

A. Upon one unvaried diet, confining a man to any one article or any one set of articles for a length of time, I do not know but that a man would starve to death upon plenty. That is a physiological question. The various secretions of the system demand a multifarious diet for the proper feeding of the system. If you were to confine a man to a single article of diet or four or five articles of diet for one year, I am inclined to say that he could not live. It is a nice physiological point. The monotonous diet issued from September till January, which continued afterward, though in larger quantities, was such as the men, without varying it, could not have lived upon without very bad effects, upon the nervous system especially. These are physiological points which I did not expect to be asked about. The diet was monotonous, consisting of corn meal, peas of not very good quality, sometimes sweet potatoes, sometimes tolerably good beef, at other times not so; sometimes good bacon, at other times raw bacon, which was not good. It is my opinion that men starved to death in consequence of the paucity of the rations, especially in the fall of 1864, the quality not being very good and the quantity deficient.

Q. Did you ever examine the question sufficiently to state the number of ounces of nutritious food necessary to sustain life and health?

A. I had a little discussion with Dr. Clayton upon that. It was after the first of January when he took charge. I was ordered to make a particular and especial report of every article that was issued, taking the number of patients then in the hospital and the attendants. I went to the commissary myself, and saw the provisions loaded up, carried in, and weighed. I took those figures and the figures of the attendants in the hospital. The calculations which I made there were that sixteen ounces of meal would make twenty-eight ounces of bread, and sixteen ounces of flour would make twenty-two ounces of bread. I gave the prisoners in that calculation the benefit of the increase. In reference to the meat, I did not make any calculation for the bones, because they were generally disposed of by the prisoners, who were glad to get them. By the first definite calculation which I made, the patients received thirty-two and some tenths ounces, and the attendants received thirty or thirty-one ounces. This was after Dr. Clayton got charge. These facts were stated in my first report to him. Six days afterward I was called upon to make a similar report, and I think then the attendants got thirty-two ounces, and the patients got twenty-eight ounces of this monotonous food. I am not prepared to say how long life could be sustained upon a monotonous diet.

Q. Did you think that the food served out was sufficient in quantity?

A. After January, 1865, the quantity was sufficient if it could have been varied. Dr. Clayton and myself concluded that thirty to thirty-three ounces for the sick was a sufficiency at that time. Many of the sick did not consume all that was issued to them, but appropriated it otherwise. There was great trading and bargaining going on all the time. I know that the patients in the hospital greatly improved after the change of administration from Dr. Stevenson to Dr. Clayton. I know that they got more provisions and were better cared for. I never made a report to Dr. Clayton as medical officer of the day but he heeded every point, and when I pointed out any deficiency he would ask me to interest myself personally and remedy it, and he would do anything that could be done.

Q. Was that the fact before Dr. Clayton took charge?

A. I cannot say that it was.

An altercation took place there between Dr. James and Captain Wirz. Upon going into the hospital one morning I learned my chief clerk was arrested, and had been ordered to be bucked and gagged; I did not see him gagged; I saw him bucked; he was sitting outside of the gate of the hospital. Upon inquiry, I found that he had by some means or other neglected to report a man that was missing; and it was a question whether the duty of reporting this man belonged to the Confederate sergeant, whose duty it was to call the roll of the sick, or to this clerk. Dr. James wrote a letter to Captain Wirz, or some other man; I saw that letter; Dr. James read it to me. I am not positive as to whom it was addressed to; but he spoke of Captain Wirz's tyranny in the punishment of this man, as he was very faithful in doing his duty. Dr. James rather felt outraged at the manner in which the man had been treated, and he made a demurrer.

Q. Describe what kind of exhalations or odors arose from that prison.

A. There are two kinds of miasma laid down by medical writers: the *kino* and the *ideo;* one consists of exhalations from the human body in a state of disease, and the other of exhalations from vegetable decompositions and saturations generally. There were both kinds there. The miasmatic effluvia emanating from the hospital was very potent and offensive indeed.

Q. In what way would it affect the healthy?

A. If I had a scratch upon my hand—if the skin was broken or abraded in the least—I did not venture to go into the hospital without protecting it with adhesive plaster. I saw several sores originating from the infection of the gangrenous effluvia saturating the atmosphere. For this reason we were all very cautious. If a prisoner whose system was reduced by inanition, which would invite and develop disease, should chance to stump his toe (some of them were barefooted) or scratch his hand, almost invariably the next report to me, so far as my charge was concerned, was gangrene, so potent was the influence.

Immediately upon the west side of the stockade, and between there and the depot, there was timber scattered; on the north side, beyond the cook-house a little, there was plenty of timber; on the south side plenty had been cut in logs and lay there, and down by the hospital there was plenty. That is a woody country, and there was plenty of wood within a mile. It was fine timber, and could have been made into shingles or clapboards. I did not see any of it used to make shelter for the prisoners. A set of sheds were being erected there, as represented on the diagram, outside of the stockade and the hospital. They were in course of erection at the time of the abandonment of the place. No patients had ever been put in them. I regret to say that the supply of wood was not sufficient to keep the prisoners from what we term freezing to death. They would not, perhaps, actually freeze to death, but a patient whose blood is thin, and his system worn down, is very susceptible to the influence of cold. In the absence of sufficient food, sufficient stimulus, and especially in the absence of fuel, many of the patients (I speak now of what I saw in my own ward) would, during the night, become so chilled that in the morning, passing round, I would remark to my steward, "Last night did the work for that poor fellow; he will die"; or, "This one will die; I cannot resuscitate him with the means in my hands, his system is so reduced." Lying upon the ground during those chilly nights, (the weather was not freezing, but sufficient to thoroughly chill the whole system,) the patient would reach a condition in which resuscitation was a matter of impossibility after he commenced going downhill from this exposure. I have seen a number die in that way.

In my judgment there was sufficient timber growing in the vicinity to supply fuel for cooking and for keeping the prisoners warm, and also to furnish shelter for them. I frequently made observation while there, that there was plenty of wood to supply every demand—shingles, boards, logs to make huts, and plenty for fuel. That is a woody country; the wood is pine wood. I judged that it could be made into boards and rails from the fact that they were pretty plenty there, and from the fact that I saw the boys splitting boards for the new hospital shed that was going up. There was no deficiency of wood.

[A diagram was exhibited to witness.]

I have seen that before; it was given to me in the Andersonville Prison by Felix De La Baume. The tents, chimneys, fence, trees, cart and mule, etc., are correct. One sketch here of "Dr. Bates" is pretty good, but rather spindle-shanked. The great point in which it is not *facsimile* is that too few men are represented. If there were forty delineated where there is one it would be more correct. These men walking on their hands and knees and on crutches, some carrying their tin cups in their mouths, represent men who could not go there otherwise. They were afflicted with scurvy as a general thing. One man represented here I recognize as a man named Ison, who was a subject of dementia; he only crept along on his haunches and feet. I recognize several others whose names I never learned, but whom I frequently saw. That man with the bucket in his mouth, I frequently saw crawling up for his rations. I see one man here representing "Dr. Bates examining the character and quantity of the beef," together with the Confederate surgeon and Ed. Young, boss of that cook-house. I also see one figure representing "Dr. Bates giving beef-bones to the cripples." It was my prerogative as officer of the day to supervise the cooking and administration of the rations, and to attend to anything that generally belonged to the hospital. When rations were being issued I would frequently go there. Those detailed to cut up the meat would put the bones in one pile and count the rations and put them carefully in another. When I would go there from twenty to one hundred or more would ask me, some of them very imploringly, for a bone. I would say, "Yes, you can have all the bones." I see that I am represented here as handing bones to those cripples. I would hand them out as here represented. The general representation in this diagram is about correct, save that there were twenty or forty men to one represented here. They were very thick about the cook-house.

[Diagram was then put in evidence.]¹

On entering the stockade, I would find dead prisoners. They were generally laid up at the gate under some sheds or boughs constituting a dead-house. They were first brought out to the gate and laid just inside of the inner stockade; they were then carried on litters to the inside of the outer stockade, and from there they were hauled away in wagons—sometimes two-horse, sometimes four-horse wagons. They were laid in the wagons. They were laid in the wagon, I believe, head foremost, one on another, regularly along in layers. I do not know how they were buried.

The dead-house of the hospital was in the southwest corner. When I first went there, what was called a dead-house consisted of some boards put up into a kind of shed. These boards were used by the inmates of the hospital or somehow else; at any rate, they disappeared. For some time the dead were laid there without any shelter. Every time I came on duty as officer of the day, which was every six days, I reported that there was no dead-house, and called the attention of the authorities to the erection of a dead-house or some place to deposit the dead, not to let them lie without shelter and exposed to the sun. This was in the hospital. They did not allow the corpse to lie long enough to cause any exhalations from putrefaction. Outside they were hauled off immediately to the graveyard; at least I saw them hauled away—I never visited the graveyard.

We needed a dead-house, so as to have some place to lay the corpses decently. At one time we got a tent erected for a dead-house, but that did not last very long. Every morning when I would go in I would find a blanket or a quilt sliced off. The men would appropriate them to wrap themselves up. At first the top commenced going, and in a few days all was gone. I remarked that it was no use to erect such dead-houses as that, except to supply the men with blankets, though I had no objection to their being erected every night, if the men could thereby get blankets. If my memory serves me right, no more dead-houses were erected. I think that tent I managed to get erected was the last.

¹ This sketch and many other exhibits originally in the record have disappeared. I caused a search to be made for them, but none can be found.

The morning after making my first tour as officer of the day, I sat down and made a report, the language of which I do not now recollect, but the substance was based upon the condition in which I found the hospital. That report was sent up, and I being a novice in military matters, for some things which I had said in that report I received a written reprimand, signed "R. R. Stevenson, by Dr. Diller," his assistant in the office. The date of that report was about the 24th or 25th of September, two or three days after I reported. I continued to make those reports, but I think they were not heeded.

Meetings of the surgeons were held to see whether these things could not be remedied. Petitions were written and partially signed, and were then destroyed for want of a proper channel by which to send them up, or some other objection. Finally there was a report made to the medical department; it was to be sent to Surgeon-General Moore or the secretary of war; I am not certain which. Dr. Eiland, Dr. McVey and some other doctors there signed it. It was not sent, as I understood. These things were talked of, and the result was a medical investigation was ordered to be made by Dr. Llewellyn and Dr. Guillot. They were to inquire how the hospital fund had been used—the hospital fund that was appropriated for the Union prisoners. During the course of this investigation medical gentlemen were called upon the stand, myself among the rest, and the account current of the hospital was examined by these two medical gentlemen, who were inspectors under orders from the secretary of war. This was after Dr. Stevenson left; he was ordered, I think, to Florence. I never saw any official opinion or report emanating from Dr. Guillot or Dr. Llewellyn.

[A paper was exhibited to witness.]
Q. Do you recognize the handwriting in that document?
A. It was written before I went to the Andersonville Prison, but I recognize it as the handwriting of Dr. Pelot, so far as I recollect his handwriting. I frequently saw him write; we made our morning report together.
Q. Were you familiar with his handwriting?
A. Tolerably so.

[The paper purporting to be a morning report, made by Dr. Pelot as medical officer of the day, was offered in evidence. Mr. Baker objected to its admission, on the ground that it was not in any way connected with the prisoner. The court, after deliberation, overruled the objection. The following report was then put in evidence:]

FIRST DIVISION, C. S. M. P. HOSPITAL,
September 5, 1864.

SIR: As officer of the day, for the past twenty-four hours, I have inspected the hospital and found it in as good condition as the nature of the circumstances will allow. A majority of the bunks are still unsupplied with bedding, while in a portion of the division the tents are entirely destitute of either bunks, bedding or straw, the patients being compelled to lie upon the bare ground. I would earnestly call attention to the article of diet. The corn bread received from the bakery being made up without sifting, is wholly unfit for the use of the sick; and often (in the last twenty-four hours) upon examination, the inner portion is found to be perfectly raw. The meat (beef) received by the patients does not amount to over two ounces a day, and for the past three or four days no flour has been issued. The corn bread cannot be eaten by many, for to do so would be to increase the diseases of the bowels, from which a large majority are suffering, and it is therefore thrown away. All their rations received by way of sustenance is two ounces of boiled beef and half pint of rice soup per day. Under these circumstances, all the skill that can be brought to bear upon their cases by the medical officer will avail nothing. Another point to which I feel it my duty to call your attention is the deficiency of medicines. We have but little more than indigenous barks and roots with which to treat the numerous forms of disease to which our attention is daily called. For the treatment of wounds, ulcers, &c., we have literally nothing except water.

Our wards—some of them—are filled with gangrene, and we are compelled to fold our arms and look quietly upon its ravages, not even having stimulants to support the system under its depressing influences, this article being so limited in supply that it can only be issued for cases under the knife. I would respectfully call your earnest attention to the above facts, in the hope that something may be done to alleviate the sufferings of the sick.

I am, sir, very respectfully, your obedient servant,

J. CREWS PELOT,
Assistant Surgeon C. S. and Officer of the Day.

Surgeon E. D. EILAND,
In charge First Division C. S. M. P. Hospital.

Q. What effect had the treatment you have described upon the mental condition and moral sensibilities of the prisoners?

A. There was among them generally an enervation of the nervous system, which ran down in consequence of this scarcity of supplies. The nervous system must of course sink under such pressure. I have seen the effect manifested in idiocy, dementia, and other mental weaknesses. I have seen several instances of that; not a great many; four or five, perhaps, came under my immediate observation. Morally, I would have expected that such abject circumstances would have produced deep humiliation and resignation, but the effect was otherwise. The moral feeling of the prisoners gradually evaporated. Instead of having a healthy influence upon their morals, it had a contrary effect. Men seemed to abandon themselves. It seemed to me at times that no man interested himself further than "I"; a well man would sometimes steal from a sick man; and if a sick man could steal anything from a well man, or anybody else, he would do so. It seemed to me that all lived for themselves, having no regard for anybody else. I judged this to be superinduced by the paucity of the rations —the starving condition of the men.

Q. From your observation of the condition and surroundings of our prisoners—their food, their drink, their exposure by day and by night, and all the circumstances you have described—state your professional opinion as to what proportion of deaths occurring there were the result of the circumstances and surroundings which you have narrated.

A. I feel myself safe in saying that seventy-five per cent of those who died might have been saved, had those unfortunate men been properly cared for as to food, clothing, bedding, etc.

Andersonville is nothing more than a railroad station. There were but a few houses there until the military shanties were put up. There were commissary stores there. There was one private store there; I think a dry-goods store. There was no grocery store while I was there. The prisoners could not obtain anything for their comfort or convenience without going into the country and foraging. They were not allowed to do that. Some of the paroled men used to do it, sometimes.

I have quoted the testimony of Dr. Bates at some length because it sets forth the phases of prison life at Andersonville in a way to bring home to the reader the reality of the struggle for existence which the prisoners were compelled to undergo, and fully explains why the mortality was unprecedented. We need have no hesitation in believing him when he says that "seventy-five per cent of those who died might have been saved, had those unfortunate men been properly cared for as to food, clothing, bedding, etc."

Do the apologists for Wirz and his co-conspirators think that the American people will ever become reconciled to the erection of a monument to Wirz whose only claim for such honor is the record of the charnel-house of Andersonville? Is it reasonable to ask the surviving Union soldiers and their friends and sympathizers to remain silent in the face of the gravely untrue inscriptions placed upon the Wirz monument?

Dr. G. G. Roy was assigned to duty at the prison on September 1, 1864, and remained until the last of April, 1865. Of the prisoners in the stockade he said: "They presented the most horrible spectacle of humanity that I ever saw in my life. A good many were suffering from scurvy and other diseases; a good many were naked; a large majority were barefooted; a good many without hats; their condition generally was almost indescribable." But let the record speak of what he saw:[1]

TESTIMONY OF DR. G. G. ROY.

I was on duty at Andersonville; I was ordered to report there for duty on the first of September, 1864, by the medical director of the army of Tennessee, Dr. Stout; I mean the rebel army.

Surgeon Isaiah H. White was chief surgeon in charge of the post at Andersonville when I went there; I do not know that there was any one particularly who was the surgeon in charge of the medical department of the stockade; so far as the chief surgeons were concerned, there were two there; Surgeon White acted as post surgeon, and confined himself to the administrative duties of the post; Dr. Stevenson was acting as chief surgeon in charge of the hospital, and of the medical department of the stockade; when I got there I found the hospital in a very deplorable condition; it was composed of tents of all sizes; I cannot say that it was laid off with any particular regularity; there was no comfort attached to it whatever; many of the tents were badly worn, torn and rotten, and of course permitted the water to leak through; the patients were not furnished with bunks or bedding, or bedclothing, or anything of that sort; when I reported for duty I was under the immediate charge of Dr. Stevenson; I was sent to Andersonville under peculiar circumstances, under positive orders to Dr. White to have organized a division, and for six days I was not put on

[1] Record, p. 91 et seq.

duty, because it took about that time to organize a division out of the divisions that were there, which were then three in number; I then took charge of the fourth division, the last that was formed; there were very few cases of gangrene coming under my treatment while I was there; I got there after most of the surgery had been done, consequently there were very few cases of gangrene; we never got vegetables suficient while I was there; my duty was to make requisitions on the chief surgeon, as he was called, Dr. Stevenson; I did so and failed to get them; after Dr. Clayton took charge of the hospital we had fewer patients, and were pretty well supplied with food and medicine; I think that would be the decision of every prisoner that was there.

I was told that there were from 30,000 to 35,000 prisoners in the stockade when I went on duty at Andersonville. They presented the most horrible spectacle of humanity that I ever saw in my life. A good many were suffering from scurvy and other diseases; a good many were naked; a large majority barefooted; a good many without hats. Their condition generally was almost indescribable. I attributed that condition to long confinement and the want of the necessaries and comforts of life, and all those causes that are calculated to produce that condition of the system where there is just vitality enough to permit one to live. In the first place, at Andersonville, the prisoners were too densely crowded. In the next place there was no shelter, except such as they constructed themselves, which was very insufficient. A good many were in holes in the earth with their blankets thrown over them; a good many had a blanket or oilcloth thrown over poles; some were in tents constructed by their own ingenuity, and with just such accommodations as their own ingenuity permitted them to contrive.

Q. Who had control of the hospital so far as its discipline was concerned? Who had command of the guards stationed about it?

A. There was always a sergeant at the gate who was under the control of Captain Wirz.

Q. Had Captain Wirz any command over you surgeons, other than that of stationing the guards about you and giving you passes to the hospital?

A. Under his orders, which I had occasion to see once, I think his power was almost absolute.

[Mr. Baker objected to witness stating the contents of the orders.]

Q. Had Captain Wirz other command over you than that of allowing you to go back and forth to the hospital on his passes? Had he control over the administration of your duties?

A. He did not exercise that control, but his orders gave him such power.

[Mr. Baker objected to witness stating anything contained in the orders. The court, after deliberation, sustained the objection.]

Q. Did the prisoner ever state to you that he had command over your action in the administration of your duties?

A. He did.

Q. State the circumstances.

A. At one time, in consequence of a difficulty between one of my assistants and Captain Wirz, we had occasion to call for these orders and the orders were presented; Assistant Surgeon Dr. James had written a communication to me about the punishment of one of the hospital attendants of his division by Captain Wire, which communication I indorsed and sent to Dr. Clayton, who was then senior surgeon; he forwarded it to Colonel Thurlow, who was then commandant of the post at Andersonville, and it was referred to Captain Wirz for remarks; when the paper was returned to Colonel Thurlow I am not able to say, but it never came back to me; no indorsement was put upon the paper, but a reply was made in a communication from Captain Wirz, which reply made it necessary for Dr. James to find out what were the orders; in other words, it made it necessary for us, as medical officers, to know the relations which we held with the officers of the post; we found from the orders that we held no power, that we had, you may say, no rights, and that if Captain Wirz felt disposed to do anything in the hospital which his orders allowed him to do, (and they gave him almost absolute power,) he could do it without consulting a medical officer.

Q. From whom did he get that authority?

A. From Brigadier-General John H. Winder.

Q. What was General Winder's status there at that time?

A. He was not there at that time.

Q. Where was he?

A. I do not know; he made his headquarters at Millen; I do not recollect where he was then, whether at Columbia, Florence or Savannah.

Q. Do you know anything of the prisoner putting men of the hospital in stocks, or exercising his command over attendants at the hospital?

A. I saw, one instance, and I am fully convinced in my own mind of another.

Q. Give the instance you saw.

A. That was the case of the young man to whom I have just alluded, the chief clerk of Dr. James, who was bucked; he was sitting outside the gate as I rode up to the hospital one morning; I inquired the cause, and was told Captain Wirz had ordered it.

Q. Do you know the reason why the man was bucked?

A. I knew it from that communication which I have mentioned.

I understood that there was a dead-line around the hospital; the understanding I had of it was that prisoners passing it should be shot; one of my patients was shot somewhere about the latter part of 1864, or the first of 1865; I don't remember exactly; the man was killed; he lived hardly three minutes; he was shot through the heart; I examined him afterwards; I did not see him shot; it happened before I arrived at the hospital in the morning.[1]

TESTIMONY OF DR. B. J. HEAD.[2]

I was assigned to duty when I first went there, but was sick and did not attend to it. I remained sick for several days. As soon as I recovered sufficiently I went and reported again to Dr. White for duty. He assigned me a division of the hospital, and I attended to that while I remained there. I found that the sufferings of the men there were very great, resulting from the diseases they were suffering under and from the want of the proper kind of dieting, remedies,

---

[1] This testimony should be considered in connection with the specific acts of cruelty by Wirz.

[2] Record, p. 362 et seq.

etc. I think I could have done more, indeed I know I could, with proper dieting than I could with the medicines that we had. When first I went there, I think for two days, not more, I examined each individual case, made my own diagnosis, and wrote out my own prescriptions accordingly. I found that the medicines had not been supplied; I asked the reason why, and they said to me I was not to practice in that way; that I had to practice according to the numbers and formulas that they had. I said, "I know nothing of these formulas and numbers and care nothing for them, and I am not going to practice in any such way." Then I went my rounds and diagnosed the cases again and made out a prescription for each case. It was very laborious; I had a good many under my charge. I sent up the prescriptions and they were again refused, and my clerk, who was what we down South call "a Yankee," told me that it was useless for me to make out these prescriptions.

Q. Explain what these formulas and numbers meant.

A. They commenced with one and, perhaps, ran up to thirty-odd. "No. 1" was good, perhaps, for diarrhœa; "No. 2" for dysentery; "No. 3" for seorbutus; "No. 4" for something else, and so on. It was taking the discretion entirely away from the prescribing physician himself. I was informed after I left that that system was abandoned. I objected to it because I could not prescribe properly for my patients. I looked upon it as utter quackery. Anybody, whether he had ever read medicine or not, could practice medicine according to the fomulas, if he could only diagnose the cases and find out what was the matter with the patients, but it was often doubtful if the prescription would suit a case in its present condition. The doctors, however, had to take that or nothing. Part of the time there was not even that, and they had nothing in the world to give their patients but a little red-oak bark as an astringent and other barks that we could get out of the woods. Frequently men would die for want of a stimulant. I could not get it; I would make requisition for it and sometimes I would get some and sometimes I would not.

Here is the testimony of a group of professional men, seven in number, which is entitled to every presumption of reliability and truthfulness. No reasonable hypothesis can be advanced which can shake the conclusions of this evidence. It is incredible that all these men would swear falsely against the government they had served. Besides, their testimony, while brought more nearly to us because of the personal contact of the witnesses with the facts narrated, is but confirmatory of Colonel Chandler's and Dr. Jones's and other reports made alone for the eye of the Richmond authorities and impartial beyond all question.

Further confirmation is found in the appearance of the prisoners who were rescued by our victorious armies, and were brought out of their confinement, restored to freedom, to pure air, and wholesome food, by their sympathetic and horrified comrades in arms.

TESTIMONY OF DR. WILLIAM BALSER.

Dr. William Balser had occasion to treat a large body of prisoners who were on their way to freedom from prison life in April and May, 1865. His testimony deals with their condition shortly after leaving Andersonville. He testified:[1]

My position is acting assistant surgeon, contract surgeon. I was stationed at Hilton Head, South Carolina, twenty-seven months. I had occasion to treat the prisoners returned from Andersonville at Jacksonville, Florida, from the 1st to the 26th of May. I was ordered there on the 28th of April. There arrived at Jacksonville on the first of May 3,250 prisoners, and the same day that I arrived 50 more arrived. They were in a most horrible condition, nearly naked. If they did have anything on it was only rags. They were covered with filth and lice. They had sores all over them, and a great many of them were living skeletons. The most prominent disease among them was scurvy and diarrhœa. The diarrhœa seemed to be a symptom of the scurvy, not the ordinary camp diarrhea that we see in our army. The men got better as soon as they got better treatment and fresh vegetables. Fresh vegetables generally increased our ordinary diarrhœa. A great number of the prisoners had their arms and legs swelled up three or four times their natural size and actually black with extravasated blood. They had ulcers three or four inches in diameter on their arms and calves of their legs. Some of them, from the effects of the scurvy, had necrosis of the jaws, so that I was obliged to pull out pieces of bone nearly an inch long. Some of them had lost the eye from ulceration of the anterior portion of the cornea. Some of them were totally blind, no doubt from extravasation of blood as well as from fluid in the posterior parts of the eye. A good many were idiotic and demented from softness of the brain, resulting, no doubt, from long suffering. Bad nourishment and exposure to the weather would cause that. There were 3,300 at Jacksonville altogether, and I do not believe there were 200 who did not require treatment, more or less. From the 1st of May to the 26th of May, when the last of them were taken away, there had died between 80 or 90. The 3,300 were not there all the time. On the 9th of May between 1,300 and 1,400 were taken away, part to the hospital at Hilton Head and part to Annapolis. On the 15th or 16th of May there was another batch taken away, so that on the 26th of May, when the hospital steamer Cosmopolitan came to take off the balance, there were only from 250 to 300 men left there. I know from the records that between 40 and 50 died at the hospital at Hilton Head. I do not believe that one-half of them will ever again be fit for their former occupations. I take it for granted that they were mostly mechanics and farmers. I do not believe that they will ever be strong enough to perform the same amount of work.

[Four photographic pictures, one of them being already in evidence, and the others being subsequently put in evidence, were here shown to the witness.[2]] I have seen cases similar to those; I have seen numbers of them, not individual cases, but, I might say, by the dozen. Long-continued, improper, and insufficient

---
[1] Record, p. 151 et seq.
[2] These photographs, sent up with the record to the War Department, have with other exhibits disappeared.

food, and exposure to the weather, produce this condition of things among these prisoners; to the sun as well as to the cold and rain storms. I also saw several cases of gangrene, produced no doubt by exposure to cold and (in the latter part of April) to the sun. From the history given by the men, their feet commenced to blister and all vitality left their limbs. I do not meet with these peculiarities of disease in treating the soldiers of our army. I have been in the service three years and eight months, and during that time I have only seen one case of scurvy in our army, and I have been where there was a chance for men to get it, on the peninsula. I did not find it necessary to make amputations in treating these returned prisoners; they were too far gone. They died three or four days after they came to Jacksonville. I made no amputations on the survivors.

I was educated as a physician in New York city. I am a regular graduate of medicine. I had been in practice two or three months before going to Jacksonville. I was in the hospital as surgeon about twenty-three months before these prisoners came to me. Those thirty-three hundred prisoners arrived between the 28th of April and the 1st of May, 1865. I knew they came from Andersonville from the statement of nearly every one of them, and from the official lists of the provost marshal general of the department of the south; official reports are sent with them. I know that all these 3,300 came from there. I know nothing about Andersonville myself, thank God.

Witnesses varied in their statements of the interior of the prison. Colonel Chandler reported the actual fact to have been that the prisoners had about six square feet to the man—scarcely enough for all to lie down at once. He probably deducted the unavailable ground. Dr. Jones estimated the area as 33.2 square feet to the man, which he said represented "the condition of the stockade in a better light even than it really was; for a considerable breadth of land along the stream was low and boggy and useless for any purpose except that of defecation." He makes no mention of the dead-line space taken out, or of the necessary passageways for admitting supplies, or space occupied by improvised shelter. Captain James M. Moore, in his official report to the war department, gave the dimensions of the prison as 1,540 feet long by 750 feet wide. This was, no doubt, by actual measurement. He gave the strip taken off by the dead-line as 17 feet, which reduced the prison to 1,506 feet by 716 feet, or 1,078,296 square feet. The evidence showed that the swamp covered about two acres and the necessary passageways another acre, or 131,880 square feet, which would leave 946,416 square feet. At times there were 35,000 prisoners at Andersonville Prison, each of whom had 27 square feet, or a space 3 by 9 feet. When there were 30,000 the space would be 31 feet, or 5 by 6.2 feet. It is not difficult to understand why these miserable creatures died as rapidly in the stockade as outside in the hospital.

Let the reader picture this compact mass of human beings, ragged, hatless, shoeless, many of them stark naked, moving about and necessarily jostling each other as they sought a change of position—the sun beating down on their devoted heads, or the rain pelting upon them, making the earth under their feet a sea of mud, as some witnesses described it. Add to this scene the physicial condition of these men, reduced to skeletons by starvation and wasting disease, and then try to realize the horrors of this death-pit!

In this narrow space the prisoner was obliged to protect himself as he might and in this 3 by 9 feet he was forced to cook most of his scanty rations and practically to live night and day. It seems incredible, that men could withstand such a life for months and survive. All the witnesses, rebel and prisoners, concurred in the belief that one, of the potent causes of death was the crowded condition of the prison, and out of all the causes of the mortality this was the least difficult of removal. The men stood ready to work their way to pure air and greater freedom of movement; the rebel authorities resolutely refused them this privilege.

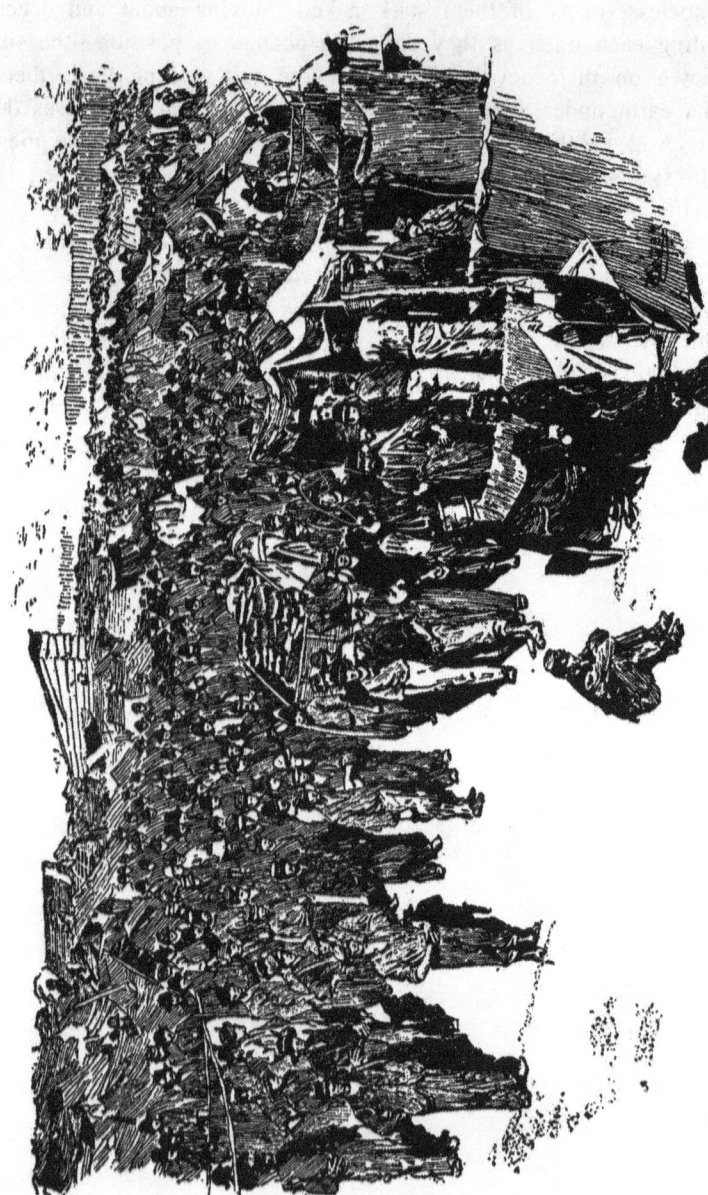

SCENE NEAR THE NORTH GATE—DISTRIBUTING RATIONS

[From an old photograph.]

CHAPTER VII.

CONDITIONS AT ANDERSONVILLE CONTINUED—TESTIMONY OF REV. FATHER HAMILTON—NO SHELTER FROM SUN OR STORMS—FATHER HAMILTON CRAWLED INTO BURROWS TO ADMINISTER LAST SACRAMENT TO DYING—PRISONERS COVERED WITH VERMIN—TESTIMONY OF CITIZENS LIVING IN THE SOUTH—PUBLICITY OF THE SUFFERING OF PRISONERS—SUPPLIES WERE OBTAINABLE AND SUFFICIENT TO HAVE SUSTAINED THE PRISONERS — PRISONERS MIGHT HAVE BEEN SHELTERED—THE PRISON MIGHT HAVE BEEN ENLARGED—MEANS OF TRANSPORTATION AVAILABLE—SUPPLIES SENT BY SANITARY COMMISSION.

REV. WILLIAM JOHN HAMILTON, a Catholic clergyman, visited the prison in May, 1864. He resided in the South, at the city of Macon, Georgia, and voluntarily went to Andersonville in pursuit of his priestly office. What he saw and experienced is confirmatory of what has already been shown. It is especially important as describing the condition in which he found the prisoners as early as May, 1864. It shows that long before the frightful and dreadful sufferings and death of July and August the prisoners were passing through a like ordeal. He testified:

TESTIMONY OF REV. WM. JOHN HAMILTON.

I am pastor of the Catholic church in Macon, Georgia.[1] I visited Andersonville three times. It was one of the missions attached to my church. I went there, I think, in the month of May, 1864, and spent a day there. The following week I went and spent three days there among the prisoners, and then returned and wrote a report on the condition of the hospital and stockade to my bishop, in order that he might send the requisite number of priests to visit the prisoners there; and I visited it again after the prisoners had been removed from Andersonville to Thomasville. I do not remember the month that occurred. It was in the beginning of this year, in the month of February or March, 1865.

Q. State to the court in what condition you found the stockade when you first visited it, and subsequently, and all the time while you were there.

A. The first time I visited the stockade I only had about three or four hours to spend there. I merely went to see what the condition of the place was. My principal object was to find out, if possible, the number of Catholics who were prisoners there, in order that we might induce the bishop to send a sufficient number of priests. I did not pay much attention to what I saw or heard there then. The following week I returned, and spent three days. I visited the stockade and the hospital, discharging my duties as a priest of the Catholic church. On this my second visit to the stockade, I found, I think, about 23,000

---

[1] Record, p. 287 et seq.

prisoners there; at least the prisoners themselves told me there were that number. I found the place extremely crowded, with a great deal of sickness and suffering among the men. I was kept so busy administering the sacrament to the dying, that I had to curtail a great deal of the service that Catholic priests administer to the dying, for the reason they were so numerous—they died so fast. I waited only upon those of my own church; they were the only persons who demanded my ministrations. When I speak of the number dying, I mean among those of my own church, and do not include others.

Q. Give the court some idea of the condition of the stockade.

A. I found the stockade extremely filthy; the men all huddled together, and covered with vermin. The best idea I can give the court of the condition of the place is, perhaps, this: I went in there with a white linen coat on, and I had not been in there more than ten minutes or a quarter of an hour, when a gentleman drew my attention to the condition of my coat. It was all covered over with vermin, and I had to take my coat off and leave it with one of the guards, and perform my duties in my shirt-sleeves, the place was so filthy.

Q. State to the court any particular case which came under your notice that would help to illustrate the condition of things there.

A. That is about the only idea I can give of the stockade.

Q. State any particular case you observed showing the destitution of the prisoners.

A. The first person I conversed with, on entering the stockade, was a countryman of mine, a member of the Catholic church, who recognized me as a clergyman. I think his name was Farrell. He was from the north of Ireland. He came over towards me, and introduced himself. He was quite a boy; I do not think, judging from his appearance, that he could have been more than sixteen years old. I found him without a hat, and without any covering on his feet, and without jacket or coat. He told me that his shoes had been taken from him on the battle-field. I found the boy suffering very much from a wound on his right foot; in fact the foot was split open like an oyster; and, on inquiring the cause, they told me it was from exposure to the sun in the stockade, and not from any wound received in battle. I took off my boots, and gave him a pair of socks to cover his feet, and told him I would bring him some clothing, as I expected to return to Andersonville the following week. I had to return to Macon to get another priest to take my place on Sunday. When I returned, the following week, on inquiring for this man Farrell, his companions told me he had stepped across the dead-line, and requested the guards to shoot him. He was not insane at the time I was conversing with him. It was three or four days after that when I was asking for him. I think it was the latter part of May, 1864. To the best of my recollection his name was Farrell. I do not know to what company, or regiment he belonged, I did not ask him. When I speak of administering the sacrament of the church to those dying, I refer to those in the stockade, and in the hospital also—in both places. I spent two days in the stockade and one in the hospital during my second visit to Andersonville. This case that I have spoken of occurred in the stockade. He had no medical treatment at all. *None of those who died in there, and to whom I administered the sacrament, received any medical treatment at all, so far as I could see.* When I went in the hospital I found it almost as crowded as the stockade was. The men were dying there very rapidly, from scurvy, diarrhea, and dysentery; and, as far as I could observe, I could not see that they received any medical treatment whatsoever, or received any medicines at all.

Q. How were they situated as to beds or bedding?

A. They were all in tents; the hospital was composed of tents arranged in avenues, and I did not see that they had anything under them at all except the ground; in some cases I think that they had dried leaves that they had gathered together. In my ministration while at the hospital, I saw one surgeon there—the surgeon in charge there at that time, Dr. White.

Q. State the circumstances.

A. I was attending an Irishman, I think, by the name of Connor, who was captured at the night assault made on Fort Sumter; at least I think he told me. so. He was captured in Charleston harbor, and he was in the last stage of dysentery. He was so bad that I had to hear his confession and give him the rites of the church sitting upon a stool. While I was hearing the man's confession, Surgeon White passed through the hospital, and seeing me whispering to the prisoner and not knowing, I suppose, who I was, ordered the guard to bring me up to his quarters under arrest. I went up there and he apologized for having done so; he having in the mean time inquired of Captain Wirz who I was, and the captain having told him that he had given me the necessary pass. I conversed with Dr. White with regard to the condition of the men, and he told me it was not in his power to do anything for them; that he had no medicine and could not get any, and that he was doing everything in his power to help them. That was the only time I ever met a surgeon there. Captain Wirz gave me the pass. I first called upon Colonel Persons, who was the. officer in command at Andersonville, arid he referred me to Captain Wirz, and Captain Wirz gave me a pass and gave me every facility in his power to visit those men. He walked down to the stockade with me and showed me the entrance. That pass held good only for that day. That was the first day I went there. It was renewed afterwards by Captain Wirz. It continued for the three days I was there. I did not have it renewed afterwards. I did not visit Andersonville again until the prisoners had been removed to Thomasville. That was the beginning of this year.

Q. Was Captain Wirz in command?

A. I did not see him. I have a mission below Andersonville, at a place called Americus, and I was going down there to give the people an opportunity of performing their religious duties. I stopped at Andersonville, intending to pass the night there if there were any prisoners still left there, but was told at the depot that the prisoners had all been removed, so I did not go up to the stockade. I do not know if there were any prisoners there or if Captain Wirz was there.

Q. What did you observe with regard to shelter in the stockade and the suffering of the men from heat there?

A. When I visited the stockade there was no shelter at all so far as I could see, except that some of the men who had their blankets there had put them up on little bits of roots that they had abstracted from the ground; but I could not see any tents or shelter of any other kind. I got the names of several prisoners who had relatives living in the south and wrote to their friends when I returned to Macon, and I had some tents introduced there; they were sent down, and the men received them.

Q. Can you illustrate to the court the condition of the prison, by stating any instance where you tried to make your way through the crowd to a prisoner who was dying?

A. Yes, sir; during my second visit to the prison, I was told that there was an Irishman over at the extreme end of the stockade who was calling out for a priest. I suppose he had heard that I had visited the prison the day before, and he was very anxious to see a priest, and was calling for one all over the stockade. There is a branch that runs right in the center of the stockade, and I tried to cross the branch, but was unable to do so as the men were all crowding around there trying to get into the water to cool themselves, and wash themselves. I could not get over the branch, and had to leave the stockade without seeing the man. The heat there was intolerable; there was no air at all in the stockade. The logs of which the stockade was composed were so close together that I could not feel any fresh air inside; and with a strong sun beaming down on it and no shelter at all, of course the heat must have been insufferable; at least I felt it so.

Q. How did it affect the priests on duty there?

A. The priests who went there after me, while administering the sacrament to the dying, had to use an umbrella, the heat was so intense. Some of them broke down in consequence of their services there. In the month of August, I think, we had three priests there constantly. We had a priest from Mobile who spoke three or four languages, inasmuch as you could find every nationality inside the stockade, and two from Savannah, and we had one from Augusta at another time. One of the priests from Savannah came to Macon, where I reside, completely prostrated, and was sick at my house for several days.

There were saw-mills in that vicinity along the railroad. I do not remember if they were near to Andersonville. I used to visit Albany, which I suppose is thirty or forty miles below Andersonville, once every month. It was my duty to go there that often, and I used to see saw-mills along the railroad in operation. I have heard that the prisoners proposed to cut wood for themselves. I have heard prisoners say so themselves. I did not keep an account of the dying men I used to attend per day to administer the last sacrament, but judging from the hours I was engaged and what I know to be the length of the service, I suppose I must have attended from twenty to thirty every day; sometimes more and sometimes less. That was about the average number—between twenty and thirty.

Q. Can you speak more particularly as to the bodily condition of those inside the stockade, their clothing and the appearance of the men?

A. Well, as I said before, when I went there I was kept so busily engaged in giving the sacrament to the dying men that I could not observe much; but of course I could not keep my eyes closed as to what I saw there. *I saw a great many men perfectly naked, walking about through the stockade perfectly nude; they seemed to have lost all regard for delicacy, shame, morality, or anything else. I would frequently have to creep on my hands and knees into the holes that the men had burrowed in the ground and stretch myself out alongside of them to hear their confessions.* I found them almost living in vermin in those holes; they could not be in any other condition but a filthy one, because they got no soap and no change of clothing, and were there all huddled up together.

I never at any time counted the number of dead bodies being taken out of the stockade in the morning. I have never seen any dead carried out of the stockade. I have seen dead bodies in the hospital in the morning. In the case of the man in the hospital of whom I was speaking a while ago, after I had heard his confession, and before I gave him the last rites of the church sacrament in "extreme unction," as we call it, I saw them placing the night guards in the hospital, and knew that I would not be able to get out after that. I told him that I would return in the morning and give him the other rites of the church, if he still lived. I was in there early the next morning, and in going down one of the avenues I counted from forty to sixty dead bodies of those who had died during the night in the hospital. I had never seen any dead bodies in the stockade. I have seen a person in the hospital in a nude condition, perfectly naked. They were not only covered with the ordinary vermin, but with maggots. They had involuntary evacuations, and there were no persons to look after them. The nurses did not seem to pay any attention whatever, and in consequence of being allowed to lie in their own filth for some hours, vermin of every description had got on them, which they were unable to keep off. This was in the latter part of May. I never noticed in the stockade the men digging in the ground, and standing in the sand to protect themselves from the sun. I did not see any instance of that kind. I have seen them making little places from a foot to a foot and a half deep, and stretching their blankets right over them. I have crawled into such places frequently to hear the confessions of the dying. They would hold from one to two; sometimes a prisoner would share his blanket with another, and allow him to get under shelter.

When I returned from the stockade after my second visit to it, at the latter end of May, I represented these things to General Cobb. I wrote to our bishop and told him that these men were dying in large numbers; that there were many Catholics there, and that they required the services of a priest, and he sent up Father Whelan. Father Whelan expressed a desire to see General Cobb before he went down to the stockade. I called upon General Cobb and told him that I had been there, and gave him a description of the place as well as I could, and he asked me what I would recommend to be done, as he intended to write to Richmond with regard to the condition of that place. After I found out from his conversation that nothing more could be done for the bodily comfort of the men, owing to the stringency of the blockade, and so forth, I advised him to parole those men upon their own word of honor, and take them down to Jacksonville, Florida, and turn them into the Federal lines. Whether that recommendation was acted on or not I do not know; he asked my opinion and I gave it. At that time, when I told him of the condition in which I found things there, it was known to the whole country, for it was published in the newspapers in the South. I do not know about its being common talk and rumor throughout the

Confederacy. I am only speaking about Macon and southwestern Georgia. The whole of southwestern Georgia is included in my mission, and I know that the condition of the prison was well known in Macon and throughout southwestern Georgia. I do not remember that I made any suggestion with regard to shelter at the time I had this conversation with General Cobb; it is very probable that I did. I cannot recollect whether he said anything about it or not.

Q. Do you remember whether he stated that he had written to Richmond or that he was about to write to Richmond to represent the condition of things at Andersonville?

A. When he asked me to give him a description of the condition of the place, he remarked; I think, that he was going to write and wished to have some information from me on the point. He remarked also that he would like me to give him a description, because he knew the relations that existed between the Catholic priest and the members of his church, and that they would be more unreserved in communicating with me than with others. . . .

I saw Captain Wirz the first time I went there. He received me with all kindness and politeness, and seemed to be pleased at my going there when I stated my purpose. I had never seen him before. I had no introduction to him more than I made myself. I told him who I was—that I was a Catholic priest come there to visit the prisoners, to find out if possible the number of Catholics there; and that I had been directed to call on him by Colonel Persons. I called on him the same as any others stranger might call on him. As well as I can remember, he said he was very well pleased to see me, and that he had expected priests would have gone there before that time. I think he had said something to the effect that he was anxious to have care and attention given to the prisoners. His action towards me showed that, and if I am not mistaken he told me so. The only time I ever conversed with Captain Wirz or saw him was when I went for my pass. I had two passes and went to Captain Wirz for them on both occasions, and those were the only times that I either saw him or conversed with him. I never met him inside the stockade or was with him there. I met him always in his office. There was no restriction upon me whatever in regard to my taking with me anything I chose into the stockade. I could take anything at all, money, clothing, or anything of that sort. I did not while I was there hear of any restrictions placed upon others to prevent them from taking in anything they chose for the relief of the prisoners. . . .

Of course I could only offer my opinion to the court as to the causes of the death of those prisoners that I saw dying in such numbers. I did not see any die from long-standing wounds either in the stockade or the hospital. I do not remember that I attended any who died from wounds. I have seen them dying from scurvy, but not from gunshot wounds. I have seen them dying from diarrhœa and from dysentery—from no other complaints or causes. Those were the prevailing complaints among the prisoners while I was there. I know only the case I mentioned, of any one being shot or dying from wounds recently received, the case of Farrel, and I did not see him shot. All I know about that is, some one said he was shot.

Q. Give us the names of the priests who attended at Andersonville besides yourself.

TESTIMONY OF CLERGYMEN AND OTHERS.

A. Father Whelan was there, a priest from Savannah, and Father Clavreul, a French clergyman from Savannah; also Father John Kirby, of Augusta, and Father Hosannah, a Jesuit from the Spring Hill College, near Mobile. Father Kirby, of Augusta, remained there two weeks, I think. They did not remain most or all of the time during the summer months. Father Whelan remained there for four months constantly, and the others left after a stay of two or three weeks. . . .

I think there are three papers published at Macon, or were there at that time. I remember reading articles in them relating to the Andersonville Prison, particularly in reference to it, describing the condition of the place. I do not think those articles appeared very frequently; I have read at least two, perhaps three. They gave an idea or correct impression to the public of what I really found there myself. It was an accurate description of the place, so far as I could judge from what I had seen myself. They gave the condition of everything. . . . The design or object of the articles seemed to be to excite the sympathy of the people, I should think. I could not say what time in May those articles appeared—before I went to Andersonville and after I returned; one article appeared before I went there and one or two after I returned. My interview with General Cobb took place about the 1st of June. I went with Father Whelan, to introduce him to General Cobb. That was not before I went to Andersonville the first time; I had been there twice. I think it was about the 1st of June that Father Whelan came up to go to Andersonville. General Cobb expressed no determination to have the state of things remedied immediately. I do not think he had power to do so; in fact Father Whelan went to him for the purpose of obtaining a document stating who he was. General Cobb said he could not give him any such pass as that, but he would give him a letter of introduction to General Winder, which he did; he wrote the letter in our presence. I do not know if this was about the time General Cobb went to Andersonville himself; I know he had not been there at that time.

Is it true, as was stated by the vice-president of the United Daughters of the Confederacy to General Ketcham, noted in a former chapter, that "the Confederacy's treatment of prisoners of war was conducted on humane principles"? Can one read the experiences of this holy man of God and discover in the treatment of prisoners witnessed by him any semblance of Christian principles? Picture Father Hamilton in his ministrations, moving about among these ragged, naked, starving, dying men. See him crawling into their burrows in the ground to give to them the consoling thought that they died with the hope which the Christian religion mercifully extends to the penitent. May not these skeletons of men have justly cried out as did Brutus at the murder of Caesar:

> "O judgment! thou art fled to brutish beasts,
> And men have lost their reason!"

TESTIMONY OF AMBROSE SPENCER.

Ambrose Spencer was a citizen of Sumter County, and resided near Americus, not far from Andersonville. His testimony is that of an intelligent man, speaking from personal knowledge and from reliable sources of information. His testimony discloses a phase of the character of Winder and Wirz which should bring the blush of shame to their apologists. Here is what he says:[1]

I reside near Americus, Sumter County, Georgia. My plantation is about nine miles from Andersonville. I have resided there for the last five years.

I visited Andersonville during its occupation as a prison very frequently. I have seen the prisoner, Captain Wirz, very frequently. I was there nearly every month, I think, during the time it was a prison. I doubt whether a month elapsed in which I was not there while it was in its crowded condition— every month except, perhaps, during March, 1865. I was there in April, 1865. I was at Andersonville constantly; nearly every month, as I have remarked. I had frequent opportunities of seeing the condition of the prisoners, not only from the adjacent hills, but on several occasions from the outside of the stockade where the sentinels' grounds were. I had opportunities of talking at different times with the prisoners, not only at Andersonville, but after they escaped, in several instances, when they came to my house. I can only answer the question by saying that their condition was as wretched and as horrible as could well be conceived, not only from exposure to the sun, the inclemency of weather, and the cold of winter, but from the filth, from the absolute degradation which was evident in their condition. I have seen that stockade after three or four days' rain, when the mud, I should say, was at least twelve inches deep on both the hills; the prisoners were walking or wading through that mud. The condition of the stockade perhaps can be expressed most aptly by saying that in passing up and down the railroad, if the wind was favorable, the odor from the stockade could be detected at least two miles.

I believe I am familiar with the surrounding country. That section of southwestern Georgia is well supplied with mills, both grist-mills, flour-mills and saw-mills. Between Andersonville and Albany (the distance by railroad being I believe, fifty miles—there is railroad communication) there are five saw-mills. One of them, a large one, is owned by a gentleman named Drew. There are four others of considerable capacity; there is one saw-mill at a distance of six miles from Andersonville, owned by Mr. Stewart; that goes by steam. There is another saw-mill about five miles from Andersonville that goes by water. There are saw-mills on the road above Andersonville. As for grist-mills there are five in the neighborhood of Andersonville, the farthest off being at a distance, I should think, not exceeding ten miles. There were two at Americus, the one farthest off being about twelve miles distant. Of these mills the water-mills are run nearly the entire year, except occasionally in the summer months; in the months of July and August they may be temporarily suspended owing to the want of water, but not for any length of time.

[1] Record, p. 355 et seq.

TESTIMONY OF CLERGYMEN AND OTHERS.

It is a very heavily timbered country, especially in the region adjoining Andersonville; it may be termed one of the most densely timbered countries in the United States. As for its fertility, southwestern Georgia, I believe, is termed the garden of America; it was termed the garden of the Confederacy, as having supplied the greater part of the provisions of the rebel army. Our section of Georgia, Sumter County, is perhaps not as rich as the counties immediately contiguous. The land is of a lighter quality, but still it produces heavily. I suppose that the average of that land would be one bale of cotton to the acre; the wheat would average about six bushels to the acre. The average of corn throughout the county, I suppose, would be about eight bushels to the acre. I am stating the general average of the whole number of acres in the county. We have land in that county that will produce 35 bushels of corn to the acre; I am stating the general average. It struck me that there was an uncommon supply of vegetables in 1864. Heretofore, at the south, there has been but little attention paid to gardens on a large scale; but last year a very large supply of vegetables was raised, as I understood, for the purpose of being disposed of at Andersonville. . . .

I know of lumber having been used at Andersonville. I was there during June and July very frequently, at the time when Governor Brown had called out the militia of the State. The militia of southwestern Georgia were stationed at Andersonville, and their tents were all floored with good lumber, and a good many shelters of lumber were put up by the soldiers. I noticed a good many tents that were protected from the sun by boards. There seemed to be no want of lumber at that time among the Confederate soldiers.

I did not take regular thermometrical observations during the summer of 1864 and the winter of 1864-65; but I had a thermometer, and every day, sometimes two or three times a day, I examined it. I generally made it a rule to look at it when I got up in the morning, again about noon, and then in the evening. So far as I remember, the range of the thermometer during the summer of 1864 was very high. I think I have seen it as high as 110 degrees in the shade. Once, and only once, I put the thermometer out in the sun on an extremely hot day in June, 1864. It ranged then, if my memory serves me aright, 127 to 130 degrees that day. Last winter, according to my experience during more than twenty-five years' residence in Georgia, was the coldest winter we have ever had there. I have seen the thermometer as low as 20 and 22 degrees above zero—from 8 to 10 degrees below the freezing-point; one night it was colder than that; it was the night of the 4th of January. It is very distinctly impressed on my memory. During the night I was waked up by my wife, who told me that somebody was calling in front of my house. I opened the side window (it was excessively cold) and asked who was there. A voice replied, "A friend." I answered that I had no friends at that time of night, and very few anyhow in that country. He said that he was a friend of mine and wanted to come near the fence to speak to me. I told him my dog would bite him if he came to the fence; he then approached and said he was an Andersonville prisoner, and asked me, calling me by name, if I lived there. I told him that I was the man and to wait a moment. I dressed myself, went out and chained my dog, and brought the prisoner in. He was nearly frozen; he could hardly stand; he had on only one shoe, and that was a poor one, and had a stocking upon the other foot. He was clad in the thin army flannel of the United States, badly worn. He had on a pair of light blue pantaloons which were badly worn. This was on a Wednesday morning; and he told me thst he had made his escape from Andersonville on the Saturday previous, that he had been apprehended and taken to Americus, where he had made his escape from the guard the night before, and was directed to my house by a negro. I asked him if he was not nearly frozen; he said he was. I looked at the thermometer then and it was eighteen degrees above zero. This was about two o'clock in the morning—between one and two o'clock.

I know that efforts were made by the ladies of my county to relieve the prisoners at Andersonville; at one time a general effort was made. All that I know is, that a gentleman named Mr. Davies, a Methodist presiding elder, exerted himself to induce the ladies to contribute clothing and provisions to the Federal hospital at Andersonville. A large amount of provisions was collected, some three or four wagonloads, if I am not mistaken, and sent up there. I believe that the effort failed. First, the provost marshal refused a pass to carry the provisions to the hospital; and when application was made by Dr. Head, who acted as the spokesman for the ladies, to General Winder, it was positively refused to them. I had a conversation with General Winder three days afterward The same matter then came up. General Winder stated, accompanied with an oath, that he believed the whole country was becoming "Yankee," and that he would be damned if he would not put a stop to it; if he couldn't one way he would in another. I remarked that I did not think it was any evidence of "Yankee" or Union feeling to exhibit humanity. He said there was no humanity about it; that it was intended as a slur upon the Confederate government and as a covert attack on him. I told him that I had understood it was done at his request; that he had requested Mr. Davies to bring this thing about. He said it was a damned lie; that he had not requested anything of the kind; that for his own part, he would as lief the damned Yankees would die there as anywhere else; that, upon the whole, he did not know that it was not better for them. That was his language, or words to that effect. Captain Wirz was not present at that time. My wife was with me at the time. There were other ladies present, but I don't think I knew any of them. They were not part of the committee.

Q. In what way did General Winder speak of the ladies and their humane effort?

A. He used the most opprobrious language that could possibly be used, language that no gentleman could listen to, especially in the presence of his wife, without resenting it in some way—language utterly unfit to be repeated in the presence of ladies. It was an intimation that he could very easily make loyal women of them by putting them in a certain condition that would bring them to it.

I was present at a conversation the day after this committee of ladies failed. It was at the depot at Andersonville. The conversation was principally carried on between the provost marshal, Captain Reed—

Q. Captain or Lieutenant Reed.

TESTIMONY OF CLERGYMEN AND OTHERS. 153

A. I believe we used to call him captain. He might have been a lieutenant, probably. He was the only Reed there. Captain Wirz and R. B. Winder were present. There were three or four officials there; I cannot recall any but those. Lieutenant Reed observed that if General Winder had done as he wanted, they might have made a good speculation out of the provisions and clothing that the ladies had brought; that he proposed they should be confiscated, but the "Old General" would not do it. Wirz remarked that if he had his way he would have a house built there, and all the ladies should be put in it for certain purposes. That was a most scandalous, infamous purpose, which I do not wish to repeat. R. B. Winder's remarks were a general concurrence. I don't know that he said anything special that I can call to mind, any more than laughingly concurring in what had been said.

I know Turner, who had the hounds, very well; his name was Wesley W. Turner.

Q. What did you ever hear him say as to his duties there and what he was receiving?

A. It was some time in the early part of 1864—March or April, I think. He had purchased a piece of land up in the same district in which my place is. I met him one day in Americus and asked him if he was going to settle that land. He said he was not; that he was making more money now than anybody in that country. I inquired how he was making it. He said the Confederate government was paying him for keeping hounds to catch escaped prisoners. I asked him if he got his pay from Richmond. He said, no, he did not trouble Richmond; that "Old Captain Wirz was his paymaster." I asked him how much he received; my impression is that he did not tell me what he received. He told me that he was making more money than anybody else in that country; better than cultivating ground. That was early in the history of that prison, I think—during March or April. It was while he was there on duty; he told me that he then had a pack of hounds and was employed there.

I know W. S. Winder—"Sid. Winder," as he is called. I saw him at the time he was laying out the prison. Between the 1st and 15th of December, 1863, I went up to Andersonville with him and four or five other gentlemen, out of curiosity to see how the prison was to be laid out. When we arrived there the limits of the prison had all been marked. They were then digging a trench to put the stockade posts in. Workmen were busy cutting down trees in and around where the stockade was. In the course of conversation I inquired of W. S. Winder if it was proposed to erect barracks or shelter of any kind inside the stockade.

[Mr. Baker objected to the reception of the evidence, on the ground that the matter narrated did not come within the time specified in the charge. The court, after deliberation, overruled the objection. The witness resumed:]

I asked him if he was going to erect barracks or shelter of any kind. He replied that he was not; that the damned Yankees who would be put in there would have no need of them. I asked him why he was cutting down all the trees, and suggested that they would prove a shelter to the prisoners, from the heat of the sun at least. He made this reply, or something similar to it: "That is just what I am going to do; I am going to build a pen here that will kill more damned Yankees than can be destroyed in the front." Those are very nearly his words or equivalent to them. That was before a stockade was erected in the trench. Captain R. B. Winder came there to the post ten or fifteen days after that—I suppose about ten days. There was nothing said at that time as to who ordered W. S. Winder there to lay out the prison. I had frequent conversations with General Winder. I used to meet him very frequently, either in Americus or going up the railroad. I saw him a good many times at Andersonville.

Q. What was the general temper and spirit of his talk with regard to those prisoners?

A. The opinion that I formed of him was anything but creditable to his feeling, his humanity, or his gentlemanly bearing. I am not aware that I ever had a conversation with General Winder in which he did not curse more or less, especially if the subject of Andersonville Prison was brought up. I can only reply to your question by saying that I considered him a brutal man. That I drew from his conversation and conduct as I observed them. I looked upon him as a man utterly devoid of all kindly feeling and sentiment.

Q. How generally, so far as you observed, were the sufferings and horrors of the Andersonville pen known throughout the South?

A. So far as my knowledge and information went, the knowledge of those sufferings was general; it was so, at least, throughout the southern part of the Southern States; I cannot speak specially in regard to the neighborhood of Richmond. The matter was discussed in the newspapers constantly, and discussed in private circles. Perhaps I might have heard more of it than most, because it dwelt more on my mind; but it was a general subject of conversation throughout the entire southern part of the Confederacy.

I went south twenty-five years ago the 8th day of last month. My residence is in Sumter County, near Americus. It is a village or town. It is called Americus. I live near the town. I have lived in Sumter County for nearly twelve years. I have been a teacher most of the time; my profession is that of a lawyer. I have been planting, farming, for the last five years, most of the time on my own farm. My farm is two lots; there are two hundred acres to the lot; four hundred acres in all. When I speak of the crops, and of vegetables there, if I judged from my own crops, my statement would be unfavorable, because I made a very poor crop that year, both of corn and vegetables. I do not judge from my own crop. The testimony I have given is what I have seen of other plantations. I believe I have travelled during the last two years almost as much as anybody has. I held a position as an agent to collect evidence of claims against the Confederate States government—to establish claims. My district comprised thirteen counties, if I am not mistaken. That is the extent of the district over which I had jurisdiction—within which I received and established claims against the Confederate government. I was appointed by General Cooper, adjutant and inspector-general. I held a Confederate office; I suppose in one sense I may be considered as having held a Confederate office. I had no commission; it was rather an agency. I travelled all through those thirteen counties constantly. I travelled mostly with my own buggy and horses; whenever I had occasion to go to places that were not on a line of railroad, in Schley, Webster, Marion, Chattahooche, Stewart, Thomas, and one or two other counties, I had to travel in my own conveyance. When I went to Mushogee, to Columbus, or to Oglethorpe, or down to Cuthbert, or to Albany, I went by railroad. I did not say I visited them several times during the last year; I said I visited each one of those counties at least twice, and some of them oftener. I did not obtain this information as to the crops while I was travelling. I did not say anything of the kind. I suppose a part of my information was obtained in that way. . . .

I know of four or five saw-mills in that vicinity. There is one located about five or six miles below Andersonville, on the railroad. Three of them run by water. There are six saw-mills that I know of. I cannot say that I visited them during the summer of 1864; I passed by all of them frequently.

Q. Do you not know that they did not hardly run during the summer of 1864?

A. No; I do not know anything of the kind. I know they did run during the summer of 1864. It is more than I can say, if they ran all the time. I have seen lumber there. I have seen large quantities of lumber at the different mills; for instance, at Drew's mill, a very large steam-mill, I have constantly seen the railroad on each side of it lined with lumber. I do not know who that lumber belonged to; at the mill five or six miles below Andersonville, I have seen a great deal of lumber, in the summer of 1864. I do not know that the Confederate government pressed that lumber. . . .

I was not concerned with those ladies at Americus in getting up contributions for the prisoners.

Q. All you know about it is from hearsay?

A. Well, I will recall that answer. My wife was personally concerned in getting up the thing. I contributed towards it. It was in February, 1865. I believe I heard of edorts being made in 1864. I know nothing about it myself. It was in September, 1864, that I had the conversation with General Winder, at which Captain Wirz was present. It was during 1864 that I went to Andersonville so often. I stated in my direct examination that I was not there so often in 1865, and that I thought I was not there at all in April, 1865.

TESTIMONY OF W. A. GRIFFIN.

W. A. Griffin was a conductor on the railroad trains from Macon to Eufaula, passing through Andersonville. His testimony went to the supply of transportation and opportunities for obtaining lumber. He testified:[1]

I reside in Nashville, Tennessee. During the last eighteen months I have been conductor on the Southwestern railroad, running from Macon, Georgia, to Eufaula, Alabama, passing by Andersonville, Georgia.

Q. What have been the means of transportation on that road for transporting materials of war, provisions, &c.?

A. We had sufficient transportation, I believe, generally from Macon to Eufaula.

Q. For all the purposes required?

A. As a general thing, I believe so.

Q. Did you run both on passenger and freight trains?

A. I ran a few trips as a freight train conductor, but as a general thing I ran passenger trains.

---

[1] Record p. 330 et seq.

156   THE TRAGEDY OF ANDERSONVILLE.

Q. Were you ever required to hold over freight trains for many trips before you were well able to carry it?

A. I knew nothing about transportation generally. As a general thing the passenger conductors rode down one day and back the next day, and then lay over one day.

Q. Did you observe many freight trains on the road?

A. Freight trains were passing. I would pass them day in and day out.

Q. Is that a timbered country?

A. There are any amount of saw-mills throughout that country along the line of the road. I saw divers of them.

Q. Was lumber being hauled over the road?

A. As a general thing there were lumber mills all the way through from Macon to Eufaula.

Q. Do you know any reason why lumber could not be carried to Andersonville?

A. I do not.

TESTIMONY OF JAMES VAN VALKENBURG.

James Van Valkenburg testified as to the condition of the crops during the year 1864 and as to the quantities of provisions stored at Macon. He testified:[1]

I reside near Macon, Bibb County, State of Georgia. I have lived there nineteen years. I was there during the Rebellion. I have been at Andersonville. So far as I know the crops have been about medium. There were certain sections of the State of Georgia last year that suffered considerable from drought, and in certain other portions the crops were exceedingly good. I am speaking of the year 1864. I should suppose as to provisions it was more than an average crop, inasmuch as no cotton was planted, and all the ground was pretty well planted in provisions. I should think the provision crop was larger than before the war. The regulation in the South requiring farmers and others to pay tithes for what they grew was, that they were to bring in one-tenth of all they raised of provisions of various kinds, corn and wheat and potatoes, and a certain proportion of their meat. I am not exactly sure what proportion, but I should think about the same ratio, one-tenth. Macon is about sixty-five miles from Andersonville, by railroad. It would be impossible for me to state what stores were in Macon during the year 1864. There were a great many storehouses where provisions were stored of various kinds—sugar, rice, molasses, meat (bacon), corn, wheat, flour, &c. I have not been at Americus as commonly as at Macon, but when I have been there, there seemed to be very large quantities. I saw a great deal of stores in various warehouses. Americus is nine miles from Andersonville; it may be a little further than that; it is possible I may be slightly mistaken on that point.

There was a large quantity of wheat grown in that section of the country; some near Andersonville. There were flour-mills there; I could not say how near Andersonville. I know there were flour-mills around there. I know my son-in-law, who lives in Americus, had a large quantity of wheat and had no difficulty in getting it ground. He told me he raised more wheat last year than

[1] Record, pp. 106, 107.

ever in his life before. Some of the flour-mills were what we called merchants' mills, and some mills doing a smaller business, merely grinding for tolls. I do not know how near to Andersonville there was a flour-mill. I know there was a large one at Macon. Georgia is considered a corn-growing country, but it is generally considered a good country for wheat also. I think some of the best wheat that is raised in Georgia is raised in southwestern Georgia. Some seasons it does not do so well. It is not so safe a crop as in the north part of the State, but when they make a crop, farmers tell me—I am not a farmer—it is better than the wheat grown in the northern part. I do not know how often they make a wheat crop.

TESTIMONY OF LIEUT. J. H. WRIGHT.

Lieutenant J. H. Wright of the Fifty-fifth Georgia Regiment, was on duty at Andersonville from February, 1864, until the following February. He assisted in enlarging the stockade. He says the prisoners themselves did the work,—about 100 white men and 30 negroes,—and completed it in a little over three weeks; that nothing was required for the work but axes, spades, and shovels, of which there were plenty. He testified:[1]

The extension of the stockade was made under the direction of Colonel Persons. I superintended the work voluntarily. The prisoners did the work themselves. I think I had about one hundred white men and thirty colored troops under my charge. Those hundred men were prisoners of war—Union soldiers. The stockade was extended about eleven acres, if I remember correctly; about one-third or a little more. If I remember correctly, the original stockade was about seventeen acres, and it was extended over a third. It took a little over three weeks, I think, to complete the job. We used nothing but axes, spades, and shovels; plenty of them were on hand at the time. I never had any want of them. Captain W. S. Winder marked out the prison and laid it out. I made requisitions for money on the authorities at Richmond when I was quartermaster. I made a requisition of $75,000 to pay off the troops that were there in April, 1864. In our service, then, the quartermasters did the duties of paymasters. That money came. Captain R. B. Winder told me the money was sent through him to me, and that he had used the money. I never received that money. I do not know how he used it; he merely told me he had used the money, and had made a requisition himself, for money, and that when he received it he would replace the $75,000, which he did—a portion of it in the latter part of September. Captain R. B. Winder told me that he had no orders to report to any quartermaster at all; that he reported directly to Richmond, and received his instructions from Richmond. He told me that all the quartermasters in that vicinity had been ordered by the quartermaster-general to furnish him what supplies he needed—to fill his requisitions. While I was there, there never was any difficulty about getting negroes. I remember the time the engineer came there to build the fortifications. I know he had a great many negroes; I do not know the number. This was in July or August; I think the latter part of

[1] Record, p. 406.

July. I succeeded Captain R. B. Winder—that is, I was left there temporarily until a man could be sent there. He left there in October. He had all the tools and matters of that kind, in his possession, sent to Millen, and all the transportation. He left me a few old horses and ambulances and wagons. I had to go to work and get up what transportation I could afterwards, myself. I got a few old broken-down mules from the convalescent camp; they generally commenced dying in a few days. I had no difficulty in getting axes when I made requisition for them. Captain Wirz made requisition on me for axes, and I had no difficulty in getting them. I think I left seventy-five axes there.

TESTIMONY OF DR. M. M. MARSH.

Dr. M. M. Marsh, in charge of the United States Sanitary Commission matters in Florida, Georgia, and the Carolinas, gave some important testimony as to the quantity of supplies the commission endeavored to send to Andersonville. The pity of it is that there is evidence that few of these supplies ever reached the prisoners. He testified:[1]

For the last two or three years I have had charge of the United States Sanitary Commission matters in the States of Florida, Georgia and the Carolinas. I was so employed from early in January, 1863, till the close of the Rebellion. I was stationed at Beaufort, S. C. While I was there, we received sanitary stores for prisoners in the custody of the rebel government and purchased also of a United States quartermaster. When we had not articles from other sources we purchased from United States quartermasters for that purpose. I forwarded clothing and provisions, sanitary stores, to Andersonville, Ga., for the use of the prisoners there. I made a memorandum of the amount of articles sent there, or had it made.

Q. Look at the paper handed you and state if that is the memorandum.

A. That is it. It is a correct list of stores sent to Andersonville, Ga. Perhaps I ought to remark that we were sending to five other points at the same time, but in making out the lists we selected only those things that were put down in our record as sent to Andersonville, Georgia.

[The paper, of which the following is a copy, was offered in evidence by the judge advocate and is attached to the record.]

Stores sent to Prisoners at Andersonville, Georgia.

5,052 wool shirts.	46 cotton pants.	4,092 pounds condensed milk.
6,993 wool drawers.	534 wrappers.	4,032 pounds condensed coffee.
3,950 handkerchiefs.	69 jackets.	1,000 pounds farina.
601 cotton shirts.	12 overalls.	1,000 pounds corn starch.
1,128 cotton drawers.	817 pairs slippers.	4,212 pounds tomatoes.
2,100 blouses.	3,147 towels.	24 pounds chocolate.
4,235 wool pants.	5.431 wool socks.	3 boxes lemon juice.
1,520 wool hats.	50 pillow cases.	1 barrel dried apples.
2,565 overcoats.	258 bed sacks.	111 barrels crackers.
5,385 blankets.	122 combs.	60 boxes cocoa.
272 quilts	100 tin cups.	7,200 pounds beef stock.
2,120 pairs shoes.	2 boxes tin ware.	Paper, envelopes, &c.
110 cotton coats.		Pepper, mustard.
140 vests.		One box tea, 70 pounds.

[1] Record, pp. 416, 417.

I do not know exactly how much more of the qualities of coffee a pound of condensed coffee contains than a pound of ordinary coffee; in regard to the beef stock, one pound is supposed to be equal to seven pounds of beef. I do not know about the coffee and milk, but I think one pound is equal to five pounds of the raw article. A portion of these articles were sent in the month of July; but a small portion of them. We began to send them quite regularly from about the 10th or the 15th of August up to about the 1st of November, 1864. I have no evidence that those articles were ever received at Andersonville; all I know respecting it is that I either personally or through some agent—I did not do it myself but in two or three instances—passed the stores over to some agent deputed by the Confederate government to receive them. This agent of the Confederate government usually, not always, gave a receipt for the articles, with a promise on my part that I should return that receipt when he obtained a receipt from the persons to whom he delivered them; if the things were sent to a prisoner personally, why he returned that prisoner's receipt, or if he delivered them to the quartermaster, he handed me the quartermaster's receipt, and when he did that I returned him his receipt. That was done in many cases. I do not know about his authority; I know that I returned his receipt to him when he produced a receipt from some party to whom he had delivered the articles. That was not always the case, however; once or twice some of the agents who were sent refused to give receipts; they said they would transmit the articles but they would not give receipts. It was a matter we cared very little about. For instance, Colonel Waddy, on one or two occasions, I know of one certainly, refused to give a receipt. He was a rebel agent. I refer now to the men who were deputed by the Confederate authorities to receive the things; sometimes one man was deputed to receive it and sometimes another.

TESTIMONY OF AUGUSTUS MOESNER.

Augustus Moesner, of Company G, Sixteenth Connecticut Volunteers, was called as a witness for the prisoner. He entered the stockade on May 3, 1864, but was on May 24th detailed as a clerk in Wirz's office. A portion of his testimony should be read in connection with that of Dr. Marsh, the agent of the Sanitary Commission. Moesner was in a position to know something about the supplies that reached the prison from the North. He testified:[1]

I have been a member of Company G, 16th Connecticut Volunteers. I was captured April 20, 1864, and taken to Andersonville. I arrived there on the 3d of May, in the evening. On our arrival we were kept under guard, and next morning Captain Wirz came to the place with several of his sergeants and we were counted off in squads and sent down to the stockade. I remained in the stockade up to the 24th of May, 1864. I was taken as a paroled prisoner to Captain Wirz's office as a clerk.

[1] Record, p. 506.

As far as I recollect we got boxes from the North three times. The first boxes we received came in May, 1864. I was just at that time in the stockade yet, but I recollect very well when those boxes were brought in. Those boxes were boxes sent from the friends of prisoners and not from the Sanitary Commission. The boxes were brought into the stockade and every one who received a box had to sign a receipt. Many things in those boxes were spoilt because they had been a long time on the road. A Union sergeant close to my tent received a box and signed for it. A few days afterwards I was paroled and came out, and we had close to our office a shanty where some provisions for the hospital were kept. I saw many boxes in there. I asked one of the clerks "what kind of boxes those were," and he told me that those were boxes for prisoners who could not be found or who had died. The things in those boxes were turned over to the hospital and the Confederate hospital steward divided them. They were in his charge and he from day to day sent some of the things in the boxes down to the hospital. The second time we got boxes was in August. We got at this time only a few boxes. Lieutenant Davis was in command of the camp. We got about sixty or seventy pairs of pants, about 100 blouses, 100 caps, and fifty pairs of shoes. I myself got a whole suit at this time. Lieutenant Davis gave all that clothing to the men who were outside at work.

Q. What reason did he assign for doing that?

A. We had at that time about 32,000 or 33,000 prisoners in the stockade, and he said it was no use to send the clothes inside, because it would not make but a single piece to one squad and it would only make trouble inside, and perhaps there might be some fighting, so he gave it to the men outside at work. The third and last time I recollect that we got some boxes was in the first part of November, 1864. We got about 300 blankets and 300 pairs of pants. They were what are known as citizens' pants, brown and gray, a mixed color, and we got gray shirts and gray drawers and stockings, but only fifty pairs of shoes.

I have endeavored to this point in the narrative of facts to conduct the reader through the prison-pen and its so-called hospital tardily, if not reluctantly, established outside the stockade. The evidence is of the highest and most convincing character, for substantially all of it is from sources which do not admit of dispute, and much of it consists of contemporaneous official records and reports which once constituted part of the archives of the Confederacy. They passed under the scrutiny of some of the higher officials at Richmond and, we are forced by the evidence to conclude, were known in all their horrifying details to the head of the Confederacy. We have a right from this array of proofs to conclude that the conditions at Andersonville were well known by the governing powers at Richmond from the inception of the prison-pen throughout all its dark and repelling history. The indifference, not to speak of any sinister design, with which these evidences of human suffering were treated will forever remain a black and ineradicable stain upon the Confederacy.

Colonel Chandler's report, aside from others of similar import previously and subsequently made, was in itself sufficient to have brought some relief to this mass of suffering and dying soldiers had there been any disposition to extend relief. Here are some of the facts which were pressed upon the attention and the eyes of the officials who had the power to act, but who did absolutely nothing to ameliorate the wretchedness of that death-pit. Colonel Chandler thus spoke to his superiors at Richmond:[1]

There is no medical attendance provided within the stockade. Small quantities of medicines are placed in the hands of certain prisoners of each squad or division, and the sick are directed to be brought out by sergeants of squads daily, at "sick call," to the medical officers who attend at the gate. The crowd at these times is so great that only the strongest can get access to the doctors, the weaker ones being unable to force their way through the press; and the hospital accommodations are so limited that though the beds (so called) have all or nearly all two occupants each, large numbers who would otherwise be received are necessarily sent back to the stockade. Many—twenty yesterday—are carted out daily, who have died from unknown causes and whom the medical officers have never seen. The dead are hauled out daily by the wagon load, and buried without coffins, their hands in many instances being first mutilated with an axe in the removal of any finger rings they may have. The sanitary condition of the prisoners is as wretched as can be, the principal causes of mortality being scurvy and chronic diarrhœa, the percentage of the former being disproportionately large among those brought from Belle Isle. Nothing seems to have been done, and but little if any effort made to arrest it by procuring proper food. The ration is one-third pound of bacon and one and one-fourth pound unbolted corn meal, with fresh beef at rare intervals, and occasionally rice.[2] When to be obtained—very seldom—a small quantity of molasses is substituted for the meat ration. A little weak vinegar unfit for use has sometimes been issued. The arrangements for cooking and baking have been wholly inadequate, and though additions are now being completed it will still be impossible to cook for the whole number of prisoners. Raw rations have to be issued to a very large proportion, who are entirely unprovided with proper utensils and furnished so limited a supply of fuel they are compelled to dig with their hands in the filthy marsh before mentioned for roots, etc. No soap or clothing has ever been issued. After inquiring, I am confident that by slight exertions green corn and other anti-scorbutics could readily be obtained. I herewith hand two reports of Chief Surgeon White, to which I would respectfully call your attention. The present hospital arrangements were only intended for the accommodation

---

[1] Record, p. 225.
[2] Unbolted cornmeal is meal from corn ground with the husk still remaining, which acted as an irritant. See Surgeon Jones' report.

of the sick of 10,000 men, and are totally insufficient, both in character and extent, and the present needs; the number of prisoners being now more than three times as great, the number of cases requiring medical treatment is in an increased ratio. It is impossible to state the number of sick, many dying within the stockade, whom the medical officers never see or hear of until their remains are brought out for interment. The rate of death has been steadily increased from 37 4-10 per mil. during the month of March last to 62 7-10 per mil. in July.

CHAPTER VIII.

TESTIMONY OF UNION SOLDIERS, PRISONERS AT ANDERSONVILLE—THEIR DESCRIPTIONS OF THE HORRORS OF THAT PRISON PEN—PERSONAL EXPERIENCES—MEN FIGHT FOR ROOM TO LIE DOWN—PRIVATE PROPERTY TAKEN FROM THEM—TESTIMONY OF MAJOR-GENERAL J. H. WILSON AND COLONEL GEORGE WELLING OF THE U.S. ARMY ON CONDITION OF PRISON AT CLOSE OF THE WAR—SIMPLE REMEDIES POINTED OUT—GENERAL WILSON CONCLUDES THAT THERE WAS SINISTER DESIGN IN THE LOCATION AND ITS RESTRICTED AREA—GOLDWIN SMITH'S OPINION OF TREATMENT OF PRISONERS ON BOTH SIDES—GENERAL SHERMAN FOUND SUPPLIES ABUNDANT IN GEORGIA IN 1864.

IF, upon the principal issues now being examined, namely: Were the prisoners in large numbers starved to death? Were the sufferings of the survivors and the death of their comrades preventable? Upon whom rests the responsibility?—the reader feels constrained to find against the prisoner and his confederates, let it be remembered that to this point in the narrative every witness except Dr. Marsh of the Sanitary Commission and witness Moesner has been either officer or soldier in the rebel service, or a resident of the so-called Confederate States. With the single possible exception of Mr. Ambrose Spencer and the two already named, not a witness thus far has spoken who was not presumably either in sympathy with the rebellion or had joined it in obedience to the pressure of local conditions. In any event, there is nothing in the testimony of these numerous witnesses to suggest bias against the Confederacy or its government. And what a picture of needless human suffering is shown!

But I am unwilling that the story of these barbarities should rest alone upon the testimony already presented. The world has the right to hear from the lips of the sufferers themselves what they endured and the cause of that suffering.

There were about one hundred witnesses of this class. Their testimony upon specific acts of cruelty to which prisoners were subjected will appear in subsequent chapters. At this place there will be given the testimony of some, but by no means all, upon the points now the subject of our inquiry.

164   THE TRAGEDY OF ANDERSONVILLE.

TESTIMONY OF ROBERT H. KELLOGG.

Robert H. Kellogg was among the more intelligent witnesses called by the prosecution. His veracity is conceded by the prisoner, who called him for the defense.

He testified:[1]

I was at Andersonville, Georgia; I entered there on the 3d day of May, 1864, and left there on the 10th of September of the same year; I went with a body of prisoners; I think there were some four hundred of us; I was taken from Plymouth, North Carolina, to Andersonville by railroad.

We entered the prison on the 3d of May, 1864; we were the first captures of the campaign. When we entered the prison there were no men there but old prisoners who had been removed from Belle Island, Libby Prison, and other places to that point. They were ragged, nearly destitute of clothing, and many of them were nearly naked; they were totally unprovided with shelter, with the exception of that which tattered blankets could afford them. They looked nearly starved; they were skeletons covered with skin. The prison at that time was very crowded, at least it appeared so to us then, although there were thousands brought there after that. We were all led in by a rebel sergeant and showed a place near the brook, which we were told would be our place, and where we were to stay; we were to fall in there every morning for roll-call. There was no shelter provided for us at that time, or at any other time while we were in the prison. We were fortunate enough to be allowed to retain our blankets, and with them we erected shelters which protected us from the heat of the sun, but not from the rain. They did protect us from the rain for a few days, but soon they became so worn as to be utterly useless against the rain. The men were in a very filthy condition; indeed, they had very poor opportunities for keeping clean. There were but two issues of soap made to the prison while I was there, from May to September, and men who were cooking over their little fires with pitch-pine knots would get smoky and dirty and would not be able to get off the dirt with mere water. When we first went there the nights were very cold indeed; that soon passed away as the season advanced, and during the summer it was intensely hot. I made a memorandum of the rainy days while there. There were twenty-one rainy days in the month of June. When my regiment went there the men were healthy; after that they gradually sickened, until I remember one morning at roll-call, out of my ninety men, there were thirty-two who were not able to stand up when the rebel sergeant came to call the roll. They were unable to stand up principally from scurvy and diarrhœa; there were a great many of the men who had their limbs contracted and swollen so that they couldn't stand up. It was on the 21st of August, and we got there on the 3d of May. A number of the men of my squad of ninety had died at that time, but the vacancies had been filled by new arrivals. Of the four hundred men captured with me, nearly three hundred are dead. They died in the prison or a few days after being paroled; and that is a larger percentage of living than there was in many a regiment. The Twenty-fourth New York Battery, which was captured at Plymouth, was nearly annihilated. I have

---

[1] Record, p. 61 et seq.

seen Captain Wirz in the prison frequently. He usually came in more often than otherwise mounted on horseback. He would ride inside the dead line and examine the prison. I never heard him give any orders. I cannot say that I ever saw him perpetrate any acts of cruelty on the men—not to my personal observation. I was in the stockade all the time; I did not go out of it with the exception of few times for wood.

I recollect the dead-line there. I do not know what the orders were in relation to it, but I know that the effect of trespassing upon it was death. I have seen the penalty enforced—I have seen sentries shoot. I cannot say that I saw men die from gunshot wounds by sentries there. I saw a man who had been shot. He was not dead then. I do not know that he died. I do not know in what part of the body he was shot. I saw him carried on a stretcher to the hospital. He was a cripple, or one-legged man. I heard the report of a gun. It was near the entrance-gate to the prison. I went up there, and I saw the man being carried to a ward in the hospital, which was then inside the prison. It had not been removed outside then. There were other cases of shooting by sentinels. I came near being shot myself once. I have seen sentinels shoot at other times than the time I have spoken of. It was the second day after my entering the prison—the 5th of May. Some men had escaped from the prison the night previous, by means of a tunnel, and the orders that morning, at roll-call, were very strict indeed. They tried to ascertain from what squad the men had gone. We understood the order to be that no one should cross the swamp. I understood the orders to be that if any one crossed from one side of the prison to the other, across the swamp, he would be shot. My squad had had its place assigned to it by the side of the brook, and but a few feet from it. I thought that it would be no violation of the order to step to the side of the brook, and wash my hands. I did so. I sat by the side of the brook, and suddenly the boys gave a cry of warning, and I heard a gun snap. I looked up, and saw that the sentinel on the stockade had leveled his piece at me, and fired; but the piece had missed. I immediately got away from that vicinity. I was not fired at on any other occasion. I never heard any threats made to shoot men. I have seen sentries fire from the sentry posts at men. I have seen them firing at men who were dipping water out of the brook, just under the dead-line. I remember, one afternoon, seeing a sentry fire his piece at a man in that way. I do not recollect whether the man was killed or not that day. I could not swear that anybody was hit that day. Shooting by sentries was a frequent occurrence; so that, after a while, we did not notice it so much as we did when we first went there.

Our supply of fuel was not regular, nor sufficient. We were allowed, several times, to go out under guards—six men from a squad of ninety, or eighteen men from a detachment of two hundred and seventy—to bring in what we could find in the woods, on our shoulders; but the quarter part of the time we had to rely upon our supply of roots, which we dug out of the ground, or grubbed for in the swamp—pitch-pine roots. I mean the swamp in the stockade. We dried them, and made fuel of them. Part of the time rations were issued raw, and part not; many times when there were raw rations issued there was no fuel issued for them. The squad of ninety men of which I was a sergeant went from the 30th of June to the 30th of August without any issue of wood from the authorities.

166   THE TRAGEDY OF ANDERSONVILLE.

The most of the men had to depend on the brook for their water, and that, at many times, was exceedingly filthy. I have seen it completely covered, almost, with floating grease, and dirt, and offal. I have gone in barefoot, when it was so dirty that I had to go out, as I was getting all over with grease and filth. It was not always so, but very frequently so. They had to depend on the stream for water, because it was all they had, except that, after they had been there some time, they dug some wells; and there were some springs along the south side of the prison, by the edge of the hill, near the swamp, but the supply from that source was entirely inadequate. It supplied the wants of a few.

The quality of the rations, as a general thing, was poor. The quantity greatly varied, so far as my observation went. There were days when we got nothing at all. I made a note of at least two such days, and have the dates here. There were other days when we got but very little. There were other days when we got enough, such as it was. There seemed to be, somehow, great irregularity in the rations. I do not know how to account for it.

TESTIMONY OF BOSTON CORBETT.

Boston Corbett was one of the prisoners. He is the person who shot Wilkes Booth, President Lincoln's assassin. Corbett was, I believe, a religious enthusiast, but his credibility was in no wise assailed.

He testified:[1]

I have been in the United States service the most of the past four years; I was captured near Centreville, Virginia, and conveyed to Andersonville, Georgia; I arrived there 12th of July, 1864.

Before we entered the stockade we remained in front of the headquarters for some time, to be told off in detachments, numbering 270, divided into 90's; while there I was excessively thirsty, and asked a man who was there near Captain Wirz's headquarters (in some small tents) for a drink of water; the reply was that he dare not give it to me; he was not a guard; he was one of our own prisoners; there were a good many of them outside, on their parole of honor. Another man in the squad was sick; and he reported himself to a lieutenant of the guard, and asked if he could not be sent to the hospital, or have some medical treatment; the officer told him no, that nothing could be done for him till the morrow, and that he must go into the stockade with the rest of us. After entering the stockade, I found nine men of my own company there, who had been taken to that place some three and a half months previously; eight of them were inside, and one had been taken to the hospital outside; I did not see him but knew of his being there; within two months' time six out of those nine men died; and before I left the stockade, out of fourteen, including five who were captured with me, there were twelve dead; but two of us returned alive. The prison was very horrible on account of the filthy condition of it; the swamp which runs on each side of the small stream that runs through the stockade was so offensive, and the stench from it was so great, that I remember the first time I went down there I wondered that every man in the place did not die from the effects of the stench, and I believe that that

---

[1] Record, p. 69 et seq.

[From a sketch made at the time by R. K. Sneden.]
VIEW FROM THE OUTSIDE OF THE SOUTH GATE

[From an old photograph.]
DIVIDING SQUAD RATIONS BY NUMBER

was the cause of the death of a great many of our men; it was a living mass of putrefaction and filth; there were maggots there a foot deep or more; any time we turned over the soil we could see the maggots in a living mass; the soldiers were not compelled in all cases to wade through it to get to the stream; in some cases I have seen them wading through it digging for roots. Having no fuel allowed to us for a considerable length of time we were obliged to go there for the purpose of digging for roots; those roots, in one day's exposure to the sun, became thoroughly dried, and the next day we could use them for fuel; this was necessary because they did not furnish us with the necessary wood for cooking purposes. In September or October, a large number of men were taken from the stockade to work outside, perhaps two or three hundred or more; they worked upon a building southward from the stockade outside of it; what the building was for I cannot say, although it was said it was to be a hospital; but I know very well if the same number of men had been employed in procuring wood outside they might have built quarters inside to protect us from the weather; it was the night rains which brought on sickness; we had no protection from the rain or the sun; I was willing to go outside and work; I would have been glad of the chance; that was the general feeling among all the prisoners; I know it was the general desire to go out; we had no opportunity to talk with Captain Wirz about it.

I have seen around the swamp the sick in great numbers, lying in a line pretty much as soldiers lie when they lie down to rest in line after a march. Going down in the morning to the stream for water, I could see here and there those who had died during the night, and in the daytime I could see them exposed to the heat of the sun, with their feet swelled to an enormous size, and in many cases large gangrenous sores, without bandages to cover them, and the sores filled with maggots and flies, which they were unable to keep off. I have seen men lying there in a state of utter destitution, not able to help themselves, lying in their own filth. They generally chose that place—those who were most offensive—because others would drive them away, not wanting to be near those who had sores. Others chose it because of its being so near to the sinks. That was the place where the worst cases generally were. In one case a man died there, I am satisfied, from the effects of lice. When the clothes were taken off his body the lice seemed as thick as the garment—a living mass. Our food was very insufficient. Even when a sergeant of a detachment received his double ration, it was not enough for him. A sergeant in charge of ninety men received a double ration for his trouble in calling the roll, reporting the sick, &c. During the first month of my imprisonment there the sick were reported, and in some cases they received medicine. During the latter part of my imprisonment they received no medicine whatever. I believe no medicine was given inside the stockade during the last six weeks or two months; during that time I myself was very sick. The doctor would come around and look at us at times. The only thing he ever gave us in the way of medicine was some sour meal-water. Twice they gave me that as belonging to the scurvy patients. They called it vinegar. It was merely water laid upon sour meal. Our own men made a better article inside the stockade, which they called sour beer. The sick were carried to the south gate at roll-call, and those who could get carried out were carried out. There was a second enclosure inside the hospital—a wooden railing with guards to keep the men from going beyond the line. There the sick would be laid. There were six detachments assigned to one doctor's care, and the sergeant would have to see that the men were in their own places. The doctor would examine them, and would select one or two of the very worst cases to be sent to the hospital, when there would be perhaps twenty or thirty sick men in the detachment, so that the number that got to the hospital was very few in comparison with the number of those that were carried there awaiting to be taken out. I had myself to carry out one of my comrades three times. The fourth time he was taken to the hospital, and he died a short time afterwards. In some cases men died while waiting at the gate to be carried out. I have seen them dead there myself. The greater part of the time the four men who were assigned to that work by the sergeant of the detachment would carry them out, and in return for carrying them out, they were allowed to gather wood outside the stockade, which they would bring in. Every man bringing in an armful of wood might sell it if he chose; and he would generally sell it to other prisoners for about a dollar. The men got so hardened to death, being so familiar with it, and seeing it so constantly before their eyes, that I have often heard those who could not get a chance to carry out a dead man, say to those who did, "That is right; trade him off for good wood." If those things are not horrible, I do not know what is. I have stated that the condition of the place was horrible; I have seen these things. Scurvy was a very general disease there; there were hundreds of cases all around. It afflicted me by swelling my feet and legs very much, contracting the cords of my leg so that it was crooked so I could not straighten it; I had to limp in walking. Others were much worse, and had to crawl on the ground or walk on crutches. The gums would get exceedingly sore; the teeth would become loose and would frequently come out. In addition to that there would be a growth of raw flesh on the gums, both inside and out. In one case, a comrade belonging to my company had such flesh grow from each side of the mouth until it formed a second growth, making it impossible for him to eat such coarse food as the corn bread that we received, or anything of that nature. My gums frequently bleed, still. Very many were afflicted in that way. There were some barrack buildings put up at one end of the stockade, sort of shed-barracks, not enclosed on the side. The sick were gathered there as an inside hospital. I think there were upwards of a thousand patients there at the time. As I went there from day to day, I found that for two days they had received nothing in the way of nourishment or as rations, except boiled beans and molasses, which caused the death of a great many. Each morning there were cords of them laid out in front of this building, dead. I noticed that whenever we had an extra cold night the number of dead laid out in front of those sheds would be very large. I mean that if they were piled up like wood they would make several cords. One morning I noticed the body of one dead man which was so very offensive that I had to step aside and go away. How long that body remained in that neighborhood I do not know, but it certainly must have been very injurious to the health of those in the barracks close by; I know that it was so.

The water that passed through the stockade was often very filthy. Sometimes it was middling clear, but generally it was not good to drink. I was often compelled to drink it, nevertheless. At times I would go to those who had wells dug. Sometimes they would give me a drink and sometimes they would not. I received such rough usage and language from them that I have turned away parched with thirst, and drank the bad water from the stream, rather than beg it from the men who had the wells. In the portion of the stockade where I was it was pretty high ground. It was called the new stockade. There were some wells dug there. Probably one of them was the well that Dr. Bates described—very deep, but with no water. We had to go down to the stream for water, or to beg it from those who had wells near the stream. There were a great many away from that stream who were unable to get at it. I have seen a man lying within a few feet of that stream who was unable to get water for himself, and I have carried water to him. I have often seen men dead near there.

TESTIMONY OF MARTIN E. HOGAN.[1]

I have been in the military service of the United States—in the First Indiana Cavalry. I have been a prisoner four times during the war; I was a prisoner at Andersonville; I arrived there on the 6th of August, 1864; at the time of my arrival Captain Wirz was sick and Lieutenant Davis was in command; to the best of my knowledge Captain Wirz took command in about a week after that.

I only know from hearsay as to the number of men in prison while I was there, about 25,000 or 30,000; the stockade was crowded; there was no space. A great many of the men were as nearly naked as could be. As to fuel, I saw none there only occasionally, when two or three wagons would come in with a stick of wood on top; I have seen the sergeants of squads go out with a squad of men occasionally and bring in wood. There was no shelter whatever, only what the men made by digging holes in the ground and by using some blankets and some of their garments. I cannot say what number of rebel troops were at the post while I was there—two or three regiments. I saw negro prisoners and negro workmen outside; there were a good many negroes who came to work every morning, building the outside stockade; I would say there were from thirty to fifty. The health of the prisoners was very bad indeed when I got there; the men were about as miserable as men could be; I was taken out the next day to the general hospital and assigned to the duty of drawing medicine for the first division; I only had access to the stockade when I was returned to it some time afterwards. At the time of my arrival there the stockade was very much crowded, so much so that you could scarcely elbow your way through the crowd in any part of the camp. I noticed that a great many of the men were lying helpless on the ground, seemingly without care, without anybody to attend to them, lying in their own filth, a great many of them calling for water, and a great many crying for food, nobody apparently paying any heed to them. I noticed a great many there almost entirely destitute of clothing lying out in the cold, with nothing to shelter them from the storm or sun—so numerous that I could not begin to say how many. I never heard Captain Wirz give any orders to shoot prisoners; I never saw any man who had been shot there.

---

[1] Record, p. 86 et seq.

At the time I arrived there, being in the heat of summer, the water that ran through the stockade was very low. There was only a very small stream running through the center of the little channel or creek; the water was muddy, and the filth of the camp, when any rain or freshet would come, washed right into it; it produced filth in every form, to the extent that the water was not fit to drink, nor in fact fit to wash in. I have often seen masses of maggots on the banks of the stream; I saw filth of every sort there.

There were thick pine woods in almost every direction; it was a timber country. There was timber within easy hauling distance, enough to supply that camp and more.

The ration consisted of corn-meal of a very inferior quality, appearing as if corn and cob had been ground together and unsifted; it was generally half baked, soft and sour. Beef of a very inferior quality came in there in small portions; the men did not get much beef. The rations were entirely inadequate to keep the men from being always hungry. They were ever crying from hunger, or calling for something to eat. The rations were cooked partly in the cookhouse. In the hospital we received the meat raw, and also the rice. There were two cook-houses outside, and they generally cooked and baked in them; I have seen bread come from both. Bread was about the only thing that was cooked outside for the hospital.

We could not get any vegetables in the prison; there was plenty of corn—large corn-fields—and other vegetables. I escaped from prison and struck for the Chattahoochee river, and there I came across very fine corn-fields within fifteen miles of the prison. I saw melons and apples, beans, tomatoes, &c.; I do not remember seeing any peaches.

The general hospital was outside of the stockade. At the time of my arrival there, Surgeon White was in charge of the post; Surgeon Stevenson arrived soon afterwards. I had nothing to do personally with Dr. White; I was under the immediate charge of Dr. Eiland, and some time afterward I was appointed Federal steward, in charge of the second division. I saw very little of Dr. White in his official capacity; he seemed to pay but little attention to the hospital. He was very seldom there that I saw. Sometimes he would ride there in his buggy. Diarrhœa and scurvy were prevalent there—scurvy seemed to be the principal disease. The limbs of those afflicted with scurvy were drawn up, contracted; they were crippled, and some could not stand at all. Such cases were very numerous indeed. There was a separate hospital some distance from the camp for small-pox cases.

I never saw any inspecting officer of the rebel government—there was nothing of that sort there. I saw one doctor who came down there searching after medical science.[1] That was the only thing of that sort I ever saw there. He did not examine into the condition of the prison. He erected a dissecting room there, and went at dissecting; that is all I saw of him. The dissecting room was just outside of the hospital, within about fifty feet of the walls. It was composed of boards nailed up roughly and a sort of canvas thrown over it. I was in there in attendance on some of the doctors while they were dissecting. I saw them dissecting several bodies there. They were the bodies of Federal

---

[1] This was probably Dr. Jones.

prisoners. I saw them saw the skulls of men in two; I saw them saw the skulls off and open the bodies in that dissecting room. It continued four or five days, to the best of my knowledge.

TESTIMONY OF JOSEPH D. KEYSER.[1]

I have been in the military service of the United States, in the 120th New York. I was taken prisoner at James City, Virginia, on the 10th of October, 1863. I was taken from Richmond to Andersonville in February, 1864; I got there in the latter part of February. Captain Winder had command until some time in March.

When we arrived at the prison it was only partially completed. We were confined to the north side of the prison, the south side not being completed. The prison had no shelter in it. The trees had all been cut down in the enclosure. There was a sufficiency of wood there, and the water at that time was very good. I arrived there among the first load—about four hundred prisoners were there at that time. There continued to be a sufficiency of wood and water for about the first month we were there. As the prisoners commenced to come there more thickly, the wood began to get scarce, and, in consequence of the rebel camp being above on the stream, the water became filthy; but we were obliged to use it, as we had no means of digging wells in the prison. Quite a number of the men were healthy when they came there, and remained so for the first few months. There was no considerable sickness from the time we arrived there until May, 1864. Then the men began to get sick quite fast, and died off quite rapidly in June, July, and August, 1864—of diarrhœa, dysentery, scurvy, and gangrene. . . .

There was not very good care taken of the sick; at least there was not much furnished to them. There were no means adequate to take care of the number of sick that were there at the time. There were only a few tents furnished, and in those there were no bunks. The patients were compelled to lie on the ground. The food was insufficient to sustain life for any great length of time, as regards its quality and quantity. When we first went there we had a sufficiency of medicines, but, as the sickness increased, the medicines became scarce, and were not adequate to supply the wants of the prisoners. I was put in charge of the sick, as hospital steward. Dr. White was the surgeon there at that time. I did not think that he took special interest in the sick. He would generally leave it to some of his assistants to look after them and attend to the condition of things. I have seen cases of small-pox there. The first case was one that broke out a few days after we arrived. They had then one tent for a hospital. Five men were confined in that tent, and that man with the small-pox was confined with them. He remained there, I think, until he died.

When we first arrived there, the rations appeared to be much larger than they were at a subsequent period. We received more bacon and corn-meal. The quality of the corn-meal was very indifferent; it had the appearance of being ground up—the cobs and corn together. The rations were cooked by the prisoners until some time in April, when the cook-house was completed. The cook-house was on the west side of the stockade, about two hundred yards from it.

[1] Record, pp. 93 et seq.

Its drainage went into the creek and passed through the stockade. There was not a very large supply of vegetables while I was there. Occasionally we had a small quantity which was cooked at the hospital and distributed to the sick. The quantity was very small and inadequate to the wants of the prisoners who were sick, especially those who were laboring under scorbutic diseases.

TESTIMONY OF ANDREW J. SPRING.

Andrew J. Spring went to Andersonville as a prisoner on May 3, 1864, and was taken out of the stockade on May 27th on detailed duty. He testified:[1]

Before I was taken out many of my own men became sick with chronic diarrhœa, and there were many cases of scurvy. Soon after I went into the stockade I found almost all my boys in there were afflicted more or less with scurvy; a great many were crippled up, so that they could not walk, and had to crawl on their hands and knees or get along the best way they could; some of them could not do even that. There was a change in their whole appearance. I was absent from there, at one time, about six weeks; there was an order issued so that we could not get into the stockade; the men who were paroled outside did not have permission to go in to see those inside the stockade; one day I was bound to go in, and I applied to the lieutenant of the guard at the gate and gave him twelve dollars in greenbacks to let me go in and stay an hour, to see our boys; I went in and spent an hour inside the stockade; a great many of the boys were very poor; there were some of my best friends whom I could not recognize until they came up and shook hands with me and made themselves known, and, even then, I could hardly believe they were the same men; I have seen idiots in the stockade; I have seen men, acquaintances of mine, who would go around there not knowing anything at all, and hardly noticing anything; I have seen men there who were crippled up so that they had scarcely any life in them at all; they would lie on the ground, to all appearances dead; at different times I went up to several who I thought were dead, but I found they had a little life in them; I was intending to help some of them, but after I helped one, I was called from one place to another, and I found that I had more than I could attend to, so I had to leave them entirely.

There was any quantity of wood in that part of the country which could have been issued to the prisoners. I saw negroes about there; I saw them cutting wood. At the time they expected Stoneman's raid down there, soon after the capture of Atlanta, I saw from 500 to 1,000 negroes chopping wood to the westward, so as to make a range for the use of their artillery. They also at the same time put up two stockades around the main stockade of the prison and made a place for the artillery to work around the prison, so that if our own men should make an attack on the prison to release the prisoners, their fire would go directly into the prison.

[1] Record, p. 111 et seq.

TESTIMONY OF JAMES CLANCY.[1]

I have been in the military service of the United States; in the 48th New York regiment. I was taken prisoner. I was at the Andersonville prison; I arrived there on the 16th of June, 1864. I remained there until the 2d of November, 1864.

I was in the stockade all the time. It was very much crowded. The men were very destitute of clothing and shelter. Quite a number were sick inside the stockade who could not be admitted to the hospital, and they died in there for the want of going to the hospital. I carried a number of my own regiment out to be admitted, but I could not get them in. I carried one man out three times before he was admitted. That was the general rule so far as I could see. They would never take any man of our regiment out until he was almost dead, and would not live more than a week after being taken to the hospital.

I do not find it possible to give more than fragments of this class of testimony and such as will disclose the various experiences through which these prisoners passed. Besides, upon other branches of the case we shall have occasion to recur to the testimony of some of these same witnesses.

TESTIMONY OF J. NELSON CLARK.[2]

I have seen soldiers become insane. One in particular wandered up and down the stream with his clothes off—the little stream of water that ran through the prison. When his meals were taken to him he had not sense enough to know that he should come out and cook them, and he remained most of the time in that water until he died. He was given clothes once or twice, but he refused to put them on. The sun was very hot and burnt his skin, and he became very thin. When I last saw him he was lying dead in the stream. I saw soldiers who had committed suicide. One morning, after I had got up, I saw a man who had hung himself about fifteen or twenty feet from my tent to a stake that was in the ground, used partly to hang our blankets on and other purposes. I suppose the man was insane. He had a wild staring appearance for a few days before, and said that he would sooner be dead than live there; he said that to some of the men alongside of him. His companions had taken him down to the stream several times to wash him off; he was very filthy, lousy and dirty, as most of them were in there; even the cleanest had lice on them. I don't recollect how many men of my company went in there with me—forty-one, I think. Twenty-two died in southern prisons, most of them at Andersonville, some at Florence.

TESTIMONY OF JOSEPH ADLER.[3]

I was in the military service of the United States two years and nine months; I was a prisoner at Andersonville; I was there from about the middle of March to the 8th of September, 1864; I know Captain Wirz. When I was captured

---

[1] Record, p. 152 et seq.
[2] Record, p. 157.
[3] Record, p. 181.

there were seventy-one of us, including a young negro boy; all that is left is about a dozen out of the seventy-one.

I was part of the time in the hospital in the capacity of nurse; I cannot state exactly how long; I think it was two or three months; I went into the hospital in the month of June, and came out of there about three or four weeks before we left Andersonville; I left Andersonville on the 8th of September; while there I had opportunities of observing, from time to time, what was going on outside the stockade; I should judge the sick were treated pretty badly; the majority of the sick men had to lie on the bare. ground; the majority of them had no blankets; they had nothing to lie on and nothing to cover themselves with; they had hardly any clothing to cover their bodies with, and most of the time the food furnished them was unfit for them to eat, and consequently they had to go without anything to eat. It rained twenty-four days in June, if I am not mistaken; I know it rained twenty days in succession; at that time there were about 200 men lying out under the open sky without any shelter whatever, without any bedding or blankets, and some of them had nothing on but a shirt and a pair of drawers, and there was no medicine at the time to be given them, and they had no attendance whatever; they had only a little water, and all they had to eat was a little corn-bread and rice soup, that I would not give to a dog. I do not recollect ever seeing Captain Wirz strike or kick any of the sick or anything of that kind; I have heard him use very abusive and insulting language.

Captain Wirz took command there in the latter part of March or the beginning of April, 1864. The first day he went in the stockade he said he had to muster us all, to divide us into squads, detachments, and divisions, and that if he did not get through by one or two o'clock in the afternoon we would get no rations that day; he did not get through, and consequently we had to go without anything to eat. I do not think it was anybody's fault that we did not get through; it was impossible to get through all the work in the time specified, and no reasonable man would have thought that it could be done.

I lost a friend while I was attending the hospital there. I made a request of Captain Wirz on that occasion. There was a man by the name of Stevenson, who belonged to the Second Massachusetts cavalry, company A, the same company that I belonged to. He died there. He had respectable clothes on, and seeing that he was a friend of mine whom I had known for a long time, I did not, as I usually did, take off his clothes and give them to the living, but I left them all on his body, and requested Captain Wirz to let the clothes remain on the body, and he told me he would; after the body was carried out of the hospital, Captain Wirz went with the wagon, and two Confederate soldiers took the clothes off the man and they buried him stark naked, without anything, not even a shirt on his body, Captain Wirz did not make use of any expressions at that time, that I can recollect.

TESTIMONY OF D. H. STEARNS.[1]

I have been in the military service of the United States; in the First Regiment United States Sharp-shooters; I was in the Andersonville prison; I got there July 8, 1864; I was put in the stockade; I remained in there one or two days;

[1] Record, p. 191.

I was removed from the stockade and put in the hospital, to act as hospital steward, which was my rank in the regiment.

Some of the men brought to the hospital from the stockade were entirely naked; some had a shirt on, some a shirt and drawers, some with drawers without a shirt; some of them appeared to have fallen into the mire that was in the swamp in the stockade, and got their clothes saturated with the filth and water, and were not yet dry. In one case, I remember, in August, a man was brought in, and the maggots that inhabited the filth had got under his clothes, and were between his body and clothes inside; a large quantity of them had collected under his clothes, and they had gone inside. They had attacked his eyes, his nose, his ears, and the openings in his body; they had penetrated the rectum, causing the man excruciating pain, so much so that, although he was much emaciated from disease, it caused him to get up after he had been in the hospital a while and go round the hospital in exertion trying to relieve himself of pain, until he was exhausted; after three or four hours he died; I could not learn the man's name; he was delirious. Among the patients brought into the hospital from the stockade were very many delirious. I saw several other cases in which men were afflicted similarly to this man with the vermin. Amputations were frequently performed in the hospital; the result of amputations there was almost invariably death; I do not remember of a single case of recovery after an operation. There were no beds in the hospital, but bunks were made in part of the hospital; they were made of boards put on poles, simply two or three boards for a patient to lie on; there were bunks in only a portion of the hospital; more were asked for on one occasion by me; I several times asked the medical officer if more could not be obtained, and was answered, that they did not know; I then asked if poles and boughs could not be procured, as wood was plenty around there; they told me in that case that the commandant, Captain Wirz, would not allow the men to go out for that purpose. I asked Captain Wirz, myself, for passes to permit the men, who had already given their parole not to attempt to escape, to go outside the hospital for that purpose. He refused me, calling me some one of his pet epithets, a God-damned Yankee son of a bitch, and told me that, if I said anything more to him about it, he would take my pass away and put me in the stockade.

TESTIMONY OF THOMAS H. HORNE.

Thomas H. Horne, a soldier of the 102d New York Volunteers, testified:[1]

I have been in the military service of the United States; in the 102d New York Volunteers; I went to Andersonville on the twenty-ninth of July, 1864. I saw Captain Wirz the day I arrived there. We had a thousand men, half of those that were taken prisoners at Atlanta; he addressed the men in the line, and said that if they did not behave themselves he would shoot them on the spot. The rebel sergeants took what they wanted from us, it made no difference what, blankets, coats, and everything else. They took money and watches from men and took blankets from some of them. I saw the rebel sergeants give the money and watches to Captain Wirz; I stood close by Captain Wirz when he took

---
[1] Record. p. 201.

them, and that is the last the men ever heard of them so far as I know. They took two or three small articles out of my knapsack; I had five shirts on which they did not take, and I had two ten-dollar bills in my mouth. They took a case-knife from me, a fork and some note paper. The men had to take off their knapsacks and haversacks and leave them on the ground to be opened; there was some one hundred dollars taken from a young man standing close by me. I saw as many as three watches taken from men right by me.

When I was first put into the stockade I tried to find a place to lie down, but it was a pretty hard matter; I went to two or three places, but it was of no use. One man said that I could not lie down there. Pretty soon I had to fight for a place to lie down on. There was no room there, and they said we had no business there. Of course I got a place after a while. The men were perfect skeletons where I lay. They were in the worst kind of a state, half-naked, filthy, lousy, too sick to get up; I lay on the ground many a night when I couldn't sleep; sometimes on account of men around me groaning in agony. When I would wake up in the morning I would see men dead all around me, perfect skeletons. One man died and lay there so long that he could not be taken out, and they had to bury him where he died.

TESTIMONY OF WILLIS VAN BUREN.

Willis Van Buren, a member of the Second New York Cavalry, testified:[1]

The prisoners, while I was there, were supplied with rations very irregularly; I have seen men in the stockade in a starving condition; at the time I went in the stockade it was so; I saw skeletons, men with the flesh all off their bones, lying and standing around and huddling over small fires—not fires to keep them warm, but fires to cook their victuals. Some were partially covered with blankets and some nearly naked. They were lying about indiscriminately in a starving condition. The place seemed a perfect hell upon earth. I frequently saw the men hunting around the sinks for food that had once passed through men's bodies, undigested food to eat.[2]

TESTIMONY OF MAJOR ARCHIBALD BOYLE.[3]

I am major of the 12th United States colored troops. I was a prisoner at Andersonville. I was captured at Ocean Pond, Florida, on the 20th of February, 1864. I was captured while in command of my regiment, which was styled at that time the First North Carolina Volunteers. I was taken to Andersonville; arriving there about the 14th of March. I stopped in the stockade at Andersonville until the 16th or 17th of June, when I was sent to the hospital. Previously to that I had been refused admittance into the hospital, and had been refused all medical attendance. I was very severely wounded. I received a flesh wound in the body and a very severe wound in the lower part of the right leg, fracturing both bones. On arriving at the hospital I was in a very reduced

---

[1] Record, p. 263.
[2] There is much testimony that prisoners hunted the swamp and other places for undigested food.
[3] Record, p. 326 et seq.

state from the effects of my wounds and from exposure and starvation, and from several other causes. My wound was in a very bad state; it was full of gangrene at the time. On the 14th of March, 1864, I came into the stockade feeling very faint. I heard there was a hospital inside the stockade, and I got some men to help me up there. I was on crutches at the time. I went in, and one of our own men, who was acting hospital steward, commenced to bind up my leg, and was binding it when Surgeon White came in and ordered him to desist, saying at the same time, "Send him out there with his niggers," or something to that effect, and using an oath the same time. I said nothing, but merely looked at him. The hospital steward finished the dressing of my leg, and it was cared for by our own men afterwards. I was in full uniform then, as I am now. At the time I was captured I had on sword, sash and belt. About the latter part of April, I should judge, I went up to the hospital, which was in the stockade at that time, and while there the hospital steward, Robinson, who was the right-hand man of Dr. White, came in and asked me if I was the major of a negro regiment; I told him I was an officer in the United States military service. He asked me what regiment, and I told him. He said, "You are the man. Now I want you to go out of this." I asked him who he was, and he told me that was none of my business. He went out himself. I stopped there. I did not consider that he had any right to order me out, so I stopped there. A little while afterwards Mr. Burns, one of our own men, who was acting as hospital steward, came in and said to me, "This man Robinson says that if I do not persuade you to go out, he will ball and chain you." Under those circumstances I went out. I afterwards learned, however, that the language he used to Burns was, that if I did not go out he would shoot me and ball and chain him. Robinson was a Confederate hospital steward; I think he was the chief steward of the post.

While I was there I demanded to have my rank recognized. I made several demands. I was used in every respect the same as private soldiers, only worse. I made a demand on Colonel Persons, when I was in the stockade; I think so, but I will not state positively. However, after I was refused treatment in the hospital, in June or July, I made two demands on Captain Wirz. The first time he said he would see me about it. This was about October, 1864. The next demand I made, he sent in after me and I went out and saw him. A day or two afterwards he sent me with a letter, under charge of an officer, to see General Winder. Captain Wirz said that he could not do anything, as he was merely a subordinate under General Winder. When I got to Millen an officer came to me and got my name, rank, and regiment. The officer commanding at Millen, Captain Bowles, put me in the stockade again and refused to put my name on the register, saying at the same time that I should never be exchanged. I left Andersonville on the 18th of November, I believe. I saw Captain Wirz frequently while I was there. He saw me frequently. I was dressed in uniform.

THE JUDGE ADVOCATE. In connection with the testimony of the witness, I desire to introduce as evidence a letter contained in Captain Wirz's letter-book.

[There being no objection, the letter was put in evidence. The following is a copy:]

TESTIMONY OF UNION SOLDIERS.

HEADQUARTERS CONFEDERATE STATES MILITARY PRISON,
CAMP SUMTER, GA., November 28, 1864.

I have the honor to forward to you under guard, in charge of Detective Weatherford, eight prisoners of war, to wit:

A. Boyle, major 35th United States. He was captured at Ocean Pond, Florida, while in command of a negro regiment; he has not been recognized as an officer, although he has made several attempts to be recognized and exchanged. I forward him to you to enable him to see the general commanding. . . .

I remain, colonel, most respectfully, your obedient servant,

H. WIRZ,
Captain Commanding Prison.

COLONEL H. FORNO,
Commanding &c.

TESTIMONY OF JOHN BURNS WALKER.

John Burns Walker, Company G, 141st Pennsylvania Volunteers, was a prisoner from June 16, 1864, to May 28, 1865.[1]

My duty as sergeant of a ninety called me to be at sick call every morning with the sick. The order generally was for such sick men as had to be carried out on blankets. I remember that on the 27th of July an order was given, I think, for 500—five from each detachment; there were over a hundred detachments in the prison at that time. The orders were generally read from the gate, but whether they came from the surgeons or from Captain Wirz, I do not know. The sick men were carried out, and about noon the surgeons were sent in. Those sick men remained in the sick enclosure until next day at noon, when they were taken out, 500 of them. They were in a dying condition. None were taken except such as were considered not fit to live until next day. I have often taken sick men when the doctor would look at them and say that they would live till to-morrow. That was Dr. Rossey, the surgeon to whom I reported at the gate. He told me to take them back. They often asked if a particular man could live to be brought again. We had no medical attendance in the stockade. I never saw the surgeons in the stockade until the stockade hospital was erected, in September and October.

TESTIMONY OF THOMAS WALSH.[2]

I have been in the military service of the United States, in the Seventy-fourth New York. I arrived at Andersonville on the 29th February, 1864, and left it about the 20th of October. . . .

I think there were altogether about sixteen or seventeen trees in the stockade when I arrived there; a portion of them were old burned up pine trees; there were six or seven other trees on the south side which I believe were afterwards cut down and used, with the exception of one or two, in making a sink in the swamp for the accommodation of the men. But the other timber there, this blackened pine wood, was cut down by ourselves and used for firewood. I think the timber was all cleared out of the stockade in less than a fortnight after I got there. I think I was in the sixteenth hundred when I arrived. Before

[1] Record, p. 349.
[2] Record, p. 373.

Captain Wirz came there I used to get out to get some pine tops; when I went out they supposed I was going to sell some things, a watch or something; when I went out the first time I sold the buttons off my coat for soap. We would not be allowed to go out for wood unless we had the privilege; that privilege was withdrawn. I was on the north side, and no man was allowed at any time to go out, even on the south side, unless he paid three dollars in Federal money to the guards. On paying that money we could go out and get wood. I know something about the enlargement of the stockade. Before the stockade was enlarged I happened to be over with a friend of mine, a young man named Kelly; he was a clerk in the hospital on the south side; I used to go over to him to get some broken victuals occasionally, little scraps of meat, a little pepper, and some corn bread, because the food I received myself was entirely insufficient to support nature. I did not hear the prisoner say anything about the enlargement of the stockade, but I heard one of the rebel sergeants say that the stockade was about being enlarged on both ends, north and south; that is, if it were enlarged on the south side it would bring it down toward the large creek down there.

TESTIMONY OF CAPTAIN WILSON FRENCH.[1]

I was lately a captain of the Seventeenth Connecticut Volunteers. I was captured February 5, 1865, in the southern part of Florida, and was taken to Andersonville, arriving there about the middle of February, 1865. I was confined in Castle Reed with sixty-four other officers. It was a short distance from the stockade. It was not within the main stockade; it was a building formerly used for a guard-house, as I understood. The quality of the rations served out was very poor, and the quantity was not sufficient to sustain life. The rations for an officer for one day were less than two-thirds of a pint of corn-meal, about the same quantity of peas, and from two to three ounces of salt meat after the bone was taken out, and perhaps a half a gill of sorghum. That composed a day's rations. When the meal was sifted there was less than half a pint of it, and less than half a pint of peas after the dirt was taken out. We did not pretend to take out the wormy ones-we cooked those; we merely took out the dirt and gravel. Had we not been allowed to buy provisions we would have starved there. We were allowed to buy provisions. We never had any difficulty in getting vegetables; we used to buy almost anything that we wanted of the sergeant who called the roll mornings and nights. His name was Smith, I think; he was Captain Wire's chief sergeant; we were divided into messes, eight in each mess; my mess used to buy from two to four bushels of sweet potatoes a week, at the rate of fifteen, dollars Confederate money per bushel. Turnips we bought at twenty dollars a bushel. We had to buy our own soap for washing our persons and clothing; we bought meat and eggs and biscuit. There seemed to be an abundance of those things. They were in the market constantly. That sergeant used to come down with a wagon-load of potatoes at a time, bringing twenty or twenty-five bushels at a load sometimes. I mean to say that if we had not had the privilege of buying what we needed, we should have starved. The quantity and quality of rations furnished us were not sufficient to sustain life, in my opinion.

[1] Record, p. 383.

I remained at Andersonville about five weeks. Our quarters were very poor. The building in which we were confined was about sixty feet long, and twenty-five feet wide, and there were sixty-four officers confined in it; so you can imagine that we were pretty closely packed together.[1] We had to do our own cooking in the building, and when first I went there we were not allowed to go outside unless to go to the sink. We had no yard to go into at all. We did not see many of the Confederate officers except the sergeant. He threatened sometimes to put us in the stocks. They were giving us from thirteen to fifteen dollars in Confederate money to one in greenbacks, and the latter part of the time they gave us twenty dollars for one. A bushel of vegetables, for which was paid twenty dollars, could have been purchased for a one-dollar "greenback" —for less than a one-dollar greenback. According to my observation, produce raised in the Southern states was cheaper than that of the North, considering the price of gold.

TESTIMONY OF J. EVERETT ALDEN.[2]

I was formerly orderly sergeant of company F, Fourth Vermont Volunteers. I was captured on the 23d of June and taken to Petersburg; thence to Richmond, there confined at Libby three or four days, and from there was taken to Andersonville. I arrived there July 12, 1864. We were immediately marched to Captain Wirz's headquarters, and there we were counted off into nineties, three of which, 270 men, constituted a detachment.

My detachment was No. 107. I think there were from 29,000 to 30,000 men there at that time. The condition of the men was very bad; some that I saw were nearly naked; some had but a pair of government drawers, and they were so emaciated, so reduced in flesh, that their bones nearly pierced their skin. Almost every morning when I went to the creek after water I would see from one to four dead bodies lying on the banks of the creek entirely naked, stripped of their clothing, by the other prisoners. As soon as a man died they would take the opportunity to appropriate his clothing, as they needed it. I should think the men whom I saw lying there were men who had died from starvation; they were very poor in flesh.

The detachment which I was in never drew any wood from the time we went there till some time towards the last of August, a period of from four to six weeks, I should think. We had some cooked rations during that time. Some of the detachments drew a small piece of wood; the wood was issued to the detachment. It was then subdivided among the nineties, and then again subdivided in small pieces among messes of thirty men each. The wood being divided into thirty pieces, the sergeant having charge of the thirty would distribute it among the men so that no one could find fault with the quantity which each got. The piece for each man was in thickness and length about the size of my arm, and it was to last for three clays. Men who drew wood would cook their rations, and as soon as they got through others would use the coals, and by blowing them they could partly cook the meal which was issued. to them and could warm the meat. I have seen men digging for roots with which to cook their rations; it was a common thing; they mostly dug for them in the swamp

---

[1] Space 3 by 8 feet to each officer.
[2] Record. p. 384 et seq.

on each side of the creek, the north side more particularly, as that was the wider. When it rained the matter from the camps would wash down into the swamp, and it was filled with maggots. They must have been from fifteen to twenty inches deep. The men were obliged to go down there and dig in that swamp to get roots, which they would dry in the sun.

I know something as to how sick men were treated by the doctors. It was my duty at seven o'clock each morning to call the sick, and immediately after roll-call to have them all fall in and march up to sick-call at the south gate. Sometimes three or four thousand prisoners would collect around this gate to gain admission outside. There was a very small space to pass through at the gate, and when there were so many prisoners there, over 30,000, two sentinels were ordered to prevent the crowd from getting close to the gate near the dead-line, and those who went out were admitted in one rank; each sergeant would call his men and march them out through the gate. When they got outside there were fifteen to twenty doctors in stalls; each doctor attended to a certain number of detachments. I have taken men out to the stall of a doctor named Williams, I think, and I have seen men crawl up there on their hands and knees with just life enough in them to get to the stall and plead to be either taken out to the hospital or to have proper medicine given them, something by which they would be relieved of their distress. Those men the doctor would order to be taken back into the stockade, as they could probably live till to-morrow. He would say, "Take him back into the stockade; he will live until to-morrow."

TESTIMONY OF SAMUEL J. M. ANDREWS.

Samuel J. M. Andrews, 17th Illinois Infantry, was a prisoner from April 27, 1864, to September, 1864. He testified:[1]

I have seen men die suddenly there; I remember distinctly seeing two men fall over and die upon the spot, or rather fall over dead; they were both at the sink and they fell forward dead while there; one of them was inside the stockade before the hospital was removed outside; the other was in the hospital after it was removed outside; one of the men was brought over to my tent; I was nursing at the time; he was brought over one day and died the next; I saw one patient in the hospital with ball and chain attached to his ankle; he was so weak that he was hardly able to walk; I saw another one with a shackle on his ankle; he said he had cut the ball off; he had no ball attached at the time I saw him, although he had shackles about his ankle; I do not know with what disease the man was suffering who had the ball and chain on him, but I should suppose from his appearance it was diarrhœa; I do not know what was the matter with the other man.

TESTIMONY OF JOHN A. CAIN.[2]

I was in the military service of the United States; I enlisted in the California Cavalry Battalion, at San Francisco.

I was taken prisoner the 22d February, 1864; I was taken to Richmond, Virginia, and remained there three or four days, long enough to be searched and have

---

[1] Record, p. 390.
[2] Record, p. 393 et seq.

everything taken from me and the rest of us. I was taken from there to Andersonville, and arrived at Andersonville on the 10th of March, 1864; it was raining very hard when we arrived there, about two o'clock in the morning. We were drawn up in line four deep, about 1,000 of us, and were marched through water about knee-deep; a great many of the men were very sick and feeble; they were forced to walk through that mud and water about knee-deep to the stockade, a distance of about half a mile; they were turned loose into the stockade; it was raining hard and we were without shelter and we did not know where to go; they were ordered to fall in the next morning to receive orders how we were to proceed while there. Being very dry I started to the swamp to get some water; in the dark I fell into a hole headlong; however, after some difficulty, I found the water and got a drink and started back; I came across several shebangs, as we called them, rudely constructed tents and covers made out of pine boughs and poles; they were a poor excuse for covering; the rain was beating on the men who were lying under them; the men were very emaciated and sick, as I thought; some were groaning. We had some little talk with them; they told us that we had no shelter and that we would have to do the best we could. I went upon the shady side of a large tree and stood up and sat down as best I could until morning; it rained until daylight. When daylight came, I can hardly describe the scene that I beheld—men lying around in all directions sick, very sick and feeble; most of them were Belle Island prisoners. It did not matter about the health of the men; it seemed to me that the healthiest of the men took sick as quick, if not quicker, than some of those who were weak. Two of my own comrades—stouter or heartier men never lived—took sick the next day; I did not know from what cause unless it was from change of water; we had to carry one of them in a blanket to the hospital. This hospital was only a few boards thrown together very temporarily to shed the rain off those very sick lying in there; they were lying in their own filth, with nobody to take care of them. When I visited the hospital to see my own comrades, men would appeal to me to help them to the sink, or to give them a drink of water, or a piece of bread or something of that kind; I very nearly got sick at the stomach and had to leave the place. About ten o'clock that day I was ordered to the other side of the stockade; the place was very steep, rising up from the swamp; it could not be called a hill—it was a bank, inclining at an angle of about forty degrees; I was allotted to a place on that bank that was very difficult for a sick man or a weak man to ascend without good help, without two men to help him; I was obliged to lie there until I was taken to the hospital. I got scurvy and diarrhœa after a while; I was obliged to lie there without shelter; we sat by a fire which a hat would cover up, made of pitch-pine roots; I sat there for twenty hours at one time in the rain; it rained a great deal during the month of April. We could not cook what raw rations we got; I very often mixed up meal and ate it raw for want of wood and cooking utensils. We got a little more than a pint of meal; that was before Captain Wirz took command; we got a little better than that after he took command. The rations consisted of about a pint of meal and a half a pound of very coarse beef; we took it to be mule flesh; it looked more like horse or mule flesh than beef; we got about a teaspoonful of salt; that was our rations for twenty-four hours; I very often ate my beef or mule flesh raw; I just picked the bones. In that condition I lay on that side of the hill until about the 23d of May, when I became so weak that I could not get up to roll-call in the morning. Captain Wirz's sergeants ordered all the sick to fall in every morning, if they had to be carried up; I very often got some of my comrades to help me up this hill, and in many instances I fainted away when I got up, One time at the top of the hill I fainted away and was conveyed temporarily to a little tent, consequently missing the roll-call; the sergeant asked where I was; they could not find me; and he ordered my rations to be stopped that day; it was neglect of some comrades for not having me up. I finally got discouraged and made up my mind to die; I did not wish to be any more trouble to my comrades, and I went over to the gate and was successful in getting to the hospital; that was a little while after the hospital was moved out of the stockade, about the 23d or 24th of May, I think. What transpired in the stockade after that I cannot say, except as I might see the victims of Wirz's cruelty come to the hospital. I was paroled as a nurse, or was allowed the privilege of nursing; we had no more liberty than any of the rest of the sick; I was very often allowed to go to the gate to help sick men off the wagons or ambulances, or to carry the men on stretchers. I had an opportunity there of seeing the cook-house and of seeing the rations taken out, and of hearing news of the inner part of the stockade.

TESTIMONY OF GENERAL J. H. WILSON.

Major-General J. H. Wilson testified with regard to army supplies in Tennessee, Georgia, and Alabama, as follows:[1]

My rank in the United States military service is captain of engineers, United States Army, and major-general of volunteers. I have been operating for the past year in Tennessee, Alabama, and Georgia, with the cavalry corps, military division of the Mississippi. During the latter part of the year 1864 and the early part of the year 1865 I have been campaigning in Tennessee, Georgia, and Alabama. I am stationed at Macon, Georgia. After passing through the mountainous region of northern Alabama I found supplies in great abundance on our lines of march—in sufficient abundance to supply a command of 17,000 men without going off our lines of march for them. On going south I marched southeast from the northwest corner of Alabama to a point called Montebello, and thence south to Selma, from Selma southward to Montgomery, from Montgomery two lines, one to Columbus, Georgia, and the other to West Point, Georgia, and thence by two converging lines to Macon, Georgia, and then all over the State of Georgia, from there to the Gulf. We found lines of railway running very nearly in the direction of the march from Montebello. The rebel government, before the invasion of the United States government, drew supplies from that part of the country, from central Alabama to southwestern Georgia, for the wants of their armies operating in the field; that was their grand region of supplies. There was a railroad communication between the parts of the country of which I have spoken, and Macon and Andersonville.

[1] Record, p. 269 et seq.

General Wilson also testified as to the location of the stockade, the facilities for making it habitable, the availibility of wood for fuel; water supply and other matters. He testified to his observations made about the time of the abandonment of the prison, and it must be admitted that the facts disclosed by the witnesses fully justified the court in taking a view of the situation similar to that expressed by General Wilson.

GENERAL WILSON'S EXAMINATION OF THE PRISON—ITS CONDITION, HIS OPINION OF ITS LOCATION, AND WHAT NIGHT HAVE BEEN DONE TO RELIEVE THE SUFFERINGS OF THE PRISONERS.

I have visited Andersonville. I have examined the state of the prison and the buildings there and the country generally in the neighborhood of it. I presume the court may have examined this drawing of the prison; it was made under my direction; it does not show quite well enough the topography. The stream here called "Little Sweet Water" is a large creek running as much as fifteen feet in width and five feet deep, and runs only about two hundred and fifty feet from the corner of the hospital enclosure. If the main enclosure had been simply enlarged so as to cross that creek, which could have been done very easily, it could have supplied all the troops that could possibly have been put there with ample water both for culinary purposes and for the purpose of police.

The timber in the neighborhood was ample, and, as a matter of course, it being a grain-growing region, the means of supply of provisions were ample, and the means of getting them there were ample. The creek on which the prison was located is not a large one, but simply a spring branch, little springs running out of the side of the hill, making a creek which I suppose will not run more water than would supply for the purposes of an army a larger command than four or five thousand men, because the water does not flow rapidly.

There is one spring inside the enclosure, but that would not supply more than a regiment of men, as troops use water and as they ought to use it. I visited the stockade some time in the last part of June or the first of July, this year. I found, I think, the remnants of some ten sheds inside the stockade, one set of five on one end of the stockade and the other on the other end. They were simply shed roofs, supported by ordinary square timber cut from woods in the neighborhood, and covered with boards, nothing else. I observed that the character of the buildings outside the stockade was temporary. They were constructed in a similar manner to those sheds, except that the sides were boarded up. The commissary was a stockade building, formed of logs; the others were generally small framed buildings, some one story and some two stories high, and made of boards. My impression is that the barracks erected for the use of the troops on garrison there were such as troops ordinarily construct for themselves—huts. There were some barracks (which had, perhaps, been used as a hospital) which were fair barracks for troops. What troops ever occupied them I could not say. I noticed the surrounding timber. It is a well-timbered region, a region abounding in fine timber of a character very easily worked—pine particularly. Northwest from the stockade there is a large pine forest, and that immediate region being a poor region, has not been generally cultivated, and this forest was undisturbed. It could have been used for getting out shelter very readily. It is just such a place as troops would like to camp in for the convenience of wood and water and such things as that, if they were going to make winter quarters, aside from mere climatic reasons. I have nothing to say in reference to that. I should say that it would require to enlarge the inner stockade one third about 1,800 feet of additional stockading to be put up, and the outer one about 2,400 feet. It would require about forty days' work for one hundred men, working as soldiers work, but one hundred men could do the work in twenty days, provided they did a full day's work and had all the appliances for transporting timber from the forest—they would not have to transport it more than a mile on the average—and all the necessary appliances for digging, &c. There was plenty of black labor to be had in that country. I found no difficulty in obtaining laborers; the difficulty was in getting rid of them. You could get all the labor required there for any purpose of that kind.

Q. State if you are able to make an estimate, allowing that 30,000 prisoners were confined in the stockade and that half of them, 15,000, were supplied cooked rations, what amount of wood would have been required to cook the rations issued to the remaining 15,000, consisting simply of corn-meal, bacon, and peas.

A. That question is somewhat complicated; it would depend entirely on the appliances used in cooking. The quartermaster's monthly allowance for wood, I think, in summer time, or from May till October, is a cord for every twelve men; that would require about 1,250 cords to 15,000 men, and that I think is a very fair estimate. A man can cut two cords of wood a day if he tries; in that timber certainly a workman would cut two cords a day, but a soldier probably would cut only one; and it is a liberal estimate, because it would not have to be split up. About thirty men per day would cut all the wood required or allowed by the quartermaster's regulations for 15,000 men, and a guard of ten, fifteen, or twenty men would be ample to protect that number of men in the work. If you take the winter allowance it would be just double. I think they allow one cord of wood per month for six men in winter time, and, as a matter of course, it requires sixty men to do the work.

There was lateral drainage in the stockade, of course, from both ends of the stockade to the creek which runs through it. There was no sewerage system that I could observe, excepting such as would naturally result from the formation of the ground. I observed no artificial drainage.

By the COURT:

I have spoken of sheds I saw in the stockade. They remained there when I was in the stockade. I found nothing in the way of habitations, huts, conveniences, &c., for the protection of the men. I understood that those sheds were used for the protection of those in the stockade whose health was worse than that of others. The men had, for protection, burrowed both in the level part of the ground and in the inclined part on the hillside, particularly in the hillside. Those constructions assimilated to tents, but they were made in the ground. I presume they must have been covered over with fragments of boards and blankets and shelter tents and such things as they could get there, but there was no evidence of anything of that kind being there. There was just as many as could be put in that space of ground, and I suppose it was very close packing, for I saw no means of passing between them. I saw the interior of some of them; I stooped down into them. I should say as a general thing that the character of them was about like the ordinary shelter made by combining two shelter tents; they might hold four men, but they would be very crowded.

Cross-examined by counsel:

I stepped down into the excavation which was used as a ground-floor or basement. I saw no tunnels running under the stockade. I was told there had been something of that kind attempted. I examined half a dozen or so of those holes; I could see them all around in riding over the ground. They all had the appearance of being houses for protection. I saw one particular kind of hole that I did not understand, circular shafts of the diameter of six feet, and sunk as far as I could see. They might be wells. They were up on the hill, which was some eighty feet above the level of the country, and they may have been made deep so as to get to water, which, if the water was at the ordinary level, would be forty or fifty feet. I examined them the last part of June or first of July.

By the COURT:

If they took crooked timber to enlarge the stockade the men would have crawled between the joints, but the timber in that country does not grow crooked; as a general thing it is very straight. They could have erected a perfectly secure stockade without squaring the timber; axes and shovels were the only things necessary. Saws and a few hammers might have been used occasionally, but axes and shovels would have done the work. Our soldiers generally worked with those, and they could make almost anything. I believe there were some few implements of that kind which fell into the hands of our troops, but what number I don't pretend to say. Afterwards I put a man in charge of the place in order to protect it, and I think he reported to me that he had found a few tools; how many he did not say. The court may have misunderstood what I said in reply to the question how long it would take to enlarge the capacity of the stockade one third. I did not mean to state the time which it would take to extend it across the creek. I think, however, that it would have taken but little longer to extend it across the creek and take in all the ground that would have been necessary for any number of prisoners that might have been put there.

I would not undertake to say that the addition of one third would have included Sweet Water creek, though possibly it might.

THE JUDGE ADVOCATE. The court will remember that Dr. Eldridge in his report said that it ought to have been extended in that direction.

WITNESS. There is no question about that, because then the prisoners would have had the use of an ample stream of running water all the time—ample for any number of troops—a stream that could not have been exhausted, instead of this little branch.

By counsel:

The larger creek is called Little Sweet Water creek. All three creeks come together within a half of a mile. I examined Little Sweet Water creek with some care; I waded into it. At the time I examined it, it was about twenty-five feet wide and about four and a half feet deep; that was just after a rain, but by inquiry of citizens in the neighborhood I learned that the stream was then at its usual stage, though probably somewhat swollen. By a rough calculation I infer that the average width of the stream was about fifteen feet and the average depth about five feet, with a velocity of probably a mile an hour; it might not be so much. It is rather a sluggish stream, though the water is clear and apparently sweet and good. At the bottom, the creek is somewhat wide, and it shelves off very gradually. It has not steep banks.

Q. You said you thought the stream was about four and a half feet deep?

A. I am striking an average of the size of the stream, in order to state the volume of water that passes through it.

By the COURT:

Q. From the construction of the stockade and the general appearance of the work, was there, in your opinion, any exhibition of intelligent engineering?

A. It was intelligent enough for the purpose, but it did not exhibit any very humane engineering. It was simply an enclosure stockade, and made safe for men to go into, with no earthly preparation that I could see for their comfort; and if there ever were 30,000 men there, as I have been told there were, that would explain very readily the cause of the deaths. There were 12,000 to 15,000 graves outside. I have been told that originally a six-horse wagon was used in hauling provisions, but that the stockade afterwards became so crowded that a wagon could not go in at all, so that a cart was used instead. Whether that be true or not I cannot say. I conceived it to be very reasonable, if there were 30,000 men inside the stockade. The improvements which suggested themselves to me were perfectly apparent to anybody.

By counsel:

Any engineer could have seen what I suggested, and any humane man could have seen that the prison was either located for a very much smaller number, or if located for that number, it was with the intention that they should not have the benefit of water or fuel, and the graves there led me to the infinance that it was intended they should not have the benefit of provisions either; the want of water, fuel, and the lack of shelter are apparent;[1] I did not notice where the stockade had been enlarged; I could not distinguish where it had been extended; I have been told that it had been enlarged, and I think that it had probably been extended towards the north; I should infer that the stream ran through the middle of it, if my inference in regard to its enlargement is correct. The stream now runs about one third of the distance from the southern end, leaving two thirds of the enclosure north of the stream and one third south; if I was to make my own inference I should simply say that if that prison had been designed for 2,500 or 3,000 men, of the size originally constructed, it would be a very good prison if it had the other appliances necessary for their comfort; there would be at least plenty of water. I should say there had never been any accommodations there for any number of prisoners. The little bake-house was probably the only thing that assimilated to any accommodations for the prisoners; there were two or three ovens in that; that was the only place that I saw that looked like intending to give the prisoners that comfort which it was necessary for them to have; it was a very good place for two thousand men, but a very bad one for thirty-three thousand. My own impression is that for an encampment of two or

---

[1] Can any other inference be drawn from the facts?

three thousand men, it would be as healthy as any one in the country. If I had been travelling through the country and had been going to make a camp, I would have made it right on the edge of Sweet Water creek; I would not have liked, probably, to have gone there to winter my command or to stay there forever.

By the COURT:

I should say that the swamp in the stockade would be very unhealthy in summer time; it has a tolerably wide bottom, quite alluvial, the water sluggish, and would be very apt to breed miasma. As to the condition of the swamp beyond the prison, I did not examine it at all. There is a little swamp in Sweet Water creek, one that would be unhealthy after taking the timber off it and letting it be exposed. The ground would have been quite as good there, and probably better, because where it was the ground washed a good deal; the men in burrowing disturbed the soil and it washed down into the creek, but the Sweet Water creek was large enough to clear itself; the ground was not so that the washing of the camps would wash into it; I hardly think so much on the "Little Sweet Water" as the other; I think the slope at the "Little Sweet Water" is more gradual and gentle; being a very large creek, it would necessarily be so. At the little creek the escarpments are very sharp and it could not clear itself very readily, particularly when covered across by the stockade, forming drains in it. I think there can be no question as to the desirability of the two locations; if you were going to put a prison there, ordinary humanity would require that it should be put across the main creek, if it were intended to accommodate such a large number of men; it would have been only three-quarters of a mile from the depot; the creek runs up in that direction and it may possibly cross the railroad.

TESTIMONY OF COLONEL GEORGE WELLING.

Colonel George Welling, who was in General Wilson's command, testified as follows:[1]

I have been in the military service of the United States for four years as lieutenant colonel Fourth Kentucky Cavalry. My regiment was ordered to Albany, Georgia. I took the command of the post about the first of May. I passed very often up and down the railroad from Albany to Macon; I stopped at Andersonville fifteen or twenty minutes at a time. I was never at the stockade. I was with General Wilson's command from the time it left the Tennessee River until we left that part of the country, about the 20th of last August. The Confederate commissaries and quartermasters who were located at Albany turned over the stores and provisions they had there. There were thirty-one thousand pounds of bacon turned over by Captain John Davis, Confederate commissary; seven hundred bags of salt; the amount of corn I do not recollect. There was a large quantity of corn and bacon in the country through which we passed. Parties after we went there proposed to supply us with any quantities needed to supply General Wilson's army. There were three grain mills in the vicinity. The mill at Albany, which was built by the Confederate government, had two run of stones. A mill some four miles from there, which I never visited, had, I understood, the same number. That mill at Albany was capable of grinding from four to five hundred bushels of corn in the twenty-four hours. This mill turned

[1] Record, p. 276.

over to us by the Confederate government at Albany had a very good bolting cloth in it, and ground very good flour. We made very good flour in it after we took possession of it. They had a bakery there with four ovens, where they baked hard bread; some of that hard bread that I have seen was very good. Albany is thirty-five miles by railroad from Andersonville. The Confederate government turned over to us some twenty-odd wagons. In the corral there were probably thirty or forty mules; a good many teams had been lent out to parties when they found we were coming there. Some of them we gathered up afterwards. [To the COURT.] I should say there were from fifty to a hundred head of mule stock there, enough to run the wagons that were turned over. Farmers along the line of march from Macon to Albany had generally ox teams with which to transport grain. They had them on almost every plantation. At Vienna there had been considerable stores, but the citizens had made a raid upon them when they heard we were coming, and had taken possession of bacon and corn and stock and had scattered it. I should judge Vienna is about forty miles from Andersonville.

GOLDWIN SMITH ON TREATMENT OF PRISONERS.

In Goldwin Smith's "Reminiscences," published in *McClure's,* September, 1910, are found some observations upon the Civil War. He was one of the most distinguished journalists of his time and had been for forty years among the foremost North American thinkers and scholars. Of prison life during the war, North and South, he said:

It seemed to me that at the North, generally, there was a remarkable absence of truculence. The determination was fixed to subdue the South and restore the Union. But I heard few expressions of thirst for revenge such as were heard the other day from loyalists at Cape Town. Prisoners of war were well treated. I visited the prison camp at Chicago and saw that its inmates were well fed and were suffering no hardships beyond that of confinement. If they died under imprisonment, it was as the eagle dies. I visited the prisoners' hospital at Baltimore, went through every part of it, and satisfied myself that the treatment was good. My visit was unannounced. On Thanksgiving Day the table was spread with the good things of the season. I record this as an answer to the charges of cruelty rife at the time in England. It was the more notable as the treatment of Federal prisoners in some of the Confederate prisons was known to be inhuman. In the Andersonville prison camp it was devilish, and such as no want of resources on the part of the captors could excuse. I saw at Annapolis the first batch of prisoners exchanged from Andersonville; they were living skeletons. No laws of war can warrant the detention of prisoners whom a captor cannot feed. They ought to be released on parole.

Here is the question stated in a nutshell. If the rebel government found itself incapable of feeding its prisoners they should have been paroled. It would have been no more reprehensible to have taken the prisoners out and shot them than to have deliberately starved them to death, as was done.

SHERMAN'S MARCH TO THE SEA—PROVISIONS ABUNDANT IN GEORGIA.

General Sherman began his march to the sea through Georgia on November 15, 1864, and subsisted his army of 65,000 men mainly from food supplies found in the country. He started with 5,000 beeves on the hoof and had 10,000 when he reached Savannah. And yet, thousands of Union prisoners of war were starving to death at Andersonville, west of his line of march and, unfortunately, too far to admit of an expedition for their relief. How futile now to put forward as a fact in defense that food for the prisoners could not be procured. I quote briefly from General Sherman's Memoirs:

We found abundance of corn, molasses, meal, bacon and sweet potatoes. We also took a good many cows and oxen and a large number of mules. In all these the country was quite rich. . . . The recent crop had been excellent, had just been gathered and laid by for the winter. As a rule, we destroyed none, but kept our wagons full and fed our teams bountifully. (Vol. 2, p. 182.)

The army camped on General Howell Cobb's plantation near Milledgeville, the Georgia state capital.

General Sherman says: "Of course, we confiscated his property and found it rich in corn, beans, peanuts and sorghum molasses. Extensive fields were around his home."

On December 16, 1864, General Sherman wrote General Grant from near Savannah:

Fortunately by liberal and judicious foraging we reached the seacoast abundantly supplied with forage and provisions, needing nothing on arrival except bread. . . . We started with about five thousand head of cattle and arrived with over ten thousand, of course consuming turkeys, chickens, sheep, hogs and cattle of the country. (p. 208.)

Again:

The property captured consisted of horses and mules by the thousand, and of quantities of subsistence stores that aggregate very large, but may be measured with sufficient accuracy by assuming that the sixty-five thousand men obtained abundant food for about forty days, and thirty-five thousand animals fed for a like period, so as to reach Savannah in splendid flesh and condition.[1]

---

[1] See map of Georgia, chap. V, which shows Sherman's course from Atlanta to Savannah, far to the east of Andersonville.

CHAPTER IX.

CONDITIONS AT PRISON (CONTINUED)—TESTIMONY OF FATHER HAMILTON AND OTHER WITNESSES CALLED FOR THE DEFENSE—HORRORS OF THE PRISON PEN CONFIRMED—WITNESSES FOR DEFENSE CORROBORATE TESTIMONY OF THE PROSECUTION IN MANY ESSENTIAL PARTICULARS—DIARY OF REV. FATHER CLAVEREUL—FATHER CLAVEREUL'S ACCOUNT A MOST PATHETIC PICTURE OF HUMAN SUFFERING.

THERE were thirty-two witnesses called and sworn for the defense. Of these, twelve were Union soldiers, prisoners at Andersonville; four were rebel surgeons who had been on duty at Andersonville, and were witnesses for the prosecution; five were rebel officers on duty at Andersonville, four of whom were witnesses for the prosecution; four were rebel officers on duty at Richmond, one of whom was a witness for the prosecution; one was a rebel officer on duty at Macon; two were rebel soldiers on duty at Andersonville, one of whom testified for the prosecution; three were clergymen who resided in the south and visited Andersonville, one of whom, Father Hamilton, was a witness for the prosecution; and Miss Rawson, who resided "on the plains of Dura, Georgia," completed the number.

The witnesses were called to meet certain of the various phases of the evidence submitted by the prosecution. At present we are dealing only with evidence bearing upon the first charge and some parts of its specifications—i. e. with the charge of conspiracy "to injure the health and destroy the lives of soldiers in the military service of the United States, then held and being prisoners of war within the lines of the so-called Confederate States and in the military prisons thereof, to the end that the armies of the United States might be weakened and impaired; in violation of the laws and customs of war."

The evidence has thus far been directed to the establishment of the prison; its management, the effect upon the prisoners there confined, and to show upon whom rested the responsibility. The acts of cruelty charged, as in furtherance of the design to kill and destroy these prisoners, such as subjecting them to cruel, unusual and infamous punishment, by "fastening large balls of iron to their feet," and binding numbers of them together "with large chains around their necks";

subjecting them "to the burning rays of the sun without food or drink"; establishing a "dead-line"; pursuing escaped prisoners with ferocious dogs, thereby maiming many—and other specifications of specific acts of cruelty, remain to be shown in subsequent chapters. There also remains the evidence relating to charge 2—"Murder in violation of the laws of war," and its specifications.

In presenting the evidence offered by the prisoner, which it is but fair should be done, it will in this connection be confined with some exceptions, to matters already dealt with.

Let us begin with the testimony of Rev. Father Peter Whelan. It bears upon some points to be considered under charge 2, but his testimony will be given substantially in its entirety.

It will be remembered that Mr. Davis, in his *Belford* article, quoted Rev. Father Whelan as saying that he was dismissed by the judge advocate, upon finding out what he would testify to, and was not allowed to be called by the prisoner. Mr. Davis must have misunderstood Father Whelan, for no one knew better than Father Whelan that the statement was not true. He was called by and testified for the prisoner, and whatever benefit it was to him as a defense, will be now given.[1] The reader cannot help contrasting his testimony with that of Father Hamilton, both men of undoubted probity—the one withholding nothing from his narrative, the other obviously disposed to minimize the horror of his surroundings, and yet unwilling to conceal the awfulness of the situation of these wretched prisoners, when questioned directly to the point. He testified:

TESTIMONY OF REV. PETER WHELAN.

My office is that of a priest; I was in Andersonville from the 16th of June, 1864, till near the 1st of October. The previous portion of the year I was at Savannah, except for some time, when I went to attend Catholics in the Confederate Camps.

Q. State how you happened to go to Andersonville, whom you saw and met there, and all about your duties there.

A. Father Hamilton had visited the place in May, seen the condition of the prisoners, and written to the bishop at Savannah to send a priest there. He asked me to go and visit the prisoners. According to his request I went; I stayed there until nearly the 1st of October, from, I may say, the 16th of June, 1864; I stayed until the vast portion of the prisoners were removed to other points; I would have stayed longer if the prisoners had been retained; my duties were those of a Catholic priest—nothing more; I had no commission from the government; I went there voluntarily, without pay or remuneration, further than merely

---

[1] Record, p. 426.

to receive rations. . . . I never saw Captain Wirz inflicting any personal violence on any prisoner; neither did I hear of it during my stay there; I might have heard reports that he used profane language, but I never saw or heard of him using any personal violence there so as to produce death; it is the highest probability that such a thing could not have occurred without coming to my knowledge. . . .

Q. When you returned to the stockade after being outside did the prisoners gather around you in crowds?

A. They often collected around me in crowds to ask questions, but I never stopped to answer; I always passed on; if I had stopped with every crowd that collected, I could not have discharged my duties as a clergyman to those who were sick and dying; I was therefore necessitated not to answer them, because they would have taken up so much of my time; sometimes they would ask me in reference to reports they had heard; I would pass on and say nothing to them. There may have been some reports to the effect that persons were torn by dogs. I may have heard of persons who had been hunted down by dogs, but whether they were torn by the dogs or not I could not positively say. If I had heard of such a thing it is more than probable I would have remembered it. I cannot say positively. Captain Wirz afforded me every facility to visit the prisoners and afford them any relief that was in my power. He never put any obstacles in my way, whether physical or spiritual. . . . He never showed any objection to give me at any time a pass to go into the stockade or hospital. I applied to him in January, 1865, about taking some provisions to the prisoners. I borrowed $16,000 and went down to Andersonville. I spoke to Captain Wirz and he freely gave me permission to purchase flour for the prisoners. I gave the money to a gentleman in Americus of the name of Wynne, and he purchased the flour and sent it to Captain Wirz. I think that he wrote a letter to Father Hamilton stating that he did so. When I applied to him about it he mentioned to me that he would have to take the flour in his own charge and see that it was cooked and distributed -in bread to the prisoners. I could not say whether it was distributed.

I administered to five of the prisoners who were hanged. There was one of them who was not a Catholic. They were arrested as raiders in the stockade, together with several more who were not condemned. There was a court-martial of the prisoners held on these men and six of them were condemned. They were put in the stocks. I visited them the evening before they were hanged and gave them all the consolations of religion that it was possible for me to do. The next morning Captain Wirz came down to carry them to the stockade to be delivered to the prisoners there. I asked him to delay their execution for another day. He said to me that it was out of his power. They were prisoners who were plundering or robbing and using violence on other prisoners. That was what I considered as what was designated raiders. They were brought in by Captain Wirz with a company of soldiers. I cannot precisely give the words that he used, but I can give the substance of them. My feelings were engrossed by the condemned men and my attention was turned to giving them all the consolation of religion before they passed off into eternity. Captain Wirz said something like this: "Boys, I have taken these men out and now I return them to you, having taken good care of them. I now commit them to you. You can do with them as you see fit." Then turning around to the condemned men he said, "May the Lord have mercy on your souls." The men were then placed on a platform or gallows. They begged of me to make an appeal to their comrades—an appeal to spare them from execution. I made it to their fellow-prisoners. There was a hollow square formed with the six men and myself inside of it. One of them broke loose. He said he would not ascend the scaffold, and he broke through the line and ran into the swamp. A number of men followed and brought him back. They were his fellow-prisoners. After the men were hanged they were cut down and buried. They carried them outside the stockade and buried them in a separate part of the graveyard, I believe. The last time I visited the graveyard I saw a place where I understood these six men were buried, separate and distinct from the rest. . . .

Q. From your intimacy with Captain Wirz while you were there can you state to the court what was his general conduct, as to kindness or harshness, towards the prisoners?

A. I think I never saw him within the stockade except the time the men were hanged.

Q. I mean generally, inside, outside, and everywhere else.

A. He was always calm and kind to me.

Q. Was he to others, so far as you saw?

A. Yes, sir; I have seen him commit no violence. He may sometimes have spoken harshly to some of the prisoners.

Q. Did you ever hear there of the atrocities that have been developed in this court, or of his personal cruelties at all?

A. I have not all the testimony before me.

Q. Did you hear of any of them?

A. I cannot say. There have been some violences charged upon him here which I never heard of being committed by him. I never heard of his killing a man, or striking a man with a pistol, or kicking a man to death. During my time in the stockade I never heard of it. I never heard, either inside or outside, during my stay there, that he had taken the life of a man by violence; that he had shot a man or kicked him to death.

Q. Or that he injured a man so that the man was laid up?

A. No, sir, I never heard positively.

Q. If any such thing occurred must you not have heard of it?

A. It is highly probable I should have heard of it.

Cross-examined by the JUDGE ADVOCATE:

My duties there were very onerous. They occupied the whole of my time. My health was somewhat impaired from it. I entered the stockade about nine o'clock in the morning. That was the time the prisoners could take most rest. I remained there sometimes till four and sometimes till five o'clock. In the morning before going in I would say my prayers and read my "office." After I came out I continued saying my prayers. I was occupied with my own business and nobody's else.

Q. How then could you see or know everything that transpired there in reference to Captain Wirz?

A. I did not say that I did.

Q. You have said that if he had committed acts of violence you would have known it?

A. I said it was highly probable I should have known it through report?

Q. Why?

A. Because if such an act of violence were publicly done it would necessarily be rumored about.

Q. Your means of knowledge were only your association with the soldiers?

A. I say it was highly probable that if such a public act as murdering a man there were done, I would have heard of it.

Q. Did you ever hear anything said there about Captain Wirz being a cruel man?

A. I heard some prisoners saying he was a violent man.

Q. What else did you hear them say about him?

A. Nothing more than that he was a violent man; that he was harsh to some and cursed them.

Q. How long were you there?

A. From some time about the 16th of June till near the 1st of October, 1864. I remained there till the prisoners were nearly all removed.

Q. Are you aware that prisoners are not in the habit of complaining of officers who have it in their power to punish them?

A. The office of keeper of a prison is a very odious one, and his actions in the performance of his duty are usually looked upon as those of harshness.

Q. Did your duties require you to curtail your religious services there?

A. Yes, sir; I had to shorten what is called the sacramentalia, and also the ceremony of baptism, and also that of extreme unction. I had to give the sacrament without the prescribed prayers.

By the COURT:

Q. State to the court whether, on the occasion of your visits there, you saw Captain Wirz within the stockade.

A. I do not recollect having seen him, so that I can speak positively, within the stockade, except on this memorable occasion. He might have been in the stockade while I was in the hospital.

Q. State whether you ever saw him in the hospital at any time.

A. No, sir; I never saw him in the hospital.

Q. Are you prepared to say that those six men who were hanged were brought to that extremity because of their being criminals, or because of their being so situated in that prison? Was there not great moral depravity there?

A. Yes; there was great moral depravity in the prison before the raiders were hanged. I heard men complaining of it. There must have been great moral depravity in it when the prisoners themselves made application to have these men tried. I cannot say whether they had been guilty of any capital crime.

Q. Do you know whether their lives might not have been spared?

A. I cannot answer.

Q. The record of the prison shows that over 900 prisoners were sent away on the day these men were hanged. Do you know any reason why these men could not have been sent away instead of being hanged?

A. I do not know that any such number of men were sent away. That is a matter which I could not decide upon because it remained with the commandant there.

. . . The food I received there was ample for my sustenance, but as I mentioned in my examination the quality was the same as that which the prisoners and the guard had. I have seen the rations and food they got, and this man got our food where it was obtained for the prisoners. He did not bring it to me cooked; he cooked it himself, and sometimes he cooked one day what would do for two days. I have heard prisoners complain of not having enough to eat; they often complained of it. I did not say the amount of food I got was the same as that issued to the prisoners as to quantity; I said as to quality. I do not know anything as to what the prisoners got.

I never received any putrid meat. I do not know but that the prisoners might have got some. The man who went to the cook-house brought this portion of food for himself and me. As to the quantity, we got enough to eat; we were satisfied with it. It was not so much my stomach I was looking after as the souls of the prisoners. I think the food taken to that bake-house was exclusively for the prisoners. . . .

Q. Have you ever heard prisoners complain of short rations?
A. I have heard them complain as to the quantity of food.
Q. Did you ever know of any starving to death?
A. I have seen persons there who were sick and the quality of food was such that they could not use it. They had diarrhœa, and the consequence was they may have died of starvation. The prisoners looked, some of them, very emaciated —those who had scurvy—and diarrhœa followed from it. They were extremely emaciated, and there was a good deal of filth in the prison. I cannot tell you to how many dying persons I have administered spiritual aid. Perhaps it might have been fifteen hundred or two thousand. I think I would be safe in saying more than one thousand. I think it would approximate to the number.
Q. Are you prepared to say that out of that one thousand none died from starvation?
A. I say that I am not prepared to say that.
Q. I ask the further question whether it is not your belief that some of them died of starvation?
A. I have mentioned that where the quality of the food was such that it could not be used, and where sick men were not able to use it, they must necessarily die from starvation.

Reverend Father H. Clavereul was sent to Andersonville by his bishop and was in the stockade from July 15 to August 20, 1864, administering to the dying prisoners such spiritual comfort as he could. He has written from his diary some experiences and some facts which cannot fail to be of interest. The record discloses, I believe, but one instance where a minister other than those of the Roman Catholic faith, deigned to visit the prison, and on a few occasions to preach to the prisoners. These noble men of God who braved disease and death in their holy calling will never be forgotten. Father Clavereul's narrative was published in 1910 by the Connecticut Association of ex-Prisoners of War. It will be accepted as true, though not made under the sanction of an oath. Father Clavereul's observations should be read in connection with the testimony of his co-worker, Father Whelan, and for that reason it is here given. He and Father Hamilton probably saw no more than was witnessed by Father Whelan. But the latter, for reasons of his own, withheld from the court what his coadjutors felt constrained, in the interest of truth, to freely disclose.

FATHER CLAVEREUL'S DIARY.

It was in July, 1864, that I left Savannah for Andersonville, being sent there to help the venerable Father Whelan, who had been ministering to the prisoners since March. Their number kept increasing owing to the advance of the Federals towards Georgia, being estimated at the time at thirty thousand. Father Whelan was already an old man, over sixty years of age. He assisted the prisoners not only by his ministrations as a priest, but also by material help, through his influence among the Catholics of Georgia. As for me, unknown and without influence, I could only weep over the miseries I hourly witnessed.

The comforts I brought them were the consolations of religion, and these, I may truly say, I gave with all the zeal and energy God's grace enabled me to impart. The following I take from my diary, written at the stockade prison, July 15th, to August 20, 1864. I must remark that some of my statements may not be entirely correct. I had during the thirty-six days I spent in the stockade, no information from the outside world, no newspapers to read. The prisoners, on the other hand, who were my only associates, were in the same predicament.

The diary opens with the names of 390 prisoners to whom I administered the sacraments of penance and extreme unction.

The sick were for a time lying within the enclosure of the stockade in the open air. It was only later on that the worst cases were taken to a hospital, where they had tents. All those whom I administered I found in a dying condition and have little doubt that they died on the very spot where I found them.

The stockade covered some twenty acres. It stood away from all habitations, in the midst of which must have been the piny woods.

All the trees had been cut down, so there was no protection left against the sun or rain. A palisade or fence twelve feet high, made of the trunks of trees set upright in the ground, formed the enclosure. Outside the stockade, eight or ten feet above the ground, was a platform, where every hour of the day and of the night one could hear the pacing of the sentries, and at each recurring hour of the night the call, "Post No. 1, 8 o'clock and all's well," taken up by No. 2, and so the entire round, and sometimes the report of a musket, telling that a prisoner had been shot within the "dead line," which ran inside the enclosure and which the prisoners were warned not to pass under the penalty of being shot. The injunction, however, was not always heeded and not infrequently some unfortunate prisoner, whilst attempting to cross over, either through recklessness or whilst demented through sickness and suffering, was found lying dead within the fatal line. I shall not attempt a description of the sufferings which we witnessed; whatever may be said or written about it, will remain always below the stern reality. Spite of the awful mortality which for some weeks reached the appalling figure of 120 and upwards a day, the number of the prisoners kept increasing, as most of the soldiers captured in the battles fought in Tennessee or Northern Georgia at the time, were sent to Andersonville; numbers of them having been wounded on the battlefield.

The food consisted of unbolted corn-meal and cow peas, with now and then vegetables sent by the country people of the neighborhood.

As most of the prisoners suffered from the scurvy, sore gums and loose teeth, they could not eat the coarse food, and thus numbers of them died with their allowance of corn bread nearby.

Starvation, however, was not the only cause of the terrible mortality which in these eight weeks must have carried off some eight thousand victims. Exposure to the inclemency of the weather was another, the stockade being entirely bare, and besides with not a tent under which to find shelter. The clothes the prisoners had on when they arrived soon became mere rags,—thousands were met without a shred of clothing, stark naked, who were busy burrowing in the ground to find protection against the rain or the scorching rays of a midsummer sun.

To the scurvy was added diarrhœa. In the middle of the stockade between banks slightly inclining, was a branch of running water.

The ground, trodden by thousands, had soon become boggy, making it impossible for many among the sick to extricate themselves from the mire. The hospital had tents but no floor, only the bare ground. There it was that most of the cases not utterly hopeless were carried. The removal took place, generally, in the forenoon after the morning inspection made by the surgeons near the entrance of the stockade.

There, for hundreds of yards back, lay stretched on the ground thousands of sick, brought by comrades; the greater number, however, lying still, the inspection over, on the very spot where they had been placed a few hours before, who, in tones of indescribable agony, were crying for water to allay their thirst, intensified by continued exposure to a broiling sun. The unchecked advance of Sherman's army upon Atlanta, the fear of a raid upon the stockade, led to the transfer of a large part of the prisoners to points more remote from the seat of war. The transfer began in the first days of September, 1864, and before the end of the month ten thousand prisoners had been removed from Andersonville to Savannah and Charlestown.

On the 20th day of August, that is, thirty-six days after my arrival at Andersonville, I was taken sick with continued vomiting.

Father Whelan decided that I should leave, and so I took the train to Savannah, whilst the heroic old priest retraced his steps to the stockade. On the 24th day of September I had sufficiently recovered to be able to resume, among the Federal prisoners in Savannah, the work I had begun in Andersonville. . . .

Referring to Andersonville, I must mention something I loathe to relate. At the entrance to the hospital there stood a wooden shed 50 x 30 feet, called the "dead house," where the bodies of those who had died within the past twenty-four hours were laid on the bare ground.

Often, toward mid-day, on my way back to our shack, (a wooden hut 12 x 8 feet, a mile from the stockade, where we ate and slept) to partake of our scant dinner of corn bread, cow peas, and parched corn coffee, I walked the narrow aisle of the dismal room, where lay in four rows, 120 corpses, the few shreds of clothing found on them at the time they died thrown over their emaciated bodies. In front of this shed were the wagons drawn by four mules to carry the dead to be buried in shallow trenches, a mile away. Not a day passed that I did not meet the gruesome sight of these wagons, piled with bodies; heads, feet, or arms dangling from the vehicle transporting them to their final rest.

I take from my diary, written at the stockade at Andersonville, the names of the Federal prisoners to whom I administered the sacraments of penance and extreme unction, from July 15 to August 20, 1864. [The names are omitted.]

Towards the end of July, Bishop Verot, with his Vicar-general, Father Dufan, came to Andersonville. During their stay of two days they shared with us in our work, attending to the dying.

In the "Annals of the Propagation of the Faith," there is an article, written by the Bishop about his visit to the Federal prisoners, stating that he had sent there two priests, without, however, mentioning their names. The prisoners confined in the stockade at Andersonville and those who were later sent to Savannah, were all enlisted men.

The only officers I saw were General Winder, in command of the stockade prison, and the unfortunate Major Wirz. It was from the latter I got the written permission to visit daily the prisoners.

Not long ago a friend wrote me from Savannah that Wirz's admirers in Georgia intended to erect a monument in his honor. Now, I think, that the poor man is no more worthy of a monument now than he was at the time deserving of being hanged. His name should be forgotten.

He was boorish, profane, although never, to my knowledge, guilty of the acts of violence and cruelty that were afterward laid to his charge, being himself the sufferer of conditions he could in no way help.

Our life at Andersonville was uneventful. After a restless night spent in our hut on bunks, and a hurried breakfast, 5 o'clock found us every morning at the entrance of the stockade, where we remained the whole long day till sundown, with one hour of recess at mid-day. A stir was occasionally felt, when for instance, long files of Federal soldiers, captured on the battlefields which were then being fought in Tennessee and Northern Georgia, were marched into the prison.

All eyes for the moment, turned in that direction. Five hundred men, sometimes more, formed in ranks at the railroad station a half mile from the stockade, and from there were marched to the prison, guards with loaded muskets on both sides of the ranks, and, near the stockade a battery of six guns was stationed on a slight eminence.

The military bearing of the men, with uniforms still brilliant and spotless, was in strong contrast with the wretchedness of the place where they were soon to be confined. A sudden change was noticeable on their countenances the moment they stepped inside, as if they then realized the horrors of the situation. They were often followed by hundreds of their companions more unfortunate still, who, because of their wounds, had to be carried from the train, unable as they were to walk or even stand. An incident that might have proved decisive, with no other result, however, but a momentary excitement, occurred in the early part of the month of August. A thunderstorm, accompanied by torrential rain and violent wind amounting to a hurricane, had torn down a portion of the stockade enclosure, leaving a gap a few hundred feet wide. I saw thousands of the men pressing on towards the gap, near the dead-line. It was a moment of awful suspense.

The guards outside stood with loaded muskets and fixed bayonets, the battery in front ready to open at the command. All seemed to wait for somebody to lead on, but no one took the initiative, and hardly an hour passed before the stockade had resumed its deathlike appearance. Amidst sufferings that the pen cannot describe, I do not remember having heard either curses or imprecations on the part of the prisoners. They seemed to think themselves the victims of circumstances forced on the authorities at Washington, who, for fear the war might be prolonged, would not listen to an exchange, no less than the Confederates themselves. The crowded condition of the place in which they were confined, the food insufficient and loathsome, their clothing in rags, their exposure to the weather, the suffering which all this entailed, rarely elicited from them a word of anger.

They seemed to look upon their misfortunes as a visitation from the Almighty. To this may be ascribed the success of our spiritual ministrations, not only with the Catholics, but with men of the various denominations, and those who professed none.

They saw, besides, that the two priests, ever in their midst, were the only clergymen who had volunteered to them their services.

The religious work among the prisoners found expression in the throngs of individuals we met here and there, bowed down in the attitude of prayer or listening to a comrade who was reading from the Bible or addressing to them words of exhortation.

Up to the time I was called to Andersonville my experience with the army had been confined to the Confederates; first, in Fernandina, Florida, when, early in November, 1861, two thousand men, infantry and cavalry, garrisoned that place. I was there when the city surrendered to the United States naval forces, after a short and desultory resistance.

A more pathetic picture cannot well be conceived than is here drawn in simple, unexaggerated, and unimpassioned language.

Even at this distance of time one cannot read this story of human anguish without being stirred by feelings of deepest sympathy for the subjects of Father Clavereul's ministrations.

TESTIMONY OF SAMUEL HALL.

Samuel Hall a lawyer residing at Macon, testified for the defense as to the crops in 1864, and stated they were poor; that the soil immediately around Andersonville was poor; it was a timber region. He cited the Eighteenth Georgia Reports, (Morgan versus Davis[1]) to show that it was lawful in Georgia to track felons and slaves. He testified, among other things, as follows: "I do not know whether sufficient vegetables could not have been taken to Andersonville Prison to have prevented great mortality there. I say this, that there might have been, with proper exertions, vegetables carried there in sufficient quantities to have alleviated some of the suffering among the prisoners."[2]

TESTIMONY OF NAZARETH ALLEN.

[Recalled for the defense.] He testified:[3]

I was connected with the First Georgia Reserves. It was formed at Macon, Georgia, in May, 1864. When we got to Andersonville we had on our own clothing that we carried there with us. We carried such clothing as we had—we had no Confederate clothing.

Our rations were corn meal and bacon, and sometimes beef. The bad rations caused sickness, I think—diarrhœa; that was the complaint generally.

I don't think I said I suffered for want of rations while out on duty; we suffered from the rain a good deal. I never suffered because I had not sufficient to eat; I got a good deal of my provisions from home. Sometimes I had to live upon the rebel rations. There was a railroad all the way from where I lived to Andersonville, and I got boxes of provisions from home all the while I stayed there, pretty much. When on picket, I lived a good deal off the citizens. I fared very well while I was on picket. I never had any difficulty in getting what I wanted to eat. I do not think any of our soldiers ever died from starvation. I never saw any cases of wasting away from lack of sufficient to eat. It was our impression that some of our men died because they had bad food. I am not a physician, but our impression was that the diet would create diarrhœa; that was my impression. We never had any scurvy among our men.

I have seen our soldiers wearing the Federal uniform. I have seen them with overcoats and boots and pants. I believe these articles of clothing came from the bodies of the dying and the dead. . . .

TESTIMONY OF CAPTAIN JAS. W. ARMSTRONG, C. S. A.[4]

I reside in Macon, Georgia. The two last years I have been a commissary officer in the service of the Confederate government with the rank of captain; I was at Andersonville. My duties there were to receive stores and issue them to prisoners and troops, and to do anything else that came into my department. I went there on the 31st of March, 1864, and remained there until the first day

[1] Record, p. 494.
[2] This case will form the subject of some remarks in a subsequent chapter.
[3] Record, p. 466 et seq.
[4] Record, p. 659 et seq.

of August, when I left, although I was responsible, I suppose, until the 21st of August. I was there again from the 10th of December until the collapse of the Confederacy. When I first went there until August 1st, the issue of rations to the prisoners, generally speaking, was bacon, corn-meal, peas, salt. The ration of bacon was one-third of a pound; of beef, one pound; of syrup, six gallons to the 100 rations; of meal, one and one-fourth pound to the ration; of vinegar, when issued, one gallon to 100 rations; salt, three pounds to 100 rations; soap, two pounds to 100 rations. The ration of the Confederate soldier was the same. The ration was altered, I think, on the 9th of August. The order was made then to issue of beef one-half pound, of peas one-half pound, of meal one-half pound, or rice in lieu of peas, salt, soap and other things. Generally, while I was there, there was not any difference--not at first.

I can recollect several boards of survey. They always condemned rations there. Captain Wirz had nothing to do with commissary supplies there at all. He had to receive them after the 14th of July, I think. Once he made a remonstrance in relation to them that I remember. I received all my orders from my superior officer in the commissary department. I issued those rations until July 14th to Captain R. B. Winder, quartermaster; after that time to Captain Wirz. The requisition from Captain Wirz to me was the ordinary provision return, known as Form 13. Captain Wirz would generally furnish me with the number of men only. Drawing every day, of course, there would be that

SOME RELICS GATHERED BY MISS CLARA BARTON AT THE PRISON GROUNDS.

number of rations; and the requisition was filled out by myself or clerks. I would till it out by my orders, and by knowing what I had on hand to issue. There was a government regulation to fill out the quantity as I had it. I was very much troubled with reference to transportation and getting the ration out; at first to a great extent. In fact it took nearly all day, and very often quite all day, to get it out--I mean to haul it away from the commissary building. The requisitions were generally made by Captain Wirz between 11 and 12 o'clock in the morning. There was not a great deal of difficulty in regard to getting the supplies from the sources from which I drew them. I was troubled very much for storage room, and could not accumulate a stock on hand. At first I occupied a room some 70 feet by 30, until some time in July; after that I occupied a house, I suppose 130 feet by 30. We would generally have on hand no more supplies than two or three days' rations; we were issuing to about 36,000 or 37,000 men. It was my endeavor to always have rations on hand for that number; I generally succeeded. The meat was generally very good when I received it. I never had any trouble on the subject of obtaining it; if I could not obtain meat I could obtain syrup in lieu of it; I could not always obtain fresh meat when I wanted it. There was not any corral there containing a large number of horses and mules connected with the department, and I do not know what horses and mules the quartermaster had; if any corral had been there I think I would have known it.

. . . I had nothing to do with the delivery of rations to the prisoners. Up to the 14th of July all the rations issued were delivered to R. B. Winder, or to his sergeants for him, and they were left subject to his control; after that time I issued them to Captain Wirz's sergeant, under his direction, of course; the sergeant was appointed by him. Captain Wirz had charge of the rations from that time, and beyond that I had no responsibility whatever. I do not pretend to know whether the rations issued by me were actually delivered to the prisoners. I was not troubled so much about procuring rations as I was from obtaining transportation and wanting storage room. I never was at any time so short that I could not issue to the prisoners. In three or four instances I issued rice instead of corn meal; but I always made up the rations. I never found it necessary to diminish the rations, except by substituting one thing for another. I always had a plenty to issue, and the only difficulty I had was in respect to storage and transportation. It was a general complaint, the transportation being short, but even then I was not obliged to withhold the rations from the prisoners; I could always substitute something in lieu of it. . . .

I issued rations to the prisoners day by day until March, 1865; they were issued in the morning for that day. It was not in the same way I issued rations to the troops; they were issued for from one to seven days. I did not issue to prisoners in the same way because we had not rations enough to issue such a quantity at the time, nor had we a place to store them; I do not think I could have issued two days' rations. I generally got the requisition between 11 and 12 o'clock in the morning. It very often took them until sundown to get all the rations out; some of the rations might run into the next day. That was changed after a while, and we issued one day for the next day; but at first they drew day by day.

Q. I want to know if it would not have been more humane to issue rations a day in advance.

A. During the latter portion of the time they were issued one day for the next. I cannot say how long before the system was changed—probably a month or more.[1]

TESTIMONY OF JOHN F. HEATH.

[Recalled for the defense.[2]]

I was at Andersonville, May, 1864, as first lieutenant company E, Third Regiment Georgia Reserves. Wagons and horses were very scarce at Andersonville.

---

[1] It is impossible to reconcile this testimony with the overwhelming proofs that no such rations as the witness describes reached the prisoners.

[2] Record, p. 448.

There were four regiments there, I think, when we got there, and they had either four or five wagons for the use of those four regiments. I saw no corral there, except a small horse lot. A few mules and horses were in this horse lot. All the horses that I ever saw were used daily; there might have been some officers' horses in the lot.

We received in my regiment a pound and a quarter of meal, very coarse at that generally. Once in a while a third of a pound of bacon. At other times a pound of beef, and that very poor, and when we did not get bacon or beef, we got a little sorghum, a kind of molasses made out of Chinese cane. I have been at the commissary often on drawing days, and have seen them drawing rations for the stockade out of the same lot that I drew from for my regiment, but to the quantity I could not say. I had to send home for provisions to live on and to buy what I could through the country.

I suppose there were some of my comrades who did not send home for provisions—who lived on the rations they got, though, in fact, most of them got provisions from home, sent to them from time to time. I could not tell how long I could have lived on the rations without having other provisions; I generally got what I could. I did not feel disposed to live on the rations. I do not pretend to say that I would have starved to death on them, but it was a very small ration.

TESTIMONY OF DR. BATES.

[Recalled for the defense.[1]]

... I may say that we had no medicines. We were not permitted to prescribe regularly, only by numbers, and they were decoctions of indigenous herbs and bark. They were numbered. For a scorbuta case we would order Specific No. 14 or 24, as the case might be. I do not know of sick or wounded prisoners being brought to the hospital from other places than the stockade. I have seen some few prisoners arrive at Andersonville who were sick or wounded. Some of the men had been reduced, some ragged, some sick, and in fact some dead or dying, when they came there. I did not see many, however, in that condition, as I was not much about the depot or headquarters.

I saw some few instances of neglect on the part of the nurses. I stated before, when I was on the stand, that in making out my morning reports I would make my calculation for the amount of commissary supplies; that there was a sufficiency. Nevertheless, I negatived that by sayting that I was not sure they got it On one occasion I detected fourteen loaves of bread that were being kept from the prisoners. It was what was known as Father Whelan's bread, which he had placed under my direction. . . .

Q. You speak of the country from Andersonville to Macon as being poor; do you mean the whole of that route?

A. I speak directly of the poverty-stricken locality of Andersonville.

Q. Did you not speak of the whole route as far as Macon?

A. If I was so understood I did not mean it.

Q. Would not that be considered a very rich Country?

A. I do not know very much about that; I never took any particular notice. I have understood that southwestern Georgia was considered the garden-spot of

[1] Record, p. 662 et seq.

the South, but I am not well acquainted with it except by stage and railroad travel, to a limited extent. I cannot give an intelligent opinion on that point.

The prime cause of the poisonous atmosphere in the hospital was the crowded condition of the patients, and their filthy condition in consequence, and the vermin, offal and filthiness generally which would accumulate where men are confined, not able to help or do for themselves, without the means at hand for cleanliness. The boxes used by the men all through the hospital were not very well attended to unless there was an officer of the day there to see to it. Everything was calculated to produce a disease-creating agency. I mean to say that this poisonous atmosphere was produced by the condition of the prison and the hospital, in regard to the numbers and the treatment which the prisoners received there; I think also the deficiency of medicines—they had no medicines. . . .

TESTIMONY OF DR. F. G. CASTLEN.

[Recalled for the defense:[1]]

I was in 1864 surgeon of the 3d Georgia Reserves, and was at Andersonville from May till the last of September.

The rations which we had for our own men were inferior, very inferior. Sometimes we got bacon, then again a coarse kind of beef, but in small quantities. The sick sent home for rations; they sometimes would write to their friends. In regard to the regular rations there was a good deal of complaint in the regiment. I heard a good deal of complaint that the rations were not sufficient. The men of my regiment, and particularly the sick, suffered a great deal from want of rations, and the poor quality of the rations. I could get no diet there suitable for a sick person. There was a good deal of sickness during the month of June in my regiment. I speak for my own regiment alone. The meat was of that inferior quality that it was an unhealthy diet the way they had to cook it. They had no means of cooking it except by boiling it. The meat would produce diarrhœa. I had a great deal of diarrhœa in my regiment. Diarrhœa was one of the principal diseases with which the men of my regiment suffered. I had no scurvy in my regiment.

The land about Andersonville is of a very inferior quality—a pine country—sandy. I would not think it suitable land for cotton. It would take five or six acres to raise a bale of cotton. I would hardly cultivate the land for that crop. My regiment never did, to my knowledge, corrupt the stream above the stockade—the stream running into the stockade; I never heard of their doing it.

We were not very much crowded in our regiment, not crowded enough to produce scurvy. The men had an opportunity of getting things from home to prevent it. There was no difficulty in that respect at all, and they got things from home. In speaking of the deficiency of food, I was speaking of the rations issued by the government. In my answer with regard to men sending home for things, I did not mean to confine it to the sick; any man in the regiment could send home and get things. It was a common thing for them to receive boxes.

Q. Were there any men in your regiment who subsisted upon the Confederate rations there?

[1] Record, p. 451.

A. I don't know whether they received them wholly or not from the commissary department. It would be impossible for me to find out that, unless I went through the regiment inquiring. I know of know cases of starvation among the Confederate soldiers, nor any cases of emaciation or wasting away. . . .

I never heard of any of our soldiers freezing to death. None of them went hungry for want of fuel to cook their rations. We could get plenty of fuel from the woods near by—as much as we wanted.[1]

When I spoke about the quality of the land at Andersonville, I meant the land immediately around that place. I never was anywhere in that country but around there. I do not speak of any other place than just around Andersonville. . . .

TESTIMONY OF DR. E. A. FLEWELLEN.

[Recalled for the defense:[2]]

I can arrive at the time during the summer of 1864 I was first at Andersonville more definitely by stating that I was there a few days before General Hood was assigned to duty in place of General Johnston—in the month of July or August—one of those two months I am confident. I am not distinct in my recollection about the number of men I found there as Federal prisoners, but there were over thirty thousand, I believe.

On my first visit I went there under a special order of the medical director of hospitals, for the purpose of inspecting the hospitals. I called Surgeon White's attention to the hospital accommodations, and the reply was that he was making efforts to fit them up—that he had not been able to get sufficient tools. I asked him if he had made efforts. He said that he had made timely, and I think he said frequent, requisitions on the quartermasters' department for tools, but that he could not get them, and he remarked further that there were at least twenty-five hundred mechanics in the stockade, who would be glad to take a parole for the purpose of working on the hospital, but that he had not been able to get tools. He went so far as to state that he had lumber there sufficient to put up one or two hospitals, (similar to the one that had just been roughly thrown up for the troops on duty,) but that he had not been able to get the tools to put them up with. The Federal hospital was a rough enclosure of plank fences; it was made up of a heterogeneous variety of tents, some comparatively new, and some almost totally worn out; I think I may safely say that I saw every style of tent in there that I have ever seen anywhere. There was little or no bedding. The bunks, if they could be called by that name, were improvised by driving forked stakes in the ground and putting railings across. I am now speaking of the Federal hospital. I saw little or no bedding—occasionally a bed-sack, very dirty. . . .

There was a good deal of difference, think, between Confederate hospitals and hospitals for Union prisoners. I never visited them officially except at Andersonville, and I did not consider that a hospital at all in comparison with what a hospital should be. I found on looking over the hospital stores that had been issued and that had accumulated in the office of the surgeon-in-chief, a large

---

[1] Will the defenders of Wirz explain why the prisoners were deprived of fuel?
[2] Record, p. 471.

lot of bed-sacks, sheets and other things necessary for the hospital. I thought it very remarkable that they were not furnished, and, of course, I called on Dr. White for an explanation. His reply was that in the first place he had not been able to get the straw to fill the sacks; that in the second place he had not been able to get bunks to put them in; and, as an additional reason, that he did not want to put them into those nasty tents and on the filthy ground—the hospital being incomplete, the bunks being fixed up with sticks, and some without sticks. He said that the sacks would soon be ruined; that they would be so filthy that they would never be fit to use when he should have succeeded in completing the hospital. I testified in my examination-in-chief as to the character of the ground; it is pine soil, black. There were no floors to the tents, simply earth floors, and if bed-sacks were placed on the ground anybody could see how quickly they would be soiled. If they were put on the bunks I have spoken of, the men climbing up and down would soil them very badly. I have no knowledge as to the chance of getting straw to fill them with, except what Dr. White stated. My recollection is not distinct as to whether I discovered any of them filled with pine straw. The Confederate hospitals were pretty short in regard to hospital clothing and necessaries of every kind; they hardly ever got what they desired, I may say there was very great suffering in consequence of that deficiency in the hospital department generally.

I called Dr. White's attention to the fact that the corn meal out of which I saw bread baked was not sifted; his reply was that he had made requisition but the sifters could not be had. When the army was at Tullahoma diarrhœa prevailed there to a very large extent; I reported the fact to General Bragg, and I attributed it very largely to the fact of the meal being used unsifted; I arrived at that conclusion from the evidences I saw of the matter passing through without digestion; I know there was great complaint about the difficulty of getting sifters in hospitals and in the army too.

Dr. Roy was recalled more particularly to testify as to matters pertaining to charge 2. His testimony will be noticed in that connection.

TESTIMONY OF REV. E. B. DUNCAN.

Rev. E. B. Duncan, a Methodist minister, visited Andersonville and ministered to the prisoners in the stockade. His testimony related to the personal conduct of Captain Wirz as bearing on charge 2. He testified in relation to the quality of the water:

I got water in the stockade. I drank some good water there; as good as I found in upper Georgia. I was very thirsty after preaching, and I mentioned that I would like to get some water; but calling to mind that the water might not be good, I thought I would not drink until I got out. Some of the men said they would get me some water, and they went out and got a bucket full of very good water, at which I was very much astonished. It was an exceedingly hot day, and I was very thirsty, and I thought it was the best water I had met; so much better than I might have expected.[1]

---

[1] Record, p. 610.

TESTIMONY OF COLONEL FANNIN.

Colonel James H. Fannin was recalled for the defense. He testified to the difficulty of obtaining tools, axes, etc.; also as to the condition of the water and the condition of the prisoners in the stockade. He testified:

I know the prison was very much crowded. It was very difficult sometimes for prisoners in large lots to march in. They would congregate around the gate. I was there one day when about twelve hundred arrived. Captain Wirz remarked that he was very sorry they sent so many men there, as they were crowding the prison so much. That was before the enlargement of the prison was completed. They were making arrangements then to enlarge it. I should think he was frequently annoyed and troubled in that way, because the prison was very much crowded—very much indeed. Large lots of prisoners came in day after day. I should think they could not be very well cared for, there were so many of them together on that small piece of ground. . . .

One of the reasons why my regiment was removed from its first encampment was because of the offensive stench arising from the prison. At that time my camp was located west of the south gate of the stockade, the one nearest Captain Wirz's headquarters. The drainage of the camp passed into the stream that led into the stockade. When we were located there the water flowing on that side of the hill would run down towards the branch.

TESTIMONY OF MAJOR FRENCH.

Major S. B. French was called for the defense; he was on duty in the commissary department at Richmond. He testified more particularly to the difficulty his department had in the winters of 1863-4 in supplying General Lee's army, which made it necessary to reduce the army ration somewhat. The situation led to the removal of the prisoners then at Richmond; and, in reply to a question whether a discussion did not arise as to the matter, he testified:[1]

Q. You say that the railroads were in such a condition as to prevent supplies of flour and other articles from being sent to Richmond?

A. Supplies of corn I should say; we did not draw flour from any southern state, except in very small quantities, because it was not raised there as a general thing. The want of facilities to transport corn was what made the corn scarce; I think entirely so. It was in the winter of 1863-64 that the commissary general thought that the prisoners had better be sent south. I think there was a very large number of prisoners in Richmond at that time; I think all of them, or very nearly all, were sent away; I do not know how many were sent away; I know that some were sent away merely by the general statement; I never saw any of them *in transitu*. I do not know whether the prisons at Richmond were emptied at any one time; I do not know that they were not; my impression is that very nearly all of the prisoners were sent away some time during the spring

---

[1] Record, p. 654.

of 1864; I am not positive about the time, I think it was during a portion of the time Grant's army was in front of Richmond. I never in the line of duty visited the southern states. I do not of my own personal knowledge know anything in regard to the supply of vegetables in the southern states, the growth of vegetables in the country surrounding Andersonville, or the growth of any particular articles of food or subsistence. The scarcity of supplies was considered general with us. . . .

If there was any reduction in quality or quantity of the rations issued to the prisoners at Andersonville, it would, as I understood, have been in violation of existing order. If so, I should think the officer in charge of the prison would be responsible if he knew the facts. . . .

TESTIMONY OF W. D. HAMMACK.

W. D. Hammack was a private in the 55th Georgia. He went to Andersonville, as he testified, February 14th and left on April 7th, 1865; he was there over a year and was detailed on July 9, 1864, and reported to Captain Wirz. He testified:[1]

I received orders to report to Captain Wirz for duty on the evening of the 9th of July. He assigned me to call the roll inside the stockade. I continued on that duty until the prisoners left to go to Millen. My instructions were to call the roll and have every man present at the roll-call. This was in the first organization of the camp. There were ninety men in a mess, and three nineties constituted a division. Each ninety had a sergeant, a Union soldier. It was his duty to have all his men at roll-call by the time that I got in to attend to the roll-call. . . . They reorganized the camp twice, I think, before they moved the prisoners to Millen, and then the order was for the men to stand in the ranks at the place where they answered the roll-call until the whole stockade was called over. That was reorganizing. That occurred twice, I think, from the time I went there until they were sent to Millen. I think no more. Our orders were that if their number was not correct, and the sergeant could not account for them, we were to just go along and leave them standing there until they got correct. I did not keep them standing ever after they were reported correct by their sergeant. I don't know what other sergeants did. I know I did not. I called the rolls of six divisions, and there were three nineties in each division—eighteen nineties altogether.

Q. Did you ever, of your own knowledge, know squads to be deprived of their rations when they reported their number as not correct?

A. Well, that was the order. I don't know that I ever knew of any squad that lost any rations on account of any men that were not present. The order was that if they could not account for the men they would lose their rations. . . .

I always supposed that the sergeants inside the stockade attended to finding the sick and the dead, and took them out if they were not able to go themselves to sick-call, though I have seen sergeants that would not take their sick to sick-call.

[1] Record, p. 498 et seq.

TESTIMONY FOR DEFENSE. 211

Q. When they carried their sick down what was the rule or practice in regard to those who were most dangerously sick?

A. There was no rule about it; they all went together; those that were sickest went along like the balance. It was the duty of the sergeants of the nineties to take those who were not accepted by the doctor back into the stockade. They did get medicine for a while; they would be prescribed for; they would be taken to sick-call in the morning and they would get medicines in the evening. . . .

Some clothes came there by the sanitary commisison, marked as such, but I do not recollect what time they came. I did not wear any of them; Captain Wirz never gave me anything in his life, except it might be a pass. I never obtained any clothing in that way; I don't know any of the Confederate soldiers that did. I have seen Confederate soldiers wear them, but they never procured them from Captain Wirz; I think all the paroled prisoners drew them. I was there when they went in to get their suits of clothes. I saw all of Duncan's squad go in for that purpose. I cannot swear that they all got them, but I know they were sent there for that purpose. I have seen men with them on; and I know that they sold them. There was a Confederate soldier named Nolan who bought a pair of those pants.

Q. Do you know in what condition the clothing of those paroled men who received the sanitary goods was? Were they destitute at the time?

A. They were not; there were men inside the stockade who needed them more than the paroled men.

TESTIMONY OF COLONEL A. W. PERSONS.

Col. Persons was recalled. He went to Andersonville in February and left in June.[1]

I think Captain Wirz reached Andersonville some time in the latter part of February, or in March. I think he took command immediately. He was interrupted, however, by the arrival of Major Griswold, who had an order to take command of the prison. That order collided with the one that Wirz had. The matter was put in abeyance. I think Captain Wirz retired for some ten or fifteen days till the difficulty was cleared up. Subsequently, Major Griswold was ordered away and Captain Wirz took command of the prison. Captain Wirz framed his local orders himself. All the general orders affecting the prison came from Richmond, from General Winder, through me.

Q. Do you know to whom his official communications were addressed and where they went?

A. That depended entirely upon the character of the communications. Some were sent to Richmond directly through the regular channel. I had an intermediate position and they went through me to Richmond to General Winder.

The reason for removing the hospital outside was that the stockade was pretty densely crowded, and there was a good deal of sickness in it. The hospital necessarily occupied a good deal of room; they had tents and flies. Captain Wirz came to me and urged me to take the hospital out. I told him I had no authority

---
[1] Record, p. 455 et seq.

to do anything of that sort. I addressed a communication, however, to General Winder, asking for permission to remove the hospital outside. My impression is, though I will not state positively, that it was declined by General Winder. Captain Wirz remonstrated, and I told him to remove the hospital—that I would take the responsibility.

I know that Captain Wirz objected to the prison being overcrowded as it was. We sent an objection to the authorities at Richmond, to General Winder, and urged him to hold up and not to ship any more there; but he paid no attention to it; they continued to come until we got about thirty-five or forty thousand. We commenced our protests at a time when we had got between ten and fifteen thousand.

Captain Wirz had no right to give any orders to the commissary; he and the commissary would confer together in making their estimates. I think the rule relative to issuing rations was issued from Richmond; I am not positive about it, but I think it was fixed by the commissary-general, and the sub-commissaries throughout the territory were all bound by it. I sent an officer to Columbus to try and get material for making sifters for bolting meal, and my officer was informed that a thing of that kind could not be had in the Confederacy. He did not get anything of the sort.

It was the duty of the quartermaster, Captain Winder, to furnish shelter, fuel, and such things for the prisoners. The quartermaster also had charge of the cooking of rations, the burying of the dead, and everything of that kind. The quartermaster at Andersonville did not have half the transportation he ought to have had. I have no idea of the number of wagons I saw there. I just know that what wagons he had there were kept going all the time, and then could not more than half satisfy the wants of the post. I have seen more than four or five wagons there. He got in some mules and wagons a short time before I left. For the first month he did not have more than four or five wagons, and they belonged to the citizens there. The cook-house was under the quartermaster's control. I do not know that I ever had any formal reports made to me for the want of shelter necessary for the prisoners. We frequently discussed the matter. I regretted that the place was so much embarrassed as not to be able to furnish things that were necessary for the health of the prisoners. Captain Wirz expressed great displeasure at the meagreness of the accommodations furnished and the inefficiency of the quartermaster's department; he frequently so expressed himself to me. Captain Wirz's complaints covered everything in respect to fuel—about not having teams to draw wood.

Q. When you were examined several days ago, you said that you recollected some fifty car-loads of lumber, for the purpose of building shelter inside the stockade, and that at the time of your relief that lumber disappeared mysteriously, and none of it went in for shelters?

A. That was my testimony.

Q. Do you still adhere to it?

A. I still adhere to it.

I cannot say that Captain Wirz did all that it was in his power to do to alleviate the sufferings of the prisoners. I know he labored indefatigably, but whether he accomplished everything he might have accomplished, of course I cannot say. All I know is that the prison was not half cared for; I know that very well. I cannot say who was responsible for its care. I think the responsibility was in sending so many prisoners where they could not be properly cared for; there is where I think it lies. Those labors were performed by Captain Wirz in the direction of his line of duty, and not expressly to alleviate the sufferings of the prisoners. I only remember that he labored a long time over that ditch inside the prison, trying to clear it out and plank it up, and reclaim the marsh and bog on either side of it, which he did not succeed in doing; he never succeeded fully in doing it.

TESTIMONY OF MAJOR GEORGE L. PROCTOR. C. S. A.[1]

I reside in Barron County, Kentucky. During the last two years I have been a major and commissary of subsistence; I was at Andersonville a portion of the time. I was on duty at Andersonville from, I think, about the 21st of August till the last of November, 1864.

I received my orders relative to the issue of commissary stores from the district commissary and from the commandant of the post; I was under his order. General Winder was commander of the post while I was at Andersonville. Captain Wirz had no command or authority over me in any way; he was not in command of the prison when I first went on duty there; Lieutenant Davis was in command. All I know about Captain Wirz's absence or sickness is that he was absent during August, perhaps until the latter part of August. Lieutenant Davis made the requisitions for the commissary during that time.

Q. Did Lieutenant Davis issue the requisitions in the same capacity and for the same purposes that Captain Wirz did after he came back?

A. I presume so; Lieutenant Davis made the requisition for the number of prisoners—the daily requisitions which were approved by the commandant of the post. I would not have issued the rations on any requisition which was not approved by the commandant; that was not the custom. The requisition for the hospital came from the surgeon in charge; Captain Wirz had nothing to do with them; they were approved likewise by the commandant of the post.

Miss Mary Rawson, who resided "on the plains of Dura," was called for the defense. Her testimony was to the effect that she visited the prison in January, 1865, and occasionally afterwards, her object being to give aid to Peter Kean of the 16th Iowa Regiment. Her testimony was to the effect that Captain Wirz treated her kindly and allowed her to send provisions to Private Kean.[2]

TESTIMONY OF COLONEL RUFFIN.

Lieutenant-Colonel F. G. Ruffin, C. S. A., was in the subsistence department of the Confederacy. It will be observed that the prisoners were removed from Richmond to get them "to the seat of plenty." He testified:

---

[1] Record, p. 668 et seq.
[2] Record, p. 607. This was probably one of those occasional incidents where the affections of the heart triumphed over sectional prejudices.

One of the objects of sending prisoners to Georgia was to get them to what we considered a good region of the country because we were drawing supplies from Georgia to feed General Lee. I reside near the city of Richmond, Virginia; I was, by promotion in the latter part of the war, lieutenant-colonel in the subsistence department of the Confederate States armies. All my duties from the commencement of the war until I resigned, a month or two before its close, were in that department and nowhere else.

Q. State to the court what you know in reference to the lack or deficiency of commissary supplies in that department.

A. I hardly know how to commence answering that; I can only say that from the beginning there was more or less scarcity; that that scarcity was apprehended from the beginning by the commissary department; that steps were being taken all the time, with more and more earnestness and energy and anxiety, as the war progressed, to obtain supplies, especially of meat, which in that section of the country had always been insufficient for the support of the inhabitants of that country; that that scarcity which did exist to a certain degree at the beginning of the war, and to a greater extent than it had existed before—because our wholesale men, apprehending the storm that was impending, had forborne to import their usual supplies of meat through that section—that that scarcity commencing in that way increased in all sections to absolute privation; I do not mean to say the point of starvation, but to the point of privation.

It was the case more or less with reference to all supplies, some of which we had not in sufficient quantities even for hospital purposes. Some of the articles of daily domestic consumption, and of regular army and hospital supplies, were not to be had at all at sometimes, and at all times in diminished quantities. Coffee, for instance, was the most important of that class of articles.

Q. Was that privation confined to any class, or did it affect rich and poor alike?

A. They were all alike so far as I know. Of course those who were well off did better than those who were very poor, as is always the case under such circumstances, but the privation applied to all classes. I was in another branch of the service, and can only speak of general causes. One of the causes, particularly towards the last of the war, as affecting us in Georgia, from which we drew a quantity of our supplies, was the raids upon our railroads.

When the army wintered from Gordonsville down along the line of the Central railroad, the rations were reduced to a quarter pound of meat per day. The same reduction was ordered everywhere else. General Bragg had drawn on the reserves which we had accumulated at Atlanta for General Lee's army, he being unable to get a supply from Tennessee, and that compelled the order for reduction. The generals all remonstrated, and said they could not keep their armies together on that. At last General Lee remonstrated; his army subsisted for some time, I do not recollect how long, on that quarter pound of meat per day, which was afterwards increased to one-third of a pound; and all his battles were fought upon one-third of a pound of meat per day. In both years from the time he wintered on the Rapidan—in 1863-'64, and then in 1864-'65. The bread ration was reduced at the same time. Our original ration had been 18 ounces of flour per day, I forget what it was in corn meal; it was presumed to be an equivalent. The bread ration, as I say, was also reduced, and when General Lee wintered from Gordonsville on the line of the Central Railroad, we were compelled to give the troops coffee in order to eke out the rations. We obtained the coffee by running the blockade at great expense and risk. The supply of coffee was very scarce. The quantity that the men got was less than they were entitled to. I only know the fact that it was much reduced, and that only men in the field had it; officers at posts, and men on post duty, or at posts, did not have it.

Q. State the whole ration. You have stated bread and meat; anything else?

A. Nothing further than sugar and coffee. Occasionally the men got issues of vegetables, principally rice and peas. What was the precise apportionment of the ration I forget. As to other items of the rations, their supply was all in reduced quantities. I cannot answer arithmetically what proportion of the whole ration our men had. I should judge-but it is a mere matter of opinion; I do not say it is a fact that I can establish; I could not without referring to documents not in my possession- but I should say the ration was less than two-thirds of the original, the meat alone being reduced to one-third of a pound. I say that cautiously; but I am very certain that I am within bounds when I say it was less than two-thirds the full ration.

The prisoners who were well, received precisely the same rations as their guards did; they got what the soldiers who were considered as being at post, and on light duty, were allowed, that is, our own soldiers. I know that was the order. My knowledge extended more or less into all other departments. I was in

BURYING THE DEAD IN TRENCHES.

Richmond, very near to the various departments of the government, for four years, and was compelled to know a good deal about what was going on in those offices. I know there was a deficiency in both those two great branches of the quartermasters' department, to wit, railroad transportation and wagon transportation, all the way through.

Q. How was it in 1864, and up to the point in 1865 when the war was closed?

A. It was much worse than it had been. We regarded the railroad system of the South at that time as completely broken down.

We found it impossible to get supplies from the Southwest in adequate quantities. My observation was not confined principally to Virginia and General Lee's army. The armies in the Southwest fared better than General Lee's army, because they were in Georgia, where there was more abundance. They could not draw from the East. After Sheridan's raid up the valley, which destroyed an immense quantity of supplies there, and threw a large portion of that community, which had before been feeding us, into the market competing against us for supplies, our supplies had to be drawn from southwestern Georgia; and then, because of the difficulties of transportation, we suffered. I know only so much of the details in the working of my department as a staff officer would be expected to know, located at headquarters.[1]

Q. With reference to the subsisting of particular brigades or divisions, or small armies, you did not pretend to know?

A. With reference to a distinct organization as an army, I had knowledge; but whether Major C. fed his brigade properly or not, was a question with which I had nothing to do. If I saw that an army was supplied with what I could get for it, my duties were discharged. The details after that I knew nothing about except incidentally; but it was not my business.

Q. For instance, you would not pretend to know how the prison at Andersonville was managed?

A. On the contrary, I would not only not pretend to know, but I insist on it that I do not know. I could not know. I would have been acting without the line of my duty if I did know it, except accidentally; and, accidentally, I do not know anything about it.

Captain C. M. Selph, was recalled for the defense. His testimony related to the efforts made to distribute sanitary goods sent south and the difficulties attending it. He testified that he knew nothing of the matter as to Andersonville.[2]

TESTIMONY OF CAPTAIN WRIGHT.

Captain J. H. Wright, recalled for the defense. He was a quartermaster of the 55th Georgia Regiment; stationed at Andersonville, and was there from February, 1864, until February, 1865.[3]

My regiment received the same rations as other troops there; the rations were inferior. We had nothing but coarse corn meal, which was frequently musty. We got one-third of a pound of bacon, and sometimes this poor Florida beef, which was always inferior or mostly so. I suppose it was the same as the Federal prisoners received. It came from the commissary, and they all drew from the same place. I never saw any difference made. It would be impossible for me to tell about the number of prisoners before the quartermaster succeeded in getting lumber or bricks for ovens, or anything for the accommodation of the prisoners. I know that prisoners were coming in constantly, and it was some time in April or May I think before arrangements were completed. There were not so many as 20,000 or 30,000. There might have been some ten or twelve thousand or perhaps fifteen thousand. I cannot give anything like a correct idea about that. They never did have a sufficient quantity of these conveniences.

---

[1] The short rations applied more especially to General Lee's forces. Supplies were more abundant in the Western armies.
[2] Record, p. 613.
[3] Record, p. 479 et seq.

The ovens never were capacitated for cooking enough for the prisoners. I have been in the stockade frequently, and the prisoners never did have their rations all cooked. I do not know if it was because bricks could not be supplied. I know they did not have it.[1]

Q. What were your efforts to get supplies for that post—lumber, nails, and other supplies?

A. I could not get any lumber at all. I do not think I ever succeeded in getting but about two thousand feet of lumber. I made every effort possible. I tried every man that had a mill near there. I went to Captain R. B. Winder every week, and made efforts to get lumber from him and General Winder.

I know that there were several inspectors sent to Andersonville. General Cobb, General Wright, and one or two others, whose names I do not remember, and Colonel Chandler came there. I never saw any improvement after their inspections.[2]

My regiment built barracks for themselves. They had no trouble in getting the wood or lumber they wanted for that purpose. The barracks did not have floors—that is, they had dirt floors. They built the barracks of split pine logs. I did not hear a great deal of complaint of the want of facilities for building those barracks. I was not able to get any lumber, but Captain Winder, when he left, turned over to me about 125,000 feet of lumber. I built all the prison hospital that is there now with it. I do not know how long it had been on hand. It came in possibly in the summer months. It was piled up and no use was made of it; and at the same time the prisoners were suffering for want of shelter. When I say I was not able to get lumber, I mean that I was not able to get any but what was on hand, and that was not sufficient. I know that Colonel Persons while there got a great lot of lumber. He got lumber towards the latter part of his stay there. He stayed there till some time in June. I know that that lumber was not used for sheltering the prisoners.

I do not say positively that the Confederate ration was the same as that given to the prisoners of war. I say that as far as I know it was; I know it came out of the same commissary. I do not know in what condition it reached the prisoners. I did not follow the rations to the prisoners. I know they did not receive the same inside the stockade. I know that when the ration was cooked and they received it inside, it was not as good as the Confederate soldiers, and not near as much. I know that the condition of the cook-house was such that it rendered the rations almost unfit for use. I know the cook-house was very filthy; they used to knead up the dough in a trough, and it seemed to me as if it was shortened with flies; it was full of flies when they worked it UP; they worked it up with a hoe, or something that looked like a hoe, and then afterwards it was baked in large loaves. You could break the loaf open and see flies in it. I never tasted it; I know the prisoners complained of it. It was not baked through and through; it did not appear to be properly done. There were no boards of survey organized at Captain Wirz's instance. I do not know at whose instance they were organized. I know I have been on boards of survey there myself; I was on a board of survey on some rotten meat and bacon; I do not

---

[1] In the cramped space given each prisoner, with scant fuel, how could he cook his ration?
[2] This was true to the end.

remember the date. It was in the summer, I think, perhaps in July. It was not a very frequent occurrence to organize boards of survey there to condemn provisions; it might have been though, and I might not have known it; I know of two boards there.[1]

Q. Do you not know that a great many provisions were issued to the prisoners of war there that would have been properly condemned by a board of survey?

A. Well, I do not know what they would have done. I have seen provisions that I would have condemned if I had been on a board. I have seen a good deal of beef at different times; I do not know the quantity, but I did not think it fit to eat. I do not remember being on but one board that condemned anything from the commissary, and that was a lot of bacon and meat. We condemned it; it was not fit for anything; it was perfectly rotten. I do not think it was issued again to the prisoners, because it was perfectly rotten and could not be used.

The order forbidding bathing above the stockade was not obeyed. The stream in which the men bathed flowed through the stockade.

Negro laborers were procured for the purpose of building trenches and laboring in the stockade. I never had any difficulty in getting all the negro labor I wanted; I never had any use for negro laborers. When requisitions were made for them I suppose they were obtainable; I think the planters volunteered and sent in their negroes by request of General Winder; I do not think he impressed them. It did not become necessary; I know as a fact that there were plenty of negroes in that neighborhood.[2]

Let the reader pause at this point, turn back and carefully consider the testimony of these twenty rebel witnesses. Not one had the hardihood to deny the existence of the awful sufferings, the needless mortality which will be found described in preceding chapters. Not one witness stated a single fact that tended to exculpate the authorities at Richmond for causing this suffering and death. Some evidence there is that Wirz was not wholly to blame, but when sifted down to its relevant and forceful elements, it furnishes no escape for the keeper of that prison from the logical and necessary consequences of his acts of omission and commission.

Witnesses testify that the same ration was supposed to be issued alike to the rebel camp and to prisoners, though these witnesses could not testify that it reached the prisoners. The camp guard had barracks; they had no difficulty in getting plenty of wood; they not only had the ration issued to them but a plentiful supply, as needed, came to them from their homes. They did not starve to death because of the treatment given them, while the prisoners did starve to death because of the treatment they received. Even the very cautious Father

---

[1] The utter inadequacy of the cooking arrangements and their unsanitary condition are frequently mentioned by witnesses.

[2] With the prisoners anxious to work and negroes abundant, why was nothing done to enlarge the stockade or provide wood?

Whelan, in his carefully guarded answers, could not deny the fact that starvation stalked through the prison pen claiming its victims. Georgia, the witnesses tell us, was the chief source of supply for the rebel armies; Andersonville was chosen as the situs of this prison for that reason, said Mr. Davis, but yet, in the midst of this region of plenty, prisoners of war, in appalling numbers were, with ingenious cruelty, permitted to starve to death.

These witnesses were called by the prisoner, presumably, to shed some ray of favorable light upon the dark picture which had been thrown upon the canvas by preceding witnesses. If there existed any facts in dispute or in palliation of the frightful sufferings, the awful mortality depicted in the course of the trial, these witnesses might be expected to furnish the evidence.

In vain will the reader look for any mitigating circumstances or extenuating facts.

We come now to a group of witnesses, twelve in all, who were called by the prisoner with a view in some degree to weaken the testimony of their companions in misery. They testified to different matters some of which bore more particularly upon the personal treatment of the prisoners by Wirz and will be referred to in that connection. At present their testimony will be confined mostly to the subjects now under examination.

Vincenzo Bardo was called to relate a circumstance involving Wirz in the charge of having caused two prisoners to be whipped who, in an effort to escape, disguised themselves by blacking their faces and going out of the stockade with some negroes. Upon being detected they were whipped and put in the stocks. It will be seen later on that Wirz gave the order, according to the witnesses for the prosecution, and it was this that Bardo was called to dispute. His testimony will be given here somewhat out of place, as he testified, among other things, that he attempted to escape because he was starving in the prison:

TESTIMONY OF VINCENZO BARDO.[1]

I have been in the military service of the United States. I arrived at Andersonville in June, 1864.

I was in the stockade; I got out of the stockade by blacking my face; I blacked my coat and from that blacked my face to go outside of the gate; I went outside with the negroes; we went down to the front of the "Dutch captain's" quarters; some of us had picks and some shovels; we went through the outside gate; we were trying to skedaddle; a lieutenant—I don't know his name

[1] Record, p. 512 et seq.

—asked me what I was doing round there; he asked me, "Are you a nigger or a white man?" Then he took off my hat and said, "You are a white man." I said, "Yes." He said, "Why the hell did you black your face?" I said that I had blacked my face to try to run away; then he took hold of me and put me in the stocks; the stocks came round my neck and my hands were stretched out; he gave me twenty-five lashes on my back; when I was taken out of the stocks I was put in the stockade for four hours; then put in the stocks again for four hours, and then I was put in the stockade again; the lieutenant left me in the stocks.

[The prisoner at the request of the counsel stood up.]

Q. Is that the man who gave you the twenty-five lashes?

A. No, sir; I know him; he is the "Dutch captain." The man who gave me the twenty-five lashes was a small man—smaller than me; he had no whiskers at all. The man wore a black hat with a feather. I think this was in August. I do not know who gave the orders to have me whipped; the lieutenant put me in the stocks himself; I do not know who ordered him to do so; I think the lieutenant was on duty at Captain Wirz's office; I do not know whether he was ordered to put me in the stocks or not; I blacked myself to try to run away; I wanted to run away because I felt very bad; I was starving; a good many around me were starving; I wanted to get away because I was starving.[1]

TESTIMONY OF FREDERICK ROTH.

Frederick Roth was called for the defense. Except as to individual acts of cruelty by Wirz his testimony strongly corroborates that of his fellow sufferers.[2]

I have been in the military service of the United States—in the 2d New York Cavalry. I was taken to Andersonville about the 20th of March, 1864. I left Andersonville on the 9th of September, 1864. I was inside the stockade all the time, except when I would get out for wood.

In some places the water was very good. In other places the water that ran through the brook was not fit to drink. There were wells and springs in the stockade. There were not enough wells in proportion to the men. I should think there were about 400 of different kinds. The springs were mostly along the swamp. In half of them the water was not fit to drink, on account of the maggots that ran all over the swamp into the water. In the wells that were deep—seventy-five feet deep—there was good water for any one that could get it.

For the first two months that I was there we got more meal than we could use. We had it there by bags full. For the last three months that I was there we had not enough to eat in what was issued to us. I know of the rations being sometimes very deficient. They would be so because some of the detachments that were not full drew just as much rations as the detachments that had their full complement. The sergeants generally drew, if they could, for their whole squad, accounting for the men some way or other. A good many drew double rations.

---

[1] This is a witness called by Wirz. May we not accept his statement that he was starving?
[2] Record, p. 604.

The first part of the time the biggest part of the trading was done by the post adjutant. He had a man inside selling for him. I have seen men going into the stockade and trading. The men traded with the guards in day-time and at night. There were a good many stores at Andersonville. Men could buy almost everything there as in this city, if they had the money. Of course, there were a few things which could not be bought there. I did not know of any eating-houses there. There were places where they sometimes boiled eggs and fried eggs, with meat which they bought from prisoners, or the quartermaster, or stole. I Cannot say that there was much money in the stockade. I know that I did not have much. This adjutant used to bring in a good deal of salt, and the guards would sell it in small quantities, in haversacks. I never saw any of the outside prisoners trading or selling to those inside the stockade.

The water of the brook that ran through the stockade was not fit to drink. The biggest part, of the men had to drink it, because they could not get any other. I have been dry myself and would not drink it, because I did not like it. Sometimes the men who had wells would give me a drink, and sometimes they would not. It depended upon their charity and their disposition to give to me. The water in the spring near the swamp was not fit to drink. The swamp overran with all kinds of filth. I suffered some on acoount of the water. I have been hot and dry, staying in the sun without shelter, and have gone down for a drink. The scum on the top of the water would be like as if there was liquor thrown on it, and I would have to wash it off or dip under it. The water would not smell, but it would not taste good. I would not like to drink it. We could see by standing on the hill that the people in the cook-house would empty slops right into it. We knew that was the way they did it. The slops from the rebel camps above went into the brook. It was pretty bad water to drink.

I suffered from hunger and exposure at Andersonville. For two weeks I did not think I would ever see Yankeedom again. I am not as strong now as I was when I was taken to Andersonville. The diarrhœa that I had there for two weeks affects me still.

I had nothing to eat some part of the time while I was at Andersonville. I should judge that that was true of a good many in camp, except those who had lots of money, or who carried on trade or business. Those who had money had the best chance to trade. If a fellow with only one or two dollars was trying to trade with a Confederate, some other fellow would come up and offer more and get it from him. Those traders ruled the camp pretty much.[1]

I saw a good deal of suffering in the stockade. I saw some men lying near the swamp; they would crawl down as near as they could. If they went near a tent they would be clubbed away down into the swamp, and then some of them got so that they could not stir, and they would lie down at the swamp until they died. Some had scurvy, which drew them up like a cripple. They could not stir, unless some one would help them. There were some who had not enough to eat, and who would go around and pick up the crumbs from the wagon that came in with rations.

I cannot recollect how many died out of my 90. I know that some died. I know that about 800 left Belle Island with me, and about 500 of them died.

[1] Many witnesses testified that there never was any difficulty in purchasing all kinds of food.

The squad that I belonged to got no rations on the 3d or 4th of July; I know that I did not. I don't know how the rest of the camp were off in regard to rations on those days. I think some of them got it, but others did not. None of the detachments right by me got any rations. Once before, in the month of April or May, rations were stopped for one day on one side of the creek, while the prisoners on the other side of the creek got the rations. I saw Captain Wirz the first time he called the roll. I think the rations were stopped once in April, because the men broke ranks; the men on one side stayed in ranks, and on the other side they did not. I saw he gave the men on one side their rations and did not give any rations to the men on the other side. There were only about ten thousand prisoners there then.[1]

Joseph Thuringer, of the 18th Veteran Reserves, was called for the defense. It appeared that he was not at Andersonville but was called to show the disposition of Wirz as to kindness in treating the witness while a prisoner at Tuscaloosa, Alabama, in 1861. It did not very clearly appear that Wirz was there but the witness thought he was the same man. He was permitted to testify to Wirz's reputation, but he said that he had never heard it discussed.[2]

TESTIMONY OF ROBERT H. KELLOGG.

Robert H. Kellogg was recalled for the defense. His testimony for the prosecution has already been given. His testimony as a witness for the defense was as follows:[3]

I was a prisoner at Andersonville. I cannot state the number of prisoners coming into the stockade there daily during the summer of 1864, while I was there, with accuracy. We received prisoners nearly every day, from 100 to 800 or 900—1,100, I believe, is the most I ever remember being received in one day; that was during the summer, while the fighting of the Army of the Potomac and Sherman's army was going on. The prisoners from the Army of the Potomac as they came in, were, as a general thing, destitute of blankets, haversacks and everything but the clothes they had on. I mean when they came into the stockade.

I was in the stockade from May 3 till September 10, 1864. During the time I was there, I cannot say that I ever knew or heard of Captain Wirz kicking, striking, or shooting a prisoner so that he died, that I remember. I have written a book descriptive of Andersonville Prison. The title of that book is "Life and Death in Rebel Prisons." I left it in the hands of Colonel Chipman, the Judge Advocate.

Q. Did you never hear of Captain Wirz ill-treating any prisoner of war in his custody?

A. I do not remember any special case of ill-treatment. I speak of nothing of that kind in my book, that I recollect now, not of my own personal observation.

THE JUDGE ADVOCATE. I am not speaking of your observation.

---

[1] This stoppage of rations is here testified to by the prisoner's witness. Many others testified to like effect. He also testified that he suffered for lack of food.
[2] Record, p. 529.
[3] Record, p. 651 et seq.

WITNESS. I don't remember having heard it. I state that in my book I no instances of personal cruelty committed by Captain Wirz, as I understood it, that I recollect. I do not say that I never heard any complaint made with regard to Captain Wirz's brutal treatment of prisoners. His character was cruel and brutal, and we all understood that perfectly well. We understood that from hearing his language, which was insulting and profane; and from the general treatment there in the prison. We saw that we were badly treated and miserably provided for; and we naturally supposed that he, as commandant of the prison, was, in a great degree at least responsible for it; we supposed, of course that somebody was responsible for it. There was discussion among us with regard to how he would treat prisoners when they arrived and afterward.

Q. What was said about that?

[Question objected to by counsel for the accused. The court, after deliberation, overruled the objection.]

THE WITNESS [continuing]: I stated before that I did not recollect any instance of cruelty. I have called to mind one that I do remember. It was the time some of Sherman's raiders were captured, and were brought into prison robbed of nearly everything. I have seen some of them with merely a shirt and pants, no hat, shoes, or coats; and I have heard statements of those men that they were searched outside before they were brought into prison, and robbed of everything, even their pocket-knives, photographs, pictures, and things of no value; and I have heard the statement of other prisoners who have come in there destitute of nearly everything, telling how they have been robbed of them. Captain Wirz was always very rough and brutal in his mode of conducting business, so far as I saw; and he was not very choice in his selection of names for the Yankees. I do not say that he did not kick, beat, or shoot to death a prisoner, but I say that I do not know it myself. Well, I don't recollect now, if I speak of instances of that kind in my own book. We all knew his reputation and character for cruelty; but I do not now remember any special act. I was there when Chickamauga was killed.

Q. Am I to understand you from your answer to counsel that you did not hear of certain things, that those things did not occur?

A. No, sir; not by any means.

Q. Am I to understand that the cruelty and brutality of this prisoner was not a matter of common talk and discussion among the prisoners at Andersonville?

A. No, sir. On the other hand it was true. We all understood him to be a cruel, overbearing, heartless man.[1]

Antonio Manoni, a private in the 7th Connecticut Volunteers, was called for the defense, but in the absence of an interpreter his examination was postponed and he was not again called.

It will be seen in subsequent pages that some of the acts of personal cruelty charged to Wirz were committed in the months of August and September, 1864. Witnesses were called by the defense to prove that

---

[1] This was the prisoner's witness. Is it hard to believe that a "cruel, overbearing, heartless man" might be guilty of acts testified to?

Wirz was sick during these months. Some of the witnesses testified that he was sick and unable to perform duty during all of August; others fixed the time as during September; still others for only a part of one or other of these months. The evidence upon the question is too indefinite and based as it is wholly upon memory of dates but little reliance could be placed upon it as showing more than that Wirz was sick on occasional days but not so as to remove him from immediate responsibility for his charge. Official documents signed by him at different times in August and September show that witnesses who testified to his being absent sick for the whole of either month or both months were mistaken. He was on active duty when Colonel Chandler was there inspecting the prison in August. Dr. Jones visited the camp in the early part of September, about the 7th he testified, and spent three weeks in his examination of first, the hospital outside the stockade, and later, the stockade itself. He gives in his report an order dated September 17, 1864, directing Captain Wirz to permit Surgeon Jones to visit the stockade. He testified that he had previously applied to Captain Wirz for permission to enter the stockade and was refused for reasons not given, and he then applied to General Winder and his adjutant gave the order. There are other incontestable proofs of Wirz's presence in both months, and any absence from sickness was not from the post or from his duties except temporarily. It would seem unnecessary to give the evidence of witnesses tending to show his absence during these two months in the face of record and indisputable evidence to the contrary. Some such testimony, however, is quoted in the course of the answers of witnesses.

TESTIMONY OF AUGUSTUS MOESNER.[1]

I have been a member of Company G, 16th Connecticut Volunteers. I was captured April 20, 1864, and taken to Andersonville. I arrived there on the 3d of May, in the evening. I remained in the stockade up to the 24th of May, 1864. I was taken as a paroled prisoner to Captain Wirz's office as a clerk.

When I was first taken out I was not well acquainted yet with the English language, and I only made some copies, and also wrote in the roll-book. Among other duties I had to carry orders down to the stockade, and to carry returns and morning reports to General Winder's headquarters, and I also had to go to the commissary with returns.

Q. Did you have anything to do with requisitions on the commissary and quartermaster? If you did, state all about it.

A. Those requisitions and returns, I think, were made out every day, and they stated the number of prisoners inside the stockade; and there was also

[1] Record, p. 536 et seq.

another requisition for those men who were detailed and men outside at work as paroled men, because they all got a second ration.

Q. Do you mean a double ration?

A. Yes, sir; double rations.

Q. How were the requisitions made out as to quantity?

A. They stated the number of men present, but the quantity of the rations was left in blank.

Q. Who would fill it up? How would the commissary know how to fill it?

A. He saw how many men were there, and as many men as he had in the requisition, so many rations he had to provide.

Q. He would make it out from his own will, or from information in his office?

A. He would do so. Captain Wirz had nothing to do with it. It was left entirely to him.

Q. What, if anything, had you to do in relation to the cook-house?

A. There was, every morning, a list made out, and on this list was put the number of the squads, and the number of the detachment, and of each detachment, how many rations the detachment had to get; because there were many squads which had not ninety men. There was not one squad which had ninety men in line; many were detailed out, and many in the hospital, and their rations had to be taken out; and so in those lists we stated how many rations every detachment had to get from the cook-house. I brought that list down to Mr. Duncan. I left it there and went back to my quarters. I do not know anything about the rations after that, or anything that came from the cook-house. I had nothing to do with that. Captain Wirz had nothing to do with that. As soon as Duncan knew how many rations he had to give out, when the rations were cooked, he would bring them down to the stockade; that was his duty. The requisitions for the hospital were made by Dr. White. We had nothing to do in our office with the hospital. I do not know that any requisitions for anything for it were made out in our office or signed by Captain Wirz.

Q. What did you have as rations while you were outside, and in what quantity, and what did you do with them?

A. The first time I was outside there as a clerk; I went every day once to the cook-house and got my rations there. I got a piece of corn bread and a piece of bacon. I could have gotten some rice or some beef, but I did not take them.

Q. Did you have any sanitary goods, or did you eat anything belonging to Union prisoners out there?

A. I never had any, because there were never any provisions sent by the Sanitary Commission. I had an extra ration. We got money for it. We sold it to Captain Wirz. He paid us eighty cents a day, Confederate money. He never took any away without paying us. I was paid every month.[1]

I do not recollect that the rations were ever stopped for the whole camp. The rations were sometimes stopped for a squad when the sergeant of the squad—Federal sergeant—reported a man missing in the line. They were stopped that the men of the squad should go and hunt up and look for the man, to find him; perhaps he might be in another part of the stockade, sick somewhere else, and

---

[1] Conceding that Wirz had nothing to do with issuing rations (which is Contrary to other evidence), it was his duty to see that it was properly done.

if he was not found he could not be treated, as they could not send a doctor to him; but afterwards if the man was found, or if the Federal sergeant reported the man as escaped, it was altered, and the squad could get their list. I know that I wrote down the lists for rations and I had to remark it if a squad were deprived of its rations, because it was left in blank, and I know that very often or sometimes, when the missing man was found it was altered and sent down to the cook-house to Mr. Duncan, who was told to give that squad rations, because the Federal sergeant could answer for the missing man and say that he was sick or was escaped. As soon as the Federal sergeant could give an answer for the man it was altered and the squad got their rations. It was done by Captain Wirz's orders.[1]

Q. Did you have any orders to keep them all day, or could you as soon as the missing man was found have the rations sent to them?

A. If Captain Wirz would not have been there in his office the sergeant would have come back and reported those missing men as found, and we had power ourselves—we clerks—to send down to Mr. Duncan and tell him to give those squads their rations.

Q. Do you say that Captain Wirz never interfered with the quantity or quality of the rations issued to prisoners?

A. Yes, sir; he did interfere. He stopped the rations. He did not stop them very frequently. He stopped them for separate squads. By squads I mean divisions of nineties. When a man was reported missing on roll-call he would stop the rations. He would stop them for the ninety, if one man was missing, until the sergeant of the squad could give an answer for the man—until he could report him in some way. He had the power to stop the rations. He had the power to direct that rations should be issued to the men; and he had the power to stop them, and he exercised the power both ways. Lieutenant Davis, at Captain Wirz's headquarters, had the same authority. There was not any one else. I know of nobody else except General Winder.

Q. Yet you stated to this court that the clerks had the power?

A. Not in this way; we had the power when Catpain Wirz was not there.[2]

TESTIMONY OF MARTIN S. HARRIS.[3]

I was a soldier in the 5th Regiment, New York Volunteer Artillery, from January 15, 1862, till I was discharged, in last June. I was confined in the stockade from July 29, 1864, until November 1, 1864. I was sergeant of a ninety in the stockade. I was a private in the army. I was appointed a sergeant by Captain Wirz before I went in, at the solicitation of the men of my own squad. The water of the creek was not fit either for cooking or drinking purposes. There were a number of wells which had been dug by members of detachments, and which were reserved by them for their own private use; no outsider, except as a matter of special favor, could obtain any water from them. The springs were abundant, especially on the south side of the creek. In September, I think—at

---

[1] Other witnesses called in defense testified that rations were stopped for the whole prison camp.

[2] This shows that Wirz had full power over the subject of rations.

[3] Record, p. 588 et seq.

any rate it was during August or September—there was a spring discovered between the dead-line and the stockade, near the north gate. The men very soon ascertained that it was water superior to any other in the stockade; and they went there, with poles with a cup or bucket attached, to dip it up. This spring was afterwards cleared out under the supervision of the police, and a trough was constructed from the spring leading to a point inside the dead-line on the prison side of it.[1]

There was abundance of fuel, both for cooking and heating purposes.[2] Salt was a luxury in the stockade.[3] I speak of my own positive knowledge when I say that salt was sold by the bakers at the bake-house to the traders inside the stockade in quantities to suit purchasers, and it was tied up in bags, and thrown over the stockade at night. The scarcity of salt affected our rations to this extent, that we had no salt at all in our bread for a long time; that is, no quantity which was appreciable; we could not taste it. Salt was conveyed into the stockade in the manner I have described, and was purchased by these traders and by them exposed for sale. . . . .

Q. Did you ever at any time while you were at Andersonville complain to any one of your comrades with regard to the fearful mortality—the great suffering, destitution and sickness among the prisoners in the stockade?

A. Yes, sir; it was a frequent subject of conversation; in fact the only subject of conversation we had was that, and anticipating the time when we would be released.

Q. And yet when you came home, among the first things you found it necessary to do was to enter into a defense of Captain Wirz?

A. What I wrote was this: not denying the horrors of Andersonville, but ascribing them to what, in my opinion, was the proper cause. I never denied them.

Q. You do not to-day deny any of the horrors that have been depicted at Andersonville?

A. Not a particle.

Q. The only question you gave any opinion on was with regard to the responsibility of the parties, and that you state now as positively as you do anything?

A. Yes, sir.

Q. You state that you have not anything to diminish with regard to the horrors of Andersonville as depicted by your comrades here?

A. Nothing at all regarding the facts.

Q. Nothing excepting on the question of responsibility?

A. Yes, sir.[4]

By the PRESIDENT:

Q. On whom, in your opinion, is the responsibility?

A. In my opinion General Winder was responsible, and also the prisoners themselves, by their conduct toward each other; the prisoners were responsible

---

[1] This is the point where several prisoners were shot in reaching for water.
[2] This statement is in conflict with the testimony of nearly all the witnesses.
[3] If there was salt for sale, why was it not furnished to the prisoners?
[4] This man received favors at the hands of Wirz. A sense of gratitude may have made him an over-zealous witness.

themselves in a great many cases for their horrible sufferings there. I never did in any instance treat any of my comrades or any of the sufferers in the stockade improperly; I treated them with as much kindness as lay in my nature. I suppose I am about the average as a kind man. I made a remark to different parties after I was exchanged, that I lived first-rate while I was with the rebel officers and had plenty to eat and plenty to drink. I made that remark at home in Brooklyn. People asked me how I fared down South, and I told them how I fared at Andersonville and how at Millen; and that was the idea I conveyed. Six prisoners comprised the whole force at Camp Lawton last winter. My experience South was diversified.

Q. I want to know whether you ever at any time remarked in the presence of any persons that while you were a prisoner in the South you had plenty to eat and plenty to drink?

A. I remarked that during a portion of my imprisonment I did live well.

Q. Did you ever make that remark to anybody with regard to your living at Andersonville?

A. No, sir; I could not do it; it was not the fact.

Q. Were cooked rations sometimes issued to the sick that were not fit for them to eat?

A. That was merely a matter of taste.

Q. Then those men who died preferred to die as a matter of taste to eating those rations?

A. The sick, those who had sore mouths, could not eat the corn bread and—

Q. What made their mouths sore?

A. Scurvy.

Q. And they preferred to die as a matter of taste?

A. They preferred to abstain from that part of the ration altogether.

Q. You use the word "abstain" as you preferred to use the term "delayed" instead of "stopped" in regard to the rations?

A. It is hardly a parallel case; they abstained from the food because it only aggravated their disease. The result of their abstaining from food was that they became greatly emaciated, and in a great many cases death ensued; death resulted from their abstinence from food, from the nature of their food, not from starvation arising from the lack of food. I said salt was thrown over the stockade in quantities to suit purchasers. At the time the salt was thrown over the stockade, the number of prisoners was estimated at 33,000; salt was a luxury at Andersonville; I consider anything a luxury which is very scarce; salt was very scarce at Andersonville; it could only be obtained by purchase; all those who could afford it purchased salt; I cannot tell how many could afford it; there was a great many in the stockade who could afford it, a great many who had money; I suppose about one-third of the prisoners had money. Each one would purchase according to his ability; men who possessed money could purchase enough for daily consumption; each would consume a spoonful perhaps; those who had money had to be economical; a spoonful of salt would be sufficient for each purchaser; that was the daily purchase; there were more than ten thousand spoonfuls of salt thrown over the stockade daily; I say that I have seen salt thrown over the stockade daily; I pretend to know of my own knowledge about this traffic; I know about this because I have been occasionally walking in the evenings down on the west side of the stockade, and I have seen this traffic going on; I presume it was going on all the time; I do not know except from what I have seen occasionally; I know where the salt came from, it came from the bake-house.

Q. You say that when the sergeant came in there, at the time the sick and others were removed, about the 31st of October, they informed the sick that they might remain, if they desired to do so, and they did remain?

A. They did remain.

Q. Preferring to stay in the Andersonville stockade to being exchanged?

A. Yes, sir.

Q. You state it as a fact that the Andersonville stockade was regarded by them as preferable to an exchange?

A. Preferable to another stockade unknown to them. Andersonville at that time was comfortable comparatively to what it had been. This was after the stockade was cleared out; some of the prisoners stayed, preferring that stockade to one that they knew nothing of; some were unable to be removed, but some to my own certain knowledge preferred to remain there—some of my own detachment; they preferred to bear the ills they had; Andersonville was preferable in their view to an exchange of stockade; I do not mean to convey the idea that Andersonville in their opinion was preferable to coming home here in the North; the idea those men had was that they would rather stay there than go to another stockade, of the horrors of which they knew nothing.

TESTIMONY OF EDWARD WELLINGTON BOATE.[1]

I was in the service of the United States; in the 42d New York Volunteers. I was a prisoner at Andersonville from February 24, 1864, till August 7, 1864; I was taken prisoner October 14, 1863. I was first taken to Belle Island.

The fare at Andersonville was about three times the quantity, both in meat and meal, that it was at Belle Island; in other respects it was better—better at Andersonville than Belle Island. I had meat at Belle Island the last month before I left twice, with an interval of a fortnight between the two times. At Belle Island we got quarter rations—a quarter of a loaf of bread, with a small bit of meat about that size, [about five inches by three].

My first rations at Andersonville were about a pound of beef, salt and fresh and two sanitary cups of meal; no coffee. We got beans at the same time. We got sweet potatoes the day of our arrival. The rations diminished. Instead of two sanitary cups of meal, we received sometimes a cup and a half. The rations got smaller as the prisoners increased. I arrived there at night, and the next morning Sergeant Duncan gave to each squad about six skillets, so far as I remember, for cooking our rations, stating that as soon as the cook-house and bakery were completed, me would receive cooked rations. The cook-house at that time was in course of completion. I think it must have been in the month of April that I got cooked rations. Our own men did the cooking at the bake-house. The bread cooked there was. bad; it was burned on the outside, and raw on the inside; this was not always the case, but generally it was; it was

[1] Record, p. 687 et seq.

badly baked. The prisoners sometimes ate the rations, and sometimes they could not eat them and threw them away; I speak now with regard to the bread.

Q. Do you know anything about efforts to get prisoners to enlarge the stockade, and what was said and done on that occasion?

A. I remember Captain Wirz having a number of men brought out—

I was then detailed to go out with them; I did not go out with them. I was in Dr. White's department at the time. A number of prisoners came before Captain Wirz; he had sent for them; he said, "Now, that stockade below is too crowded for you, and I have no labor to increase the size of it; all the black labor is engaged on farms, and I have hardly enough men, in fact, to guard you; I ask you to come out; I will give you axes; come out and increase the stockade to any extent that is necessary for you."

The reply was, "Captain Wirz, we do not want to come out to work, for we have been told by recent prisoners who have arrived in the stockade, that if we go to work for rebels our pay will be stopped, and we will be tried and probably sent to the Dry Tortugas."

[To the Court:] I heard this conversation myself. Captain Wirz said, "Your government are not such rascals or such fools as to blame or punish you if I can give you ten feet of room instead of four, if you come out and work for it."[1]

There was an average of a barrel of whiskey a day sent to the hospital and stockade for the prisoners. Eggs were sent to the hospital, not the stockade. Tea, sugar, and matters of that kind were sent to the hospital daily.[2] I know that eggs were selling at Andersonville around there at $3.50 per dozen. I will not speak in regard to the eggs, but I will speak in regard to the vegetables. Dr. White, not Captain Wirz, gave the order, "Bring all you can find of these things and I will pay you any price." They came in very limited quantities, but I heard Captain Wirz offer to pay any price that they demanded, and tell them to bring him all the articles of that character that they could find round the country.

I know that there was a very bad smell through the camp. I would not offer an opinion advisedly upon it. I have expressed an opinion in reference to that swamp that it was unhealthy. I said it was "filled with untold impurities." That was true.

I said that the food there was "unfit for human beings." That was true at the time I was referring to. At the time I understood so from my companions who came out of the stockade and who joined me in the commission referred to here. They told me that the food was bad, not fit for human beings. I know myself that the bread baked there was unfit for human beings. That is so. That was my opinion and I repeat it.

I have said that that stockade was "without shelter of any kind." Using the phrase "from the fierce tropical sun and the heavy rains." That is partially true. There were several hundreds in that stockade without shelter. I used the expression that their clothes were "miserable" and "insufficient even for the purposes of common decency." That was true.

[1] The testimony is that the prisoners helped to enlarge the stockade.
[2] The surgeons at the hospital testified that there were not stimulants enough for cases under the knife. Dr. Bates testified that the cry of the patients was for food.

Q. Did you ever make use of the expression "the confinement of 35,000 human beings within an area of some 17 acres, with a pestilential swamp running through the camp"?

A. That should be 27 acres. I wrote it so in figures, and the printer made the mistake. With that change it is true. I wrote this expression: "Our sick when removed to hospital being utterly devoid of any sort of accommodation, and often three weeks at a time without a particle of medicine." That is not fully true. There is a slight exaggeration in it. They were not three weeks altogether at a time without medicine; but they might be a week. With that change it is true. I used this expression, "the despair, the mental imbecility, the madness which have been the result to so many of those unhappy prisoners." It is literally true. I lost my health at Andersonville. My eyesight was impaired. I did not lose it at Andersonville; I lost it at Belle Island, from the suffering endured there lying out without shelter.

Q. Was it contributed to at Andersonville?

A. Yes, it was not benefited.

Question repeated.

A. Yes. When I arrived at New York I had an attack of my lungs, I presume arising from my confinement in the South. I made that statement believing it to be true. In speaking of my sight being impaired, I made use of the expression "only one degree removed from total blindness"; at a certain time my sight was so bad that that was true.

Q. Did you use this expression in regard to it: "all the result of eleven long weary months spent in the bull pens of the Southern Confederacy?"

A. I referred to that.

[Mr. Baker claimed that the whole sentence on which the witness was being questioned should be read to him.]

WITNESS. I admit the whole document. I admit that I wrote that letter. Every line of it is true with the exceptions I have named.

TESTIMONY OF BENJAMIN F. DILLY.[1]

I reside in Allentown, Pennsylvania. I was in the service of the United States for three years and seven months, in Company F, 54th Pennsylvania. I was taken prisoner on the 2d of February, 1864; I was carried to Belle Island, Richmond. I remained there until the 16th of March, 1864; I was then taken to Andersonville; I was there one year. I went there on the 23d of March, 1864, and came away on the 23d of March, 1865. I was in the stockade at Andersonville for three weeks. I was allowed to go in and out of the stockade until August. I was detailed as a clerk at the headquarters of Captain Wirz; I was admitting clerk. . . . I was connected with the hospital department from the latter part of August till the 23d of March, 1865.

Every man traded who had means. Hams, fresh pork, bacon, flour, meal, peanuts, sweet potatoes, white potatoes, thread and needles, cigars, tobacco, and anything of that kind were traded in. That was going on both inside and outside. Articles were bought outside and taken into the stockade. I know about trading over the stockade between prisoners and rebels; prisoners would walk

---

[1] Record, p. 672 et seq.

up to the dead-line and ask some of the guards if he had anything to trade; if he had he would show it, and the prisoner would throw up the money on the end of a string and the guard would let down the article.

There were a number of small wells inside the stockade while I was there—there were no large ones while I was in the stockade. I suppose there were 75 or 100 on the south side. The number increased, but the men who owned the wells would not allow their comrades to drink from them. Very good water was in the wells, better water than we had outside. That water would not supply more than one-fifth the wants of the stockade, I suppose. . . . The creek water when I was inside the stockade was very bad, excepting some portions of it—the upper end of it, and even there the water was bad; the water was good enough except for the grease on it that came from the cook-house.

Captain Wirz made an effort to impress 500 slaves to enlarge the stockade. He could not get the slaves, and he sent to Richmond for orders in regard to it; he also sent into the stockade for men—the men refused to come out. The excuse was that they would compromise themselves in the eyes of their government. The sick men could not do it, and the well men refused to do it; at last they got some men out—some 150. I understood that Captain Wirz's orders were to place the men three deep if they did not come out. He placed so many men in the stockade that they were forced to come out at last.

Captain Wirz said that that rice and corn meal were not fit for niggers; that he would not feed his slaves on them, and that the man who sent that corn meal to Andersonville should be court-martialed—that he was robbing the Confederate government. I do not know anything about the conduct of cooks in the cook-house in reference to rations, more than that they traded the rations off to the slaves for vegetables. Captain Wirz's detectives found fifteen bags of hams and bacon in the woods. The slaves were men whom I saw working around on the fortifications. There were some 500 slaves working on the fortifications at Andersonville.

I saw suffering inside the stockade certainly; they all suffered more or less. They could not eat the food; it was not fit to eat. It would be hard for any man to eat the corn bread they had there. There were plenty of sick men in there. I saw plenty of men dying in there. I never saw anybody naked in there, although their clothes were good for nothing—nothing but rags. I saw men there without hats, without shoes, and without pants; but I have never seen them without all these things at one time. I have seen men without pants.

August Gleich was called for the defense. He belonged to the 8th Pennsylvania Cavalry; was at Andersonville from March until November, 1864. He entered the stockade March 10th and was paroled and went to work for Wirz April 8th. He testified that Wirz was absent sick the whole of August and this was the principal fact brought out by him. He also testified that he "never heard that Captain Wirz shot or injured a man so that he died. I heard it spoken of while I was at Andersonville. All I can tell is that he would curse a man for nothing at all hardly; that is about all he would do."[1]

[1] Record, pp. 585, 587.

TESTIMONY OF FREDERICK GUSCETTI.

Frederick Guscetti was called for the defense. He belonged to the 47th New York Regiment and arrived at Andersonville March 28, 1864, and remained there until August, when he was paroled for work outside. He tells of a desperate attempt made to escape which presumably was brought out to show the kindness of Wirz in overlooking it.[1]

I attempted to escape once on the 4th of July; they did not give us anything to eat, and in the evening I told some of my friends to tie me up in a blanket and I would go out as a dead man; they put me in a blanket, put a cloth over my face and carried me into the hospital; in the hospital they put No. 61 on my breast; they put me into the dead-house and kept me there until the last wagon came that night; they then took me away during the night; I knew that the orders were to carry away twenty-five bodies at a time, I counted so many dead and placed myself so as to be about the twenty-fourth or twenty-fifth; the next morning the men came in to carry away the dead; they counted out twenty-four and then it came to my turn; a negro, named "Abe," lifted me up and threw me on the wagon—a canvas-covered wagon like a tent—to go to the dead-house; when I was carried to the dead-house the negroes took my clothes off, so that I had nothing on but a pair of drawers, and I had no chance to get away; they carried me out in a wagon too near the kitchen; I had not eaten the whole day before, and did not feel strong enough to go away; I slipped down from the wagon with the intention of waiting until night, and then going to some farmers near by and getting clothes somehow; I was lying down when about ten o'clock I saw Turner with the dogs run around the stockade; I was afraid of him, of course; I then saw him go away; he was going to headquarters; afterwards I saw him with Captain Wirz on horseback; I heard afterwards that their object was to discover a hole which had been made the night before; in passing around there the dogs found me out and jumped towards me; I did not move; I knew that they would not bite me if I did not run away. Captain Wirz came up and said: "What the hell are you doing here?" I told him I was trying to run away; he asked me if I thought I could run away without any clothes on; I then told him all about how it was; he took me down to the hospital and asked the steward, or some one of the men in the hospital, to give me some clothes; he then put me into the stockade; he said that he had a mind to put a ball and chain on me for it; but after all he sent me back into the stockade. That was my first attempt to run away; I do not think a great many of the prisoners liked to pass off for dead, but many were running away all the time—as often as they could.

On the fourth of July rations were stopped for a whole day. I cannot say why they were stopped. I think the prisoners would have died if the rations had been stopped two or three days in succession.

Rations were stopped inside the stockade on the 4th July. They were not stopped altogether at any other time; they were stopped from some squads. I

[1] Record, p. 513 et seq.

234   THE TRAGEDY OF ANDERSONVILLE.

once saw that they did not bring anything at all inside; that was the 4th of July. No one at the south gate certainly got anything that day. On other days I know that some squads or messes did not get their rations; they were squads who could not find men who were absent. Sometimes a man would be found sick in his tent who had not received any rations for one or two days. The camp police often found men so, and often bucked and gagged sergeants for allowing it. I have known some men to be without rations for two days. On that 4th of July I got nothing to eat; I ran away because I did not like the prison; there was very poor eating in the prison. I could stand it myself, because I was always very healthy. Out of ninety-one countrymen of mine only four died. We were healthy and used to that kind of living, but I know that a great many other men died.

Q. Did you allow yourself to be put into the dead-wagon, laid along with corpses, and left in the dead-house all night for the purpose of escaping from a place where you got enough to eat?

A. Yes; that dead-house was a horrible place. I was lying alongside of dead bodies; some of them had gangrene, and some had their legs off.

Q. And you subjected yourself to all that suffering merely to escape from a place where you got enough to eat?

A. I told you that I did not have enough to eat, but I could stand it.

It appeared that the witness was very much interested in behalf of the prisoner and this interest was shown as tending to discredit him. He was shown a clipping from a New York paper and admitted that it was written and sent by him for publication.

The record shows the following[1]

To the Editor of the New York News:

Captain Henry Wirz, at present on trial before a military commission at Washington, is *a poor man*, having a wife and three children depending on the charity of friends for their support. He is entirely without the means of drfraying those expenses which are unavoidable for a person who must singly and alone defend himself against the prosecution of the government. The sentiment in favor of a fair and perfectly just trial of any and all the state prisoners is so universal, that some of the personal friends of Captain Wirz take this method of appealing to all such as may feel interested in knowing that the accused has not wanted a fair and full opportunity for presenting the whole of his case in its true aspect before the tribunal charged with deciding his fate. Hence they ask for contribution of funds for that purpose, to be sent to the editor of this paper, to be by him forwarded to the consul-general of Switzerland at Washington.

It is hoped that the countrymen of Captain Wirz, and the adopted citizens generally, will feel it a duty devolving upon them especially, without allowing other considerations to prejudice his case.

All acquainted with facts in the case, and willing to testify for Captain Wirz, are requested to forward their names and address to L. Schade, Esq., attorney at law, Washington, D. C., with a statement of what they can testify to.

F. GUSCETTI.

(Western papers please copy.)

Q. How did you happen to take such extraordinary interest in this case?

A. I was always, myself, treated well by Captain Wirz, and when I wrote

[1] Record, pp. 525-7.

TESTIMONY FOR DEFENSE. 235

this article, or had it written, I was in company with several other men who had been treated well by Captain Wirz, They said they could not come here as witnesses for him. I implicated nobody in the letter, but stated what I wished to see, that he should be tried justly.

The remaining witness of this class was George Washington Fechtner. I think any one who may read the extraordinary story he narrated will conclude that he should have been named Ananias instead of George Washington. Counsel for the prisoner would gladly have checked this glowing account of the modern bazaar and commercial emporium he made out of the prison pen.

Recalling the report of Colonel Chandler and the graphic description given by Dr. Jones of this prison and the numerous witnesses who depicted the horrors of that dreadful place, the story of Fechtner reads like the outpourings of a disordered brain.[1]

TESTIMONY OF GEORGE W. FECHTNER.

I was in the Union army in September, 1862; I was taken prisoner on the 15th of September, 1862, by Colonel Jesse, a Confederate colonel; I was held as a spy, having been identified by one of his men as such; I was taken to Knoxville, East Tennessee, and from there to Grenada, Mississippi; I was held in that country nine months for trial; finally I made my escape but was recaptured by the Mississippi home guard, and taken to Columbus, Mississippi, and from there I was sent to Richmond, under the name of Charles W. Ross; I gave another name for the purpose of saving my life; I had been on trial as a spy; I arrived at Andersonville the first of June, 1864; none of my comrades who were captured with me were punished as spies, except one who was hung.

When I arrived at Andersonville I was put in the stockade.

Q. What did you do in the stockade?

A. I was prison sutler part of the time, and I was chief of regulators and magistrate for the southwest part of the camp. My duty as magistrate was to punish men for stealing; I punished some by flogging, some by setting them to work, and some by sentencing them to be washed. They were so very dirty that they had to be washed once in a while, and it was a punishment to them.

THE JUDGE ADVOCATE. I must object to this course of testimony as immaterial and irrelevant.

MR. BAKER. You will find that this witness will give a new complexion to matters inside the stockade; that instead of all the horrors we have heard of, he will show that it was a little more comfortable and agreeable.

THE JUDGE ADVOCATE. Very well, I will not object to that.

Q. State what you did as a magistrate.

A. In the southwest part of the camp all the men guilty of stealing were brought before me for trial; they were prosecuted by the men from whom they had stolen; they would steal tin cups, clothing, food and anything they could get their hands on. The police there were organized for the defense of the

---

[1] Record, p. 557 et seq.

camp; they were composed of companies, thirty men to a company. (To the Court.) They were organized for the regulation and defense of the men in the camp; the system of robbing men in the streets gave rise to the regulators; this system of robbing was carried on by a number of men who had banded themselves together for the purpose of taking by force that which was not their own, money, watches, clothing, and anything they took a fancy to. The police were first organized by a number of men, who were prominent in the camp, going round and secretly taking the names of able-bodied men who were willing to take part in putting down the robbers. After they were sufficiently strong it was done openly; the raiders then tried to put down the regulators; they styled themselves "the regulators." This led to an outbreak; assistance was called for from Captain Wirz, which was furnished immediately; and the raiders were taken out; eleven of them were tried, six were hung, and five sentenced to wear a ball and chain. There were sixteen companies of police; they were organized by the chief of police; a man named Keese was the first chief; he was appointed by the regulators themselves; the regulators elected their own captains, and these captains elected the chief; complaints were made daily concerning robberies; I would dispose of them to the best of my ability. For stealing a tin cup, if the man was healthy, he was flogged; if he was not healthy he was made to sit in a tent all day long, or he was taken down to the creek and washed; the men of the regulators executed my orders—the police.

There were quite a number of storekeepers of different kinds there; I would be safe in saying there were a thousand of different kinds in the stockade;[1] they would keep their stores in their tents; they dug holes in the ground to put them in; they got the stores from the post adjutant—the rebel sutler; they got the largest part of them from him; they got a good many stores through the hospital, and by paying the guards at the gate $5 or such matter for leave to go into the country to buy them. All kinds of trades that are calculated to make men comfortable were carried on there, such as shoemakers, tailors, watchmakers, &c. There were two watchmakers there, five or six shoemakers, and five or six tailors. The streets were full of soup jobbers; there were about thirty eating-houses there; they consisted of tables made out of rough boards and long benches; coffee, tea, ham and eggs, biscuit, butter, and honey could be got there; there were at least five hundred bakers in the stockade; they would bake biscuit, bread, pies, cakes. They would get the flour from the post-adjutant and from the cook-house and through the hospital; it would be smuggled in from the cook-house on wood wagons; it would be concealed below the wood and brought in. When the wood would be unloaded the flour would be taken out and delivered to the men it was sold to; it was always sold previously to being taken in; the bakers would manage to carry on their business very easily; there was always plenty of wood for sale and plenty of flour to be had, and plenty of saleratus; I had a 50-pound keg of that; I had a store after I had been there a while, styled "the novelty store." I had a greater variety to sell than any other man in the camp; some of the articles I had for sale were potatoes, onions, peas, beans, apples, peaches, grapes, pears, plums, chickens, watermelons, saleratus, flour, red and black pepper, honey, butter, and beer; I had sorghum, about a barrel.

[1] Thus there was a storekeeper for every 25 or 30 men.

I had to pay for a barrel of sorghum $1,300 of Confederate money; that would be $325 in greenbacks. I had to pay $70 of Confederate money per pound for tea. We got the apples from the post adjutant; they cost us at the rate of $60 a bushel, potatoes the same, onions the same; flour cost us $70 a sack of 98 pounds; I had large quantities of tobacco; it was generally in 25-pound boxes, which would sell at $22.50; we got ale from the post adjutant; we bought it directly from him; he always came inside with loads of these goods; I had ginger and capsicum, and different kinds of roots and herbs in my store; I would buy them from the paroled men detailed in the hospital; I would get apples, grapes, and watermelons sometimes from the post adjutant; sometimes from the men who were on working squads; they would get them when out at work and would bring them in and sell them to the traders inside; we could get outside whenever we wanted to by giving the sergeant at the gate $5, generally to take us out to the country to a house where those articles were kept for sale; it was about five miles outside the limits; have very often helped sick prisoners, acquaintances of mine; I would give them medicine for scurvy and diarrhœa; a dose of medicine there for diarrhœa would cost about $1.25 in greenbacks; they would come around there to my tent every day when I told them to do so. There were clothing merchants there; there were only two that I particularly know of; but there were a great many on the streets selling clothing of different kinds, shirts, pants, shoes, overcoats, caps and hats. Clothing was very cheap there; a good pair of army shoes could be got for 75 cents or a dollar; a very good overcoat for $4; pants for $2; shirts were about the dearest things there were there, they averaged about $3. There were quite a number of money brokers there; they would buy and sell State money, Confederate money, gold and silver; there were about 50 of that class there; they would also deal in bounty certificates and watches, and would buy and sell bank checks. There were bank checks to buy and sell; they would be brought in by new prisoners; they would buy these bounty certificates at a great discount and run the risk of getting their pay on them; there was no place there for paying those bounty certificates; they would risk getting their pay when they returned North; it was not known there whether the certificates were genuine or not; most of them were on the State of Massachusetts; they gave about 50 per cent for bounty certificates. I should judge there was half a million of greenbacks circulating there when the Plymouth prisoners were brought in; Confederate money was brought in in any quantity. There were a number of barber shops there where men could, get shaved, their hair cut and whiskers dyed, and some of them carried on the doctoring business. Only one carried on the doctoring business that I know of personally. They would buy their dyeing articles to work with, their soap and other things, from new arrivals. Those things were brought in in large quantities. During the month of June there was an arrival of fresh prisoners nearly every day, who were brought from the neighborhood of Petersburg and Richmond. There were quite a number of arrivals in July; not so many in August. Those who were brought in in those months were generally able-bodied men, very healthy, well clothed, and had plenty of greenbacks. They had also a number of little articles which soldiers wear. There were two watchmakers there that I know of. They repaired watches and jewelry. I have been at their shops. I saw upwards of 50 watches in one

238   THE TRAGEDY OF ANDERSONVILLE.

man's shop, and a number of articles, such as breastpins and rings, left to be repaired. This man kept a journeyman; the work was too heavy for himself. They had a full set of tools. They had a tent to work in. The tents were generally made of blankets stretched upon poles. Those poles were brought into camp by working parties. There were pole merchants there. I should say there were about 30 pole merchants. The working squads brought poles in—men who were taken out every morning to work and who were sent into camp in the evening; they would bring in such things as they could secure every day, fence rails, poles, and boards. The bakers could carry on their baking business very easily; everything that was needed to carry it on was to be had in the camp. Wood was for sale in large quantities. They constructed ovens of mud, some very large and others very small. They would buy the wood from wood merchants and also from the messes in camp. I cannot say how many wood merchants were there; they were passing around on the streets all the time. A common-sized cord stick was worth two dollars in greenbacks. There were about five hundred bakers there. The tailors had the business of making pants out of cornsacks taken from the commissary wagons. There were a number of tailors— five or six I was acquainted with. They were always busy making pants for men who wanted a clean pair of pants to put on once in a while, to make themselves feel like being at home. They stole the sacks out of the commissary wagons.

I had a store. I first bought a lot, and erected a shanty on it. I dug a cellar at the bottom of the tent, which was made of boards. In the night-time I would keep my goods in the cellar and in the day-time I would display them on the street. I would buy the boards from men who belonged to the working parties; they would bring them in when they came in at night. There were about three thousand tents or buildings of that sort inside the stockade, as near as I can judge. About half of the area outside the dead-line was covered with tents. We had real estate owners there; every man owned the ground his tent was on. There were some real estate agents for the purpose of buying and selling lots. They would buy lots whenever they could find them for sale, and pay for them according to the locality. I bought a lot on a side street, six feet square, and gave a dollar for it. I bought another on a principal street, also six feet square, for which I gave five dollars. There was not anything on it. I erected a shanty in both places. I bought the boards, which were for sale there every day. There were lumber merchants there. I occupied the shanties. I occupied them for stores and for dwelling both.

There were gamblers there; quite a number of them. They would deal faro, honest john, euchre, seven up, and poker. There was an organized gang of gamblers there; also some detached gamblers who would make use of tents during the day-time to gamble in, and who would have runners hunting out men who wanted to gamble. There was a great deal of money won and lost every day; there were a good many "chuckle-up" dealers, men who had a little board with numbers on, and boxes of dice. There was money there, so that that could be made profitable; I should judge there were a hundred "chuckle-up" dealers on the main street, and they had a crowd around them at all hours of the day.

There was a great deal of suffering there on account of exposure to the weather. I cannot say that anybody suffered from hunger. The rations that I got when I first went there were sufficient for me to live on; after the first week I did not eat the rations at all. If anybody had money there he could get what he wanted to eat. There were about a thousand dealers, stores and such like, there I think.

[To the Court.] The adjutant's name was Selman; he was a Confederate officer. He belonged outside; he had a board shanty erected inside, and had two Federal prisoners to take charge of it. That was the sutler's storehouse. He would have large quantities of flour, tobacco, beans, and peas, salt and rice, and small quantities of onions, potatoes, apples, and such things. Things that were liable to spoil would be brought in in small quantities, and anything not liable to spoil would be brought in in large quantities. I would obtain grapes by the quart every day.

There were at least four hundred wells and springs in the camp. The water was always plentiful. The water was very clear and good until the month of June. During June the water was very muddy.

Q. How did they get water out of the wells?

A. There were strings and ropes in the camp, and boot-legs were cut up and leather strings made. There were buckets; six buckets were issued to each squad of ninety men, and there were also buckets for sale. All the buckets that were wanted could be obtained for money. There was one man there who made bogus greenbacks; followed it as a business; he made a living at it; he had men to pass them off at so much a dollar. Those greenbacks would be thrown over the stockade to the guards in exchange for goods. He manufactured them with a green and a red pencil and paper. I have seen some of them; I had one passed on myself, a ten-dollar bill. None of these men were ever tried or punished. The making of them was countenanced because it was for the benefit of the prisoners.

It is hardly necessary to look back over the testimony of these twelve witnesses. Most of them were in some way favored by their keeper and showed a willingness to shield him so far as they could. The reader, however, will fail to find in their testimony, any facts diminishing the force of the evidence which unerringly described the actual conditions surrounding the prisoners and located the responsibility for these conditions. No one can attach the slightest credence to Fechtner's testimony. It is at variance with all the evidence and describes an utterly impossible condition in the prison. It must strike the reader as remarkable that counsel would submit to the court an account so grotesque and unbelievable.

CHAPTER X.

TREATMENT OF PRISONERS (CONTINUED)—CRUEL AND INHUMAN PUNISHMENTS INFLICTED—BALLS AND CHAINS USED AS MEANS OF PUNISHMENT—PRISONERS CONFINED IN THE STOCKS AND LEFT EXPOSED TO THE WEATHER—THE "DEAD-LINE" AND ITS ATTENDANT PERILS—FEROCIOUS DOGS USED TO HUNT DOWN ESCAPING PRISONERS—PRISONERS TORN AND MUTILATED BY THESE DOGS—PRISONERS DIE FROM EFFECTS—IMPURE AND DEADLY VACCINE MATTER USED FOR VACCINATION OF THE PRISONERS, CAUSING MANY HORRIBLE DEATHS—WIRZ BOASTS OF HIS SERVICE TO THE REBELLION IN SLAYING PRISONERS—REVOLTING MANNER OF HANDLING AND BURYING THE DEAD—TESTIMONY OF REBEL WITNESSES CONFIRMS TESTIMONY OF WIRZ'S CRUELTY TO PRISONERS—REPORT ON PRISONS BY UNITED STATES SANITARY COMMISSION AND COMMITTEE OF HOUSE OF REPRESENTATIVES.

IN the preceding chapters evidence has been presented bearing upon the charge of conspiracy, more particularly in respect to the general management of the prison. Attention will next be given to the more personal treatment of prisoners by Wirz. It serves to emphasize the guilt of the persons responsible for retaining him in control, when, as we shall see, such treatment consisted of cruel and inhuman punishment inflicted for light and trivial causes and in violation of the laws and customs of civilized warfare. The system of control and discipline of the prison, in its entirety, must be the measure by which guilt or innocence is to be adjudged. I have endeavored to show upon what evidence the court found the parties named in charge 1, to be guilty as charged; of "conspiring to destroy the lives and injure the health of Union soldiers, by confining the prisoners in unhealthy and unwholesome quarters, by exposing them to the inclemency of the winter and to the dews and burning sun of summer; by compelling the use of impure water, by furnishing insufficient and unwholesome food; by neglecting to furnish tents, barracks or other shelter for their protection from the inclemency of winter or the burning rays of the sun in summer; by neglecting to provide proper lodging, food or nourishment for the sick, or necessary medicines and medical attendance for the restoration of their health, and permitting the sick to languish and die for want of proper care and treatment; by permitting the bodies of the dead to remain in the prison among the emaciated sick and languishing living, until the said bodies became loathsome

CRUEL AND INHUMAN TREATMENT.

and filled the air with fetid and noxious exhalations, thereby greatly increasing the unwholesomeness of the prison." The reader is to judge whether, in the foregoing chapters, these specifications have been proved. Evidence will now be given in support of the further specification to charge 1, namely—"That the prison keeper, in pursuance of the general design, subjected the prisoners to cruel and unusual punishment upon slight and trivial pretenses, by fastening large balls of iron to their feet, and binding large numbers of the prisoners closely together with large chains about their necks and feet, and being so confined subjecting them to the burning rays of the sun; that he confined them in stocks, often without food or drink, for hours and even days, by reason whereof many sickened and died; that he established a dead-line within the stockade about twenty feet from the inner face thereof, which was marked by insecure and shifting stakes and strips of boards, and at places an imaginary line, and gave orders to the guards to shoot any persons who might touch, fall upon, or under, or cross said dead-line, by reason of which many persons were killed; that he used and kept ferocious dogs, dangerous to life, to hunt down prisoners who made their escape and encouraged said beasts to seize, tear and mangle the bodies of fugitive prisoners, whereby many were slain; that he used poisonous vaccine matter for the vaccination of said prisoners, whereby many died."

Reserving for, the present the summing up of the evidence, a phase of the case is approached, less sweeping in its resultant mortality but none the less significant of the prevailing spirit and apparent motive which actuated the perpetrators of the crimes charged against them.

It will not be found practicable to group the evidence as to any particular form of cruelty or punishment to which prisoners were subjected by Wirz or by his orders, nor can the witnesses be conveniently classified. Neither will attempt be made to give all the evidence introduced by the prosecution, embracing the subject we are now to consider. Enough testimony will be shown, however,—much of it by witnesses who were in the rebel service,—to support the specifications above alluded to. Some of the witnesses who will be quoted testified on other matters as already shown.

TESTIMONY OF COLONEL GIBBS.

Colonel Gibbs, of the Confederate army, whose previous testimony will be remembered, testified:[1]

---
[1] Record, p. 22 et seq.

Q. Did you ever know him [Wirz] to interfere in any way with the hospital?

A. I never knew him to interfere with the medical treatment of the prisoners in the hospital. The only instance of interference I have ever known was the punishment of a paroled man, employed as a nurse, I think, who had failed to report the escape of a prisoner.

Q. What did Captain Wirz do with him?

A. The man was put in the "stocks" for a little while, till Dr. James interfered and demanded his release.

I know of there having been established a dead-line at the prison. I do not know if Captain Wirz had anything to do with the construction of it. Its object was to keep the prisoners from approaching the stockade. I cannot tell what Captain Wirz's orders were in regard to it. I presume there were orders, but do not know what they were. I never heard them. I never gave any, and I never heard Wirz give any. The existing regulation at all the military prisons I know of was that any one crossing the dead-line was to be shot; I believe that was the regulation at Andersonville.

I know that there were dogs kept at the prison. They were intended, on the escape of prisoners, to track them, so that they could be recaptured. They were used in that way. I do not know how they were subsisted, except in this; that after the prison became almost empty of prisoners, when there were none left but a few sick, the dogs were subsisted by corn meal furnished by the commissary. I heard they were mustered into the Confederate service as horses, but I do not know of my own knowledge that they were. A man named Turner had them in charge; I do not know his given name, or what became of him.

I have seen at the prison an instrument called "the stocks." The prisoner did not tell me anything about the use of them; he never spoke to me about them at all. I do not know of any man being put in them, except the one of whom I spoke.

The prisoner never told me about any other instrument of torture or discipline used for the purpose of enforcing discipline. There was a ball and chain at the place. I have heard him speak of an instrument called the "chain-gang." He said there had been such a gang at Andersonville.

Q. Do you know who was in the habit of giving orders in that prison for executing any sentence?

A. I do not know of any sentence having been pronounced.

Q. Do you know who put in the stocks the man you spoke of?

A. It was done by order of Captain Wirz; I know he was not ordered to do it by any superior officer.

The hounds were in charge of a man named Turner; they were certainly not bloodhounds according to my understanding of what bloodhounds are; I think they were ordinary plantation dogs, a mixture of hound and cur, and anything else—the ordinary plantation dogs; I think there were about six or seven kept there; they were not kept in the prison, but about an eighth of a mile from it, in a building which had been used as soldiers' quarters; I believe they were a part of the discipline of the prison; I do not know by whose order the dogs were kept there; I do not know who established them there at all.

Q. Did you ever know of Captain Wirz giving any orders in reference to them?

A. Mr. Turner was under the orders of Captain Wirz.

Q. Would he not have been under the orders of any other person who was in Captain Wirz's place?

A. That I cannot say; I could not say under whose orders he might have been before I went there.

Q. You never knew of Captain Wirz using them at all?

A. I never knew of his using them himself; I know that Mr. Turner, who kept them, was under Captain Wirz's orders.

Q. Was Mr. Turner a person in the employ of the prison?

A. He was a detailed soldier.

Q. How large dogs were they?

A. They were of various sizes, little and big.

Q. Were they ferocious dogs or were they harmless?

A. I do not think they were harmless dogs.

Q. Were they dangerous dogs?

A. I do not know about that.

Q. Were they anything more than the ordinary farm dog?

A. They were the ordinary plantation dog.

Q. Not all ferocious or dangerous?

A. Well, I do not know about that.

TESTIMONY OF DR. BARROWS.

Dr. A. V. Barrows, a paroled prisoner, detailed for duty in the hospital, testified:[1]

I had in my ward cases of vaccination. I had what I call vaccine sores; they were in the arms usually; sometimes in the axilla. They were the result of vaccination, and had every symptom of "secondary" syphilis, in my opinion. A person can be impregnated with that disease by inoculation; it is so put down in medical history. I should say I have seen two or three hundred cases of that description in the course of my stay there. The sores were as large as my hand, and were produced by vaccination. In my opinion, the matter used must have been impure. I considered it as poisonous, judging from the effects and results; there was every appearance of "secondary" syphilis in the sores. Amputations were necessary from that cause, and I do not remember of one living; there may have been, but I do not remember such a case at the present time. I have seen men die from the effects of that vaccination in the months of June, July, and August; more particularly, 1864. I have had conversations with the surgeons about that matter, and some of them have admitted that, in their opinion, it was poisonous matter. I do not know that I called Dr. White's attention to it specially. I was not considered as a privileged character there, and had not opportunities to report. He had means of knowing it, and must have known it; he visited the hospital very often.

The "stocks" is a frame about six feet high, with boards that shut together, leaving just room enough for a man's neck, and arranged so that his arms are

---

[1] Record, p. 45 et seq.

fastened at full length each way, and his feet just touch the ground. I have seen cases where the men could have the privilege of standing on their feet with their whole weight on the feet; and I have also seen them where they could merely touch the ground with their toes. I have seen men punished with the stocks both ways. There was a different kind of stocks from those I have described. There was one kind for putting the men's feet in the stocks, and balls and chains on their hands, with their feet elevated. The men would be lying, or I do not know but they might sit up. I do not remember any other description of stocks but that.

I have seen six men in the chain-gang, and I remember seeing eighteen men in it at one time; a heavy chain ran from one to the other, and round their necks, chaining them all together in a circle as it were. They were connected with handcuffs on their hands, and balls and chains to their feet, and those chains running from their feet connected in some way with the circular chain that ran from one to the other. That is as near as I can describe it. A 32-pound ball was attached to the chain, or a smaller ball, perhaps ten or twenty pounds. I am not able to state the exact size. The prisoners were confined in the chain-gang at all hours of the day. I have known of some men being there for a week, and some two weeks, at different times. The time would vary. The men would have to be there as long as Captain Wirz saw fit to let them remain there. They were without shelter in the sun or rain. The effect upon the men at best must be to weaken them—reduce their strength. I cannot testify that I saw any prisoners die from being confined in the chain-gang. I have no doubt of the fact, although I did not see the men die.

I have seen the hounds used at the prison. I think the first time I saw them was in the forepart of the month of June, 1864. At that time some one had made his escape from the hospital. They were brought to the hospital and taken round the hospital to see where the man went away, and they took the trail, and caught the man, and he was brought back and put into the stocks. I have seen Captain Wirz on horseback with the party who were running the hounds. I could not say that he was running them. Turner had command of them, and I have seen Wirz order the men off—I mean the men who had charge of the hounds. I have heard him give orders to Sergeant Smith, I think his name was, to start the hounds, as some one had got away from the hospital, or something to that effect, at a good many different times.

I remember a man making his escape from the hospital in July, and being overtaken by the hounds; a large portion of his ear was torn off, and his face mangled, and he was afterwards brought into the hospital. That man got well. This was in July or August, 1864; I do not remember the exact date. I remember, also, that, at the end of August, or in September, 1864, a man who had been bitten badly by the dogs in trying to make his escape, was brought into my ward and died. The wound took on gangrene and he died. He was a Union prisoner. I am not certain whether he was trying to escape from the stockade or the hospital. I cannot state the exact date when he died. It was either the last of August or the forepart of September. If my memory serves me right, I should say he died four or five days after he was torn by the dogs. I know the wound took on gangrene and he died. I do not think he died di-

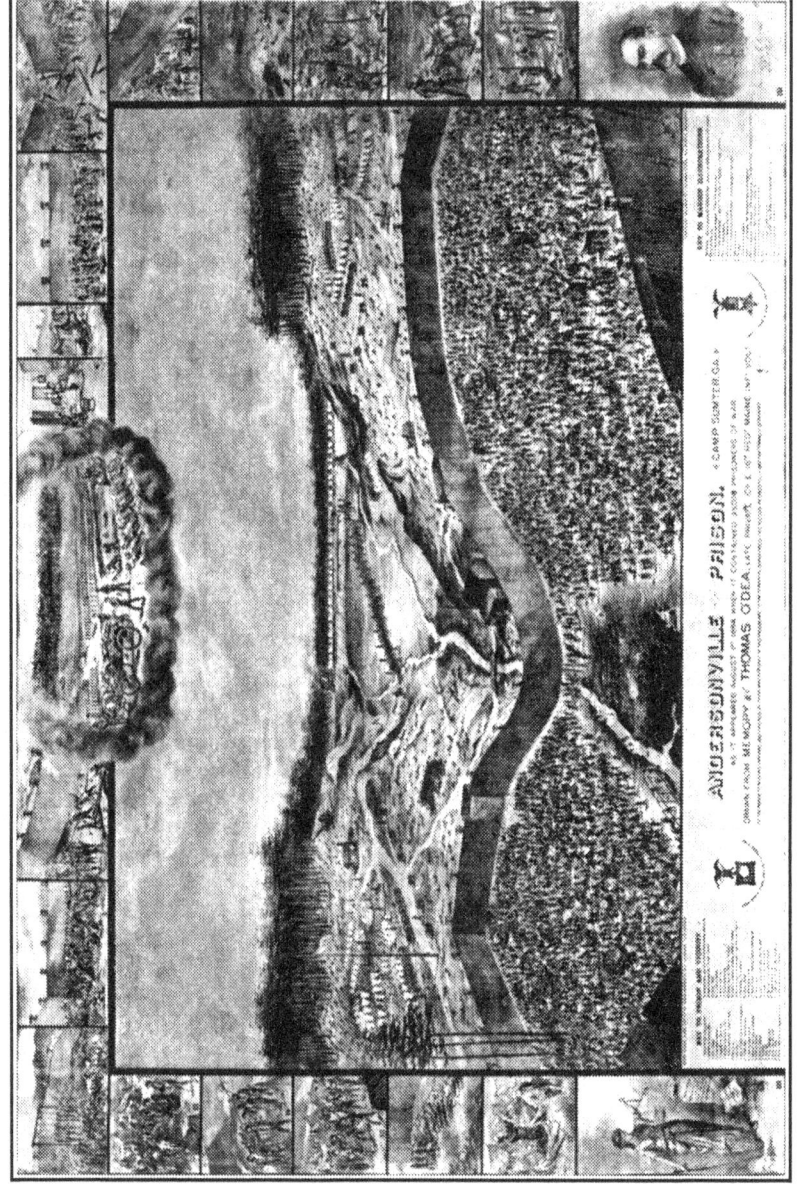

rectly from the effects of the wound. I think he did indirectly—it was from the effects of the gangrene. The gangrene was manifested in the wound, and in no other part. He was bitten through the throat on the side of the neck, and gangrene set in, and he died. The gangrene was the result of the bite, in my opinion.

I have often heard Captain Wirz tell the guard at the hospital, that if any of those "Yanks" tried to get away to shoot them. We had no dead-line established there. I remember one of our soldiers being shot in the hospital. He was a man from my ward; I don't remember his name. It was in August, 1864. He was cold. There was a fire inside the enclosure on the south part of the hospital. It was swampy there, and there was no ground for the guard to stand on, and they were stationed inside the hospital at one portion of it. Where this shooting happened the board fence came down to the swamp, and there the guards were on the other side. This was a patient in my ward. He got up to go warm himself by this fire beside the fence, perhaps five or six feet from it. A Confederate soldier put his gun barrel through the fence and shot him, breaking his thigh. His limb was amputated by Dr. White. Within five to seven days he died. He was shot inside of the hospital. This happened some time in August, 1864, I think.

I remember once, when we were expecting a raid from Kilpatrick, I was up at Captain Wirz's headquarters; he was standing by the battery; I heard him give orders to the gunners if the prisoners huddled together in a heap in the stockade to fire the artillery upon them; that was at the time of Sherman's march, about the time he took Atlanta; there was a good deal of excitement in the stockade as well as out; the troops were drawn up in line around the stockade all the time; there were from 33,000 to 36,000 prisoners there at that time, as I understood; it was difficult for the prisoners to avoid being huddled together; there were so many that when they lay down at night they would cover every foot of the ground; that, I believe, was before the stockade was enlarged; it was enlarged some two acres; I will not be positive whether it was before or after; but previous to its enlargement, the stockade was terribly crowded, so that the prisoners, when they lay down, would cover the whole space, I think.

I know about rations being cut off from prisoners in the stockade. I remember being at the bake-house or cookery when I heard of it. Some of the men had been trying to tunnel out. I think the whole thirty thousand prisoners were deprived of rations until these men could be found out. They were twenty-four hours without rations at that time, and there was a great deal of disturbance in relation to it.

When I first went there, the dead were carried from the hospital over to the outer gate of the stockade, where they were laid, lying in a row, three or four rods from the front entrance. Those who died in the stockade during the night were brought out the next morning, and from there they were hauled to the burying ground. I cannot tell you exactly how long the bodies were allowed to remain there. They were not hauled away immediately. For instance, if dead bodies were taken out at night they remained there over night till the next morning. As to the dead-house at the hospital, I remember at one time some dead bodies lying there some three days. I made a complaint to Dr.

CRUEL AND INHUMAN TREATMENT. 247

Cridelle, who commanded the division in which my ward was, and he made a complaint to higher authorities, I do not know to whom, and the bodies were hauled away. The stench was terrible; worse than any dissecting room I was ever in. It was in August, and was very hot weather. I could plainly discover the effect of it upon the atmosphere of my tent, which was ten or fifteen rods from the dead-house. I called the attention of a number of surgeons to it, Dr. Kilpatrick, Dr. Cridelle, and others. I think Dr. Cridelle entered the complaint to higher authorities. I think that is the only time I ever knew dead bodies to remain there such a length of time. I have known of persons who died in my ward in the night and were not found perhaps till next morning. Often in making my morning call through my ward I have found men dead, lying beside a comrade asleep. It was a very common occurrence in the hospital. I do not know how it was in the stockade. I remember when there have been as many as from seventy-five to one hundred who died during the day in the stockade, and who were never taken to the hospital. That was in the month of August. These men died without coming outside the stockade. There were surgeons who went to the outer gate, and who were called stockade surgeons. Those who were able to come out to that gate received medical treatment, as far as the medical officers would give it to them.

At the time when they were removing the prisoners from Andersonville to Savannah, I suppose, and other places, I was up at Captain Wirz's headquarters one day; they were taking the prisoners from the stockade to the railroad; I don't remember the month; there was one man who was sick, unable to walk, and he fell back; I could not hear Captain Wirz's language to him, but I saw Captain Wirz knock him down and stamp on him; I think it was in September, 1864; he had a revolver, but I could not say whether he struck him with his revolver or his hand; I was perhaps four rods from him.

I remember hearing Captain Wirz make the remark that he was of more service to the Confederate Government, by being in command of that prison, than any four regiments at the front.

TESTIMONY OF BOSTON CORBETT.

Boston Corbett, a Federal prisoner, testified:[1]

I observed outside the stockade some forts, some guns near the headquarters, and around the building near the headquarters I noticed several men with heavy balls and chains. They were exposed to the heat of the sun. The heat was so great that I have the marks upon my shoulder yet.

I have seen the stocks when I went to help to carry a comrade to sick-call, but I do not recollect seeing any one put in them. They were exposed to the sun so that any one in them would have to be exposed to the heat of the sun.

I know of hounds having been kept there for hunting and recapturing prisoners who tried to escape. In the month of October, 1864, we were allowed in certain instances to go outside the stockade, under rebel guard to bring in wood for fuel. For some months previously we had not been allowed such a privilege. I told some of my comrades that the first time I got outside the stockade I should try to escape. Being one of a party of twenty who went out in that way, after going

---
[1] Record, p. 72 et seq.

some short distance from the stockade, perhaps half a mile (more or less), I watched an opportunity and made my escape from the guards. I got some short distance and secreted myself. While I was there they came in pursuit of me, but my hiding-place was sufficiently secure, and they could not find me, although I heard my name called and heard men passing close by me. I lay there perhaps an hour or two, when I heard the yelping of dogs in the distance. The man with the hounds evidently thought that I was further off, and he had taken them to a considerable distance. I heard them in the distance; then nearer and nearer, till they finally approached me, and one actually rubbed his nose against my face. I was ready for a spring, and intended to grapple with him; but the dogs, instead of tearing me, made a circle and kept running about me until the hunter came. He immediately called the dogs off and told me that I would have to go back with him. He put up his pistol and talked pretty clever to me. He said, "The old captain told me to make the dogs tear you, but I have been a prisoner myself and know what it is to be a prisoner, and I would not like to do that." Speaking kindly to me, he took me back to headquarters. The first question of Captain Wirz was, "Why did you not make the dogs bite him?" evidently showing that he had given the order which the man had told me he got. The answer of the man showed me that he was under the command and inferior to Captain Wirz. He replied, "I guess the dogs hurt him enough," and that seemed to satisfy Captain Wirz, who ordered me to be taken back to the stockade.

That dead-line was a slight wooden railing, about the height of this railing, [some three feet]; it was on little upright posts, running inside of the stockade, about twelve or fifteen feet from it, as I thought then; but I have heard since that it was further than that—that it was twenty feet; I judged myself that it was from twelve to fifteen feet. At the place where the stream entered the stockade the dead-line was broken down for some weeks, and during that time there were several men shot there. I have seen several carried away from there who were said to have been killed in that way. The horrors of that prison were so great that one man went over the line, and refused to leave it until he was shot dead. So great was the horror and misery of that place that I myself had thoughts of going over that dead-line to be shot in preference to living there. But it immediately occurred to my mind that it was a Christian's duty to bear whatever was thrown upon me, otherwise I should have undoubtedly gone over—preferring death to life. I think that in every case of shooting I knew of they were men who had to go to that place to get water. The nearer to the stockade the clearer the water was, consequently men would go in search of it as far as they dared to go to get clear water; and, in some cases, they would get on the line without knowing it, because there was no actual line on the spot, and they would have to look to the right or to the left to see where the line ought to be. I believe that, in many cases, new prisoners who had not been warned about the dead-line crossed it, and were shot without knowing where the dead-line was, as no warning would be given except, as I have said, by our own men. I used to make it a particular portion of my business when new prisoners came to show them the dead-line, because when I went there at first myself I would have been shot if one of our own men had not dragged me back.

I have been within hearing of the sentinels who shot men on that line or passing it. I never heard them halt a man, or give him any intimation. The instance that occurs to my mind is this: one of the rebel sentinels had just shot one of our men; one of the other prisoners seeing it, remonstrated with him, threatening retaliation if ever he got a chance; the rebel hastily reloaded his piece, took aim at the man, and told him if he heard another word out of his head he would shoot him dead; whereupon, of course, the man said no more. I do not recollect ever hearing the sentinels say anything in reference to their orders. I do not know the number of prisoners I have seen killed or shot by the sentinels on duty. I often, very often, heard the report of a musket. I knew by what was said that a man was shot, but I did not see it; but I saw several cases myself. It was a very common occurrence.

TESTIMONY OF MARTIN E. HOGAN.

Martin E. Hogan, of the 1st Indiana Cavalry, testified:[1]

I saw hounds that were used about there; I have been captured myself and brought back by them—not, however, by the hounds used in that hospital—I was brought back by an outside pack of hounds. They were patrols of hounds around the stockade for eighteen miles. The pack there I saw every morning. They were under the charge of a man named Turner. I have seen the prisoner when they were trying to strike the trail of escaped prisoners, riding around on his gray mare and assisting.

I escaped from the prison about the 8th of October, and was captured about two days afterwards and brought back. After some of the most profane abuse from Captain Wirz that I ever heard from the lips of man, I was ordered into the stocks. I was fastened at the neck and ankles and left for sixty-eight hours without any food. I got food, but I heard him give the order that I should not have any. Comrades who were paroled stole the food to me. I have seen very many in the stocks. There were three comrades with me when I tried to escape, and they were fastened in the stocks at the same time that I was. I have seen men in them for various offenses. I have seen one man put into the stocks for being abused by a Confederate, and because he had manhood enough to assert his rights. I did not see any chain-gang there; that was before I arrived there.

TESTIMONY OF JOSEPH D. KEYSER.

Joseph D. Keyser, 120th New York, a prisoner from February, 1864, testified:[2]

I have seen Captain Wirz at his office. I have frequently heard him give orders to the guard to shoot anybody who passed over the dead-line. I have seen men immediately after they were shot. I have seen the sentinels who shot them immediately after they had shot them. My reason for supposing they had shot them was, because I knew of no fire-arms being in the hands of our prisoners around where the men lay who were shot. In one instance—I think it was in April or May, 1864—we had received our express-boxes from the North, and some of the

---

[1] Record, p. 88 et seq.
[2] Record, p. 95.

men had thrown out under the dead-line pieces of mouldy bread and cake. This man had one hand on the dead-line, and was reaching under to obtain some of those pieces of mouldy bread or cake to eat, and was fired on by the guard and shot through the head. He was killed instantly. He was on the north side of the stockade; his body lay partly under the dead-line after he was shot. In the other case I did not see the man shot, but I saw him immediately after he was shot. He was brought to the hospital; he had been shot by one of the guard, it was said. I did not see him shot. I did not see him on the ground before he was taken up—not until he was taken to the hospital.

I have seen a pack of hounds at that prison. I have seen Captain Wirz and a man named Turner bring them down to the hospital and start them round it, to see whether they could find the trail of any prisoner who had escaped during the night previous. I never saw them attack any prisoner—I never saw any person who had been bitten by them.

As a general thing I thought that Captain Wirz was rather overbearing, and very profane and abusive in his language toward our men, on the slightest provocation. I never saw him buck any man—I have seen men bucked by his orders. I heard the orders given. I have heard orders given for men to be bucked.

Dr. F. G. Castlen, a rebel surgeon on duty at the prison, testified:[1]

I saw one man who had been bitten by the dogs. I saw the dogs bite him. I saw the dogs running down the swamp below my camp. I went down, and when I reached the brow of the hill, I heard the dogs baying; going down, I saw this man up the tree. I heard some one order him down. I don't know who it was. He came down, and I saw the dogs seize him. Captain Wirz was there with the hounds.

The prisoners were being removed to Savannah in August or September. I don't know which. It was the last part of August, or the first part of September, I think. The prisoners, at the time of this assault, were standing in front of Captain Wirz's headquarters. There was not a large crowd around the prisoners. I did not see a large crowd; there were a good many prisoners. There was no disturbance that I saw, except this man falling out of ranks. I was at that spot half an hour, I suppose. Captain Wirz struck the man with his right hand. I do not know whether Captain Wirz was or was not to blame for the awful condition of the prison. I never saw any other acts of violence by Captain Wirz, excepting what I have described. I never knew of any other.

It was about the first of August that I saw Captain Wirz pursue a prisoner with the hounds. He was between quarter and half a mile from the prison. I did not see him set those dogs on that man. I don't know who set them on. I did not see him in the water up to his knees trying to prevent the dogs from biting that man. I did not see him making any attempts to keep the dogs from biting that man. I did not see him seize that dog. I was from twenty to thirty feet from him, I suppose. It was woody in the swamp, but not outside. The man was in the swamp. When he came down from the tree the dogs seized him, and they bit him after he came out of the swamp. I do not know that Captain Wirz set the dogs on him after he came out. I do not know that the biting of the dogs was

[1] Record, p. 108.

accidental. I just saw them bite him. The dogs were common fox-hounds. There were some five or six in that pack, I believe. I don't think I ever saw that pack but once; that was the only time. I know of no other pack but that one.

I have seen the prisoner, Captain Wirz. I do not know what his duties were officially at Andersonville. I saw acts of cruelty committed by Captain Wirz on one or two occasions. At one time the prisoners were being removed, I think to Savannah. One prisoner was out of the ranks; Captain Wirz jerked and struck him, I think, once or twice; don't remember how many times, but I think once or twice.

TESTIMONY OF ANDREW J. SPRING.

Andrew J. Spring, private in the 16th Connecticut Volunteers, was taken to Andersonville in May, 1864. He testified:[1]

I saw the hounds exercised; I saw them several times when they were taking men's trails, but I saw them one time when they caught a man; I think it was about the last of August or the first of September that I saw a man who had been brought in by Captain Wirz, and this man Turner, who had charge of the dogs. The man was bitten very badly. Captain Wirz went over the hill. The man was brought around by the bakery. I was well acquainted with the guard, at least by sight, and I asked him where the man was caught. He said he was caught over here by Captain Wirz and Turner, the man who had charge of the hounds; that the man was in a tree and was shaken down out of it.

I saw a chain-gang there; I have seen them every day; there were thirteen of them in it at one time; they were in two ranks; each man had a chain and shackle around each ankle, a chain going from the front side of the ankle to the next one before him, both legs shackled so that they could step but eight or ten inches at a time. The men had to keep step with each other. Each man had a small ball (I do not know the weight of it) outside the leg, which he had to carry in his hand when he traveled, and also a 64-pound ball to every four men. There was a large shackle around the neck with a large chain, much larger than that fastened to the legs, around their necks, reaching around the circle. I have known one man to be reduced so low that he was taken from there and sent to the hospital; I cannot tell his name; I cannot tell what date; he was taken to the hospital and soon after died. I should think this was some time about the middle of August. These men were put in the chain-gang for trying to make their escape.

I saw a man shot there. I never saw the prisoner give orders to shoot men. There was one man shot there on the 15th of May, from the first sentry-box next the south gate. The man who was shot was inside the dead-line, or I suppose he was. I saw the man shot and I saw him after he was shot. I was on the north side of the stockade. I saw the smoke of the gun and went directly over. The man lay inside the dead-line. About the time I got over there Captain Wirz was in the sentry-box with the guard. Directly after that Captain Wirz came inside the stockade. He drew out his revolver and swore he would shoot all the men there if they did not get away from the gate, and the men scattered. I do not know that I saw any communication between Captain Wirz and the

---

[1] Record, p. 112 et seq.

sentinel. When he stood in the sentry-box he was close to the sentinel; the sentry-box was not more than four feet square. I saw another man shot there. A short time after that—perhaps six or eight days—there was a man who was asleep under his blanket in the middle of the day. The stockade being so crowded, he had to lie near the dead-line. This man, while he was asleep rolled over under the dead-line. As soon as he rolled under it he was shot. That was in May, I think, from the 20th to the 25th. The ball went into his back and killed him instantly. I do not think he knew what hurt him. I do not know his name. I did not see the prisoner at that place then. The ball struck the first man I spoke of in the temple and went down into his breast. He was taken off to the hospital, which was then inside the stockade, and he died on his way to the hospital. He was not a sound man; he was a cripple, a one-legged man.

I have seen our darky prisoners hauled up there and receiving from fifty to seventy-five lashes a number of times; [to the Court:] I mean our negro soldiers. I can speak of one of them in particular; one of them was sick and refused to go to work. The man who had charge of the gang at that time—I forget his name—reported the matter to Captain Wirz. Captain Wirz came along and ordered the negro to be taken up to the stocks and whipped; I forget the number of lashes the man got; I saw them given to him. I believe that the man who whipped him was named Humes; he was generally called quartermaster, but was nothing but a private soldier, as I understood, to issue rations from the bakery to our men in the stockade. He used to go in with the wagon and issue the rations.

TESTIMONY OF NAZARETH ALLEN.

Nazareth Allen, a rebel soldier on duty at Andersonville, testified:[1]

I have seen the stocks, and seen men in them; I have seen several put in the stocks, and some ten or twelve in the chain-gang; I know that one prisoner died in the chain-gang or stocks; I won't be certain which, but I think in the stocks; I think it was some time in August, 1864; I do not know what his sickness was; he appeared to be sick when I saw him; I saw him only once or twice, and afterwards I saw him dead; I don't recollect how long afterwards; I was passing there almost every day for several days; I cannot say how long he was confined in the stocks; there were several in the stocks; I do not know why this man was placed in the stocks; I think it was for trying to escape. The stocks were between Captain Wirz's headquarters and the stockade, on the road you would take in going to the stockade.

Once I saw a prisoner step out from the ranks to speak to Captain Wirz for an exchange into a mess, when they were counting them out; he had made an agreement with one of his fellow prisoners to go into the other mess. He lacked one or two of getting to him, and he stepped out to speak to him. Captain Wirz ordered him back and threatened to shoot him. He did not shoot him; he threatened to shoot and he cursed him.

[1] Record, p. 117, et seq.

CRUEL AND INHUMAN TREATMENT. 253

I don't know how many hounds there were; I have seen about eight at a time. They were common plantation hounds; they are hounds trained to run people; I guess these dogs were trained to run people; they ran them. I did not see them trained; they were common-sized dogs, about half as high as this railing [about four feet high]. They were common hounds, such as you find on all the plantations of the South; I think they were nothing more or less. They did not appear to be particularly ugly or savage, more than a common hound, so far as I saw. I never saw them pursuing any one; I have heard them at it; heard them crying in the woods. They made a noise like a hound; I cannot exactly imitate it. I have seen a hound pursue game. I have never heard them cry in the same way when they were not pursuing game as they do while pursuing it. There is a particular sound when they are pursuing; I cannot describe that particular sound; it is a more ferocious sound than when they are pursuing in sport. I never saw a man bitten by those dogs.

TESTIMONY OF CAPTAIN HEATH.

John F. Heath, a rebel officer, testified:[1]

I reside in Macon, Georgia. I have been in the Confederate service. In 1861 I was in the 20th regiment Georgia Volunteers. I was commissary, with the rank of captain. In April, 1864, I was in the Georgia Reserve Corps. I was on duty at Andersonville from May till October, 1864. I know the prisoner; I have seen him at Andersonville. I understood that he commanded the prison at Andersonville. I never received any orders from him directly. I was never on duty at the prison but one day. There were thirteen prisoners sent over from headquarters to be ironed. I think it was in August; I was officer of the day. They were sent over to me from the provost marshal's office, to have them ironed; they were not ironed on that day; I think on the second or third day afterwards twelve of them were ironed. The men were sent over under guard, with an order from Captain Wirz. There was one man chained in the gang of twelve, who was sick at the time he was chained. I could not say to my certain knowledge what became of him. I know that I saw him several days afterwards very sick; every man who was chained with him objected to it. The man had the diarrhœa; I should judge so from the looks of his clothes, and he was very lousy; I could see from a distance the lice crawling over him. His comrades objected to being chained with him, because of his condition. Their objections were not heeded; he was chained with them. I do not know that their complaint ever went to Captain Wirz; they objected to being chained by the side of such a man. He was the last of them I think that was chained. They had to all travel at the same time and for all purposes. I cannot say to my certain knowledge what became of the sick man. I think this took place in the month of August, 1864.

At the time that these thirteen men were to be ironed, one of them got away; we called him "Little Frenchy"; a hound was put upon his track. I ran down to the little swamp, between a quarter and a half mile off. Just as I got to the swamp I heard a shot from a pistol, and I saw the man in a tree. Captain Wirz came up and ordered the man to come down. The man begged the dogs should not be let hurt him. He made the man come down, and with that the

---

[1] Record, p. 121.

dogs rushed at him. I could see the dogs run up and grab him by the legs. Captain Wirz did not try to keep the dogs off from the man; he could have done so. I do not know who fired the pistol; I only heard the report. The prisoner was sent with a gang two days before to be chained. He was not chained afterwards. I saw him two or three days afterwards in the guard quarters, without the chains upon him; I saw him sitting and walking about in there, as I passed. I did not notice his wounds; I was not near enough to him to see whether he had wounds or not.

I have seen Captain Wirz kick two or three prisoners. I cannot tell for what reason, except that he got a little excited. At one time, I think it was when they were moving from Andersonville, I saw him kick a prisoner. To the best of my recollection it was the case of a man who was trying to get out of a squad to which he did not belong. I think it was in September, 1864.

TESTIMONY OF WILLIAM DILLARD.

William Dillard, a rebel soldier on duty at Andersonville, testified:[1]

I guarded twelve prisoners in the chain-gang one day and night. One of them was sick and very low, and had to run out every five or ten minutes, and the others were wanting him turned out of the gang because he wanted to run out so much. I think he was taken out about dark. I cannot say how long he had been in the chain-gang. I know he was in from the morning when I went on guard. He was in a sick condition all that day. I cannot say what sort of a day it was. It was in August. I cannot say what became of the prisoner, except from hearsay. I do not know where he was taken after he was released from the chain-gang. It was all the man could do to stand alone when he was taken away from there. I never saw him after that. I heard what became of him from some of the boys next day.

Hounds were kept there to catch prisoners trying to make their escape and our own men also. I saw them catch a man called "Frenchy." I was walking my post and I suppose some 300 yards off. I saw Captain Wirz and Reid, the provost marshal, and the man with the dogs, hunting up and down before they started on the man's track. After a time the dogs got on the trail and treed the man, and after that I saw Captain Wirz come down and heard a pistol or gun fired and saw the smoke rise. I was more than 300 yards from where they were with the dogs. I heard the men halloo and the dogs making a fuss. I saw the smoke rise from the gun. I could not tell from what person the smoke seemed to rise. It was in the bushes and I could not see. I could not say whether the man was hurt by the dogs only from hearsay. I saw the dogs running down the branch before they treed him. I did not see them when they were at him at all.

I have seen several men in the stocks. I have seen some fastened by their feet and lying exposed to the heat of the sun and to the rain. I saw one man fastened by the neck and with his arms extended, who had no hat on; I do not know how long he was in there. I never saw any one in the stocks when they were sick, that I know of.

[1] Record, p. 124.

CRUEL AND INHUMAN TREATMENT.

TESTIMONY OF CALVIN HUNEYCUTT.

Calvin Huneycutt, a rebel soldier, testified:[1]

I reside in Bibb County, Georgia; I was in the Confederate service from April, 1864, till April, 1865; I was on duty at Andersonville about five months, I reckon; I went there in May, 1864, and stayed until September or October, I believe.

I know Captain Wirz; I have heard him abuse the prisoners and draw his pistol to shoot them; but I never saw him shoot any one. I have seen him kick them, in July, I believe, for not standing up in ranks, when Captain Wirz was counting them off; the man was sick; he looked like it; I do not know what was the reason he did not stand up only that; he was not trying to escape. I have heard Captain Wirz threaten to shoot prisoners at the time he drew his pistol; it was when they were brought there to be put into the stockade; he was counting them off. There was one who did not stand up in the ranks, and the captain drew his pistol and said he would shoot him if he did not stand upright; he kicked him a little, not much; the soldier looked sick; I do not know what was the matter with him.

I recollect the man they called "Frenchy" trying to escape; he was caught by the hounds; I saw him after he was caught; he was torn by the hounds pretty badly, in the leg; I think it occurred in August; I do not know whether he was put in irons; I saw him when he was brought up to Captain Wirz's headquarters. Captain Wirz was with him, as well as I can recollect, and the man who kept the hounds; I saw where the hounds tore the man; it had the appearance of a dog-bite.

I guarded the prisoners in the chain-gang for one or two days and nights; I do not know how long the men were kept in the chain-gang without being relieved; they were in there every time I saw them; I do not know that they were exactly the same men; I do not know how long any one man was kept in the chain-gang; I have no idea; they were kept there while I was on guard; I was on guard twice a day and a night at a time; they were in there during that time; they were not changed during the time; I know of an instance where one of them became very sick in the chain-gang; I know that the rest of the men who were chained to him complained of his being sick and wanted him loosed, he bothered them so much in going out; I do not know how long he was kept in the chain-gang, nor what became of him. I did not see the chains taken off; I do not recollect any others confined in the stocks or chain-gang who were sickly; I think that one of them had six men in it and the other had twelve in it; I recollect that they cut the chains off one prisoner and he got away one night and he escaped, but they caught him and brought him back; I mean the man himself cut off the chains; I do not know of any instance when the rebel authorities had to cut off the chains by reason of their affecting the prisoner.

I saw one of the prisoners whipped; I did not count the strokes, but to the best of my knowledge it was about twenty-five or thirty. I do not know who it was that was whipped; he was a white man, a prisoner of war; I saw a man come from Captain Wirz's headquarters, who took him out and whipped him;

[1] Record, p. 127 et seq.

I do not know his name; he was an officer; the whipping commenced right straight away after he came out; the officer walked down and carried the man off with a couple of guards; I did not hear the officer say anything at the time. He did not say by whose order the man was to be whipped; I was not close to him; I was about thirty yards away; the man was stripped and whipped on the bare skin, right upon his back; he was not tied up; he was whipped with a common size hickory, about four feet long; I do not know whether it was green or seasoned; they afterwards carried the man back and put him in the stocks; I never knew what they did with him after that; the man had blackened himself and tried to escape with the darkies when they went in carrying rations; I do not know of anything that was said at that time.

The prisoners who died were buried in a trench, side by side, with the dirt thrown over them, with no covering, without any box; I should judge the trench was about two or three feet deep; I was standing on post one day when they were taking bodies out; they had been there so long that when they were brought out and put in the wagon they burst, something broke inside, and ran out of their mouths and noses and smelled very badly.

TESTIMONY OF JAMES MOHAN.

James Mohan, a rebel soldier, testified:[1]

I have been in the Confederate service only as a private. I was afterwards elected a second lieutenant in the 3d Georgia Reserves. I was on duty at Andersonville for about five months—May, June, July, August, September, and up to, I believe, the 13th of October, 1864. I was not much around the stockade. I was appointed assistant provost marshal for a time, and my business was with my own men, running up and down the trains, examining passports, etc. I had nothing to do with the prison except sending over prisoners that arrived there, and prisoners that had escaped and were caught and brought to the provost marshal's office. I would send my guard over to Captain Wirz's headquarters with the prisoners by order from the provost marshal. I did not receive any orders at all in regard to the treatment of prisoners. The disposition of them was to turn them over to Captain Wirz; that he had sole charge of them. I received orders on that subject from the provost marshal. He was under General Winder. Captain Wirz was then commander of the inner prison; he had charge of all the prisoners that came down there. I had something to do with putting chains on prisoners. The prisoners were brought from Captain Wirz's headquarters to the provost marshal's office by a guard. The provost marshal ordered me to take charge of the guard up to the blacksmith's shop. I went up there with the prisoners to take charge of the guard, and to see also that the prisoners got their irons on. There was a verbal order on that subject. A sergeant of Captain Wirz came over with the prisoners from his office. It was to see that these men had balls and chains put on them and linked together with a sort of a collar around their neck and a chain attached to it. I took over thirteen men. The collars were not ready that day and I sent the men over again to Captain Wirz's quarters. I told a lieutenant under me to take them over and to state to Captain Wirz that the irons were not ready. Those were

[1] Record, p. 130 et seq.

CRUEL AND INHUMAN TREATMENT.   257

the orders I received from the foreman of the shop—to tell Captain Wirz that the irons were not ready. The next day the men were sent over there, but I did not take them. I saw them coming down the hill with balls and chains on them, linked together.

When I was sending the prisoners over to Captain Wirz's headquarters a young man whom they called "Frenchy" escaped. He was not put in the gang afterwards. The gang consisted of twelve men. In the evening "Frenchy" was recaptured. When this lieutenant who was under me carried the men over it was found that there were only twelve men. Wirz got on his horse and rode over. He said: "that damned Frenchy has escaped again; send for the dogs." The dogs came and got on the trail of him and recaptured him in the woods, or rather by the stream that ran by the stockade. Captain Wirz did not ride off with the dogs; he got off his horse and walked. He went alongside the dogs; that is, when the dogs got down across the stream, the dogs went one way and he went another, along with Captain Reed, the provost marshal, searching for this man. I was standing on a platform at the depot and I saw where he stood, and heard the howling of these dogs around the tree. It seemed as if the prisoner was up there. I did not see him. I looked around again to see where Captain Wirz was and I heard the report of a pistol and saw the flash. I should judge the flash came from Captain Wirz. After firing, they captured the prisoner and took him to the guard tent. I know that he was injured. I saw him a day or two afterwards. His pantaloons were torn on the leg and he looked sickly. I don't know whether his flesh was torn; I did not see. I cannot tell why he was not put in the chain-gang. I heard he was badly bitten from some of my brother officers there, after the affair happened, when we were talking about it. The dogs were common hounds. I believe there were a couple of them called catch-dogs; the others were hounds. The technical name is fox-hound. They call some of them track-hounds there. I believe there are track-hounds and catch-dogs; I am not much acquainted in the dog line. One is very vicious by nature. I don't think the other is very dangerous. The catch-dog is vicious.

I very frequently heard Captain Wirz remark that he wished the prisoners were all in hell and he with them. Sometimes they would offend him or something like that in his office—he would say it if any prisoners would make him angry around his quarters or around the stockade, or anywhere else where he was. There were a large lot of paroled prisoners outside—four or five hundred, I presume. I did not hear him make use of any other remark.

I was officer of the guard when I first went down there. That was before my assignment as assistant provost marshal. I received instructions from Captain Wirz's adjutant at the stockade. He read the instructions to the guard and turned the papers over to me, or when I was relieved the next morning, to the officer who relived me. The instructions in regard to the dead-line were that we were not to allow any of the prisoners to cross it; that if they crossed it they were to be fired on by the sentinels. That was the substance of the instructions. I did not have occasion to observe the condition of the prison very well while I was on duty there; it was a place I never liked to go into.

TESTIMONY OF O. S. BELCHER.

O. S. Belcher, private 16th Illinois Cavalry, was a prisoner from March until September. He testified:[1]

I heard Captain Wirz say that he could kill more Yankees there than they were killing at the front. I suppose he was excited and angry with some of the men who had said something to him. He got so at the last that he dare not come over on our side of the prison at all. He could not come unless he had 300 or 400 men with him.

I saw men shot on the dead-line or crossing it; I have seen a number of men shot. I have seen 25 or 30 killed in that way, shot in different places around the stockade; some were over the dead-line, and some were shot who were not near it.

TESTIMONY OF JAMES K. DAVIDSON.

James K. Davidson, 4th Iowa Cavalry, was a prisoner at Andersonville from March, 1864.[2]

Many prisoners died in the stockade. The hospital was then within the stockade; the dead men were carried on stretchers out to the gate, and from there they were hauled to the graveyard in wagons. Part of the time I was employed outside the stockade chopping wood, and part of the time driving a wagon from the hospital to the graveyard; I drove a wagon to the graveyard a little over a week; not two weeks, I think; there were two teams of us driving; we would each have from 50 to 75 men per day; we would throw them in the wagon just as we would wood; sometimes there were 20 or 25 at a load; we drove the same wagons back to the stockade loaded—sometimes with wood for the prisoners, sometimes with rations. We would go by way of the depot sometimes and get rations in the same wagon in which we carried dead bodies; those were the orders, I believe, from the quartermaster or the man who had charge of the teams; I believe his name was Duncan; I think he was an officer; he had charge of the cook-house.

I have heard Captain Wirz say that he was killing more damned Yankees there than Lee was at Richmond. That was said in August; he was in my wagon at the time; I had been to the graveyard with the dead men.

I have seen men who were starved to death, thousands of them, inside the stockade; I saw men eating food that they took from the ground; I have seen men pick up and eat undigested food that had passed through other men; they would find it all through the camp; it came from men who were not able to go to the slough, and they would find it all through the camp.

I saw the chain-gang; I have seen from twelve to fourteen men in the chain-gang; it was a common thing to see the men in the chain-gang; I never saw men in the chain-gang under a tent; they were kept out in the hot sun; I saw one man die in the chain-gang; I believe he was buried with the iron collar round his neck; this was in August, I think, the first part of the month; I do not know the man's name.

[1] Record, p. 136.
[2] Record, p. 140 et seq.

CRUEL AND INHUMAN TREATMENT.

I saw hounds there; there were six to nine that I saw every morning; they were used for catching prisoners, I suppose; they had them after them several times; there were two kinds of dogs, the hound and the catch-dog, as he was called; I guess he was a bull terrier or something of that kind; he resembled that somewhat; I don't know why he was called a "catch-dog." He was more ferocious than the hounds; I saw one man who had been bitten by the dogs; he was bitten in the legs; the calf of his leg was torn and pretty nearly off; I saw Captain Wirz there at the time; I did not see what became of the man; I don't know whether he died or got well; I do not know his name.

I saw two men shot there by the guards; I do not know the names of either of them; it was down on the east side of the stockade near the branch; the man had been washing his clothes and was hanging them on the guard line to dry; one of the garments blew over the dead-line; he reached through to pick it up, when the guard fired and shot him; I think it was the last of March or the first of April, 1864. The other case happened on the north side of the stockade; the man reached through the dead-line to pick up some crumbs of bread that had been thrown out there, and he was shot; he was killed. The other man was killed instantly; he was shot in the breast; the second man was shot in the head; I do not know his name; I heard shots fired of which I did not see the effects; I suppose the shots were fired by the sentinels; it was a very frequent occurrence.

No conversation at all led to the remark that he was killing more Yankees than Lee. I believe that same morning he had been out with the hounds and caught a man. He told me he was killing more damned Yankees than Lee was killing at Richmond. That was all that was said. I did not make any reply. I did not say anything before he made that remark. I do not recollect whether he said anything to me before he made that remark. It was just a sudden outbreak on his part.

TESTIMONY OF P. V. HALLEY.

P. Vincent Halley testified:[1]

I have been in the military service of the United States, in the 72d New York Volunteers. I was taken prisoner. I was at Andersonville. I arrived there the first or second of March, 1864.

I heard orders about putting prisoners in the stocks or the chain-gang. At one time when some prisoners who had escaped were taken to Captain Wirz's headquarters—I was there at the time—he ordered the men to be taken to the forge and irons put on their feet.

I heard Captain Wirz threaten to shoot a man. I think it was in May. Captain Wirz was in the stockade, and one of the men did not fall in quick enough, and Captain Wirz drew his revolver and threatened to shoot any man who did not fall in when ordered; sometimes he used his right hand. I did not know at the time that anything was the matter with his right hand; he used his right hand as frequently as his left, so far as I saw. I have seen him use his left hand; he wore his revolver on the left side.

I saw a man who had been shot; the first man I saw shot was, I think, on the 10th of May; I am not certain; he was shot while getting some water

---

[1] Record, p. 159 et seq.

260   THE TRAGEDY OF ANDERSONVILLE.

in the stockade. The guard fired on him and shot him in the thigh, I think; I do not know the man's name; it was on the 10th of May, I think; it was at the creek; I cannot say positively whether he died or not, I know that he was severely wounded; part of his body was over the dead-line; he was leaning over to get some cleaner water than was in the stockade; I saw one man in August who had been shot through the brain; he was carried to the hospital; I do not know his name; he was entered on the register "unknown dead." Captain Wirz was not present at the time I saw these men shot; I was once at Captain Wirz's headquarters when the guard was there; he told his guard that the first man who crossed the dead-line to shoot him down.

I knew Captain Wirz there; he took command of the prison about two weeks after I got there; I heard him give orders; I heard him one time send for the keeper of the dogs to put them on the track of prisoners who had escaped; I saw prisoners who had been bitten by the dogs; they were taken to the hospital; they had been recaptured and were brought in there; they had the marks of the dogs on their persons; both of them were bitten about the legs; one of them was bitten severely.

I saw cases of vaccination; I saw, I think, about 150 cases of vaccination, and in many of them after vaccination gangrene set in, and the sores were about three inches in diameter. They varied from an inch to four inches in diameter; in some instances men's arms had to be amputated from that cause; some of the cases of amputation recovered and some did not; I do not remember anything about the proportion of recoveries.

TESTIMONY OF EDWARD S. KELLOGG.

Edward S. Kellogg testified:[1]

I was in the military service of the United States. I was in the 20th New York Regiment. I was captured. I was taken to Belle Island. From thence I was taken to Andersonville. I arrived there the 1st of March, 1864.

I saw the cripple they called "Chickamauga" shot; he was shot at the south gate.[2] He was in the habit of going off, I believe, to the outside of the gate to talk to the officers and the guard, and he wanted to go off this day for something or other. I believe that he was afraid of some of our own men. He went inside the dead-line and asked to be let out. They refused to let him out, and he refused to go outside the dead-line. Captain Wirz came in on his horse and told the man to go outside the dead-line, and went off. After Captain Wirz rode out of the gate the man went inside the dead-line, and Captain Wirz ordered the guard to shoot him, and he shot him. The man had lost his right leg, I believe, just above the knee. They called him "Chickamauga." I think he belonged to the Western army and was captured at Chickamauga. I think that was in May. I will not be certain as to the time.

I saw other men shot while I was there. I do not know their names. They were Federal prisoners. The first man I saw shot was shortly after the dead-line was established. I think it was in May. He was shot near the brook, on

---
[1] Record, p. 161 et seq.
[2] This "Chickamauga" case is mentioned many times and particularly under the charge of murder.

CRUEL AND INHUMAN TREATMENT. 261

the east side of the stockade. At that time there was no railing; there was simply posts stuck along where they were going to put the dead-line, and this man, in crossing, simply stepped inside one of the posts, and the sentry shot him. He failed to kill him, but wounded him. I don't know his name. I saw a man shot at the brook; he had just come in. He belonged to some regiment in Grant's army. I think this was about the first of July or the latter part of June. He had just come in and knew nothing about the dead-line. There was no railing across the brook, and nothing to show that there was any such thing as a dead-line there. He came into the stockade, and after he had been shown his place where he was to sleep he went along to the brook to get some water. It was very dark, and a number of men were there, and he went above the rest so as to get better water. He went beyond the dead-line, and two men fired at him and both hit him. He was killed and fell right into the brook. I do not know the man's name. I saw other men shot. I do not know exactly how many. I saw several. It was a common occurrence.

I saw sanitary stores there. While I was in the hospital I saw some blankets and some pants and shirts; I think very few. They were issued to the men in the hospital-our own men. I saw them on other men than our own men. I saw a pair of pants on a rebel at one time; his name was Dance.

I was in the hospital. I went into the hospital August 6, 1864, and remained there until February 1, 1865. I was bucked six hours at one time while there. There was a man escaped from my ward. I was steward of the 17th ward, and I failed to report the man who escaped. Sergeant Smith came round and called me outside the gate and said that Captain Wirz had ordered him to buck me till dark. This was about nine o'clock in the morning. He proceeded to buck me, and I was left there till three o'clock in the afternoon. There was another man bucked with me; his name was William S. Wood, belonging to the 120th, and master of the ward. He was bucked by Captain Wirz's order.

When they bucked me they took a string and tied my wrists together in the first place; they sat me down on the ground next, put my hands over my knees and put a stick over my arms and under my legs, my hands being tied together. I never saw a man bucked in our army, and I have been in the service four years. I have heard of it. I had no squad. I was steward of the 17th ward in the hospital. The time I was bucked one man got away. Several others got away afterwards. They failed to escape, and were brought back. I did not consider it my duty to report them, but it was the rule. I did not comply with the rule, and for non-compliance I was punished. There were very few in the hospital that were able to run away. I don't know whether there were any.

TESTIMONY OF JOSEPH R. ACHUFF.

Joseph R. Achuff testified:[1]

I have been in the military service of the United States three years and nine months. I was a prisoner at Andersonville about six months. I was taken there on the 28th of March, 1864, and kept there until about the middle of August, 1864. I was taken from Andersonville to Charleston, South Carolina, in August, 1864. I attempted to make my escape while at Andersonville. I

---

[1] Record, p. 163 et seq.

was recaptured by the hounds. Three of us got one rebel to take us out for wood. We gave him twelve brass buttons to take us out. When we got out about a quarter of a mile from the stockade I jumped on his back and the other boys took his gun from him, and off we went. We went to the Flint River, and crossed it five times, and then rowed down the river a piece. We did not know the hounds were after us until we heard them yell. Then we scattered. I ran into the swamp. The first thing I noticed there were five hounds upon me; seven rebels, armed, came up on horseback. They were in sight at the time the hounds came on. They never took off the hounds for about fifteen minutes, and I had to fight the hounds with my fist. I had not even a club, or a chance of getting one. I had no clothes on but a pair of pants made out of two rebel meal sacks. I was bareheaded and barefooted. I fought the hounds with my fists about fifteen minutes. They tried to catch me by the throat, but I kept them off. They caught me by the legs, and I carry the marks there to-day. One of the men on horseback blew a horn, which called the hounds off, and I was marched back afoot. I was taken to Captain Wirz. He ordered me into the stocks. I was put into the stocks with my head fastened by a board, and my arms stretched out. They pretended to have us in the shade, but I was kept in the broiling hot sun. For thirty-six hours I had nothing to eat, and but two drinks of water out of that dirty creek. When I appealed to Captain Wirz about it he told me to dry up, or he would blow my damned brains out, that I deserved to be hung. After I was taken out of the stocks, I was ironed. I had shackles fastened around each leg, an iron ring, and a bar of iron between my legs. This kept my legs separated about eighteen inches, so that I had to shuffle along. There was nothing done to cure my legs. Scurvy fell into the wounds, but still I was kept in irons.

Parties going into the stockade with each other would become separated and lose sight of each other. We would go in there, and when the "nineties" would not be full the men would be scattered among them to fill up these "nineties." That is the way we came not to know, half the time, where our comrades were. They would be carried off to the hospital or carried off somewhere else and we would never see them again. The stockade was the filthiest place that could be imagined. The filth was fully six inches deep. When I went in there it was in the night and was raining. The men were sitting around fires that were no bigger than a spittoon. Maybe there would be a dozen men crouching over such a fire. We thought they were all negroes. They were half naked, with no shelter and with nothing to eat. Some of the men were lying out doors and some were lying in shelter tents on the ground. If they had a blanket they were fortunate; if not, they lay on the ground without any. The water that ran through that stockade a horse would not drink. It was the filthiest stuff, with grease upon it. I complained to Captain Wirz and asked him if he could not stop the grease from the cook-house from being allowed to flow in there. He said it was good enough for me. I made that complaint about the latter part of June. I am not sure about the month.

CRUEL AND INHUMAN TREATMENT. 263

TESTIMONY OF DANIEL W. BUSSINGER.

Daniel W. Bussinger testified:[1]

I have been in the military service of the United States. I was in the 10th Pennsylvania Reserves. I was captured on the 21st of May, 1864, at Spottsylvania Courthouse. I was taken to Libby Prison, and from there to Andersonville, Georgia. I arrived at Andersonville on the 7th of June, 1864.

Captain Wirz was in command of the prison when I went there. The weather was very warm when I got there. We were counted off in front of Captain Wirz's headquarters. It was very warm weather and we were forced to stand out for four hours while the sergeant called the roll and took our names. Some of the boys were sun-struck and fell down and we volunteered to carry them into the shade. Captain Wirz gave orders to the guards that if any man stepped out of the ranks he was to be shot; at the same time we were in want of water, but they would not give us any. I asked some from one of the guards, and Captain Wirz gave orders to the guards that any man who asked for water would be shot. He said they were damned Yankees and did not need any water. When the men fell down and fainted, Captain Wirz said that if it lay in his power he would make the victory complete; that the men who fell down there and fainted deserved to die there.

I heard shots fired into the stockade very frequently. I have heard shots fired over the stockade by men outside of the guards, I suppose. They were not fired at any person, but were fired over the stockade. I never heard Captain Wirz give any orders as to firing into the stockade. I have seen men shot there. In the early part of July one man was shot down there at the run. That was the first case. In the middle of July a man was shot belonging to the 118th Pennsylvania Volunteers. I am not able to give his name. I saw him shot. He was shot at the run getting water. He was killed. Captain Wirz was not present. The man was not on the dead-line; he was getting water. The water that came into the stockade was very greasy, and the man wanted to get the best water he could, and in doing so he approached too near to the dead-line and was shot. That was the first instance I saw. The man was carried to the south gate after he was shot. He remained there about two hours and was then carried off to the dead-house. The prisoner was at the stockade while the man lay there. I did not hear him say anything. I saw a man shot on the 18th of July, in the northeast part of the stockade. I do not know his name. He belonged to the 118th Pennsylvania. He was shot through the hip; he was lying in his tent at night when he was shot. He was carried out next morning to the doctors, and I saw him lying there waiting for his turn to be carried out. He was not dead. I am not able to state whether he died or not. I did not see Captain Wirz there. I saw another man shot by the dead-line. I cannot say at what time. The prisoner was not present. Captain Wirz was present when the first one was brought up to the south gate to be carried out. I did not hear him make any remarks.

The men were very emaciated. I have seen them searching for food that passed through men, not digested, down in the sink and in the marsh. I have seen them searching in the filth that was thrown away; they would pick up

[1] Record, p. 169 et seq.

anything dropped from the wagon that brought the rations, bits of corn bread, or any scraps thrown from the raiders' tents; anything in the way to be eaten was picked up by such men. I have seen them eat this undigested food. They would wash it and eat it.

Two men were buried inside the stockade after the men began to go away. There was one dead man who lay in the barracks about four days. He became putrid and was not carried out. Whose fault it was I do not know. He was buried there.

Another man was buried there very near the raiders' tent; I saw his grave. I am not able to state why these men were buried inside the stockade. I suppose the one who died up at the barracks would have been carried out if the men had not gone away. That was the only way we could get wood, and when the men began to go out the wood became plenty. The man was not in a condition to be carried out when he was buried; his body was decayed. I mean by the raiders' tent, the tent of the desperadoes who infested the camp there, plundering their comrades of rations or anything else they could find. They were some of the men who were afterwards hanged. There was an organized band of them of about five hundred.

TESTIMONY OF H. B. TERRELL.

Horatio B. Terrell testified:[1]

I was in the United States service; in the 72d Ohio Infantry. I was taken prisoner on the 12th of June, 1864, and was taken to Andersonville on the 19th of June, 1864. I have often heard the prisoner use violent language to prisoners when they were being counted off. He said that if more than four damned Yankees got into a rank, he would make four out of them very quick. I remember that he came into the stockade one day during the winter and one of the men showed him his rations of corn bread, and asked him politely if he could not give us a little more. Captain Wirz turned around, drew his pistol and said, "God damn you, I will give you bullets for bread." I do not recollect in what hand he held his pistol. I presume he held it in his right hand from the fact that if he used his left hand, I should have remembered it distinctly.

Our rations were stopped about ten or twelve days altogether when I was at Andersonville, not continuously. They were stopped about the 4th of July, I think for two days.

A good many sick men were not able to go to the swamp, and had their comrades dig holes for them by the side of their tents. In this way a good deal of the ground along the edges of the tents were soon perforated with these holes. This made it unhealthy and spoiled the water to some extent which was in our wells. The whole ground in the swamp was perfectly poisonous from the filth and urine that had accumulated there, and any prisoner having the least scratch on his foot and going there, would get it poisoned, so that his foot would swell up and would gangrene in a short time. Frequently they lost their limbs and sometimes their lives.

The dead-house was at the hospital during the first part of the time I was there. I carried out two men at different times and brought in wood on my re-

---

[1] Record, p. 171 et. seq.

turn. But soon afterwards it was changed and put nearer the stockade, so that we only had to take the dead just outside the south gate, and that cut off the supply of wood. I counted forty-six corpses one day in the dead-house at the hospital. After they moved the dead-house nearer the stockade I saw what I should judge to be from seventy-five to one hundred dead men lying there in the sun. I have seen them carried away in wagons. We could see them plainly from the interior of the stockade when they took them away. About every day they would take them away. One man would go to the heels of a corpse and the other to the head, and they would swing him into the wagon. They would pile them in just like dead hogs from the slaughterhouses. I suppose there were eighteen or twenty to a load.

I never saw any articles of value taken from the prisoners at Andersonville. I know of money being taken by the guards for permitting prisoners to go out. There was money taken about the middle of March, 1865, when an exchange apparently was agreed upon. The rebel sergeants came in, and Selman, the rebel sutler, and Mr. Barr, the rebel quartermaster, and they told the boys that if they would give so much money, they should be the first to go out, and those who gave money were the first men who were taken out for exchange. Some that I know of paid twenty dollars and some paid less. These persons were under Captain Wirz's command. They were in every day to call the roll. These propositions were tolerably open. They did not stand up and proclaim it, but they went to a good many who they supposed had money and told them of it. I know of men who gave money, and I know of men who gave a lot of brass buttons to get out. I do not know of the prisoner having received any for that purpose.

TESTIMONY OF FRANK MADDOX.

Frank Maddox testified:[1]

I belong to the 35th United States (negro regiment). I was at Andersonville, Georgia, as a prisoner. I was there about eleven months. I was taken there April 1, 1864. I left there February 2, 1865. When I was taken there I was put in the stockade and stayed there about two months, until my wounds got well enough to allow me to work. I was then taken out and put to work. I was wounded in the hip and foot. I was wounded at Olustee, Florida. When they took us out of the stockade, they put us to work, pulling up stumps around the stockade, cutting wood, and doing first one thing and then another. We were in and out until the 2d or 3d of September. We were then taken out and put to burying the dead. I did not assist in building the fortifications. We helped to enlarge the stockade. We commenced on that, I think, the 1st of June. I know Captain Wirz, I heard Captain Wirz make threats as to what he would do with us. One morning, I think it was in February, they sent us to the swamp to ditch. It was very cold, and the boys did not want to go. Captain Wirz told the sergeant in charge, if we did not go, to take a club, and kill the last "damned one of us, and let the buzzards eat us." I am speaking of the colored men. My wounds hurt me while I was at work; they had not healed up. I did not complain. I saw no use in complaining. Those who did complain did not get

---

[1] Record, p. 176 et seq.

anything done for them. I heard men complain to Captain Wirz about their sufferings from cold. When I was there in April it was very cold and we had no wood and nothing to lie upon, except the ground. One morning the sergeant asked him to let us out and get some wood. He said he was not going to do it; that he did not care a damn if we all died. The sergeant intimated to us that Captain Wirz gave the men a thirty days' furlough every time they shot a Yankee. He would never treat us boys as Captain Wirz wanted him to treat us. He wanted him to be whipping us and knocking us about, and he did not do it. Captain Wirz ordered him to do it. I have seen him many times when he gave the orders. I looked right at him when the words came out of his mouth. I never saw colored men put in the stocks or the chain-gang. When they wanted to punish them, they put them across a log and whipped them half to death and put them back to work. . . .

Captain Wirz never inflicted any punishment of any kind on me but he did on others. One he had whipped. I was up at his office in the morning to get an order for rations for the boys who would be out at work. He thought I was the man and commenced to curse me. The sergeant told him I was not the man, and called up Isaac Hawkins and asked him what he had been doing. He told him nothing. Captain Wirz hauled back and knocked him to the side of the tent, and told Turner to take him, strip him, and give him five hundred lashes, calling him "a damned Yankee son of a bitch." They gave him two hundred and fifty lashes, and the sergeant who was boss over us, and counted them, told Turner that he had given him five hundred, when he had only given him two hundred and fifty. The man was then loosed, and taken to the blacksmith shop, and had about two feet of chain put on him, and was sent to the graveyard to work, being told that if he stopped five minutes during the day, he would get two hundred and fifty more. The man was whipped on the bare back. He was stripped naked and put across a log, and. they whipped him from his feet up to his head, across his back. They whipped him all over. He was whipped with a leather strap about as wide as my forefinger, attached to a staff about two feet long.

I know of a white man coloring himself and trying to escape. The man came out in the morning when we did. He had blackened himself and intended to get out to work where we were, so that he could get a chance to get away. They found him out, and Captain Wirz told the sergeant to take him, strip him, and give him thirty-nine lashes on his naked back, and he did so. He then ordered the man to be put in the stocks. Captain Wirz said the man had blacked himself to be a nigger, and, God damn him, he would give him a nigger's law. That was thirty-nine lashes. He was whipped, but I don't know whether they put him in the stocks or not. I went off to work.

I saw twelve men in the chain-gang for about a week. They had iron collars on their necks, and the chain connecting them all together, a ball and chain on their feet, and a large ball in between every four men.

CRUEL AND INHUMAN TREATMENT.

TESTIMONY OF JOSEPH ADLER.

Joseph Adler testified:[1]

I was in the military service of the United States two years and nine months; I was a prisoner at Andersonville; I was there from about the middle of March to the 8th of September, 1864; I know Captain Wirz; when I was captured there were seventy-one of us, including a young negro boy; all that is left is about a dozen out of the seventy-one.

I was part of the time in the hospital in the capacity of nurse; I cannot state exactly how long; I think it was two or three months; I went into the hospital in the month of June, and came out of there about three or four weeks before we left Andersonville; I left Andersonville on the 8th of September; while there I had opportunities of observing, from time to time, what was going on outside the stockade; I should judge the sick were treated pretty badly; the majority of the sick men had to lie on the bare ground; the majority of them had no blankets; they had nothing to lie on and nothing to cover themselves with; they had hardly any clothing to cover their bodies with, and most of the time the food furnished them was unfit for them to eat, and consequently they had to go without anything to eat. It rained twenty-four days in June, if I am not mistaken; I know it rained twenty days in succession; at that time there were about 200 men lying out under the open sky without any shelter whatever, without any bedding or blankets, and some of them had nothing on but a shirt and a pair of drawers, and there was no medicine at the time to be given them, and they had no attendance whatever; they had only a little water, and all they had to eat was a little corn-bread and rice soup, that I would not give to a dog. I do not recollect ever seeing Captain Wirz strike or kick any of the sick or anything of that kind; I have heard him use very abusive and insulting language.

I lost a friend while I was attending the hospital there. I made a request of Captain Wirz on that occasion. There was a man by the name of Stevenson, who belonged to the 2d Massachusetts Cavalry, Company A, the same company that I belonged to. He died there. He had respectable clothes on, and seeing that he was a friend of mine whom I had known for a long time, I did not, as I usually did, take off his clothes and give them to the living, but I left them all on his body, and requested Captain Wirz to let the clothes remain on the body, and he told me he would; after the body was carried out of the hospital, Captain Wirz went with the wagon, and two Confederate soldiers took the clothes off the man and they buried him stark naked, without anything, not even a shirt on his body, Captain Wirz did not make use of any expressions at that time, that I can recollect.

I heard complaints made to Captain Wirz with regard to the condition of the rations and other things. Before I was detailed to go into the hospital, I went to see a friend of mine who was in another part of the stockade. He was almost dead with diarrhoea, in fact so weak that he could hardly get up alone. He had very little clothes on, only a shirt and a pair of drawers, and he had to lie on the ground with his drawers down. He was not able to go to the place where we went to do our business. I and seven other persons had dug a tunnel in

[1] Record, p. 181 et seq.

order to make our escape if we could. There was another man, a Union prisoner, who had found out that we had dug the tunnel and were ready to start that evening; he went to Captain Wirz and told Wirz if he would give him something to eat he would tell him some good news. The captain said he would, and then he told the captain. The captain came in with six Confederate soldiers and filled up the tunnel. After the tunnel was filled up he went out of the stockade and came right back again on a gray horse. He had a loaf of corn bread in his hand, and as he went past the sick man that I was with the sick man saw him and got up as well as he could and said, "Captain, please give me something to eat, a piece of that bread; I am hungry; I have had nothing to eat for two days; I was too sick to go and get my rations, and there was no one to get them for me." The captain had a little riding whip in his hand, but the end of it was rather thick, and he turned round and struck the man over the head with it. The man fell right on the ground and swooned away, and it was an hour before he came to himself again. The next day he was carried to the hospital, and two days after I heard he was dead. Afterwards, when I was detailed in the hospital, I tried to find him out but could not. I was told he was dead.

I saw men in the stocks. I know of one man who was lying senseless in the stocks for three hours before they would take him out. Captain Wirz was nowhere to be found. The order was to leave him in till Captain Wirz ordered him taken out. The captain was nowhere to be found, and the guards did not dare to take him out, and he lay five or six hours in the stocks senseless until Wirz came and they took him out. He was in there for trying to make his escape.

I heard Captain Wirz give orders to the guards in regard to the dead-line. One day I went down to the brook to wash myself all over. The dead-line which crosses the brook was torn down, and there were two or three men reaching out in order to get some good water, because the water was rotten, filthy, muddy, and greasy. Captain Wirz was at the sentry-box with the sentry looking over the stockade, and as he saw the men just dipping their hands a little beyond, inside the dead-line, he asked the sentry why he did not shoot that man; he was over the dead-line; no matter whether his whole body was over the dead-line, or only part of it, it was his business to shoot him, and if he did not shoot him he would have him punished. The sentry put up his musket, aimed at the man, and shot him right in the right breast. The man fell into the water, and we dragged him out and took him up to his quarters. That was some time in the month of July, 1864. I don't know what day. I am certain I recognized Captain Wirz by the sentry. I heard his voice; I do not know what the result of the wound was. The man was taken to the hospital, and that was the last I saw of him. The ball entered the right breast. I do not know if it passed through him. I do not recollect young Brown of a Pennsylvania regiment. There were other persons witnessing that occurrence. I know of other instances of shooting by sentries. There was a man by the name of "Chickamauga," a cripple. I saw that occurrence. The man went inside of the dead-line. He was a kind of idiot; he had not his senses at all and the boys teased him a good deal. He went to Captain Wirz and asked Wirz to let him go out of the stockade because

A TYPICAL SOLDIER OF THE UNION, THE FIGURE SURMOUNTING THE CONNECTICUT MONUMENT AT ANDERSONVILLE.

the boys teased him so. Captain Wirz would not let him, so he went inside the dead-line and some of us tried to get him out of it by speaking to him, but he would not come and we dared not go inside because we were afraid we would be shot too. Captain Wirz ordered the sentry to shoot at "Chickamauga." The sentry hallooed to him first and told "Chickamauga" to go outside of the deadline; that if he would not go out he was obliged to shoot him, and "Chickamauga" would not go out and then Captain Wire walked up to the sentry and asked him what he talked so much for, why he did not take his musket at once and shoot the man down, so he took his musket at once and shot the man down dead. It was about six weeks after I went into the stockade, after I went to Andersonville. I cannot state exactly what time it was because sometimes we would not know one date from another there.[1]

TESTIMONY OF W. H. JENNINGS.

William Henry Jennings testified:[2]

I was in the military service of the United States, in the 8th United States Colored Troops. I was captured at Olustee, Florida; I was wounded there through the legs. I was at Andersonville as a prisoner nearly a year. I was taken in February, 1864. I saw Captain Wirz while I was at Andersonville. When I got off the ears I saw him. We were taken up to his quarters, and then sent to the stockade.

I was placed on duty about a month after I was put in the stockade. I was set to digging a ditch outside the stockade. My wound was then bleeding. I was wounded through the thigh of the left leg. I received no medical attendance. My wound was not dressed while I was there. I was not employed at the graveyard, nor had anything to do with the dead. I could not walk.

I was whipped in March, 1864. I got thirty lashes by order of Captain Wirz. I was whipped for not going to work one morning; I was unable to do so. I had caught a heavy cold, working in the water in the swamp. My wound was just the same as when I had been wounded; nothing had been done for it. The lashes were ordered by Captain Wirz, and laid on by Turner, the man who ran the hounds. The whipping had no effect on my wound. They whipped me on my bare back. They made me bend over. Afterward they took me and put me in the stocks. I was kept there a day and a night. I did not get any food or drink while in the stocks. After that I was taken and put back in the stockade. When I was taken down, I could not walk. I do not know of any other instance of whipping, only what I have heard. I never heard the rebel sergeant give any orders with regard to whipping.

TESTIMONY OF D. H. STEARNS.

D. H. Stearns, private, 1st Regiment United States Sharpshooters, was taken to Andersonville as prisoner, July 8, 1864. He testified:[3]

I saw the chain-gang; I have seen from eight to twelve men at a time chained together; I saw them in July and August, almost daily, as I was passing from

---

[1] These cases may be considered under the charge of murder.
[2] Record, p. 187.
[3] Record, p. 191.

the hospital to the dispensary for medicine. I noticed on one occasion a man who was very feeble, scarcely able to stand; the gang were walking at the time, and those nearest him had to assist him in moving; I cannot tell what became of him; I was told he died; I do not know his name; it was in August, I should think; I cannot tell certainly.

I saw the prisoner, Captain Wirz, while I was there. I saw him when I first arrived there. The first time I saw him, I heard some person cursing, and heard a blow; I turned around and saw one of our prisoners who seemed to be recovering from the effects of a blow. I saw the prisoner standing near him. I should consider from the motion that he had struck the man, and the man was recovering from the effects of the blow. Captain Wirz was still cursing him, telling him that, if he did not stand up, and stand still, he would shoot him. At that time, or soon after, another man had fallen out of the ranks, being unable to stand from the effects of the heat, and Captain Wirz ordered him to get up and get into the ranks. The man did not do so quickly, and Captain Wirz ordered one of the guards to shoot him. The guard raised his musket, but the man got back in the ranks. When he threatened to shoot his man if he did not stand up in the ranks, he drew his revolver. I am certain that he used his right hand, because if he had used his left I should have noticed it.

It was during the fore part of August that I saw those men in the chain-gang. I don't think I saw them after the tenth. I saw the chain-gang also in July, after the tenth. Sometimes they were the same men, but in different numbers. I saw them nearly every day from some time about the 10th of July to the 10th of August. They were near the southwest corner of the stockade, outside, not near the hospital,—between the hospital and Captain Wirz's headquarters. I have not heard the description of other witnesses as to where they were. I have no means of knowing whether it was the same lot described by other witnesses. I have noticed changes in the chain-gang; a difference in the number. I have seen as many as twelve, perhaps more. I cannot tell what day it was that I saw twelve.

TESTIMONY OF ALEXANDER KENNEL.

Alexander Kennel testified:[1]

I was in the military service of the United States from September 26, 1862, till June 24, 1865, in the 7th Ohio Cavalry. I was a prisoner at Andersonville from February 27, 1864, till September 7, 1864, and from December 25, 1864, till April 19, 1865.

I know the prisoner, Captain Wirz. I have seen men who were balled and chained, and also men who were bucked and gagged by his orders; I have seen them put in the stocks. One special act which I know of occurred last February. In that case a man was taken out of the stockade in the evening about 4 o'clock, and kept in the stocks all night. He was turned into the stockade the next morning at nine o'clock, and he died in less than eight hours. He died in the stockade. He was apparently as healthy as any of the prisoners in the stockade. He was kept all night in the stocks, which were outside the stockade. It was supposed that he died from the effects of the stocks. It was a very cold night.

[1] Record, p. 193.

I talked with him an hour before he died. He was impressed with the belief that he was chilled to death that night in the stocks. He did not expect to live, from his conversation. He did not eat anything after he came into the stockade. He told me that he was kept in the stocks from the time he was taken out until about eight o'clock in the morning. He was chilled so thoroughly that he was insensible. I helped to carry him to the gate after he died. I did not know his name; I never inquired it. He belonged to a Pennsylvania regiment. I am certain that it occurred about the 15th of February, 1865.

In one case I had a conversation with a man in the hospital who had been taken out of the chain-gang, and I saw his body carried to the dead-house three days after I had the conversation with him. He told me in that conversation that he had not been able to walk since he had been taken out of the chain-gang. He died in the hospital. That was in August, 1864. I cannot tell how long after he had been taken from the chain-gang that he died. It was about the 13th of August when I had this conversation. The man was very much emaciated, and was sore in the ankles where the ball had been put on. There were no other marks on his person, that I saw. I can speak of no other instances, except of men whom I have seen confined in the stocks for some time.

TESTIMONY OF L. S. POND.

L. S. Pond testified:[1]

I was in the military service of the United States; in the 2d New York Heavy Artillery. I was a prisoner at Andersonville. I was there about four months—from the 28th of June, 1864.

I saw the prisoner commit acts of cruelty towards sick men. He came into the stockade one day, I think it was in the month of August (I had a memorandum of every circumstance that happened, but I lost it; I never tried to commit them to memory). The men were ordered to fall into ranks to be counted off. We were playing what we used to call "roots" with them. That is, we used to go into three or four different squads if we could, so as to get an extra ration. There was a very sick man there who could not stand upon his limbs, and Captain Wirz ordered him to fall in to be counted off. The man could not fall in, and he told him so. Captain Wirz kicked him three or four times, and said: "I will learn a damned Yankee who tries to 'play roots' upon me."

TESTIMONY OF SIDNEY SMITH.

Sidney Smith testified:[2]

I was in the military service of the United States. I was in the 14th Connecticut when I was taken prisoner. I was taken to Andersonville. I was there from the 23d of May, 1864, to the end of September, 1864.

I know Captain Wirz. On the 7th of September, 1864, I saw him knock a man down with a revolver. I do not recollect in which hand he held the revolver. The soldier was taken back inside the stockade, and I never saw him since. It was the day the prisoners were taken to Savannah. I belonged to the eighty-ninth detachment, and tried to get out with some of the first ones, and went outside for

[1] Record, p. 195.
[2] Record, p. 199 et seq.

CRUEL AND INHUMAN TREATMENT. 273

that purpose. I "flanked" out. There I heard this remark from Captain Wirz, that the first flanker he would catch he would shoot him. A flanker means a man going into a wrong detachment. This soldier who was knocked down with a pistol was out there with a detachment to which he did not belong. The roll was called and he was left out, his name not being on the roll. Captain Wirz knocked him down and told him he was a flanker, and he was sent back to the stockade.

Complaints were made about our rations and treatment. I have signed one letter myself, and sent it, stating that we suffered a great deal. It was dropped in the letter-box. There was no notice taken of it. We never received any answer. I never heard Captain Wirz make use of any language with reference to it. I never spoke to him myself.

I saw prisoners who were shot by sentries. I have seen a man shot going for water, leaning over the dead-line. I have seen the sentries fire, and I afterwards saw the man carried from the place wounded. I have heard sentries say that they got thirty days' furlough for shooting prisoners. My tent was right close by the dead-line, and I asked the sentry once if it were so, that they got furlough for shooting men. He said yes, they got thirty days' furlough. Almost every time a man was shot the sentry was relieved and taken from his post. The corporal of the guard would come up and inquire what the firing was about, and would bring another man and would relieve the sentinel. I saw Captain Wirz at sick-call. I have seen him standing once at the gate when the sick men were crowding and pushing at the dead-line. Captain Wirz said to one of the guards, "Give them the bayonet, the damned Yankees." The sentinel did not charge bayonet on them. At that time I saw a sentry shoot one of the sick men at the gate. It was in August, 1864; I cannot state the date. The sick men behind were pushing the men in front, and some of them got over the dead-line. The sentinel stepped back one step and aimed. One man thought the sentinel aimed at him, and he took the gun to prevent him shooting him; at the same time the sentry fired and split the man's arm open, and at the same time hit another man in the hip. I did not see Captain Wirz there. No warning was given to prisoners about the dead-line. On the 23d of May we were drawn up in line in front of Captain Wirz's office, and had to wait there for about three hours in the sun until he came to count us off. All that time the rebel soldiers would not dare to give us water. We asked for water, and they said they had orders not to give us any. Captain Wirz came and made us fall in and counted us off in detachments. I never was told about the dead-line, and when I saw it I thought it must be just a pleasure walk for the prisoners to exercise in. I was not there half an hour before I was told what it meant.

TESTIMONY OF WILLIAM GROUSE.

William Crouse testified:[1]

I have been in the military service of the United States; in the 7th Pennsylvania Reserves. I was taken prisoner on the 5th of May, 1864. I was taken to Lynchburg, where I stayed two weeks, and from Lynchburg to Andersonville, where I arrived on the 20th of May, 1864. I stayed there till the 15th of September, 1864.

[1] Record, p. 217.

I knew the prisoner there. I saw him knock a man down. I cannot tell the man's name. That was in July, 1864. Captain Wirz knocked him down, that is all. I did not hear him say anything. He just knocked him right down. That man was a Union prisoner. That is all I know about it.

I saw men in the stocks. I saw them in July and August, 1864. I saw a man die the day after he came out of the stocks. I do not know his name. It was about July, 1864. I should judge he had been in the stocks about two weeks. I saw him die. He died in the next tent to me.

I do not know of any event that transpired about that time by which I can fix the date of that man dying, who had been in the stocks. I remember seeing six men hung there. They were hung on the 13th of July, 1864. It was two or three days before that.

TESTIMONY OF JAMES E. MARSHALL.

James E. Marshall testified:[1]

I have been in the military service of the United States, in the 42d New York. I was a prisoner at Andersonville from the latter end of February, 1864, up to September, 1864. I often saw Captain Wirz while I was there. I suppose I know him.

I know of prisoners being shot by the guards. The first instance I saw was at the northeast corner against the hospital. It was at the time the dead-line was being marked out, but it was not then finished. I saw a man shot there. It was in the early part of April. I saw the man shot by the sentry. The mark of the dead-line was there, but the rail was not nailed on the top. The sentry did not say anything at the time. The man died afterwards in the hospital. He was a sick man in the hospital then. He was not a German. I recollect an instance where a German was killed. He passed me, and when he had got about five yards from me he was shot by the sentry. That was at the northeast part of the stockade, in the month of May, 1864, I believe. The man had laid his left hand on the dead-line, and stooped on his knee to pick up a piece of mouldy bread that was within the dead-line, when the guard shot him. The ball passed through his back. It killed him dead. The sentry said something about a furlough. When the man fell he was not outside of the dead-line, and some of us made the remark in the camp that that guard would get a furlough for shooting the man. The sentry said he would damned soon have another one; that he would shoot some more. Captain Wirz came up and we had to go away. When Captain Wirz heard the firing of the gun he would often come up. He told the sentry to make the prisoners go away from there; they had gathered around the man after he was shot. The sentry was relieved.

When Captain Wirz first came to take charge of the camp he was forming the men into detachments, and they did not fall into ranks properly according to his wishes. He stopped the rations that day. They had not had rations since the day previous. That was in the early part of April, when Captain Wirz first came to the camp; the first time I saw him.

I saw the dogs at Andersonville. They were kept for hunting men who escaped from the prison. I know of their hunting men. I saw one man who was torn.

[1] Record, p. 252.

CRUEL AND INHUMAN TREATMENT. 275

His leg was torn. He afterwards died in the hospital. That was in May, 1864. I cannot state the day of the month. It was some time in the latter part of May. I know that the man was bitten by the dogs, because I and several others looked at his leg. He was taken to the hospital. I afterwards saw the man, but he was dead when I saw him. He died from the wounds. He died some twenty days after he was bitten. He died some time in the early part of June, in the hospital.

TESTIMONY OF W. M. PEEBLES.

William M. Peebles, a rebel soldier at Andersonville, detailed as a clerk: Some of his testimony has already been quoted. He testified further:[1]

I saw several men in the stocks. I did not learn their names. They were Federal prisoners. I was passing around one day during a hard rain, and I saw a prisoner in the stocks. He seemed to be near drowning. I rode up and put an umbrella over him. I passed up to Captain Wirz's headquarters and told him that the prisoner was there and might drown. He remarked, "Let him drown," using an oath. His words, as well as I remember, were "Let the damned Yankee drown; I don't care." In a few minutes some one from his headquarters went down and released the prisoner—took him out from the stocks. It was during a very hard rain. The man's head was kind of erect, and it was raining down in his face. He looked as though he would drown. That was what caused me to make the report.

TESTIMONY OF W. W. CRANDALL.

W. W. Crandall, private in the 4th Iowa Infantry, testified:[2]

I saw hounds used about there. They were not what I would call fox-hounds; they were rather heavier, I should think, but I am not well posted enough in dogology to tell you what kind of dogs they were. They were called hounds; there were two kinds, however. I saw there three different packs. One or two in each pack, I think, they were more of a bulldog. They called them catch-dogs. I have seen the dogs there, and have seen men brought in by them. Some of the men were bitten considerably. I saw one man with the calves of his legs torn badly. He was a Union prisoner. I cannot now recollect his name. He belonged to the same detachment as I, but not to my ninety. He was brought in there and a ball and chain put upon each foot. He was kept in that condition several weeks. He was kept there until I went to Captain Wirz and pleaded with him to take the balls off. He said to me that he could not do it. I then watched for the surgeons, and when one of them came in one morning to examine the sick I asked him to take the balls off. He went with me and examined the man. The man's leg had become badly swollen and very blue. It had a bluish putrified look. I told the surgeon that I thought the man would die unless the balls were taken off. He said he could not conscientiously take off but one. He did allow one to be taken off. The man finally died, as I supposed. I buried a man whom I thought I recognized as the same man, but he was so badly emaciated that I might be mistaken, but I think I was not. The man escaped, I think, about the 1st of

---
[1] Record, p. 254 et seq.
[2] Record, p. 256 et seq.

May. He was brought back the next day, I think; it may have been the next day but one. Those balls and chains were put on at once and kept on him for perhaps three weeks, then they took one ball off. He retained the other when I was taken outside, on the 23d of June. Then about the middle of July (it might have been the last of July; I cannot fix the date, but it was some time from the middle to the last of July,) I buried a man whom I recognized, or thought I recognized, as the same man. I examined the body particularly because several of us were acquainted with him, and we all thought he was the same man.

I buried dead at Andersonville. I assisted in burying the dead from June 23, 1864, until September 8th. I was detailed for that duty. It would be pretty hard to tell the number of prisoners that I buried who had been shot, because it became so common a thing that we did not fix the number. I should say at least thirty, possibly forty, and it may be more. I cannot tell the exact number. I am speaking of the period from June 23d to September 8th. The bodies would be brought in and the remark would be made, "Here is another man shot." It became so common an occurrence that I did not take any notice, so that I cannot speak as to the number. I would see, during those months, all that were shot, that were buried. I might not hear of them. The duty I was doing was covering up the dead. I became so accustomed that I paid little attention, and unless some remark was made to call my attention, I might not see them.

I know of a man being put in the stocks for asking to see his brother. His name was Austin; he was paroled in the same squad I was. I was on the banks of the railroad when a lot of prisoners came in. This man Austin made the remark, "There is a brother of mine; I am going to see him." He went down to the squad, and I saw him a short time afterwards in what we call the "spread-eagle stocks." He was there from two to four hours. That was in the latter part of July. I asked another man who was there what it was for, and was told it was for asking to see his brother. The man had told me that was what he was going for. I do not know who ordered the man to the stocks, no further than what I have stated. The stocks in which that man was placed were just above the south gate of the stockade. They were the ordinary stocks. There were two kinds of stocks there, but they were both near together. There were what we called the foot stocks, and also, as the boys termed them, the "spread-eagle" stocks, which held a man by his ankles, his neck, and his hands.

TESTIMONY OF JOHN FISHER.

John Fisher (colored) testified:[1]

I am a soldier in the United States army. I am in the 8th United States Regiment. I was a prisoner at Andersonville. I was taken on the 20th of February, 1864, and taken there in May, 1864. I received very bad treatment there. I was bucked and gagged, and whipped with thirty-nine lashes. I was bucked because I would not go to work. Captain Wirz ordered me to be whipped; so the man said who was in charge of the squad. He went to see Captain Wirz, and when he came back he said Captain Wirz ordered me to be whipped. He gave me thirty-nine lashes. This was in October, 1864. I was bucked and gagged at the same time. That was the only time. I have seen the prisoner there many a time. I

---

[1] Record, p. 279 et seq.

saw him draw a pistol to shoot a prisoner named George Brown. He was going after some shovels, and could not run as fast as Captain Wirz wanted him. Captain Wirz drew his pistol and said if he did not run he would shoot him. I saw no others whipped there. I saw others after being whipped. They were Isaac Hawkins, Abe Woodward, and George Washington. That was in September. Two of them were whipped at the graveyard. I was not present when they were ordered to be whipped. I did not see them while they were being whipped. I just saw them after they were whipped. They had marks upon them of the strap with which they had been whipped. They were not badly whipped; the blood was not drawn.

TESTIMONY OF J. H. GOLDSMITH.

John H. Goldsmith testified:[1]

I have been in the military service of the United States, in the 14th Regiment, Illinois Infantry. I was taken prisoner on the 4th of October, 1864, at Atwood, Georgia; I arrived at Andersonville on the 11th day of October, and remained there until the 18th day of March, 1865. Captain Wirz was in command of the prison all the time I was there.

On or about the 1st of March, 1865, Captain Wirz put me in charge of the rations to be issued to the prisoners inside of the stockade, and to the paroled men outside. I had charge of the rations up to the time I left the prison. The rations consisted of half a pound of meal of very poor quality, half a pound of beef, half a pound of peas and two gills of molasses. The ration of molasses was on each alternate day, and of beef the same day. When they took the beef and molasses together, there was one quarter of a pound of beef and one gill of molasses. The beef was very poor; some called it "jackass." It was salt; we got some fresh once or twice a week. It was poor meal, with cob and grain all ground together. [The sample of meal produced by De la Baume was here shown the witness.] That is just the quality of meal, as a general thing. Captain Wirz used to give me the orders always for drawing rations, when I had charge of the rations. He used to make out tickets for me to draw from Captain Armstrong. I drew what he made out the tickets for. The ticket specified the articles and the quantity—it limited the rations. The rations issued to our prisoners was just one-half the quantity issued to the rebel troops. There were three days there that he increased the rations of meal and of peas to one-fourth pound per day. At the end of three days he put the ration back to the old standard again. He said the Yankees were getting too damned saucy, and that he would bring them to their milk.

I was out on parole most of the winter, from the 21st of November, 1864, until the time I left. My duties outside the stockade were writing for Captain Wirz. Part of the time I attended to the death list, making out the records of the prisoners. I had no particular duties assigned to me, but to assist in writing. The death list was the list of those who died each day in prison. I was engaged in that duty every morning. I recorded the names of those who were shot. I did not keep the causes of death there, but merely stated the day they died, without stating the disease. I have had to write out orders for Captain Wirz to punish men—orders to the guard to fire upon them in case any of them attempted to speak to the guard.

[1] Record, p. 298 et seq.

278   THE TRAGEDY OF ANDERSONVILLE.

There were orders issued for the discipline of the prison, warning men not to attempt to speak to the guard, as they had got orders to fire upon them if they did so. I have heard verbal orders given to rebel sergeants to punish those who had command of detachments inside in case they failed to report any man that was missing. They were to be punished by being placed in the stocks or by being bucked and gagged.

I have heard Captain Wirz say he was doing more good there than if he were in the field, and that he could whip more men than Johnston's army could. He did not make that statement more than once that I recollect. That was made about the latter part of January, 1865. I cannot recollect his saying "killing"; he said he could whip more men.

I have seen orders signed by the prisoner in relation to furloughs. I made out a furlough once for a man who killed one of our own men; he received a furlough for thirty days. His name was Scott; he belonged to the 4th Georgia Reserves. The man he killed was Henry Lochmire, belonging to some Pennsylvania regiment, I cannot recollect what regiment. It was in the latter part of February, 1865.

TESTIMONY OF JASPER CULVER.

Jasper Culver testified:[1]

I was connected with the 1st Wisconsin Infantry. I was captured at Chickamauga and taken to Richmond and Danville, and afterwards to Andersonville. I arrived at Andersonville on the 16th of March, 1864.

I know the prisoner. I saw him frequently. When I first arrived at the prison it was in charge of a man named Selman. At least I saw him counting off squads and seeming to have a great deal to do there. Soon after I went there Captain Wirz came there and took charge. I first saw him come into the stockade with Selman in the evening. Selman gave his orders to the men to fall in the next morning in four ranks. Next morning they beat roll-call and we fell in as he directed. Captain Wirz came and counted us off in detachments of 270 men, and divided these into nineties, appointing a sergeant over each ninety. He then gave his orders not to break ranks, to remain in ranks until he got through counting the prisoners. We did not stay in ranks, except for some time, as we supposed we were all through. I was down towards the gate afterwards, about noon, and heard Captain Wirz going about using rough language. He said we should not receive any rations, and he would learn us to stand in ranks as we were ordered, and we did not receive rations that day. That was the first day that he took command. I saw him shortly afterwards when he was counting off. I was standing near by and happened to be looking towards him. A man seemed to be walking past him, and Captain Wirz turned around and struck him three or four times and knocked the man down. I saw the man afterwards. He seemed to be quite sickly and delicate. He could hardly walk. Some time after that rations were stopped from the northern side of the stockade. That was some time in April, 1864, I think. Next day he came over and said he would give us rations, (I was on the south side,) but that the fellows on the north side would not get rations because they did not do as he had ordered them to do. He said that they had broken ranks, and he would not give them any rations; and he did not.

[1] Record, p. 301 et seq.

CRUEL AND INHUMAN TREATMENT.

I was not kept in the stockade all the time I was there. I was put on duty in the bakery on the 29th of June, 1864. That was the bakery on the stream just above the stockade. My duties there were to unload the meal that came there and carry it into the bakery, and also to load the bread into the wagons for the stockade. The meal was generally very coarse, as if it was ground cobs and all. Other sacks seemed to be very good meal. A great many sacks came there in which the meal was mouldy and wet, as if it had been stored in a damp place. Some of it would come in large mouldy chunks of meal. Sometimes it could not be used at all. It was not used. It was just thrown out by those who were making it up.

[The sample of meal exhibited by De la Baume was here shown to the witness.]

That is a fair sample of a large portion. There were sometimes some sacks better than that, but very seldom. It was generally of that quality. I have sometimes noticed sacks coarser than that. I used to help in loading the bread into the wagons. The bread was baked in cakes about eighteen inches long, ten inches wide and two inches thick, made of this meal. Ten of those loaves or "cards" were sent out to a detachment of two hundred and seventy men for one day. There was some baked in larger pans, about two and a half feet long, fifteen inches wide and two inches thick, made of this meal. There were four or four and a half of them sent to each 270 men. They were generally very poorly baked. The center of them was almost always raw. They never could be baked properly. Those large "cards" that were baked in the night and sent in in the afternoon frequently became sour and stringy; it became stringy from the sour dough and the heat of the bread, and it was impossible to eat it.

I saw the chain-gang. When I first went outside of the stockade on the 29th of June, 1864, I saw twelve men in the chain-gang chained together under guard. Next morning they came down to the bakery to wash. I gave them some water and pails to wash and also carried their rations to them from the bakery. I saw them almost every day for over a month or six weeks that they were together. They were placed in two files with a thirty-two pound ball chained to each outside leg of the file on the right side and on the left leg of the left file. Then they were chained with what seemed to be two 100-pound balls, at least they called them 100-pounders. There were three men of each file with chains attached to each one of these 100-pound balls. They had also a band of iron riveted around each man's neck, and a chain attached from one man to another. In that condition they were kept. I believe there were six men in each file. The file leaders were not attached to the other file. If one man moved the whole twelve had to move. One of the file leaders was very poorly and seemed as though he could hardly carry himself without carrying ball and chain; those in the gang with him complained about his being sick. He caused a great deal of trouble by reason of his having diarrhea, and they all had to go with him whenever he was called. I afterwards saw this sick man out of the chain-gang, but he had the ball upon his legs, also the band upon his neck. He afterwards died in the guard-house. I saw our men who were on parole take the irons off him after he was dead. He was taken from the chain-gang, but the 32-pound ball was left upon his leg and the band upon his neck, and they were left upon him until he died. I think he died three or four days after he was relieved from the chain-gang. I think he died some time in

July. I do not know his name or his regiment. I never made inquiries about it. I think the same occurrence was testified to by one witness. I think I heard a different one testified to, although I do not recollect of any other occurrence of a man dying in the chain-gang but this one. I heard these men complain to us who had been out on parole that he was a great trouble to them.

I have often seen men in those stocks that are spoken of. I have seen men in them very frequently. I never knew of men dying in the stocks. It was a common occurrence to see men standing in those stocks, and also men lying down in the stocks that were made to hold men in that way. They had to lie upon their backs with their feet about a foot from the ground; they lay in that position all day in the sun. I know of one man in particular; he was a man who used to drive one of the wagons that drew rations into the stockade. He also used to help draw the dead with the same team. This man, for something or other, was put in there. I saw him lying on the ground all of one day in the sun. I cannot think of his name, although I did know it.

I do not recollect "Chickamauga's" name. I recollect hearing them say he be-belonged to the 96th Illinois. I was at my tent and saw a crowd around the gate. I walked down towards the gate and saw Captain Wirz on his gray horse inside the gate. I walked up towards the crowd. Just as I got there Captain Wirz came to the gate and I asked him what the trouble was, and he said that the boys were having some fun with "Chickamauga." I turned around to go back towards my tent, when I heard the report of a gun and saw the guard just drawing back his musket and I saw the smoke of the gun. I turned around to go back again near the dead-line, and saw this cripple lying just inside the dead-line. He seemed as if he was not quite dead; he was writhing in the agonies of death. I turned with some of the boys who took him up and were conveying him to the hospital. I walked along with them and looked at him. After I got some distance away, I looked around and saw Captain Wirz upon the sentry-box with the sentry. I did not hear anything said or any remarks made by him to the sentinel. I went off to my tent pretty thoroughly disgusted.

I heard Captain Wirz make a remark with reference to what he was doing there. He was just inside the gate one day; there was quite a crowd there talking. I heard one of the boys making the remark that he would rather be at the front with Sherman or Grant than to stay there. Captain Wirz made the remark that he was doing more for the Confederate government there than any general in the field, and he made some other remark which I did not hear distinctly. It was just inside the gate.

TESTIMONY OF J. L. YOUNKER.

John L. Younker testified:[1]

I was in the military service of the United States, in the 12th United States Infantry. I enlisted March 31, 1862, for three years. I was a prisoner at Andersonville from June 16, 1864, to September 12, 1864.

I know about the use of hounds there for pursuing and capturing prisoners. There was a man, I suppose about fifty years of age, who was in charge of twelve bloodhounds; whenever he was on duty he always rode on a mule. He

---

[1] Record, p. 315 et seq.

generally went round the stockade every morning, and if he found the track of any prisoners he went in pursuit. There was one man, belonging to an Indiana regiment, who was taken sick and sent to the hospital. From the hospital he tried to make his escape; he was recaptured by the bloodhounds and sent back to the stockade in the evening. He had an acquaintance in the next hole to mine. The man's right ear was almost off; he was bitten in several places in the legs. He was all scratched, and had hardly any clothing on. I took a piece of my old dirty shirt and helped to tie up his wounds. Then he gave up to a friend of his a likeness of his mother which he had, and said that he should send her this if he should never recover, because he believed he would die. The next morning he was dead. He gave this picture to one of my comrades. He was a resident of the northern part of Ohio, and he said that the man should deliver the picture to his mother, as he should never recover, that he should die. In that same conversation he said something as to how he had been injured. We questioned him, and he replied in a feeble voice that he had got about thirty-five or forty miles, and was strongly pursued by the hounds; that, as he was very weak, coming out of the so-called hospital, he tried to climb up a bush, but was pulled down by one of the dogs, and so disabled that he could proceed no further. We had to stir him up once in a while, give him a regular shake, so that he might answer a few more questions, because he was expiring. I saw him after he was dead. That was a few days before the six raiders were hung, which was on the 11th of July. That bloodhound affair struck my mind. Shortly afterward, I was taken out on detail into the graveyard, and I one day met the old bloodhound man, and I asked him, "Why in the world are you committing such cruelties against us Yankees?" "Why," said he, "it is the order of Captain Wirz. I would not do it, but he told me to fetch back one of you Yankee sons of —."

I was on duty as a grave-digger. The prisoners were buried in trenches 180 feet long, 7 feet wide, and 3 1/2 feet deep. That was the order we had from Captain Piggot, superintendent of the graveyard. They were laid side by side on their backs; and we generally covered them with some pine slabs or puncheons as they were called, until these got so scarce that we could not get enough to cover the bodies, so we just put them in without anything covering them but the ground. The bodies when they came there for interment were about half mortified. We could hardly touch them to pull them out of the wagons onto the old stretcher without their skin remaining in our hands; and they were full of vermin of all descriptions. Two teams, drawn by four mules each, were employed in bringing the dead to the graveyard. They were covered wagons like our army wagons. They were hauling steadily from morning till night almost. The dead were placed right on top of each other in the wagons. They had hardly any clothes on.

The first act of cruelty which I saw committed by Captain Wirz was on the day of my arrival. We were marched from the railroad depot in front of his headquarters, which consisted of an old log cabin. He was most noted to me by the revolver which he carried in his belt, and the foreign accent with which he spoke the English language. I and about fifteen more were on the extreme left of the line. We were counted out, as I was told by the guard, to fill up old detachments, and the rest of the men were all counted in nineties. Captain Wirz fussed around there, threatening and cursing. I thought he was a pretty rough customer. After the other men were all marched into the stockade we were marched in front of his headquarters and remained there. Captain Wirz and several other rebel officers went inside. One of the guards seemed to be a little friendly to me, and he told me the condition of the prisoners in the stockade; that they had no shelter or anything. I had been robbed in Richmond of everything I had. I saw an old piece of tin under the log house, and as I am a blacksmith by profession, I thought I might make myself a pan out of that tin if I had it. I reached for it. At the same moment Captain Wirz came out. He commenced cursing and said to the guard, "Why don't you shoot that Yankee son of—. I will keep you in line. Damn you, I will put you in the stockade, and let you rot like a great many have done before." So I did not get the tin. I went in without it.

My rations were stopped. Whenever Captain Wirz wanted to find out something in regard to tunneling, or if a man was absent from roll-call—some poor fellow who might have gone to the sink in the center of the stockade where the little brook was, and become unable to return—our rations were stopped. On the 4th of July, 1864, we did not get a bite.

I have seen men in the stocks. The stocks were of various kinds. Some just held the feet ten or twelve inches higher than the ground, so that the man could either sit or lie down, exposed to all kinds of weather. Others held a man round the neck with his arms stretched out. As a man stood there in that way it appeared to me (I can find no other expression for it) just like the image of Christ crucified.

TESTIMONY OF WILLIAM BULL.

William Bull testified:[1]

I have been in the military service of the United States, in Company A, Means's Independent Loudon Rangers, from the State of Virginia. They were loyal. I was a prisoner at Andersonville. I arrived there the 3d of June, 1864. When I got there I was put in the stockade, where I remained eight months. I then got out on parole, and was out three months and twenty-three days. I left the stockade the 24th March, 1865.

I saw several men shot on the dead-line. For the whole eight months I was there, I think I saw in the neighborhood of eight or nine men shot. I do not know the names of any of them. The first man I saw shot was the afternoon that I entered the stockade—the third of June, 1864, at the north gate. Captain Wirz came in at the head of the detachment. He put three guards on the stoop, and ordered them to fire at the crowd to make them keep back, As we came along in he kept telling them to keep back, and he told the guard to fire. At last one of the guards did fire and shot a man. The ball struck him in the stomach. The sentry was not fifteen feet from him when he fired. There were three sentries together; only one sentry fired. The next man I saw shot was about two months after that. He was inside the stockade, at the stream which ran through it. I think the man had come in the same day. He went down to the brook to get water, stooped over to get a drink, and was killed. He was shot right through the head. The ball went in at the right ear and came out at the other side. I do not know that man's name or regiment. I do not know by whose orders he was shot.

---

[1] Record, p. 328 et seq.

CRUEL AND INHUMAN TREATMENT. 283

All the orders I ever heard given there were given by Captain Wirz. I heard none given at that time. There was no one on the post but the sentinel. The next man I saw shot was in September, 1864. I was lying in the stockade about six feet from the dead-line, asleep. I lay right next him, within three or four feet of him. It was the habit at night to call out the hour. This guard was asleep, and when it came round to him to call the hour the guard below him kept hallooing to him to wake up. He woke up and fired right down into the camp, and shot a man through the knee. The man died two or three days afterwards. I do not know his name; he belonged to an Illinois regiment. I should judge this was about the middle of September. The next man I saw shot was about the 15th of July about three or four days after the execution of these men at the south gate. It was doctor's call in the morning, and the crowd was rushing up. The orders from the doctor were to fire on the crowd if they did not keep back. This man was so sick that he fell over on the guard, who fired at him and shot him through the right shoulder. I do not think he died. I recollect one being shot back of the hospital, inside the stockade. He was a crazy man. He was shot right through the head. He ran over the dead-line and asked the guard to shoot him. That was in January, 1865, a few days before I came out on parole. He was killed instantly. I did not see Captain Wirz present at the time. I do not recollect, now, seeing any other men shot.

On the 3d of June, 1864, the day I went to Andersonville, we were drawn up in a line. A young fellow named Doherty, belonging to my company, started after some water. Captain Wirz was counting at the head of the men, and the young fellow asked Sergeant Smith, who was standing right by, if he could go and get some water. Smith said he had no objection. Captain Wirz came along and asked where that damned Yankee was going. He caught hold of him, kicked him three or four times, and put him back in the ranks. I do not know any other incident of that character.

TESTIMONY OF J. H. BURNS.

Jas. H. Burns testified:[1]

I was in the military service of the United States, in the 10th Connecticut, Company I. I was a prisoner at Andersonville for nearly eight months, from February 23, 1864, to the 7th of September. I saw Captain Wirz while I was there.

I have known him ill treat prisoners in his custody. I saw him order the guard to shoot a man named Chickamauga for going inside the dead-line.

I was put in the stocks once myself, under his orders, for trying to make my escape. I heard him order the guard to put me there. I was kept there twenty-four hours or thereabouts, with nothing to eat or drink. That was either on the 13th or 14th of July, 1864.

I saw Captain Wirz come in there one morning to call the roll—one morning in July, 1864. He came in and knocked some of my comrades around, and used harsh language to them. He drew his revolver upon me one morning, but he did not use it. I have known him fire into a crowd of prisoners. One morning a stone or brick was thrown at him as he came into the camp, riding on his horse. He

[1] Record, p. 331.

immediately drew his revolver and fired into the crowd of prisoners in the stockade. I never heard any complaints made to him to my knowledge. I remember no instance of death resulting from shooting or otherwise by Captain Wirz. That is all I remember now about what I saw and suffered down there.

He stopped the men's rations once on the 3d or 4th of July; at least it was said that it was he who stopped them. Next day the meat was brought in in a condition not to be used. That was said to be under his orders.

I was in prison at the time a shot was fired over it. There was a solid shot fired over the camp one day. The prisoners had rushed down near the gateway to see some new prisoners who were coming in. There was a solid shot fired over the camp, going toward the northwest corner of the camp. I do not know the date, but I should judge it was in July, 1864. The guns pointed toward the stockade. All the artillery that we could see was turned toward the camp. I saw eight pieces to my knowledge bearing on the camp. I saw them in that position for three months.

I heard Captain Wirz tell the guard, "Shoot the first Yankee that undertakes to make his escape or anything of the kind. The more we shoot the less we will have to feed or fight." That was one morning that I was going after wood. It was in the month of June.

TESTIMONY OF A. G. BLAIR.

A. G. Blair testified:[1]

I was in the military service of the United States, in the 122d New York. I was taken prisoner on the 23d of May, 1864, at the battle of the Wilderness. I was taken to Libby Prison first, and from that to Andersonville, where I arrived about the first of June. Captain Wirz was in command of the prison when I arrived there.

I have heard a great many questions asked Captain Wirz about rations whenever he would come into the camp. His reply was generally an oath, saying that we would get all the rations we deserved, and that was damned little.

Q. Did he ever say he would not give you rations if he could?

A. I never heard him make that exact remark.

Q. Did he make any similar remark?

A. Several days during the fore part of my imprisonment there we had no rations. The report came from good authority that he was the cause of it, he being in charge of the camp.

[Interrupted by counsel for the accused.]

Question repeated.

A. I have not heard those words from his mouth.

Q. Did you hear any similar language used by Captain Wirz to that which I repeated to you? If so, state what the language was.

[Objected to by counsel for the accused on the ground that witness had already answered in the negative. After deliberation the objection was overruled.]

A. On one occasion when he was asked by several of the prisoners who had not had any rations for twenty-four hours, when they were to have any, he made the

[1] Record, p. 343 et seq.

remark that if the rations were in his hands we would not get any. That was in the beginning of July, 1864, just before or after the 4th.

I have seen him stand at the gate when sick men were carried out. The men were very anxious to get out of the sun into the shade, and they would rush out to a small passage-way made in the large doors coming out, to suit him. I have seen him shove the well, and the sick who were being carried, over on their backs; or sometimes he would order the guards to do it. The condition of the men taken out of camp into the hospital was hopeless—all that I ever saw taken out.

I escaped from Andersonville in the latter part of July or the fore part of August, and got about thirty miles from the stockade when I was captured and brought back to the camp. I was kept over night, and then was put in the stocks. The first day that I was taken out of the stocks I was not put in the stockade that night. I was put in the stocks the next day, and then was returned to the prison with three other comrades. I do not recollect the exact number of hours I was kept in the stocks; I should think five or six hours.

Q. Did the prisoner give any orders in reference to your being put in the stocks?

A. Just before I was put in the stocks I saw him give some orders from his headquarters, and I supposed that those were the orders.

I saw prisoners shot on or near the dead-line, on several occasions. I was down, in the fore part of my imprisonment, to get water at the creek. That was the only resource for obtaining water, except you had a right in one of the wells. The crowd was very great there. It was absolutely necessary sometimes either to get over the dead-line or to thirst. I have seen men on five or six occasions either shot dead or mortally wounded for trying to get water under the dead-line. I have seen one or two instances where men were shot over the dead-line. Whether they went over it intentionally, or unconsciously from not knowing the rules, I cannot say. I think that the number of men shot during my imprisonment ranged from twenty-five to forty. I do not know that I can give any of their names. I did know them at the time, because they had tented right around me, or messed with me, but their names have slipped my mind. Two of them belonged to the 40th New York Regiment. Those two men were shot just after I got there, in the latter part of June, 1864.

Q. Did you see the person who shot them?

A. I saw the sentry raise his gun. I hallooed to the man. I and several of the rest gave the alarm, but it was too late. Both of these men did not die; one was shot through the arm; the other died; he was shot in the right breast. I did not see Captain Wirz present at the time. I did not hear any orders given to the sentinels, or any words from the sentinels when they fired; nothing more than they often said that it was done by orders from the commandant of the camp, and that they were to receive so many days' furlough for every Yankee devil they killed. Those twenty-five or forty men were shot from the middle of June, 1864, until the 1st of September. There were men shot every month. I cannot say that I ever saw Captain Wirz present when any of these men were shot. I had no chance of seeing him unless he was in the stockade. The majority of those whom I saw shot were killed outright; expired in a few moments.

Q. Can you give a detailed description of those you saw killed and of the dates?

A. In regard to the dates I cannot give you any detail. I lost dates there, and did not know when Sunday came. I came very near being shot myself. A very large crowd had gathered at the stream of water, and I was reaching over the dead-line in order to get some water. I could not get it anywhere else, as I had no right to the wells. A bullet came, I should judge, within two or three inches of my right ear, striking one man through the arm, and mortally wounding another. These men were in their tents, unoffending.

Q. Were all these twenty-five or forty men shot by the sentries for crossing the dead-line or being near it?

A. Some were across it, and others not. I saw a man shot who was three feet inside the dead-line. I saw one shot on the 10th of July, just the day before the men whom we called the raiders were hung.

Q. Describe the circumstances that led to the men being shot.

A. I do not know, except from the great desire of sentries to get furloughs.

Q. Did you ever hear any order given by the prisoner in reference to firing grape and canister on the prisoners in the stockade?

A. He gave an order; I aid not hear it; but there was an order given—

(Interrupted by counsel for the accused:)

Q. What order did you ever hear him give?

A. Captain Wirz planted a range of flags inside the stockade, and gave the order, just inside the gate, "that if a crowd of two hundred (that was the number) should gather in any one spot beyond those flags and near the gate, he would fire grape and canister into them."

Captain Wirz gave this order I was speaking of to the crowd of prisoners around the gate. He merely told them he would fire upon them if they gathered there. I did not hear him give the order to the men outside. He warned us that if we gathered there in numbers he would fire upon us.

Q. Then it was not an order, but simply a warning?

A. Yes, sir.

TESTIMONY OF J. B. WALKER.

John Burns Walker testified:[1]

I was in the military service of the United States, in Company G, 141st Pennsylvania Infantry. I was a prisoner at Andersonville from June 16, 1864, till May 26, 1865.

I was wounded on the evening of May 28, 1864, at Hanover Junction, Va., and was taken to Richmond on the 30th; from there to Danville, and by Columbia to Andersonville, where I arrived on the 16th of June. . . .

I know the name of a prisoner who was shot by a sentry and killed. I have a memorandum from which I can state it with certainty. On the 4th of September, 1864, a prisoner belonging to the 7th Indiana Infantry, whose name was Morris Prendiville, was asleep in his tent about 10 o'clock in the evening. His quarters were near mine. I heard the report and went out. There was a little commotion at the quarters where the prisoner was shot. When I got opposite the tent I found something under my feet, and on looking down I found the man's brain and blood on the path. His feet were toward the dead-line, about three feet from it; his head was toward the path. He had been wounded in

---

[1] Record, p. 348 et seq.

CRUEL AND INHUMAN TREATMENT. 287

battle and afterwards brought to Andersonville. He had been there only a few days when he was shot. I reported the case next morning to Captain Wirz. I left a report at the gate; I never heard anything more of it. He was shot in the head, the ball scattering his brains about. I know the man's name was Prendiville, because I wrote it on a paper and pinned it on his breast; I wrote the cause of his death—that he was shot by the guard—and I pinned the paper on his shirt bosom. I made a memorandum at the time for myself, and I have it here. I wrote this on the morning after the man's death.

[Witness produced the memorandum, which was read, as follows:

"Morris Prendiville, Company H, 7th Indiana Regiment, infantry; shot through the head on the night of the 4th of September, 1864, by the rebel guard. He was asleep in his tent, directly opposite the post. The guard had no cause to commit the crime."]

THE JUDGE ADVOCATE: I desire to call the attention of the court to the following extract from the hospital register: "11,230, Prendiville, M., private 7th Indiana, Co. H, complaint unknown; admitted September 6th; died September 6th; died in quarters."

WITNESS [continued]: I do not know the names of any others who were killed. On the 5th of August, 1864, five men were shot. I did not take their names. Four of them were shot at the branch, and one of them near the northeast corner, inside the stockade. Three of them were shot at one time; one was killed and two were wounded. Such shooting was a frequent occurrence at that place.

My rations were stopped while I was at Andersonville; on the 3d of July the sergeants came in and told us that we were going to have a fine time on the 4th of July, that we would have an extra ration. The 4th of July came and we had no rations at all. The rations were frequently stopped. The crime of any man not being able to report, or any sergeant not being able to report the number of men, was considered a sufficient cause for stopping our rations. I generally managed to substitute men for those whom I could not account for. Sometimes it was not possible for all the men to be present. Sick men had to leave and go to places where it was necessary for them to go, and they would not be able to get back in time. I generally found men from other squads who had been counted, and filled up the vacancies with them.

We were not doing anything when the sergeant came in on the 3d of July and spoke to us in regard to our rations. We had not been attempting to break out that day. I used to hear about a plan to break out, but I never could find any organization. Such an attempt was not the cause for stopping our rations. I never knew of any organization to break out; I knew of some tunneling. I guess the rations were not stopped because there had been tunneling. I do not know; I know that we had the promise of a good day on the 4th, and we did not get it. I did not hear at that time anything about tunneling out.

TESTIMONY OF C. H. RUSSELL.

Chas. H. Russell, recalled for the prosecution, testified:[1]

I saw acts of cruelty committed at Andersonville by a man named Duncan; I believe his name was James Duncan. I understood that he was a rebel quarter-

---
[1] Record, p. 366.

master. He used to come in with the wagon bringing in the bread. He issued it out to the sergeants of detachments. . . .

I saw Duncan in this courtroom; I see him now.

[Witness pointed out the man to whom he referred.][1]

About the 10th day of June, 1864, he came in with some bread, and I with six other men of my detachment was detailed to go down and help him to bring up the bread. A fellow belonging to my 100—I don't know his name; he belonged to a Tennessee regiment—came down with me, and while we were getting the bread, or rather while we were standing by, for our turn had not come, a piece of crust broke off and this man stooped down to pick it up; as soon as he did so, Duncan jumped out of the wagon and struck him, and kicked him twice or three times severely. The man died three or four days afterwards in a tent in the stockade. Before that occurred he was just as healthy as I was, and I thought his chance of getting out was fully as good; he had as good a tent as mine was. Another instance was three or four days afterwards, about the 15th of June. My tent was close to the gate where the wagon stopped and where the bread was issued. This Duncan was issuing bread again. A poor fellow, about half-witted, who stayed on the north side of the stockade, came over there. He went to get some bread. I did not see the commencement of the affair, and could not tell whether he wanted to steal some or not; at all events, I saw Duncan jump out of the wagon and kick him and knock him down. The man jumped up and Duncan knocked him down again, then picked him up and threatened to throw him inside the dead-line and let the guard shoot him. The man went away and that was the last I saw of him. The first occurrence which I have narrated occurred about the 10th of June. I do not know the man's name whom I saw Duncan kick; he belonged to a Tennessee regiment. I do not know the name of the second man. I saw him about the camp, but I never knew his name; he was a half-witted fellow. That is all I know about acts of cruelty committed by Duncan.

TESTIMONY OF W. W. CRANDALL.

W. W. Crandall, recalled for the prosecution, testified;[2]

I knew a man at Andersonville named Duncan. That [pointing him out in court] is the man. He had charge of the cook-house there. During the first time I was there he used to come into the stockade with rations. During the latter part of the time they said he was acting as detective. In the first days of October, 1864, I was in the ball-and-chain-gang. I saw him and another man named Barr bring a man to put in the stocks. His name was James Armstrong. He belonged to an Ohio regiment; the number of the regiment I cannot tell. They put him in what they called the "spread-eagle stocks," and after putting him in they took from him his money and a picture. I heard Armstrong plead with Duncan for the picture, saying either that it was a picture of his sister or of his mother, He did not get it. He was left there three or four hours, when Duncan came back alone and took him out, saying that he was

---

[1] Duncan was subsequently tried by military commission and convicted of participation in the Andersonville horror.

[2] Record, p. 367.

going to send him away on the cars. I heard Armstrong at the time ask Duncan if he could not give him back that picture. The answer was, "You may consider yourself damned fortunate to get away at all, and that you are not put in the ball-and-chain-gang with those other boys." I did not notice anything that he took except the money and picture. I do not know how much money.

The man told me the amount while he was still in the stocks. I think he stated the sum was about eight or nine dollars in greenbacks. I do not know of any other special acts of cruelty by Duncan.

TESTIMONY OF S. M. RIKER.

Samuel M. Riker testified:[1]

I have been in the military service of the United States, in the 8th New Jersey Volunteers. I was taken prisoner the 22d of June, 1864. I was taken first to Richmond and from there to Andersonville, where I arrived on the 10th of July.

I saw the prisoner the day I arrived there. I went there with some six hundred Union prisoners, and was taken immediately to Captain Wirz's headquarters. We were compelled to stand there under the burning sun, without shade, and without water, between three and four hours. The men were formed in four ranks and were ordered to remain so. They would leave the ranks in order to get water, if possible, from boys passing with canteens for soldiers. They were cautioned frequently not to do it. One man who stepped out was struck on the head with the butt of a gun by one of Captain Wirz's sergeants, whose name I do not know. The man was insensible for some time. Many of the men standing there fainted away from exposure and the heat of the sun. It would probably be called sun-stroke. They were carried and laid under trees, and were not taken into the stockade with us. Soon after we were all turned into the stockade. Next day raw rations were issued to us. We had no wood to cook them, and of course were hungry for a long time before we got enough used to the ways of the stockade to obtain wood and materials for cooking. . . .

I know of two cases of shooting in the stockade. The men were not acquaintances of mine, not men that I knew. I kept a diary while there, but being obliged to keep it in lead-pencil it is so blurred and rubbed out that I cannot read it, and cannot give the names. The men were shot in July, near the place where they used to get water to drink from the stream. The persons shooting them were younger men, who were on guard. The first man I saw shot was shot in the breast. I saw him after he was carried away. He died a few minutes afterwards. He was shot by a mere boy, probably not more than fourteen years old. That was about the middle of July, soon after I was taken into the stockade, which was on the 10th of July. It was on the 11th that the six raiders were hung. I saw the next man shot in the latter part of July. It was at the same place as the other, or very near it, where he was getting water.

[1] Record, p. 368.

TESTIMONY OF C. E. SMITH.

Charles E. Smith testified:[1]

I am in the service of the United States. I belong to Company K, 4th United States Cavalry. I went to Andersonville on the 2d of May, 1864, and remained till the 12th of September.

I saw four men shot in the stockade. I saw three shot together, the one ball taking effect on the three of them. One of them was killed instantly, another died in about an hour, and the third died in about two days afterwards. I think that was about the 10th of June. I do not know the men's names. They were shot at the creek by the sentinel on post. Only one sentinel fired. I saw a man shot on the north side of the stockade. He was reaching under the deadline to pick up a piece of bread which some other man had thrown out of his haversack. The sentinel shot him from his post. I think this was about the 10th of May. I got there a very few days before. The man died instantly. I think the man was in his right mind, except from starvation and hunger. Captain Wirz was present at the first shooting. The man was stooping at the dead-line for water, when Captain Wirz told the sentry to fire at him. The sentinel hesitated and would not do it. Captain Wirz drew his own revolver and said to the sentinel that if he did not shoot them damned Yankees he would shoot him. It was after that remark, by Captain Wirz, that the sentinel fired and hit these three men.

I heard Captain Wirz order men to be vaccinated. He came in one day with the doctor. They had been vaccinating three or four days. He came to our detachment that morning and gave the sergeant orders that every man should be there and vaccinated. They went in to vaccinate, and they vaccinated most of the ninety. I was vaccinated myself, and I went to the brook and washed it, and sucked the blood out of my arm and stopped it. Other men who were vaccinated at the same time came near losing their arms, and I do not know but what they did lose them after I left. There came big sores in the arms where the matter was put in, and the flesh rotted away, and there came big sores under the arms. I cannot say that I saw any cases where the sores did not spread in that manner. I saw mostly all of them with very large sores, bigger than a silver half-dollar. I never saw them get well while I was there, except they did the same thing that I did to get it out of their blood. Captain Wirz said that any man who would refuse to obey his orders would have a ball and chain put on. That order was carried out. There was one man named Shields, belonging to the 2d Iowa Infantry, who refused to be vaccinated. They took him out and put a ball and chain on him until he consented to have the matter put on his arm. I saw him after he was vaccinated. He went and washed it out, and got well shortly afterwards.

I know very well that the prisoner could use both hands. I and some of my comrades were digging a tunnel, when he and some more of the rebels found it out, and came in with prodding irons to find out where it was. They confiscated our blankets and what little meal we had, and took all away from us. I know he could use his right arm very well then.

[1] Record, p. 369.

Our rations were stopped there for the 3d, 4th, and 5th of July; we got no rations at all. I have seen men, in a starving condition, on the bank of the swamp picking up beans which had passed through men, and go wash and eat them.

TESTIMONY OF CHARLES T. WILLIAMS.

Charles T. Williams testified:[1]

I was in the 1st New Jersey Cavalry. I arrived at Andersonville Marsh 12, 1864, and remained in the stockade till August 30th of the same year. I was then taken out to the hospital, and stayed there till March 25, 1865. Dr. White was in charge of the hospital when I went there. Afterwards Dr. R. R. Stevenson, after him Dr. Clayton. The treatment was better under Dr. Clayton. He was post surgeon, and Dr. G. G. Roy had charge of the interior of the hospital. The treatment was better under them.

I saw men in the stocks. I cannot tell by whose order. I have heard Captain Wirz order men into the stocks, and seen the sergeant on the way to put them in. It was on March 25, 1865, when we were down to Captain Wirz's headquarters, being about to arrive there. One of the men did not answer to his name. Captain Wirz ordered the sergeant to go and put the man in the stocks. His name was Darling. I don't know how long he remained in the stocks. I never saw him afterwards.

I have seen the chain-gang. I was in the stockade at the time, and was not very near them. I do not know why the men were put in the chain-gang.

I saw the hounds. They were used for tracking the men when they made their escape. I saw men who had been caught by them. I have seen them brought back by them. I never saw any men bitten by them. There was one catch-dog, and the others were what they call plantation dogs; The catch-dog was a sort of bull-dog, and the others were more of a hound.

I was at Andersonville station three or four times, I was there in March, 1865, just before leaving, and also last December. Never prior to that. I saw a storehouse there. I should judge it was about 125 feet long, and thirty or thirty-five feet wide.

I saw men shot by the sentinels. I saw two men shot in the stockade, and one in the hospital. I cannot give any exact date. I cannot tell what month it was; it was such a common occurrence that I never took the dates or months. I saw one man shot at the south gate, as we called it, on the west side of the stockade, the southwest corner, and I saw one man shot at the north side. This man shot at the gate was a cripple; they called him "Chickamauga." The next case, the man, I don't know his name, was shot at the dead-line on the north side of the stockade. I do not know in what month. The man was killed. Captain Wirz was not present at the time the man was shot at the north side. I did not hear anything said by the person who shot him as to why the man was shot. He was shot because he reached over or under the dead-line to get a piece of bread that lay there. He died. I saw one man shot in the hospital. He went up to the fence to speak to the guard. He wanted to do some trading. The guard fired at him. I do not know whether any one ordered the guard to shoot. I don't know his name. He was a cripple afflicted with scurvy, who had to go on

[1] Record, p. 208.

crutches. He was killed. I do not remember the month in which that occurred. I called Dr. Bates's attention to it at the time, and took him down and showed him the man.

TESTIMONY OF THOS. WALSH.

Thos. Walsh, private, 74th New York, was taken to Andersonville, February 29, 1864, leaving October 20th. He testified:[1]

When I arrived at Andersonville the prison was not completed. There was a portion between the north and south gate on the east side that was not quite finished. After it was finished there was a kind of boundary marked out with sticks put into the ground so as to denote it; afterwards there was some kind of slabs of wood put around, about two and a half feet high, supported at intervals of about six, eight, or ten feet, with props. I do not know who directed it to be laid out. We got directions not to go inside that boundary mark, or otherwise the parties doing so would be taken out, bucked and gagged; I do not know who gave that order; I have seen men taken out myself by some of the sergeants of the rebel guard; they were bucked and gagged for stepping over that line. That was immediately after Captain Wirz came there. Afterwards the dead-line was established; it was immediately after Captain Wirz came there that the dead-line was established. The directions to the sergeants who used to call the roll every morning were, that no person should enter the dead-line, as, if he got in there, he would be shot.

I kept a diary, while I was there, in a testament. [Witness produces it.] I was a prisoner in Richmond three months previously to going to Andersonville, and I kept a short diary in pencil; a great portion of it is obliterated, but it is readable; I have got all the dates down.

Q. Refer to your memorandum of the 26th of March, 1864.

A. It reads, "There were no rations served out to-day." This is my memorandum which I kept in this testament. On the 27th it reads, "Rations were not served out until three o'clock; a numher is sick, weak, and hungry; what a sad thing for us all." There were no rations issued on the 1st of April. On the 2d of April they were issued about five o'clock in the afternoon; I think they consisted of meal and of what I considered mule flesh; about a pint of meal and about two or three ounces of mule flesh. I have a memorandum for the 8th of April, that the "adjutant and Dutch captain were both placed under arrest." I do not see anything about rations under that date. The memorandum for the 19th of April is, "We had no meal to-day, a little molasses and a few grains of rice." There were no rations issued on the 3d of July. On the 4th of July we got rations, but had to throw half of it away, it was so full of maggots.

I find, for the 27th of April, the memorandum: "There was a man shot in the leg for infringing beyond the boundary." I do not know his name. I do not know whether he died or not. I have down in my memorandum, on Monday, the 2d of May, "Our friend, the cavalry fellow, shot." [To counsel for accused:] I entered everything in my testament; it was written down, then and there, on the spot. I recollect the facts.

Mr. Baker: Then I shall not object.

[1] Record, p. 373 et seq.

CRUEL AND INHUMAN TREATMENT. 293

I do not know the man's name; but I knew him well, because he had been confined with me in the same building in Richmond, and we came on the same train to Andersonville. The man has been mentioned several days here. We used to call him the shaky man. He was a simpleton almost. Some boxes had arrived from Richmond that had been sent to the prisoners. Some of the men very incautiously threw some of the mouldy pieces of bread inside the dead-line. It was almost in a line with the street where we had our shanty. This poor man, after the shot had been fired, I saw lying upon the ground, with his hand stretched out inside the dead-line and part of his head inside the dead-line. The blood was oozing from him. He was then dead. It may have been two or three minutes before I got up to him. I did not see Captain Wirz present. On the 13th of July a man belonging to the 20th Indiana, 3d Army Corps, was shot on the dead-line. I suppose he was shot by one of the sentries overhead. After the shot had been fired I ran out; saw him recover his piece, and saw the smoke rise. I did not see the man myself, but I heard from his friends that he was dead. A man was shot about the 6th of August. I understood that the man had arrived the same day; that he had gone down to the stockade to get some water; that he had put his hand, with his tin cup or vessel, under the dead-line, and was shot. I heard the shot fired myself from the sentry box. I was on the north side, and had a perfect view down; I could see the water flowing down tinged with his blood; the water was not more than three or four inches deep there. I do not know that man's name or regiment. I do not know whether Captain Wirz was present or not; I did not see him. I have often heard three or four shots fired at night and during the day; but it was impossible for a person, unless he was close, to see when a man was shot. There were twenty-six or twenty-seven thousand people there on the enlargement of the stockade, about the first of July, and I believe there were thirty-five thousand there altogether at one time. One day there was a conversation outside, where I was on parole, about one of the prisoners attempting to get out, or getting into the dead-line, and the guard snapping his gun at him. The reason the guard gave for not shooting was, that he had snapped three or four caps and the piece had not gone off. Wirz said, I believe, that the man ought to be shot himself. I did not see the captain then, for he was outside, but I knew his voice.

"Chickamauga" was shot on Sunday, the 15th May, (Whit-Sunday). The entry in my memorandum is: "The singular cripple shot dead at the stockade." I knew "Chickamauga." He was confined in the same building with me in Richmond, and came at the same time to Andersonville.

I have a memorandum for the 18th of May, in reference to artillery being fired over the stockade; it reads: "General order read that if any attempt be made to break out of the stockade or the gate, the artillery to fire indiscriminately on the stockade." The rebel sergeant of our squad read the order. The order was signed by Captain Wirz; all the orders were signed by him.

On the 28th of May the entry is: "The captain is vigorously looking out for tunnels, and has succeeded." I recollect a shot being fired over the stockade; it was a shell. I have got the date down here. I recollect it very well; I think it: was shortly before I left. There were some prisoners coming in at the time, and whenever prisoners came in there was a crowd gathered about them. In fact, the place was so packed that I could hardly call it a crowd; but they got a little closer together. This shot was fired from the battery that overlooked the entire stockade.

I believe the hospital was removed about the 30th of May. The patients were in a most deplorable state. They were lying on the bare ground in shelter tents, with a strip running along, and open at each end. The wind could pass through it. The dead were put out in front of those tents, in view of the dying men themselves. I have known myself, in my own squad, that men were always in dread to go to the hospital, because they were sure to die, and I do not recollect one man that ever went into the hospital who ever came out again, except one man; his name was Kelly; he belonged to my squad; he came out, but was sent back, and he died.

I never saw the prisoner strike or maltreat any one. I have heard him threaten to shoot men for falling out of the ranks. The time he came there when our rations were first stopped he ordered us all into line and said we were to remain there until he had counted the entire stockade. I think there were about seven or eight thousand men there at the time. It was very warm, and it was almost impossible, from the weakness of the men, for them to stand until he had counted them all. Some of the squad—and I was one myself—went back to their shanties, when Captain Wirz came rushing back with a revolver in his hand and said: "May God Almighty damn me forever and ever if I don't shoot the first man who attempts to leave the ranks." On these occasions there were two sentries in each sentry-box, and directions were given that we should not leave the ranks until the second sentry went down. I have myself, even in defiance of those orders, gone into my shanty, not being able to stand the heat.

TESTIMONY OF J. R. GRIFFIN.

J. R. Griffin testified:[1]

The first portion of the past year I was an officer in the Confederate service, colonel of the 8th Georgia Cavalry, Army of Northern Virginia. For the past four months I have had an interest in trying to improve and beautify the Andersonville graveyard; that is, I have aided a brother of mine in trying to improve it. About the 20th of May last, being somewhat disabled, I went down for the purpose of observing matters at Andersonville. I heard that there had been a great deal of distress there; that was the reason I went there. I was ordered by General Wilson to go there to look after the prison. I arrived there about the 20th of May, 1865. I arrived under orders from General Wilson to protect the property there, to improve the graveyard, and to cover bodies that had been somewhat exposed, which I did I found the graveyard in rather a bad condition. It had been disturbed by cows, and part of the graves torn up to some extent, which I had covered. Two of the bodies were exposed; the bodies were placed in lines, and the dirt having been in some instances taken off them in part, the graves were somewhat offensive; that is, of the last bodies buried. No measures had been taken by the rebel government to care for that graveyard that I know of.

I saw no reason at all to believe that the uncovering of those bodies was intentional; it was from want of care. There was no person there to take care of the

[1] Record, p. 384.

graveyard. That was three or four weeks, probably, after the Andersonville prison had been broken up.

TESTIMONY OF J. E. ALDEN.

J. Everett Alden, orderly sergeant, Company F, 4th Vermont Volunteers, testified:[1]

I have a memorandum, which I made at the time, of the number of men shot by the sentinels while I was there; I remember the number aside from the memorandum; there were seven; I can state the particulars without reference to the memorandum as to the shooting of two of them; I do not think I can as to all the rest. On July 22, 1864, there was a man killed; I do not know his name or his regiment; he was shot through the groin; he was not killed instantly; he was taken outside to the hospital; the guard shot him; he was over the dead-line; he was a sergeant, and he was anxious to get outside with his men, as he had some who were very badly off; he wanted to be the first to get outside to the door, and he crowded up; the sentinel repeatedly told him to keep back; a sergeant came up to the gate, with whom he was acquainted, and he motioned to him if he could come out; the sergeant beckoned to him to come out, but the guard did not notice it; the man crowded past, and the guard raised his gun; he could not lift it high enough to shoot him through the body, but he shot him through the groin; I did not see the man afterwards; he was a sergeant in charge of a squad. I do not know his name or regiment; I must have been some eight feet from him. Captain Wirz was not present at that time; at least I did not see him. The next instance was July 26th; I cannot tell where that man was shot; he was shot inside the stockade by a sentinel. On the 4th of August two men were shot; I do not know where they were shot; I do not know their names; they were shot inside the stockade. The next instance of shooting was on the 6th of August; I do not know who the man was who was then shot; I do not know whether any of the others, except the first one I have mentioned, died; I merely made a memorandum at the time the event occurred. The next instance was on the 25th of August; I saw that man; the camp was all quiet; it was in the evening, a bright, moonshiny night, between the hours of ten and twelve; I heard a musket fired; I spoke to the man lying alongside of me, and said there is a man shot, and I am going to see who it is; I arose, and when I got three or four rods, several others joined me and we moved toward the dead-line; I was about a hundred yards from the dead-line at that time, and was looking towards the sentinel; he raised his gun and shot again; that was the second shot at the same man, I suppose; as I got down where I could see a third shot was fired; the man was inside the dead-line, up close to it, and the words he used were, "See if you can kill me now"; I should think, by the conversation, that the officer of the guard was in the sentry-box; the man was shot through the head, the ball passing lengthwise of his body; I inquired round there who the man was, and they said he was a man who was tired of living, and wanted the sentinel to shoot him; I think he was shot in the leg by the first discharge; the last ball proved fatal. The man died in the course of ten minutes; I do not know his name or regiment; it was in the north end of the stockade. The creek does not run exactly in the center of the camp. It was

[1] Record, p. 385 et seq.

in the larger part of the stockade towards the end—about the middle of the stockade. I find also that one man was shot on the 5th of September; I do not know any of the circumstances. On January 1, 1865, I saw a man shot; I saw him after he was dead; he was struck in the head; the sentinel that shot him was near the south gate; I know the circumstances of the shooting; it was the last time I was put in the stockade; I left there in September and went in there again towards the last of December. There were boards piled up near the dead-line in the stockade, and men who were destitute of anything to lie upon thought that if they could get those boards they would make a floor to keep them from lying on the ground; after it was dark several made attempts to get them, and were successful. This man did not prove quite as much so as the rest; he had hold of the end of a board and was dragging at it. It was a very cold night, about ten or eleven o'clock; the sentry had gone down from his box to warm himself by the fire, and the fellow took the opportunity to get the board, but in doing so he made somewhat of a noise, which alarmed the sentinel, who crept to a crack and saw the man getting the board, and then he slyly went upstairs and shot the man without any warning. I should think the boards were within ten or fifteen feet of the stockade; five feet from the dead-line, perhaps; I do not think the dead-line was over twenty feet from the stockade.

I have seen acts of cruelty committed by Captain Wirz. Last September the hundred to which I belonged were ordered to get ready and march out of the stockade. As we marched out—it was at night, and there were fires on each side of the gate, so that they could see to count the men off as they passed out—a large fellow, named, I think, Williams, a rebel sergeant, had a large stick, or club, in his hand. Captain Wirz was outside of the gate, and this Williams got the men in four ranks, so that they could be counted, while another man counted them at the gate. The men were so impatient to get outside the stockade that they crowded down as near the gate as they could get, and a great many who did not belong in the hundreds flanked out. At last Captain Wirz became very much enraged because the men crowded down on him, and did not give him a chance to get them into four ranks, so that he could count them. He told the sergeant to knock them down, if they did not keep back out of the way. He struck down between the files, but hit nobody.

TESTIMONY OF ROBERT TATE.

Robert Tate, private, 52d Pennsylvania Volunteers, testified:[1]

I saw Captain Wirz commit acts of cruelty while I was at Andersonville. I saw him kick men who were not able to stand on their feet at roll-call. About the first of May one case occurred. It was a man who was very sick and weak. The orders were to fall into line in the morning at seven o'clock at roll-call, and the men were kept standing there in the heat of the sun until about twelve o'clock. This man fell down out of the line and his comrades rolled him out alongside under one of the sheds there. Captain Wirz came along and saw the man there and asked him what he was doing there. The man told him he was sick and could not stand in line. Captain Wirz said, "God damn your soul, I will keep you into line." He kicked the man and rolled him back to the line; the man lay there and was not

[1] Record, p. 388.

able to stand up. In the course of two days the man died. I don't know what his name was nor his regiment.

The prisoner fired his pistol at me one day for being out of line at roll-call. I had a very sore leg and could not stand more than about half an hour at a time. I got weak and left the line and went into the shade of a tent and lay down there; directly Captain Wirz came out. I heard the sound of his footsteps and hastened to get back into line so that he could not see me, but he saw me and said: "Hold on there, you Yankee son of a bitch." I commenced running; he said: "Hold on"; I kept running; he fired his pistol. I got back into line and tried to hide myself. Captain Wirz came along and wanted to know where that man was, and said that he would not issue any rations till the man was found. I stepped out and said: "Captain Wirz, I have a sore leg." He said: "God damn. I wish the legs would rot off of every damn son of a bitch in the stockade, and I would have no more trouble with you." The ball from his pistol did not strike me.

I know the rations were stopped on the 1st of April, 1864; I do not know the cause; I think it was on account of some trouble at roll-call. There were too many men in the stockade and Captain Wirz could not get the exact number of the prisoners; and he swore that he would not issue rations till he got the exact number of the men in the stockade. He said that we got more than we deserved; that if he had his will, he would not give us anything to eat.

I knew some Libby prisoners who were put in the stocks; I don't know of any who died while in the stocks; I don't know of any who died immediately after being taken out. I have known them to die in the course of three weeks afterward. I have known a man to be kept in the stocks forty-eight hours without anything to eat or drink, except what was smuggled to him; that was Captain Wirz's order, not to give him anything to eat or drink for forty-eight hours. His name was B. F. Russell; he belonged to the 17th Pennsylvania Cavalry, Company A.

TESTIMONY OF S. J. M. ANDREWS.

Samuel J. M. Andrews testified:[1]

I was in the military service of the United States; I belonged to the 17th Illinois Infantry; I was a prisoner at Andersonville from April 27, 1864, till some time in September, 1864.

I saw a good many cases of vaccination while there; I should think two or three hundred; almost all that I saw had large sores upon their arms, and some on other parts of their body, from the size of a dollar to that of the palm of my hand; some had two on the same arm, some one on each arm; almost invariably, so far as I knew, amputation was the result; death was the final result in almost all cases of amputation; I have known instances in which men suffering from these sores became insane; I have seen two or three such cases; I observed one in particular; the man was in the same tent as I was in the hospital; he seemed to be completely insane; his agony and suffering was so intense that that seemed to be the cause of his insanity—the suffering which he endured from these sores.

I have not recovered from the effects of that confinement there; I am still troubled with the effects of what I suppose to be scurvy; my mouth and gums occasionally bleed without any apparent cause.

[1] Record, p. 390.

298   THE TRAGEDY OF ANDERSONVILLE.

Among the witnesses to the cruelties described in this chapter, are eight who were in the rebel service at Andersonville. Their testimony is direct and positive. They saw the acts of cruelty committed which were charged against Wirz. Such testimony cannot be neutralized or disputed by the negative testimony of others who testified that they neither heard of nor saw such acts committed.

I will not admit, even by implication, that the testimony of the prisoners is not entitled to full credence. But it is fortunate that they are so completely corroborated by witnesses whose testimony the defenders of Wirz will not have the hardihood to doubt.

Here as elsewhere in this history of the Andersonville atrocities the findings of the court may rest upon rebel testimony.

REPORTS MADE ON CRUELTIES INFLICTED ON UNION PRISONERS OF WAR.

The Wirz Military Commission was not the only official body that investigated the horrors of Southern prison-pens. Sworn testimony was the basis of the reports which I venture to include in this volume in part.

The U. S. Sanitary Commission appointed in May, 1864, a committee to investigate as to the treatment of Union soldiers, prisoners, in Confederate prison-pens, and that committee—consisting of Drs. Valentine Mott and Edward Delafield, and Governor Morris Wilkins, of New York, and Dr. Ellerslie Wallace, Hon. John J. Clark Hare, and Rev. Treadwell Walden, of Philadelphia—said in their report made some months later:[1]

It is the same story everywhere; prisoners of war treated worse than convicts, shut up either in suffocating buildings, or in out-door inclosures, without even the shelter that is provided for the beasts of the field; unsupplied with sufficient food; supplied with food and water injurious and even poisonous; compelled to live on floors often covered with human filth, or on ground saturated with it; compelled to breathe an air oppressed with an intolerable stench; hemmed in by a fatal deadline, and in hourly danger of being shot by unrestrained and brutal guards; despondent even to madness, idiocy, and suicide; sick, of diseases (so congruous in character as to appear and spread like the plague) caused by the torrid sun, by decaying food, by filth, by vermin, by malaria, and by cold; removed at the last moment, and by hundreds at a time, to hospitals corrupt as a sepulcher, there, with few remedies, little care, and no sympathy, to die in wretchedness and despair, not only among strangers, but among enemies too resentful either to have pity or to show mercy. These are positive facts. Tens of thousands of helpless men have been, and are now being, disabled and destroyed by a process as certain as poison,

[1] See Lossing's "Pictorial History of the Civil War," Vol. III, p. 593.

and as cruel as the torture or burning at the stake, because nearly as agonizing and more prolonged. This spectacle is daily beheld and allowed by the rebel government. No supposition of negligence, or indifference, or accident, or inefficiency, or destitution or necessity, can account for all this. So many, and such positive forms of abuse and wrong cannot come from negative causes. The conclusion is unavoidable, therefore, that these privations and sufferings have been designedly inflicted by the military and other authority of the rebel government, and cannot have been due to causes which such authorities could not control.

Lossing, in comment on this report, says:[1]

Such was the verdict of a committee of men whose ability, honor, integrity and fidelity, to the duties demanded by truth and justice, no man can rightfully question. It is the testimony of eye and ear-witnesses which no one, competent to speak, has ever dared to deny. We read with feelings of horror of the cruelty of the British in India, in blowing their Sepoy prisoners to atoms from the muzzles of cannon. That act was merciful compared to the fiendishness exhibited toward Union prisoners in the late Civil War. We read with feelings of horror of the tortures formerly inflicted upon prisoners by the savages of our wilderness. These were mild sufferings compared with those to which the conspirators and their instruments subjected the soldiers of the Republic when they fell into their hands.

With this Report in hand, United States Senator Howard in a speech in the Senate, said, "The testimony is as clear as the noonday sun, that their barbarities were deliberately practiced upon our men for the double purpose of crippling and reducing our armed force, and of striking terror into the Northern population in order to prevent enlistments. There does not remain ground for a doubt that the rebel government designedly resorted to the slow process of torture and death by starvation, and to freezing and starving united, operating minute by minute, hour by hour, day by day, week by week, and month by month, until the man became a living skeleton and idiot, no longer able to recognize his wife, his children, or his friends; no longer of any value either to himself or to his country; and this for the purpose of weakening our military arm and deterring our people from prosecuting the war."

A committee of the House of Representatives, appointed July 10, 1867, and consisting of John P. C. Shanks, of Indiana; William A. Pile, of Missouri; Abner C. Harding, of Illinois; Aaron F. Stevens, of New Hampshire, and William Munger, of Ohio, to investigate "treatment of prisoners of war and Union citizens by the so-called Confederate Government," said:[2]

The subsequent history of Andersonville, has startled and shocked the world with a tale of horror, of woe, and death, before unheard and unknown to civilization. No pen can describe, no painter sketch, no imagination comprehend its fearful and unutterable iniquity. It would seem as if the concentrated madness of earth and hell had found its final lodgment in the breasts of those who inaugurated the Rebellion and controlled the policy of the Confederate Government, and that the prison at Andersonville had been selected for the most terrible human sacrifice

[1] See Lossing's "Pictorial History of the Civil War," Vol. III, p. 593.
[2] House of Representatives, Fortieth Congress, Third Session, Report No. 45.

which the world had ever seen. Into its narrow walls were crowded thirty-five thousand enlisted men, many of them the bravest and best, the most devoted and heroic of those grand armies which carried the flag of their country to final victory. For long and weary months here they suffered, maddened, were murdered, and died. Here they fingered, unsheltered from the burning rays of a tropical sun by day, and drenching and deadly dews by night, in every stage of mental and physical disease, hungered, emaciated, starving, maddened; festering with unhealed wounds; gnawed by the ravages of scurvy and gangrene, with swollen limbs and distorted visage; covered with vermin which they had no power to extirpate; exposed to the flooding rains which drove them drowning from the miserable holes in which, like swine, they burrowed; parched with thirst and mad with hunger; racked with pain or prostrated with the weakness of dissolution, with naked limbs and matted hair; filthy with smoke and mud; soiled with the very excrement from which their weakness would not permit them to escape; eaten by the gnawing worms which their own wounds had engendered, with no bed but the earth, no covering save the clouds or the sky; and these men, these heroes, born in the image of God, thus crouching and writhing in their terrible torture, a loathsome, horrible sight, the mutilated, murdered victims of a cool and calculating barbarity, stand forth in history as a monument of the surpassing horrors of Andersonville, as it shall be seen and read in all future time, realizing in the studied torments of their prison house the ideal of Dante's Inferno and Milton's Hell.

CHAPTER XI.

TESTIMONY OF WITNESSES FOR DEFENSE UPON THE SPECIFICATIONS OF ACTS OF CRUELTY AND OF MURDER IN VIOLATION OF THE LAWS OF WAR—MAN SHOT ON DEAD LINE—HUNTED DOWN BY DOGS—PUT IN STOCKS AND CHAIN GANG—WIRZ KICKED AND ABUSED PRISONERS—VERY PROFANE—HIGH TEMPER—CARRIED PISTOL—THREATENED TO USE IT—SOME ACTS OF KINDNESS SHOWN—WITNESSES NEVER HEARD OF HIS KILLING OR TREATING A PRISONER CRUELLY.

IT would seem unnecessary to quote further from the Record in support of the specifications now being considered. It remains to notice the exculpatory evidence introduced by the defense either in palliation or denial of the mass of proof introduced by the prosecution, and also as bearing on the charge of murder to be particularly noticed in the next chapter.

Some of the witnesses called for the defense were not examined on these subjects and will not be quoted. Those who testified to facts tending to mitigate or explain or deny the cruelties of Wirz, will now be given opportunity to speak in his behalf.

Nazareth Allen, a rebel soldier, recalled for the defense, testified that Captain Wirz rode a gray or white horse; that he never "knew of him having a sorrel or roan horse."

I never knew a man to get a furlough for shooting a Union prisoner. I have heard some little talk of it, but I never knew of its being done; I just heard a little sort of rumor. I do not know anything about it. I never heard of any particular man who got such a furlough.[1]

TESTIMONY OF CAPTAIN ARMSTRONG

Captain Armstrong, C. S. A., on duty at Andersonville from March to August and again from December to the end. His duty was to receive stores. He testified:

I never knew or heard of any Confederate soldier getting a furlough for shooting a Union prisoner. I never knew or heard of Captain Wirz shooting, killing, or in any way injuring a Union prisoner while I was there.

I was not familiar with the business going on at Captain Wirz's headquarters, or at the headquarters of the commandant of the post. I would not know anything about granting furloughs if there had been any granted.

While I was there, previous to August, I was not familiar with Captain Wirz's conduct. After that time I became more intimate and better acquainted with him.[2]

[1] Record, p. 471.
[2] Record, p. 661.

TESTIMONY OF DR. BATES.

Dr. Bates, surgeon at Andersonville, recalled, testified:

I never heard of Captain Wirz shooting, beating, kicking or otherwise maltreating Union prisoners while I was at Andersonville.

Captain Wirz was never absent from duty when he was sick, to my knowledge.[1]

Q. You spoke of Captain Wirz looking feeble at one time; for how long a time was that his appearance?

A. Well, sir, I did not see him for some time after that. I did not make it an object to go over. I saw him occasionally after that, and he looked better. Captain Wirz I suppose began to improve perhaps in October; I did not see him very often. I do not know whether he was ever released from duty because he was sick; I never saw anything to indicate that.

TESTIMONY OF DR. CASTELEN.

Dr. Castelen, rebel surgeon, testified:

I never knew or heard anything about furloughs being granted to any of our men for shooting Union soldiers.

I saw Captain Wirz's horse two or three times. I never saw him have a sorrel horse. I never saw Captain Wirz with any kind of a horse but a gray horse.[2] I never knew or heard of Captain Wirz shooting or beating a man with a revolver, or in any way maltreating a man so as to kill him; if such a thing had been done I should not have heard it except from rumors in the camp; I might have heard of it in that way. I was at Andersonville from May, 1864, till the last of September.

My duties did not require me to visit Captain Wirz very frequently. I don't think I visited Captain Wirz while I was there. My duties did not require me to visit the stockade or prison. I know no more about the stockade or Captain Wirz than what I stated in my evidence when I was first on the stand.

TESTIMONY OF DR. FLEWELLEN.

Dr. E. A Flewellen, inspected the prison hospital in August; again in November and again in January. He was recalled for the defense and testified:[3]

Q. At any time while you were at Andersonville did you hear of Captain Wirz shooting, beating with a pistol, or in any way maltreating Union prisoners?

A. I never heard anything of the kind.

Q. If such a thing occurred would you not have been likely to hear of it?

A. I made an honest effort while I was there to arrive at all evils connected with the prison hospital, and indirectly with the prison itself, and I should have thought the officers I conferred with very derelict in their duty if they had not reported anything of the kind that they knew; I made an honest effort to get at the facts.

[1] Record, p. 664. Wirz's illness and absence from duty were urged as in the nature of an alibi.
[2] Witnesses for the prosecution testified to having seen Wirz riding a white or roan horse.
[3] Record, p. 474.

MONUMENT ERECTED BY THE STATE OF MASSACHUSETTS.

TESTIMONY OF DR. ROY.

Dr. G. G. Roy was recalled for the defense. He went to Andersonville, September, 1864. He testified:[1]

During the month of September Captain Wirz was sick; I did not see him except on one occasion; that was at his house. I was called to take charge of a number of assistant surgeons to go and attend a collision that occurred, which happened just about half a mile below Captain Wirz's house. He was sick two-thirds of September, if not all of it. During that month he was sick most of the time; in other words he was not on duty. My going to his house was altogether accidental; I did not attend him professionally, but I had to pass there in going a half mile below his house to reach this train that had run off the track. There were a number of killed and wounded. I stopped at his house, and, if the court will excuse the expression, I took there a drink of whiskey and a cup of coffee. He was not in bed; he was unable to be at his office in Andersonville.

I have sometimes in the hospital dressed the wounds of men who had been injured, but generally my assistant did that. I never dressed one who had been wounded with a pistol or a revolver there at Andersonville; I never knew of any such case; I never knew or heard of Captain Wirz shooting or beating a man to death while I was at Andersonville.

I had knowledge of the condition of Captain Wirz's arm while I was at Andersonville; I saw it often. I tried to treat him, but he would not let me do so; not, I believe, because he had not confidence in my treatment, but he thought it might get well of itself; that was his expression.

The prisoner at the request of Mr. Baker removed a portion of the covering from his right, arm.

Q. Examine the prisoner's arm and see what is its present condition, and state what was its condition then as compared with its present condition?

A. From my knowledge of his arm and my professional knowledge, I do not think he would be able to strike a man and knock him down with that arm. I should not think he would be able, in any way, to strike a man down with anything in the hand of that arm. He might defend himself with that arm in its disabled condition, in a certain way; I mean he might feebly defend himself, but it would not be such a defense as I would like to have. I think he could not with that arm or hand grapple or shake any one. I have not seen Captain Wirz's left shoulder; I have not examined it.

I never knew or heard of any Confederate soldiers getting a furlough for shooting a Union prisoner while I was there.

I was not with him except on certain occasions, which I can mention. I can remember some other occasions when I met him, besides at the depot; but so seldom that they did not impress me. I would say to the court that I rented a house two miles from Andersonville, and I had there my wife and children. I usually visited the hospital between eight and nine o'clock. I always had an officer of the day, who was responsible for the administration of the hospital during the day and night. In coming to the hospital I did not go by Captain

---

[1] Record, p. 656 et seq. We have official reports signed by Wirz in September and he gave Dr. Jones passes into the prison while he was there.

Wirz's headquarters by nearly a quarter of a mile. I went directly to the hospital and attended to my duties. Very frequently I would stay there after I got through my duties, to see the prisoners play cricket, and things of that sort, just to look at their amusements. I very seldom saw Captain Wirz except at the depot.

I never saw Captain Wirz engage in any effort to defend himself against attacks of prisoners or anything of the kind. I have never seen him defend himself in any respect. I have never seen him in any belligerent motion whatever. My opinion with regard to the disability of his arm is simply a scientific one; judging from its nature and appearance, that it would not be a very serviceable arm in such a contest, and that is all I know about it.

Captain Wirz's headquarters, when I first arrived at Andersonville, were in a tent adjoining Dr. White; I met him very frequently then because I had to pass right by his tent door to go over to the depot. I cannot answer how long that tent was there; it was there a week and a fortnight,—I think, probably a month; it was in the month of September. I met him very seldom, because he was brought in in an ambulance; he came to his office to look over his records, and was carried directly back. I cannot say if that was the case during all that month; it was so, so far as my knowledge goes, most of the time during that month.

Q. When you say that he was sick, you do not mean to say that he was so sick that he did not come to camp?
A. He came there. He was reported as being unfit for duty by the surgeon who was attending him; I believe it was Dr. White or Dr. Stevenson. So far as I know he did not come in camp every day in an ambulance. Let me make an explanation. Captain Wirz occupied half of a house owned by a man named Boss, about two miles from Andersonville. During the month of September he was most of the time unable to perform any active military duty. There was no one, so far as I know, to occupy his place in his office, because his duties were very peculiar; and he came down in an ambulance whenever he was able, whenever his fever was off him or whenever he was able to look over his list, which was made out by a man named Martin, who was a paroled Federal prisoner and who was his clerk. . . .

Rev. Mr. Duncan testified that he preached to the Union soldiers on several occasions and while there he "never heard of Captain Wirz shooting, killing, kicking or otherwise injuring a prisoner; I heard nothing on that score."[1]

The testimony of Rev. Father Whelan has been given in a previous chapter.

TESTIMONY OF REV. W. J. HAMILTON.

Rev. Father Hamilton was recalled for the defense. He testified also quite fully for the prosecution. His testimony for the defense was brief and is as follows:[2]

[1] Record, p. 610.
[2] Record, p. 425.

I have been at Andersonville frequently; I had an opportunity of observing the conduct of Captain Wirz while I was there to a very limited extent. It seemed to me that he was disposed to do everything in his power for their spiritual comfort, and as far as I could see for their bodily comfort also. He gave me every facility in the pursuit of my object.

I had no complaints made to me by prisoners of ill-treatment on the part of Captain Wirz; I never heard of any prisoner dying from any such treatment from the hands of Captain Wirz, nor from any personal violence from him; I never knew of a prisoner being torn by dogs there; nothing of the kind. In declining to answer the question put to me the other day by the Judge Advocate, I did not decline on the ground that the answer would in any way prejudice Captain Wirz or make against him.[1]

TESTIMONY OF COLONEL FANNIN.

Colonel Fannin, recalled for the defense. He was asked about furloughs being granted for shooting prisoners and replied: "I am satisfied it was never done." He testified further:[2]

There never was an application of that kind made to me that I know of; if there had been such an application I think I would have recollected it; I was never requested by any one to give a guard a furlough because he had shot a Union prisoner; I recollect on one occasion there was a man applying for a furlough who, it appeared, had shot one or two Union prisoners for crossing the dead-line at night, and it was remarked by some one, when he made the application, that he was a good shot and that he ought to be furloughed; but there was no furlough granted and no application made on that ground; the reason that remark was made was that a great many prisoners had crossed the dead-line, and had traded a good deal with the guards; they used to tie their watches to strings and exchange them with the guards for potatoes; the remark was made in this way to show that this man had not been bribed, and had not been trading with the prisoners. . . .

Captain Wirz had control of the guards after they were turned over to him, until a new guard was furnished to take their place. I do not know whether he ever inflicted punishment on them or not. He could arrest them, I suppose, if they did not do their duty, and I understood he did arrest some and prefer charges. He was recognized as a captain in the rebel army. I saw that he signed himself as assistant adjutant-general, and gave transportation, but not until this year. He was a staff officer of General Winder's.

Q. Could he not exercise the same power as General Winder, by reason of his being a staff officer; and did he not so issue transportation?

A. He did issue transportation on the railroad from Andersonville to other points. I obtained a furlough from him once; I said he could not give a furlough to a soldier unless when he was in command of the post. Then it was

---

[1] Many rebel witnesses as well as prisoners testified to the facts met only by this negative witness.
[2] Record, p. 433 et seq.

necessary for him to approve a furlough. He did approve a furlough for me when he was in command of the post. I presume he gave other furloughs when he was in command of the post; I never saw it; I understood that General Winder was in supreme command while there.

I knew Captain Wirz had command of the prison; I was not a familiar associate of Captain Wirz; I did not see him every day. He was not an associate of mine. His business and place of business were entirely different from mine.

Q. Did not the officers shun him, regarding him as a man not fit for their association?

Objected to, and modified so as to apply only to witness.

I did not associate. a great deal with Captain Wirz. Our business was different; I had other friends at the post. I had plenty to associate with; I did not select him while there as an associate. I was in the stockade three times, I think, while I was on duty there. I was in the stockade I think in June, 1864, when Colonel Persons was in command, and I think the other time I was there was in 1865, when Colonel Gibbs was in command. The only time I was in the stockade in 1864, was once in June, I think; I was not familiar enough in Captain Wirz's headquarters to know all that was going on there. My business was elsewhere. Part of the time my office was half a mile from his, and part of the time it was not more than two or three hundred yards, but all this year my office was away from his nearly half a mile; I cannot say that I knew what was doing in there. I have never known an application for a furlough on the grounds of a soldier having shot a Yankee prisoner. So far as I am concerned, I do not know that any application was ever made to me on that score. I would not influence a man to shoot prisoners unnecessarily. I certainly would not hold out that inducement.

Q. Then you would not very likely have found it embodied in the application as one of the reasons why a furlough should be granted?

A. So far as that is concerned, I do not think a man would state that in his application.

Q. From what you know of General Winder's power there, and of Captain Wirz's influence as staff officer, would not his or their approval have secured a furlough for any soldier?

A. General Winder's certainly would; there is no doubt of that.

I never knew Captain Wirz to commit any act of cruelty towards prisoners of war of my own personal knowledge. I never saw it. I have been near the post when prisoners arrived and were being carried off. Some of them would get out of place when standing in ranks, and I have heard Captain Wire curse men for being out of their places and say that he would shoot them if they did not get into line. I have seen him draw a pistol on the men. He was a profane man. I have heard him swear and curse a good deal. A great many men in his office seemed to be getting on with him very well. I have heard him talk sociably with them, and I have heard him swear and curse them sometimes. I did not say that I never heard of any act of cruelty on his part. That was not what I intended to say. I have heard a good deal sworn against him on the stand here, and when at Andersonville I heard of men being in the stocks, and I have seen them in the stocks. I have seen men in the chain-gang.

TESTIMONY OF SAMUEL HALL.

Samuel Hall, recalled for defense, testified:[1]

Q. What do you know about Captain Wirz being sick in August, or at any time?

A. Well, the first time I ever saw Captain Wirz in my life, I think, was in the month of August. He had the appearance then of having recovered from a spell of sickness. He was feeble and emaciated. When he was taken sick, or how long he was sick, I don't know.

Q. What is the law in relation to the employment of dogs to search for prisoners and such like in the State of Georgia?

A. There is no law on the subject of hunting prisoners in Georgia. Dogs are used for tracking, felons, violators of the law, and for tracking runaway slaves. By the laws of Georgia you cannot pursue anybody with ferocious, savage dogs.

THE JUDGE ADVOCATE. We do not want a judicial opinion. Tell us the authority.

A. It is a statute of the State and a decision of the supreme court on that statute to which I refer. It is the 18th volume Georgia Reports; the case of Morgan versus Davis. I argued the case before the supreme court for the counsel for the plaintiff in error, who was absent.

[The Judge Advocate objected to the testimony as irrelevant and immaterial, to say nothing of placing men who fought for their country on the level of common felons. Mr. Baker contended that the evidence was proper. He wanted to show by this witness that dogs might be by the laws of Georgia used to track colored people and prisoners.]

THE WITNESS. I stated distinctly that I knew of no law covering this case.

[Mr. Baker said that he wished to get from this witness such facts as he could get bearing on that point, and that he would finally show that by the laws of the United States, the use of dogs for such purpose was authorized; that the United States government was the first to authorize and command the use of hounds to track human beings in this country.]

GENERAL THOMAS. I suppose you mean in Florida.

MR. BAKER. I shall trace it to several places, and I shall follow that up by showing that these people were bound by law to do what they were commanded to do by their superior officers.

[After deliberation, the decision of the court was announced, sustaining the objection. Examination resumed:]

I do not know any laws in reference to the recapture of prisoners. There was a law forbidding the inhabitants to entertain or harbor our prisoners. There was a State law against it, making it a capital felony. I have never seen prisoners who were brought back to Andersonville searched there. I never witnessed any searching there. The fact never came to me officially. I only know of that from what others told me. I know nothing in the world about the effort of Captain Wirz to exchange the prisoners, or anything of that sort, except what Captain Wirz told me.

I was not often at the prison; I was at the post frequently.

[1] Record, p. 492.

VIOLATION OF RULES OF WAR. 309

Q. Did you at any time know or hear of Captain Wirz shooting or beating a prisoner with a pistol, or killing him in any other way?

A. No, sir; I never heard about that. It was not my business to search into it. Any testimony that I can give on that subject is merely negative. I saw Captain Wirz riding a white mare.

Q. You know how to prove that a thing was not done; is it not always proved by negative testimony?

[The Judge Advocate objected. It was for the court, not for the witness, to decide that. Objection sustained.]

I do not know how often I was at Andersonville. I may have been there twenty times. I never went there unless I had business. All my observations there were based upon these twenty visits-I do not think they exceeded that number. I did not always see Captain Wirz when I went there. I cannot say the number of times I saw him. I most generally saw him there. I know nothing in the world about the management of that interior prison.

TESTIMONY OF W. D. HAMMACK.

W. D. Hammack, a rebel soldier on duty at Andersonville, testified:[1]

I never saw or knew of Captain Wirz going with the hounds at any time. I never saw the dogs sent after Confederate soldiers. Turner had a pack of dogs at the post and there was a pack in the country; I have seen those hounds, but I do not think they belonged to the post. Those dogs of Turner's were common fox dogs. I suppose I never knew anything about a man who had been bitten by dogs dying at Captain Wirz's headquarters. I never heard of such a thing; not while I was at Andersonville.

Captain Wirz's horse was a gray mare; I never saw him ride a sorrel or roan horse. I never knew of such a horse belonging to him being about his quarters, not of his.

I never knew Captain Wirz to shoot or beat a prisoner so that he died while I was there. I never heard of it while I was at Andersonville.

I never shot a prisoner of war or saw one shot; I never saw any of the sentries fire when I was up on the stoops; I heard the report of guns very frequently; I cannot say whether from the stockade or from around the post. I know they were fired about the post.

Q. You say you have known frequent occasions when prisoners of war had been brought out of the stockade who had been shot?

A. No, I do not say I knew it frequently; I have seen, I think, four or five fetched out of the stockade, to the best of my knowledge.

I never heard of soldiers procuring furloughs for shooting Union prisoners. The first thing I ever heard about it was when Furlow's battalion came there. I heard some of their men speaking about it. Then it got into the reserve regiments—that if a man shot a Federal prisoner he would get a thirty days' furlough. But I do not think any man could say where the report started from. I do not think it could be traced back. I do not know anything at all about the fact, only what I heard men say. I was not on duty in the adjutant's

[1] Record, p. 502 et seq.

office; I don't know how our men got furloughs if they got any; I did not see the applications. I do not know anything about them officially.

Captain Wirz never shot or beat or kicked a prisoner of war while I was on duty there to my knowledge. I have not told any person since I have been a witness in Washington, that I have seen him kick and abuse prisoners of war. I have said that I have seen him take hold of men like any officer would, when the men were standing in full ranks, and draw them to their places if they were not exactly right. He generally spoke short to them. He did not speak kindly to anybody; he always spoke short. He was very profane, one of the profanest men I ever saw. He had a very severe temper. I never saw him mistreat a prisoner of war, unless you call it mistreating to take hold of a man and draw him up to his place. I am not positive that he cursed him at the same time, but it is more than likely he did, because that was his natural style of conversation. I saw men in the stocks. I saw them wearing ball and chain. I do not think I ever saw anything else of the kind. I never saw men tied up by the thumbs; I never saw them whipped.

I have seen a pistol in his hand a good many times. I do not know that I ever saw him draw it; I know he would draw it for a whole squad, and would threaten to shoot them if they did not do so and so; but I do not think I ever saw him draw it on one man.

TESTIMONY OF COLONEL PERSONS.

Colonel Persons, recalled for defense, testified:[1]

I certainly know that General Winder ordered dogs to be employed. I do not remember whether I told Captain Wirz, or served him with the order; I am safe in saying, however, that he had notice of the fact that that was General Winder's order. I do not understand that the dogs were bloodhounds; they were the rabbit dogs that we use down there for running rabbits, and which are sometimes used for running negroes—a very ordinary pack of hounds. I never saw the pack of hounds that Turner had. There was a pack from the country of four or five, owned by a man named Harris; that is the one I have reference to. Harris's pack was not used at the same time Turner had his there. I never saw Turner or his dogs. These were dogs owned by a citizen out in the country. Citizens would frequently bring in prisoners without any orders from any one at the post; it was purely a voluntary matter on their part. I never knew of Captain Wirz being absent with the hounds hunting prisoners. I never knew him to be absent for that purpose.

Captain Wirz could not in any way give furloughs to the guards for shooting Union prisoners. I never heard of a guard obtaining a furlough for shooting a Union prisoner, and do not believe that there was any, while I was at the post. I think I would have heard of it if any such thing had happened. Things might have been smuggled through without my knowing it, as a matter of course, but I think I should have detected it. If it was given to them as a reward, I think I would have heard of it. We had to send furloughs for approval to General Winder if they exceeded seven days. I granted seven days' furloughs. General

---

[1] Record, p. 456 et seq.

Winder was at Richmond. I do not know positively anything about Captain Wirz relieving the guards whenever they shot a prisoner.

I never knew or heard of Captain Wirz in any way shooting, or beating with a pistol, or kicking to death, any prisoner while I was there. I never knew of his killing them in any way or brutally treating them. If he had used any extraordinary violence it strikes me I would have heard of it, but I never did. Captain Wirz rode a gray mare—a white animal, almost perfectly white. I never saw him on any other than a white horse.

I never saw a chain-gang or stocks in my life. I did see a dozen men or so chained together, but that did not constitute the chain-gang which I have heard spoken of. I saw them chained togther; I do not know what it was for. I presume that was not the chain-gang mentioned here. I only know the chain-gang by reputation.

I understood the chain-gang—I do not know positively about it—to be a number of men linked together in such a way as to allow them to move around. Those men that I saw were chained together in the shape of a square, so they could not move. I never saw those in the chain-gang. It was not done by my order; I don't know by whose order it was done. I never exercised the right to punish prisoners of war; I never had it under my letter of instructions. I do not know who had the right to punish them. Captain Wirz was commander of the prison; he exercised the right, and I presume he had it. Captain Wirz's orders came through me, but he never received any order to punish prisoners through me. If he punished them it was at his own instance, and I presume he was responsible.

TESTIMONY OF MAJOR G. L. PROCTOR.

Major Geo. L. Proctor, C. S. A., commissary at Andersonville, testified:[1]

While I was at Andersonville I never knew or heard of Captain Wirz shooting or in any way killing a man.

I never knew or heard of a Confederate soldier getting a furlough for shooting a Union prisoner; I knew nothing outside of my department, and I heard nothing of it.

TESTIMONY OF CAPTAIN WRIGHT.

Captain Wright, C. S. A., recalled for defense, testified:[2]

I have seen the dogs there. I never saw Captain Wirz go with them. I do not know whether dogs were used there before Captain Wirz came; J remember of their bringing prisoners in who had been captured with dogs; I don't know whether it was before Captain Wirz came there. It was before Turner's dogs were employed. I think it was before any dogs at all were employed at the post. This man Harris brought them in—no one connected with the post. I knew two planters around Andersonville that had hounds. I know that this man Harris brought in prisoners. He is the only farmer that had hounds, that I know of, that did so. Confederate soldiers were hunted by Turner's hounds. I

---
[1] Record, p. 669.
[2] Record, p. 480 et seq.

do not know whether he ever captured them or not. I know that he started after them. Turner applied to me to be paid for his hound running. I refused to pay him. He then went to the commander of the post—Colonel Forno, I think, was in command then. He decided that Turner was not entitled to it, being a detailed man; that he was only entitled to his detailed pay of twenty-five cents per day extra.

Q. What do you know about complaints being made on the part of Captain Wirz on account of the bad condition of affairs there?

I cannot now think of any specific act on the part of Captain Wirz to ameliorate the condition of the prison. I know that I carried different things into the stockade to the prisoners—vegetables and other things. Captain Wirz never prevented or tried to prevent me from doing so. I always showed him what I had to carry in, and he would give me a pass to take it in.

I never knew or heard of Captain Wirz promising a guard a furlough for shooting Union soldiers. I never knew of any one getting a furlough for that cause. Captain Wirz gave transportation in the name of General Winder; he used to sign the orders for transportation there.

Q. Can you explain that?

A. We had an order from Richmond forbidding any one to issue transportation except on the orders of chiefs of bureaus and commanders of armies and departments. That locked up our post so that we could not issue any transportation at all until General Winder got an order allowing him to issue transportation. After he left there Captain Wirz signed orders for transportation, as assistant adjutant-general.

I know that Captain Wirz was crippled in his right arm. I do not think he could use it. It was injured in some way. I do not know whether it was broken or not. I know that his right arm was injured. I have never seen him dressing it.

I was quartermaster to my regiment part of the time, and then quartermaster for all the troops there. I had nothing at all to do with the stockade or with Captain Wirz. I have seen him passing every day is the reason I know so much about it. I was not a familiar associate with Captain Wirz. I used to see a good deal of him after I was made quartermaster of the post. He would come around to the quartermaster's office; his office was not more than thirty steps from mine. He went there for anything he wanted. I did not know anything about his business. I know nothing more than what I heard about the rigors he imposed on the prisoners in the stockade. Whenever I would go to the stockade I would most commonly see him. I have seen him go into the stockade a good many times; I used to go into the stockade frequently myself. I had friends there to whom I carried vegetables. I do not pretend to know what Captain Wirz did while he was there. I know nothing of my personal knowledge as to what he did to the prisoners inside the stockade.

Q. Do you know of your personal knowledge what he did to prisoners outside the stockade?

A. Well, I know that he has had them put in the stocks, and in the chain-gang and such things as that; that is about all I know.

I know that Captain Wirz had prisoners chased by dogs. I didn't say that no dogs were used there until Turner's were brought there. I say that dogs were used there without being hired; that there were prisoners brought in that had been captured by dogs.

Q. Do you not know that no dogs were used there till Captain Wirz came from Richmond?

A. I do not know about that, whether it was before or after. I could not say positively, because I do not remember, but I remember the first prisoners that were caught by dogs. I do not remember the date; I do not know whether Captain Wirz was there or not. I went there in February; I cannot say how long it was after I went there; it appears to me Captain Wirz was there. I know that Harris was employed there for that purpose; I will not say positively, but I think it was after he brought prisoners in. He brought the first. I do not know that he was employed by Captain Wirz. I saw him about Captain Wirz's headquarters every time he came with prisoners. It was generally known that he was in that business of chasing prisoners with dogs. Turner, the hound runner, applied to me for pay. He told me Captain Wirz had promised him $30 apiece for the captured prisoners, and that he was needing the money. I told him I did not believe he was entitled to it and would not pay him without a special order from the quartermaster general. It was a technical question raised by me, he being a detailed soldier. I never paid him at all. I do not know whether he was paid or not. He afterwards appealed to the commandant; he applied to Colonel Forno, and he came and reported to me that he was entitled to twenty-five cents a day. Colonel Forno talked about it afterward. At the time Turner applied to me he said Captain Wirz had promised him $30 a head. He did not tell me when Captain Wirz employed him.

I do not pretend to know all that went on at headquarters with regard to granting furloughs. I was not a staff officer at headquarters. I had nothing to do with furloughs—who received them, and what cause was assigned for them. I know nothing about it only from what I heard. I heard of a furlough being granted to a Confederate soldier for shooting a Union prisoner; I never knew it. I heard such rumors in camp among our own soldiers.

Q. You say he was crippled in his right arm. Do you not know that he uses his right hand to write with, to use the pen?

A. Yes, I think he uses the pen with his right hand. I do not think he could use his right arm well. I have heard him complain of it. I never noticed him riding with the reins in his right hand. I never noticed which hand he used. I have seen him riding when he carried a pistol and held the reins at the same time. I do not know which hand he used to hold the reins or pistol with. I don't think he had the reins and pistol in the same hand; I never noticed his being incapacitated entirely to use his right hand. I do not know how much he used his right hand. I never noticed particularly about his using it. His being crippled in the right hand never struck me as being remarkable from his use of it. I never saw him have occasion to use it except in writing, and it is my recollection that he then used his right hand.

Q. You say you never saw but one chain-gang?

A. Well, it might not have been the same chain-gang that I saw. The time I saw the prisoners in the chain-gang might have been before General Winder came there. I did not say whether it was or was not; I cannot say positively when it was. I do not remember the date, for I never charged my mind with it.

I never heard of prisoners of war escaping over or breaking through the stockade; all I know is that where the stockade crossed the branch the ground was boggy and marshy, and the stockade was not fixed tightly in the ground. I know it was washed down, and I thought that was a weak spot.

The foregoing comprises the testimony of the witnesses for the defense, except those who were prisoners.

Vincenzo Bardo was called for the defense, not to disprove the fact that he was whipped and put in the stocks for attempting to escape, but to shield Wirz from the responsibility for the outrage. His testimony has been given in a previous chapter.

TESTIMONY OF EDWARD W. BOATE.

Edward Wellington Boate was called for the defense to show among other things that Captain Wirz endeavored to relieve the situation by calling upon the prisoners to assist, and was refused on grounds which seem improbable on their face and contrary to the facts elsewhere established. The condition of the prisoners, their short rations and sufferings generally, he describes much the same as other witnesses.

He testified:[1]

During the time I remained in the stockade, I never knew or heard of Captain Wirz committing any assault on any prisoner there. I never heard of such a thing as Captain Wirz shooting, beating, or in any way injuring a man so that he died, until this trial.

Q. What do you know about an outbreak there?

A. I did not know anything about an outbreak; but I heard that there was to be such a thing. I know that Captain Wirz sent for the sergeants and addressed them. [To the Court:] It was at his headquarters. They were brought out. He said to them: "Men, I am aware that there is an outbreak on foot, and I desire to warn you. I do not wish to take any advantage of your position, but if you attempt it, I will be obliged to open the artillery here upon you. I advise you, therefore, as sensible men, not to attempt anything of the kind." On that occasion one of the soldiers said: "Captain Wirz, will you help us to get exchanged out of this place? Will you forward a petition for us?" He replied, "certainly," and said in addition to that, "I suppose you are short of stationery down in the stockade; come in and help yourselves to as much paper and stationery as you require." On that occasion Private Higginson, who has since been made a major, came in and took away a quantity of paper from Captain Wirz's office.

This witness also testified to the fact that a petition to the Federal government was prepared by the prisoners with the consent of Wirz for their exchange, and that certain prisoners were chosen to take it

[1] Record, p. 689.

to Washington. The witness was not permitted to testify to what he claimed was a copy of the petition printed in a Northern newspaper.[1]

THE JUDGE ADVOCATE. The only practical point in the evidence offered by the defense is that Captain Wirz and General Winder made efforts leading to the coming of certain persons here to Washington. What these persons did has nothing whatever to do with this case. When it has been shown that General Winder or Captain Wirz expressed a wish or intention on that subject, that is all there is in the matter. Whether our government acted rightly or wrongly on the subject can be no defense with them. If the evidence which is offered be allowed to come in, the court may be required to sit some time longer to determine whether the government of the United States is to blame in the matter. Mr. Tracy has been here as a witness for the government, and he would have been retained for the defense if he had been asked, or would have been subpœnaed subsequently if such a request had been made. But now, here at the close of the trial, we are called upon to meet points which seem purposely to have been reserved for this occasion.

[Colonel Stibbs inquired of Mr. Baker what was the object in offering the proposed evidence.]

MR. BAKER. To show that the committee came forward and that they did their duty; that they were a committee for a legitimate purpose, and that they tried to carry out that purpose. I propose afterward to show that Colonel Ould tried to do the same thing in another way.

GENERAL THOMAS. It is perfectly well known that our government would not consent to the exchange of prisoners so long as the rebel government refused to recognize the United States colored troops as prisoners of war, and murdered them. Our government was certainly right in the position which it took, and would not have been justified in taking any other.

MR. BAKER. I know that there is a great question in reference to that, but I want to avoid all that.

Q. Did you know anything about letters from our prisoners offering to take the oath of allegiance to the Southern Confederacy?

A. Captain Wirz showed me several letters. Sometimes there were as many as twenty from our men in the stockade—at least, I believe so; I did not see them written—offering to take the oath of allegiance. He told me, "Destroy these letters, I don't like a deserter, North or South."

TESTIMONY OF W. W. CRANDALL.

W. W. Crandall was recalled for the defense to show that Lieutenant Davis was in command of the prison during most of August, 1864. This was to disprove some of the acts of cruelty charged to Wirz as having been committed by him during that month.

He testified:[2]

Lieutenant Davis was at Andersonville during most of the month of August— from among the first days of August; I cannot tell accurately when his com-

[1] Record, p. 695.
[2] Record, p. 413.

mand commenced, but, from among the first days of August until about the 27th, 28th, or 29th of that month, he was reported to be in command, and gave orders to us, and we looked upon him as our commander the same as we had previously looked upon Captain Wirz; we had nothing to do with Captain Wirz during that time.

TESTIMONY OF B. F. DILLEY.

Benjamin F. Dilley, Company F, 54th Pennsylvania Volunteers, testified:[1]

I never heard of such a thing as a prisoner being shot in the stockade; there was an alarm there one night. I never knew or heard of Captain Wirz giving a furlough to Confederate soldiers for shooting Union prisoners; I never heard of anything of that kind. I never heard it mentioned at Andersonville. While I was there my desk was within two feet of his—about the same as these two desks here—all the time.

Q. Would it have been possible for any furlough of that kind to be given without your knowing it?

A. Oh, it could be done, of course. I do not think it could be done without our knowing it. I do not think Captain Wirz had authority to give a 30 days' furlough. He gave furloughs for eight days, when the colonel commanding the post was absent. It was about harvest time, and the men wanted to go home and attend to their grain when these furloughs were given. There was not any other time that I know of that furloughs were given by Captain Wirz. I never heard tell of such a thing as a furlough being given for shooting a Union prisoner.

The prisoner called "Frenchy," who was brought back by dogs, was not seriously hurt; he was merely scratched; he laughed over it himself. I think he said he gave Wirz a good tramp after him. One of our men attended to him. He was not what I would call seriously wounded, and he did not die.

In the light of so much testimony from the lips of both rebel witnesses and others of the shooting of prisoners by the guards, it seems remarkable that this witness never heard of it. The other statement of the witness is equally incredible.

TESTIMONY OF AUGUST GLEICH.

August Gleich, for the defense, testified:[2]

I was in the Union army for three years and a half; I belonged to the 8th Pennsylvania Cavalry; I was taken prisoner October 12, 1863, at Sulphur Springs, Virginia; I was then carried to Richmond; I remained in Richmond till the 4th of March, 1864, and then I went to Andersonville; I arrived at Andersonville March 10, 1864; I remained there bill November 16, 1864.

When I arrived at Andersonville I was put in the stockade; I was not in the stockade all the time; I was paroled the 8th of April. I wrote a note to Captain Wirz asking him if he would not take me out of the stockade; I told

---

[1] Record, p. 673.
[2] Record, p. 585 et seq.

VIEWS IN ANDERSONVILLE CEMETERY. LOWER PICTURE WAS TAKEN BEFORE IMPROVEMENTS WERE COMMENCED.

him I would be willing to chop wood; at the same time he had sent in for hands to come out and cut wood for the men inside to cook their victuals with, so I told him that I would be willing to go out and cut wood; the next day he sent for me and I went out into his office; he looked at me and told me that I was too weak yet to cut wood, and he asked me if I could not do anything else; I told him that I could make myself useful among horses, so he told me to go to the stable, an officers' stable; I went there and I remained there till the time I left; there were horses at the stable belonging to officers, and Captain Wirz's mare was there; I took care of her; there were about eighteen horses in that stable; some of the horses were General Winder's, some belonged to Captain Piggott, to Captain White and Lieutenant Davis, and Captain Wirz's mare was there and two or three government horses. Captain Wirz had a gray mare; he never had any other.

Captain Wirz was sick once while I was at Andersonville; I think it was in the month of August; Captain Wirz's horse stopped there in the stable while he was sick; nobody rode her then except Sergeant Smith; he sometimes rode her. Captain Wirz was sick about a month at that time; Lieutenant Davis was in command while Captain Wirz was sick.[1]

I drew clothing twice while I was at Andersonville; once in August and the next time in November. The first time I drew government clothing; the second time Sanitary Commission clothing. The first time I got pants, a blouse, shoes, and a cap; the second time I got a blanket, pants, drawers, and shirt, no shoes; there were not many there, only about 40 or 50 pairs. There was an order given in relation to the Union soldiers selling things. Captain Wirz told us that if we would sell anything to the guard he would put us in the stocks, and if he saw the guard or any citizen having anything from us he would punish him for it.

The letter that I wrote to Captain Wirz was written in English; I am sure it was not written in German. I told Captain Wirz in the letter that I was a prisoner and was sick and very bad off; had the scurvy badly; that I would be willing to go out and chop wood. He had called for men to do that. I wanted to go out; I was glad to get out; I was very bad off. I had the scurvy. I was very poor then; I was sick. I did not have enough to eat. I wanted to go out of the stockade because I did not have enough to eat. I understood that if I were outside I would get double rations, that was another reason why I went out.

Q. Do you remember all about the dates of occurrences there, the particular days of the month, &c.? Did you charge your memory with anything of that kind?

A. No, sir; I never did.

Q. Then how do you happen to remember so particularly about the time when Captain Wirz was sick?

A. I know it was the month of August. I know it was the month of August because we drew clothing then, and I put that down in my brain; I had nothing for a whole year. I do not know the date exactly. I am certain it was in

---

[1] We know from reports made by him and by Colonel Chandler that this witness was mistaken.

August. I am certain Captain Wirz was not sick in July. I don't know whether he was sick in September or not; I know he was riding around all the time in the month of July.

At the time I drew clothing I was not naked, but I had not much. I was no better off than those inside the stockade. When I came out of the stockade I had a pair of drawers and a shirt, that was all. I continued to wear those about a week, and then I got a pair of pants which were given to me by Captain Reed, the provost marshal. About three or four weeks afterwards I drew a suit of clothing. Lieutenant Davis was in command then. In November I drew another suit. While I was outside I had two full suits of clothing served out to me besides a pair of pants which Captain Reed gave to me. Others, who were outside, got them. I had a double ration while I was outside.

I never heard of a man being injured by Captain Wirz; I heard it spoken of while I was at Andersonville. All I can tell is that he would curse a man for nothing at all hardly; that is about all he would do. At the time of roll-call he might pull a fellow around if he would not stay in his place; I have seen him do that. He would pull them around roughly. I never saw him draw his pistol on a man; I have seen him knocking them around in the line. I never heard any of my comrades or any of the prisoners say that Captain Wirz had injured them by beating them or anything of that kind; I never heard a word said about that.

TESTIMONY OF FREDERICK GUSCETTI.

Frederick Guscetti, private in 47th New York Regiment, was called for the defense to show the disposition of Wirz towards the prisoners. He was also called to explain the death of a prisoner, called "Chickamauga," and to dispute witnesses whose testimony, hereafter to be given, fixed the responsibility directly upon Wirz.

He testified:[1]

I am an Italian; I speak six or seven languages; I have been in the military service of the United States, in the 47th New York Regiment; I was taken as a prisoner to Andersonville. I was then taken to Tallahassee, Florida; I arrived at Andersonville, March 28, 1864.

I was in the stockade from March 29 till August 28, 1864; I was then paroled; I was taken out by a sergeant and brought up to the headquarters of Captain Wirz; I was at Captain Wirz's headquarters from the 28th of August, when I was taken out, till the 15th or 16th of November; I first saw Captain Wirz five or six days after I was taken to Andersonville; there was from 7,000 to 9,000 prisoners there then, perhaps more; when I was paroled I was sick, and one of the doctors asked Captain Wirz to take me out; the captain told him he should not do so, but the next day he sent orders to take me out; I was brought to his headquarters; he told me to stay there and said to me "When they want you, you will go to the hospital and do what they ask you." The first time a man

---
[1] Record, p. 513 et seq.

was shot by the sentry outside, he was taken out; the sentry shot him as he was coming to the river; he shot him with two bullets, one through the body and one through the leg;[1] I was inside at that time; Captain Wirz came in in the morning and I told him that three or four of us would like to go and see that man; he said that he would allow nobody to go; after a little while, when he was going out of the gate, I told him again; he said "Well, if they go under guard they can go." Dr. White came and I told him that Captain Wirz had said we might go; I and two other men went to see the man in the hospital; afterward when I was in the hospital I used to go with the guard to bring men from the stockade to see men in the hospital; this was done four times, I think. One morning a man came up and told Captain Wirz that he was a preacher, and Captain Wirz told me to go with him into camp; we went in. The man stopped to talk with several of the prisoners; the men were asking him when they would be exchanged.

The man came in and bought watches; when he came out I told Captain Wirz that that man whom he had sent me in with did nothing but buy watches; Captain Wirz sent him with Sergeant Smith down to General Winder; I don't know what occurred afterward.

Chickamauga was a Canadian who used to be in a tent where I was. Several of us were digging a tunnel in order to get out. Some five days after a rebel officer came in and came to where the hole was and said "Here is a tunnel"; his men came in and broke it up. We suspected that somebody had reported the matter, but we did not know for sure. About two days and two nights afterwards we began another tunnel. We were about five days on it when one morning an officer came in and broke up the hole. A third time we made a hole. We then suspected that somebody was reporting our holes. We looked around and in the morning we saw Chickamauga pass the dead-line and go where the letter-box was. We did not know what he was going to do. About ten minutes afterwards a lieutenant with a red sash, the officer of the day, came in with a guard and went right to the place where we had put the sand. We had worked the matter so well that we never thought anybody could suspect it, but he went right up to it and said, "Here is a tunnel." A big Canadian who was there said to him, "Lieutenant, who told you that we made a hole there?" The lieutenant said, "Well, that cripple told me." The cripple was then between the dead-line and the gate; we began to curse him. There were about fifty or sixty men where we were, Canadians, Frenchmen, and others, all mixed together. There was a low shanty there, and some of the men said they were going to hang Chickamauga up there. He was afraid to come inside of the dead-line again, into the camp. He asked the officer to take him out; the officer said that he had not the power to do it; at his instance Captain Wirz came down inside the south gate on his white mare, and told him to go inside, that he would not take him out. The man said that he would not come in, that the men wanted to hurt him. Captain Wirz replied, "I have nothing to do with that, I cannot help that; go inside the dead-line or you will be shot."

---

[1] The crippled soldier known as "Chickamauga" was shot by a guard, as the evidence showed with reasonable certainty upon the direct order of Wirz. He admitted the killing but denied that he ordered it.

The man would not go in. Captain Wirz took out his pistol and said, "If you do not go inside the dead-line I will shoot you." The man bared his breast and said, "I do not care; shoot me if you want to." Captain Wirz put the pistol away and turned his horse to go out; some of our men said, "Bully for you," meaning bully for Captain Wirz. We knew that the man was a spy, and as Captain Wirz went out, as he was shutting the gate, some of our men took hold of this Canadian, "Frenchy" as he was sometimes called, and pulled him inside the dead-line. Almost everybody who was not an American or a German was called "Frenchy." This man was now inside the dead-line, but in a few moments he passed out again, past the dead-line, and sat down about one yard from the dead-line—inside of the dead-line. The guard told him twice to go away; he said he would not do it. The guard then took up his musket and said he would shoot him if he would not go in. He said "Go in, or I will shoot you." The man said "I don't care," and he opened his blouse again. The guard shot him. The men were all around there at the time. We told him to come inside, as we were not fools enough to cross the dead-line to bring him out. There were a great many men around there; it was generally understood what Chickamauga had done in the morning, that he had acted as a spy, and the men cursed him of course. Captain Wirz was outside the gate when the man was shot; the gate was shut.

Q. Did you hear any orders given to the sentry?

A. When Captain Wirz got outside I do not believe that anybody could hear him say anything.

THE JUDGE ADVOCATE. State what you did or did not hear.

WITNESS. Nobody could hear.

Q. Why could they not hear?

A. The stockade was about fifteen feet high and two or three feet thick, and the dead-line was about eight or ten steps from the stockade.

Q. Did the crowd around there make any noise by talking or hallooing to each other?

A. I did not remark a noise. The men always made a noise. The men were around me and some of them were cursing this man. Some of them wanted to bring him inside, but they would not cross the dead-line.

I never saw any clothing or boxes in the stockade; boxes came, but not into the stockade. They came to the headquarters of Captain Wirz. I saw some of the boxes brought into the stockade for the prisoners. I saw them come in in May; about thirty came that I saw. They were small boxes, such as are sent by express; such as Northern people sent to the men. Boxes were not frequently coming in that way. I saw about thirty in the month of May and three in July. There may have been more, but I did not see them. There was a letter-box, and they put a notice in the letter-box for the men who had boxes. The men would then report to the sergeant at the gate. I know that they received their boxes in that way. When nobody came to answer a letter which was put into the letter-box then the boxes were sent to the hospital. I did not know when I was in camp what they did with them, but when I was out I saw that when nobody applied for boxes they were sent to the hospital—the Federal prison hospital.

I know that Captain Wirz's right arm was crippled. When he used to ride on horseback, he could not use his right arm to get into the saddle. He always used his left arm, and when he was very badly sick I had to give him a chair to mount on horseback, and I also had to lift him on his horse.

There were two Canadians who were both called "Frenchy." This man used to be near my tent. He ran away four times and was captured and sent back into camp. He passed without punishment three times, and the fourth time there was a ball and chain put upon his feet. He made his escape again; I did not see him until he was brought back. I heard Captain Wirz order him to be placed, with twelve other paroled prisoners, in a chain-gang; when he was brought down to the smith, he managed to run away. The officer, Lieutenant Hill, I believe, did not remark his escape until he came to the smith, when he found there was one man less; he went to Captain Wirz and told him that one man had run away. Captain Wirz looked at the men and said "Frenchy has run off again"; he sent for Turner to find out where Frenchy was; the dogs found out his track and followed and caught him; he was brought back with Turner's dogs; Captain Wirz was along with them; Captain Wirz had on a pair of white pants which were very muddy; the captain told him he would not send him back to the stockade, but would send him to the guard-tent, and he called Sergeant Smith and sent Frenchy to the guard-tent. Afterwards I came down to him and asked him about running away; I said "You cannot run away any more; you have too much watching." He said: "I do not care; I will try again." Frenchy had on a pair of raggish pants; he did not say whether he was torn by the dogs or not; I asked him if he was hurt, and he told me "That did not hurt me"; that means in French, in which he expressed himself, that it did not hurt him much. He said that he did not care for Captain Wirz, that the dog who barked did not bite much; that was the expression he used. I did not see that he was torn at all; he was lying down in the guard-tent; he ran away again, but I did not see him; I heard that he ran away near Macon; I once saw Turner come in with his dogs and twelve Confederate soldiers.[1]

I witnessed the death of Chickamauga. Some of the men were saying that this man was a poor cripple, and they pitied him, and some there who knew who he was—a great part—cursed him. There was not a great deal of noise. I do not know their purpose or intention, but I know they got him out of the deadline and back into the camp. That was before Captain Wirz left the camp. The guard snapped his piece once before he fired. The guard pulled up his piece and cocked it again; he looked out, pointed it at Chickamauga, and shot him through the head. I next saw Captain Wirz about eight or ten days afterwards. I did not see him again on that occasion. After Chickamauga was shot, I followed on, first to about the middle of the camp, to see where he went, and then I got back to my tent. I was badly lamed at that time. After the shooting, I saw a man with the sentry at the sentry-box from my tent. It was long enough after that for me to make fifty steps. It took me about five minutes to go to my tent. I looked back from my tent, and saw some one besides the sentry at the sentry-box. I do not know who it was. I cannot say whether Captain Wirz went to the sentry-box or not—I am not sure. I saw the sentry at the

---

[1] This was the testimony of the witness on cross-examination.

sentry-box. Captain Wirz was not beside him; the sentry was alone. In about five minutes afterwards I looked up to the sentry-box and saw a man there besides the sentry. I looked up after the sentry fired. I heard here in court that Captain Wirz went up to the sentry-box immediately after the shot was fired. I cannot say that it is the fact. I cannot swear that Captain Wirz did not go up to the sentry-box at that time. I swear that I do not know. I swear that I heard men say so here in the court, but I don't know it myself.

Q. Do you swear that you did not hear his voice after he went out of the stockade?

A. As soon as the gate was closed I could not possibly hear his voice.

Q. Do you say it was not possible for anybody to hear from inside the stockade?

A. I do not know as to other ears. I said it was not possible for me to hear it.

Q. Was it possible for anybody else to hear him?

A. Believe it was pretty hard.

Q. Do you swear that he did not give orders to the sentry to fire at Chickamauga?

A. I swear that I did not hear him.

Q. Do you not recollect that the sentry said that he would not fire, and that he refused to fire?

A. I do not know, and I cannot swear that the sentry did say something, and I could not tell what he said.

Q. Did he hesitate to fire? Did he refuse or appear to regret to fire?

A. I did not see anybody order him to fire. Before he fired, he did look down this way and that, and then he fired. I was called, in the army, a blind man. I have big eyes, but a very short development of sight. I am not a blind man, but I am very short-sighted. I could not tell at a distance of fifty feet whether it was Captain Wirz. I cannot see at that distance whether a man has a beard or not, or whether he is a negro or a white. When I wear shortsighted glasses, I can see pretty well. I had no glasses on at that time. I see a man there—[pointing to where the prisoner sat]—I see a man there with a black beard, but I cannot swear that it is him. There is a man standing in the light among the audience. I know him because he is a friend of mine, but I could not recognize a person with whom I was not acquainted. I would not rely upon my recognizing a man, with whom I was not very familiar, at twenty feet distance.

The Judge Advocate, to show the interest of the witness, introduced the letter written by him to the New York *News,* which appears on a previous page.

TESTIMONY OF M. S. HARRIS.

Martin S. Harris, 5th Regiment, New York Volunteer Artillery, was a prisoner from July 29th to November, 1864, at Andersonville. He was called for the defense and testified:[1]

---

[1] Record, p. 588.

I never heard, while at Andersonville, of any actual personal violence by Captain Wirz; I have heard of his cursing a man. Captain Wirz rode an old gray mare. I never knew him to ride a sorrel or a roan horse; he was always on the gray mare when he was mounted at all; sometimes he came in on foot. Captain Wirz never wore an out-and-out rebel uniform; it was generally a mixture.

I have suffered from excessive marches and exposure. I suffered at Andersonville. The heat of the sun was a great cause of my suffering; in the exercise of my duties, during the greater part of the day, I was continually exposed to the intense heat. That was the chief cause. I also suffered from diarrhœa. I never suffered from lack of water. The confinement was the principal cause of suffering—confinement and exposure to the sun and sickness. I arrived at New York May 16, directly from Annapolis. I have done nothing since I left the army. I have written two letters to the New York Daily News with regard to this trial. Their purport was a plain statement of facts. I wrote those letters merely to see justice done to a man I thought wrongly accused. I selected the New York News because I was acquainted with the editors; they are personal friends of mine. The editors are Ben Wood and Mr. Peloi. Ben Wood has not been a personal friend of mine a great while. My relations with him are not intimate at all. I state that he is a personal friend of mine because I am acquainted with him, and for no other reason. I do not know that that paper has been in sympathy with the Rebellion during this war. I know that the paper has been called a copperhead sheet.

Q. During the publication of your letters in the New York News, in the interest of this accused, how many times did you see Ben Wood?

A. Twice, I think; not more than that. I talked with him, on those occasions, but a few moments about this case; I did not talk about anything else; I met Ben Wood in his office; he did not send for me; I went there to make a correction in the publication of my article; it was on that business purely that I went there. I published two articles in the Daily News—two relative to the Andersonville affair. I do not know how I came to be subpœnaed in this case. I received a subpœna; how it came about is more than I can tell you. I did not write a letter to the counsel in this case, nor to anybody else; I signed my initials, M. S. H., to the communication I wrote to the News. I wrote for the Brooklyn Eagle an article relative to the Andersonville business; I am not aware that that paper has been more bitter than the News against the government. I have been a long time down South and have not read many papers lately. I had been home a few weeks before I commenced writing letters; probably four or five; the writing of those letters was the first literary labor I performed after I got home; I saw that attacks were being made by the press on Captain Wirz, anticipating his trial; and also, anticipating his trial, I commenced his defense. I consider the Brooklyn Eagle a first-rate paper; it is democratic in its principles. I am not aware that it ever attacked the present government. I pretend to say that at that day I did not know it had been in opposition to the administration. I do not consider it at all remarkable that I selected the News and the Brooklyn Eagle. I knew their complexion. That is what my impressions were concerning the papers; I knew they were not in hostility to the present administration. I did not know anything about them beyond that; I never heard them discussed. I have heard the New York *News* spoken of; I never heard its character for loyalty questioned. I am not acquainted with the editor of the Brooklyn *Eagle,* personally; I sympathize with the political views of that paper, and also with the New York *News* in its present course; that was one reason why I selected those sheets.

Q. I now want to know whether in the letters written by you to the New York *News* and Brooklyn *Eagle,* touching the trial of Henry Wirz, you entered into this case beyond what you now state was your purpose?[1]

A. I said nothing about the trial of Wirz; the trial had not commenced.

I said something about the approaching trial in those letters. I portrayed the sufferings of the prisoners at Andersonville in those letters as fully as I could. The only feature in my letter differing from the statements of the witnesses for the prosecution was with regard to the responsibility and nothing else; that is true of all the letters I wrote.

When I arrived at Andersonville I was treated like all the rest; I could perceive no difference. When we were brought up in front of Captain Wirz's headquarters we were divided into squads of ninety men each. The men of my squad wished me to act as their sergeant. Captain Wirz came to me with a sheet of paper and told me to take the names. That constituted me sergeant of the squad. Captain Wirz did not display any violence of temper on that occasion. I have never seen Captain Wirz display any temper except inside the stockade; he displayed it there frequently. Almost every week or so he would come in on his gray mare, and the men would collect around him by hundreds, and would pester him with questions about exchange. At such times he would go off in a rage. I never saw Captain Wirz draw his pistol on the prisoners; I have seen his pistol in his belt; I never saw him with his pistol in his hand. I am sure of that.

The dead-line was removed about the 10th of September, immediately after the removal of the first detachment of prisoners; it was all taken down, and all restriction with regard to that dead-line removed. That I state positively. After that time there was no shooting on the dead-line until the dead-line was reconstructed. I do not know why it was reconstructed unless it was—

THE JUDGE ADVOCATE. If you do not know why, you need not state.

It was reconstructed about the middle of October. There was no shooting to my knowledge after the dead-line was put up. I never saw any man shot; I never knew a man to be shot after the 10th of September on the dead-line. So far as I know there was no shooting on the dead-line. I have heard of prisoners being shot on the dead-line previous to the removal, but I never witnessed anything of the kind. I never heard of men being shot after the 10th of September.[2]

There were a great many wells there, but no persons were allowed to use them except those who built them, or had an interest in them. Those who had built the wells, or had an interest in them either by purchase or otherwise, kept the water for their own use. They would watch the well and prevent all except their own company from using it unless they purchased the privilege.

There were occasional instances where the bacon would come in raw; the rations were generally served cooked; I do not think there was need of wood;

---

[1] This is the witness alluded to by Mr. Davis as "M. H. S." in his *Belford* articles.
[2] Many cases are proved to have occurred after this date.

that is the reason there was sufficient wood, because there was no necessity for it, the rations being cooked; raw rations were occasionally issued. The bread, while I was there, was always baked; the beans were always baked; the rice was always baked; there was occasional issues of raw beef and bacon; I could not say that this was true of the whole camp; I attended to my own duty; I do not know anything extensively beyond my own detachment; I do not pretend to state, with any certainty, observations beyond my own ninety.

Q. Was it not a fact that in the crowded state of that prison it was impossible for a man to know, with any certainty, what was going on beyond his own immediate vicinity?

A. Some had greater facilities than others for acquiring general information, those engaged in trade; I was not of that class, and did not make this general observation. I do not say the prisoners had sufficient to eat, I say they had enough to sustain life provided they could eat it. They could not eat their ration always; some prisoners died for want of proper food; I saw a great many deaths of that kind there, for lack of proper food, but not from lack of quantity; from the lack of proper food a great many did die; I have seen a great many die from hunger because they could not eat the food which was provided for them; raw rations were seldom issued to prisoners who were sick; raw rations were issued to the sick sometimes, but very seldom.[1]

I saw vaccine sores in the arms of several men; their arms were in a horrible condition. I never saw any vaccinated; I knew they had been vaccinated because of the nature of the sores on their arms—they were vaccine sores. I did not see any besides those. I never received any order in regard to having my men vaccinated.

TESTIMONY OF FREDERICK ROTH.

Frederick Roth testified:

I have been in the military service of the United States—in the 2d New York Cavalry. I was captured on the 19th of October, 1863, near New Baltimore, Virginia. I was taken to Richmond, Belle Island, and from there to Andersonville. I was at Belle Island five months. I was taken to Andersonville about the 20th of March, 1864. I left Andersonville on the 9th of September, 1864. I was inside the stockade all the time, except when I would get out for wood.

In some places the water was very good. In other places the water that ran through the brook was not fit to drink. There were wells and springs in the stockade. There were not enough wells in proportion to the men. I should think there were about 400 of different kinds. The springs were mostly along the swamp. In half of them the water was not fit to drink, on account of the maggots that ran all over the swamp into the water. In the wells that were deep—seventy-five feet deep—there was good water for any one that could get it.

For the first two months that I was there we got more meal than we could use. We had it there by bags full. For the last three months that I was there we had not enough to eat in what was issued to us. I know of the rations being sometimes very deficient. They would be so because some of the detachments that were

[1] Rebel witnesses testified that the cooking facilities were entirely inadequate to do the necessary baking.

not full drew as much rations as the detachments that had their full complement. The sergeants generally drew, if they could, for their whole squad, accounting for the men some way or other. A good many drew double rations.

I never heard, while at Andersonville, of Captain Wirz killing or shooting or beating or kicking men to death. I have heard of it since I came to Washington. I have heard him curse men and threaten to shoot them.

TESTIMONY OF AUGUSTUS MOESNER.

Augustus Moesner, Company G, 16th Connecticut Volunteers, testified for the defense:[1]

Q. What do you know about little boys being taken out of the stockade and what was done with them?

A. There were about forty or fifty boys inside the stockade, who had been taken prisoners, and Captain Wirz requested Dr. White to take some of them to the hospital as helps to the nurses or cooks there, because it was no use to keep those boys as prisoners of war; they would only get sick and die inside the stockade or they would get spoilt there, and, if it was in his power, he would send them to our lines, because it was no use to take boys as prisoners of war.

Captain Wirz took them out of the stockade and sent them to the hospital. One of them, a small little boy, who seemed to be ill, he took in our office and told us clerks to nurse him, and we had him there. When the boys were taken out they were sent to the hospital to assist the nurses and cooks, and some of them were sent to get blackberries for the sick.

Q. What was the rule in regard to men under punishment that got sick?

A. Well, sir, when a man who had been ordered to wear a ball and chain complained that he was sick, a doctor was sent for, and if he found that it was so, the ball and chain would be taken off and the man would be sent to the hospital if necessary; also, when new squads of prisoners came in, and there were men among them who claimed to be sick, the doctor who was officer of the day was sent for, and he had to see if the men were really sick or not; if they were they were sent to the hospital. I recollect also that once there was a man amongst them who told me he was a hospital steward in our army; I spoke to Captain Wirz about it, and the man was immediately sent to the hospital as a steward; he was paroled and was not sent into the stockade at all. Some of the hospital attendants serenaded Captain Wirz and Dr. Stevenson, and I understood Dr. White too.

Q. Did you at your headquarters or did Captain Wirz have anything to do with vaccination? If so, state what.

A. When I was first sent in the stockade there was a sergeant near my tent whose arm was very sore; he told me that it was caused by vaccination; but I was only a short time inside the stockade. When I was outside Dr. White gave an order, as the small-pox was increasing among the prisoners, that all men who came as new prisoners to Andersonville, who had not been vaccinated, should be vaccinated. One day a prisoner was brought out to Captain Wirz by one of the doctors, and the doctor reported to Captain Wirz that the prisoner refused to be

---

[1] Record, p. 540 et seq.

vaccinated; but the order had been given by Dr. White and not by Captain Wirz, and Wirz told him that he had nothing to do with it; that it was by the order of Dr. White that men who came there, and had not been vaccinated, were to be vaccinated, and that he (Wirz) would not care a damn whether they died of small-pox or not.

Q. Do you know anything about Frado or "Frenchy," who was brought in by the dogs? If you do, state what you know about it.

A. Frado was a Frenchman; he was a man who escaped seven times; he escaped once when I was inside the stockade; he went out by tunneling; there were four of them together; I saw him brought back with a ball and chain on him; a short time afterwards he escaped again; I do not know in which way, but he had taken off his ball and chain; and so he escaped several times.

Q. What do you know about his being brought back by Captain Wirz?

A. He was brought back once when he had made his escape.

Q. What condition was he in?

A. Those men who should make the chain-gang were sent to the blacksmith's shop, and he went there.

Q. If you saw him come back, what condition was he in and what did they do with him?

A. He was brought back and sent to the stockade; his pants were torn up; Captain Wirz was very muddy; he had white pants on but they were muddy away up to his knees; they brought Frenchy inside the stockade, and the next day he was brought out again by one of the Confederate sergeants to our office, and he said that it was because he had said to the sergeant inside the stockade that he wanted to try the dogs once more; Captain Wirz told him that he saw it was of no use to put him in irons, because he had slipped off the irons, and he sent him to the guard-house and kept him there; I saw only that his pants were torn up; I did not see that the dogs had hurt him; I did not hear him say anything himself on that subject; I saw him afterwards at Millen, and also at Annapolis, when we were exchanged; they kept him at the guard-house after he was taken out of the stockade until he was sent to Savannah; I think about a month—over a month.

I never saw, knew, or heard of anybody dying at Captain Wirz's headquarters who had been bitten by dogs.

I never saw, knew, or heard about Captain Wirz shooting, beating, or killing men in any way while I was there; I never saw, knew, or heard in any way of Captain Wirz carrying a whip while I was there. He never did.

Thirty or forty boxes were in that first lot which I saw, while I was in the stockade. I don't know whether that was the same lot Guscetti told about; I don't recollect what he said. The first boxes we got were sent from the North by friends of the prisoners in the month of May. They came inside. The boxes were of different size. Some were so long [about a yard], and others were smaller.

Q. Then they were from a foot square to two or three feet square? Those are the only boxes you know to have gone into the prison with provisions?

A. Yes, sir. I saw them when they came inside the stockade. I saw them all distributed. The boxes had been opened before and examined. The second time that I saw boxes arrive was in August. Then we got clothing sent by our government

MONUMENT ERECTED BY THE STATE OF MICHIGAN

merit-blue pants, shoes, caps and blouses. They were distributed to those on duty outside. In addition to double rations, we also got the clothing that came. That clothing was not distributed to those inside the prison, and the reason stated was that the quantity was so small that there would be too much fighting about it. There were many men in there who needed clothing. That was the only reason assigned for not sending that clothing into the stockade, and the clothing was distributed to those who needed it outside. I got some of that clothing. I got blue pants, and I sold them and bought a blanket, because I had none, and I had been lying on the ground with nothing to cover me. I sold that pair of pants for five dollars. I sold them to a rebel sergeant. I have seen rebel sergeants wearing those Federal clothes; I saw them wearing blue pants and overcoats. I don't know where they always got them. I don't know anything about it.

I stated that when men were in the chain-gang they were put under a fly. I saw them under it; I have seen them out from under it; I saw them in the morning going down to the cook-house to get their rations. I do not recollect that I saw them out from under that fly at any other times.

I know all about the orders issued in regard to the chain-gang; I know that they always issued from General Winder's headquarters, because Captain Wirz told me. All that I know about it is what Captain Wirz told me, and he told me that the orders came from General Winder. I cannot swear that I ever saw a written order on that subject. I cannot swear that I ever heard General Winder give a verbal order to Captain Wirz on that subject. I don't know anything about it except what Captain Wirz told me.

Q. Did Captain Wirz always tell you when he was executing an order of this kind that it came from General Winder?

A. He was nearly always talking about it. He did not report to me when General Winder sent an order of that kind. He did not always tell me from whom the order came.

Q. Then there were men put in the chain-gang when you did not know for what reason, or on whose order?

A. I know so far as Captain Wirz told me. But he did not always tell me. I do not know about those cases in which he did not tell me; I do not know anything about those.

Q. Did not Captain Wirz always direct the officer to put the men in the chain-gang?

A. The prisoners were sent to the blacksmith shop. Captain Wirz sent them there.

Q. He sent them there to be ironed?

A. I did not hear him give these orders. He went over to General Winder, and after he came back he said these men were to be put in the chain-gang. He very frequently said that General Winder had given him the order—not always. The men could be put in the stocks by Captain Wirz's order.

Q. Do you know any reason why he could not also order them put in the chain-gang?

A. They were mostly paroled prisoners; at least the first who were put in the chain-gang were paroled prisoners. Captain Wirz had the power to inflict other punishment besides putting men in the stocks. He had the power to put the ball and chain on them. Nothing else. I never saw a man bucked and gagged while I was at Andersonville. I don't know whether he could issue the order on that subject. I don't know how far his power went. My observation in reference to bucking and gagging has been just as good as in reference to anything else. I think my knowledge and opinion on that point are just as good as on anything else. I know of Captain Wirz ordering men to be whipped; I have heard him give the order to whip a man. That is another thing he had power to do; he gave the order. No men were tied up by the thumbs; I say positively that I never knew a man to be tied up by the thumbs while I was there. I am as positive in reference to that as anything else. I think that no man was tied up by the thumbs there. Captain Wirz had the power and exercised the power to direct that prisoners be caught by the hounds. He had that power. He put them in the stocks. I don't recollect any other punishments than what I have mentioned. Although Captain Wirz had the power to inflict all these other punishments, he had no power to put men in the chain-gang, so far as I know, and I know about that just as I know about everything else.

The chain-gang commenced about the first of July and ended the latter part of July; of that I am as positive as of anything else. I did not hear of a man's dying in the chain-gang with the chain on them; I never heard of it. I swear positively that I never heard of a man's dying in the stocks.[1]

---

[1] This statement is in conflict with the testimony of rebel and other witnesses.

VIOLATION OF RULES OF WAR. 331

I say Captain Wirz's right arm was crippled. In a battle in Virginia he was wounded. I do not know that he was hurt by being thrown from a stage-coach. He never told me that. He told me he was wounded. He told me once his whole story, and he said his arm was crippled by a piece of shell somewhere in Virginia; I do not know where,—in 1861 or 1862. I have seen Captain Wirz on horseback very often. He mounted the horse on the right side. He held the reins in his left hand.[1] I never recollect seeing him hold a pistol; he had a pistol generally in a belt around his waist. I do not swear positively that I never saw a pistol in his hand, I am as sure of that as of everything else. I have seen Captain Wirz write. He wrote with his right hand. He ate with his right hand. I don't recollect seeing him do anything else with his right hand. It did not attract my attention especially what hand he used.

I never heard of Captain Wirz shooting, kicking, or beating a Federal prisoner while I was at Andersonville. I swear positively to that; I saw him pushing prisoners into the ranks, but not that they could be hurt. He would take them by the arm and push them into the ranks and say "God damn it! couldn't you stay in the ranks where you were put?" He would not push them in violently—a gentle push. He was violent in these moments, cursing and swearing, as he always was with us, but he seemed harder than he was. I never saw him take any one by the throat, but by the shoulder or arm. Not with both hands; with one hand. I don't know which hand. I have seen him often go up the line of prisoners; I have seen him counting them, and I never saw him with his pistol in his hand on any of these occasions; it was his custom; he had his pistol in his belt. I saw him in the stockade while I was there; I saw him once at the south gate and once on horseback with Lieutenant Colonel Persons, and I saw him once in the stockade while I was outside. I saw him riding among the prisoners only once after I was taken out. On none of those occasions I never saw him carry a pistol except always in his belt. I swear positively that I never heard of Captain Wirz kicking or shooting a prisoner, nor in any way maltreating him except as I have stated.

Q. You swear positively that you never heard of a man's being torn by the hounds.

A. I saw that Frenchy had his pants torn. That is the only instance of hounds tearing the soldiers' clothes or flesh that I ever heard of, and I know as much about these things as about anything else.[2]

During the month of August Captain Wirz was so sick that he did not come to the office. He was sick previously and sick afterwards while he was still in command. In the first days of August he was on duty yet, perhaps up to the 4th or 5th day of August, and about the last day, the 30th or 31st, he came back.

Q. Between the 4th and 30th of August you swear positively that Captain Wirz did no official act?

A. He was not on duty. He was confined to his house and was partly on furlough. I heard he was on furlough from Lieutenant Davis; I did not see him going off, nor see him returning. I know he was confined to his bed by hearing it; I did not see him.[3]

---

[1] Can a horse be mounted from the right side while the rider holds the reins in his left hand?
[2] The evidence is overwhelming that men were wounded by the dogs.
[3] Record evidence disputes this.

TESTIMONY OF FREDERICK ROTH.

Frederick Roth, 2nd New York Cavalry, was a prisoner from March to September. He testified:[1]

I recollect seeing Lieutenant Davis first the day I left Andersonville—the 9th of September, 1864. I think he went in the same train with us. I did not see him till I got to Savannah. I never heard, while at Andersonville, of Captain Wirz killing or shooting or beating or kicking men to death. I heard of it since I came to Washington. I have heard him curse men and threaten to shoot them.

I do not know anything about Captain Wirz, except that for the first month or two he would come in and call the roll. Captain Wirz would curse and damn men because they would sit down, or would not stand up long enough. Some men would have to go off about their business, and if he was not there just at the right time Captain Wirz would send him outside. I do not know what was done with them, but some said they were put in the stocks or bucked and gagged. That is all I know about Captain Wirz. I never saw Captain Wirz lay hands upon any one. He used to have a pistol in his hand most of the time, and he would make the men stand in line. I cannot say that I ever saw him make sick men stand up in line.

[1] Record, p. 604.

CHAPTER XII.

TESTIMONY OF WITNESSES TO THE CHARGE OF MURDER—PRISONERS SHOT BY WIRZ —PRISONERS SHOT BY HIS ORDER—PRISONERS KILLED BY THE DOGS—MANY INSTANCES OF WIRZ'S BRUTALITY—MEN KILLED BY BEING SHOT IN STOCKS AND CHAIN GANG.

IN giving the testimony for the defense, in the preceding chapter, relating to the more specific acts of cruelty and inhuman treatment under the specifications of charge 1, the testimony of witnesses introduced to refute the evidence taken in support of charge 2— murder in violation of the laws of war—is also presented. It was not found practicable to segregate this testimony. Indeed, the evidence under charge 1 is very closely related to that directed towards charge 2, and might well be considered with it.

However, as the charge of murder, if established, was to be expiated alone by Wirz, it has been deemed best to separately group some of the inculpatory testimony. Some testimony under this charge appears in previous chapters.

The evidence as to charge 2 is directed to the killing of prisoners by means of the stocks or chain-gang; by the dogs; by Wirz's orders, and by his own hand. Such testimony as bears upon these specifications, in addition to the testimony already stated, will be given as found in the record without any attempt to classify it or group it around particular instances where death follows the act or acts. That is to say, the testimony bearing upon any particular homicide will not all be placed in a separate group.

Dr. A. V. Barrows was for four years hospital steward of the 27th Massachusetts Regiment, and served previous to his capture several months as assistant post surgeon at Plymouth. He reached Andersonville on May 27, 1864, and was by Captain Wirz placed in charge of two wards in the hospital. He escaped to Pensacola, in our lines, in October, and was mustered out, since which time he had been practicing medicine at his home. In his evidence, already quoted, he testified that a man escaped from the hospital in July and was overtaken by the dogs and brought back to the hospital. "A large part of his ear was torn off, and his face mangled. That man got well." Another instance occurred at the end of August or in the fore part of September; the exact date he could not remember. "He had been badly bitten by the dogs in trying to make his escape, and was brought into my ward and died. The wound took on gangrene and he died. I should say he died in four or five days after he was torn by the dogs. I know the wound took on gangrene and he died. I do not think he died directly from the effects of the wound. I think he died indirectly—it was from the effects of gangrene. The gangrene was manifested in the wound, and in no other part. He was bitten through the throat on the side of the neck, and gangrene set in and he died. The gangrene was the result of the bite, in my opinion." He also declared, as will be seen by turning to his testimony, that a prisoner in the hospital was shot by the guard under circumstances clearly without cause, and that the man died within five days. He also testified that he saw Wirz on one occasion knock down and stamp upon a sick prisoner.[1]

TESTIMONY OF SAMUEL D. BROWN.

Samuel D. Brown testified:[2]

I saw Captain Wirz while at Andersonville. I knew him to commit acts of cruelty—once especially. On or about the 15th of May, 1864, I wrote a letter to my parents and took it to the south gate where the letter-box was. As I came up near the gate I saw a cripple—a man with one leg, on crutches; he had lost one leg above the knee. He was asking the sentinel to call Captain Wirz. He called him, and in a few minutes he came up. I stopped to see what was going to be done. The Captain came up and the man asked him to take him outside of the prison, as he had enemies in the camp. I presume it was Captain Wirz. I did not know him so well then. Captain Wirz was the man that was called. This cripple asked him to take him out; he said his leg was not healed, and that he had enemies in camp who clubbed him. Captain Wirz never answered him, but said to the sentinel, "Shoot that one-legged Yankee devil." I was there and heard the order, and saw the man turn on his crutches to go away. As he turned the sentinel fired, and the ball struck him on the head and passed out at the lower jaw. The man fell over, and expired in a few minutes. The sentinel fired at the prisoner with a musket. The prisoner was perhaps two feet inside the deadline, which was twenty-five or thirty feet from the stockade and almost parallel with it; so that the man was probably thirty feet away from the muzzle of the gun. I would recognize the man who gave that order. I recognize the prisoner at the bar as him. The sentry was relieved; I saw him taken down out of the stand outside. That was the last I saw of him. Report says that he got a thirty days' furlough. I have witnessed other acts of cruelty.

I have no means of verifying the date of that occurrence, any more than what I have stated. It was on the 15th of May that I wrote this letter. I put it in the office the same day. On the 26th of last December I came home, and I was there six or eight days when I "lifted" the letter at the office—the letter I had myself mailed at Andersonville. That was the only letter I wrote there.

[1] Record, p. 43 et seq.
[2] Record, p. 78.

TESTIMONY OF J. D. BROWN.

J. D. Brown testified:[1]

I am a brother of the young man who has just testified; I have been in the military service of the United States; enlisted on the 31st day of January, 1862, and served till the 13th June, 1865; I was a prisoner at Andersonville from the 20th day of April, 1864, to the 9th September, 1864; I was in the Andersonville prison, or not exactly in the prison, all the time; from the 3d of May to the 9th September I was in the prison.

I saw Captain Wirz there; I see him now, the prisoner at the bar; that is the same man; in one instance, about the 27th of July, 1864, I saw Captain Wirz in the sentry-box with the sentinel at the cook-house, near the brook; the prisoners were there getting water from the brook, and men would accidentally reach under the dead-line to get water, and Captain Wirz ordered the sentinel, if any men reached through the dead-line to get water, to shoot them down; he had barely said the words when a prisoner reached through under the dead-line with his cup to get some water, and the sentry fired; the ball took effect in the man's head and he was killed; I was about three feet off; I was just passing the brook from one side of the stockade to the other; the sentinel had in his hand the ordinary musket—a soldier's musket; after the ball had entered the prisoner's head he dropped, and in a very short time expired; I was close by when he died; I saw him after he was dead; I saw him borne away to the gate to be taken out; this happened about the 27th of July, 1864. I know of one other instance; as to the date I am not so well posted as I am in regard to the others, but it was some time about the middle of August, 1864; from the same sentry-box Captain Wirz ordered the sentinel to shoot men again that were getting water from the brook; the men were much crowded, as they always were at that place, getting water, and I was crossing the brook again; I had some friends on the north side of the stockade, and I stopped on the south side; Captain Wirz was in the sentry-box with the sentinel; he gave the order to the sentinel and the sentinel fired, and the ball took effect in the man's breast; I did not see the man die, but it was a fatal wound; there was no doubt of that; I saw where the ball entered the breast; I could not say that it passed through him; the man was lying on his back. I am sure I recognized Captain Wirz on that occasion; he had been sick, or it was so reported at the time, and I did not know he was on duty; I am certain it was Captain Wirz.

Martin E. Hogan's testimony is given in previous pages. He testified further:[2]

I saw Captain Wirz at the time the prisoners were being removed from Andersonville to Millen take a man by the coat collar because he could not walk faster. The man was so worn out with hunger and disease that if he had got the whole world I do not think he could move faster than he was moving. Captain Wirz wrenched him back and stamped upon him with his boot. The man was borne past me, bleeding from his mouth or nose, I cannot say which, and he died a short time afterwards. When I speak of Captain Wirz, I mean the man sitting

[1] Record, p. 79.
[2] Record, p. 89.

there [pointing to the prisoner]. I have no doubt of his identity. I should know him anywhere. The prisoners commenced to move from there from the 5th to the 8th of September, 1864, and this occurred inside of a week from that time. It was some time in the early part of September. I cannot say within two or three days what date it was.

The following proceedings took place and will explain themselves:[1]

Upon the meeting of the court on the 30th of August, General Thomas stated that the prisoner, as he had been informed by his counsel, had last night been confined with handcuffs which had injured his wrists. While he (General Thomas) was well aware that the court had no control or responsibility with regard to the treatment of the prisoner outside of the courtroom, yet, as the prisoner while in prison might need to write for the purpose of preparing his defense, it might be worthy of consideration by the court whether such rigorous treatment as confinement with handcuffs might not be dispensed with.

The Judge Advocate stated that the treatment referred to had been resorted to as a matter of precaution and at the suggestion of one of the counsel of the prisoner (Mr. Baker), who had stated on the evening of his proposed retirement from the case that he believed there was great reason to apprehend that the prisoner might commit suicide before the next morning.

It was not unusual for prisoners charged with offenses such as are alleged against Captain Wirz to be kept in close confinement and with handcuffs.

The court was responsible for the treatment of the prisoner only while he was in the presence of the court, and could not with propriety direct the nature of his treatment while in custody of the prison-keeper. The government did not propose to apply the *lex talionis*. Doubtless, if the court desired it, Colonel Colby would exempt the prisoner from any such treatment in the future. If the prisoner's wrists had been injured by the handcuffs, it was no doubt unintentional, and was altogether unknown to Colonel Colby.

GENERAL THOMAS. I mentioned this matter simply because it had been suggested to me by one of the prisoner's counsel. I distinctly stated that the court had nothing to do with the prisoner while not in its presence.

Mr. Baker said that on the evening referred to, the prisoner was in a state of mind so distracted that it was a matter of grave apprehension as to what he might be tempted to do, as he at that time said to his counsel that if they left him then, he would never again come into the presence of the court. Counsel had stated this at the time to the Judge Advocate, and had added that he did not know but that it was necessary to confine the prisoner closely. But that suggestion was intended to be limited to that particular time, and probably ought not to have been made at all.

The prisoner made no complaint himself of any harsh treatment; the guards and others in charge of him had been uniformly kind. The fact that he had been injured last night by the handcuffs was doubtless one of those accidents for which no one was to blame. But for the sickly condition of the prisoner the handcuffs would not have injured him. He (Mr. Baker) was sorry that his colleague had brought the matter to the attention of the court. He presumed that the same thing would not occur again.

[1] Record, p. 98.

MONUMENT ERECTED BY THE STATE OF INDIANA.

338   THE TRAGEDY OF ANDERSONVILLE.

THE JUDGE ADVOCATE. The government must take its own course with regard to its prisoner.

MR. BAKER. It will not occur as a consequence of any suggestion of mine.

THE JUDGE ADVOCATE. Certainly not.

TESTIMONY OF O. S. BELCHER.

O. S. Belcher testified:[1]

I have been in the military service of the United States; in the 16th Illinois Cavalry. I was a prisoner at Andersonville from the 8th March to the 8th September, 1864.

I saw Captain Wirz order one man shot there one day, and the guard shot him; I did not see him do it, but I heard him. It was a man that was a cripple and went on a crutch. Captain Wirz was in the stockade and this man went up to him, and wanted him to take him outside. Captain Wirz would not do it, and finally this cripple went over the dead-line, and said he would rather be shot than stay there, and begged the guard to shoot him. The guard would not shoot him, and Captain Wirz went outside the stockade. There was a large crowd inside the stockade; pretty soon I heard Wirz halloo to the sentry on the post. He was outside the stockade in a little kind of canal which they used to drive into the stockade. I heard him tell him if the man did not go back over the dead-line, the guard was to shoot him. The guard told the man to go back; he did not, and was shot. The ball took effect in the jaw and passed down through the breast. A few minutes after Wirz came on the top of the stockade and threatened that if we did not go to our quarters, he would fire upon us and shoot some more of us. The man that was shot was called "Chickamauga." That happened at the south gate. I do not exactly remember the month. I think it was some time in June. We never paid any attention to such things there in regard to dates. It was hard for us to tell whether we were going to live to get out. The crippled man had lost one of his legs; he went on a crutch.

I saw Captain Wirz use his revolver. After he took command, we were called up and counted off in hundreds. I was sergeant of a hundred. There was a man belonging to my hundred who had got away. Captain Wirz had threatened that if any man left the ranks, he would shoot him. This man left the ranks. He was sick, and was not able to stand up. They kept us standing there in the hot sun all day, and would not allow any of us to go to get water or anything else. This man started to go out of the ranks and Wirz pulled out his revolver and fired at him. The ball went through the top of his hat, but did not hit him.

James K. Davidson's testimony has already been given upon several matters, including the shooting of prisoners by the guard, and the boast of Wirz that he was "killing more Yankees than Lee was at Richmond." He testified further:[2]

I saw Captain Wirz shoot a man; it was about the first of April, I think, shortly after he took command there; Captain Wirz was coming in the south gate

[1] Record, p. 135.
[2] Record, pp. 142, 146.

one day; a sick man, as I took him to be, a lame man, asked Captain Wirz something, and Captain Wirz turned round and shot him; the man died.

Captain Wirz shot this man that I have spoken of on the south side of the branch, up pretty near the gate, on the inside of the stockade. I think it was in April. I don't think it was later than the 10th of April. Captain Wirz had not been there a great while. He shot the man with a revolver. I cannot tell the man's name, nor to what company or regiment he belonged. I never saw the man before that. I saw him after he was shot, when they were carrying him out of the gate. He was dead. Captain Wirz had on white clothes then. I would not call it a Confederate uniform; I would call it a citizen dress. He had on his head a gray cap. I never saw him wear anything else. His coat was not made in uniform style. I believe he had brass buttons on his coat; I am not certain. It had a turndown collar. I never saw Captain Wirz shoot more than one man, and that was near the south gate, inside the stockade. He was not within the dead-line.

TESTIMONY OF OLIVER B. FAIRCLOUGH.

Oliver B. Fairclough testified:[1]

I was in the military service of the United States; in the 9th New York Cavalry. I was taken prisoner October 10, 1863. I was first taken to Libby Prison, Richmond. I remained there until some time in February, 1864. I was then taken to Andersonville. My treatment in Libby Prison was better in every respect than at Andersonville. I was in the stockade at Andersonville all the time.

Captain Wirz took command about six weeks after I went there, and he was in command there all the time afterwards, from that time until the time I left. He attended roll-call when he first went there, until the number of prisoners became too great for one man to superintend the roll-call. His manner at roll-call was very overbearing and abusive. He generally saluted the prisoners by calling them "damned Yankee sons of bitches." He often abused the prisoners. It was of frequent occurrence. I know a person, whom he kicked. He was my father. One morning Captain Wirz came to roll-call when my father was lying in a helpless condition. He was affected with scurvy. His legs were drawn up so he could not straighten them, and also his arms. While he lay in that condition Captain Wirz came up to him several times and told him he wished him to fall in at roll-call or he would kick him. He did finally kick him, and abuse him in language most shamefully. He said, "You God-damned Yankee son of a bitch, if you don't fall in at roll-call I will not give you anything to eat for a week." He stopped my father's rations. On such occasions as I have referred to twenty-four hours was the longest period at one time. The kicking caused my father to have a very severe pain in his side. I saw him beat other prisoners; I saw him knock a man down with his pistol for entering a complaint about the rations being so poor. My father died while in prison, about a month after the occurrence I have narrated. I have a statement of his made at the time of his death. He made a verbal statement to me at the time he died. He called me by name and said he died from sheer starvation, and asked me not to tell my mother,

[1] Record, p. 154.

his wife, the awful condition in which he was compelled to die. After he had spoken those words I wrote them down, and held his hand upon the paper, and he signed his name. I did not guide the pencil, I merely placed his hand upon the paper. He was perfectly rational until the last.

[A paper being exhibited to the witness, he identified it as the one just referred to in his testimony. The Assistant Judge Advocate proposed to offer it in evidence. Mr. Baker objected.]

THE COURT. How long before he died did your father sign that paper?

A. He did not live, I think, ten minutes after he signed it.

[The court, after deliberation, overruled the objection, and the paper was admitted in evidence. The following is a copy:]

CAMP SUMTER, ANDERSONVILLE, August 27, 1864.

Oliver, I die from sheer starvation, and don't for the world tell your mother of the awful condition I am compelled to die in.

RICHARD FAIRCLOUGH.

I saw a man shot who was lying in his tent near the dead-line. The sentinel who shot him fired at another man and missed him, and shot this man who was lying in his tent. I saw the sentinel when he shot. I immediately went to the tent where the man was lying and saw him lying there, and afterwards saw him die. I went directly to where the sentinel was and asked why he did not halt men before shooting, as there were a great many in camp who did not understand the meaning of the dead-line. He told me that Captain Wirz held out as an inducement to them a thirty days' furlough to every man who would shoot a Yankee. I said no more to him.

TESTIMONY OF WILLIAM WILLIS SCOTT.

William Willis Scott testified:[1]

I am in the military service of the United States; in the 6th West Virginia Cavalry. I was a prisoner at Andersonville. I was captured June 26, 1864. I remained at Lynchburg, I think, three weeks, and I arrived at Andersonville, I think, the middle of August.

I know Captain Wirz very well. I saw him commit acts of cruelty on prisoners. In one case I was coming down after a bucket of water. I belonged away up in what they called the new stockade on the north side. Captain Wirz was coming in. A sick man was sitting on the side of the bank. He asked Captain Wirz if he could get out; Captain Wirz turned around, gave him a kind of sour look, and said, "Yes, God damn it, I will let you out," and with the revolver he struck the fellow over the head and shoulders several times. The fellow went to his tent then. On the third morning, I think, I made it my business to go down and see him. He was dead. He had died the night before. I saw him. I suppose he died from the effects of the beating with the pistol. He was pretty badly bruised around the head and face. I think he beat him with the butt of the revolver which he had in his hand. I don't remember which hand he used. He knocked the man down the first blow. I think this was about the 25th or 26th of August, 1864. I cannot give the man's name. I did not inquire about that. I just came down to see if he was much the worse for his treatment, and I did not inquire any further.

[1] Record, p.194.

TESTIMONY AS TO MURDER.   341

I saw Captain Wirz on one occasion coming in between the stockade and the dead-line; one of his own guards was up above, and a stone or a brickbat, I cannot tell which, was thrown down and hit Captain Wirz on the back. His own guard threw it; I saw the guard throw it. Captain Wirz wheeled around on his horse and there was near him one of our prisoners coming out of his tent. He shot and struck the man on the head. He made no inquiries before firing. He never made any inquiries nor looked. He just rode on. He cut off the skin of the fellow's head along with some of the hair. He was only stunned a little; he got up and went into his tent. Captain Wirz did not make any inquiries at all.

TESTIMONY OF PRESCOTT TRACY.

Prescott Tracy testified:[1]

I am in the military service of the United States. I am a lieutenant. I was commissioned last year. My previous position in the army was sergeant. I was taken prisoner. I was at the Andersonville prison. I was taken on the 22d June, 1864, in the last charge we made on Petersburg. I was taken to Andersonville, I think, the last of June of that year. I was put in the stockade when I got there, by Captain Wirz. I was in there until the 17th of August of the same year. I was pretty near starved to death.

I saw the prisoner [Wirz] very often. I never saw him commit acts of cruelty upon prisoners himself, but I saw him give the orders to do it, to shoot a man. I could not give the day exactly; I know that it was a Wednesday, that is all I know. In the month of August the man was shot. His name was Roberts. I cannot tell what regiment he belonged to. He was what we called "fresh fish," just come in by the north gate, and, not knowing the rules and regulations, he went to take a drink at the creek, and, it being muddy there, he slipped and fell in so that his head went about six inches inside the dead-line. Captain Wirz was behind me, perhaps the distance of this room or a little more, and he hallooed to the sentry, "God damn your soul, why don't you shoot that Yankee son of a bitch?" That was the expression he made use of. The sentinel fired and shot the man through the top of the head and the ball came out at the back of his neck. The sentry did not say anything at the time; he only just fired. I lay down, for I was afraid of getting shot myself. This was in August, the forepart of August. I could not tell the date, because we did not know one day from another there. The man did not live; he died right in the creek, and we pulled him out and buried him that same afternoon. I never saw any other man shot. I heard the reports. of guns, but I never saw a man shot. I saw one laid out, but did not see him shot. He was shot and dead, and we were going to bury him, and he was what is called laid out. I do not know the circumstances under which he was shot.

I saw men in the stocks. I could not tell you when I saw some. I never saw men die in the stocks, but I saw men die afterwards. I saw men die on the south side of the stockade from the effects of being in the stocks. I do not know their names. They were stretched out in the stocks; then pieces of wood across their necks and across their feet, and their hands were stretched out as far as they could go and tied down, and there they lay with the sun pouring right down on them. They died the next morning after they were in the stocks. The first case I

[1] Record, p. 212 et seq.

saw was a man belonging to the 3d Pennsylvania Cavalry. He was stretched out full length with his head up before the sun, with a piece of wood right across his neck, and another across his two feet, and there he lay from nine in the morning until nearly six in the afternoon. The next time I saw him he was a corpse; it was the next morning; I helped to carry him out. I cannot remember the date. We could not remember one day from another there. We could not tell Sunday from Monday. It was in August, the fore part. I never saw any one else die after being in the stocks. When the man died he was out of the stockade, in a little shanty made of trees. He was not brought back after he was in the stocks.

[To the Court:] Captain Wirz was behind me, about the length of this room, when the man was shot. I hallooed, "Roberts, Roberts, for Christ's sake get out of that!" That was the expression I made use of, and Captain Wirz was behind me with one hand behind his coat. He was outside the dead-line, on the street, or the road down to the creek, coming down from the north gate. Before I had time to get the man out, or speak to him a second time, he was shot. Captain Wirz was inside of the stockade, on the road down towards the south side of the stockade. He was walking down the street at the time. I am sure I saw him, I can swear to it, and if he will look me in the face he knows it.

TESTIMONY OF FELIX DE LA BAUME.

Felix De La Baume testified:[1]

I was in the military service of the United States, in the 35th New York Volunteers. I was a prisoner of war at Andersonville from July 8, 1864, till April 19, 1865.

I know the prisoner, Captain Wirz. On the 8th of July I arrived at Andersonville, with three or four hundred other prisoners, most of them sick and wounded. We were brought up to Captain Wirz's headquarters, were drawn up in line four ranks deep, and kept there for a considerable length of time, without any business being transacted. The guards had orders to let hone of us go to the water. One of the prisoners was attacked with epilepsy or fits; he fell down; some of his friends or neighbors standing near him ran down to the creek after water. I don't know whether they had permission of the guard; I suppose so, because the guard was tied up by the thumbs for permitting them to do so. First I heard a shot fired, without seeing who fired it. After hearing that shot fired, I looked down to the left and I saw Captain Wirz fire two more shots, wounding two men. One of them was carried up near his headquarters, and, in my opinion, was in a dying condition. The other was wounded, too, but I did not see him again. I never saw him afterwards. The one who was carried up near the headquarters was wounded somewhere in the breast. Captain Wirz had a revolver in his hand. I was perhaps twenty paces distant from him. I am not positive about the distance. The prisoner whom he shot was not very far from him. I am certain I saw Captain Wirz discharge the pistol in his hand. I did not myself see the man who was brought up to headquarters die; but he was evidently in a dying condition, judging by his appearance; I never saw him again. We were not allowed to speak to the guard, and I could not make any inquiries. Captain Wirz asked the lieutenant of the guard, "Where is the guard who allowed this man to

---

[1] Record, p. 282 et seq.

fall out of the ranks?" The guard was pointed out, and Captain Wirz ordered him to be tied up by the thumbs for two hours. After this Captain Wirz pointed out the man, and said, "That is the way I get rid of you damned sons of bitches." I myself saw the man fall down; he had epileptic fits, and I was informed that the men ran after water for him. We had not received any water all night; they kept us all night in the cars; on the way down from Macon to Andersonville we had no water. When we passed the creek we wished to get some water, but we were not allowed to have any. We were kept there at the headquarters of Captain Wirz for about two hours, without receiving a drink. We were then divided into squads and transported into the stockade. I was taken out with four other men to be put into the 71st detachment, and was shortly afterwards taken away from the headquarters into the stockade. All I can state as to whether the man died from that gunshot wound is that he was, in my opinion, in a dying condition; I judged so from his heaving up and down and from his gasping for breath. I have seen many men on the battlefield in the same condition, and they always died shortly afterwards. The blood was running out from his breast or the middle of his body somewhere. All I heard about it afterwards was from a rebel sergeant; I think his name was Colby; he said the man died; he told me that some time after I was in the stockade.

In the month of December, 1864, when it was so very cold, we did not receive any wood in the hospital. I obtained sometimes a pass from Edward Young, who was chief cook there, and from Jim Lane, who was also a cook; they were Federal prisoners. On those passes I used to go outside of the hospital enclosure to gather up some wood, so as to have some fire in the tent where I stopped. Going out one day, I saw a man named Edler, a private in the 39th New York Volunteers, who was captured on the 6th of February near Martinsburg. I saw him tied, with an iron collar round his neck, to a post. As I had the pass of another man, which was always punished when it was found out, as soon as I saw Captain Wirz standing near him I went off, so as not to be captured myself, because if Captain Wirz had found out that I had the pass of another man he would have punished me too. I heard this man Edler say something to Captain Wirz, whereupon Wirz said, "One word more, and I will blow your damned brain to hell," holding a pistol towards his head. I have drawn a representation of that scene. [A drawing being exhibited to witness:] I draughted this from recollection. This figure represents a guard standing over the man. That is a true representation. There was a guard, a captain, and some other man. I only represented one guard, but there were some more rebels about there.

The man was afterwards sent back to the hospital, of which he was an inmate. As he belonged to my regiment I took an interest in him, and as soon as he came back to the hospital I went to his tent to make inquiries, but his neck and his tongue were so much swollen that he was unable to speak, and was evidently in a dying condition. The nurse, named Butsell, told me that the man was punished for having gone out on a forged pass. The man died two or three days afterward; I only visited him once while in that condition; the second time I went there he was dead; I cannot say whether the swollen neck and tongue still continued. The first time I was there his neck and tongue were very much swollen; when I came there again he was dead. I don't think he died from the effects of that iron collar round his neck alone; if he had been a stout, healthy man, he might have stood it; but he was very far reduced already, almost to a skeleton, by starvation, before he was put in the irons. His neck or tongue was not swollen before he was put in the irons. He was able to speak before he was put in the irons. This circumstance happened near the end of December, 1864, after Christmas. I have seen men bucked and gagged. In going out on these passes of which I have spoken, I had several opportunities of seeing men bucked and gagged. I have drawn a representation of the front and side views of that bucking and gagging operation. [A drawing being exhibited to witness:] That is a correct representation. I drew it from my recollection. One of the figures here represents a sentry standing over the man. The other person standing by was one of the rebel sergeants.

I remember about the hounds. In the month of September, 1864, I was allowed to go out after wood. At that time Captain Wirz allowed squads of twenty-five to go out after wood about a mile distant from the stockade. At that time I myself was not able to carry any wood, but I availed myself of the opportunity to go out to have some fresh air. I went out with a man named Louis Holm, of the 5th New York Cavalry. We were both starved; we had had nothing to eat in consequence of being unable to cook our meal which we received. When we came out Holm made a proposition to me that we should hide ourselves and try to get away from the guard and go to some farm to obtain something to eat. We were too weak to run off; we did not intend to run off or "skedaddle," because we could not walk far; but we wished to obtain some food from some of the farmers; we always heard that the farmers around there were good Union men, and always aided our prisoners whenever they could do so without being detected. Holm and I hid ourselves in a very large tree in a kind of a mud-hole among the bushes, and remained there for over an hour; then we heard the dogs bark. An old Indian had once told me that in case of being overtaken by bloodhounds I should pretend to be dead and the hounds would not attack me. So I told Holm to remain quiet in the bushes and not make any noise, but he was so much frightened by the dogs that he tried to get up a tree, so as not to be torn to pieces by them. While he was trying to get up the tree the dogs came up and caught hold of him by one of his legs, biting quite a large hole. I have drawn a representation of that scene. [A paper being shown to witness:] That is the drawing; the man climbing the tree represents Holm, and I am represented lying under the tree. That represents the character of the dog; it was a dog looking like this. My comrade was torn by the dogs very badly; we were brought in by a sergeant and by the men who had the dogs. At that time they had only two dogs out, and one of them captured us. They brought us in to Captain Wirz's headquarters, and one of the sergeants—I don't remember his name—spoke a few words for me and the other man. Captain Wirz did not punish us, but sent us back to the stockade and gave orders to the sergeant of the detachment not to let us go out any more.

I have noticed persons with ball and chain attached to them. I saw one man in the stockade in the month of August, 1864; the south side of the stockade was where I saw him first. He was insane, for I asked him why he had the ball and chain on, and he told me that he was Samson and they wanted to try his strength. He was a lunatic. I have drawn a representation of that man as confined with

Monument Erected by the State of Wisconsin.

the ball and chain. [A drawing being shown to witness:] That is my representation.

I have seen a great many men shot in the stockade near the dead-line, inside the dead-line; I mean between the dead-line and the inner stockade, having crossed the dead-line, between the dead-line and the inner stockade. There was a man of my company named Le Vois, a Frenchman, who was robbed in Richmond of his gold watch and chain and all his jewelry, in consequence of which he became insane. A few days after coming to Andersonville, he went inside the dead-line near the gate of the north side. He opened his shirt and called on the guard there, who was an old man, to shoot him, saying that he wanted to be killed. The old guard, who was a very sensible man, told him to go out of the dead-line, and hallooed to some of his comrades, telling them to call him out; but he would not come out, and we were all afraid to go inside the dead-line to bring him out. He went to the next guard, and the next guard shot him, killing him instantly. The guard who killed him was a young boy, about 15 or 16; and he said to the old guard, "If I had not killed the Yankee son of a bitch, I would have reported you to Captain Wirz for not shooting him; but I am satisfied; I now get my furlough." This occurred in the month of August, 1864, in the first part of the month, I believe. When we were there we did not know one day from another, and I cannot state the day definitely. I know positively of two whom I myself saw killed on the dead-line by the sentries; one was Le Vois, and another was a corporal of the 125th New York; I do not know the name of the corporal. Le Vois belonged to Company E, 39th New York Veteran Volunteers. I know the corporal that was killed belonged to the 125th New York Volunteers. I had seen him before, because his regiment belonged to my brigade. He was killed while reaching under the dead-line for clean water; I do not know to what company he belonged.

TESTIMONY OF CHARLES E. TIBBLES.

Charles E. Tibbles testified:[1]

I have been in the military service of the United States, in the 4th Iowa Infantry. I was a prisoner at Andersonville. I went there on the 28th of March, 1864, and escaped on the 7th or 8th of September.

We were taken there in the night. It was very dark and rainy. The captain ordered us to report at the same place at 9 o'clock next morning; we did so; we formed in line in two ranks, and were counted off; we were then ordered to stand in line until the whole of the prisoners were counted off—all the men in the prison; we did so. We were in line about two hours. I think there were only some six thousand there at that time. I presume we were kept there until all were counted; we all dispersed at the same time. I do not know whether Captain Wirz had been engaged in counting before that time. I know Captain Wirz personally. The next morning after we went there, a man walked along the front of our line, about ten feet from the line. Captain Wirz turned around and saw him and caught him by the throat. He drew his pistol and told him he would blow his damned brains out if he did not keep away. I also saw him draw his pistol on several other men. I never saw him shoot any one.

After we had been there some time burying the dead—I think it was in the latter part of July—Captain Wirz issued orders to us that we would not be

[1] Record, p. 294 et seq.

allowed the mile as the agreement stated, but only from the graveyard to our quarters, and we were guarded every night. Thinking that as he broke his agreement I was not bound by mine, I made my escape on the 7th or 8th of September, and was recaptured by the hounds about forty miles from Andersonville. We were on a fence when the hounds came up, and we fought them off. The hound keeper told us to get down, and we said we would not until he would call the hounds off. They said they had orders to let the hounds bite us, and they drew revolvers and said they would shoot us if we would not come down. We told them to shoot; that we would rather die anyhow than go to Andersonville. [To the Court:] There were four of us. There were six rebels. They whipped the hounds off and we got down and were marched back to Andersonville. On arriving at Andersonville we were brought up in front of Captain Wirz's headquarters. The houndkeeper said, "Here are these Yankees, Captain." Said he "I will attend to them in a minute," and he ordered his revolver to be brought to him. The orderly brought his revolver. After he made his revolver ready, he came out, holding his revolver I think, in his right hand—came in front of us, looked at us a little bit, and said, "Where is Crandall?" referring to another man who escaped the same day. We told him we did not know anything about him. He turned to the houndkeeper and said, "If you will bring me Bill Crandall I will give you five hundred dollars out of my own pocket. I will learn him how to run away." Then turning to us, he said, "You young sons of bitches of Yankees, I'll make you smell hell before night." He then, turning to the sergeant, said, "These men's sentence is to work in the graveyard hard every day, on half rations, to be sent into the stockade at night, and not to be exchanged when the other prisoners are exchanged. Take these men and see that my orders are fulfilled, and if they do not work, or if they refuse to work, put them in on top of the dead and cover them up, and if you don't do it, I will serve you the same way." The sergeant took us to the graveyard, where we worked all day. That night we were taken back and put in the stockade. The next day Captain Wirz came to us and said he had received orders to send us all away, and that he would put a special guard over us. He started us to Florence, South Carolina, and that was the last I saw of Captain Wirz. That was in September. This man Crandall is the same who testified a day or two since—William Crandall.

TESTIMONY OF GEORGE CONWAY.

George Conway testified:[1]

I belonged to the 3d New York Artillery; I was a prisoner at Andersonville from the night of the 17th of March to the 7th of September, 1864.

I saw a man shot one day; he came down after water; no one was allowed to put their head or any part of their body under the dead-line. This man probably not being acquainted with the rules, as many of them were not who came in there after the rules were read, put his hand in under the dead-line to get a cup of water and the cup dropped from his hand; he put his hand in under the dead-line to raise it up again and Captain Wirz shot him, the ball taking effect in his head. He died almost instantly. [To the Court:] Captain Wirz shot him; he was standing in the sentry-box. This occurred about the time the raiders were hung; I could not say whether it was before or after. It was about that time.

[1] Record, p. 323.

I am certain I recognized Captain Wirz; I knew him well at that time. He had a revolver in his hand, I believe. Those were the circumstances. He was getting a cup of water out of the brook when the cup dropped from his hand. I do not know the name of that man; I never saw the man before till I saw him that time. The man died.

TESTIMONY OF D. S. ORCOTT.

D. S. Orcott testified:[1]

I was in the military service of the United States, in the 11th Pennsylvania Cavalry, Company L. I was taken prisoner and taken to Andersonville. I arrived there on the 22d of July, 1864.

We arrived there about 10 o'clock on the 22d of July, 1864, and were marched up before Captain Wirz's headquarters, and were kept standing there in the hot sun for three hours without any water. We had been seven days on the road and the men were dry, and he would not allow us to have any water. One of the men stepped out of the ranks and asked for a drink of water. Captain Wirz told the guard not to allow him to go out. He told the guards that if any of the men attempted to leave the ranks to kill them, to shoot them. One man stepped out and Captain Wirz came along and said, "Kill the damned Yankee son of a bitch." The guard hit the man over the head with his gun and knocked him down. His head was cut open and he lay there; he could not speak. I could not tell the appearance of the wound. I was not close enough to him, but I could see the blood flowing freely. The man did not die while I was there. There was a man of my regiment who got sun-struck and was left out there. He came into the stockade afterwards, and he told us that the man died two or three hours after we left. He did not state any declarations of the man at the time he died. I do not know the name of the man who was killed. He belonged to the 5th Pennsylvania Cavalry. I think he was a private. The date this occurred, as near as I can tell, was the 22d of July.

I heard the prisoner, Captain Wirz, say something about giving land to the Federal prisoners there. While we were standing in front of Captain Wirz's headquarters, a wagon came out with a load of dead in it, and one of the boys spoke up and asked what was in that wagon. Captain Wirz said it was "Yankees going out to get their land warrants." He said, "We are going to give you all land warrants of the same kind, six feet of land, or land enough to bury you," or something like that.

TESTIMONY OF CHARLES H. RUSSELL.

Charles H. Russell testified:[2]

I was in the military service of the United States. I was orderly sergeant, Company E, 1st Wisconsin Cavalry, at the time of my capture, on the 9th day of May, 1864. . . . I was sent to Andersonville, where I arrived on the 27th of May, 1864.

After I had been in the stockade about two weeks, a number of men from my regiment who were there, and who had been fed on sour bread, wanted me to

---
[1] Record, p. 325.
[2] Record, p. 345.

speak to Captain Wirz about it, and to see if he wouldn't give them better bread. I took a sample of it to him one day, when he came in the stockade, and I showed it to him. He turned himself and said, "I don't want to know anything about it." I insisted on his looking at it. It was all moldy and sour. That made him angry. He had his pistol in his hand, and he wheeled around and presented it at my head, cocked. There was a big crowd around there, and the boys began to sing out, "Go in for him." He got scared, and wheeled around and rode out of camp. I think it likely he would have shot me if he had dared to.

I have seen two men shot myself for crossing the dead-line, and three after they were shot.

Q. State the circumstances of the shooting of those whom you saw shot.

A. I saw a man shot at the creek one morning in June. We were down after water. There was a big crowd there. The ground near the creek was very slippery, where the boys were running in and out and spilling water. A fellow there, who looked very weak and sick, tried to get some water, but he slipped and fell, sticking his arm under the dead-line-nothing but his arm. I was within six feet of him when the guard raised his gun and fired and shot him down. The man did not speak a word afterwards.

I do not know that man's name nor his regiment. I did not see Captain Wirz present at that time. About the 20th of July, I think, there was a man shot on the south side, at a little spring where they dug a hole in the ground about eight feet from the dead-line, on the south side of the creek. He was there getting water, and there was quite a number getting water at the same time. They were crowding around to see who would get the water first. This man got crowded outside the dead-line, and the guard fired on him and shot him. The guard stood on the first post, on the south side of the creek. Captain Wirz came along shortly afterwards, and went up the stand where the sentry was, and I saw him shake hands with the sentry. Shortly afterwards the sentry went down, and another soldier took his place. He shook hands with the sentry and called him a "bully fellow," or something of that sort. I heard nothing said about furloughs at that time. At one time I was detailed to go out and get some wood. There was a Confederate soldier who made it a practice of going out in the woods where the boys went for wood, and trading with them there, out of the sight of his officers. He said that there was an order out that they would get furloughs for every Yankee they killed.

TESTIMONY OF HUGH R. SNEE.

Hugh R. Snee testified:[1]

I was in the military service of the United States—in the 39th Illinois Regiment. I was a prisoner at Andersonville about five months. I was captured May 16, 1864, and I made my escape about the 9th of September following. I made my escape by smuggling myself out with a few prisoners who were to be exchanged on special exchange arranged between General Sherman and General Hood. When they called the roll of these men who were to be exchanged, it was after dark; that time being chosen on account of the heat, as men would faint during the day. When they called the roll, they said they wanted none but able-bodied

[1] Record, p. 352.

men. After I got out I fell into line. Others came out who could not walk. There were two men belonging to a western regiment—I think one belonging to an Iowa regiment; I am not certain as to that; they fainted before they got to the brook that ran, I think, between Captain Wirz's headquarters and the depot. They fell out of the ranks, and the guard shoved them to one side. A man ran back and wanted to know why they were out. They made the remark that they wished to get out of prison. The man said, "I will help you out damned soon." We were hurrying along at the double-quick. I heard six discharges from a pistol; I supposed it to be a revolver, and I heard a cry, as if somebody was hurt. Presently a rebel officer, a lieutenant I think, came along, and he made the remark that it was a brutal act. Some one asked who did it, and he said the captain. I have no means of knowing that they were killed, except that this lieutenant said that only one of them was killed. He said, "One of them is dead." I have heard Captain Wirz's voice on several occasions. I cannot say positively if the voice I heard at that time had the accent of his voice. I thought at that time that it was his voice. We passed him soon afterward, perhaps not over fifteen minutes. He was sitting in his chair in front of his headquarters, and General Winder was sitting not a great distance from him. I suppose it was calculated that we were passing in review before them, and they were counting us. We were ordered to march in particular order so that we could be counted. That is all I know about that particular affair.

TESTIMONY OF AMBROSE HENMAN.

Ambrose Henman testified:[1]

I am a private in Company L, 4th United States Cavalry. I was a prisoner at Andersonville from the 23d of April, 1864, till the last of July, 1864. I saw the prisoner [Wirz] there.

I saw one man shot after I was there nine or ten days. It was about the 6th or 7th of May, I think, at the northwest corner of the stockade. The man put his hand under the dead-line to get a crumb of bread, when he was shot by the guard. I do not know the man's name or regiment. I think he was an idiot, a crazy man.

I saw a man shot at the south gate, about the last of May, 1864. The man had several names—"Pretty Polly," "Fortune Teller," and "Chickamauga." Captain Wirz was present at the time he was shot. Pretty Polly, as I called him, went up to the gate. Wirz was at the wicket-gate, having the gate open. Pretty Polly asked him to let him out. Captain Wirz drew his revolver and told him that he could not get out. Pretty Polly seemed to be afraid of the raiders inside, as they called them. Wirz drove him back from the dead-line and closed the gate and walked out. Chiekamauga walked inside the dead-line and sat down, saying he would rather be shot by their men than be killed by our own men. Wirz ordered the sentinel to shoot him. The sentinel hesitated, and before the sentinel fired Wirz went up to the sentry-box with his revolver drawn. But before he got there the sentry fired at the man and shot him down, the ball striking him in the chin and passing through the breast. I heard nothing about furloughs. I spoke to Captain Wirz at the time, after the man was shot, and asked the privilege of

---

[1] Record, p. 372.

taking him from the dead-line. He gave me permission, telling me to take him and go to hell with him.

I picked him up and carried him back about four rods from the dead-line. He lay down there and died. The men crowded around there so much to see him, that Captain Wirz ordered the sentinel to fire again. I saw Captain Wirz up in the sentry-box. I did not see him before he went to the sentry-box. I could not see over the stockade. I saw him at the gate before the man was shot. He drew his revolver and ordered him back. There was some crowd. Captain Wirz went to the sentry-box. He gave orders to the sentinel before he went up to shoot "the Yankee son of a bitch." The sentinel was only a few feet from where the crowd stood.

TESTIMONY OF GEORGE W. GRAY.

George W. Gray testified:[1]

I am in the military service of the United States; in the 7th Indiana Cavalry, Company B.

Q. How long have you been in the service?

A. In my last term two years and one month; I was taken to Andersonville on the 10th of June, 1864, and remained there until November.

About the last of August I made my escape from Andersonville, and was overtaken by a lot of hounds; before the catch-dog could get at me I took a tree. After I took the tree the hounds circled around and barked until the catch-dog came up; when the catch-dog came up some Johnnies came up also, and demanded that I should come down. I told them to tie that dog and that I would come down, but not before. They said they would tie one of the other dogs. I said no, that they should tie up the catch-dog; they tied him and I came down. The hounds did not touch me. I knew they would not—for the reason that I used to catch niggers myself with them, and so knew all about them. I was brought back to Andersonville prison and taken to Wirz's quarters. I was ordered by him to be put in the stocks, where I remained for four days, with my feet placed in a block and another lever placed over my legs, with my arms thrown back, and a chain running across my arms. I remained four days there in the sun; that was my punishment for trying to get away from the prison. At the same time a young man was placed in the stocks—the third man from me. He died there. He was a little sick when he went in, and he died there. I do not know his name; if I heard it, I have forgotten it. This occurred about the last of August or the first of September, 1864. I am certain he died. The negroes took him out of the stocks after he was dead, threw him into the wagon, and hauled him away.

Q. Do you know anything about the prisoner [Wirz] having shot a prisoner of war there at any time.

A. He shot a young fellow named William Stewart, a private belonging to the 9th Minnesota Infantry. He and I went out of the stockade with a dead body, and after laying the dead body in the dead-house Captain Wirz rode up to us and asked by what authority we were out there or what we were doing there. Stewart said we were there by proper authority. Wirz said no more,

[1] Record, p. 397 et seq.

but drew a revolver and shot the man. After he was killed the guard took from the body about twenty or thirty dollars, and Wirz took the money from the guard and rode off, telling the guard to take me to prison.

Q. Are you sure about that?

A. If I was not I would not speak it.

Q. By whose orders did you come out with the dead body?

A. It was my determination—I don't know whether it was Stewart's or not—to get away again. For that reason we went out. We begged for the dead body.

Q. Do you know whether that was the time that Lieutenant Davis had something to do with the prison?

A. I recollect now that Lieutenant Davis ordered the sergeants of each detachment to detail men to carry out of the stockade the dead bodies of men belonging to that detachment.

Q. State what Captain Wirz had in his hand when he shot that soldier.

A. He had a revolver; whether a navy pistol or not I don't know; it was a large pistol.

Q. How near was he to him?

A. About eight feet from him, I think.

Q. Where did the ball take effect in your comrade?

A. In the breast. He died right there where he was shot.

Q. Were you at the time attempting to make your escape?

A. No, sir; but it was my intention if I could, to do so. I was not attempting it at that time, nor was Stewart.

Q. How far were you from the dead-house?

A. About fifty yards—about half the distance from the stockade to the dead-house; a little off and to one side of it.

Q. You do not know whether Lieutenant Davis had a partial command there?

A. I think that in September Captain Wirz was relieved temporarily by Lieutenant Davis on account of ill health, about two weeks, probably.

Q. Of the fact of Wirz committing this particular offense, you are certain?

A. I am, sir.

Q. Did you state the time when Stewart was shot?

A. It was about the middle of September, after I got out of the stocks.

Q. When testifying with reference to the man on the white horse, you said something about not being able to identify him; had you any difficulty afterwards in identifying Captain Wirz?

A. The first time I knew such a man in the prison, I heard Lieutenant Davis call the name at the gate. He said, "Captain Wirz, come down this way." I looked at the man and asked the boys if it was not the commander of the Andersonville prison.

[The Judge Advocate called upon the prisoner to stand up for identification. The prisoner, who was lying on a lounge, partly raised himself, turning his face to the witness.]

Q. Do you recognize that man as the person who shot your comrade?

A. That is the man.

[The prisoner attempted to say something in contradiction of the witness, but was not permitted by the court. The Judge Advocate requested the prisoner to stand up on his feet. The prisoner having complied with the Judge Advocate's request, the witness looked at him and said, "I think that is the man."]

Q. The person whom you have been talking about, you were afterwards in the habit of recognizing in the prison as Captain Wirz?

A. Yes.

Q. Do you recollect whether the man who shot your comrade had a foreign accent?

A. I took him to be a German or a foreigner by his talk, for this reason: When I was put in the stocks he said to me, "Cott tam you, I fix you." For that reason I took him to be a foreigner or a Dutchman.

I knew a young man being brought to the stockade after being caught by the hounds. I went out to see him and asked him what was the matter. He told me he was caught by bloodhounds and torn very badly. Part of his cheek was torn off, and his arms and hands and legs gnawed up so that the man only lived some twenty-four hours after he came into the stockade. That was in October, 1864, I think. I do not know the date exactly when I left Andersonville. I got to Savannah, Georgia, in December, 1864. I do not know the name of the man who was bitten by the dogs and who died in the stockade.

I saw an officer riding on a white horse the day I arrived at Andersonville. I believe it was the same day. We got there, I think, on the ten o'clock train, and I think it was about the middle of the day. I saw that man afterwards. I could not at that time tell whether it was Captain Wirz or not, because I never had heard his name. I will not be positive whether it was Captain Wirz at that time or not. I knew him about two weeks after I went to the prison. I saw him when I first went there, at the prison-gate. The next place I saw him was inside the stockade, at the time Lieutenant Davis called him to one side and took him the other road. I cannot say whether it was or not the same man whom I first saw on the gray horse. I would not wish to say.

CHAPTER XIII.

Resumé of the Foregoing Chapter—Some Comment upon and Deductions from the Evidence Mortuary Statistics—Johnson's Island and Andersonville Compared—Table of Deaths by Months—Number of Dead at Andersonville, 13,171—Deaths in Twenty-five Federal Prisons in 1864 Compared with Andersonville—Stockade and Its Terrors Described—Condition of Prisoners Known at Richmond—Hospital and Prison Co-ordinated to Destroy Life—The Conspiracy—Charge of Murder—Photograph of Johnson's Island Prison—Statement of Soldiers on Duty There and at Fort Deleware Prison.

OF the participants in the trial of Captain Wirz, two only are living—General J. H. Stibbs, one of the judges, now residing in Chicago, and the writer.

In vindication of his verdict, General Stibbs has recently, in an address, given some interesting details of the trial. As for myself, I am performing not only what I regard as a duty I owe to the government and to the members of the court, the justness of whose findings is now being assailed, but I am giving the true story of the darkest page of the Rebellion, and I am seeking to make abortive and innocuous the misleading and altogether unwarranted implications arising from the erection of a monument to the memory of Wirz, and to refute the charges and statements placed indelibly upon that monument.

The reader will have discovered that the evidence is first directed to the charge of conspiracy, which had for its purpose, in violation of the laws of war, the weakening of the Federal armies by the various means specified,—by starving large numbers to death, and rendering unfit for service such as fortunately survived the ordeal of their treatment; by crowding them into insufficient and unwholesome quarters, exposed to the changing temperatures of heat and cold, unprovided with any kind of shelter or clothing; by depriving them in these congested quarters of sufficient pure water to drink, or even water with which to bathe or perform the most ordinary offices necessary to personal cleanliness; by leaving large numbers of the sick without medical attendance, who died in their quarters from sheer neglect; and by failing to exercise any sort of police control over this turbulent and despairing mass of human beings, encouraged thereby to rob and prey upon each other in their desperate struggle for existence.

Is it necessary to look beyond the testimony and reports given and made by rebel officers and soldiers for support of the findings of the court? Turn back and read what Colonel Chandler reported and testified to; read again the awful picture drawn by Dr. Jones and the testimony of the five or six rebel surgeons on duty there; read what officers and soldiers stationed there said of the prison and its horrors. Is it necessary to look to the testimony of the sufferers themselves?

But we may look to their testimony; and, looking there, what do we see? A picture of such helpless, hopeless misery and suffering as would wring the most callous heart and should bring the blush of shame to those who seek to immortalize one of the arch perpetrators of this monstrous iniquity.

THE STOCKADE.

Notice next with what ingenuity the prison was planned and prepared. A sluggish stream coursed through the enclosure. Above was located the cook-house, from which the garbage, grease, and offal were cast into this stream to find their way down into the prison. Still farther above were located the camps for the soldiers constituting the prison guard. Near the stream were located the army sinks for the use of the soldiers, and into it the drainage from the camps passed, contaminating the water in its course through the prison. And now turn to the evidence, documentary and oral, from rebel sources and from the lips of the surviving Union soldiers, and note the picture of the morass into and through which the prisoners had to wade to dip up the scant and infected water they were to use. The testimony is recorded; it cannot be blotted out; much of it cannot with propriety be here repeated. Indeed, its publication as part of this record is justified, and to be tolerated in print only because it came from the lips of living witnesses who were sworn to tell the whole truth.

Originally built with scanty space for ten thousand prisoners, the stockade was denuded of all timber which might have been some protection from the sun's rays or could have been made use of for firewood, and was soon filled with double its estimated capacity. Instead of enlarging it to increase its habitability, it was contracted in size by the establishment of a dead-line twenty feet from the walls of the stockade and completely around its interior. This dead-line became the scene of frequent slaughter of the occupants of the prison, not one of whom was shown to have encroached upon it with any purpose to reach the stockade wall or effect his escape. It may be truthfully said of the killings near or on this fatal dead-line, which occurred almost daily, that they were, all of them, wanton and reckless sacrifices; and be it noted, in no single instance was a guard ever rebuked, much less tried, for his crime. On the contrary, there is evidence tending to show that guards were rewarded for killing prisoners at the dead-line.

Mr. Davis in his *Belford* articles refers to Dr. Jones as eminent in his profession and of great learning and probity. I have no hesitation in quoting him, for his testimony is not to be gainsaid. Nor can we discredit other of the rebel surgeons whose testimony is before us.

Dr. G. G. Roy was asked this question: "What was the condition of the men sent from the stockade to the hospital? Describe their appearance and condition." He replied: "They presented the most horrible spectacle of human suffering that I ever saw in my life. A good many were suffering from scurvy and other diseases; a good many were naked; a large majority barefooted; a good many without hats. Their condition generally was indescribable. I attributed this condition to long confinement, want of necessaries and comforts of life, and all those causes which are calculated to produce that condition of the system where there is just vitality enough to permit one to live. The prisoners were too densely crowded; there was no shelter except such as they constructed themselves, which was very insufficient. A good many were in holes in the earth, with their blankets thrown over poles; some were in tents constructed by their own ingenuity, and with just such accommodations as their own ingenuity permitted them to contrive. There were, you may say, no accommodations made for them in the stockade."

Upon their arrival, the prisoners were paraded in front of Wirz's quarters and counted off in detachments consisting of two hundred and seventy men, divided into three squads of ninety, and a prisoner designated as sergeant of each ninety. A number was given each detachment, and the members of the nineties were enrolled as belonging to the detachment thus constituted. They were thus turned into the stockade to shift for themselves, but were required to answer to their names at roll-call each day in their respective nineties.

One of the indefensible means resorted to in securing a daily census of the prison was to punish the squad of ninety by stopping their rations unless all were accounted for at roll-call. In that mass of thirty-odd thousand, if one man could not be found, or if, unknown to his comrades, he had died and was unaccounted for, the remaining

MONUMENT ERECTED BY THE STATE OF RHODE ISLAND.

eighty-nine suffered the penalty, and the evidence was that this happened frequently. There was evidence that on several different days —notably on the 3d or 4th of July, 1864—the entire prison was deprived of rations. Witnesses testified to the suffering which resulted from the great irregularity as to time of issuing rations. Often the rations did not reach the prisoners until late in the day, and were then but sufficient to partly allay hunger, and left nothing until another day's rations came.

TERRORS OF THE PRISON PEN.

The terrors of the prison pen were greatly augmented by the utter lack of police control. There was in fact none whatever, except such as the prisoners themselves could enforce. Robbery of the weak by the stronger was common; the dying saw around them eager, wolfish faces of men ready to fight over their scanty clothing; the more fortunate possessors of a well levied heavy toll for a drink of water begged by some thirsty fellow-prisoner. Men fought like perishing animals for meat bones or crusts of bread; they crawled with crippled limbs, drawn up by scurvy, with cup in teeth, to the slimy creek for water; they burrowed in the ground like rodents of the plain to escape the scorching rays of summer and the cold of winter. The appeal to brutish instincts was so strong and insistent that the law of the jungle became the law of the prison with many, and there were enacted tragedies such as Dr. Jones described, where murder was stealthily committed for the miserably inadequate and wholly selfish motive of possessing the ragged garments of the victims.

This lack of police supervision brought its harvest of suffering and death in many ways, and its effect reached a climax in a manner forever to condemn the prison management, by the prisoners taking the law into their own hands, and by drumhead court-martial trying, condemning, and executing on the gallows six of the supposedly most desperate characters. How can the prison authorities or their apologists ever explain or justify a condition such as made this violent proceeding seem to the prisoners to be a necessity for self-protection? Who shall say that when Wirz refused to hear their plea for mercy and coldly turned these unhappy wretches over to a tribunal lacking every semblance of a judicial investigation, with their fates sealed, that he does not stand guilty before God and man? Let us not for a moment hold the members of this improvised court responsible for resorting to means desperate and cruel to bring about some sort of safety to person in the prison. Necessity drove them to it; but Winder and Wirz and the prison management created the necessity.

Father Whelan, whose testimony was relied on as tending to exculpate the accused in some degree, was pointedly asked if he was willing to testify that prisoners did not die from starvation, and he replied that he could not do so, and that, being unable to eat the rations given them, many must have died from starvation.

If it were known to the prison authorities that because of the quantity of the rations, or because of their quality, prisoners, even in small numbers, were dying of starvation,—and that it was known to them is established to a moral certainty,—every consideration of humanity as well as the rules of civilized warfare demanded of the enemy that such condition should be speedily remedied. But it was not remedied, nor was it attempted to be remedied. On the contrary, the conditions so fatal were allowed to increase, and with this increase the death-roll was swollen to frightful proportions. That this was a result reasonably to be expected can admit of no doubt, for not only the prison records proclaimed it, but the more humane and conscientious officers on duty at the prison forewarned the prison authorities that such result was inevitable unless remedial measures pointed out by them were adopted.

If a guardian charged with the duty to feed his ward deliberately starves him to death, it is murder. In time of war captive prisoners become wards of the enemy. Except when forced to do otherwise in retaliation,—and only in retaliation,—prisoners of war are entitled to such humane treatment as may be consistent with their safe-keeping and as may be reasonably within the power of the enemy to give. It is never allowable to kill them outright, when once captured, much less to subject them to slow death by torture or starvation. When I say that this rule of conduct in time of war was flagrantly violated at Andersonville, I state not alone a conclusion or inference from the evidence, but I state what was the opinion, given under oath, of the rebel surgeons on duty there. If it be cruel, if it be monstrous to lay so atrocious a crime at the doors of these prison authorities, I but repeat the sworn testimony of men who were there, and who speak from personal observation and personal experience.

Acting Assistant Surgeon J. C. Bates, who had been a medical practitioner since 1850, testified: "I feel myself safe in saying that seventy-five per cent of those who died might have been saved had those unfortunate men been properly cared for as to food, clothing, bedding, etc."

Vattel, who wrote upon international law over a century and a half ago, said: "As soon as your enemy has laid down his arms and surrendered his person, you have no longer any right over his life, unless he should give you such right by some new attempt, or had before committed against you such a crime deserving death. Prisoners of war may be secured, but cannot be made slaves, unless for personal guilt which deserves death, nor be slain, unless we be perfectly assured that our safety demands such a sacrifice."

What shall be said of the scores shot at the dead-line, some of them but reaching across it for a cup of water or piece of bread; what of those who died from being put in the stocks and chain-gang or pursued by the dogs; and what of the thousands who perished in the stockade and hospital for want of being properly cared for?

CONDITIONS KNOWN AT RICHMOND.

It does not admit of a moral doubt that the conditions at Andersonville were well known to many of the responsible heads of the rebel government at Richmond from the beginning to the end of that prison, with all its accumulating horrors; nor can it be doubted that they were known to the Confederate President. It was generally known throughout Georgia, and was the subject of newspaper comment. It was reported over and over again to the authorities at Richmond. Let it not be forgotten that Mr. Davis defends the selection of Andersonville as the site for this prison on the ground that it was in "a productive farming country; had never been devastated by the enemy; was well watered; was near Americus, a central depot for collecting the tax in kind and purchasing provisions for our armies."[1]

Will not the inquiry suggest itself to the intelligent reader as to why these facilities were not taken advantage of to safeguard the comfort and provide subsistence supplies for the prisoners sent to this land of plenty?

There is no escape from the conclusion that there was design in withholding from the prisoners the supplies that abounded and were available. It may be hard for us at this distance of time, confronted too by evidences that a feeling of good-will exists between the North and the South, and especially between the surviving soldiers of the two armies, to conceive the disclosures in this volume to have a possible basis of truth. But however abhorrent, however humiliating the thought, however dark and repelling the shadow cast over great names,

[1] *Belford Magazine,* January, 1890.

the truth stands recorded in these pages, and the horrors of Andersonville will forever remain one of the most tragic chapters in a most wicked and causeless rebellion against the best government that man has ever instituted.

THE HOSPITAL.

But let us pass out of this horrible human corral, where men died by inches under slow processes of starvation and lost all moral sense and moral responsibility, many of them demented, in their effort to sustain life,—let us visit the hospital, in the hope of finding conditions ameliorated. What do we find there?

There was a small stream running across one corner of the hospital stockade, the upper portion of which was used by the patients for washing, and the lower portion as a sink (privy). Let Surgeon Jones speak:

This part of the stream is a semi-fluid of human excrement, and offal and filth of all kinds. This immense cess-pool fermenting beneath the hot sun emitted an overpowering stench. North of the hospital grounds the stream which flows through the stockade pursues its sluggish and filthy course. The exhalations from the swamp, which is loaded with the excrement of the prisoners confined in the stockade, exert their deleterious influences on the inmates of the hospital.

It would seem that the prison pen and the hospital were so located, relatively, as to co-ordinate in the work of destruction to the occupants; each was to contribute its share to the death-roll. Look at the picture of the hospital as drawn by Dr. Jones:

The patients and attendants [the attendants were prisoners], near two thousand, are crowded and but poorly supplied with old and ragged tents; a large number without any bunks in the tents lay upon the ground, ofttimes without even a blanket. No beds of straw appear to have been furnished. The tents extend to within a few yards of the small stream, which was used as a privy and loaded with excrement. I observed a large pile of corn bread, bones, and filth of all kinds, thirty feet in diameter and several feet in height, swarming with myriads of flies, in a vacant space near the pots used for cooking. Millions of flies swarmed over everything and covered the faces of the sleeping patients, crawled down their open mouths, and deposited their maggots upon the gangrenous wounds of the living and mouths of the dead. Mosquitoes in great numbers also infested the tents, and many of the patients were so stung by these pestiferous insects that they resembled those suffering from a slight attack of the measles. The police and hygiene of the hospital were defective in the extreme. Many of the sick were literally incrusted with dirt and filth and covered with vermin.

When a gangrene wound needed washing, the limb was thrust out a little from the blanket or board or rag upon which the patient was lying and water poured over it, and all the putrescent matter allowed to soak into the ground-floor of the tent. I saw the most filthy rags, which had been applied several times and imperfectly washed, used in dressing recent wounds. Where hospital gangrene was prevailing, it was almost impossible for any wounds to escape contagion under the circumstances.

This was the condition existing as late as in the middle of September, six months after the prison was established. All this time the Great Reaper was inexorably gathering in his toll of dead American soldiers; all this time the boast of Wirz, that he was performing the service of the generals at the front in slaying the enemy, was being realized; all this time General Winder was enforcing the policy he declared to Colonel Chandler, that it was better to leave the prisoners "in their present condition until their number had been sufficiently reduced by death to make the present arrangements suffice for their accommodation."

The treatment of the sick was not less barbarous than was the treatment of the dead revolting, and Dr. Jones speaks of the latter "as calculated to depress the already despondent spirits of the living." He said:

The dead-house is merely a frame, covered with old tentcloth and a few brushes, situated in the southwest corner of the hospital grounds. When a patient dies he is simply laid in the narrow street in front of his tent until he is removed by the Federal negroes [negro soldiers] detailed to carry off the dead. If the patient die during the night, he lies there until morning; and during the day the dead were frequently allowed to remain for hours in those walks. In the dead-house the corpses lay on the bare ground, and were in most cases covered with filth and vermin.

The reader will recall how the dead-wagon was loaded, tier upon tier, until twenty or thirty were piled in like so many swine. This, too, in the presence of the sick and dying. Little wonder that it was calculated to "depress the despondent spirits of the living."

When Dr. Bates was assigned to duty he expresses himself as "shocked at the appearance of things. The men were lying partially nude, and dying and lousy; a portion of them in the sand and others upon boards which had been stuck upon props pretty well crowded, a majority of them in small tents. They could not be furnished with any clothing except the clothing of the dead, which was generally appropriated by the living. There was a partial supply of wood, but not sufficient to keep the men warm and prolong their existence. As a general thing, the patients were destitute, filthy, and partly naked. The clamor all the while was for something to eat."

Like testimony came from the lips of many others. But why recall these horrors, which must have made upon the reader a lasting impression as he progressed through their unfolding in previous pages? Other abhorrent features of this so-called hospital will not be forgotten, and need not be referred to again.

It is true that medical science has advanced much since the Civil War, and armies in the field and in hospital receive more skillful treatment now than then; but it would be an unwarranted impeachment of the intelligence of that day to suggest that the hospital we have been examining was managed as it might or should have been, or that it was conducted with a view to prolong the lives of its unfortunate patients. There has never been a time in the history of the human family when it was supposed that man, sick or well, could exist without nourishment. Yet here was a hospital where "the clamor all the while was for something to eat"; and this, too, in a region to which the prisoners were sent because, as Mr. Davis said, "it was a productive farming country," and because, as Commissary-General Ruffin testified, "it was the seat of plenty."

The stockade and the hospital were the chief causes of the mortality, and it was the professional opinion of surgeons on duty there "that seventy-five per cent of those who died might have been saved had these unfortunate men been properly cared for as to food, clothing, bedding, etc."

There were many deaths from violence, through ignominious punishments inflicted in violation of the laws of war. These, in the aggregate, seem insignificant when compared with the thousands who died in the prison pen and hospital, but the manner of their taking off shows the reckless abandon of Winder and Wirz in their successful execution of the conspiracy.

THE CONSPIRACY.

It is not my purpose to halt now to show, what is settled law, that criminal intent may be presumed to have accompanied the criminal act. The law upon this point is fully given in the address of the Judge Advocate, hereinafter partly given, to which the reader is referred. Nor will I undertake to point out here all the facts and circumstances leading to the conclusion reached by the court. The policy pursued by the rebel authorities throughout the tragedy of the Rebellion is plainly manifested in the letter of Colonel Robert Ould, Commissioner of Exchange, as early as March 17, 1863, written to

General Winder at a time when the rebel government was exchanging Libby and Belle Island prisoners for prisoners held in the North by the Federal government. He said: "The arrangements I have made works largely in our favor. We get rid of a set of miserable wretches, and receive some of the best material I ever saw." This was a year previous to the opening of the Andersonville drama, but the proofs abound that our soldiers in rebel prisons continued to be treated as they were later at Andersonville. All through this record is evidence of this fact. Indeed, it was attempted to be shown in defense of Wirz and the prison management at Andersonville, that prisoners came there from Libby, Belle Island, Florence, Salisbury and other places in the South in a dying condition.

In his letter of May 5, 1865, to General Wilson, Wirz wrote: "I do not think that I ought to be held responsible for the shortness of rations, for the overcrowded state of the prison (which was of itself a prolific source of fearful mortality), for the inadequate supplies of clothing; want of shelter, etc. Still, I now bear the odium, and men who were prisoners seem disposed to wreak their vengeance upon me for what they have suffered; I was only the medium, or I may better say the tool, in the hands of my superiors."

Could confession go further? Is there not here an admission of the main facts adduced at the trial? Does not the record disclose who were the superiors referred to who must share the responsibility of this great crime? And will the law acquit a co-conspirator, who was a willing tool in the perpetration of the conspiracy? Was Wirz under any such physical coercion as should shield him?

Again he appealed to the court in his address: "Am I the person who, from my position at Andersonville, should properly be held accountable for the crowded condition of the stockade, the want of shelter, the unwholesomeness of the food, the impurity of the water, the inadequate hospital accommodations, and the lack of medicines and medical supplies, all of which combined and led to the dreadful mortality which prevailed at that place?" Again: "A poor subaltern officer should not be called upon to bear upon his overburdened shoulders the faults and misdeeds of others." Again: "It is not for me to suggest where the culpability or responsibility lay."

No, it was not for him to say; for in this responsibility he was a willing sharer. There does, indeed, seem to have been a failure of justice that he alone should have suffered vicariously "for the misdeeds of others." But the righteousness of the verdict resides in the fact that, though not alone in guilt, he still was guilty.

NEGATIVE TESTIMONY.

There is testimony by persons who were on duty at Andersonville, and in a few instances by the prisoners themselves, that they never knew or heard of Wirz having killed a prisoner, and some testified that they never saw him commit, or heard of his committing, any personal act of cruelty upon the prisoners. From this negative testimony the inference is sought to be drawn that he was not guilty of any such crimes. These witnesses all agree that Wirz was a very profane man, a man of high and ungovernable temper; that he cursed the prisoners, and often was rough in his personal treatment of them; that he carried a revolver, and was known to have threatened to use it; that he consigned prisoners to the stocks and chain-gang for no other offense than that of attempting to escape, as was their right and duty to do if they could; that he was the prisonkeeper and directly responsible not only for their safety, but for their subsistence and comfort. Some of these witnesses thought that had Wirz been guilty of personally causing the death of a prisoner by his own hand or by his order they would have heard of it; others admitted that they had little or nothing to do with the prisoners or their care, and that the crimes charged against Wirz might have been committed by him and they not have known it. But before we can discard and disbelieve the sworn testimony of eye-witnesses we must be able to say that these witnesses were willful perjurers, and this we must conclude from the inherent improbability of the testimony. It does not present the case of conflicting testimony generally met with in criminal trials, for there was no conflict. The case is not an ordinary one such as arises in a peaceful community suddenly aroused by the perpetration of a murder. We are not dealing with some great crime committed in a well-organized city of thirty thousand inhabitants, where its infrequency promotes publicity and the shock passes wavelike from house to house.

What was the situation at Andersonville? Need I recall the picture so often described by the witnesses? Men were shot almost daily on the dead-line; the victims of disease and starvation were being carted off to the burying-ground in wagonloads by hundreds, almost a thousand in a week at times, buried without ceremony in nameless graves, unhonored and unsung; scenes of horror surrounded the prison; human life was little valued, and death had no terror and attracted scant notice. When men were dying by hundreds daily, from causes no less criminal than if caused by direct violence, is it strange that an individual homicide, committed by Wirz or any one else, should have been unknown to some in the camp or in the prison?

But it is urged in defense that Wirz showed a spirit of mercy and kindness in certain instances. He extended to Father Whelan and Father Hamilton the courtesy of allowing them to administer spiritual comfort to the dying, although Father Hamilton found it impossible, by curtailing the sacrament, to reach all the dying, they perished so rapidly. Could Wirz have done less and have claimed the right to the human name? He made recommendations which would have helped matters if carried out; but they were recommendations which he had the power himself to execute, and he should have done so, but did not. These things showed that there was some human kindness in his nature, but they are not wholly incompatible with guilt and in themselves are insufficient to raise a reasonable doubt that he committed the crimes charged against him.

CHARGE OF MURDER.

It has been suggested that the evidence of murder lacks credence because the witnesses could not always give the name of the victim or identify him in any way, nor give the precise date of the homicide. This is true of some, but not all of the instances. I will not attempt an analysis of the testimony touching individual cases; this was thoroughly done by the Judge Advocate in his address to the court, which the reader may consult. It is not necessary to a full justification of the sentence of the court that more than one deliberate and intentional homicide of an unoffending prisoner should be established to a moral certainty; and that one such case was shown, and more than one, cannot be doubted, without an absolute rejection of the testimony as unworthy of belief. The witnesses were before the court; their manner of testifying was under observation; the effect of the cross-examination was open to scrutiny; and the surrounding circumstances also cast their weight upon the issue. Can we say,—has any one the right to say—that the witnesses absolutely perjured themselves, and that the members of the court, all of them men of high rank and unimpeachable character, willfully violated their oaths to give the accused a fair and impartial trial upon the evidence adduced before them?

MONUMENT ERECTED BY THE STATE OF NEW JERSEY.

Witnesses generally stated that they took but little note of time; that they did not know one day from another; some lost even the recurrence of the month.

Identification might be possible, as it was in some of the cases, but in others the victim might not at the moment be near any of his known comrades, and the evidence was that the prisoners became so begrimed with dirt and emaciated by suffering that they were past recognition. And who was to prosecute an inquiry after the man was killed? His body was carried out of the prison pen and carted off with the other dead of the day to the cemetery. What motive was there for investigating these occurrences or fixing them in the memory of the witnesses? Was not Wirz the sole arbiter of his own conduct? Out of all the cruel killings by Wirz and the prison guards, or by the treatment or lack of treatment of the sick in the hospital and in the prison, was there ever a court of inquiry called or any investigation of a judicial character? Is there any inherent improbability in the testimony that charges the killing by Wirz's own hands, in view of the known character of the man, of the boasts he made that he was doing better service than any general in the field, and of the indifference with which he saw the prisoners dying by thousands from the treatment they were receiving?

The specifications under charge 11 relate particularly to the conduct of Wirz personally towards the prisoners, embracing acts of violence resulting in death at his hands, directly or by his order. In judging the evidence connecting him immediately with these homicidal acts, we may, and should, to a right understanding of the evidence, take into consideration all his acts in connection with the prison management. His disposition toward the prisoners, his cursing them, his violent and ungovernable temper, his threats of bodily injury, his depriving them of rations, punishing the innocent for breaches of discipline by others, his modes of cruel and inhuman punishment for trivial and wholly inadequate infractions of rules, the frightful mortality in hospital and prison, much of which it was within his power to have avoided,—indeed, in large degree, his responsibility for the indescribable horrors of the prison life at Andersonville,—all bear upon and help to shed light upon and render probable the evidence directed to the charge of murder. It is a legal and logical deduction from this continuous and unbroken series of cruelties resulting in the death of many thousands, of which he was a willing instrument, that such a man was quite capable of being guilty of personal and individual acts of cruelty which caused immediate death.

If the general management of the prison had been humane, and everything had been done for the comfort and welfare of the prisoners which reasonably could have been expected under the circumstances; had there been no chain-gang, no stocks, no shutting off of rations as punishment, no brutal pursuit of escaping prisoners by ferocious dogs, no indiscriminate killing at the dead-line,—in short, had the prison been conducted by Captain Wirz with some regard for the principles that govern civilized nations in time of war,—it would be hard to believe the witnesses who testified to the facts upon which he was found guilty under charge 11—the charge of murder. But, unfortunately, Wirz could come before the court with no such record in his favor. All his conduct tended to make probable his guilt of the specific homicides laid at his door. It is true, under the rules of criminal procedure, that where one is on trial for some specific crime, evidence of other and different crimes is not admissible to prove the crime charged. But where an unbroken series of crimes appears, and all point to a common purpose, and all tend to a like result, in all of which the accused is criminally implicated, it is competent evidence as tending to establish his guilt of one or more individual crimes intimately connected with the series.

SOME MORTUARY STATISTICS—JOHNSON'S ISLAND FEDERAL PRISON COMPARED WITH ANDERSONVILLE—TABLE OF DEATHS BY MONTHS —NUMBER OF DEAD AT ANDERSONVILLE, 13,171.

It has been frequently stated in Southern papers that more deaths of rebel soldiers occurred in Union prisons than of Union soldiers in rebel prisons. This statement is based upon a report made July 18, 1866, by General Hitchcock to Secretary Stanton, in which it appears that the number of rebel prisoners during the war is given as 220,000, and the deaths were 26,436, or 12 per cent, and that the number of Union prisoners is given as 126,952, and the deaths were 22,576, or 17.78 per cent. General Hitchcock calls attention to the fact that the reports from Southern prisons were exceedingly irregular, and that no reports had been received from the Florence and other Southern prisons. "The reports," he says, "received from all prison stations in the South are believed to be very incomplete, with the exception of those received from Andersonville, Ga.; Salisbury, N. C.; Cahaba, Ala.; and Danville, Va." He states one instance given by the Christian Commission, showing that there were 676 Union soldiers died of which no report was made to his office. It is not possible to approximate the actual deaths occurring in rebel prisons, while the deaths in Union prisons were carefully recorded and reported. It is not to be forgotten that at least two thousand of the Andersonville prisoners, after their release, died before reaching their homes, from causes directly traceable to the cruel treatment given them while in prison.

General Hitchcock's letter follows:[1]

OFFICE COMMISSARY-GENERAL OF PRISONERS,
WASHINGTON, D. C., July 18, 1866.

HON. E. M. STANTON, *Secretary of War:*

SIR: In answer to the resolution of the House of Representatives of the 12th instant calling for a report of the number of deaths among Union soldiers while in Southern prisons, and also the deaths among rebel soldiers while held as prisoners of war, I have the honor to state that from the records of this office it appears that 26,436 deaths have been reported among the rebel prisoners of war, and 22,576 Union soldiers are reported as having died in Southern prisons. These numbers should be seen in comparison with the number of prisoners respectively held North and South, to wit: In the North there were about 220,000, while in the South there were little more than half the number, to wit, about 126,952, as per reports received. It also should be noticed that while we have accurate reports of the deaths which occurred among rebel prisoners in the North, the reports from Southern prisons were exceedingly irregular, as appears by the report of the Christian Commission, showing that there were 676 Union soldiers died of which no report was made to this office. Add to which no reports of deaths were made from localities in the South, as Florence, S. C., and other places. The reports received from all prison stations in the South are believed to be very incomplete, with the exception of those received from Andersonville, Ga.; Salisbury, N. C.; Cahaba, Ala.; and Danville, Va. The number of deaths included in the Christian Commission report chiefly refer to battle-fields, with the exception of the 676 whose graves were found at prison camps.

Very respectfully, your obedient servant,

E. A. HITCHCOCK,[2]
Major-General U. S. Vols.; Commissary-General of Prisoners.

[1] War of the Rebellion, series 2, vol. 8, pp. 946, 947.
[2] The statistics do not sustain Governor Woodrow Wilson, who states that the number of dead in the prisons of the two armies were about equal. The relative per cent was 11% rebel and 18% Union. History of the American People, vol. IV, p. 307.

RESUME AND COMMENTS. 371
SOME FURTHER COMPARISONS.

Rebel prisoners on hand at the beginning of each month in the twenty-five prisons of the North for the year 1864:[1]

	Prisoners.	Died.	Total.
January	35,489	801	36,290
February	34,983	779	35,762
March	33,860	675	34,535
April	33,798	413	34,211
May	33,592	357	33,949
June	44,310	436	44,746
July	49,564	715	50,279
August	50,838	793	51,631
September	56,931	879	57,810
October	57,098	772	57,870
November	55,243	818	56,061
December	50,825	1,084	51,909
Total		8,522	545,053
Average per month		710	45,421

There were accessions during the month and transfers to other prisons, exchanges, escapes, and releases. But the beginning of the month plus the accessions, less the transfers, gives the number, when added to the deaths, as the number actually accounted for. The number at the beginning of the month plus the deaths would give the ratio of prisoners to number of dead.

Average number of prisoners per month in twenty-five Northern prisons during year	45,421
Total deaths	8,522
Average per month	710

In Andersonville there died:[2]

In June	1,187
In July	1,731
In August	2,994
In September	2,677
Total	8,589
Average number of prisoners at end of each month[3]	24,489
Average deaths per month for four months	2,147

More died in this one prison of the South in four months than died in the twenty-five prisons of the North for the entire year of 1864,

---
[1] War of Rebellion, vol. 8, series 2, p. 994.
[2] Superintendent Bryant's table, p. 375.
[3] Dr. Stevenson's Book, p. 403.

and the average number of prisoners in Northern prisons was nearly double the average number in Andersonville prison for these four months.

JOHNSON'S ISLAND AND ANDERSONVILLE PRISONS COMPARED.

One of the Northern prisons frequently brought into comparison with Southern prisons, by apologists for Andersonville, is Johnson's Island. We have the statistics of Johnson's Island.[1] I give here a table of prisoners and deaths by months for twelve months, from April, 1864, to March, 1865, inclusive, at Johnson's Island, covering most of the life of the Andersonville Prison:

1864,	Prisoners.	Deaths.
April	2,251	4
May	2,114	4
June	2,313	1
July	2,244	1
August	2,570	1
September	2,717	5
October	2,697	2
November	2,754	4
December	3,231	9
1865.		
January	3,256	7
February	3,025	6
March	2,456	2
Average number of prisoners per month for the 12 months,	2,636	
Average number of deaths per month for the 12 months ..	3.8	

The average number of prisoners per month at Andersonville for the period stated, as reported by Dr. Stevenson,[2] was 12,527. The average number of deaths per month for that period, as given by Superintendent Bryant, was 1,049. The statistics show that at Johnson's Island the average deaths per month were 1.5 per cent, and at Andersonville they were 8.3 per cent per month.

I do not wish to convey the idea by these comparisons that there was no unusual suffering among rebel prisoners of war, or that the mortality was no greater than might ordinarily have been expected among a like number suddenly thrown into confinement. There was suffering and there were many deplorable deaths. But what I claim and what the records of our prisons will show is—that sufficient and nourishing food was supplied; barracks and shelter from heat and

---

[1] War of Rebellion, vol. 8, series 2, p. 994.
[2] Dr. Stevenson's Book, p. 403.

MONUMENT ERECTED BY THE STATE OF IOWA.

cold were provided; bedding and lodging facilities, rough, to be sure, but yet reasonably comfortable, were furnished; and there was an honest effort to provide and enforce sanitary and police regulations and to secure some sort of orderly management and discipline in the prisons and prison enclosures. Frequent official inspections were made by the officers appointed for that purpose and defects in sanitation pointed out and remedied. The war department records contain instances of military trials of guards who had recklessly or heedlessly fired upon prisoners. The treatment of the sick was in strong contrast with that given in Southern prisons, of which we had just cause for complaint. And the highest proof that there was a vast difference between the treatment given the prisoners generally by the respective governments resides in the undisputed fact that a large proportion of rebel prisoners were ready for service at any moment of their discharge, while the prisoners confined in Libby, Belle Island, Florence, Andersonville and other prisons of the South were so reduced in vitality as to be practically *hors de combat,* and with little promise of being recruited in health for any future service in the army. This fact is indubitably shown by the letter of rebel Commissioner of Exchange Ould, to General Winder, which elsewhere appears in this volume, and, that this result was part of the policy being carried out, is an irresistible inference from the evidence herein recorded. There is in truth no logical force in the claim, if it be admitted, that the rebel prisoners were inadequately fed or cared for. It is not pretended that our soldiers were starved in rebel prisons as a retaliatory measure, and such a claim, if made, would necessarily dispute the other claim made that they were well fed. The treatment of rebel prisoners in the North is wholly irrelevant and can neither palliate nor excuse the treatment of Federal prisoners in the South. The subject has been referred to for no other reason than that there are persons who would find some excuse for the crime of Andersonville if the facts would warrant the belief that similar atrocities in kind and number, could be laid at the door of the Federal government. But the facts warrant no such belief. Had conditions existed in Northern prisons such as are shown to have existed at Andersonville and other prisons of the South, no power could have restrained the public press from exposing and denouncing the inhumanity of such a policy, and public sentiment would have made its enforcement impossible.

RESUME AND COMMENTS. 375

The superintendent of the cemetery, Mr. Jas. M. Bryant, in a letter to me of date June 13, 1910, sends the following compilation of deaths for each day of each month. He says: "The enclosed figures are not absolutely correct, but are a very close approximation":

DAILY RECORD OF DEATHS IN ANDERSONVILLE MILITARY PRISON PEN.

Day.	February, 1864.	March.	April.	May.	June.	July.	August.	September.	October.	November.	December.	January, 1865.	February.	March.	April.
1	..	1	27	19	18	49	74	105	81	25	6	10	4	5	1
2	..	2	21	7	21	45	74	104	49	26	5	6	6	2	..
3	..	1	21	27	30	43	74	112	41	28	5	6	7	6	..
4	..	1	21	13	31	51	74	96	65	35	7	5	6	6	..
5	..	7	27	29	27	42	90	97	46	33	4	5	7	2	3
6	..	4	22	12	34	32	103	105	49	35	9	7	8	8	..
7	..	6	16	22	25	60	71	64	54	22	6	3	8	2	2
8	..	6	15	20	32	22	96	109	50	22	5	6	8	6	1
9	..	3	23	19	35	41	93	77	35	13	5	7	6	..	1
10	..	..	24	31	45	57	85	100	63	12	6	5	11	2	1
11	..	4	9	21	28	38	103	98	105	13	2	7	2	..	1
12	..	3	27	17	30	54	81	111	75	11	12	8	3	12	..
13	..	4	15	24	30	34	110	78	60	20	11	5	10	8	..
14	..	3	27	26	55	57	113	102	78	13	4	5	5	4	1
15	..	5	19	29	80	42	120	83	23	22	6	7	2	8	..
16	..	4	13	28	24	55	108	100	53	21	5	9	7	3	2
17	..	4	20	21	56	66	113	106	46	16	3	6	5	4	2
18	..	6	17	23	31	69	89	127	53	19	5	6	3	6	1
19	..	9	17	24	49	50	101	92	55	10	5	7	7	3	2
20	..	11	22	25	43	66	107	98	41	6	4	6	3	4	1
21	..	10	10	21	49	67	86	107	40	9	3	8	3	3	2
22	..	11	15	21	42	63	122	37	51	16	3	6	8	1	2
23	..	28	27	31	45	36	127	82	51	10	2	7	4	..	2
24	..	12	15	29	50	69	102	77	67	12	7	3	1	3	..
25	..	17	19	25	53	63	98	74	22	8	3	3	..	5	2
26	..	20	19	27	53	65	103	49	71	13	10	10	5	..	..
27	1	19	15	18	45	71	93	83	40	9	6	13	2	1	..
28	..	18	24	28	45	80	89	75	37	9	2	5	6	..	1
29	..	21	16	21	42	85	106	69	27	3	3	4	..	3	..
30	..	19	13	20	39	69	95	60	40	6	7	6	..	..	..
31	..	23	..	45	..	96	92	..	27	..	4	6	..	..	..
Monthly Total	1	282	576	723	1,187	1,731	2,994	2,677	1,595	499	165	197	147	108	28
Grand Total	1	283	859	1,582	2,769	4,500	7,494	10,171	11,766	12,265	12,430	12,627	12,774	12,882	12,910

DEATHS AT ANDERSONVILLE PRISON, 13,171.

Surgeon Isaiah White, when on duty there, in an official report to the end of July, reported 4,585 deaths. Captain Wirz reported the deaths for August at 2,993, and Dr. Jones reported the deaths for August as 2,992, less than either Stevenson or Bryant, making to the end of August 7,577, as against 7,494 compiled by Superintendent

Bryant. In his book, Dr. Stevenson states the deaths for September at 2,794 (Mr. Bryant's figures give 2,677), making the total, as shown by official reports and Dr. Stevenson's table, to October 1st, 10,371.

Dr. Stevenson made an official report to General Winder for October in which the dead are given for that month as 1,595, the same as by Mr. Bryant. This brings the total to the end of October to 11,966. For the remaining six months Dr. Stevenson in his book states the dead at 1,205, and Mr. Bryant at 1,144. Taking Mr. Bryant's figures for these last months, we have a total of 13,110. Using Dr. Stevenson's figures, we have 13,171.

There cannot be any doubt that the dead exceeded thirteen thousand. Both Dr. Stevenson and Mr. Bryant have failed to get the correct figures for the period to the end of August as to which we have the official reports. In his table Dr. Stevenson gives the total to August 31st at 7,156, whereas the official reports show the correct figures to be 7,577, a difference of 421. Mr. Bryant's table shows 83 less than the official figures. There are but 12,912 graves identified or marked, including 443 marked as "unknown." The actual deaths, as I have shown, were 13,171.

The question arises, Where are those 259 nameless bodies to be found? The evidence was that men died and were buried who received no medical treatment and whose identity was lost. The reports show 443 of these unidentified dead whose graves are known. But as to names marked "unknown"! Where are the bodies of these additional 259? They lie scattered somewhere among the bodies of their comrades, and are not even designated as "unknown." We are told, by Dr. Jones and other witnesses, that numerous post-mortem examinations were made "in the interest of science." Can it be that the dissection of the dead so dismembered the bodies as to leave them unrecognizable? Who shall answer for this desecration, this mutilation of the dead, thus leaving in painful uncertainty the fate of men supposed to have been tenants of that wretched prison pen?

Four hundred and forty-three bodies of Union soldiers lie in Andersonville Cemetery whose identity has been lost, but their graves are marked. Two hundred and fifty-nine others died there, and not even the place of burial is known or their remains marked in any way!

There is no angle, no perspective by which to view Andersonville that does not present the same criminal mismanagement; the same revolting, condemnatory picture of suffering and death which no

LAKE VIEW OF JOHNSON'S ISLAND.

Photographed 1863. The timber shown in background was cut off in 1864 and barracks extended about as appears in small picture, which latter is a photograph of a sketch made by a rebel prisoner in the summer of 1864. "A" and "B," guard barracks; "C," hospital; "D," prison barracks; "E," blockhouse; "F," prison sutler.

consideration now put forward can for one moment offer excuse or palliation.

The monument to Wirz may stand with its misleading and false inscriptions. The children in the schools of the South may be taught, as the young lady informed General Ketcham they were being taught, "how atrocious was the conduct of the Union officials and how humane and just was the conduct of the Confederate officials," but the truth of history can never be effaced.

The cruelty, the sufferings needlessly and wickedly inflicted upon helpless Union prisoners may be *forgiven,*—the thirteen thousand victims of that needless suffering at Andersonville may be counted among the hundreds of thousands who willingly gave their lives to save the Union,—but it is not in the nature of man to *forget* such sacrifices.

Mr. Scott Doane, a prominent citizen of Red Bluff, California, was on duty as guard at Johnson's Island Prison. He has furnished me a photograph of that prison and a photograph of a sketch of the prison drawn by a Confederate soldier who was a prisoner there. Mr. Doane states that the prison grounds contained fourteen acres. There are 43,560 square feet in an acre and in fourteen acres 609,840 square feet. The table I have given at page 372 shows that the average monthly number of prisoners at Johnson's Island was 2,636. The largest number was in January, 1865, there then being 3,256. The prisoners thus had 187.3 square feet to the man. Taking the average number, each man had 231.4 square feet. But the barracks were two stories, which added to the available space. Compare this with Andersonville, where each man had but 27 square feet—a space 3 by 9 feet.

Now look at the well-appointed barracks as shown in the picture of Johnson's Island and turn back to page 245 and look upon the picture sketched by O'Dea. Imagine that mass of crowded human beings without shelter of any kind and given but 3 feet by 9 feet in which to live and surrounded by a moving throng equally restricted in their movements. Compare this scene with the ample quarters given the rebel prisoners at Johnson's Island. Is it not amazing that at this late day the school children of the South are being taught, as Miss Baster says is being done, "telling how atrocious was the conduct of the Union officials and how *humane* and *just* was the conduct of the Confederate officials."

Mr. Doane's letter follows:

RED BLUFF, CALIF., Sept. 28, 1911.
GEN. N. P. CHIPMAN,
    Sacramento, Cal.
Dear Sir and Comrade: Yours of the 24th ult. came duly to hand. About Johnson's Island Military Prison: The sketch was made by a Confederate prisoner in the summer of 1864 and was photographed soon after. I got one of the photos at that time and carried it in my pocket for many years. It is *very correct* as to the inside of the prison, so much so that many of us who had been familiar with the post for years throught it a photograph taken in the usual way and not from a sketch. You will notice that there are six buildings in each of the two rows and one in the center between the rows. Each of these thirteen buildings was about 30 x 120 feet, two stories of about ten feet each in height. They were ceiled up with matched lumber all through the same as the barracks for the garrison. The two long, low buildings to the left of the barracks were for bathing and washing clothing. I have a photograph of the upper left-hand corner of the prison as shown in sketch, which gives a good view of one of the prison barracks and some of the garrison buildings, also the prison wall, etc. The size of this photo is about 6 x 8 inches, and will just fill one full page of your book. It is an unquestionable evidence of the comfortable way in which the prisoners were housed. I will lend it to you if you think you can make use of it.

About the size of the prison inclosure: It was always called 14 acres, and my estimate would be that it was about 60 rods the way the rows of buildings run and about 35 to 40 rods the other way.

From the time I was first stationed at this prison in September, 1862, to the time of my discharge from the army in June, 1865, there was *only one* prisoner killed by the guards. That was during an attempted wholesale scaling of the walls at night in the winter of 1864-5, in which about two hundred prisoners took part. Not one succeeded in making good his escape.

I was at various times employed at headquarters, examining the correspondence to and from the prisoners; in the commissary department, dealing out rations to both prisoners and garrison, and know that all were served alike, except that prisoners had a *little* less in quantity than our men, who were constantly engaged in active duty. I also for a time had charge of the examining and delivery in prison of goods sent by flag of truce and from friends in the north, amounting to about a two-horse wagon-load per day. This latter duty took me into the prison every day, so that I had a chance to know fully what their condition was, and can truly say that they were treated with humanity and justice, and that they had everything provided for their health and comfort, the same as Federal soldiers. In case of death a squad of Confederates went out under guard and buried their comrade with such services and ceremony as they saw fit.

If there is any further information on this subject that will be of service to you that I can give, will be pleased to serve you. If you wish to have a cut made for your book of the prison sketch, I can send you the original photograph, which is much better than the copy I sent you.

    Very sincerely yours in F. C. & L.,
            SCOTT DOANE.

I have no hesitation in placing before the reader another letter bearing upon the treatment of rebel prisoners of war while in Federal prisons. Mr. A. D. Cutler, treasurer of the Cutting Packing Company, San Francisco, has written me his observations at Fort Delaware. He was in a position to know whereof he speaks and his reputation as a man of honor and integrity is so well established that his statements may be received as importing verity. He writes:

SAN FRANCISCO, August 25, 1911.

GEN. N. P. CHIPMAN.

Dear Sir: I notice in your recent publication of the trial of Wirz comparison and conclusions between Northern prisons for Confederates and Andersonville.

My regiment (Sixth Massachusetts Infantry) was on duty at Fort Delaware, one of the largest of the Northern prisons, during September and October, 1864. There were about 9,000 Confederates confined there, the greater part of them from the battlefields of the Richmond campaign. They were fed, clothed, sheltered and treated every way with the utmost kindness when well, and when sick there was no perceptible difference between their clothing, fare, accommodations and treatment and that of our own men. They usually arrived from recent battles, often wounded and sick and generally dirty and ragged. When destitute they were supplied from new but condemned clothing of which a quantity was supplied by our Quartermaster's Department for that purpose, while blankets and quarters were practically the same as furnished our men.

A considerable knowledge of the facts qualifies me to say that their treatment at this post was above that of our men in the *average* Federal hospitals from Washington to Florida. There was but little illness and their wounded recovered rapidly. Had it not been for an influx of smallpox, the percentage of mortality among them would not have exceeded that of the garrison.

The pleasantest relations existed between the garrison and prisoners, and so far as regulations allowed, there was satisfactory and in some cases agreeable intercourse.

Of course there were infractions of prison rules and regulations and extreme cases were punished with the necessary severity, even to the shooting of prisoners who attempted to escape. In such cases there was always, however, a prompt and rigid investigation of all the circumstances by a court as to the necessity for so extreme a penalty and our officers and men were always held to a strict accountability for such doings. The usual punishment for minor offences was by enforced labor in improving the post with new buildings, renovating old buildings, cleaning old quarters and hauling military stores around the post.

There was a large, commodious chapel at the post to which prisoners were welcome with our men and at which there were services twice each Sunday. Its administration was non-sectarian and non-partisan, as may be believed when I recall that Stonewall Jackson's father-in-law, Rev. Dr. Jenkins, preached there on one occasion and labored zealously among the prisoners.

My experience from February to June, 1865, at Hilton Head, S. C., so far as the condition and treatment of Confederate prisoners is concerned, was practically the same as at Fort Delaware, although the number was inconsiderable, a few hundred at the most, but seldom as many. While the quarters and hospital accommodations were limited compared to Fort Delaware, they were on a par with those of our men, and their rations practically the same,—at least, I recall no difference either of quality or quantity. So far as their health was concerned, I am, at this late date inclined to believe they had an advantage over our men, in being acclimated and immune as to certain ailments common to our Southern coast.

In May, a large number of Federal prisoners, perhaps several thousand, were brought to Hilton Head by steamers from Confederate prisons in the interior of Georgia, presumably from Andersonville and Macon, en route to the North. They were landed temporarily only until transportation north could be arranged and also to fit them out with clothing and otherwise place them in a fit condition for the voyage. It was also necessary to separate the dead from the living and to retain at Hilton Head those unable to travel. The condition of these men as a whole is difficult to describe and our people to-day, the two generations since the war especially, would not, in fact could not, understand how or why such conditions should have existed, or, if known, allowed to continue. Nothing of the kind would be tolerated in these days among civilized nations.

I have read carefully the testimony of the witnesses at the Wirz trial as to the condition of our men while prisoners at Andersonville, and none of them exaggerate or exceed that of hundreds of the men I saw landed at Hilton Head in May, 1865.

In fact, although 46 years have passed, the picture was so startling that my recollection of it is complete and vivid and will never be effaced.

I have in mind one among them from my native town, who returned there and lived a quarter century after, but never recovered mentally, although physically competent, after a year or more of home nursing.

I am positive that in all my varied experiences in such matters there has been no parallel to what I saw there and that the appearance and actual condition of the men—dead and living alike—confirms and substantiates the testimony of witnesses for the prosecution at the Wirz trial.

The picture is still vivid in my memory—the river boat tied up at the long wharf, the men landing and being brought to land in ambulances, the groups standing and others (both the dying and the dead) lying beside them on the sandy beach—all as though it occurred yesterday and no language is adequate to describe their condition.
Yours truly,
A. D. CUTLER.

Believing that every fact that can throw light upon the question relating to the accuracy of the number of Union dead at Andersonville Cemetery, and also thinking that it would be of interest to know what States contributed to this melancholy record, I am able in this second edition to give the following statement, furnished by Superintendent Bryant:

Number by States of Union Soldiers Reported as Buried at Andersonville National Cemetery.

Maine	252	Kansas	4
Vermont	248	Wisconsin	260
Connecticut	306	Alabama	16
New York	2,529	Territorial Infantry	2
New Jersey	189	U. S. Army	368
Delaware	42	U. S. Colored	28
North Carolina	19	New Hampshire	153
Kentucky	444	Massachusetts	800
Indiana	652	Rhode Island	74
Missouri	105	Pennsylvania	1,863

Maryland	189	Minnesota	86
Virginia and West Virginia	285	Michigan	662
Tennessee	730	Mississippi	8
Ohio	1,072	District of Columbia	7
Illinois	924	U. S. Navy	121
Iowa	209	Undesignated	180

A recapitulation by Superintendent Bryant is as follows:—

Total number, supposed to be correct	12,806
Total unverified by State Adjutants-General	1,010
Total who survived the war	56
Total duplicates found to date	6
Total	13,878

This makes an apparent excess of fourteen over number carried as buried at Andersonville. There have been a few disinterments since the cemetery was established, and in making up the figures it was not thought necessary to separate these from the total; it would have required considerable labor and the error is too small to warrant it.

The following explanatory letter will be read with interest:

ANDERSONVILLE, GA., NATIONAL CEMETERY,
October 7, 1911.

HONORABLE N. P. CHIPMAN,
  Presiding Justice District Court of Appeals,
    Sacramento, Cal.
      (Through depot quartermaster, U. S. Army, Jeffersonville, Indiana.)

Sir: Referring to your letter of August 30, 1911, requesting authority to have a photograph made of the Illinois Monument, and to be furnished with a list of the dead in this cemetery from each state, you are respectfully informed that the photograph was mailed to your address some days ago and letter of advice mailed same day.

I enclose a list of the dead here, as near correct as it is practicable to make it at this time. You will notice that a large number appear as "not verified," "survived the war," "died elsewhere" and "duplicates."

It must not be understood, however, that the 1010 appearing as "unverified" are not buried here. It means that the soldier's name cannot be found in the records of the state to which credited. Probably the wrong state appears on our records and that he belonged to another state. In fact, we have found several such errors, and in the course of time we hope to eliminate the greater portion of them.

At the beginning of the work of verifying our records we prepared lists of each state and submitted them to the various state adjutants-general, who compared them with the muster rolls and made notations opposite each name of any correction required. In this manner we found that several supposed to be buried here are yet alive or have died in recent years. Some were found to have died elsewhere. Two men from the Sixteenth Connecticut Infantry, killed at the battle of Antietam, September 17, 1862, appear on our list and their graves are marked with the regulation headstone.

In several cases we have got into communication with men reported as having died at Andersonville, but who are yet alive, and have learned how some of the errors occurred.

RESUME AND COMMENTS.

Mr. Silas D. Burdick, formerly of Company C, Eighty-fifth New York Infantry, appears as being buried in grave No. 10,924. His name is recorded and a headstone marks his grave, yet he is still living at Cuba, N. Y., and is one of the commissioners for the erection of the New York monument in this cemetery. Thinking it would interest you, I enclose a letter from this gentleman. Be sure and return it promptly. Quite a number of similar letters are on file, and when we get through with the work of gathering material for corrections and the job is finished, there will not be many errors left.

There are a number of errors that can never be corrected; so many men gave the Confederate authorities fictitious names when captured and placed in prison, in addition to which there were quite a large number in Sixteenth Connecticut and Eighty-fifth New York, captured at Plymouth, N. C., who were deserters from the Confederate army, and for their protection in case of recapture were given the names of former members of those regiments who had been lost in battle, discharged for disability or for other causes. These men when captured gave the names by which they were known in the Union army. When they died they were buried under those names. Consequently, when the list is compared with the muster rolls, it is learned that the soldier was mustered out at the end of the war, or was killed in battle elsewhere, or died and was buried at another point.

By taking these cases up with the commissioner of pensions we have, in many cases, got a history of the matter, and if the soldier supposed to be dead yet lives, his postoffice address.

The nature of this letter and the fact that absolute correct information cannot be supplied at this time renders it desirable, if not necessary, to forward through the quartermasters department.

Very respectfully,
Your obedient servant,
J. W. BRYANT, *Superintendent*

Mr. Burdick's letter here follows:

CUBA, N. Y., R. 2., Aug. 26, 1909.

J. W. BRYANT,
    Andersonville, Georgia.

My Dear Sir and Comrade: In answer to your letter of August 23, 1909, in reference to error in records, I will explain how my name is on tombstone 10,924. It happened thus, I think: On leaving Andersonville prison-pen, September 9, 1864, I gave my blanket to Addison A. Burdick of my company (C, 85th). In the corner of the blanket was my name on a sampler, which my mother had made in 1862 and sent me so that I could identify my blanket if lost or stolen, or that others might recognize my body if I should be killed or should die away from my company. I sewed the sampler onto the blanket. When we were to leave Andersonville the rebels told us we were to be taken to Savannah for exchange and as Addison was not able to walk to the station and, further, had no blanket, I gave him mine. I think he was alone so far as any of the Eighty-fifth boys were concerned at the time of his death, and no doubt was carried out in his blanket and the person who made the record, seeing the name on the corner of the blanket, supposed that was his name.

On May 30, 1890, a party of ten, five men and their wives, members of the Eighty-fifth New York, visited Andersonville. The men had all been prisoners at Andersonville and were much interested in revisiting the place. I found my name on the grave of Addison A. and after studying the subject for some time I came to the conclusion I have given you. You may recall our party, as my wife read the poem on that day, which she had written for that occasion. With this I send you a roll of the Eighty-fifth dead who died in rebel prisons. No other regiment in the service lost as many men in prison as ours. A few errors crept in in this way.

At the time of our surrender there were two companies of loyal North Carolinas, many of whom had been conscripted into the rebel ranks, but having a chance had deserted and then joined the Union forces. After our capture, as many of these men as possible took the names of men of the Eighty-fifth who were away from the regiment or had been killed during the battle. Eugene Shippy of Company D was on detached duty, but he is recorded as having died at Andersonville. I have made a pretty careful study of our regiment and still have never been able to get a complete record of the losses of the regiment while prisoners of war.

I and my wife remember you with pleasure, on account of the courtesies you showed us at the time of our visit in 1890.   Yours in F. C. & L.,

S. G. Burdick, Co. C, 85th N. Y.

RULES IN TIME OF WAR.

Let us stop for a moment and consider some of the principles upon which civilized nations long ago agreed should govern belligerents when engaged in war.

The War Department promulgated a code of rules for the government of the army which was prepared by Francis Lieber, LL. D., an eminent authority on international law. These rules or instructions were embodied in General Orders No. 100, Washington, April 24, 1863. They are but codified from the best writers on the customs and usages of civilized people to be observed in time of war. I quote certain paragraphs found in section 2 of the Orders:

56. A prisoner of war is subject to no punishment for being a public enemy, nor is any revenge to be wreaked upon him by the intentional infliction of any suffering, or disgrace, by cruel imprisonment, want of food, by mutilation, death, or any other barbarity.

57. So soon as a man is armed by a sovereign government, and takes the soldier's oath of fidelity, he is a belligerent; his killing, wounding, or other warlike acts are not individual crimes or offenses. No belligerent has a right to declare that enemies of a certain class, color or condition, when properly organized as soldiers, will not be treated by him as public enemies.

58. The law of nations knows no distinction of color, and if an enemy of the United States should enslave and sell captured persons of their army, it would be a case of the severest retaliation, if not redressed upon complaint. The United States cannot retaliate by enslavement; therefore, death must be the retaliation for this crime against the law of nations.

71. Whoever intentionally inflicts additional wounds on an enemy already wholly disabled, or kills such an enemy, or who orders or encourages soldiers to do so, shall suffer death, if duly convicted, whether he belongs to the army of the United States, or is an enemy captured after having committed his misdeed.

Turn back and read rule 56 and reflect how flagrantly and mercilessly it was violated. Witness our brave men in the stocks and chain-gang with heavy balls of iron riveted to their feet, suffering the disgrace and ignominy accorded common felons; see them blistering in the sun in cruel imprisonment, without semblance of shelter, or brought back torn by dogs when making a justifiable attempt to escape; consider their physical suffering for want of food and water; think of all the barbarities to which they were subjected in the face of the rule of conduct laid down for belligerents. Read again rules 57 and 58. The law of nations knows no distinction of color and to have enslaved captured persons who had taken the oath of fidelity to the United States and had been armed by its sovereign authority as soldiers, was a crime against the law of nations and punishable by death. We have seen how captured negro soldiers were driven with the last to perform menial services. In a subsequent chapter we shall see how serious a matter it became to refuse them the right of exchange and to claim the right to return them to slavery when captured. Now read rule 71 and ask yourself if a case was not made out against Wirz and all equally guilty with him, bringing him and them within the purview of the principle there laid down? These rules were made for the government of the Federal army and are cited to show the restraints which all civilized nations seek to place upon their soldiers in the field and to hold them to the observance of conduct in some sort of keeping with the demands of a Christian civilization.

The subject will be further called to the reader's attention in the chapter on Exchange of Prisoners, as well as elsewhere in the course of these pages.

CHAPTER XIV.

SOME INTERESTING FACTS AS TO THE PREPARATION OF THE CASE FOR TRIAL—PERSONNEL OF THE COURT—PROCEEDINGS AT CLOSE OF THE TRIAL—JURISDICTION OF THE COURT DISCUSSED—THE LAW AND FACTS AS TO CONSPIRACY STATED—REVIEW OF THE RECORD BY THE JUDGE ADVOCATE-GENERAL-APPROVAL OF THE SENTENCE BY THE PRESIDENT—EXECUTION OF THE SENTENCE—LAW OF NATIONS SYSTEMATICALLY VIOLATED—CONDITIONS SURROUNDING PRISONERS WHO WERE WITNESSES—BURIAL OF WIRZ'S BODY.

THE rule of procedure in military courts requires the address of the accused and of the judge advocate to be submitted in writing, the accused to first address the court, and the judge advocate to close. When the court called upon counsel for the prisoner to state at what time they would be ready, they asked for an adjournment of two weeks. The judge advocate stated that he would be ready in two days after the address of the prisoner was in his hands. In criminal courts counsel are always supposed to be ready to go to the jury upon the close of the evidence. An adjournment such as was asked would have been without a parallel. The court was of the opinion that the time asked by counsel was unreasonable, and, after some parleying, offered to give the prisoner's counsel twelve days; but they declined to accept the offer, and left him without the benefit of their argument. According to military usage, the duty was cast upon the judge advocate to sum up for both the government and the prisoner—a most embarrassing task, which, in view of the circumstances, was practically impossible for the judge advocate to do, in fairness to the prisoner. There were three stenographic reporters of the court, who were regularly employed in the House of Representatives when in session—Mr. Henry G. Hayes, Mr. D. Wolfe Brown, and Mr. Nelson Hinks. They were among the most accomplished reporters of that day. The judge advocate appointed Mr. Hayes to assist the prisoner in the preparation of his address to the court, which was accomplished to the satisfaction of Wirz.

THE PERSONNEL OF TEE COURT.

General John H. Stibbs, the only surviving member of the court except myself, has recently published an interesting lecture which he gave on Andersonville Prison. In it he makes reference to the per-

THE COURT AND THE TRIAL. 387

sonnel of the court, which may interest the reader. I will be pardoned for retaining what he was pleased to say about me:

The military commission that met and tried Wirz held their sessions in the Court of Claims rooms in the capitol building, Washington, D. C., and was made up as follows: At the head of the table sat Major-General Lew Wallace, the president of the court. Any of you who did not know him must have known of him. He was at that time a man of mature years, a lawyer by profession, and of recognized ability. On his right at the table sat Major-General G. Mott, who subsequently became governor of New Jersey. He was a man then of forty-five or fifty, a lawyer, and a man of excellent judgment and discretion. Opposite him sat Major-General Lorenzo Thomas, the adjutant-general of the United States army. He was then fully sixty-five years of age, had been for many years connected with the regular service, and was an acknowledged authority on military law and the rules and usages of war. On General Mott's right sat Major-General John W. Geary, who, after his discharge from the military service, was made governor of the great state of Pennsylvania, a man aged fifty or more, and possessed of more than ordinary ability. Opposite him sat Brigadier-General Francis Fessenden, of Maine, son of old Senator Fessenden, a man aged about thirty-five, a lawyer, and one who in every sense might have been called an educated gentleman. On General Geary's right sat Brevet-Brigadier-General John F. Ballier, of Philadelphia, Pa., an educated German, aged fifty or more, and who had commanded the 98th Pennsylvania Infantry. On his right sat Brevet-Colonel T. Allcock, of New York, a man of forty or more, and a distinguished artillery officer; and finally, on the opposite side of the table, was placed the boy member, your humble servant. Possibly it might have been truthfully said of me that I was too young and inexperienced to fill so important a position, I being then only in my twenty-sixth year; but I had seen four years of actual warfare, had successfully commanded a regiment of Iowa men, and I thought then, as I think now, that I was a competent juror. The judge advocate of the commission was Colonel N. P. Chipman, who early in the war served as major of the 2d Iowa Infantry. He was severely wounded at Fort Donnelson in February, 1862. When sufficiently recovered to return to duty he was promoted and became chief of staff for General S. R. Curtis, and later on was placed on duty in Washington. He was a lawyer by profession, a man of superior education and refinement, and withal one of the most genial, kind-hearted, companionable men I have ever had the good fortune to meet.

The average, good, level-headed citizen, while considering the verdicts rendered in an ordinary criminal case, is generally ready to say, "The jury are the best judges of the evidence; they heard it all as it was given, had an opportunity to judge of its value and estimate the credibility of the witnesses, and their judgment should be accepted as correct and final." It seems to me the American people, and especially the future historian, should be equally fair in dealing with the Wirz commission, and I believe they will, as I do not see how it would be possible for an intelligent, unprejudiced, fair-minded reviewer to conclude that such a court could or would have rendered a verdict that was not in full accord with the evidence presented. I assure you no attempt was made to dictate or influence our verdict, and, furthermore, there was no power on earth that could have swerved us from the discharge of our sworn duty as we saw it. Our verdict was unanimous; there were no dissenting opinions, and for myself I can say that there has been no time during the forty-five years that have intervened since this trial was held when I have felt that I owed an apology to any one, not even to the Almighty, for having voted to hang Henry Wirz by the neck until he was dead.

The trial was a long one and taxed the physical and nervous forces of all who took active part in it to the verge of exhaustion. The preparation of the case for trial was itself a great labor. An extensive correspondence in all parts of the Union became necessary, and it was largely through this means that much important evidence was obtained. It may be of interest to the reader to relate two or three instances. The report of Dr. Jones came to my knowledge by the merest accident. I learned that he had visited Andersonville and had a report ready for delivery. I sent an officer to his home in Georgia with instructions to subpoena him and to make sure to get possession of the report. In both he was successful, Dr. Jones making no attempt to conceal or destroy the document so anxiously desired.

The report of Colonel Chandler, another most important document, was picked up in the streets of Richmond and carried home by a Union soldier as a souvenir of the war. This I traced with some difficulty, and it was fully identified, and its use by the rebel government clearly shown.

The letter of Robert Ould, in which, speaking of the effect of his policy as commissioner of exchange, he said they were getting rid of a lot of miserable wretches (victims of Libby and Belle Isle) and receiving in exchange some of the best material he ever saw, was first brought to my attention by General Benj. F. Butler, who had had much to do with Colonel Ould in matters of exchange. After considerable correspondence, I traced the letter to the hands of Samuel F. Hunt, at that time living I think in Cincinnati, Ohio, and through him it was brought to the light.

It is due the prosecution to explain somewhat further the course pursued in subpoenaing witnesses for the government. When it became generally known that Wirz was under arrest at Washington, to be tried for his complicity in the sufferings at Andersonville, and that I was to have charge of the case, hundreds of letters came pouring in from all parts of the North filled with accounts of personal experiences and personal observations.

It was known at Washington that there had been great suffering at Andersonville, but the full extent of it was not known, as the sufferings at Libby and Belle Isle were known, until the close of hostilities and the prisoners began to return in large numbers. Their condition was such as to challenge inquiry, and this inquiry led to the arrest of Wirz, and, through correspondence with the prisoners, I learned not only of the general facts but of the personal acts of cruelty and the personal responsibility of Wirz. Before subpoenaing witnesses of this class I required of them a statement verified by their affidavit of the facts they could testify to. From these statements I selected and subpoenaed the persons who seemed to relate the facts with least apparent bias.

Upon the principal facts, aside from the charge of murder, the evidence was cumulative and might well have been greatly shortened. But the facts were so startling, and in some respects so apparently unbelievable, exhibiting treatment of our soldiers in a manner so atrocious, that I was unwilling to rest the case short of proofs irrefragible and impossible of refutation in the future. The wisdom of thus fortifying the record, if at the time thought unnecessary, is now manifest, in view of the fact that a respectable body of citizens has recently in the most public manner denied that the verdict spread upon the record in the Wirz trial has any basis of truth.

THE JURISDICTION OF THE MILITARY COMMISSION—SOME PRINCIPLES OF LAW GOVERNING TRIALS FOR CONSPIRACY TO COMMIT CRIME—THE EVIDENCE OF CONSPIRACY AS REVIEWED BY JUDGE ADVOCATE.

Before reaching the concluding pages of this remarkable and important trial, the reader should be given some answer to the inscription placed upon the Wirz monument—that he was tried by an illegal court. In the proceedings of the Daughters of the Confederacy, as shown on preceding pages, it was declared that Wirz "was judicially murdered." This very grave charge rests alone on the claim that the court was without authority to try the prisoner. In the earlier pages of this volume the circumstances attending the arrest of Wirz were fully given, showing that there was no violation of any parole or promise by the government. The point now to be considered is, Had the court any authority to try Wirz for the alleged crimes?

I will content myself with some extracts from the argument of the judge advocate made to the court,[1] to show that the power is the same as that exercised, about the same time, by the military commission which tried the assassins of President Lincoln:

[1] Record, p. 723 et seq.

JURISDICTION OF THE COURT.

Among the numerous special pleas filed by the counsel, denying the right of the court to try the prisoner, there is but one, I believe, which has not been abandoned. This is the plea to the jurisdiction.

I can hardly suppose that any member of this commission entertains a doubt on this point; yet I do not feel at liberty to pass unnoticed a question so seriously made, and about which honest and loyal men differ. If there be neither law, safe precedent, nor right, upon which to base this proceeding, then it is a serious assumption of power, and alike dangerous to yourselves and the prisoner, and one in the exercise of which the order of his excellency the president will not protect you. While I have yet to read the adverse opinion of a single lawyer given outside the court-room, who speaks from the standpoint of one who knows from the teachings of experience how strong has been, and is still, the necessity of checking and punishing crimes against the laws of war, committed in rebellious districts, during and in aid of rebellion against the government, yet it must be conceded that there is a color of reason in the argument, and it is because with great persistency your right to proceed is denied that I shall presume to address myself to this question.

As we recede from a state of actual war and approach a condition of profound peace, we doubtless travel away from the corner-stone upon which the military commission as a judicial tribunal rests; but that your right to try the case before you is disturbed by a mere suspension of hostilities on the part of rebels in the field, while the spirit of rebellion is still rampant, I do not for a moment suppose, and in a very brief résumé of the argument on the subject I hope to make it so appear. As I view this question of jurisdiction, it is one of both law and fact, to determine which each case must rest upon its own merits. It involves a question of law in determining whether a court of this kind can be legally constituted, and a question of fact as to whether the present case can be thus tried; for a military court may be properly constituted, yet the case brought before it not properly triable by it.

If this be true, the subject may be disposed of in the examination of the following questions: 1st. Has the president of the United States the constitutional power to convene a military commission for the trial of military offenses committed in time of war? 2d. Is this case triable by military commission?

First. I believe it is not claimed by any that the power assumed by the president in convening this commission for the purpose named in the order dwells in him, except in time of war and great public danger, or during insurrection or rebellion. Your jurisdiction is a special one, resting upon no written law, but derived wholly from the war powers of the president and Congress, which are themselves of course derivable from the constitution. If it can be shown to safely rest upon these, you become invested not only with a right but with a high duty to sustain it in obedience to the proper order of your commander-in-chief.

On an examination of the opinions expressed against the right claimed, you will discover the whole argument to rest upon the negative declarations or prohibitory clauses of our fundamental law, denying to Congress the exercise of certain powers, as for example: "No person shall be held to answer for a capital or otherwise infamous crime unless on presentment or indictment of a grand jury," &c.; "in all criminal prosecutions the accused shall enjoy the right of a speedy and public trial by an impartial jury," &c. (Amend. Const., arts. V, VI.) "The trial of all crimes, except in cases of impeachment, shall be by jury." (Const., art. II, sec. 2.) Whatever else may be brought into the argument, these and kindred clauses are the real source of complaint whence a misguided loyalty, a super-technical judgment, have found reason for withholding their approval of the measures adopted by the government through the military commission, to aid in suppressing a rebellion for its overthrow. And hence you are told gravely the act of the president is a usurpation of power, this court without a legal existence, your proceedings a nullity.

For a moment, let us try and ascertain the purpose of those who framed the constitution, and by fair interpretation arrive at the true meaning of that great chart of liberty.

Alexander Hamilton wrote at the time the constitution was being canvassed before the people for final adoption: "The circumstances that endanger the safety of nations are infinite, and for this reason no constitutional shackles can wisely be imposed on the power to which the care of it is committed. . . . This is one of those truths which to a correct and unprejudiced mind carries its own evidence along with it, and may be obscured, but cannot be made plainer by argument or reasoning. The means ought to be proportioned to the end, the persons from whose agency the attainment of any end is expected, ought to possess the means by which it is to be attained." (Federalist, No. 23.)

Mr. Madison, in speaking of the impossibility of anticipating the exigencies which might arise, and the futility of legislating for what could not be anticipated, at the same time insisting that the powers as granted to the president and Congress are now ample for every emergency, says: "It is vain to impose constitutional barriers to the impulse of self-preservation. It is worse than in vain, because it plants in the constitution itself necessary usurpation of power." (Federalist, No. 41.)

Many years later, and after its adoption, with such light flooded upon it as the great minds of those early days could shed, Mr. Adams, in unequivocal phrase, enunciated the same idea. In speaking of the authority of Congress in time of war, he says: "All the powers incident to war are, by necessary implication, conferred upon the government of the United States. . . . There are then, in the authority of Congress and of the executive, two classes of powers, altogether different in their nature and often incompatible with each other, the war power and the peace power. The peace power is limited by regulations and restricted by provisions prescribed within the constitution itself. *The war power is limited only by the laws and usages of nations.* This power is tremendous; it is strictly constitutional, but it breaks down every barrier so anxiously erected for the protection of liberty, of property, and of life."

These are bold words, uttered when Civil War was not impending, when a powerful rebellion to overthrow this great nation could hardly have been anticipated; the opinion of a great mind and a pure patriot, with judgment free from the tyranny of partisan clamor, they come to us with all the force of law itself.

Do you find difficulty in reconciling these constitutional incompatibilities? Your statute punishes assault and battery, yet a law underlying the statute, not expressed, says you may resist force with force; and this well-grounded rule will allow you to defend yourself even to the slaying of your antagonist. Necessity knows no law inadequate to its demands, and self-preservation antedates all law. Who shall say that a government in whose perpetuation rest the hopes of the world, a constitution broad enough and liberal enough to protect the rights of all over whom it reaches—a people whose confidence in the perfection of their form of government four years of internecine war have not shaken—who shall say that these are denied nature's first law? No, these law-givers and wise men of olden and modern times spoke truly when they laid down the doctrine that the principle of self-preservation belongs to nations no less than to individuals, and that it is not in the power of a nation to code away this right.

The supreme court of the United States has, in numerous decisions, declared that Congress and the executive possess the right to do whatever the public safety may require to suppress rebellion or repel invasion. (4 Wheaton, 420; 12 Wheaton, 119-128; 8 Cranch, 15.) This opinion was entertained by the fathers of the constitution and is found embodied in congressional legislation as early as 1792, reiterated in 1795 and 1807, which seem to have been statutes made to meet just such emergencies as this war brought upon us. (See 1 Stat. L., pp. 264, 424; 2 Stat. L., p. 419.)

In 12 Wheaton (Martin *vs.* Mott) Mr. Justice Story, in an opinion sustaining the constitutionality of these laws, says: "The president is the exclusive judge of the exigency, and his action must be conclusive of the exigency." Thus taking from the supreme court the right to impeach the president's judgment. This same opinion is sustained in Luther *vs.* Borden, 7 Howard, 42-43.

I suppose it will not be denied that war changes the relations of all parties brought into antagonism as belligerents by it. No one can attack me without forfeiting his right for redress if I injure him by proper resistance without resorting to the forms of law to make him keep the peace; and no one can levy war upon our government without placing himself beyond the aegis of the constitution.

It must be remembered when objection is made to the exercise of this necessary power of the president that what might be a good plea for a loyal citizen who has committed a civil offense against the criminal statutes of the land is not a good plea for a traitor who is on trial for the commission of a military offense against the laws of war.

As we are endeavoring to determine whether the president can by right exercise the power to organize a court for the trial of military offenses committed by those not in the military service, it may not be necessary to pursue this line of argument further. Let me, however, place by antithesis some things expressly prohibited in the constitution, but which it is generally conceded may be done in time of war.

"The United States shall guarantee to every state a republican form of government, . . . and shall protect each of them against invasion," (Const., art. IV, see. 4); yet the whole power of the government has been concentrated in one grand invasion of the South for four years.

"The right of the people to be secure in their persons, houses, papers, [&c.,] against search, [&c.,] shall not be violated; and no warrant shall issue, but upon probable cause, supported by oath," &c., (Amend. Const., art. IV;) yet, I suspect, an action of trespass would not lie against the officer who broke open certain escritoires, bringing to light the proofs of conspiracies entered into by leading rebels South and North to poison, burn, and assassinate.

"No soldier in time of war shall be quartered in any house without the consent of the owner, but in a manner to be prescribed by law," (Amend. Const., art. III;) yet it was hardly expected that our generals in an enemy's country would consult the statutes "in such case made and provided."

"The right of the people to keep and bear arms shall not be infringed," (Ibid., art. I;) yet the general or executive who would, fearing to violate this right, permit the Knights of the Golden Circle, or any other hostile combination, to organize or menace the government could hardly defend himself before his country.

"The freedom of speech shall not be abridged," (Ibid., art. I;) yet who would hesitate to say that the inciter of treason by speech is no less a traitor than he who raises his hand against the government?

"Private property shall not be taken without just compensation," (Ibid., art. V;) yet during the Rebellion millions of dollars' worth have been' seized and used for military purposes without any process of law whatever, and millions more have been libelled under the confiscation act of Congress and converted to public use without just compensation.

Who so bold as to deny the principle upon which this has been done?

Article IV, section 11 of the constitution provides for the recapture of slaves escaping to free states, and, the supreme court of the United States has said, also pledges the Federal government to protect the rights thus secured to slave-owners against and in violation of which rises like a pillar of fire the proclamation of freedom, apotheosizing its author—the crowning glory of his administration; the highest proof that our cause is approved in the *forum conscientice.*

How can there be such antagonisms in our *magna charta?* How are these things defensible? They are the "incompatibilities" of which Mr. Madison speaks. We see here the harmony, at the same time, the conflicts between the war powers and the peace powers of which Mr. Adams speaks, and there is presented in strong light the adaptation of means to ends, which Mr. Hamilton insists upon; and above all, that inherent power which spurns all barriers and grounds itself upon great first principles, dwells always with the source of all power and is inseparable from it—the people—and declares as fearlessly as it battles, that in times of war and great public danger laws and constitutions are silent if they stand in the way of the nation's life.

But it is said that Congress may have the power to create military commissions, yet as it has not done so, or conferred that right upon the president, it is, therefore, an unwarrantable assumption.

It seems to me that, as the constitution expressly confers no power of this kind upon Congress, it matters little whether Congress or the president exercise it; and if one can do so, with equal right can the other. The whole question still rests upon necessity, to meet which the neglect of one will not excuse the other. Still, inquiring whether this can be done in any case, let us recur a moment to opinions cotemporaneous with the constitution.

We began our struggle for independence under the articles of confederation, and it is well known that the colonies reserved all rights to themselves, not *expressly* delegated to the Confederacy. Then, as now, there were traitors, whose

Monument Erected by the State of Ohio.

THE COURT AND THE TRIAL. 395

crimes partaking of the nature of military offenses, were made punishable by military courts. If you will examine the legislation of the country, it will be found that from 1775 down to the present time, authority has been conferred upon military courts to try civilians for the commission of certain offenses. (See acts of Congress, 7th November, 1775; 17th June, 1776; 27th February, 1778; 23d April, 1800; 10th April, 1806; 13th February, 1862; 17th July, 1862.) Congress conferred this jurisdiction on both courts-martial and military commission, until during this war, however, resorting to the court-martial.

Now, it has been frequently decided by the supreme court that a court-martial is a tribunal provided for in the rules and articles of war, but with a jurisdiction limited to military persons, as well as military offenses, so that it is as much a usurpation to try a civilian by court-martial as before a military commission.

Admitting this, we find ourselves strongly fortified by those early enactments, especially in the light of the decisions of the supreme court. Stewart *vs.* Laird (1 Cranch, 299) decides that "a cotemporary exposition or construction of the constitution acquiesced in for a period of years fixes it beyond the reach of doubt," and we are compelled to conclude that the power assumed grows out of a necessity of which Congress or the president must judge at the time.

Many things are proper to be done in time of war, which in time of peace become high crimes. No criminal code and no civil criminal tribunal can reach these; they are incident to and grow out of a state of war.

Every student of history, whether or not he may have studied law, understands this. It is a timid loyalty, a yielding to doubtful and hasty clamor, that, during this war, questioned a practice sanctioned by all nations and which began on this continent contemporary with the constitution.

But, again, a declaration of war institutes a code of laws for the government of the belligerents, known as the laws of nations. And this is true of an insurrection, as well as of a foreign war, so that we are to look more to the custom of nations than to our own constitution for guides. We have enumerated some of our constitutional guarantees intended to protect all persons, but it will hardly be pretended that rebels, traitors, assassins in aid of rebellion, banditti, guerrillas, and spies, could plead them or derive any immunity by them. The true guide and the higher law is the law of war and the customs of civilized nations. From a recent opinion of the present attorney-general, given in support of the commission for the trial of the president's assassins, taking this view, I extract the following: "A military tribunal exists under and according to the constitution in time of war. Congress may prescribe how all such tribunals are to be constituted, what shall be their jurisdiction and mode of procedure. Should Congress fail to create such tribunals, then, under the constitution, they must be constituted according to the laws and usages of civilized warfare, and they may take cognizance of such offenses as the laws of war permit. That the laws of nations constitute a part of the laws of the land is established from the face of the constitution, upon principle and by authority." (See, also, 1 Opinions of Attorneys-General, p. 27; 5 Wheaton, 153.)

He then proceeds to show that an army has to deal with two classes of enemies, one of which is the open active belligerent or soldier in uniform, who observes the law of war; the other is a violator of the laws of war, and usages of civilized nations, who, when caught, may be shot down as an enemy to the human race, or tried by military courts and subjected to such punishment as the laws of war authorize. Here, as before, we see that the only safe rule is to place in the hands of the commander-in-chief of the army, or his subordinates acting under proper orders, full and exclusive discretion as to the means to be used to protect the existence of his army, subject only to be held responsible for the abuse of the discretion so conferred. And whether he resort to military commission, court-martial, drumhead court, summary and instantaneous execution, right, reason, and wise public policy must sustain him so long as he keeps within the code of civilized nations.

I do not think it necessary to notice the distinction made between martial law and military law, your guide being, as I conceive it, the law of nations rather than either. I might remark, however, that *military law* is a part of the law of the land in times of peace and war; but *martial law* is an incident of war, and may or may not be declared. I do not rest your right, however, to sit as a military commission, upon the action of the president in this particular. He may not have declared martial law to be in force, still your existence be legal. He may not have suspended the writ of *habeas corpus,* still your jurisdiction be undisturbed. To declare martial law is one act of the war power; to suspend the writ of *habcas corpus* another; to order this court to try the prisoner before it, another.

It is an error to suppose there must be an enemy menacing you *pendente lite,* a declaration of war, a suspension of trial by civil tribunal before you can proceed. The civil courts may be in never so complete operation, the enemy in a remote part of the country, and the place of trial in the midst of a peaceful portion of the land; still, if there be a necessity, and the offense be properly punishable by the laws of war, the duty at once falls upon the proper *officer* to meet that necessity as the public safety may require. I believe this view to be sustained by the best military writers, and a legitimate sequence of the argument in support of military commissions. The practice of European powers confirms this opinion, the right having never been seriously questioned, but its abuse being provided for by bills of indemnity.

If further precedent be required it is amply presented in the action of President Washington during the "whiskey insurrection" of 1794 and 1795; of President Jefferson during the Burr conspiracy of 1806; of General Jackson in 1814, at New Orleans, and afterwards in Florida, in all of which cases, though of infinitely less moment compared with the exigencies growing out of the present war, it was enunciated that whatever the existing necessity demands must, be done. (See Halleck's International Law, pp. 371, 380, and cases cited.)

Second. Having presented sufficient reasons for concluding that the president has usurped no authority and violated no law in constituting you a military court for the trial of military offenses, it remains to notice whether the present case comes within the scope of your jurisdiction. Here I think we will have less difficulty, as it is more a question of fact than law.

This prisoner is charged with the perpetration of offenses many of them unknown to common law or statute law; they were committed by a belligerent, in his own territory, in the exercise of a commission assigned him by the enemy, and in the execution of the orders of his superiors, given in violation of the laws of war.

The government he served never did and never can try him; no civil tribunal is possessed of power; the duty then, as I think, devolves upon you. But it is said the war is over, there is no longer any necessity for military tribunals, and however proper in times of war and public danger to assume the functions of civil courts, there is now no reason for doing so.

If it were necessary I would traverse the fact. The war is not over. True, the muskets of treason are stacked; the armies of the Rebellion are dissolved, some of the leaders are in exile, others are in prison; but by far the largest portion, sullen, silent, vengeful, stand ready to seize every opportunity to divide the loyal sentiment of the country and with spirit unbroken and defiant, would this day raise the standard of rebellion if they dared hope for success. This opinion of the war still existing is not mine alone. The attorney-general in his return to Judge Wylie's writ of *habeas corpus,* issued for the surrender of the body of Mrs. Surratt, spoke of it in that sense.[1]

Congress in many of its enactments provided for a state of war after a cessation of hostilities. The whole policy of the government towards the Southern states sustains this idea.

The president, by suspending Judge Wylie's writ in the Burch case on the 16th of September, since this trial began, his adherence to President Lincoln's proclamation of martial law, and his declining to take any action that might be construed into a proclamation of peace, all show beyond doubt that the time of public danger has not passed. But, however this may be, with the fact you have nothing to do. The president, by constituting you a court to try this prisoner, has, by that act alone, declared the presence of a public danger, and that a necessity exists to still cling to military tribunals for the punishment of military offenses; and it is beyond your power to dispute his judgment. You may perhaps pass upon the question as to whether you are a court, but as to the emergency requiring you to try and punish this prisoner if guilty, the president is the sole judge. The supreme court has so decided, as we have before seen.

I hope then, gentlemen, you may find it not against your consciences or judgment to proceed to a final verdict in this case, and that you may illustrate the wisdom expressed in the judicial opinion of one of our most eminent jurists, given in 4 Wheaton, 316: "The government of the Union is a government of the people, it emanates from them, its powers are granted by them, and are to be exercised for their benefit; and the government which has a right to do and act, and has imposed upon it the duty of performing the act, must, according to the dictates of reason, be allowed to select the means."[2]

SOME OBJECTIONS BY THE PRISONER NOTICED—A FAIR TRIAL WAS GIVEN HIM.

Having thus disposed of the question of jurisdiction, I ask indulgence a moment to notice some of the objections which have been made by the counsel for the prisoner in the progress of the trial.

[1] In the Supreme Court of the District of Columbia.
[2] Was not Chief Justice Marshall the first person to announce that this is "a government of the people, by the people, for the people?"

I am not prepared to believe that this court would stultify itself by declaring that their action, after argument pro and con as to the admissibility of evidence, overruling of motions of pleas or sustaining the same, was wrong, and that they now desire to correct it; however, as the conduct of the case has been somewhat criticized, and as the counsel, who declined to argue the defense, intimated that a large part of the address would have been directed to those objections, and has asked that they be not wholly overlooked; I think it is not entirely out of place to review at this time, very briefly, the points of objection. It has been frequently asserted in court by counsel that the whole power of the government was concentrated upon the prosecution of this prisoner, and that he, single-handed and without the aid of the government, has been conducting the defense. It is well known that witnesses for the defense receive a per diem and their actual expenses in coming to the court and returning to their homes. The records of this court will show that every subpœna asked for has been given, except in the cases of a few rebel functionaries who, for reasons stated at the time, were not subpœnaed. Of this, however, there should be no complaint, as the facts which those witnesses were expected to establish were shown by other witnesses, and as a proposition was made by the judges advocate to admit that those witnesses thus excluded would testify here as to the same facts, a proposition which was declined by the counsel.

The records of this court will also show that there have been 106 witnesses subpœnaed for the defense, of whom sixty-eight reported. Of these, thirty-nine, many of them soldiers of our army and sufferers at Andersonville, were discharged without being put upon the stand, the counsel, for reasons known only to himself, declining to call them. Besides this the government has, without a precedent, furnished, at great expense, to the prisoner a copy of the record from day to day during the progress of the trial. The government has also given his counsel the benefit of its clerical force, and, in short, shown the prisoner indulgences which should forever close the mouth of one whose treatment of its soldiers was in such striking contrast, that he must have felt the more deeply his guilt. Again, it has been frequently complained of during the trial, that the court has excluded the declarations of the prisoner, made in his own behalf, and has refused to allow him in other instances to show what he did. I think the court will remember that in every case the whole of any particular transaction has been given for and against the prisoner, and that the *res gestæ,* properly so called, has never been excluded.

All the prison records in possession of the government which could throw any light upon this case are in evidence.

The prisoner has been allowed to show acts of kindness wherever they could, with any legal propriety, be given, as, for instance, the taking of drummer boys out of the stockade because of their youth, the allowing Miss Rawson to administer to the wants of one soldier, the giving of passes to ministers of the gospel to enter the stockade, his letters and reports with reference to the wants of the prison, his kindness to the prisoners whom he detailed for duty outside the stockade, and many other things, all of which, we shall show hereafter, are not incompatible with the idea of his guilt. But even admitting more than is claimed or proved for the prisoner, in regard to his urging Winder and the rebel authorities to do certain things, the law is clear that if a party remain in a conspiracy, though protesting against it and seeking to escape from it, or if he continue in an unlawful enterprise, insisting that he does not mean to do harm, yet if harm results or serious and criminal consequences follow, he is nevertheless responsible.

If in the course of one year's pursuit of an illegal business, a stupendous crime indeed, the perpetrator could show less than this prisoner has shown in his favor, he would not be entitled to the human name.

It would be strange indeed if this record of five thousand pages, of sixty-three days of weary, laborious trial, presented no wrong rulings, no improper exclusion or admission of evidence in a greater or less degree pertinent to some issue made; but I assert with all confidence and with honest belief, that the interests of this prisoner have not been and cannot be affected injuriously by such action in any instance that can be named.

It must not be forgotten, and to do this I call the special attention of the counsel and of the court, that nowhere in this record can there be found the exclusion of a scintilla of evidence bearing on the defense to the charge of murder, and to which this prisoner is more especially called to answer. There is another fact to which I would also call the attention of the counsel and the court, and it is this: that if after a careful examination of the evidence there be found sufficient legal proof, legally spread upon the record, you must proceed with your finding without regard to any illegal evidence, and not, as the counsel would insist, declare the whole vitiated. This is sustained by reason and by law, wherever it comes up to the true standard, which after all is but the perfection of human reason. The only instance in which appellate courts remand cases for new trial is where, from the bill of exceptions presented, they cannot determine whether the jury were or were not misled by the evidence improperly admitted; but where they find that the errors complained of were not material, or where the verdict is sustained after disregarding the errors, no courts will subject the parties to a second trial, or interpose to save the complainant.

Out of place as this may be in the order of my argument, I have deemed it just to say this much.

CHARACTER OF TESTIMONY.

It is argued that the evidence presenting the horrors of Andersonville is not of that class which is entirely reliable; that those who were in the Rebellion have been brought here forcibly by the government, and made to testify in anticipation of reward by pardon or through fear of being themselves punished, and that the evidence of soldiers who were sufferers at Andersonville were highly colored, testifying as they did under the sense of the injuries inflicted upon them while prisoners, and warmed to enthusiasm in the enumeration of their wrongs.

I need say only in reply, that the careful observer of this trial must have discovered how utterly powerless has been the language of witnesses to describe the condition of affairs at Andersonville; that where science has spoken through her devotees, where inspectors have tried to convey a correct idea, where the artist has sought to delineate, or the photographer to call the elements to witness, they have all uniformly declared that with all these appliances, nothing has presented in their true light the horrors of that place.

The evidence before you is of the highest character. It consists of many kinds, from many directions, from persons speaking in the interest and for the good of the rebel government, from persons under a strong sense of the wrongs done those miserable wretches, from disinterested observers neither in the one nor the other army, and from the injured themselves. And yet there is a most striking concurrence in all this testimony all agreeing that history has never presented a scene of such gigantic human suffering. If I can succeed in presenting to your minds a faithful picture of Andersonville as it was, or make such an analysis and grouping of the testimony as to show to the civilized world a tithe of its horrors, the suffering endured, I shall have accomplished all I can hope, and shall have done more than I fear I am able to do.

THE CONSPIRACY CHARGE.

The record of the trial presents a question far more important than the inquiry whether Wirz was innocent or guilty. It presents a question of guilt or innocence of many others—some of them high in authority—and involving the president of the Confederacy. The evidence has been laid before the reader. The charge of conspiracy was a grave one—the gravest and most important involved in the trial. It was due the court that the law and facts should be placed before it in some proper sequence. This was done by the judge advocate, and it is due the reader that he should have the opportunity of judging whether the court found support in the evidence for its conclusions. Upon this branch of the case the judge advocate addressed the court citing the evidence which will be recalled by the reader as set forth in preceding pages. I quote:[1]

We now come to a consideration of the third branch of the subject. Having presented a faithful representation—faithful because the witnesses have given it—of the condition of the stockade and the hospital, we shall proceed to unfold the extent of the conspiracy, the purposes of the conspirators, and the cruel and devilish means resorted to to accomplish their ends.

I confess to you, gentlemen, that I enter upon this branch of the argument with regret and reluctance. I confess that, to a greater or less extent, our nationality, and the good name we bear, are involved in the issue; but I do not fear to present to the world, on this account, this great conspiracy of treason, this confederation of traitors, though it shock the moral sentiment of the universe; for, however much we may deplore the fact that its head and front were Americans, once prominent in the councils of the nation, they have forfeited all rights; they have ceased in any way to represent the true spirit of Americanism; they are outlaws and criminals, and cannot by their crimes taint our fair escutcheon. It is the work of treason, the legitimate result of that sum of all villainies, and which, by many, very many, proofs during the past four years, has shown itself capable of this last one developed. When we remember that the men here

---

[1] Record p. 599 et. seq.

charged, and those inculpated, but not named in the indictment, are some of them men who were at the head of the late rebellion, from its beginning to its close, and as such chiefs, sanctioned the brutal conduct of their soldiers as early as the first battle of Bull Run; who perpetrated unheard-of cruelties at Libby and Belle Isle; who encouraged the most atrocious propositions of retaliation in their Congress; who sanctioned a guerrilla mode of warfare; who instilled a system of steamboat burning and firing of cities; who employed a surgeon in their service to steal into our capital city infected clothing; who approved the criminal treatment of the captured prisoners at Fort Pillow, Fort Washington, and elsewhere; who were guilty of the basest treachery in sending paroled prisoners into the field; who planted torpedoes in the paths of our soldiers; who paid their emissaries for loading shell in the shape of coal, and intermixing them in the fuel of our steamers; who ordered an indiscriminate firing upon our transports and vessels and railroad trains, regardless of whom they contained; who organized and carried to a successful termination a most diabolical conspiracy to assassinate the President of the United States—when we remember these things of these men, may we not without hesitancy bring to light the conspiracy here charged?

Before entering, however, into a discussion of the evidence, let me present the law governing in cases of conspiracy. I quote from the very able argument of John A. Bingham, delivered for the prosecution in the trial of the conspirators for the assassination of President Lincoln, whose law propositions and authorities given cannot be gainsaid:

If the conspiracy be established as laid, it results that whatever was said or done by either of the parties thereto, in the furtherance or execution of the common design, is the declaration or act of all the other parties to the conspiracy; and this, whether the other parties, at the time such words were uttered, or such acts done by their confederates, were present or absent.

The declared and accepted rule of law in cases of conspiracy is that—

"In prosecutions for conspiracy it is an established rule that where several persons are proved to have combined together for the same illegal purpose, any act done by one of the party, in pursuance of the original concerted plan, and in reference to the common object, is in the contemplation of law, as well as of sound reason, the act of the whole party; and therefore the proof of the act will be evidence against any of the others who were engaged in the same general conspiracy, without regard to the question whether the prisoner is proved to have been concerned in the particular transaction." (Phillips on Evidence, p. 210.)

The same rule obtains in case of treason: "If several persons agree to levy war, some in one place and some in another, and one party do actually appear in arms, this is a levying of war by all, as well those who were not in arms as those who were, if it were done in pursuance of the original concert, for those who made the attempt were emboldened by the confidence inspired by the general concert, and therefore these particular acts are in justice imputable to all the rest." (1 East., Pleas of the Crown, p. 97; Roscoe, 84.)

In Ex parte Bollman and Swartwout, 4 Cranch, 126, Marshall, Chief Justice, rules: "If war be actually levied, that is, if a body of men be actually assembled for the purpose of effecting, by force, a treasonable purpose, all those who perform any part, however minute, or however remote from the scene of action, and who are actually leagued in the general conspiracy, are to be considered as traitors."

In United States vs. Cole et al., 5 McLean, 601, Mr. Justice McLean says:

"A conspiracy is rarely if ever, proved by positive testimony. When a crime of high magnitude is about to be perpetrated by a combination of individuals, they do not act openly, but covertly and secretly. The purpose formed is known only to those men who enter into it; unless one of the original conspirators betray his companions, and give evidence against them, their guilt can only be proved by circumstantial evidence." . . .

It is said by some writers on evidence that such circumstances are stronger than positive proof. A witness swearing positively, it is said, may misapprehend the facts or swear falsely, but that circumstances cannot lie.

The common design is the essence of the charge, and this may be made to appear when the defendants steadily pursue the same object, whether acting separately or together, by common or different means, all leading to the same unlawful result. And where *prima facie* evidence has been given of a combination, the acts and confessions of one are evidence against all. . . . It is reasonable that where a body of men assume the attribute of individuality, whether for commercial business or the commission of a crime, the association should be bound by the acts of one of its members in carrying out the design.

It is a rule of the law, not to be overlooked in this connection, that the conspiracy or agreement of the parties, or some of them, to act in concert to accomplish the unlawful act charged, may be established either by direct evidence of a meeting or consultation for the illegal purpose charged, or more usually from the very nature of the case, by circumstantial evidence. (2d Starkie, 232.)

Lord Mansfield ruled that it was not necessary to prove the actual fact of a conspiracy, but that it might be collected from collateral circumstances. (Parsons's case, 1; W. Blackstone, 392.)

"If," says a great authority on the law of evidence, on a charge of conspiracy, "it appears that two persons by their acts are pursuing the same object, and often by the same means, or one performing part of the act, and the other completing it, for the attainment of the same object, the jury may draw the conclusion there is a conspiracy; if a conspiracy be formed, and a person join in it afterwards, he is equally guilty with the original conspirators." (Roscoe, 415.)

The rule of the admissibility of the acts and declarations of any one of the conspirators, said or done in furtherance of the common design, applies in cases as well where only part of the conspirators are indicted and upon trial. Thus upon an indictment of murder, if it appear that others, together with the prisoner, conspired to commit the crime, the act of one, done in pursuance of that intention, will be evidence against the rest. (2d Starkie, 237.) They are alike guilty as principals. (Commonwealth *vs.* Knapp, 9 Pickering, 496; 10 Pickering, 477; 6 Term Reports, 528; 11 East., 584.)

Let us see what the evidences are of a common design to murder by starvation these hapless, helpless wretches. First, then, who are officers, high and low, civil and military, whom the evidence implicates in this great crime?

As I shall show you by the testimony, there are associated in this conspiracy, as directly implicated and as perpetrators, the prisoner at the bar, and others named in the charges.

Remote from the scene, but no less responsible than these named, nay, rather with a greater weight of guilt resting upon them, are the leader of the Rebellion, his war minister, his surgeon-general, his commissary and quartermaster-general, his commissioner of exchange, and all others sufficiently high in authority to have prevented these atrocities, and to whom the knowledge of them was brought.

Chief among the conspirators and the actual participators in the crime, the immediate tool, first and last, of the rebel government, we shall see was General Winder.

It is proper, therefore, that we should know who he was, and the precise relations which he bore to the government which he represented. We learn from many sources that he had for a long time prior to the organization of the Andersonville prison been at the head of the military prisons in and around Richmond, holding also the position of provost marshal of that important center of the Rebellion.

We learn from the witness J. B. Jones (record, p. 2531; manuscript, p. 1219) that his rule as provost marshal was almost a reign of terror; that his authority was so great he could arrest men indiscriminately even in distant states, and that he was constantly sustained and supported by Jefferson Davis and his confidential adviser and premier, Mr. Benjamin.

The witness Cashmeyer (record, p. 2840-41; manuscript, p. 1221), the confidential detective and constant companion of General Winder till the close of the Rebellion, says: "Their relations [those of Davis and Winder] were very friendly indeed, and very confidential; I often heard General Winder say so; I often saw him go there and come from there."

About the time that General Winder's reign of terror was at its climax, and there was great opposition felt and expressed towards him, both in and out of the rebel congress, a combined effort was made to have him relieved and sent away, Generals Bragg and Ransom being prominent in the movement. At this time Cashmeyer says: "President Davis was his [Winder's] especial friend. When the order relieving General Winder came from the war department, he took it and went up to Mr. Davis; President Davis indorsed on it, as well as I can recollect, that it was entirely unnecessary and uncalled for."

Some time after this it was thought wise by the rebel authorities to organize the Andersonville prison, and the whole matter was placed in the hands of General Winder by the orders issued from the war department for the purpose. General Winder himself did not go to Andersonville till about the first of June, but he sent forward, as we learn from the testimony of Cashmeyer (record, p. 2842; manuscript, p. 1221), of Spencer (record, p. 600; manuscript, p. 1056), of Captain Wright (record, p. 790; manuscript, p. 1177), and others, his son, Captain W. S. Winder of his staff, as his special executive officer, and as we learn from the testimony of Colonel Persons (record, p. 613; manuscript, p. 250), "with absolute discretion in the location of the prison." This was in the latter part of December, 1863.

Shortly after, another officer of General Winder, a nephew of his, Captain R. B. Winder, a quartermaster, arrived at Andersonville and assumed the duties of his office. Captain Wright, in speaking of him (record, p. 2447; manuscript, p. 1177), says: "He told me that he had no orders to report to any quartermaster at all; that he reported directly to Richmond, and received his instructions from Richmond."

Subsequently in the month of March, 1864, General Winder sent still another of his staff officers, the prisoner at the bar, who, as we learn from his report, made May 8th (see exhibit 16; manuscript, p. 658), was assigned to the command of the prison on the 27th of March.

Of him, Colonel Persons says (record, p. 602 and following; manuscript, p. 249): "He came direct from Richmond, my understanding was, by order of General Winder; I saw an official order to that effect; I received a communication about the time Captain Wirz reached there from General Winder; it stated that Captain Wirz was an old prison officer, a very reliable man and capable of governing prisoners, and wound up by saying that I would give him command of the prison proper."

404   THE TRAGEDY OF ANDERSONVILLE.

From the return of staff officers made by General Winder after he had himself arrived at Andersonville, and who he says were "acting under the orders of Brigadier General John H. Winder, commanding the post at Andersonville, Georgia, commanding the camps and stockade containing Federal prisoners of war and the guard troops for the same, the prison for Federal prisoners of war at Macon, Georgia," &c, we find that Dr. Isaiah H. White, also on his staff, was assigned to duty at Andersonville, by orders of the war department at Richmond, as chief surgeon in charge of the prison hospital; he arrived at Andersonville about the same time as the two Captains Winder.

This comprises the original corps of officers sent from Richmond to carry out the hellish purposes of the rebel government, and which, as we shall see as we advance, was most faithfully done by them. Can there be any doubt as to what the original purpose of the rebel government was? Let us go to the very origin of the prison.

Ambrose Spencer testifies (record, pp. 2472-74; manuscript, p. 1056), as follows: "I saw Captain W. S. Winder: at the time he was laying out the prison. . . . I asked him if he was going to erect barracks or shelter of any kind; he replied that he was not, that the damned Yankees who would be put in there would have no need of them. I asked him why he was cutting down all the trees, and suggested that they would prove a shelter to the prisoners, from the heat of the sun at least; he made this reply, or something similar to it: *That is just what I am going to do; I am going to build a pen here that will kill more damned Yankees than can be destroyed in the front.* These are very nearly his words, or equivalent to them."

How was this plan, thus emphatically avowed, carried out? The stockade was located across a stream which General Wilson of our army says (record, p. 1839; manuscript, p. 822) "would not run more water than would supply for the purposes of an army a larger command than four or five thousand men,"—"a sluggish stream," as Dr. Jones calls it,—which with the springs along its banks, sufficient probably to supply a regiment more, was the only water originally intended for the prisoners.

From the inside of the prison everything was taken which could in any way contribute to the comfort, convenience, or health of the prisoners, and was never replaced by shelter, neither during the burning heat of the summer, which Dr. Thornburg tells you was not much short of 150 degrees in the sun, nor the cold which followed in the winter, sufficiently severe, as is shown by several witnesses, to freeze and which did freeze many prisoners to death.

It will be remembered, too, that not 400 yards distant, below the site selected for the stockade, was a stream of water which General Wilson says was ample for any number of troops, a stream that could not have been exhausted, and which, after careful examination, as he says, was found to flow a volume of water equal to fifteen feet by five feet, with a velocity of a mile an hour (record, p. 1876; manuscript, p. 822), and which Colonel Persons says (record, p. 610; manuscript, p. 250), it occurred to him would have been a preferable place to the one where the prison was located, adding, "I suggested it to W. S. Winder, I believe; I recollect distinctly it was one of the Winders."

The mere location of the prison in the absence of other facts would not perhaps, of itself, convey a criminal intent; but when we remember what followed, and certain other facts which will be presented, it becomes a very important link in the chain of evidence leading to the guilt of the parties alleged. It will be remembered that the immense bake-house, the only accommodation of that kind furnished for the prisoners until late in the year, was located so that all the filth and garbage, and offal of that place, which is described as itself almost as filthy as the stockade, passed directly through the prison.

This, it is testified to by many, could with equal convenience have been located elsewhere, and this was suggested to Captain R. B. Winder, the quartermaster, at the time of its erection. Immediately below the stockade, as appears from the evidence of Dr. Jones, Dr. Roy, and others, trees were felled in the stream and brush thrown into the swamp, so that the filth escaping from the prison, which ought to have been allowed to pass rapidly off, was here caught, spread over the surface and disseminated in the soil, till, as these medical gentlemen say, it became a prolific source of disease, and sent back into the prison a horrible stench.

These preparations of death did not cease here, but with incredible malice, or with recklessness equally criminal, the troops arriving at the post for the purposes of defense were encamped above the stockade and along the stream in such a manner that, as many witnesses testify, all the washings of the camps and overflowings of the sinks during storms swept into the stockade. Into this horrible pen were the prisoners of war ushered, and here were they confined in hopeless captivity. Here, too, for many months, with all these surroundings, and everything calculated to make it certain death for the sick, was the hospital retained; and not until after earnest protests from many officers, not until after frequent representations through official channels to the rebel government, through General Winder, who was still in Richmond, not until after, as we learn from the testimony of Colonel Persons, humanity impelled him to take the responsibility, was the hospital removed outside, and this he tells us (record, p. 3059; manuscript, p. 1304), was done in violation of General Winder's orders, and was tardily acquiesced in some weeks after by an order from Richmond.

About the time of this clamor for the removal of the hospital, considerations of humanity pleaded with equal fervor for an enlargement of the stockade. Prisoners had been sent forward, under orders from Richmond, with such rapidity and in such numbers that they could only be turned into this place like cattle, until at the time we speak of, within an enclosure of little more than twelve acres, excluding the swamp, unfit for occupation, and the dead-line space, the frightful number of over 18,000 were confined. Protest after protest went up through many sources to General Winder at Richmond. Colonel Persons says (record, p. 2061; manuscript, p, 1305): "We sent an objection to the authorities at Richmond, to General Winder, and urged him to hold up, and not ship any more prisoners there, but he paid no attention to it."

This seething mass of humanity, with scarcely room to stand upon, crying for help, the more conscientious officers of the post doing all in their power to alleviate their sufferings, the commanding officer. notifying the rebel government what they must have known all the time, that the mortality was great, and must be still greater unless something should be done, Colonel Persons was aroused upon this subject, as he had been upon the matter of removing the hospital, and here again he took the responsibility, as he tells us (record, p. 621; manuscript, p. 258), to order an enlargement of the stockade about one-third, which was done under the direction of Captain Wright by the prisoners themselves, Colonel Persons says (record, p. 3063; manuscript, p. 1306) that when he saw they did not intend holding up, but continued to ship more prisoners, and saw that the prison was overcrowded, he directed the enlargement of the prison, and he says: "After I had finished the extension, or, perhaps, after I had got it partly finished, orders came giving me permission to do it."

There can be no doubt that during all this time the precise condition of affairs at Andersonville was well understood at Richmond. General Winder, to whom the entire business of organizing and conducting the prison was assigned, remained in Richmond as the representative of the prison at that place. He was in constant correspondence with the officers on duty at Andersonville, as is fully shown by what has just been stated. That he frequently conferred with the officers of the war department is not only reasonably inferable but is absolutely certain.

General Cobb, in his letter to the adjutant-general of May 5, (see exhibit number 15; manuscript, p. 649), says: "I presume the character of the prison is well understood at Richmond, and therefore give no description of it."

The introduction of his letter, showing that his presumption was well founded, is as follows: "Under your order to inform myself of the condition of the prison at Andersonville, with the view of furnishing from the reserve corps the necessary guard for its protection and safety, etc."

Dr. Eldridge, in his report, forwarded to Richmond at the same time as General Cobb's, in speaking of the necessity of removing the hospital outside and endeavoring to meet the objections made at Richmond, says: "Such an enclosure as I should suggest—a plank fence ten feet high—would require but very few additional guards, as the guard appears to be the objection urged at Richmond to a separate enclosure."

On the 8th of may, 1864, the prisoner at the bar made a report to Major Turner, who, as an officer on duty pertaining to prisons, connected with the war department (see exhibit 16; manuscript, p. 658), in which the condition of affairs at Andersonville at that date was fully set forth. This report reached Richmond during the same month, and was submitted to the war department by General Winder, with the following indorsement: "Approved and respectfully forwarded. Captain Wirz has proven himself to be a diligent and efficient officer, whose superior in commanding prisons and incident duties I know not."

We all know, as officers of the army, that the furnishing of subsistence, of the material used by quartermasters, and of hospital supplies and medicine, was all done either through the chiefs of those several departments at Richmond, acting under the supervision of the secretary of war himself, or by virtue of the orders of these chiefs and of that secretary.

It is not credible that such an immense prison as that at Andersonville, used as a receptacle for prisoners from all parts of the South, was unknown to the Richmond government, and that the whole management, the subsistence of the prisoners, their comfort, their safety, everything was left in the hands of this heretofore obscure man, now on trial. But it is said that during these straitened times the prisoner and the other officers charged were doing all in their power to alleviate the sufferings, so well known at Richmond and at Andersonville.

Without stopping now to inquire what could have been done, and what is shown by a cloud of witnesses to have been in their power, notice a moment what *was* done, and whether or not it was in furtherance of the conspiracy. Captain R. B. Winder, as we learn from Captain Wright's testimony (record, p. 2747; manuscript, p. 1177), came to Andersonville untrammelled by any orders, reported to no one, but received his instructions from the quartermaster general. He told Captain Wright that "all the quartermasters had been ordered by the quartermaster general to furnish him with what supplies he needed to fill his requisitions."

With powers thus ample he erected a few scanty, miserable sheds at one end of the stockade, which were then used as a hospital, and were not sufficient for the sick; he built a cook-house which was a prolific source of suffering and death, and which was not of sufficient capacity to prepare rations for more than 5,000 men properly. He built a hospital enclosure with some sheds within it, covered but not sided; he furnished the prisoners with wood for cooking purposes, as we learn, at the rate of three cord wood sticks to a squad of ninety; he managed to transfer to his private till a large amount of money sent him by his government, as intimated in the testimony of Captain Wright; he folded his arms while Colonel Persons enlarged the stockade and removed the hospital, work which belonged exclusively to him; he did this, omitting to do many things that were not only in his power, but which it was his duty to do, leaving the post finally in the latter part of the summer, taking away nearly everything, as Captain Wright says (record, p. 2749; manuscript, p. 1178), that pertained to his department. Not, however, until by his acts of omission and commission he had become answerable for the deaths of hundreds of these unfortunate prisoners.

Captain W. S. Winder remained true to his purpose, as declared to Mr. Spencer, and in more ways than one demonstrated how true was his declaration: "I am going to build a pen here that will kill more damned Yankees than can be destroyed in the front."

Dr. Isaiah H. White, an important adjunct to this scheme, and indispensable to its faithful execution, was at the head of the hospital. whence he reported to his superior officers at Richmond, from time to time, the dreadful and increasing mortality.

The prisoner now before you, despite all his pretended protests at the time, despite the individual and widely separated instances of humanity which have been paraded here, remained, as he truly said in his letter to Major-General Wilson, which was the first item of evidence introduced in this trial, "the tool in the hands of his [my] superiors." (See exhibit number 1; manuscript, p. 1.) He had introduced himself to the prisoners by stopping their rations the first day he was on duty; he had instituted, between that time and the time of General Winder's arrival, a system of the most cruel and inhuman punishments; he had made his name a terror among the prisoners, and his society a reproach to his comrades upon whom he inflicted it; he had established the dead-line and all its accompanying horrors; he had given the prisoners a foreshadowing of the stocks, of the balls and chains, of the chain-gang, of starvation as a punishment, and all that black catalogue of cruelty and suffering unknown even to a "Draconian code"; he had declared to several of the prisoners engaged in the burial of the dead, "This is the way I give the Yankees the land they came to fight for"; he had scores of times told the prisoners, when maltreating them, that he intended to starve them to death; he had boasted that "he was doing more for the Confederacy than any general in the field"; he had paraded the chain-gang for the amusement of his wife and daughters; he had with drawn pistol told a prisoner who dared to complain of the rations, "Damn you, I'll give you bullets for bread." Are you not prepared then to believe that at the time of General Winder's arrival the prisoner was in the execution of the common design, with a knowledge of its object, and acting in harmony with its chief instrument, General Winder?

This is Andersonville in part, the sufferings of the prisoners in part, and something of the evidence of the conspiracy begun and continued up to the time of General Winder's arrival.

We shall see now whether the law governing this question, after a recital of the facts which follow, does not direct you to find a verdict of guilty.

You will remember that when Colonel Persons was on the stand, he told you that, assuming to do what the law and the army regulations made it the duty of the quartermaster to do, and which in this case Captain Winder had wholly neglected to do, he sent to the different saw-mills along the line of the railroad for lumber, moved, as he tells you, by a feeling of humanity and a desire to alleviate, in some may, the sufferings of the prisoners. He says (record, p. 608; manuscript, p. 252): "I had concentrated there, I suppose, about five or six trainloads of lumber; I suppose nearly fifty carloads."

I quote further from the record the following:

Q. Were you permitted to erect a shelter?
A. I was in the act of doing so, was just carrying the lumber, when I was relieved.
Q. By whom?
A. By General Winder.
Q. Had he arrived on the same day?
A. He arrived there about that time.
Q. Was our plan carried out?
A. I went into the stockade several times after I was relieved from duty and I saw no shelter there. I saw forty or fifty houses springing up outside of the grounds. The lumber disappeared in that way.

At this time, the journal of the prison shows there were over 19,000 prisoners in the stockade. This was the first official act of General Winder on his arrival. It was the third time Colonel Persons had given mortal offense, and he was no longer to be tolerated. What could more strongly present the unmitigated diabolism of that friend of President Davis, that man upon the order relieving whom the rebel chief wrote, "It is entirely unnecessary and uncalled for"? This was the man who found a ready advocate in the rebel premier, Mr. Benjamin, and who was not only sustained from first to last by his chief, but was rewarded for official conduct that will place his name amongst those of the most infamous of any age or clime.

General Winder's second act was to establish himself comfortably and at a respectful distance from the prison, where he remained from the first of June until early in the fall. Notice now, as we advance, how the sufferings of this prison increased; how everything from which torture and death could result was resorted to; how all those methods of inhuman punishment instituted by the prisoner were approved and sanctioned by General Winder, and that, during the whole period of his command, not a single act is recorded which does not prove him to have been not only "a brutal man," as Mr. Spencer says he was, but that he was the chief instrument in the hands of a wicked, treasonable conspiracy to murder the prisoners of war in his custody. He came there with authority unlimited, with discretion to do whatever circumstances required to carry out the purposes of his command. In an appeal published by him to the citizens of the surrounding counties (see exhibit 27; manuscript, p. 707) he calls for "2,000 negroes properly supplied with axes, spades, and picks, and supported by the requisite number of wagons and teams," for the purpose of rendering more hopeless the imprisonment of our soldiers, holding over the people of that vicinity the terrors of impressment, which, in this appeal, he claims to have authority to make; yet, with all this power, with all these appliances at hand, and within reach of his call, not a single shelter did he ever erect; not a ditch did he dig to drain that horrible cesspool below the stockade, and within it; not a tithe of the wood absolutely necessary did he cause to be taken into the stockade; not once did he visit that place over which he had supreme control; not a well did he cause to be digged within it; not an order did he issue to abate one jot or tittle of the frightful rigors of that prison pen; not a kindly or humane sentiment has he shown during that whole time to have uttered towards these prisoners in his custody. On the contrary, he scattered to the four winds, as we have seen, that immense pile of lumber accumulated by Colonel Persons for the purpose of erecting shelter in the stockade; he approved all that had been done by his subordinate, the prisoner, even recommending him for promotion; he legalized the detail of Turner, who was a Confederate soldier, to take command of a pack of hounds to run down prisoners, and afterwards permanently detached him from his regiment for that purpose; he authorized and ordered the hanging of six prisoners of war within the stockade, which, by all the laws of war, was no more nor less than murder, so far as he was concerned; he brutally refused the philanthropic ladies of Americus twice in their attempts to render assistance to the sick at the hospital, even intimating on one of those occasions, to those ladies of the highest respectability, that a repetition of their humane efforts would bring upon themselves a punishment too infamous to be named.

Is it still contended that there was no conspiracy; that these things evinced no common design to destroy; that of all these things the Richmond government was in blissful ignorance? Let us see. On the 21st of July, 1864, General Winder addressed a letter to the war department at Richmond (see exhibit 17; manuscript, p. 662), dated Andersonville, in which he uses the following language before quoted: "You speak of your indorsement of placing the prisoners properly. I do not exactly comprehend what is intended by it; I know but of one way to place them, and that is, to put them into the stockade, where they have between four and five square yards to the man."

Is it possible that he did not comprehend what was intended by the war department? Can it be that he knew of but one way to place those prisoners properly?

His government did not dare to speak more definitely, nor was it necessary, to such a man as General Winder, occupying the position he did, and with the letter of Robert Ould in his private desk, written as early as March, 1863—a private letter to himself and indorsed by his own hand. The *one* way was the way given in his original instructions; it was the way understood by W. S. Winder, when he said it was the intention to kill more Yankees at Andersonville than they did at the front; it was the way meant, and well understood by General Winder, when he said to Mr. Spencer that, for his own part, he would as lief the damned Yankees would die there as anywhere else; that, upon the whole, he did not know that it was not better for them (record, p. 2467; manuscript, p. 1054), and which he afterwards disclosed to Colonel Chandler in the remark: "It is better to leave them in their present condition until their number has been sufficiently reduced by death to make the present arrangements suffice for their accommodation."

It was the way well understood by the rebel government, when, in the face of the protests of humane officers, and in the face of the official reports of the mortality of that place, they continued to forward prisoners, trainload after trainload, to an already overcrowded prison. It was the way dictated to the agent of that government, Robert Ould, and revealed by him in his letter to Winder (see exhibit, manuscript, p. 1920) when he declares, speaking of exchanges: "The arrangement I have made works largely in our favor. We get rid of a set of miserable wretches, and receive in return some of the best material I ever saw," adding, "This, of course, is between ourselves."

It was the way understood perfectly by General Howell Cobb, when, in a speech at Andersonville, he pointed with terrible significance to the graveyard, remarking: "That is the way I would care for them."

It was the way well understood by the prisoner at the bar, who is shown to have uttered sentiments similar to those expressed by W. S. Winder on more than a hundred occasions. It was the way, and the only way, ever indicated by the chief of the rebel government and his secretary of war, else why did he, with this frightful picture before him, deliberately fold General's Winder's letter, indorsing it "Noted filed.—J. A. S."

Let us advance another step in the evidence connecting the Richmond government with these atrocities. Colonel D. T. Chandler, of the rebel war department, pursuant to an order of his chief, of July 25, 1864, directing him to make an inspection at Andersonville, and other places in the Confederacy, submitted a report dated Andersonville, August 5, 1864, and which reached the war department August 17, 1864. This officer, from whose report we have already quoted, gives a graphic description of the sufferings of the prisoners of war, and in earnest terms beseeches his government that no more be sent forward to that place, and that immediate steps be taken to relieve the sufferings of those prisoners already there; making many practical suggestions for their comfort which he thought could be readily carried out. In a supplemental report, also dated August 5th, and which was received in Richmond with the report first named, he says:

My duty requires me respectfully to recommend a change in the officer in command of the post, Brigadier-general John H. Winder, and the substitution in his Place of some one who unites both energy and good judgment with some feelings of humanity and consideration for the welfare and comfort, as far as is consistent with their safe-keeping, of the vast number of unfortunates placed under his control; some one who, at least, will not advocate *deliberately*, and in cold blood, the propriety of leaving them in their present condition until their number has been sufficiently reduced by death to make the present arrangements suffice for their accommodation, and who will not consider it a matter of self-laudation and boasting that he has never been inside of the stockade—a place the horrors of which it is difficult to describe, and which is a disgrace to civilization—the condition of which he might, by the exercise of a little energy and judgment, even with the limited means at his command, have considerably improved.

In his examination touching this report, Colonel Chandler says:

I noticed that General Winder seemed very indifferent to the welfare of the prisoners, indisposed to do anything, or to do as much as I thought he ought to do, to alleviate their sufferings. I remonstrated with him as well as I could, and he used that language which I reported to the department with reference to it —the language stated in the report. When I spoke of the great mortality existing among the prisoners, and pointed out to him that the sickly season was coming on, and that it must necessarily increase unless something was done for their relief—the swamp, for instance, drained, proper food furnished, and in better quantity, and other sanitary suggestions which I made to him—he replied to me that he thought it was better to see half of them die than to take care of the men.

And to show that he cannot be mistaken in what he avers, Colonel Chandler speaks of Major Hall, his assistant, having first reported to him similar language used by General Winder to him, and remarks: "I told Major Hall that I thought it incredible, that he must be mistaken. He told me no, that he had not only said it once, but twice; and, as I have stated, he subsequently made use of this expression to me."

Let us now see what the rebel government had to do with this report. As I before remarked, it reached Richmond on the 17th day of August. Immediately on its reception, as we learn from Captain C. M. Selph, of the rebel war department, it was carefully briefed, and extracts made and sent to the heads of the different bureaus, the commissary-general and the quartermaster-general; a report of Dr. White's, an enclosure of Colonel Chandler's report, being sent to the surgeon-general. The entire report was then laid before the secretary of war, Mr. Seddon, and there cannot be a shadow of doubt that it was immediately, and fully, and seriously considered; nor can there be any doubt that Mr. Davis and his war minister conferred together with regard to this momentous subject.

Captain Selph, speaking of a conversation between himself and Colonel Woods, a staff officer of Jefferson Davis, in regard to the prison at Andersonville, says: "During that conversation I obtained the impression that President Davis had some knowledge of it." (Record, p. 1161; manuscript, p. 659.) "This," he says again, "was subsequent to the receipt of Colonel Chandler's report."

To the question, "Would a paper of this kind, on a subject of this magnitude, find its way to the president of the so-called Confederate States in the ordinary course of proceedings?" he answers, "Yes, sir; I think it would."

It will not do to say that this report was buried among the multitude of papers that arrived daily in the war office, or that lay upon Mr. Seddon's table with piles of other papers unnoticed. Mr. J. B. Jones, private secretary to Mr.

Seddon, says (record, p. 2836; manuscript, p. 1218) that he remembers when the report was received, but only read the headings enough to see the purport of it; and adds that he thinks it was sent for by the secretary of war. Mr. R. T. H. Kean, chief of the bureau of war, says that he saw it lying on the secretary's table. He also speaks of a conversation between himself and the assistant secretary of war, Judge Campbell, in which the report was spoken of, and in which Judge Campbell, speaking of the fearful mortality, remarked, "This looks very bad." Captain Selph also testifies that the report excited general comment in the department.

But we are not left with this evidence alone. This report was not sent in like ordinary inspection reports, but special attention was drawn to it by three officials. On the day of its receipt, it was submitted to the secretary of war, as the following indorsement proves, beyond doubt:

ADJUTANT AND INSPECTOR-GENERAL'S OFFICE, August 18, 1864.

Respectfully submitted to the secretary of war. The condition of the prison at Andersonville *is a reproach to us as a nation.* The engineer and ordnance departments were applied to for implements, and authorized their issue, and I so telegraphed General Winder. Colonel Chandler's recommendations are coincided in.
By order of General Cooper:
R. H. CHILTON,
Assistant Adjutant and Inspector-General.

The report passed through the hands of R. B. Welford, a confidential clerk employed in the war department for his legal abilities, who also made a brief analysis, strongly commending Colonel Chandler's recommendation, Mr. Welford's analysis being again indorsed, and the whole laid before the secretary by J. A. Campbell, assistant secretary of war, with the following indorsement:

These reports show a condition of things at Andersonville which calls very loudly for the interposition of the department in order that a change may be made.
J. A. CAMPBELL,
Assistant Secretary of War.

What more could have been needed, or what more done, to bring authoritatively and strongly before the proper authorities at Richmond the subject of the Andersonville sufferings? Here were an intelligent inspecting officer of high rank, Colonel Chandler, the chief of the inspector's bureau, Colonel Chilton, the chief of the bureau of war, Mr. Kean, a confidential clerk, Mr. Welford, and the assistant secretary of war, Judge Campbell, all pressing in the strongest terms the necessity of an immediate interposition by the department, and not hesitating to declare the prison at Andersonville "a reproach to them as a nation." These appeals might have moved hearts of stone, but addressed as they were to these representatives of a government based upon wrong and injustice, that had its origin in a treasonable conspiracy to overthrow the best government on the face of the earth, however much they may have moved the hearts of those representatives as individuals, they seem to have felt it their duty to adhere to a purpose so cruelly and wickedly begun and thus far so faithfully carried out; and they dared not, or would not—for it is certain they did not—abandon, even then, this atrocious conspiracy. Mr. Kean says he is not aware the report was ever acted upon. Captain Selph says the same, and we learn from his testimony that the report remained with the secretary, never having come back to the inspector-general's department, where it properly belonged, till

THE COURT AND THE TRIAL. 413

about the time Mr. Breckinridge succeeded Mr. Seddon—some time in 1865—when Colonel Chandler having returned and demanded that some action should be taken on the report or he would resign, it was brought to light and laid before Mr. Breckinridge, who would have acted upon it, as Captain Selph thinks, but for the rapid change of affairs in the Confederacy, and the dissolution of their government soon after.

And here let me diverge a moment and follow a portion of this remarkable report to the surgeon-general's office. We find indorsed upon exhibit 24 (manuscript, p. 695) the following:

> Surgeon White was authorized some time since to send his requisitions for supplies directly to the medical purveyor. Not having supplies is his own fault; he should have anticipated the wants of the sick by timely requisitions. It is impossible to order medical officers in place of the contract physicians. They are not to be had at present.   S. P. MOORE, *Surgeon-General.*

This is the flippant indorsement of the surgeon-general, and the only evidence showing his notice of the condition of things at Andersonville, and this is all that he seems to have done in the matter, while Dr. White was allowed to remain in charge of the hospital, which, as described by the surgeons who were on duty with him, seems to have been little else than a dead-house. . . .

It is strange, truly, that the surgeon-general passed over the matter with so slight a notice of it, when we remember that, several weeks previously, it is shown that he had the whole matter before his office and took action upon it, which makes him no less culpable than the others we have mentioned. He had called into his counsels an eminent medical gentleman, of high attainments in his profession, and of loyalty to the rebel government unquestionable. Amid all the details in this terrible tragedy, there seems to me none more heartless, wanton and utterly devoid of humanity, than that revealed by the surgeon-general, to which I am about to refer. I quote now from the report of the same Dr. Joseph Jones, which, he says, was made in the interest of the Confederate government for the use of the medical department, in the view that no eye would ever see it but that of the surgeon-general.

After a brief introduction to his report, and to show under what authority it was made, he quotes a letter from the surgeon-general dated "Surgeon-General's Office, Richmond, Virginia, August 6, 1864." The letter is addressed to Surgeon I. H. White, in charge of the hospital for Federal prisoners, Andersonville, and on September 17th reecived the following pass:

> SIR: The field of pathological investigation afforded by the large collection of Federal prisoners in Georgia is of great extent and importance, and it is believed that results of value to the profession may be obtained by careful examination of the effect of disease upon a body of men subjected to a decided change of climate and the circumstances peculiar to prison life. The surgeon in charge of the hospital for Federal prisoners, together with his assistants, will afford every facility to Surgeon Joseph Jones in the prosecution of the labors ordered by the surgeon-general. The medical officers will assist in the performance of such post mortems as Dr. Jones may indicate, in order that this great field for pathological investigation may be explored for the benefit of the medical department of the Confederate armies.   S. P. MOORE, *Surgeon-General.*

Pursuant to his orders, Dr. Jones, as he tells us, proceeded to Andersonville, and on September 17th received the following pass:

ANDERSONVILLE, September 17, 1864.

CAPTAIN: You will permit Surgeon Joseph Jones, who has orders from the surgeon-general, to visit the sick within the stockade that are under my medical treatment. Surgeon Jones is ordered to *make certain investigations which may prove useful to his profession.*

By order of General Winder:

Very respectfully,

W. S. WINDER, *A. A. G.*

Captain H. WIRZ, *Commanding Prison.*

When we remember that the surgeon-general had been apprised of the wants of that prison, and that he had overlooked the real necessities of the prison, shifting the responsibility upon Dr. White, who he must have known was totally incompetent, it is hard to conceive with what devilish malice, or criminal devotion to his profession, or reckless disregard of the high duties imposed upon him—I scarcely know which—he could sit down and deliberately pen such a letter of instructions as that given to Dr. Jones.

Was it not enough to have cruelly starved and murdered our soldiers? Was it not enough to have sought to wipe out their very memories by burying them in nameless graves? Was it not enough to have instituted a system of medical treatment the very embodiment of charlatanism? Was this not enough, without adding to the many other diabolical motives which must have governed the perpetrators of these acts, this scientific object, as deliberate and cold-blooded as one can conceive? The surgeon-general could quiet his conscience, when the matter was laid before him through Colonel Chandler, by indorsing that it was impossible to send medical officers to take the place of the contract physicians on duty at Andersonville. Yet he could select, at the same time, a distinguished gentleman of the medical profession and send him to Andersonville, directing the whole force of surgeons there to render him every assistance, leaving their multiplied duties for that purpose! Why? Not to alleviate the sufferings of the prisoners; not to convey to them one ounce more of nutritious food; to make no suggestions for the improvement of their sanitary condition; for no purpose of the kind; but, as the letter of instructions itself shows, for no other purpose than "that this great field for pathological investigation may be explored for the benefit of the *medical department* of the Confederate armies." The Andersonville prison, so far as the surgeon-general is concerned, was a mere dissecting-room, a clinic institute to be made tributary to the medical department of the Confederate armies. But let me return from this digression. One can hardly believe all these things of a government pretending to struggle for a place among civilized nations, yet horrible as it seems, the facts cannot be resisted. Do I injustice to the leaders of the Rebellion? Have I drawn inferences that are unwarrantable? Is it indeed true that these men, high in authority, are not responsible? I think not; motives are presumed from actions, and actions speak louder than words. What was the action of Jefferson Davis and his war minister upon these reports? The papers were pigeonholed in the secretary's office, not even being dignified by being placed upon the regular files in the proper office, while General Winder, the chief accomplice, instead of being removed immediately, and broken of his commission, and tried for violation of the laws of war—for cruelty, inhumanity, and murder; instead of being held up by

THE COURT AND THE TRIAL. 415

that government as a warning to others, giving a color of justice to their cause, was promoted, rewarded, and given a command of wider scope and greater power, but still in a position to carry out the purposes of his government towards prisoners of war. History is full of examples similar in character, where a government, seeking to carry out its ends, has selected as tools men not unlike General Winder, and history, faithful in the narration of the facts, is faithful also in fixing upon the government who employed such persons, and sustained and rewarded them, the responsibility for the acts of their agents. James II had his Jeffreys, Philip II his Duke of Alva, Louis XIV his Duke de Louvois, the Emperor of Austria his Haynau, and *Jefferson Davis his Winder.* The closest scrutiny of the immense record of this trial will show that, up to the very close of that prison, there were no steps taken by the rebel government, by General Winder, or by any of the officers of his staff clothed with proper authority, to alleviate in any material particular the great sufferings of that place. You will remember the uniform testimony of the medical officers, as well as of the prisoners who remained there during the winter of 1864 and 1865, that there was no perceptible change in the condition of the prison, and an examination of the hospital register, and the death register, will show that the mortality was even greater during that period, in proportion to the number of prisoners confined, than it was during the months of its most crowded condition. From the prison journal, kept by the prisoner himself, we find that in September, the mean number of prisoners being 17,000, the deaths were 2,700; in October, the mean strength being about 6,700, the number of deaths was 1,560—nearly one out of every five; in November, the mean strength being 2,300, the deaths were 485; while those who remained to the very close, till the prison was broken up, are described by General Wilson and others as having been "mere skeletons" "shadows of men." Nor must it be forgotten that the marks of this cruelty were so indelibly stamped upon its victims that thousands who survived are yet cripples, and will carry to their graves the evidence of the horrible treatment to which they were subjected. The surgeons of our army who treated those shadows of men when they arrived within our lines at Jacksonville and Hilton Head tell you of hundreds who died before they could be resuscitated; of others permanently disabled; of others who, upon their partial recovery, were started on their way homeward, being again treated at Annapolis. Dr. Vanderkieft, of our army, speaks of the condition of those prisoners while under his treatment at that place. He says: "They were reduced, suffering from chronic diarrhcea and scurvy; some of them in a dying condition; some of them died a few days after they arrived; and those who did recover were obliged to remain a long time in hospital before they were able to return to their homes."

And with that certainty with which science reasons from effect to cause oftentimes, after describing the condition of the men as it has been brought out in this testimony, he concludes, "The symptoms and condition of the patients presented cases of starvation." Nor must it be forgotten, in the summing up of the cumulative proofs of the Andersonville horrors, that numerous photographs of returned prisoners were introduced here, and identified by Drs. Vanderkieft, Balser, and others, as representing eases no worse than hundreds and thousands they had seen. So impressive indeed and so strong seemed this evidence of rebel cruelty, that the counsel for the prisoner sought, in his cross-examination, to show that they were fancy sketches[1]. Are we told that these things are improbable, and cannot be believed, because it is said that Mr. Davis is a *good man*, not capable of such cruelty? Are we told that no direct order of his is shown, and therefore, notwithstanding all these facts and circumstances narrated, he must be acquitted of all blame? The law governing cases of conspiracy does not require us to show a direct order; circumstances from which guilt may be inferred are sufficient. The rebel chief did not find it necessary to issue direct instructions, nor indeed could it reasonably be expected. He was too wary, too sagacious for that Michelet relates an anecdote of Louis XV, not malapropos:

The illustrious Quesney, physician to Louis XV, who lived in the house of the latter at Versailles, saw the king one day rush in suddenly, and felt alarmed. Madame D. Haussett, the witty femme de chambre, inquired of him why he seemed so uneasy. "Madame," returned he, "whenever I see the king, I say to myself, there is a man who can cut my head off." "Oh!" said she, "he is too good."

The lady's maid thus summed up in one word the guarantees of monarchy. The king was too good to cut the man's head off; "that was no longer agreeable to custom; but he could with one word send him to the Bastile, and there *forget* him. It remains to be seen whether it is better to perish with one blow, or suffer a lingering death for thirty or forty years." Mr. Davis was not capable of being the instrument of death. He was *too good* to be keeper of a prison and withhold from starving men their scanty rations; but he could send them out of his sight, away from the prison in plain view of his own residence, into the dense forests of Georgia, and there forget them. If Jefferson Davis be ever brought to trial for his many crimes—and may Heaven spare the temple of justice if he be not!—it will not do for him to upbraid and accuse his willing tools, Winder and Wirz, as King John did Hubert for the death of Prince Arthur; they will turn upon him and say, "'Here is your hand and seal for what I did. And in the winking of authority, did we understand a law."

THE LAW OF NATIONS.

Before advancing further in the argument, let us define briefly the laws of war, which, it is alleged by the government in its indictment against this prisoner and his co-conspirators, have been inhumanly and atrociously violated. One would suppose that an enlightened conscience need not consult the opinions of writers upon law or ethics to determine the violation of rules governing civilized warfare with sufficient certainty to condemn the treatment of prisoners at Andersonville; yet, as the averment is traversed by the prisoner, and it is insisted that no violation of the humane principles governing nations in war is shown, I must trespass upon the court a moment before proceeding. In the forum of nations there is a higher law, a law paramount to any rule of action prescribed by either of them, and which cannot be abrogated or nullified by either. Whatever the peculiar forms or rights of this or that government, its subjects acquire no control or power other than is sanctioned by the great tribunal of nations. We turn then to the code international, where the purest morals, the highest sense of justice, the most exalted principles of ethics, are the corner-stones, that we may learn to be guided in our duties to this prisoner.

[1] It is to be regretted that these photographs were not preserved, for had they been they would have strongly corroborated the testimony of witnesses.

Grotius derived the *jus gentium* from the practice of nations, and living in an age when the greatest cruelties were practiced in the operations of warfare, his rules as laid down often seem to have been the inspiration of barbarity itself, rather than laws which should govern nations; yet even he, in Books 3 and 4, insists that all acts of violence which have no tendency to obtain justice or terminate the war are at variance both with the duty of the Christian and with humanity itself.

Manning, an author of great force and clearness, says:

At the present day a mild and humane treatment exists with regard to prisoners of war, which is perhaps in some degree attributable to the deference paid to the writings of Vattel, who appeared to have been the first author who established the true principle upon which prisoners should be treated. He says that, "as soon as your enemy has laid down his arms and surrendered his person, you have no longer any right over his life unless he should give you such right by some new attempt, or had before committed against you a crime deserving death." "Prisoners of war," he says, "may be secured but cannot be made slaves unless for personal guilt which deserves death, nor be slain unless we be perfectly assured that our safety demands such a sacrifice."

After having discussed at some length this subject, he sums up the whole question thus:

It may be remarked in conclusion that the same principles which have been appealed to in the preceding chapter afford also a clue to the right treatment of prisoners of war. The usages of former ages proceeded upon the supposition that any violence was allowed in warfare and that the rights of the victor unon the vanquished were unlimited, and that having the right to deprive his antagonist of life, the captor had a right to impose any treatment more lenient than death upon his prisoner. But we have seen that so far from the rights of the belligerent being unlimited, the law of nature strictly limits them to such violence as is necessary, that thus, when an antagonist no longer resists, there can no longer be any right to use violence towards him; and that whenever the purposes of warfare are not frustrated by the granting of quarter, the belligerent cannot refuse to give quarter without a direct violation of the law of nature, which warrants no further hardships towards prisoners than is required by the purposes of safe custody and security.

Another author remarks:

Prisoners of war are indeed sometimes killed, but this is not otherwise justifiable than it is made necessary either by themselves, if they make use of force against those who have taken them, or by others who make use of force in their behalf and render it impossible to keep them; and as we may collect from the reason of the thing, so it likewise appears from common opinion, that nothing but the strongest necessity will justify such an act, for the civilized and thinking part of mankind Will hardly be persuaded not to condemn it till they see the absolute necessity of it. (Rutherforth's Institutes, page 525.)

Kent, in speaking of the barbarous usages of war, checked and done away with by the progress of civilization, says:

"Public opinion, as it becomes enlightened and refined, condemns all cruelty and all wanton destruction of life and property as equally useless and injurious, and it controls the violence of war by the energy and severity of its reproaches. . . . Grotius, even in opposition to many of his own authorities and under a due sense of the obligations of religion and humanity, placed bounds to the ravages of war, and mentioned that many things were not fit and commendable, though they might be strictly lawful; and that the law of nature forbade what the law of nations (meaning thereby the practices of nations) tolerated. . . . Montesquieu

MONUMENT ERECTED BY THE STATE OF PENNSYLVANIA.

insisted that the laws of war give no other power over a captive than to keep him safely, and that all unnecessary rigor is condemned by the reason and conscience of mankind. . . . Vattel has entered largely into the subject, and he argues with great strength and reason and eloquence against all unnecessary cruelty, all base revenge, and all mean and perfidious warfare; and he recommends his benevolent doctrine by the precepts of exalted ethics and sound policy, and by illustrations drawn from some of the most pathetic and illustrious examples."

To the same effect writes Wheaton and Halleck.

So strongly did the principles here laid down impress themselves upon our government, that during General Jackson's administration Mr. Livingston, then secretary of state, instructed Mr. Buchanan, our minister in Russia, to insert in the treaty proposed to be negotiated stipulations "in order to restrain citizens or subjects of the one or the other of the high contracting parties respectively from infringing any of the known rules of modern warfare," and among other things mentions "for injuries offered to the bearers of flags of truce, for the massacre of prisoners who have surrendered, for the mutilation of the dead, for other breaches either of this treaty or of the laws of nations; for preserving peace or lessening the evils of war."

The object of this, Mr. Livingston said, was "to express a national reprobation of the doctrine which considers a state of war as one of declared hostilities between every individual of the belligerent nations respectively. . . . To massacre an unresisting and unarmed enemy, to poison his provisions and water, to assassinate a prisoner, and other similar acts, are universally acknowledged to be breaches of international law, and to justify retaliation and an increase of the horrors of war." (Ex. Doc. No. 111, 1st sess. 33d Congress, H. R.)

It would seem that these teachings, so long recognized, so long practiced by civilized nations, ought to have found some advocate even among the councils of treason. Whatever the form of government may have been to which the leaders of the Confederacy, so-called, aspired; whatever of wrong and injustice they sought to embody in their system, with whatever of oppression and tyranny they sought to grind down their subjects, the moment they asked a place among the nations they were bound to recognize and obey those laws international which are and of necessity must be applicable alike to all. With what detestation, then, must civilized nations regard that government whose conduct has been such as characterized this pretended Confederacy. An ordinary comprehension of natural right, the faintest desire to act on principles of common justice, would have dictated some humane action, would have extorted from some official a recognition of international rules of conduct. It was not retaliation, for they had the example of our government, in sending to their homes on parole whole armies that had been captured; it was not punishment, for these unfortunate prisoners had been taken in honorable battle; it was not ignorance of the law, for they had constantly with them all those great lights just quoted, and if these failed to convince, they could have found recorded back of these, "If thine enemy hunger, feed him," and still further back they might have found an example worthy of imitation, which I cannot refrain from here giving. A large number of Syrians had been by a cunning piece of strategy taken captive, and became prisoners of war, whereupon the following dialogue occurred: "And the King of Israel said unto Elisha, when he saw them, my father shall I smite them? Shall I smite them? And he answered, thou shalt not smite them; wouldst thou smite those whom thou hast taken captive with thy sword and with thy bow? Set bread and water before them, that they may eat and drink and go to their master. And he prepared great provision for them; and when they had eaten and drunk he sent them away and they went to their master. (2 Kings, ch. vii.)

No gentlemen, it was not retaliation, punishment, nor ignorance of the law; it was the intrinsic wickedness of a few desperate leaders, seconded by mercenary and heartless monsters, of whom the prisoner before you is a fair type.

CRUELTIES PRACTICED TOWARDS PRISONERS.

Thus far we have not pretended to enter with any particularity into the questions of the cruel treatment of prisoners. There may be two objects, or two reasons, for at this time dwelling more in detail upon the conduct of the prisoner. These are, first, to connect him more certainly with the conspiracy, and, second, to enable us more understandingly to examine the second charge. Here, as at other points in the argument, I desire only to present the evidence, avoiding all embellishment and all argumentation, for this case must be decided upon the facts proven, and not the coloring of counsel.

I cannot hope to recapitulate all the facts bearing upon this point, as it will be remembered that each day's record bears witness to an accumulation of horrible details which there can be no necessity for now repeating, and to give all of which would require almost the entire proceedings to be duplicated. We may, however, perhaps to some purpose, present briefly the proofs of each phase of cruelty alleged.

The judge advocate then takes up the evidence of the numerous forms of cruelty inflicted on the prisoners—the stoppage of rations, which must have contributed greatly to the mortality; the dead-line, with its numerous victims; the stocks, the chain-gang, and other means of punishment; the use of ferocious dogs to run down escaped prisoners. Upon this last of the methods of prison government some remarks of the judge advocate should be read. I quote:

In this connection, as further illustrating the barbarous treatment of our soldiers and the cruelty of the prisoner at the bar, as well as the systematic violation of the laws of war at Andersonvillle, it seems proper to notice the method adopted for recapturing prisoners.

The court will remember that the counsel for the prisoner laid great stress on the fact that a law existed in the state of Georgia authorizing the use of dogs for the capture of fugitive slaves, and an attempt was made to prove by Judge Hall, the witness who testified to this fact, that a justice of the supreme court of that state had made a decision sustaining the law. The court very properly excluded the evidence, but I will give the prisoner the benefit of the decision. It was made by Justice Lumpkin, and is another evidence of the extent to which a naturally strong mind may be warped and turned from a strict view of justice when compelled to square it with a system of slavery. The case referred to is Moran vs. Davis, (18 Ga.). The facts were substantially these: A negro ran away, was pursued by dogs, and in trying to escape from them plunged into a creek and was drowned. The slave had been hired to the man who pursued him, and the owner brought suit for the value of the negro. The court below held "that the hirer or overseer had no right to chase the slaves with such dogs as may lacerate or materially injure the slave; should he do so he will be responsible to the owner for all damage that may ensue to the slave." Exceptions were taken to the rulings of the court, and on appeal Justice Lumpkin reversed the decision, remarking, "The South has already lost 60,000 slaves, worth between twenty-five and thirty millions of dollars. Instead, therefore, of relaxing the means allowed by law for the security and enjoyment of this species of property, the facilities afforded for its escape, and the temptation and encouragement held out to induce it, constrain us willingly or otherwise to redouble our vigilance and to tighten the cords that bind the negro to his condition of servitude, a condition," he adds with a flourish of rhetoric and a shameful distortion of Scripture, "which is to last, if the apocalypse be inspired, to the end of time."

Unfortunately for the argument of counsel, prisoners of war are not property, neither are they slaves, and with all his adroitness he can hardly torture this case to his purpose, especially in view of the fact that the decision was given in support of a relic of the dark ages now happily passed away.

When two nations are at war, neither has a right to prescribe a code of laws for the other; a moment's reflection will show the injustice of such a thing; but both are governed by a higher law than that prescribed by either—that is, the law governing civilized nations; and it seems to me that no refinement of reasoning is necessary to show that Judge Lumpkin's decision, given in the interest of barbarism, is plainly in violation of the rules of enlightened civilization. Dogs were kept at Andersonville from the organization to the close of the prison, and of this the rebel government had notice from several sources. Dr. Eldridge reported it, as we learn from exhibit 15A. The prisoner also reported it, as we learn from exhibit 13. Benjamin Harris and a man named W. W. Turner were employed and paid for this despicable business. The first named, a citizen, was a professional negro catcher who kept a pack of hounds for that purpose; the other was a detailed soldier, detailed by order of General Winder, and paid as an extra duty man. (See testimony of Colonel Fannin, Captain Wright, and Ambrose Spencer.) These hounds were fed with provisions taken from the cook-house and furnished the prisoners of war, taken, too, from the scanty supply issued by the commissary for those prisoners. (See testimony of Jasper Culver.) They were mustered into the military service of the rebel government the same as cavalry horses. (See testimony of Colonel Gibbs, commandant of the post at Andersonville. (They were of two kinds, "tracking hounds" and "catch dogs," and if anything were wanting to show the deliberate purpose to injure prisoners by resorting to this means of capture it will be found in the presence of these packs of hounds of "catch dogs," which are described by many as fierce and bloodthirsty. If there had been no desire to injure, why were they used at all? They have none of those qualities peculiar to the tracking; they run only by sight, and, as has been testified to, always remained with the pursuer until approaching a prisoner. The tracking hounds would have been sufficient to discover the prisoners, and as they are usually harmless, would have served the purpose of the pursuer and at the same time inflicted no injury upon the pursued. The evidence, however, convinces one that this was only another means of putting prisoners of war out of the way. The prisoner at the bar frequently accompanied Harris and Turner in their chases after prisoners, and, as we shall see hereafter, gloated over the pain inflicted by those bloodthirsty beasts. Cannot we safely stop here and ask that the prisoner at the bar be recorded as one of the conspirators? I know that it is urged that during all this time he was acting under General Winder's orders, and for the purpose of argument I will concede that he was so acting. A superior officer cannot order a subordinate to do an illegal act, and if a subordinate obey such an order and disastrous consequences result, both the superior and the subordinate must answer for it. General Winder could no more command the prisoner to violate the laws of war than could the prisoner do so without orders. The conclusion is plain, that where such orders exist both are guilty, and *a fortiori* where the prisoner at the bar acted upon his own motion he was guilty. You cannot conclude that this prisoner was not one of the conspirators because he is not shown to have been present and to have acted in concert with all the conspirators. If he was one of the conspiracy to do an illegal thing, it matters not whether he knew all his co-conspirators or participated in all that they did. It is not necessary to prove any direct concert or even meeting of the conspirators. A concert may be proved by evidence of a concurrence of the acts of the prisoner with those of others, connected together by a correspondence in point of time and in their manifest adaptation to effect the same object. (Starkie's Evidence, pp. 323-324.) These rules of law place beyond doubt the guilt of the prisoner, for in every respect there is plainly discoverable "a correspondence of time and a manifest adaptation to effect the same object," in all that he did; and these principles apply not only to the prisoner, but to all others on duty at Andersonville, whose acts concurred with those of others of the conspiracy and were adapted to effect the same object.

The prisoner at the bar appeals to you through his letter of May 7th, directed to General Wilson, and asks, "Shall I now bear the odium (and men who were prisoners here have seemed disposed to wreak their vengeance upon me for what they have suffered) who was only the medium, or I may better say the tool, in the hands of my superiors." Strongly as it may strike you that strict justice would require the punishment of the arch-conspirator himself; strongly as this wreck of a man, with body tortured by disease and over whom already gather the shadows of death, may appeal to your sympathies, you cannot stop the course of justice or refuse to brand his guilt as the law and evidence direct. While I would not dignify the chief conspirators in this crime without a name by associating with them the prisoner at the bar, yet he and they, so closely connected as they are, must share the same fate before the bar of a righteously indignant people. Nothing can ever separate them, and nothing should prevent their names going down to history in Common infamy.

I have said that Phillip II had his Alva, that Jefferson Davis had his Winder. I might add that the Duke of Alva had his de Vargas, and Winder his Wirz.

As the Duke of Alva rises out of the mists of history the agent of a powerful prince, so Winder stands out with fearful distinctness no less perfect for his willing obedience to the government he served than for his skill to devise and ability to select agents as capable to execute the refinements of cruelty. Nor does the parallel cease here; has not history repeated itself in making Wirz a man cast in the same mould as the infamous de Vargas, a hand to execute with horrible enthusiasm what his superior had the genius to suggest?

Motley tells us, in his "Rise of the Dutch Republic," of these men Alva and De Vargas, whose spirits, after the Pythagorean theory, seemed to have centuries afterwards infused themselves into the bodies of this prisoner and his immediate superior, Winder. He says of the subordinates of Alva: "Del Rio was a man without character or talent, a mere tool in the hands of his superior; but Juan de Vargas was a terrible reality—no better man could have been found in Europe for the post to which he was thus elevated. To shed human blood was in his opinion the only important business, and the only exhilarating pastime of life."

"He executed the bloody work with an industry which was almost superhuman and with a merriment which would have shamed a demon; his execrable jests ringing through the blood and smoke and death cries of those days of perpetual sacrifice. There could be no collision where the subaltern was only anxious to surpass an incomparable superior."

After pointing out the evidence as to the quantity served as a ration, the judge advocate concluded his argument upon the charge of conspiracy as follows:

Thus we have shown from evidence of the highest character, that the defense based upon want of supplies within the reach of the rebel authorities, and which is popularly believed to have been the real cause of the sufferings of Andersonville, is entirely overthrown, and without foundation in fact; and the same may be said of every question entering into the defense incident to the matter of supplies. With whatever truth the straitened circumstances of the South may be urged to exculpate those in charge of other prisons, certainly, so far as Andersonville is concerned, no one will hereafter with seriousness dare to urge it.

Having shown with certainty that supplies were abundant and available, I cannot omit to mention what amount was actually issued as the only means of sustenance to the prisoners. I quote Dr. Bates, whose acknowledged credibility on the part of the accused in his statement to the court makes it unnecessary to support him by the many witnesses who testify to the same point; but the court will remember that his estimate is several ounces more than the prisoners themselves testify to having received. He says: "I wish to be entirely safe and well guarded on this point. There might have been less than twenty ounces to the twenty-four hours; but I do not think it could have exceeded that."

The ration, it will also be remembered, consisted of one unvarying diet of corn bread and salt meat, with an occasional issue of peas, and with no vegetables whatever. In comparison with this scanty allowance which the concurrent testimony of all the witnesses shows was the immediate cause of the great mortality at that prison, I desire to call your attention to some interesting and instructive facts, showing the amount of food necessary to sustain life. I quote from a work on the economy of armies, by medical inspector Lieutenant-Colonel A. C. Hamlin, United States Army:

The data of French's shows that eighteen ounces of properly selected food will be sufficient, and the observations of Sir John Sinclair are to the same effect, yet Dr. Christison maintains that thirty-six ounces are required to preserve the athletic condition of prisoners confined for a long term. To preserve the athletic condition with these small quantities, the nutrient substance must be of known value.

In the public establishments of England the following quantities are given: British soldier, 45 ounces; seaman, royal navy, 44 ounces; convict, 57 ounces; male pauper, 29 ounces; male lunatic, 31 ounces.

The full diets of the hospitals of London give, Guy, 29 ounces, with one pint of beer; Bartholomew, 31 ounces, with 4 pints of beer or tea; St. Thomas, 25 ounces, with 3 pints of beer or tea; St. George, 27 ounces, with 4 pints of beer or tea; Kings, 25 ounces.

The Russian soldier has bread 16 ounces; meat 16 ounces: Turkish soldier has bread 33 ounces, meat 13 ounces; French soldier has bread 26 ounces, meat 11 ounces; Hessian soldier has bread 36 ounces, meat 6 ounces; English soldier has bread 20 ounces, meat 16 ounces.

The United States soldier receives ¾ pound of bacon, or 1¼ pound of fresh or salt beef; 18 ounces of bread or flour, or ¾ pound of hard bread, or 1¼ pound of corn meal; with rice, beans, vegetables, coffee, sugar, tea, etc., in proportion.

When we remember that there seems to have been no difference made in the rations issued to the sick in the hospital and prisoners confined in the stockade; that, as we have seen by the testimony of Dr. Jones, the mortality was proportionately the same in both places, and all the surroundings so prolific of disease, added to the fact that for months the prisoners had barely room to stand upon, we are prepared to comprehend the force of the illustrations above given and those which I shall now give. The number of patients treated in the hospital at Andersonville is shown by the hospital register to have been something less than 18,000, the number of deaths a little short of 13,000, and to this number must be added 2,000 more, who, as we have shown with reasonable certainty, died before reaching their homes, making in all 15,000, and this falls far short of the maximum number, giving, as we see, the frightful ratio of mortality of over 83 per cent.

Quoting from the same learned author we find that "the average mortality of the London hospitals is nine per cent; in the French hospitals in the Crimea, for a period of twenty-two months, mortality was fourteen per cent. The city of Milan received during the campaign in Italy 34,000 sick and wounded, of whom 1,400, or four per cent, died. The city of Nashville, Tennessee, received during the year 1864, 65,157 sick and wounded, of whom 2,635, or four per cent, died. During the year 1863 Washington received 67,884, and of these but 2,671, or less than four per cent, died; and in 1864 her hospitals received 96,705 sick and wounded (49,455 sick, 47,250 wounded), of whom 6,283, or six and four-tenths per cent, died. The mortality of the rebel prisoners at Fort Delaware for eleven months was two per cent; at Johnson's Island during twenty-one months 134 deaths out of 6,000 prisoners."

This is the record of history, against the charnel-house of Andersonville. Let the mouths of those who would defend these atrocities by recrimination, charging the United States government with like cruelty, forever hereafter be closed.

Fort Delaware and Johnson's Island, with their two per cent of dead. Andersonville with its eighty-three per cent! Look upon that picture and then upon this, and tell me there was no design to slay! Let no mind, be it warped ever so much by treason and treasonable sympathies, doubt this record, for "If damned custom have not brazed it so that it be proof and bulwark against sense," it must believe; it cannot deny these things,

May it please the court, I have done with the argument under charge first. I leave it with you to answer by your verdict whether this charge of conspiracy, solemnly and seriously preferred, can be frittered away and disposed of without a single explanatory line in defense. I place before you, gentlemen, on the one hand the protestations of this accused, who speaks for himself and his co-conspirators; on the other the testimony of Dr. Bates, where he declared, as you well remember, with faltering tone and feelings overpowered, "I feel myself safe in saying that seventy-five per cent of those who died might have been saved had those unfortunate men been properly cared for."

I leave it with you to say whether the prisoner at the bar can acquit himself and his associates in crime by declaring the charge here laid to be, as he has told you, "a myth," "a phantasy of the brain," "a wild chimera, as unsubstantial as the baseless fabric of a vision."

CONDITIONS SURROUNDING WITNESSES.

In his argument upon the charge of murder the judge advocate called attention to the conditions surrounding the witnesses at the time of which they testified. He said:

I have thus hastily passed over the evidence touching this class of murders. I shall presently endeavor to individualize the instances mentioned and to reconcile and unite the separated, and in some instances apparently complicated, circumstances. But, before doing so, let me suggest that on the review of this evidence, while the testimony must be and ought to be subjected to the closest criticism and scrutiny, and while the court should be convinced, beyond a reasonable doubt, of the guilt of this accused, still I submit it as worthy of grave consideration that there are many circumstances peculiar to prison life, as it was at Andersonville, which make the ordinary test applied in tribunals of law for the verification of testimony altogether inappropriate in this case. The court will not forget that there existed at Andersonville a condition of affairs for which it would would be impossible to find a precedent. The prisoners were deprived, to a great measure, of facilities for ordinary intelligence or for communication with each other and the outer world. They were subjected to the closest and most cruel confinement and discipline. Most of them were constantly racked with the pangs of hunger or disease, or engrossed from hour to hour in a struggle with death in which the odds were fearfully against them. Their companions were constantly dying around them, either from emaciation, disease, or acts of violence, so that, as the prisoners themselves have declared in the presence of the court, they became so habituated to these horrible surroundings, that the death of a comrade, under what would ordinarily seem the most frightful circumstances, made in many cases but a slight impression upon their minds; and certainly they would not charge their memory with dates or circumstances, even should they be able to fix the time, and it will be remembered that many of them state that they lost all knowledge of the days of the week and the month. Besides, they never expected to emerge from that scene alive, and never hoped that a day would come when their persecutor should be arraigned before a tribunal of justice, and they themselves be summoned as witnesses to his iniquitous acts. It is not to be expected that, under these circumstances, witnesses should evince such precision as to dates and minute particulars as might be expected in an ordinary trial for the investigation of offenses disturbing but rarely the tranquillity of civilized society. A court of justice never requires higher evidence than the best of which the case will admit; for, as has been well remarked by a distinguished legal writer, "The rules of evidence are adopted for practical purposes in the administration of justice, and must be so applied as to promote the end for which they were designed." (1 Greenleaf's Evidence, sec. 83.)

But I have no apology to offer, no defense to make for the testimony upon which the prosecution relies for the conviction of this accused under the charge now being examined.

In every case where you are asked to hold the prisoner responsible for the death of any one of those in his custody, you will find the evidence direct, positive, and clear; you are not asked to find this prisoner guilty upon vague, uncertain, doubtful testimony, but you are asked to apply the rules of evidence properly applicable to cases occurring under the peculiar circumstances to which we have alluded, always remembering that your duty is to arrive at the truth in the most direct manner possible.

After having given to the court his analysis of the evidence bearing upon the charge of murder, the judge advocate concluded his address as follows:

I have thus, without regard to the evidence under charge first, presented the evidence under charge second, as spread upon the record, showing that this accused, while acting as commandant of the prison at Andersonville, deliberately, wantonly, and maliciously destroyed the lives of eighteen prisoners of war in his custody. I confess myself too much overcome with the melancholy details of this trial and the frightful disclosures to dwell longer on so sad a theme. If this accused still answer that, admitting the facts charged, he did these things in the exercise of authority lawfully conferred upon him, and that what he did was necessary to the discipline and safety of the prisoners, I answer him in the language of Lord Mansfield, given in an important case:

In trying the legality of acts done by military officers in the exercise of their duty, particularly beyond the seas, where cases may occur without the possibility of application for proper advice, great latitude ought to be allowed, and they ought not to suffer for a slip of form, if their intention appears, by the evidence, to have been upright. It is the same as when complaints are brought against inferior civil magistrates, such as justices of the peace, for acts done by them in the exercise of their civil duty. There the principal inquiry to be made by a court of justice is, how the heart stood, and if there appear to be nothing wrong there, great latitude will be allowed for misapprehension or mistake. But, on the other hand, if the heart is wrong, if cruelty, malice and oppression appear to have occasioned or aggravated the imprisonment, or other injury complained of, they shall not cover themselves with the thin veil of legal forms, or escape, under the cover of a justification the most technically regular, from that punishment which it is your province and your duty to inflict on so scandalous an abuse of public trust. (Wall *vs.* MacNamara.)

May it please the court, I have hastily analyzed and presented the evidence under charge second. If we had not travelled through the history of those long weary months of suffering, torture, starvation, and death, and become familiar with each day's roll of those who passed away, the mind could not contemplate this last though briefer roster of the dead without feelings of utmost horror. Mortal man has never been called to answer before a legal tribunal to a catalogue of crime like this. One shudders at the fact, and almost doubts the age we live in. I would not harrow up your minds by dwelling further upon this woeful record. The obligation you have taken constitutes you the sole judges of both law and fact. I pray you administer the one, and decide the other, meting out to those involved in this crime of the universe all justice; without fear, favor, or partiality, and without regard to position, high or low, of those proved guilty.

The address of the judge advocate was made under strong conviction not only of the prisoner's guilt, but that a crime of monumental proportions had been committed in which many others besides the prisoner were involved. He spoke at a time when the atmosphere was surcharged with the enormity of the terrible consequences which had accompanied the Rebellion, and which were weighing heavily upon the hearts of the loyal people of the country.

It was too soon after the arms of rebellion had been laid down for the North to forgive or forget. Our President had been cruelly assassinated; many of the leaders of the Rebellion were in confinement under charges of high treason; the public mind was feverish and in a condition of high tension. The crimes with which Wirz and his co-conspirators stood charged, were of such a character as to arouse in the minds of those who had suffered by the Rebellion, a spirit of deep resentment, and to demand speedy punishment where guilt was shown.

Under such circumstances and in such atmosphere, a prosecuting officer may well be excused for some extravagance of speech, some comments and criticisms which, in after years, may seem unnecessarily, even unwarrantedly, harsh and severe.

Recalling those days, now forty-five years past, remembering the vivid impressions the evidence of the frightful sufferings and needless mortality at Andersonville made upon my mind, I cannot bring the judgment of my maturer years to doubt the righteousness of the verdict, nor can I find it in my heart to offer apology for the ardor and zeal with which I prosecuted the prisoner.

The court made the following findings and pronounced the following sentence:

The court, being cleared for deliberation, and having maturely considered the evidence adduced, find the accused, Henry Wirz, as follows:[1]

Of the specification to charge I, "guilty," after amending said specification to read as follows:

In this, that he, the said Henry Wirz, did combine, confederate, and conspire with them, the said Jefferson Davis, James A. Seddon, Howell Cobb, John H. Winder, Richard B. Winder, Isaiah H. White, W. S. Winder, W. Shelby Reed, R. R. Stevenson, S. P. Moore, — Kerr, late hospital steward at Andersonville, James Duncan, Wesley W. Turner, Benjamin Harris, and others whose names are unknown, citizens of the United States aforesaid, and who were then engaged in armed rebellion against the United States, maliciously, traitorously, and in violation of the laws of war, to impair and injure the health and to destroy the lives, by subjecting to torture and great suffering, by confining in unhealthy and unwholesome quarters, by exposing to the inclemency of winter and to the dews and burning suns of summer, by compelling the use of impure water, and by furnishing insufficient and unwholesome food, of large numbers of Federal prisoners, to wit, the number of about forty-five thousand soldiers in the military service of the United States of America, held as prisoners of war at Andersonville, in the state of Georgia, within the lines of the so-called Confederate States,

[The remaining portion of the specification was found as charged.]

Of charge I, "guilty," after amending said charge to read as follows:[2]

Maliciously, willfully and traitorously, and in aid of the then existing armed rebellion against the United States of America, on or about the 27th day of March, A. D. 1864, and on divers other days between that day and the tenth day of April, 1865, combining, confederating and conspiring together with Jefferson Davis, James A. Seddon, Howell Cobb, John H. Winder, Richard B. Winder, Isaiah H. White, W. S. Winder, W. Shelby Reed, R. R. Stevenson, S. P. Moore,—Kerr, late hospital steward at Andersonville, James Duncan, Wesley W. Turner, Benjamin Harris and others unknown, to injure the health and destroy the lives of soldiers in the military service of the United States, then held and being prisoners of war within the lines of the so-called Confederate States and in the military prisons thereof, to the end that the armies of the United States might be weakened and impaired; in violation of the laws and customs of war.

Of specification first to the charge II, "guilty," adding the words "or about" immediately before the phrase "the ninth day of July."

Of specification second to charge II, "guilty."

Of specification third to charge II, "guilty," after striking out "June," and inserting instead "September."

[1] Record, p. 805.
[2] Record, p. 807.

Of specification four to charge II, "not guilty."

Of specification five to charge II, "guilty," after striking out the phrase "on the thirtieth day," and inserting instead the phrase, "on or about the twenty-fifth day."

Of specification six to charge II, "guilty," after striking out the word "first," and inserting "fifteenth," and also striking out the phrase "on the sixth day," and inserting instead the phrase "on or about the sixteenth day."

Of specification seven to charge II, "guilty," after striking out the word "twentieth," and inserting instead the word "first," and also after inserting "or about" immediately before the phrase "the twenty-fifth day."

Of specification eight to charge II, "guilty."

Of specification nine to charge II, "guilty."

Of specification ten to charge II, not guilty."

Of specification eleven to charge II, "guilty," after striking out the word "first," and inserting instead the word "sixth"; after striking out also the phrase "incite and urge" and the phrase "encouragement and instigation," and by adding the words "or about" after the word "on," where it last occurs in the specification; and also after striking out the phrase "animals called bloodhounds," and inserting the word "dogs"; and also striking out the word "bloodhounds" where it afterwards occurs, and inserting the word "dogs"; and also striking out the words "given by him."

Of specification twelve to charge II, "guilty."

Of specification thirteen to charge II, "not guilty."

Of the second charge, "guilty."

And the court do therefore sentence him, the said Henry Wirz, to be hanged by the neck till he be dead, at such time and place as the President of the United States may direct, two-thirds of the members of the court concurring herein.

LEW WALLACE,
N. P. CHIPMAN,   *Major-General and President of Com.*
    Col. and Add. A. D. C., Judge Advocate.

And the court also find the prisoner, Henry Wirz, guilty of having caused the death, in manner as alleged in specification eleven to charge II, by means of dogs, of three prisoners of war in his custody and soldiers of the United States, one occurring on or about the 15th day of May, 1864; another occurring on or about the 11th day of July, 1864; another occurring on or about the 1st day of September, 1864, but which finding as here expressed has not and did not enter into the sentence of the court as before given.

LEW WALLACE,
N. P. CHIPMAN,   *Major-General and President of Com.*
    Col. and Add. A. D. C., Judge Advocate.

OPINION OF THE JUDGE ADVOCATE-GENERAL.

Military records are first examined by the judge advocate-general and his opinion and recommendation taken. All sentences involving death penalty go to the president for final action. The Wirz record had careful scrutiny, and went to the president with an elaborate written opinion of the judge advocate-general. Some extracts only will be here given:[1]

It is not necessary for the purposes of this review to go into an elaborate discussion of the question involved in the findings on the first charge. From the document of the proceedings, containing more than 5,000 pages, presenting a mass of evidence bearing upon these questions, no brief summary can be made which would do justice to the subject. The argument of the judge advocate sets forth an able and exhaustive examination of the material legal points raised and proof established by the trial, and forms a part of the record. It may be relied on as giving a full and just exposition of the matters which entered into the deliberations of the court, and, as particularly applicable to this branch of the case, reference is respectfully invited to pages 4838 to 5148. The opinion is expressed that the conspiracy, as described in the findings above recited, was clearly made out, and that the conclusions arrived at by the court could not, in the light of the evidence this record contains, have been avoided.

Language fails in an attempt to denounce, even in faint terms, the diabolical combination for the destruction and death, by cruel and fiendishly ingenious processes, of helpless prisoners of war who might fall into their hands, which this record shows was plotted and deliberately entered upon, and, as far as time permitted, accomplished by the rebel authorities and their brutal underlings at Andersonville prison. Criminal history presents no parallel to this monstrous conspiracy, and from the whole catalogue of infamous devices within reach of human hands, a system for the murder of men more revolting in its details could not have been planned. Upon the heads of those named by the court in its findings the guilt of this immeasurable crime is fixed, a guilt so fearfully black and horrible, that the civilized world must be appalled by the spectacle.

There remains yet to be noticed the matter involved in the second charge. The homicides alleged to have been committed under this charge, and which the court found were committed, are of four classes: First. Those cases of death which resulted from the biting of dogs. (Specification 2.) Second. Cases of death which resulted from confinement in the stocks and chain-gang. (Specifications 5, 6, 7.) Third. Cases of prisoners killed by guards, pursuant to *direct* orders of Wirz, given at the time. (Specifications 8, 9, 12.) Fourth. Cases of prisoners killed by Wirz's own hand. (Specifications 1, 2, 3.)

That all the deaths embraced in these four classes resulted from the causes and in the manner set forth in the specifications, is conceived to be very clearly established by the evidence adduced by the prosecution, and it is not deemed necessary, in the absence of any contradictory testimony directly bearing on these instances, to recite the evidence applicable to each, except, it may be, briefly, that relating to the fourth class (Specifications 1, 2, 3) and some acts of a similar character.

The testimony supporting the first specification is that of Felix De la Baume, a Union soldier, who states that on or about the 8th of July, 1864, he was one of a detachment of prisoners taken to Wirz's headquarters to be enrolled, before

---

[1] Record, p. 808.

being sent into the prison; that one of his comrades was attacked with epilepsy, and some of his companions, by permission of the guard, ran to the creek for water; that he, the witness, heard a shot fired, and, on turning, saw Wirz fire two more, wounding two prisoners, one of whom the witness never saw nor heard of afterwards; and the other of whom he saw carried up to Wirz's headquarters, in a dying condition, the wound being in the breast.

There is also the testimony of George Conway, who states that on or about the 11th of July, 1864, he saw Wirz shoot a Union prisoner within the stockade as he was stooping to pick up his cup, which had fallen under the dead-line, and that the man died almost instantly.

Which of these two cases (either being, it is conceived, sufficient to sustain the allegation) the court relied on, does not, of course, appear.

In support of the second specification, Martin E. Hogan testifies that some time in September, when the prisoners were being removed from Andersonville to Millen, he saw Wirz take a prisoner, who was worn out with hunger and disease, by the coat-collar, and, because he could not walk faster, wrench him back and stamp upon him with his boots; that the man was borne past him (witness) bleeding from his mouth and nose, and died in a short time.

The third specification is supported by the testimony of George W. Gray, who states, that about the middle of September, 1864, he and a comrade named William Stewart, a private belonging to a Minnesota regiment, went out of the stockade, in charge of a guard, to carry a dead body, and that after laying it in the dead-house they were on their way back to the stockade, when Wirz rode up to them and asked, "by what authority they were out there"; that Stewart replied, they were out there by proper authority; whereupon Wirz drew his revolver and shot Stewart, the ball taking effect in his breast and killing him instantly; and that the guard then took from his body some twenty or thirty dollars, which Wirz received and rode away.

Further evidence in regard to Wirz killing certain prisoners was presented, but the dates given by the witnesses show the murders to have been other than those alleged in the specifications. They will be referred to as illustrating the character of the prisoner, and establishing a frequency and repetition of like crimes.

James H. Davidson testified that in April, as he remembered, Wirz came into the stockade one day, and a lame man went up to him and asked him a question, whereupon Wirz "turned around" and shot him, and he died.

Thomas C. Alcoke states that one day (the witness seems to have no knowledge or recollection of dates) Wirz came into the stockade and a man asked of him permission to go out and get some fresh air; that Wirz asked him what he meant, and that after a few more words had passed between them, Wirz "wheeled around," pulled out a revolver, and shot him down, the ball taking effect in his breast, and death occurring about three hours afterwards. It also appears by this witness that when he remonstrated Wirz told him he "had better look out, or he would be put in the same place," and that soon after Wirz came in with a guard and put him in irons.

Hugh R. Snee testified that some time in September, 1864, a party of Union prisoners were to be exchanged under an arrangement between General Sherman and the rebel Hood; that they were taken from the stockade after dark, as the heat in the day was so great that the men would have fainted; that none but able-bodied men were selected, it being stated when they were called out that any one who could not walk eighteen miles a day would be shot; that notwithstanding this the men were so anxious to escape imprisonment that some too weak to perform the day's travel came out. The witness states that three, who belonged to some western regiments, were able to go but a short distance before they fainted and fell out of the ranks, and were pushed one side by the guard; that thereupon a man ran back, and speaking in a voice he thought at the time to be that of Captain Wirz, wanted to know why they were there; that they replied, they wished to get out of prison; whereupon this man said, "I'll help you out, God damn you." Witness then heard six pistol-shots, followed by a cry as if some one was hurt, "and immediately after, a rebel lieutenant came past remarking that it was a brutal act; that one of them was dead," and, when asked who did it, replied, "The captain."

The most prominent features of the defense under this second charge will now be considered:

An attempt was made to prove that during the whole of August and parts of July and September the prisoner was sick and confined to his bed, and could not have committed the crimes charged to him in those months. In his statement to the court, however, he made no reference to his absence—doubtless for the reason that the testimony was of too general and loose a character to set up as contradictory to the explicit statements of numerous witnesses as to the dates when the crimes recorded in the finding were committed, corroborated as those statements were, by official papers, bearing his signature, showing that at different times during those months he was in the performance of his ordinary functions as commandant of the prison.

It was claimed that deaths resulting from the use of dogs, in the capture of escaped prisoners, were not crimes fastened upon Wirz, he not being present at the pursuit and therefore not responsible. But it appears to have been the fact that this use of dogs was under Wirz's special direction; that the pursuit of prisoners was in many instances initiated under his immediate orders, and in some eases captures were made under his personal supervision. It was also clearly proved that a part of each pack were ferocious dogs, dangerous to life, so as to make it probable that the men on whose track they were sent would be killed. A man overtaken by these beasts, and desiring to surrender, could not, by coming to a stand, save his life; the instinct of the dogs was for human blood, and to surrender to them was death. A most shocking illustration will be given. Two soldiers had escaped, but were overtaken; the party who captured them returned with but one (who was so mangled that he died), and the chief of the party, known as Turner, exulted in accounting for the other, stating that they allowed the dogs to tear him in pieces, and left him in the woods.

As applying to the question of criminal responsibility involved in this class of homicides, the judge advocate referred the court to the well-settled principle of law, that it is not essential that the hand of the party should be the immediate occasion of the death, but that if it be shown that means were used likely to occasion death, and which did so occasion it, the party using such means is to be held responsible for the consequences.

There is but one of this class of homicides which enters into the findings of "guilty," under this charge. A discussion of the legal points involved is conceived to be needless, inasmuch as the charge is sustained by a conviction on nine other distinct allegations of murder.

As to the deaths resulting from the use of stocks and chain-gangs, the defense urged that the men were placed therein for the purposes of discipline; that they were commonly used for such purposes; and that their use at this place was attributed to those higher in authority than Wirz, to whose orders he was subject. Upon this point it is to be observed that prisoners were put in these instruments of torture as punishment for having escaped, or having made attempts to escape from their captors, which attempts, whether successful or not, it was their right and duty as prisoners of war to make. Any punishment inflicted upon them, therefore, by their captors was a violation of the laws of war, and deaths resulting from such unlawful punishment are murders. This would be the judgment of the law apart from some of the peculiar circumstances which surround these crimes, and which so decidedly indicate their true character, prominent among which is the often declared animus of the prisoner, showing conclusively that in these and kindred barbarities he was deliberately seeking to sacrifice the lives of his victims. It was shown that these stocks and chain-gangs were under Wirz's immediate and direct control; that he exercised full authority in committing prisoners to both. While it may be, and probably is, the fact that his action in this matter was sanctioned by the rebel Winder when he was on duty at that place, it does not relieve the prisoner of responsibility for the result.

Relating to the three homicides embraced in the third class, the prisoner makes no special defense, except as to the killing of the man known as Chickamauga. He urges in his final statement, that his order to the guard to shoot this man was only intended as a menace. It is clear, however, from the testimony, that his order in this case, as in the others, was peremptory, and, according to his own version, it was not a command that could be construed by any subordinate as merely a menace; moreover, it was distinctly proved to have been accompanied by a threat that he would shoot the guard if the guard did not shoot this crippled soldier. He states further, and it is so found by the record, that this poor man desired to be killed, it would seem, because he was suspected by his comrades of having given information to the prison-keepers of some attempts of prisoners to escape from the stockade. This fact, however, in no degree palliates his murderous guilt.

Of the homicides embraced in the fourth class (those committed directly by his own hands) the prisoner's statement notices but one, that of Stewart, sworn to by the witness Gray. It is asserted that the testimony of this witness is a pure fabrication. There is nothing found in the examination of the record which casts a doubt on his veracity, and the court seem to have discovered nothing in his manner on the stand to raise the question of his credibility.

As to all those cases not heretofore specially mentioned, the defense insists that the allegations were too vague and indefinite, and that the testimony is insufficient to sustain them, and also that it is altogether improbable that such murders could have been committed without coming to the knowledge of various witnesses, who stated that they had never heard of such crimes at Andersonville. No evidence being submitted which contradicts the concurrent and explicit statements of the witnesses who gave positive testimony of their perpetration, these murders are fastened to Wirz's hands.

Many points were raised by both sides relating to the admission of evidence as the trial progressed. These were fully debated at the time. No discussion of them here is deemed necessary, it not being found that competent proof material to the prisoner's defense on the specific offenses of which the court pronounced him guilty was excluded.

Much latitude seems to have been given him. He was allowed to show special acts of kindness to prisoners, and to introduce declarations made by himself in explanation of his acts. Letters and official reports, and oral testimony of his personal efforts, offered as indicating his interest in, and a care for, the comfort of the prisoners, were also admitted. It is shown that every witness asked for by the defense was subpoenaed, except certain rebel functionaries, who, for reasons stated at the time, did not appear on the stand. But the judge advocate proposed that if the counsel for the defense would set forth, according to the common rule, by affidavit, what he expected and had reason to believe any witness who did not so appear would testify, it would be admitted of record that such witness would so testify. This proposition was not accepted. One hundred and six witnesses were subpoenaed for the defense, of whom sixty-eight reported, but thirty-nine of these, many of them soldiers of our army, and sufferers at Andersonville, were discharged by the prisoner's counsel without being put upon the stand.

A review of the proceedings leads to the opinion that no prejudice to the legal rights of the prisoner can be successfully claimed to have resulted from any decision which excluded testimony he desired to introduce. The trial is believed to have been conducted in accordance with the regulations governing military courts, and the record presents no error which can be held to invalidate the proceedings.

The annals of our race present nowhere and at no time a darker field of crime than that of Andersonville, and it is fortunate for the interests alike of public justice and of historic truth that from this field the veil has been so faithfully and so completely lifted. All the horrors of this pandemonium of the Rebellion are laid bare to us in the broad, steady light of the testimony of some one hundred and fifty witnesses who spoke what they had seen and heard and suffered, and whose evidence, given under oath and subjected to cross-examination and to every other test which human experience has devised for the ascertainment of truth, must be accepted as affording an immovable foundation for the sentence pronounced.

The proof under the second charge shows that some of our soldiers, for mere attempts to escape from their oppressors, were given to ferocious dogs to be torn in pieces, that others were confined in stocks and chains till life yielded to the torture, and that others were wantonly shot down at Wirz's bidding or by his own hand. Here in the presence of these pitiless murders of unarmed and helpless men, so distinctly alleged and proved, justice might well claim the prisoner's life. There remain, however, to be contemplated crimes yet more revolting, for which he and his co-conspirators must be held responsible. The Andersonville Prison records (made exhibits in this case) contain a roster of over thirteen thousand dead, buried naked, maimed, and putrid, in one vast sepulchre. Of these, a surgeon of the rebel army who was on duty at this prison testifies that at least three-fourths died of the treatment inflicted on them while in confinement; and a surgeon of our own army, who was a prisoner there, states that four-fifths died from this cause. Under this proof, which has not been assailed, nearly ten thousand, if not more, of these deaths must be charged directly to the account of Wirz and his associates. This widespread sacrifice of life was not made suddenly or under the influence of wild, ungovernable passion, but was accomplished slowly and deliberately, by packing upwards of thirty thousand men, like cattle, in a fetid pen—a mere cesspool, there to die for need of air to breathe, for want of ground on which to lie, from lack of shelter from sun and rain, and from the slow, agonizing processes of starvation; when air and space and shelter and food were all within the ready gift of their tormenters. This work of death seems to have been a saturnalia of enjoyment for the prisoner, who amid these savage orgies evidenced such exultation and mingled with them such nameless blasphemy and ribald jests, as at times to exhibit him rather as a demon than a man. It was his continual boast that by these barbarities he was destroying more Union soldiers than rebel generals were butchering on the battle-field. He claimed to be doing the work of the Rebellion, and faithfully, in all his murderous cruelty and baseness, did he represent its spirit. It is by looking upon the cemeteries which have been filled from Libby, Belle Isle, Salisbury, Florence, and Andersonville, and other rebel prisons, and recalling the prolonged sufferings of the patriots who are sleeping there, that we can best understand the inner and real life of the Rebellion, and the hellish criminality and brutality of the traitors who maintained it. For such crimes human power is absolutely impotent to enforce any adequate atonement.

It may be added, in conclusion, that the court before which the prisoner was tried was composed of officers high in rank, and eminent for their faithful services and probity of character, and that several of them were distinguished for their legal attainments. The investigation of the ease was conducted throughout with patience and impartiality, and the conclusion reached is one from which the overwhelming volume of testimony left no escape. It is recommended that the sentence be executed. J. HOLT,
Judge Advocate-General.

ORDER OF THE PRESIDENT.
[General Court-martial Orders No. 607.]
WAR DEPARTMENT, ADJUTANT-GENERAL'S OFFICE,
WASHINGTON, November 6, 1865.

I. Before a military commission which convened at Washington, D. C., August 23, 1865, pursuant to paragraph 3, Special Orders No. 453, dated August 23, 1865, and paragraph 13, Special Orders No. 524, dated October 2, 1865, War

Department, Adjutant-General's Office, Washington, and of which Major-General Lewis Wallace, United States Volunteers, is president, was arraigned and tried Henry Wirz.

[Here follow the charges, specifications, findings, and sentence.]

II. The proceedings, findings, and sentence in the foregoing case having been submitted to the President of the United States, the following are his orders:

EXECUTIVE MANSION, November 3, 1865.

The proceedings, findings, and sentence of the court in the within case are approved, and it is ordered that the sentence be carried into execution, by the officer commanding the department of Washington, on Friday, the 10th day of November, 1865, between the hours of 6 o'clock A. M. and 12 o'clock noon.

ANDREW JOHNSON, *President.*

III. Major-General C. C. Augur, commanding the department of Washington, is commanded to cause the foregoing sentence, in the case of Henry Wirz, to be duly executed, in accordance with the President's order.

IV. The military commission, of which Major-General Lewis Wallace, United States Volunteers, is president, is hereby dissolved.

By command of the President of the United States:

E. D. TOWNSEND,
Assistant Adjutant-General.

Official:

E. D. TOWNSEND,
Assistant Adjutant-General.

LETTER OF THE COMMANDING GENERAL, DEPARTMENT OF WASHINGTON, REPORTING THE EXECUTION AND BURIAL OF HENRY WIRZ.

HEADQUARTERS DEPARTMENT OF WASHINGTON,
WASHINGTON, D. C., November 11, 1865.

SIR: I have the honor to report that the sentence and orders of the President in the case of Henry Wirz, as promulgated in General Court-martial Orders No. 607, dated War Department, Adjutant-General's Office, Washington, November 6, 1865, have been duly executed (between the hours of 10 and 11 A. M.) yesterday, November 10, and his body has been interred by the side of Atzerodt, in the arsenal grounds.[1]

I am, general, very respectfully, your obedient servant,

C. C. AUGUR,
Major-Gen. Vols., Commanding Department.

The ADJUTANT-GENERAL of the Army.

[1] Later removed to Olivet Cemetery near Washington.

Monument Erected by the State of Illinois.

CHAPTER XV.

THE CARTEL SUSPENDED — EXCHANGING OF PRISONERS INTERRUPTED — CAUSES THEREFOR—VIOLATION OF CARTEL BY REBELS—RIGHT TO EXCHANGE DENIED TO NEGRO SOLDIERS AND THEIR OFFICERS—WHEN CAPTURED TREATED AS FELONS—SUFFERINGS OF PRISONERS DUE TO TREATMENT THEY RECEIVED, NOT BECAUSE CARTEL WAS SUSPENDED—REBEL COMMISSIONER ROBERT OULD, MANEUVERING TO GET EXCESS OF PRISONERS HELD BY FEDERALS AND USE THEM AT CRITICAL PERIOD OF WAR—ACTION OF OUR GOVERNMENT FULLY VINDICATED—REPORT OF GENERAL HITCHCOCK, FEDERAL COMMISSIONER OF EXCHANGE, COVERING ENTIRE SUBJECT—LETTER OF GENERAL GRANT, PART OF WHICH IS INSCRIBED ON THE WIRZ MONUMENT—INTERVIEW WITH COLONEL JOHN MCELROY, A PRISONER AT ANDERSONVILLE—THE EVOLUTION OF SLAVES TO THE STATUS OF UNITED STATES SOLDIERS—SOME INTERESTING FACTS ABOUT THE NEGRO AS A SOLDIER.

THE slavery question not only led to the Civil War, but, in the midst of the struggle to preserve the Union, it was largely instrumental in causing the suspension of the cartel and breaking off a general exchange of prisoners of war. It will not be without interest to trace briefly the evolutionary processes through which, prior to President Lincoln's proclamation of freedom, large bodies of the slaves of the South passed, and by which they attained recognition of their liberty by our government, and were mustered into military service, and partly in consequence of which the exchange of prisoners was interrupted.

The secession of the Southern states from the Union and the taking possession by them of the forts, buildings, arsenals, custom-houses, and other public property of the government within their borders, necessarily made the army for the restoration of the Union an army of invasion of the rebel territory. The border slave states of Maryland, Kentucky, Tennessee, Missouri, and a considerable portion of West Virginia refused to join in the Rebellion, but to reach the armed forces of the enemy the Union armies were compelled to pass over this slave territory, and they necessarily came in contact with the system of slavery and with slave-owners. Many of these latter were loyal to the Union, but still many others had either gone south to join the enemy or were disloyal, and, though remaining in loyal territory, secretly gave such aid and comfort to the enemy as they could with safety to their persons and property.

Prior to President Lincoln's inauguration, the newspapers and public men of the South had proclaimed that war was inevitable, and that the purpose of the North was to free the slaves. Naturally, as the armies of the North passed into slave territory, the negroes flocked to the camps in the hope of enjoying that freedom which they had been taught to hope was the purpose of the North to give them. And this was the situation from Maryland to Missouri—touching thousands of helpless men, women, and children. A similar condition also arose along the Atlantic Coast wherever our army, with the aid of the navy, was able to maintain a footing—notably along the eastern shore of Virginia and at points on the Carolina coast and the coast of Florida.

So anxious was the government to give the loyal slaveholders and the world generally the assurance that its object was to restore the Union, and not in any way to interfere with slavery, that every effort was made to prevent the coming of slaves into our lines, and when there to compel them to return to their masters.

On August 30, 1861, General Fremont, commanding the western department, at St. Louis, Missouri, issued a proclamation declaring martial law throughout the state of Missouri, and ordering all persons found with arms in their hands to be tried by court-martial and, if found guilty, to be shot, besides confiscating all property of such persons and liberating their slaves.[1]

This led to a retaliatory order by General Jeff. Thompson on September 2, 1861, in which he declared that "for every member of the Missouri state guard or soldiers of our allies, the armies of the Confederate States, who shall be put to death in pursuance of said order of General Fremont I will hang, draw, and quarter a minion of said Abraham Lincoln."[2]

On September 2, 1861, President Lincoln wrote General Fremont, pointing out the embarrassing nature of his order, and asking him on his own motion to withdraw it.[3] Fremont refused to voluntarily modify his order, and the President promptly did so on September 11th.[4]

General Halleck, who later succeeded to the command of the department, on November 20, 1861, issued general orders No. 3, directing that "no such person [slave] be permitted to enter the lines of any

[1] War of Rebellion, vol. 1, series 2, p. 221.
[2] War of Rebellion, vol. 1, series 2, p. 181.
[3] War of Rebellion, vol. 1, series 2, p. 766.
[4] War of Rebellion, vol. 1, series 2, p. 778.

camp or of any force on the march and that any now within such lines be immediately excluded therefrom."¹

The following resolution was introduced in the House of Representatives December 9, 1861:

Whereas, Major-General Halleck of the western department has issued an order prohibiting negroes from coming within the lines of our army and excluding those already under the protection of our troops; and whereas, a different policy and practice prevails in other departments by the direct sanction of the administration; and whereas, said order is cruel and inhuman and in the judgment of this house based upon no military necessity; . . . That the president be respectfully requested to direct General Halleck to recall said order or cause it to conform with the practice in other departments of our army.²

On December 11th this resolution was laid on the table by a vote of 78 to 64.

On November 23, 1861, at Fort Holt, Kentucky, the commanding officer issued an order reading: "No officer or soldier will be allowed to arrest, secrete, or harbor or in any way interfere with persons held to service [negroes], property of citizens in slave states."³

General Grant addressed a letter to Colonel Cook, commanding at Fort Holt, on December 25th, calling attention to General Halleck's order No. 3, and said: "I do not want the army used as negro-catchers, but still less do I want to see it used as a cloak to cover their escape. No matter what our private views may be on this subject, there are in this department positive orders on the subject, and these orders must be obeyed."⁴

A similar policy was enforced in other parts of Kentucky.

General W. T. Sherman, then commanding at Louisville, Kentucky, wrote to Colonel Turchin on October 15, 1861, as follows: "Two gentlemen unknown to me, but introduced by Mr. Guthrie, say some negro slaves have taken refuge in our camp and are there sheltered. The laws of the United States and of Kentucky, all of which are binding upon us, compel us to surrender a runaway negro on application of negro's owner or agent. I believe that you have not been instrumental in this, but my orders are that all negroes shall be delivered upon claim of the owner or agent. Better keep the negroes out of your camp altogether unless you brought them along with your regiment."⁵

---

[1] War of Rebellion, vol. 1, series 2, p. 778.
[2] War of Rebellion, vol. 1, series 2, p. 784.
[3] War of Rebellion, vol. 1, series 2, p. 779.
[4] War of Rebellion, vol. 1, series 2, p. 794.
[5] War of Rebellion, vol. 1, series 2, p. 774.

THE EXCHANGE OF PRISONERS.

In the armies of the East commanders were confronted with the same problem and surrounded with like embarrassments. The negroes were put to work and otherwise cared for while the permanent solution of the difficulty was in abeyance.

General Benj. F. Butler was in command at Fortress Monroe, Virginia. A better lawyer than military tactician, he was, I believe, the first to make the point—the theory on which slaves were held, i.e. as property—that when captured or otherwise coming into our possession they became contraband of war, and the appellation of "contrabands" was thereafter applied to them. It has always seemed to me that a much broader principle was applicable to these unfortunate human beings, which would carry with it, under the existing circumstances, a right to freedom, and to be treated by us as entitled to such right, and not merely as property contraband of war. And the status of absolute freedom was finally given them by our government and resolutely and to the end maintained.

The following correspondence will illustrate that as early as in May, 1861, at Fortress Monroe, Virginia, the question had become a serious problem in the conduct of the war:

HEADQUARTERS DEPARTMENT OF VIRGINIA,
FORT MONROE, May 27, 1861.

LIEUTENANT-GENERAL SCOTT.

SIR: . . . Since I wrote my last despatch the question in regard to slave property is becoming one of very serious magnitude. The inhabitants of Virginia are using their slaves in the batteries and are preparing to send the women and children south. The escapes from them are very numerous and a squad has come in this morning to my pickets bringing their women and children. Of course these cannot be dealt with upon the theory on which I designed to treat the services of able-bodied men and women who might come within my lines, and of which I gave you a detailed account in my last despatch. I am in the utmost doubt what to do with this species of property. Up to this time I have had come within my lines men and women with their children, entire families, each family belonging to the same owner. I have therefore determined to employ as I can do very profitably the able-bodied persons in the party, issuing proper food for the support of all and charging against their services the expense of care and sustenance of the non-laborers, keeping a strict and accurate account as well of the services as of the expenditure, having the worth of the services and the cost of the expenditure determined by a board of survey to be hereafter detailed. I know of no other manner in which to dispose of this subject and the questions connected therewith. As a matter of property to the insurgents it will be of very great moment, the number that I now have amounting as I am informed to what in good times would be of the value of $60,000. Twelve of these negroes I am informed have escaped from the batteries on Sewall's Point, which this morning fired upon my expedition as it passed by out of range. As a means of offense therefore in the enemy's hands these negroes, when able-bodied, are of the last importance. Without them the batteries could not have been erected, at least for many weeks. As a military question it would seem to be a measure of necessity to deprive their masters of their services. How can this be done? As a political question and a question of humanity can I receive the services of a father and mother and not take the children? Of the humanitarian aspect I have no doubt; of the political one I have no right to judge. . . .

Very respectfully, your obedient servant,
B. F. BUTLER,[1]

WASHINGTON, May 30, 1861.

MAJOR-GENERAL BUTLER:

SIR: Your action in respect to the negroes who came in your lines from the service of the rebels is approved.

The department is sensible of the embarrassment which must surround officers conducting military operations in a state by the laws of which slavery is sanctioned. The government cannot recognize the rejection by any state of its federal obligations nor can it refuse the performance of the federal obligations resting upon itself. Among these federal obligations, however, none can be more important than that of suppressing and dispersing armed combinations formed for the purpose of overthrowing its whole constitutional authority. While therefore you will permit no interference by the persons under your command with the relations of persons held to service under the laws of any state, you will, on the other hand, so long as any state within which your military operations are conducted is under the control of such armed combinations, refrain from surrendering to alleged masters any persons who may come within your lines. You will employ such persons in the service to which they may be best adapted, keeping an account of the labor by them performed, of the value of it, and of the expense of their maintenance. The question of their final disposition will be reserved for future determination.
SIMON CAMERON,
Secretary of War. [2]

General Dix, at Baltimore, on August 25, 1861, wrote to General McClellan as follows:

HEADQUARTERS DEPARTMENT OF PENNSYLVANIA,
BALTIMORE, MD., August 25, 1861.

MAJ.-GEN. G. B. MCCLELLAN,
Commanding Army of Potomac.

GENERAL: Early this morning three negro men came to Fort McHenry representing themselves to be runaway slaves from Anne Arundel County. I declined to receive them into the fort on the ground that I could neither harbor them as fugitives from service nor arrest them for the purpose of restoring them to their

---

[1] War of Rebellion, vol. 1, series 2, p. 754.
[2] War of Rebellion, vol. 1, series 2, p. 754.

masters. In a former letter I stated the view I take in regard to my duty in such cases, and having no instructions from the government I acted on it and directed the negroes to leave the fort.

I am, very respectfully, your obedient servant,
[JOHN A. DIX,]
Major-General Commanding.[1]

Colonel Harvey Brown, commanding at Fort Pickens, department of Florida, wrote Assistant Adjutant-General Townsend at Washington on June 22, 1861, as follows: "I shall not send the negroes back, as I will never be voluntarily instrumental in returning a poor wretch to slavery, but will hold them subject to orders."[2]

General T. W. Sherman wrote the Adjutant-General from Port Royal, South Carolina, on December 15, 1861:

GENERAL L. THOMAS,
Adjutant-General U. S. Army, Washington, D. C.

SIR: For the information of the proper authorities and for fear lest the government may be disappointed in the amount of labor to be gathered here from the contrabands, I have the honor to report that from the hordes of negroes left on the plantations but about 320 have thus far come in and offered their services. Of these the quartermaster has but about sixty able-bodied male hands, the rest being decrepit and women and children. Several of the 320 have run off. Every inducement has been held out to them to come in and labor for wages and money distributed among those who have labored. The reasons for this apparent failure thus far appear to be these:

First. They are naturally slothful and indolent and have always been accustomed to the lash, an aid we do not make use of.

Second. They appear to be so overjoyed with the change of their condition that their minds are unsettled to any plan.

Third. Their present ease and comfort on the plantations as long as their provisions will last will induce most of them to remain there until compelled to seek our lines for subsistence.

Although comparatively few have thus far come in it is therefore probable that in time many will, and if they are to be received and taken care of some provision should be made to cover them. They are a prolific race and it will be found that for every able-bodied male there will be five to six females, children and decrepit. It is really a question for the government to decide what is to be done with the contrabands.

Very respectfully, your obedient servant,
T. W. SHERMAN,
Brigadier-General Commanding.[3]

---

[1] War of Rebellion, vol. 1, series 2, p. 766.
[2] War of Rebellion, vol. 1, series 2, p. 755.
[3] War of Rebellion, vol. 1, series 2, p. 785.

The following confidential letter will show with what hesitating policies the negro question was being treated and indicates the embarrassment of the President in dealing with it:

[Confidential.]   HEADQUARTERS OF THE ARMY,
               WASHINGTON, July 16, 1861.

BRIGADIER-GENERAL MCDOWELL, *Commanding, &c.*

SIR: The general-in-chief desires me to communicate to you that he has received from the president of the United States a second note dated to-day on the subject of fugitive slaves in which he asks: "Would it not be well to allow owners to bring back those which have crossed" the Potomac with our troops? The general earnestly invites your attention to this subject, knowing that you with himself enter fully into his excellency's desire to carry out to the fullest all constitutional obligations. *Of course it is the general's wish the name of the president should not at this time be brought before the public in connection with this delicate subject.*

     I remain, very respectfully, your obedient servant,
                SCHUYLER HAMILTON,
          Lieutenant-Colonel and Military Secretary.[1]

Thus we see that an officer in Florida positively refused without orders to return negroes to slavery. And yet we find that about the same time such orders were sent to General McDowell with the sanction of the president.

On January 7, 1862, in his instructions to General Burnside, who was about to embark with the navy on an expedition along the southern coast, General McClellan cautioned him that in making any proclamation to "say as little as possible about politics or the negro. Merely state that the true issue for which we are fighting is the preservation of the Union and upholding of the laws of the general government, and stating that all who conduct themselves properly will as far as possible be protected in their persons and property."[2]

But it soon became apparent that it was practically impossible to hold the slaves back or prevent their coming, and to drive them out of camp and away from protection and support meant starvation in some cases and in others their restoration to families whose heads were in active rebellion, with arms in their hands, fighting the very soldiers who were engaged in restoring to them their slaves.

Secretary of War Cameron, on December 6, 1861, very clearly put the situation before Congress, as follows:

---

[1] War of Rebellion, vol. 1, series 2, p. 760.
[2] War of Rebellion, vol. 1, series 2, p. 798.

It is already a grave question what shall be done with the slaves abandoned by their owners on the advance of our troops into Southern territory, as at Beaufort district of South Carolina. The number left within our control at that point is very considerable and similar cases will occur. What shall be done with them? Can we afford to send them forward to their masters to be by them armed against us or used in producing supplies to sustain the Rebellion? Their labor may be useful to us. Withheld from the enemy it lessens his military resources and withholding them has no tendency to induce the horrors of insurrection even in the rebel communities. They constitute a military resource, and being such, that they should not be turned over to the enemy, is too plain to discuss. Why deprive him of supplies by a blockade and voluntarily give him men to produce them?

The disposition to be made of the slaves of rebels after the close of the war can safely be left to the wisdom and patriotism of Congress. The representatives of the people will unquestionably secure to the loyal slaveholders every right to which they are entitled under the constitution of the country.

SIMON CAMERON,
Secretary of War. [1]

The Congress was not indifferent to the exigencies nor unmindful of the anomalous position the army was being placed in by being called upon to return negroes to slavery. A resolution was introduced in the House of Representatives and adopted on December 23, 1861, and on March 13, 1862, it was enacted into law as an army regulation. The resolution was as follows:

Resolved, That the committee on military affairs be instructed to report to this house a bill for the enactment of an additional article of war for the government of the army whereby the officers in the military service of the United States shall be prohibited from using any portion of the forces under their respective commands for the purpose of returning fugitives from service or labor, and providing for the punishment of such officers as may violate said article by dismissal from the service.[2]

SLAVES MUSTERED IN AS UNITED STATES SOLDIERS.

General Hunter had established a hold upon the coast of South Carolina. He took the bull by the horns, and not only set the negroes at work, but organized them into companies and armed them. This called for an inquiry from Congress, through Secretary Stanton, to which General Hunter replied in a characteristic letter. Hunter was a trained soldier, a stern, fearless, and uncompromising patriot, who saw farther into the causes and purposes of the Rebellion than many others of that day. His letter[3] is a valuable contribution to the con-

---

[1] War of Rebellion, vol. 1, series 2, p. 783.
[2] War of Rebellion, vol. 1, series 2, p. 791.
[3] War of Rebellion, vol. 1, series 2, p. 820.

flicting sentiment of the period on the relations of the slaves to the war, and is good reading at this time. It is as follows:

HEADQUARTERS DEPARTMENT OF THE SOUTH,
PORT ROYAL, S. C., June 23, 1862.

HON. EDWIN M. STANTON,
Secretary of War, Washington, D. C.

SIR: I have the honor to acknowledge the receipt of a communication from the adjutant-general of the army, dated June 13, 1862, requesting me to furnish you with the information necessary to answer certain resolutions introduced to the House of Representatives June 9, 1862, on motion of the Hon. Mr. Wickliffe, of Kentucky, their substance being to inquire:

1. Whether I had organized or was organizing a regiment of "fugitive slaves" in this departments?
2. Whether any authority had been given me from the war department for such organization; and
3. Whether I had been furnished by the war department with clothing, uniforms, arms, equipments, etc., for such a force?

Only having received the letter covering these inquiries at a late hour on Saturday night I urge forward my answer in time for the steamer sailing to-day (Monday), this haste preventing me from entering as minutely as I could wish upon many points of detail such as the paramount importance of the subject calls for. But in view of the near termination of the present session of Congress and the widespread interest which must have been awakened by Mr. Wickliffe's resolutions, I prefer sending even this imperfect answer to waiting the period necessary for the collection of fuller and more comprehensive data.

To the first question therefore I reply that no regiment of "fugitive slaves" has been or is being organized in this department. There is, however, a fine regiment of persons whose late masters are "fugitive rebels"—men who everywhere fly before the appearance of the national flag, leaving their servants behind them to shift as best they can for themselves. So far indeed are the loyal persons composing this regiment from seeking to avoid the presence of their late owners that they are now one and all working with remarkable industry to place themselves in a position to go in full and effective pursuit of their fugacious and traitorous proprietors.

To the second question I have the honor to answer that the instructions given to Brig.-Gen. T. W. Sherman by the Hon. Simon Cameron, late secretary of war, and turned over to me by. succession for my guidance, do distinctly authorize me to employ all loyal persons offering their services in defense of the Union and for the suppression of this Rebellion, in any manner I might see fit or that the circumstances might call for. There is no restriction as to the character or color of the persons to be employed or the nature of the employment—whether civil or military —in which their services should be used. I conclude therefore that I have been authorized to enlist "fugitive slaves" as soldiers, could any be found in this department. No such characters, however, have yet appeared within view of our most advanced pickets—the loyal slaves everywhere remaining on their plantations to welcome us, aid us, and supply us with food, labor and information. It is the masters who have in every instance been the "fugitives," running away from loyal slaves and loyal soldiers, and whom we have only partially been able to see—

chiefly their heads over ramparts or rifle in hand dodging behind trees in the extreme distance. In the absence of any "fugitive-master law" the deserted slaves would be wholly without remedy had not the crime of treason given them the right to pursue, capture and bring back those persons of whose protection they have been thus suddenly bereft.

To the third interrogatory it is my painful duty to reply that I have never received any specific authority for issues of clothing, uniforms, arms, equipments and so forth to the troops in question. My general instructions from Mr. Cameron to employ them in any manner I might find necessary, and the military exigencies of the department and the country being my only but in my judgment sufficient justification. Neither have I any specific authority for supplying these persons with shovels, spades and pickaxes when employing them as laborers, nor with boats and oars when using them as lightermen; but these are not points included in Mr. Wickliffe's resolution. To me it seemed that liberty to employ men in any particular capacity implied with it liberty also to supply them with the necessary tools, and acting upon this faith I have clothed, equipped and armed the only loyal regiment yet raised in South Carolina.

I must say, in vindication of my own conduct, that had it not been for the many other diversified and imperative claims on my time and attention, a much more satisfactory result might have been hoped for, and that in place of only one, as at present, at least five or six well-drilled, brave and thoroughly-acclimated regiments should by this time have been added to the loyal forces of the Union.

The experiment of arming the blacks, so far as I have made it, has been a complete and even marvelous success. They are sober, docile, attentive and enthusiastic, displaying great natural capabilities for acquiring the duties of a soldier. They are eager beyond all things to take the field and be led into action, and it is the unanimous opinion of the officers who have had charge of them that in the peculiarities of this climate and country they will prove invaluable auxiliaries, fully equal to the similar regiments so long and successfully used by the British authorities in the West India Islands.

In conclusion I would say it is my hope—there appearing no possibility of other re-enforcements, owing to the exigencies of the campaign in the Peninsula—to have organized by next fall, and to be able to present to the government, from 48,000 to 50,000 of these hardy and devoted soldiers.

Trusting that this letter may form part of your answer to Mr. Wickliffe's resolutions,

I have the honor to be, most respectfully, your obedient servant,

D. HUNTER,
Major-General, Commanding. [1]

It thus will be seen, by gradual and inevitable progressive steps, thousands of negro slaves became free and were so recognized before the immortal proclamation of universal freedom. From slavery to

---

[1] No one can fail to admire the bold frankness of this letter and the obviously practical view of the situation taken by General Hunter. It will be recalled that many eminent men in the South advocated arming the slaves in defense of the Rebellion—most remarkable, indeed, as it would have been asking the slaves to fight for the privilege of having their fetters more strongly riveted upon them.

the proud position of a United States soldier, an honored defender of the Union, was indeed a remarkable transformation and a most striking departure from the earlier reception given to fugitive slaves.

The organization of negro companies and regiments to aid in the preservation of the government which was then protecting them and their families in the enjoyment of their liberty, and whose former masters were in the armies of the Rebellion, seeking to destroy that government, was justifiable on principles of international law, of self-preservation, and on the part of the slaves was as an acknowledgment of a reciprocal obligation due for the protection and freedom bestowed upon them. And when once enlisted as soldiers, they became entitled to the same protection from our government, should they become prisoners of war, taken in honorable battle, as any other of our prisoners.

And this brings me to one of the causes for the breaking off of the general exchange of prisoners which had theretofore taken place under the cartel.

The rebel congress passed an act outlawing any white officer who when taken prisoner was in command of negro troops and prescribing as penalty the fate of a felon. The negro troops themselves were to be restored to their masters or put to hard labor. This brutal and barbarous policy was to some extent enforced. In some instances negro troops and their officers were shown no quarter when captured and were murdered in cold blood. The Fort Pillow massacre will be recalled. The right of exchange was denied them, officers were ignominiously treated, and the enlisted men were, as at Andersonville, put to work on fortifications or other defensive work, were treated with great severity,—at times punished by whipping,—and at no time and in no instance given recognition as soldiers. When this policy became known to the Federal authorities a most vigorous protest was sent through the officers of exchange; threats of retaliation were made, and, pending the settlement of the question upon a basis that would accord equal treatment to all United States prisoners of war, general exchanges, which had been going on under the cartel, ceased.

TEE NEGRO AS A SOLDIER.

In a very interesting and instructive lecture delivered at Boston by Brigadier-General Andrew S. Burt, U. S. A., retired, on December 12, 1910 and published in the New York *Evening Post* December 17, 1910, he shows what splendid soldiers the negroes made and how valuable their services became in the struggle to maintain the Union; and that now, in time of peace and in garrison duty, they have shown themselves to be model soldiers. There were 187,000 negroes enlisted during the Civil War, many more than most people realize. I quote:

They participated in 213 battles and engagements, and never permitted the Union colors to be dishonored by cowardice or treachery.... The glorious achievements of the negro soldiers in the war for independence were forgotten in the second war with Great Britain, and when they drove back General Packenham, and kept him out of New Orleans in 1812, it was hailed as a new discovery of the military capacity of our people.

When the Civil War came on, it was not until the second year of that death-grapple that the negro soldiers were permitted to enlist and then on half-pay; but before the terrible struggle was concluded they had written a new chapter in heroism and one which will never perish. Their brilliant achievements at Forts Wagner and Olustee, Fort Hudson and Milliken's Bend, made them welcome into the flower of the army—the Army of the Potomac—in the closing months of those bloody conflicts in front of Richmond and Petersburg. In the battles of Wilson's Wharf, Deep Bottom, Chapin's Farm, and Hatcher's Run they won for themselves immortal glory. On May 24, 1864, Gen. Fitzhugh Lee, then in the prime of youthful vigor, at the head of 4,000 dismounted Confederate cavalry, attacked Wilson's Wharf, defended by two negro regiments under Gen. Wild, but the chivalry of the South was compelled to retire precipitously before the desperate counter, charges of the negroes.

A government that would withhold its protection from such men and such of its defenders would be unworthy fighting for. It cannot for a moment be admitted that our government was wrong in the stand it took upon this issue. It would have been a dastardly betrayal of its duty to defenders of the Union to have yielded its position and conceded to the rebel government the right to treat our officers as felons and enslave our soldiers. It is cowardly and atrocious at this day to attribute blame to our government for the wanton cruelties to prisoners at Andersonville, in its stand taken with reference to colored troops and their officers, the justice and humanity of which no one not blinded by hatred and prejudice can gainsay.

But this was not the only ground on which our government justified its action, though in itself all-sufficient. Exchanges were proceeding without serious interruption, although, as the rebel commissioner, Ould, said in March, 1863, they were sending to us miserable wretches and receiving some of the best material he ever saw. The facts are very clearly stated in a report made to the secretary of war by General Hitchcock, our commissioner of exchange. His statement of the case will be received with that confidence in its truth and fairness which his high rank, his known uprightness of character, his devotion

Monument Erected by the State of Connecticut.

THE EXCHANGE OF PRISONERS.   451

to the cause of the Union, and his familiarity with the subject must inspire. His report to the secretary of war covers the whole ground, and is a most convincing vindication of the course taken by our government, and is a complete defense of General Grant's attitude in dealing with the subject of exchange, and should be carefully read.[1]

SUSPENSION OF THE CARTEL—REASONS THEREFOR.

WASHINGTON CITY, D. C., November 22, 1865.
HON. EDWIN M. STANTON, *Secretary of War.*

SIR: I have the honor to submit the following statement as my general report for the current year on the subject of the exchange of prisoners of war; in doing which I find it necessary to revert to some facts of a precedent date in order that the subject may be better understood.

At an early period of the Rebellion a cartel for the exchange of prisoners was agreed upon in conformity with the authority of the president, as communicated to General Dix by the secretary of war in the following despatch, which contains on its face an important limitation, carefully guarding against any recognition of the rebel government, the object having expressly in view the humane purpose of extending relief to prisoners of war:

WAR DEPARTMENT, WASHINGTON CITY, July 12, 1862.
MAJ.-GEN. JOHN A. DIX, Fort Monroe.

The president directs me to say that he authorizes you to negotiate a general exchange of prisoners with the enemy.

You will take immediate measures for that purpose, observing proper caution against any recognition of the rebel government and confining the negotiation to the subject of exchange. The cartel between the United States and Great Britain has been considered a proper regulation as to the relative exchange value of prisoners.   EDWIN M. STANTON, *Secretary of War.*

The agreement, signed by General Dix on the part of the government, and General Hill on the part of the rebels, was duly announced in public orders by authority dated war department, adjutant-general's office, Washington, September 25, 1862, a copy of which is hereunto annexed.

So long as the cartel for exchange of prisoners was respected in the South it was faithfully observed by the government, and there is no doubt that its faithful execution would have been continued by the government until the end of the war, unless properly revoked by competent authority, if the rebel authorities had not most distinctly violated its terms, under circumstances, indeed, of great aggravation.

The first indication on the part of the rebels of a disposition to disregard the cartel became public through a message by Jefferson Davis to the rebel congress, in which, after alluding to the proclamation of the president announcing emancipation, he makes use of the following language: "I shall, unless in your wisdom you deem some other course more expedient, deliver to the several state authorities: all commissioned officers of the United States that may hereafter be captured by our forces in any of the states embraced in the proclamation, that they may be

[1] War of Rebellion, vol. 8, series 2, p. 799.

dealt with in accordance with the laws of those states providing for the punishment of criminals engaged in inciting servile insurrection." [1]

This announcement of Mr. Davis was made January 12, 1863, and received the modified approval of the rebel congress, as shown in the following sections of an act approved May 1, 1863, to wit: [2]

Sec. 4. That every white person, being a commissioned officer, or acting as such, who, during the present war, shall command negroes or mulattoes in arms against the Confederate States, or who shall arm, train, organize, or prepare negroes or mulattoes for military service against the Confederate States, or who shall voluntarily aid negroes or mulattoes in any military enterprise, attack, or conflict in such service, shall be deemed as inciting servile insurrection, and shall, if captured, be put to death, or be otherwise punished at the discretion of the court.

Sec. 5. Every person, being a commissioned officer or acting as such in the service of the enemy, who shall during the present war excite, attempt to excite, or cause to be excited, a servile insurrection, or who shall incite, or cause to be incited, a slave to rebel, shall, if captured, be put to death, or be otherwise punished at the discretion of the court.

Sec. 7. All negroes and mulattoes who shall be engaged in war or be taken in arms against the Confederate States, or shall give aid or comfort to the enemies of the Confederate States, shall when captured in the Confederate States, be delivered to the authorities of the state or states in which they shall be captured, to be dealt with according to the present or future laws of such state or states. [3]

When the message just referred to became known to the president, he saw at once the necessity of meeting it, and gave instructions to retain such rebel officers as might be captured, in order to be in a position to check the rebel government and restrain the execution of its avowed purpose, in violation of the cartel.

This proceeding, initiated by the rebel government in violation of the cartel, ultimated in the cessation of exchanges, which, as the history of the matter shows, became unavoidable, and was entirely due to the rebel government.

Coincident with the proceedings with regard to the exchange of prisoners of war, the rebels inaugurated a system of seizing unoffending citizens of the United States and subjecting them to maltreatment, in various ways, in order to effect a particular object, which became apparent when a demand was made for their release. For this purpose quite a number of citizens of Pennsylvania were carried into captivity by General Lee when he penetrated into that state in 1863.

When a demand was made for the release of this class of prisoners it was met by a most positive declaration that no citizen prisoner in rebel hands should be released unless the government would enter into an agreement with the rebel authorities not to arrest any one on account of his opinions or on account of his sympathy with the rebel cause; and this declaration was repeated again and again by the rebel authorities whenever the government demanded the release or exchange of said citizen prisoners.

It will require but the slightest glance at this subject to convince any one of the utter impossibility of acquiescing in the demand of the rebel authorities as a prerequisite to the release of the citizens thus held in bondage. Such an agree-

---

[1] The state laws made such offense a felony with a felon's punishment.
[2] Joint resolution. See War of Rebellion, vol. 5, series 2, p. 940.
[3] The rebel congress attached the death penalty for the alleged crime of commanding negro troops in aid of the suppression of the Rebellion.

ment on the part of the United States would have been a virtual acknowledgment of the independence of the rebel government, and would have foreclosed all proceedings of the United States against all persons whomsoever, engaged in the crime of treason and rebellion. It was absolutely impossible to acquiesce in the demand of the South on that point, and this is the reason why this class of prisoners was beyond the reach of the government, except through the power of its armies, which finally settled the entire question by putting an end to the entire Rebellion itself.

At the commencement of the cessation of exchanges the rebels held a few prisoners of war over and above the number of rebels held by the government, but the capture of Vicksburg and Port Hudson threw the balance largely the other way; and, as the prisoners captured by General Grant and General Banks were left in the South on parole, the rebel authorities determined to make use of them, not merely in violation of the cartel, but in open contempt of the laws of war. They first ordered that body of men to be assembled at a place called Enterprise, in Mississippi, on pretense of facilitating measures for their supplies, but in reality for the different purpose, as we are now compelled to believe, of throwing them into the rebel ranks to meet the anticipated conflict which, it was seen, was near at hand in East Tennessee, and which accordingly took place at the memorable battles of Chiokamauga and Chattanooga; in which battles many of the captured prisoners, paroled in the South by Generals Grant and Ranks, took part without having been duly exchanged, although the rebel authorities made an *ex parte* declaration of exchange in their favor without proper authority, which was protested against by the United States.

It must be understood that the rebels might at any time have resumed the system of exchange agreed upon in the cartel by receding from the assumed right of disposing of captured Union officers as required in the act passed by the rebel congress, before alluded to, and agreeing to the exchange of colored troops; but they would never agree to acknowledge the right of colored troops to treatment due to prisoners of war; and as the government of the United States had exercised the right of employing colored troops as a part of the force against the rebels, their claim to such protection as the government could give was one which did not admit of discussion.

When the rebels discovered that the suspension of exchanges was operating against them they resorted to the horrible expedient of subjecting the prisoners they held to starvation and exposure to the elements, without the protection of quarters or tents, after first robbing them of their money and most of their clothing, and without regard to seasons or their inclemencies, in the hope of forcing the government into a system of exchanges which should have the effect not only of leaving in their hands all the colored prisoners they had taken, but of throwing into their ranks the entire body of prisoners held by the Federal power, then greatly in excess over the prisoners held by the rebels.[1] This fact is proved by the declarations of the Richmond papers at the time when a few exchanges were made, that the rebel agent, Colonel Ould, had not sent over the lines the number of prisoners equivalent to those received, but only a proportionate number, the ratio being

[1] Andersonville and its horrors justify the view thus taken of the treatment given Union prisoners.

determined by Colonel Ould, in view of the number of prisoners held in the South against those held in the North, the claim to hold in reserve the colored prisoners in the South having never been abandoned. This fact was further established by the official records of the commissary-general of prisoners, by which it appeared that, after sending several boatloads of exchanged prisoners each way, the rebels were constantly falling in debt. Upon observing this fact, and noticing the publications in Richmond, I called upon the commissary-general of prisoners for a tabular statement of the result, and the statement showed an indebtedness in our favor of over 500 men, which statement was handed to the secretary of war, who thereupon directed an order to General Grant to assume the entire control of the matter of exchanges, with authority to give such orders as he might think proper on the subject. General Grant at once reverted to first principles, and directed that Colonel Ould or the rebel authorities should be notified that colored troops should be treated as prisoners of war when captured; and, as the rebels were not willing to accede to this requirement, no further exchanges were made.

Upon the receipt at the war department of the first intelligence of the inhuman treatment to which our prisoners were subjected at Richmond,[1] the secretary of war, without a moment's hesitation, gave instructions to our agent of exchange at Fort Monroe to send forward supplies from the public stores for their relief, and large quantities of provisions and clothing were accordingly sent for distribution among the prisoners, and every possible effort was made to afford that sort of relief, even at the hazard of large portions of the supplies being wasted, or, what was worse, misappropriated to the benefit of our enemies, who, it soon appeared, made use of these supplies for their own advantage, leaving our prisoners still to suffer.[2] But even this did not destroy the hope of the secretary that some portion of the supplies would, at least, be permitted to reach its destination, and the orders to send that relief were left in force until the rebels themselves, shamed, perhaps, by the scandalous state of things, then likely to become historical, refused to receive any further supplies through the agents of the government.

In the mean time the sympathies of friends in the North were naturally awakened, and large quantities of supplies of all kinds were sent to Fort Monroe, whence they were forwarded for the relief of the prisoners at Richmond; but the moment they passed beyond the control of our agents they fell into the hands of the most unprincipled and shameless scoundrels that ever disgraced humanity. It is in proof that large quantities of supplies furnished by the benevolence of the North for the relief of suffering humanity in Southern prisons were piled up in sight of the objects for whose relief the supplies were sent, but beyond the line of the prison guards; and while the prisoners were thus in sight of their own boxes they were not only forbidden to touch them but compelled to witness depredations upon them by the guards themselves, who feasted upon their contents, leaving the victims of war a prey to that merciless barbarism which will make one of the darkest pages in the history of a rebellion which will itself remain an astonishment to all posterity for its almost causeless existence.

Many have supposed that it was in the power of the government to afford relief to the prisoners in the South by a resort to retaliatory treatment of rebel prisoners

---

[1] This was in 1863, and before Andersonville Prison was created.

[2] This was true at Andersonville.

in the North. It is difficult to meet a suggestion of this kind by an appeal to the instincts of civilized humanity, because the mere suggestion supposes the absence of those instincts, and implies a willingness to see the public sentiment degraded into barbarism, which would have put the nation itself on the footing of savages, whose only excuse for their barbarity is their ignorance and their exclusion from the civilized world. The day must come when every true American will be proud of the reflection that the government was strong enough to crush the Rebellion without losing the smallest element of its humanity or its dignity, and stands before the world unimpeached in its true honor and glory.

It may be observed that no one imagined, prospectively, the horrors that came to light at Andersonville, the full enormity of which only became known at the close of the military events which ended the war. Had they been known when at their worst the government would have had the choice of but three measures: First, the rebel prisoners might have been sent South, we to receive in return such white prisoners as they might have held, leaving the colored troops to their fate; second, a resort to retaliatory measures; or lastly, for the country to wage war with increased zeal to bring it to a legitimate end. No man can doubt which of these plans the Northern people would have approved if submitted to them, and the government only assumed to represent the people in the question.[1]

It ought to be mentioned here, as a beautiful illustration of the moral sublime, that among the many memorials, some of them very numerously signed, which reached the war department, praying for relief to Federal prisoners suffering in the South, in nearly all of them there was an express protest against a resort to retaliation. And what was the real effect of the barbarity upon the prisoners in the South? Certainly it was most deplorable and shocking upon individuals for the time being; but no one whose moral eyes are open can fail to see that it became in many ways a signal step, under the guidance of Providence, for bringing the rebel cause to destruction. It strengthened the feeling in the North in favor of warlike and determined measures against the Rebellion; it sent thousands into the army who took the field resolutely determined to punish the authors of a great crime against humanity. The enemy might almost literally have felt that it is "a terrible thing to fall into the hands of the living God."

An erroneous opinion appears to have been circulated, more or less widely, with regard to the number of colored Federal troops who fell into the hands of the enemy, which makes it important to state that the actual number thus exposed to injurious treatment was very much greater than has been commonly supposed. This will sufficiently appear from the fact that, on the 21st of January, 1865, Lieut. O. O. Poppleton, adjutant of the 111th U. S. Colored Infantry, addressed a letter, dated at Nashville, Tenn., to Major-General Butler, in the following words, to wit:

I have the honor to enclose herewith a copy of a Mobile paper (rebel) containing, over the signature of D. H. Maury, Major-General, C. S. Army, the names of 569 soldiers belonging to the One hundred and sixth, One hundred and tenth, and One hundred and eleventh Regiments of U. S. Colored Infantry, who were taken prisoners by a force of the enemy under Maj.-Gen. N. B. Forrest at Athens

[1] After having read this scathing indictment of the rebel authorities and this exposure of their perfidious conduct, can the reader view with complacency the attempt to charge upon General Grant the responsibility for the sufferings at Andersonville?

and Sulphur Branch Trestle, Ala., on the 24th and 25th of September, 1864, and placed at work on the defenses of Mobile, Ala., by order of the rebel authorities. Lieut. William T. Lewis, adjutant One hundred and tenth U. S. Colored Infantry has a paper of later date than this, containing the names of nearly 300 more soldiers of the same command also at work on the defenses of Mobile.

This is an official report from the adjutant of the One hundred and eleventh Regiment Colored Infantry, showing that there were then, in January, 1865, at work on the fortifications about Mobile 569 colored soldiers belonging to three regiments only; and a reference is made to another paper as being at that time in the hands of another officer, an adjutant also of one of those regiments, embracing the names of "nearly 300 more soldiers of the same command," making in all over 800 colored soldiers of the United States army at work under rebel officers on the fortifications around Mobile alone.

When the government determined to employ colored troops in its armies the principle was recognized that they were entitled to protection; and accordingly it was claimed that the class of troops referred to should receive such treatment from the army as was due to other troops employed in the defense of the government. The assertion of this principle did not depend upon the number of colored troops who might at any time be in the hands of the enemy. Every consideration of honor and humanity required the assertion of this principle as due to the troops employed in the service of the government; and accordingly, in various communications, when the subject required it, the government agents connected with the duties of exchange of prisoners invariably set forward the principle. But this did not prevent the exchange of prisoners, man for man and officer for officer; the difficulty on this subject was due, first, to the message of Mr. Davis to the rebel congress, already referred to, declaring his purpose to deliver to Southern state authorities such white Union officers as might be captured for trial under state laws unknown alike to the laws of Congress and to the laws of war, as also stated above, in the fact the rebel authorities released from the obligations of their parole a number of rebel prisoners and placed them in their ranks without exchange.

During the brief period prior to the capture of Vicksburg the rebels held more prisoners of war than the government; but after the date of that event the case was reversed, and from that time forward the government made every effort to obtain exchanges—man for man and officer for officer—but without avail, the rebel authorities persistently resisting applications for exchange unless the government would release all rebel prisoners, after they had openly violated the cartel themselves, claiming that the government should deliver to them all rebel prisoners, while they on their part declared their purpose of withholding from exchange such colored prisoners as they might have in their possession.

It is important to observe here that while this controversy was pending we actually held in prison depots in the North about 70,000 prisoners of war, over and above which we had a just and valid claim for more than 30,000 men who had been captured and paroled in the South, chiefly at Vicksburg and Port Hudson, and who had never been properly exchanged; making in all at least 100,000 men whom the rebel authorities wished to draw from us in exchange for about 40,000 of the white troops of the United States, the effect of which would have been to throw into the army of General Lee an effective force of about 60,000 or

70,000 men, in fine health and able in all respects to be put immediately into the field against General Grant's army, or with which General Lee might have obtained a disposable force of some 50,000 or more men for the purpose of entering the states of the North, and thereby possibly compelling General Grant to raise the siege of Richmond or expose the Northern states to devastation by the enemy.[1]

It was the desire of the rebel agent of exchange to avoid making special exchanges, in the hope of drawing from us the whole of the rebel prisoners of war we held in return for inferior numbers held by the enemy. To accomplish that object the rebel commissioner or agent of exchange not only declined to make exchanges on equal terms in any considerable number, but refused to make special exchanges, except under extraordinary influences brought to bear by the friends of interested parties; and in repeated instances the rebel agent took care to indorse upon special applications the express declaration that he neither made nor countenanced such applications.

In consequence of this state of things, and while there was a hope of effecting general exchanges, only a few applications of a special character were forwarded over the lines; but when it became apparent that a general exchange could not be effected I received your instructions to forward all special applications for exchange, in order, as you explained the purpose at the time, to afford every possible opportunity to extend relief to as many individuals as might have the good fortune to secure Southern influences for that object; and great numbers of such applications were sent over the lines, most of which, however, were never heard from afterward.

Another fact I beg to state in connection with this subject, as a further illustration of the efforts of the department to extend relief to Federal officers and soldiers imprisoned South, to wit: The rebel authorities resorted to the system of placing individuals in close confinement, in alleged retaliation for what on our side was but the legitimate operation of the laws of war in the punishment of spies and other offenders against those laws. In the endeavor to afford relief in a particular case of this kind the rebel agent seized the opportunity of proposing the mutual release and exchange of all prisoners in close confinement, although at that time we had no rebel prisoners thus confined except by due course of law. This proposition was manifestly unfair, and a recovered letter from the rebel agent has shown that he knew it was so. Nevertheless, the proposition was accepted by your orders, and although it effected the release of some criminals belonging to the rebel army, it carried relief to a number of Federal officers and soldiers in the South, who thus obtained liberation, the concession on your part having had in view the relief it promised, and to some extent, effected, in favor of a few of our officers and soldiers.

The recovered letter alluded to was dated at City Point, March 17, 1863, and addressed to Brigadier-General Winder, in the following words:

SIR: A flag of truce boat has arrived with 350 political prisoners, General Barrow and several other prominent men amongst them. I wish you to send me at 4 o'clock Wednesday morning all the military prisoners (except officers) and all the political prisoners you have. If any of the political prisoners have on hand proof enough to convict them of being spies, or having committed other offenses

[1] Does not General Hitchcock make perfectly clear that the course our government pursued was the only one consistent with national honor and the plainest principles of justice?

which should subject them to punishment, so state opposite their names. Also, state whether you think, under all circumstances, they should be released. The arrangement I have made works largely in our favor. We get rid of a set of miserable wretches and receive some of the best material I ever saw. Tell Captain Turner to put down on the list of political prisoners the names of Edward G. Eggling and Eugenia Hammer-mister. The president is anxious they should get off. They are here now. This, of course, is between ourselves. If you have any female political prisoner whom you can send off safely to keep her company I would [like] you to send her. Two hundred and odd more political prisoners are on their way. I would be more full in my communication if I had time.

Yours truly,

Ro. Ould, *Agent* of *Exchange*.[1]

It should be noticed in this report that when the subject, of exchange became embarrassing, because of the unwillingness of the enemy to exchange man for man, he demanding all of the rebel prisoners we held in exchange for the white prisoners held by him, Major-General Halleck, by the direction of the secretary of war, made an effort to obtain exchanges on equal terms. For this purpose he sent a flag of truce to General Lee, then in force on the Rapidan, and 'proposed that species of exchange; but General Lee declined to act upon the proposition, and answered, evidently in accordance with instructions from Richmond, that the subject of exchange was in the hands of a commissioner and he preferred to have nothing to do with it.

As a further effort to obtain this class of exchanges the secretary authorized various commanders, distant from Washington, to open communications with the enemy, and to effect exchanges whenever they could be made on equal terms. In the midst of these difficulties I was painfully impressed with the impossibility of effecting exchanges on equal terms with Judge Ould; and having understood that General Butler was of the opinion that, if empowered to do so, he could make exchanges, I addressed a note to the secretary of war and proposed to withdraw from the position of commissioner of exchange in favor of any officer who could accomplish so desirable a result; upon which, however, the secretary did not see fit to make an order. A few days after this I was sent for from the war office, where I found the secretary in conversation with General Halleck on the subject of exchanges. The secretary then informed me that General Butler had expressed the opinion above stated, and that several members of Congress had expressed a similar opinion with regard to General Butler's ability to effect exchanges, if empowered to do so. I at once said to the secretary, "If General Butler is of opinion that he can make exchanges, I think, sir, you had better let him try." He then said that it was his wish that I should go to Fort Monroe and confer upon General Butler the requisite power by his authority, and he thereupon wrote, in the presence of General Halleck and myself, the following order:

War Department, Washington, December 16, 1863.

Major-General Hitchcock, *Commissioner of Exchange of Prisoners.*

General: You will proceed immediately to Fort Monroe and take any measures that may be practicable for the release, exchange, or relief of U. S. officers and soldiers held as prisoners by the rebels.

You are authorized and directed to confer with Major-General Butler on the subject, and may authorize him, as special agent, commissioner, or otherwise, to

---

[1] This is the letter I discovered and introduced at the trial—N. P. C.

procure their release or exchange upon any just terms not conflicting with principles on which the department has heretofore acted in reference to the exchange of colored troops and their officers, and not surrendering to the rebels any prisoners without just equivalents. You may, if you deem it proper, relieve General Meredith and direct him to report to the Adjutant-General for orders.
Yours truly,
EDWIN M. STANTON, *Secretary of War.*

Within half an hour after the writing of the above order I was on my way to Fort Monroe, and on the morning of the 17th of December I reported to General Butler. After stating the limitations under which he would be authorized to make exchanges I requested him to prepare instructions for himself, giving him the authority he desired, in accordance with the orders of the secretary, stating that when ready I would sign them in the name of or with the authority of the secretary. In two or three hours thereafter I called again upon General Butler and made the instructions he had prepared official. They contained the following paragraphs:

You are hereby instructed not to make any exchange which shall not return to you man for man, officer for officer, of equal rank with those paroled and sent forward by yourself, regarding of course for motives of humanity in the earlier exchanges; those officers and men on either side who have been longest confined.

Colored troops and their officers will be put upon an equality in making exchanges, as of right, with other troops.

You are permitted, in conducting the exchange, to waive for the present the consideration of the questions of parole and excess now pending between the Confederate belligerent authorities and this government, leaving them untouched as they stand until further interchange of views between those authorities and yourself.

The above instructions to General Butler will show precisely the animus of the secretary of war on the subject of exchanges. He was perfectly willing and anxious to make exchanges, man for man, officer for officer, and gave, as must be seen, the fullest power to General Butler to effect those exchanges. General Butler in his conversation with me expressed no desire to have any other instructions or powers committed to him, and appeared to be very confident of his ability to accomplish the desired result, giving me in detail many reasons for that confidence. I returned to the city of Washington, and within a few days the public prints announced General Butler's first attempt to make exchanges and the result. General Butler sent a boatload of prisoners under a flag of truce to City Point, where they were offered for a like number of Federal troops. It appears that when this was reported to the rebel government violent indignation was expressed by the rebel authorities on the alleged ground that General Butler was an outlaw by the proclamation of Mr. Davis, and that it was an insult to employ him to accomplish any result requiring any sort of intercourse between him and the rebel authorities; but it was concluded that, inasmuch as a certain number of their troops were actually within their lines as returned prisoners of war, they should be received, and a like number of Federal prisoners should be exchanged for them; but notice was given to our agent that no more prisoners would be received in that manner, and it was reported at the time that General Butler was informed that a flag of truce even should not protect him within the rebel lines.

When this was reported in Washington the president himself, in the presence of the secretary of war, declined to give any order on the subject, unwilling to concede to the rebels the right to dictate what agents this government should employ in its public business; but it was plain to be seen that the real object of the rebel authorities was to avoid making equal exchanges of man for man and officer for officer, their purpose. being to deliver to us, as before stated, only a proportionate number of prisoners held by them as against those held by us; and because General Butler's instructions required the exchange of man for man, made the employment of General Butler in the business of exchange the pretext for refusing those equal exchanges. This was evident, because, in point of fact, General Butler did not personally appear in the business—that is, he did not accompany the flag of truce—and if there had been any disposition on the part of the rebels to make equal exchanges they knew those exchanges would be made through the agency of another officer and not personally by General Butler; and thus the real purpose of the rebels becomes manifest, their object being to draw from us all of their own troops in our hands, giving us in exchange only such white troops of the Federal forces as they might hold.

After this experiment by General Butler matters remained in suspense for some time, no exchanges being made.

At length two Federal officers who had escaped from rebel prisons gave me their opinion, in this city, that if we would send to City Point for exchange a body of 300, 400, or 500 rebel officers, demanding a like number in return, the feeling in the South, they believed, would be such that the rebel authorities would not dare to refuse the exchange; and if that succeeded, they would not dare thereafter to refuse to exchange private soldiers. I thought very well of this suggestion and addressed a note to the secretary of war, communicating it and recommending its trial. The secretary at once accepted the suggestion and directed General Canby, then on duty in the war office, to require General Butler to make that trial. But General Butler thought proper to send a mixed boatload of officers and men.

Here, then, was another effort to make exchanges on equal terms. The enemy accepted the prisoners sent over the lines but did not return a like number. This fact was publicly stated by the newspapers at Richmond and was confirmed by official reports received at the office of General Hoffman, the commissary-general of prisoners, after several boatloads had passed. When the purpose of the rebel commissioner became apparent, not to make exchanges man for man but only in proportionate numbers, the fact, with the evidence for it, was submitted to the secretary of war, and then it was, as stated above, that General Grant was instructed to take the subject under his own supervision, with the result already alluded to.

After General Butler took charge of the duties in connection with the exchange of prisoners I was not officially advised of his proceedings, because he, being of senior rank to myself, made no reports to me; but in August, 1864, there was published in the journals of the day a letter, over the signature of General Butler, of the highest importance in connection with this subject. No official copy was furnished to me and I have never seen the letter of Judge Ould to which it refers, the authenticity of which, however, is sufficiently vouched in the letter of General Butler, which commences, addressed to Judge Ould, in these words:

SIR: Your note to Major Mulford, assistant agent of exchange, under date of the 10th of August, has been referred to me. You therein state that Major Mulford has several times proposed to exchange prisoners respectively held by the two belligerents, officer for officer and man for man; and that the offer has also been made by other officials having charge of matters connected with the exchange of prisoners, and that this proposal has been heretofore declined by the Confederate authorities. That you now consent to the above proposition and agree to deliver to you (Major Mulford) the prisoners held in captivity by the Confederate authorities, provided you agree to deliver an equal number of officers and men.

This letter, cited by General Butler, from Colonel Ould shows conclusively by whom the proposition for an equal exchange was originally made. It shows also that it had been repeatedly made by the government and had been as repeatedly refused by the rebel authorities.

The matter had been placed in General Butler's hands, and he answered Judge Ould's letter, asking some preliminary explanations, which I believe were never made, and the opportunity of a final action upon Judge Ould's letter was thus cut off by himself.

The reasons that induced General Butler's action may no doubt be seen, in part at least, in the letter he addressed to Judge Ould, which was published in the journals of the day. I have never heard that the matter was referred to the secretary of war, and have never understood that he gave any order in the premises.

We learn from General Butler's letter that Judge Ould did not reach his conclusion in reference to Major Mulford's proposition until a period of eight months had elapsed.

It is impossible to approach the subject of this report without being solemnly impressed by a sense of the horrors inflicted upon the prisoners of war in the South; but in making the report I have felt imperatively called upon to confine myself to facts connected immediately with the subject of exchanges, leaving inferences to be drawn by others. I attach hereto such official letters and telegraphic despatches as have either originated in my office or have reached me as may throw light upon the subject of this report.

I have the honor to be, very respectfully, your obedient servant,

E. A. HITCHCOCK,
Maj. Gen. of Vols. Commissioner for Exchange of Prisoners.

On October 20, 1863, General Halleck at Washington wrote General Grant, then at Louisville, Kentucky, after General Rosecrans' defeat at Chicamauga:[1]

It is now ascertained that the greater part of the prisoners paroled by you at Vicksburg (July 4th), and General Banks at Port Hudson, were illegally and improperly declared exchanged, and forced into the ranks to swell the rebel numbers at Chickamauga. This outrageous act, in violation of the laws of war, of the cartel entered into by the rebel authorities, and all sense of honor, gives us a lesson in regard to the character of the enemy with whom we are contending. He neither regards the rules of civilized warfare, nor even his most solemn engagements. You may, therefore, expect to meet in arms thousands of unexchanged prisoners released by you and others on parole, not to serve again until duly exchanged.

[1] General Sherman's Memoirs.

The inscription on the Wirz monument, giving a quotation from General Grant's letter of August 18, 1864, was placed there for the obvious purpose of fixing upon him the responsibility for the sufferings of our soldiers. It is due to the truth of history and to General Grant's memory that the correspondence, of which his letter forms a part, should be read. It will thus appear that General Grant was consistently adhering to a policy which would not only have been base treachery to the negro troops to abandon, but, as he points out, inhumanity to our soldiers in the field. The correspondence is as follows:

CITY POINT, VA., August 18, 1864.

MAJOR-GENERAL BUTLER, *Commanding, etc.*

I am opposed to exchanges being made until the whole matter is put on a footing giving equal advantages to us with those given to the enemy. In the mean time I direct that no flags of truce be sent to the enemy nor any arrangements or agreements entered into with him without my first being fully advised of what is being done and yielding my consent to it.

The steamer New York will not be permitted to proceed to Aiken's landing until I receive a report of the full object of the mission and the load she now has on board.

U. S. GRANT,
Lieutenant-General.[1]

BUTLER'S HEADQUARTERS, August 18, 1864, 7 P. M.

LIEUTENANT-GENERAL GRANT:

Telegram received. No exchange has been made or will be made which will give the enemy any advantage. To show that my views and the lieutenant-general's are in exact accordance, I will send letter written to General Hitchcock to-day upon this subject with the indorsements referred to.

I have exchanged nobody but wounded men since the first of May, except surgeons, non-combatants, and a few cases of special exchange. A full report will be made to the lieutenant-general of all that was intended to be done in the matter.

BENJ. F. BUTLER,
Major-General, Commissioner of Exchange.

[Enclosure.]

HDQRS. DEPT. OF VIRGINIA AND NORTH CAROLINA,[2]
IN THE FIELD, VA., August 18, 1864.

MAJOR-GENERAL HITCHCOCK,
  Commissioner of Prisoners, Washington, D. C.

GENERAL: I have one or two indorsements from you which say in substance that "it is desirable to have all our prisoners exchanged." I agree [to] that if all means all. But does the government intend to abandon the colored troops? That is

---

[1] War of Rebellion, vol. 7, series 2, p. 606. General Hitchcock's report shows very clearly why it would have been inhumanity to our soldiers in the field to have yielded to the rebel demands.

[2] War of Rebellion, vol. 7, series 2, p. 606.

the only question now pending. All others can be settled. From my conversation with the lieutenant-general he does not deem it desirable to move from the position taken on that question. I will again call the subject to the attention of Mr. Ould and obtain an interview with him if possible.

I have the honor to be, very respectfully, your obedient servant,

BENJ. F. BUTLER,
Major-General and Commissioner of Exchange.

CITY POINT, VA., August 18, 1864.

MAJOR-GENERAL BUTLER, *Commanding, etc.*

I am satisfied that the object of your interview had the proper sanction and therefore meets with my entire approval. I have seen from Southern papers that a system of retaliation is going on in the South which they keep from us and which we should stop in some way. On the subject of exchange, however, I differ from General Hitchcock. *It is hard on our men held in Southern prisons not to exchange them, but it is humanity to those left in the ranks to fight our battles.* Every man we hold, when released on parole or otherwise, becomes an active soldier against us at once either directly or indirectly. If we commence a system of exchange which liberates all prisoners taken, we will have to fight on until the whole South is exterminated. If we hold those caught they amount to no more than dead men. *At this particular time to release all rebel prisoners North would insure Sherman's defeat and would compromise our safety here.*

U. S. GRANT,
Lieutenant-General. [1]

When General Hood moved up the Chattanooga Valley upon Resaca, which was held by a small force under Colonel Clark R. Weaver, he sent a demand for surrender October 12, 1864, in which he stated that if the commander yielded without resistance "all *white* officers and soldiers will be paroled in a few days. If the place is carried by assault, no prisoners will be taken." In the face of the "no quarter" threat of General Hood, Colonel Weaver replied, much as General Corse had done shortly before at Altoona: "In my opinion I can hold this post. If you want it come and take it."

This incident is referred to as illustrating that the policy not to treat negro troops or their officers as prisoners of war was then in force.

HEADQUARTERS ARMIES OF THE UNITED STATES, October 2, 1864.[2]

GENERAL R. E. LEE, *Commanding Army of Northern Virginia.*

GENERAL: Your letter of yesterday proposing to exchange prisoners of war belonging to the armies operating in Virginia is received. I could not of a right accept your proposition further than to exchange those prisoners captured within

---

[1] War of Rebellion, vol. 7, series 2, pp. 606, 607. Note.— The inscription on the Wirz monument is that portion of General Grant's letter marked in italics.

[2] War of Rebellion, vol. 7, series 2, p. 909.

the last three days and who have not yet been delivered to the commissary-general of prisoners. Among those lost by the armies operating against Richmond were a number of colored troops. Before further negotiations are had upon the subject I would ask if you propose delivering these men the same as white soldiers?

Very respectfully, your obedient servant,

U. S. GRANT,
Lieutenant-General.

General Lee declined to decide the question, and the Richmond authorities adhered to their refusal to treat captured negro soldiers as prisoners of war.

Looking back upon this painful controversy, the surviving veterans of the Union army, as well as all fair-minded persons must feel that our government took the only course open to it consistent with national honor and national safety.

Colonel John McElroy, of Washington City, editor and proprietor of the *National Tribune,* an able and prolific writer of Civil War subjects, was a prisoner at Andersonville. In my quest for information upon certain points, I sought an interview with him. I do not offer his opinions and statements of fact as evidence, but coming from one so well informed, and himself an eye-witness of many things to which his attention was invited, I do not hesitate to commend them to the careful consideration of the reader. Those who know Colonel McElroy will accept his statements as importing verity.

CHIPMAN.—Did you ever hear of a report made by the Confederate Congress upon the treatment of prisoners—a public document printed by the Confederate government? Mr. Brooks, past department commander, told me last night that he had seen such a report and had once had it, but I had never heard of it.

McELROY.—The only things that I know were the report made by the inspector-general, C. S. A., and the proceedings of the grand jury of Sumter County, Georgia.

C.—Where are the proceedings of that grand jury to be found?

McE.—I do not know where to find them, but I think I made reference to it in my book on Andersonville and must have had it in an authoritative form at that time.

C.—You were about to tell me some important facts that I should not overlook. Will you state them?

McE.—The main element in the whole consideration of the prison question is the fact that the exchange definitely stopped July 4, 1863. Prior to that time there had been a cartel in operation by which prisoners were to be paroled and reported to their respective sides. This cartel was abused in ways that any one can see it would be, and finally modified to an agreement that all captures should be reduced to possession and delivered to the respective authorities at City Point or Vicksburg. After the capture of Vicksburg and Port Hudson, General Pemberton applied to

THE EXCHANGE OF PRISONERS. 465

General Grant for a guard to take the prisoners outside his lines and deliver them to the Confederate authorities. General Grant refused this from reasons of good policy, the strongest being his belief that as a large portion of Pemberton's forces had been drawn from the country which was now in our possession, if these men were turned loose they would go back home and take no further part in the war. In fact, General Grant furnished transportation to all those who wished to go back to their homes.

C.—Well, then, what Pemberton was seeking to bring about was to have his soldiers return to the army and not return to their homes?

McE.—Yes. We all know that where the rebel armies advanced they conscripted every able-bodied man and put him into the ranks. This was the recognized policy of the Southern Confederacy and the real reason of many of their forward movements. Naturally, these men, if they could escape and go back home, living under the protection of the Union army would remain out of the Confederacy. At the battle of Gettysburg Lee captured a great mass of Union prisoners and made a proposition to Meade to exchange them, but Meade pointed out this clause in the cartel compelling the reduction to possession, and then properly refused to receive them, they not having been reduced to possession since Lee was at least one hundred miles from his own lines. A great many of the prisoners—in fact the great body of them—understood this clearly and refused to accept the paroles which were offered them. There is a statement that General Couch, then commanding the district of the Susquehanna, not understanding the situation, did accept the paroles of a number of the Pennsylvania militia. There had come in at the same time the question of the colored troops to complicate the situation. Immediately upon the formal announcement of the policy of the government to accept negro troops the so-called Confederate government had responded with a law that the enlisted men among the colored troops who were captured should be returned to their lawful owners, and if these could not be found they should be sold at auction, while their white officers should be turned over to their several states to be dealt with according to the laws punishing those who incite servile insurrection. In one notable instance, that of Milliken's Bend, a number of captured officers were formally hanged, *in terrorem,* in front of General Dick Taylor's army at Richmond, Louisiana, which paraded to witness the execution. These officers were in command of colored troops. You will find in the war records that General Grant addressed a note to General Dick Taylor asking if this were true. Taylor denied it, in spite of the fact that it had been witnessed by the entire division and the deaths of the officers who were so executed. This may be found in the Rebellion records under proper index. You will find in the "Volunteer Army Register" for 1865 (part 8, p. 152), published from the adjutant-general's office, the following note in the casualties of the 5th U. S. Colored Heavy Artillery: "Capt. Corydon Heath, taken prisoner June 7, 1863, and murdered by the enemy at or near Monroe, La., June —, 1863." Possibly Captain Wm. A. Skillen, Sidney, Ohio, if alive, can furnish some facts relative to this.

C.—Did that policy with regard to exchange continue as it stood at that period?

MONUMENT ERECTED BY THE STATE OF MAINE.

McE.—Our government insisted that all the men who wore its uniform and bore its commissions should be treated alike as prisoners of war, and consequently those who had been taken in the operations subsequent to July 1, 1863, were held in possession in abeyance to this discussion. The year 1863 ended with the Confederates having about 15,000 Union prisoners in their possession, and this government having about 25,000 Confederates in its prisons. A still further complication arose on account of an order by Robert Ould, the Confederate commissioner of exchange, declaring all those prisoners captured at Vicksburg and Port Hudson to be duly exchanged. The Confederate secretary of war then ordered them into the field, and it is estimated that 10,000 of them fought us at Chickamauga when Jefferson Davis made the crowning effort to crush Rosecrans.

C.—Had Ould any authority for making this declaration?

McE.—The only basis that I can remember for this action was the alleged acceptance of paroles of Pennsylvania militia by General Couch. I should have said that in the cartel as modified there was a provision for exchange of man for man and the parole of the surplus. This question of surplus immediately began to be of interest from the preponderance of prisoners in our hands and with Davis and Ould, insisting that they would not exchange man for man unless the surplus in our hands was paroled. My remembrance is that on February 11, 1864, General B. F. Butler, who had been appointed to the command of the department of Virginia and North Carolina, and became ex-officio commissioner of exchange, owing to City Point being in his department, wrote a letter in which he said: "For the sake of humanity let us return these men to their homes. Leaving the questions in dispute in abeyance, I will send up to-day 500 prisoners for which you can return a like number, and this can continue until all these men are returned to their homes." My remembrance is that perhaps two or three squads of 500 each were so exchanged, when Davis interposed with this demand that the surplus be paroled. As the operations which began on both fronts May 4, 1864, advanced, the disparity in the number of prisoners reduced to possession on both sides increased daily in favor of the government. According to the letter sent to the House of Representatives by Secretary Stanton, enclosing one from Major-General Hitchcock, then commissioner of exchange, we had by that time accumulated 220,000 rebels in our prisons, while they had 127,000 of us. This must have been in February or March of 1865. This disparity bears upon the question of paroling the surplus. This great disparity in our favor made Grant, who I am convinced stood firmly all the time for an exchange of man for man, determined against the paroling of the surplus, which would put at least 100,000 fresh, well-fed, well-rested troops in front of his army or that of Sherman, and he very properly said that hard as the lot of us prisoners was it was much better that we should suffer than to have such a prolongation of the war as would result. This, then, will explain the letter which Grant wrote in August, 1864, part of which is inscribed on the monument to Wirz.

C.—What was the relative condition of the prisoners, federal and rebel, as to numbers in the beginning of 1864?

McE.—My remembrance from statements which I saw in the public press is that the year 1863 ended with the Confederates having 15,000 Union soldiers in prison, while the government had 25,000 Confederate soldiers. According to the report of General Hitchcock, the year 1864 ended with the government having 220,000 Confederate prisoners, while the Confederates had 127,000 Union soldiers in prison.

C.—Andersonville was established February 24, 1864. I wish you would give me generally a statement as to the different places where our prisoners were at that time imprisoned, and approximately the number at the different prisons when Andersonville became an establishment.

McE.—When it was seen that there was to be a prolonged discussion over the question of exchange, it was decided to be too dangerous to have such a body of prisoners in Richmond, and besides there was a difficulty in supplying them, as the resources of the Confederacy were taxed to supply Lee's army. There were also small bodies of prisoners at Danville, Virginia, and Cahaba, Alabama, east of the Mississippi. The prisoners west of the Mississippi were collected in a prison called Camp Ford, at Tyler, Texas. Therefore it was decided to build a general prison remote from our armies, and Andersonville, Georgia, 120 miles south of Atlanta, and in the midst of the unsettled piny regions, was selected as a general prison in which all of the prisoners east of the Mississippi could be gathered. This prison was opened when not yet finished, February 24, 1864, I being in the first squad of about 800 which marched in from Richmond.

C.—At that time how many prisoners were in Richmond?

McE.—There must have been about 10,000. When we entered the prison we found that it consisted of a heavy stockade 1,100 feet north and south and 700 feet east and west, extending on both sides of a small creek which ran through a swamp in the center. We were turned in there without shelter or cooking utensils. Seeing that we had to stay there, we immediately began erecting shelters. Everything inside of the prison had been cut off except two pine trees in the southwest corner. We took poles from the rank growth in the swamp and bending them over like a wagon-cover fastened them together with grapevines and briars and then thatched them with the long-leaf-pine leaves, which we took from the trees which had been cut down. This was an exhibition of ingenuity which much astonished the Confederates. The records show that March, 1864, ended with 4,603 prisoners inside this stockade. This may be found in the American Cyclopœdia (vol. 1, p. 474). We got along tolerably well, though this ground was not larger than what is usually taken for the camp of a full regiment of infantry, of 1,000 men. The end of April saw this number increased to 9,577. The operations on both fronts began May 4, 1864, and by the end of the month there had been gathered into the prison 18,454.

C.—You mean the operations in the Wilderness?

McE.—I mean the operations in the Wilderness and the advance on Atlanta. The end of June saw 26,867 there. There was then not room enough to lie down, and the Confederate authorities increased the prison by a stockade enclosing about seven acres more on the north side of the creek. The original area had been estimated at thirteen acres, and it was now increased to twenty-odd acres. This was reduced, however, by a dead-line twenty feet from the stockade running around the whole interior of the stockade. By the end of July there were 31,678 in the prison, and at the end of August there were 31,693. I think the record for August is too low. We were divided into squads of ninety, three squads to a detachment, which were numbered consecutively. These detachments were kept full. One day, through curiosity, I counted 137 sergeants coming up to draw rations for their detachments. This would show 36,990. Atlanta fell September 1st, and brought our armies into such close proximity that it was necessary to remove the prisoners. There had been some efforts made by the cavalry of Sherman's army to reach and release us before Atlanta fell. The dispersion of the prisoners began September 7th, I going out with the first squad to Savannah. It is my impression that probably 8,000 or 10,000 were sent to Savannah in September. Everybody who was able to walk was taken out of the prison before the middle of the month, and September ended with only 8,218 in the prison. Those not taken to Savannah were sent to Florence, South Carolina. In October those of us at Savannah were sent to a new stockade built near Millen, at the junction of the railroad from Augusta to Savannah with that running to Macon, where we remained until some time in November, when Sherman having begun his march the prison at Millen was broken up. We were taken back to Savannah, and some 5,000 of us sent down the coast to a place called Blackshear. There 1,000 of us were taken out and paroled and sent back to Savannah, where it was represented to us we should meet our ships and be exchanged. A partial exchange had been declared of 10,000 sick. As Sherman had passed on, leaving Andersonville behind him, the three or four thousand at Blackshear were taken across the country back to Andersonville and remained there until the close of the war. The squad in which I was was taken to Charleston and thence to Florence, where we found 8,000 or 10,000 of our former companions in Andersonville. In the mean time the prisoners who were being taken from the armies in Virginia were collected at Salisbury. Salisbury had been maintained as a prison from the beginning of the war, but no considerable number confined there until late in 1864. Those of us in Florence remained there until toward the close of the war. As Sherman advanced a large portion of them were taken out of Florence and sent up into North Carolina, but there was no safe place for them up there, and all were finally delivered to our authorities at Wilmington, North Carolina, after the capture of that place. The few thousand who went back to Andersonville had their number augmented somewhat by the prisoners captured by Hood, and were kept there until the 17th of April, 1865, when the last of them were sent to Florida and reached our lines in front of Jacksonville.

C.—On several of the monuments erected in the cemetery is inscribed the statement "Death before dishonor," apparently the sentiment which arose in the prison times. I wish you would explain that.

McE.—All the time that we were in prison there were Confederate emissaries among us trying to incite discontent with our government and encouraging the sending of delegations to Washington demanding our exchange. The bulk of the prisoners understood the situation very clearly and refused to join in these demonstrations and clubbed severely men who were promoting them.

C.—There is to be found in the Rebellion records a paper signed by a large number of sergeants of squads petitioning the government and setting forth the condition there to some extent, which was carried to Washington I believe by permission of the rebel authorities. What is your recollection about that? Did it represent anything like the universal sentiment?

McE.—It never was allowed to be generally known. As an illustration of that, while we were in prison at Savannah, the rebels came into the stockade and had a stand erected for speaking. When the stand was completed a shyster from New York, a very despicable fellow, named Pete Myers, got up on the stand and began a harangue to the effect that our government had abandoned us, had denounced us as "coffee-boilers" and "blackberry-pickers," and he proposed that we pass a resolution to the effect that if we were not exchanged within thirty days that we would join the Confederate army. That was at Savannah, after we had left Andersonville, and immediately the whole camp was thrown into a fever of excitement, and had it not been for the Confederates guarding Myers and helping him at once out of the prison he would have been beaten to death. At Millen, where I was a sergeant of a squad, an order came in for us to make out a list of all the men whose terms of service had expired and who had been born abroad. Thinking that it might help us to exchange I made out my list, making every man foreign born. The next thing was an order for all those whose names appeared on the list to fall in. We were marched outside the prison, surrounded by a strong guard, when a man on a stump told us the old story of our government having abandoned us; that we had done our duty faithfully to it; that it was apparent to all of us that the Confederacy was about to succeed; and that if we would join its ranks we would receive the same treatment in bounty lands and other considerations that their soldiers were to get. Before he had finished his speech a sergeant named Tom Lynn sprang out in front of his detachment and ordered it to about face, and we all marched back into the prison. I remember the incident particularly, as the rebels were determined to punish us for it. We had with incomprehensible labor split off slabs and made shelters for ourselves. The guards followed us directly into the prison, drove us up into a corner, and began to destroy these shelters which we had erected. The feeling was very bitter, but the comrades stood firm.

C.—What was the physical condition of the prisoners when they left Richmond?

McE.—It was tolerably fair. Those who went from Belle Isle had been much reduced by the scanty fare and the inclement weather there, to which they had been exposed without shelter. Those of us who had been in the buildings in Richmond were in better condition.

C.—It is stated in excuse for the mortality at Andersonville, that the prisoners when brought there were on the verge of death, and that the mortality did not result from their treatment at Andersonville.

McE.—In reply to that I will say that of the 45,000 men who so much as set foot in Andersonville, in round numbers 14,000 died. The bulk of these men were active, fit-for-duty soldiers who had been taken either in battle or on picket or in some other active service. The worst part of Andersonville lasted only about four months. That is from the time of the great crowd coming in in the middle of May until the middle of September. During that time, one out of four of these strong, healthy, present-for-duty men died, without taking into account those who were broken down there and died while being removed to other prisons or in those prisons. My remembrance is that we would be put on the cars and ride for a day or night and when we got off every car would have men who had died. We would camp in the woods or some place and move on leaving dead men lying all around.

Those men have not been counted in the record of the mortality of Andersonville. I notice in the record in the American Cyclopædia that 149 died of gunshot wounds. This seems to me a great understatement. The orders were very stringent about approaching or touching the dead-line. The only water that came into the prison was from the creek which previously passed through the camps of the five or six thousand rebel guards, and further became polluted by passage through the swamp lying in the center of the prison. It seems to me that every day, and sometimes twice during the day, the guards would kill a man who was reaching up under the dead-line to get water less foul than that below.

C.—Colonel Chandler in his report concerning the prison management says that he heard no complaint as to the want of good drinking-water—that he inquired particularly of the soldiers if they had plenty, and so far as he could learn there was no complaint.

McE.—Those of us of the older prisoners immediately began digging wells, and some of these were dug down as deep as thirty feet in the clay, and we used water from these wells. The newer prisoners of course did not have these and had to drink water from the creek.

C.—Can you explain Providence spring?

McE.—I do not know anything about Providence spring of my own knowledge. It appeared in August. In the early part of that month I had made an effort to escape, and being barefoot at that time and running through the briars in the swamps, had hurt my feet so that I was unable to get around as I had formerly done, and I remained so lame that on September 7th, when we went out of the prison, I was still hobbling along with a stick. The spring broke out while I was in that condition, so I never saw it.

C.—Some criticism is made of the findings of the court as to the individual murders committed by Wirz, on the ground that names of parties and definite statements as to dates could not be given, and it is urged that convictions under such circumstances are wholly without foundation. What explanation can you give of the conditions existing there that would make it probable that men might be killed and witnesses who saw it not know personally the person who was killed?

McE.—You must remember that here were 30,000 or more men gathered from all the armies of the United States, coming in sometimes singly, sometimes in squads, and we did not know each other usually, more than the number of our regiments. For example, they all knew me as "Little Illinoy," as I belonged to an Illinois regiment. We were all in there in absolute barbarism. All that we wanted was to live until we could escape. There was no thought of records, organization, or anything, and we were all looking forward to the next day when we might either escape or be exchanged. I was engaged in digging tunnels and planning escape and getting what rations I could, and such things as that. The first man that I knew to be killed there was a poor half-witted German who we called "Sigel." This, it seems to me, was only a few weeks after we got into prison. Somebody had got hold of some biscuit that were moldy and had thrown them under the dead-line. Sigel came along and reached under the dead-line for them and was killed. I remember they came to me and said, "Let's go up there and look up that fellow that killed him. We may meet him later."

C.—Give your explanation of the condition of things that led up to the trial and execution of some of our own soldiers by their comrades.

McE.—While we were in Richmond there were a number of acknowledged thieves, criminals, and bounty-jumpers who had deserted to the rebel army. The rebels did not want them, but were holding them there. After we had been in Andersonville a few days they brought these men down and put them over on the south side of the creek to themselves, and they immediately began preying on us. These noted thieves stayed in a little bunch by themselves, and we older prisoners knew them. We had several fights with them, and confined ourselves after that to taking care of ourselves. We called these scoundrels "Raiders." I was in command of fifty men formed for our own protection in the southwest corner of the stockade. Great numbers of prisoners would come in, and a great many from the Army of the Potomac would bring in blankets, watches, and money, and these thieves would watch for them and rob them. I have known them to kill as many as three of our men in one of these fights. The great mass of the prisoners could not be made to understand that it was only a small body that was doing this robbing, and they thought that we were all thieves. Finally a man who was commissary-sergeant of Company M of my regiment, decided to put them down, and got Wirz's permission. At this time, when we were digging tunnels and making other efforts to escape, Wirz had put up a row of poles around the inside of the stockade and issued orders that any assembly of more than 100 men passing these poles would be the signal for the artillery opening upon them without warning. Sergeant Key got him to allow us to make a fight against these men, and assembled us to the number of about 500. The "Raiders" had a big tent which they had made of blankets taken from the other prisoners, and on the second of July we armed ourselves with clubs and went up and attacked them. There were about 400 or 500 of them, and we arrested about 125. Wirz agreed to take charge of these. Then Wirz said that he would not take care of so many, and we turned back all but a few. We found in the meanwhile that the camp had understood what we were doing and were with us, and when these men that were turned back came in they had to run the gauntlet, and several were killed. I remember one man particularly who was a well-known criminal. The fighting for the day was over, and I had gone up to my quarters at the end of the street on the north side, taking no part in the gauntlet running. A sailor, one of the worst of the criminals, cut his way through the gauntlet and started up the street toward me. I picked up my club. A man was standing there holding a rail, and just as the sailor came in front of him he dropped the rail across the back of his neck and killed him. The others were given as fair a trial as we could by a court-martial consisting of thirteen sergeants chosen from the new prisoners. All the men accused were brought before this court, where they had the benefit of counsel and were confronted by the witnesses of their crimes. The decision of the court was that six should be hanged, and this was carried out by us on the 11th of July, 1864, which resulted in introducing order into the camp and terrorizing these criminals, who had before held the camp in terror. Wirz simply gave us permission to carry out the execution, but had his whole garrison under arms with the artillery turned upon us. He brought the condemned in to us and told us that it was none of his business; that we had tried them and condemned them ourselves,

THE EXCHANGE OF PRISONERS.

and he washed his hands of the whole affair. Subsequent developments showed that every one of these men whom we had hanged had a long record of criminality both in the Confederate army and in our own. They were men who had deserted back and forth from the Confederate army to the Northern army.

The men merely rotted to death in Andersonville. We got nothing to eat but corn meal without salt, and no meat. The men literally rotted with what we called "scurvy," and what is now known as pellagra, due to insufficient quantity of one kind of food. The record of the rebel surgeon-general says that there were 10,000 men at one time in there dying of scurvy. The rebel medical department applied to the rebel secretary of war for a commission to go to Andersonville and study the effect of crowding such an immense number of men together without sufficient food in such foul surroundings, but my remembrance is mostly of scurvy. It would begin usually with a man's ankles stiffening and his legs swelling. Then his gums would protrude beyond his lips, his teeth would drop out, ulcers would appear all over him, and he would simply rot to death.

CHAPTER XVI.

ANDERSONVILLE CEMETERY MADE BEAUTIFUL—EXPEDITION IN SPRING OF 1865 TO PROVIDE FOR ITS PERMANENT CARE—REPORT OF CAPTAIN JAS. M. MOORE, U. S. A.—IMPORTANT AND INTERESTING REPORT OF CLARA BARTON, FOUNDER OF THE RED CROSS SOCIETY, TO THE AMERICAN PEOPLE—REPORT OF DORENCE ATWATER, WHO KEPT THE DEATH REGISTER, TO THE RELATIVES OF THE MARTYED DEAD—INTERESTING LETTER OF SUPERINTENDENT OF CEMETERY-INSCRIPTIONS ON STATE MONUMENTS—PATRIOTIC WORK DONE BY WOMAN'S RELIEF CORPS AT PRISON PARK—A PARTING WORD WITH THE READER BY THE AUTHOR—BILL PENDING IN CONGRESS TO APPROPRIATE MONEY BY GOVERNMENT TO ERECT MONUMENT TO CONFEDERATE NAVY—DISCUSSION IN UNITED STATES SENATE—VIEWS EXPRESSED IN PUBLIC PRESS—DANGEROUS STEP FOR GOVERNMENT TO THUS GIVE OFFICIAL SANCTION TO REBELLION AND TREASON.

> Peaceful he sleeps, with all our rights adorn'd,
> Forever honor'd and forever mourn'd—*Illiad*.
> And here were men (coequal with their fate),
> Who did great things, unconscious they were great.—*Lowell*.

There are eighty-four national cemeteries in the United States under the supervision of the quartermaster's department of the army, in which are buried 350,000 soldiers.

Not all, but most of these contain the bodies of soldier-patriots who gave up their lives during the Civil War that this government of ours should not perish. The major part of these cemeteries are nearby or on the battlefields where their tenants fell in defense of the nation's flag and nation's honor. If their spirits visit the scenes of their valor and could speak to us, would they name a spot for the resting-place of their earthly remains of more glorious memory or more to be preferred than the hallowed ground where they so nobly died? We may well conceive, too, that they would behold with pride and satisfaction the loving tenderness with which the nation they helped to save is protecting, beautifying, and making forever sacred these last resting-places of its patriotic dead.

The spirits of the thirteen thousand martyrs at Andersonville Cemetery have not the satisfaction of feeling that their earthly bodies lie in some one of the great battlefields where in life they bravely fought, but they will find at Andersonville the assurance of their country's appreciation for their sufferings and sacrifices. All that art and nature can do to dispel the gloom and sadness which hung over that valley of despair in 1864, and to brighten and make attractive the resting-place of these heroes, is being done by our government; and thanks to the noble efforts of the Woman's Relief Corps, auxiliary of the Grand Army of the Republic, the prison grounds and ample surrounding area have been acquired as a national park, and by these patriotic women conveyed to the nation.

More than ordinary interest attaches to these grounds and I find satisfaction in giving such illustrations as I have been able to obtain showing how completely the scene has changed. I also feel quite sure that the reader will be glad of the opportunity to read the reports of an expedition promptly sent to Andersonville by the quartermaster-general, upon the order of the secretary of war, to take possession of the cemetery and initiate the necessary steps for its permanent improvement.

This expedition was under the direction of Captain Jas. M. Moore, assistant quartermaster United States army, with whom went Miss Clara Barton, widely known for her Red Cross work of mercy and charity during the Civil War, and Dorence Atwater, who had been a prisoner at Andersonville and had kept the death register. Each of these made a report of more than ordinary interest, which I am glad to include in this volume. Captain Moore's report is an official document addressed to the head of his department. Miss Barton's is semi-official, but is addressed to the people of the United States. Dorence Atwater's statement is rather the story of a personal experience, which would seem incredible as exhibiting a species of arbitrary power by our government of which he was the victim, and which can only be accounted for, if not justified, by some imperative necessity of which we can now but speculate. It is addressed to the surviving relatives of the martyred dead at Andersonville.

Miss Barton's account of the expedition, read in the light of the testimony found in this volume, shows how an observant and sympathetic mind can discover the true situation by *a priori* reasoning. She saw everywhere effects of which the cause could unerringly be traced.

The inscriptions on the monuments erected by state authority cannot fail to touch the hearts of all who read them.

REPORT OF THE EXPEDITION TO ANDERSONVILLE, GEORGIA, DURING THE MONTHS OF JULY AND AUGUST, 1865.

ASSISTANT QUARTERMASTER'S OFFICE, WASHINGTON, D. C., September 20, 1865.

GENERAL: In accordance with Special Orders No. 19, quartermaster general's office, dated June 30, 1865, directing me to proceed to Andersonville, Georgia, for the purpose of marking the graves of Union soldiers for future identification, and enclosing the cemetery, I have the honor to report as follows:

(Inscription)
LIZABETH A. TURNER
Past National President Woman's Relief Corps, Auxiliary to the
Grand Army of the Republic.
Life Chairman Andersonville Prison Board.
Died at Andersonville April 27, 1907.
Erected by the Woman's Relief Corps to Memorialize Her
Work in Hallowing These Grounds.

ANDERSONVILLE CEMETERY, AND CONCLUSION.

I left Washington, District of Columbia, on the 8th of July last for Andersonville, Georgia, via Savannah, with mechanics and material for the purpose above mentioned.

On my arrival at Savannah, I ascertained there was no railroad communication whatever to Andersonville—the direct road to Macon being broken, and that from Augusta, via Atlanta, also in the same condition. I endeavored to obtain wagon transportation, but was informed by the general commanding the department of Georgia that a sufficient number of teams could not be had in the state to haul one-half my stores; and, as the roads were bad, and the distance more than four hundred miles, I abandoned all idea of attempting a route through a country difficult and tedious under more propitious circumstances.

The prospect of reaching Andersonville at this time was by no means favorable, and nearly one week had elapsed since my arrival at Savannah. I had telegraphed to Augusta, Atlanta and Macon almost daily, and received replies that the railroads were not yet completed.

At length, on the morning of the 18th of July, the gratifying telegram from Augusta was received, announcing the completion of the Augusta and Macon road to Atlanta, when I at once determined to procure a boat and proceed to Augusta by the Savannah River.

The desired boat was secured, and in twenty-four hours after the receipt of the telegram alluded to, I was on my way with men and material for Augusta. On my arrival there I found the railroad completed to Macon, and that from Macon to Andersonville having never been broken, experienced little difficulty in reaching my destination, where I arrived July 25th after a tiresome trip, occupying six days and nights.

At Macon, Major-General Wilson detailed one company of the 4th U. S. cavalry and one from the 137 regiment U. S. colored troops to assist me. A member of the former company was killed on the 5th of August, at a station named Montezuma, on the Southwestern railroad.

The rolling stock on all the roads over which I traveled is in a miserable condition, and very seldom a greater rate of speed was attained than twelve miles an hour. At the different stations along the route the object of the expedition was well known, and not infrequently men wearing the garb of rebel soldiers would enter the cars and discuss the treatment of our prisoners at Andersonville; all of whom candidly admitted it was shameful, and a blot on the escutcheon of the South that years would not efface.

While encamped at Andersonville, I was daily visited by men from the surrounding country, and had an opportunity of gleaning their feelings towards the government; and with hardly an exception, found those who had been in the rebel army penitent and more kindly disposed than those who had never taken a part, and anxious again to become citizens of the country they had fought to destroy.

On the morning of the 26th of July, the work of identifying the graves, painting and lettering of head-boards, laying out walks, and enclosing the cemetery was commenced, and on the evening of August 16th was completed, with the exceptions hereafter mentioned.

The dead were found buried in trenches on a site selected by the rebels, about three hundred yards from the stockade. The trenches vary in length from fifty to one hundred and fifty yards. The bodies in the trenches were from two to three feet below the surface, and in several instances, where the rain had washd away the earth, but a few inches. Additional earth was, however, thrown upon the graves, making them of a still greater depth. So close were they buried, without coffins or ordinary clothing to cover their nakedness, that not more than twelve inches were allowed to each man; indeed, the little tablets marking their resting-places, measuring hardly ten inches in width, almost touch each other.

United States soldiers, while prisoners at Andersonville, had been detailed to inter their companions, and by a simple stake at the head of each grave, which bore a number corresponding with a similar numbered name upon the Andersonville hospital record, I was enabled to identify and mark with a neat tablet, similar to those in the cemeteries at Washington, the number, name, rank, regiment, company, and date of death of twelve thousand four hundred and sixty-one graves, there being but four hundred and fifty-one that bore the sad inscription "Unknown U. S. Soldier."

One hundred and twenty thousand feet of pine lumber were used in these tablets alone.

The cemetery contains fifty acres, and has been divided by one main avenue running through the center, and subdivided into blocks and sections in such a manner that, with the aid of the record, which I am now having copied for the superintendent, the visitors will experience no difficulty in finding any grave.

A force of men is now engaged in laying out walks and cleaning the cemetery of stumps and stones, preparatory to planting trees and flowers.

I have already commenced the manufacture of brick, and will have a sufficient number by the first of October to pave the numerous gutters throughout the cemetery; the clay in the vicinity of the stockade being well adapted to the purpose of brick-making.

Appropriate inscriptions are placed through the grounds, and I have endeavored, as far as my facilities would permit, to transfer this wild, unmarked, and unhonored graveyard into a fit place of interment for the nation's gallant dead. At the entrance gate, the words "National Cemetery, Andersonville, Ga.," designate this city of the dead.

On the morning of the 17th of August, at sunrise, the stars and stripes were hoisted in the center of the cemetery, when a national salute was fired, and several national songs sung by those present.

The men who accompanied me, and to whom I am indebted for early completion of my mission, worked zealously and faithfully from early in the morning until late at night, although suffering intensely from the effects of the sun. Unacclimated as they were, one after another was taken sick with the fever incident to this country, and in a brief period my force of mechanics was considerably lessened, obliging me to obtain others from the residents in different parts of the state.

All my men, however, recovered, with the exception of Mr. Eddy Watts, a letterer, who died on the 16th of July of typhoid fever, after a sickness of three weeks. I brought his body back with me, and delivered it to his family in this city.

Several of the 4th United States cavalry, detailed by General Wilson, died of the same fever shortly after joining their command at Macon.

ANDERSONVILLE CEMETERY, AND CONCLUSION.

Andersonville is situated on the Southwestern railroad, sixty miles from Macon. There is but one house in the place, except those erected by the so-called Confederate government as hospitals, officers' quarters, and commissary and quartermasters' buildings. It was formerly known as Anderson, but since the war the "ville" has been added.

The country is covered mostly with pines and hemlocks, and the soil is sandy, sterile and unfit for cultivation, and unlike the section of country a few miles north or south of this place, where the soil is well adapted to agricultural purposes, and cotton as well as corn are extensively raised. It is said to be the most unhealthy part of Georgia, and was probably selected as a depot for prisoners on account of this fact. At midday the thermometer in the shade frequently reaches one hundred and ten degrees and in the sun the heat is almost unbearable.

The inhabitants of this sparsely-settled locality are, with few exceptions, of the most ignorant class, and from their haggard and sallow faces the effects of chills and fever are distinctly visible.

The noted prison pen is fifteen hundred and forty feet long, and seven hundred and fifty feet wide, and contains twenty-seven acres. The dead-line is seventeen feet from the stockade, and the sentry boxes are thirty yards apart. The inside stockade is eighteen feet high, the outer one twelve feet, and the distance between the two is one hundred and twenty feet.

Nothing has been destroyed; as our exhausted, emaciated, and enfeebled soldiers left it, so it stands to-day, as a monument to an inhumanity unparalleled in the annals of war.

How men could survive as well as they did in this pen, exposed to the rays of an almost tropical sun by day and drenching dews by night, without the slightest covering, is wonderful.

The ground is filled with holes where they burrowed in their efforts to shield themselves from the weather, and many a poor fellow, in endeavoring to protect himself in this manner, was smothered by the earth falling in upon him.

A very worthy man has been appointed superintendent of the grounds and cemetery, with instructions to allow no buildings or structures of whatever nature to be destroyed, particularly the stockade surrounding the prison pen.

The stories told of the sufferings of our men while prisoners have been substantiated by hundreds, and the skeptic who will visit Andersonville, even now, and examine the stockade, with its black, oozy mud, the cramped and wretched burrows, the dead-line and the slaughter-house, must be a callous observer, indeed, if he is not convinced that the miseries depicted of this pen are no exaggerations.

I have the honor to be, general, very respectfully, your obedient servant,

[Signed] JAMES M. MOORE,
Captain and Assistant Quartermaster, U. S. Army.

Brevet Major-General M. C. MEIGS,
　Quartermaster-General, U. S. Army, Washington, D. C.

REPORT BY MISS CLARA BARTON.

REPORT OF AN EXPEDITION TO ANDERSONVILLE, GEORGIA, JULY, 1865, FOR THE PURPOSE OF IDENTIFYING THE GRAVES AND ENCLOSING THE GROUNDS OF A CEMETERY CREATED THERE DURING THE OCCUPANCY OF THAT PLACE AS A PRISON FOR UNION SOLDIERS IN REBEL HANDS.

To the People of the United States of America:

Having by an official invitation been placed upon an expedition to Andersonville for the purpose of identifying and marking the graves of the dead contained in those noted prison grounds, it is, perhaps, not improper that I make some report of the circumstances which induced the sending of such an expedition, its work, and the appearance, condition and surroundings of that interesting spot, hallowed alike by the sufferings of the martyred dead and the tears and prayers of those who mourn them.

During the search for the missing men of the United States army, begun in March, 1865, under the sanction of our late lamented President Lincoln, I formed the acquaintance of Dorence Atwater, of Connecticut, a member of the 2nd New York Cavalry, who had been a prisoner at Andersonville and Belle Isle twenty-two months, and charged by the rebel authorities with the duty of keeping the death register of the Union prisoners who died amid the nameless cruelties of the first named prison.

By minute inquiry I learned from Mr. Atwater the method adopted in the burial of the dead, and by carefully comparing his account with a draft which he had made of the grounds appropriated by the prison authorities, I became convinced of the possibility of identifying the graves simply by comparing the numbered post or board marking each man's position in the trench in which he was buried with the corresponding number standing against this name upon the register kept by Mr. Atwater, which he informed me was in the possession of the war department.

Assured by the intelligence and frankness of my informant of the entire truthfulness of his statements, I decided to impart to the officers of the government the information I had gained, and accordingly brought the subject to the attention of General Hoffman, commissary-general of prisoners, asking that a party or expedition be at once sent to Andersonville for the purpose of identifying and marking the graves and inclosing the grounds, and that Dorence Atwater, with his register, accompany the same as the proper person to designate and identify. The subject appeared to have not only been unheard, but unthought of, and from the generally prevailing impression that no care had been taken in the burial of our prisoners the idea seemed at first difficult to be entertained, but the same facts which had served to convince me presented themselves favorably to the good understanding and kind heart of General Hoffman, who took immediate steps to lay the matter before the honorable secretary of war, upon whom, at his request, I called the following day, and learned from him that he had heard and approved my proposition, and decided to order an expedition consisting of men and materials, under charge of some government officer, for the accomplishment of the object set forth in my request, and invited me to accompany the expedition in person, which invitation I accepted.

ANDERSONVILLE CEMETERY, AND CONCLUSION.

Accordingly, on the 8th of July, the propeller Virginia, having on board fencing material, headboards, the prison records, forty workmen, clerks and letterers, left Washington for Andersonville, under the command of Captain James M. Moore, assistant quartermaster U. S. army; Dorence Atwater and myself, via Savannah, Georgia, arriving at the latter place July 12th. Having waited at Savannah seven days and then resumed the journey by way of Augusta, Atlanta and Macon, the entire party reached its destination in safety about noon on the 25th of July.

We found the prison grounds, stockade, hospital sheds and the various minor structures almost in the same condition in which they had been evacuated; and care is taken to leave those historic monuments undisturbed so long as the elements will spare them.

There is not, and never was, any town or village at this place except what grew out of its military occupation. Andersonville station, on the railroad from Macon to Eufala, Alabama, was selected as a depot for prisoners, probably on account of its remoteness and possible security, and the prison itself, with the buildings which sprang up around it, constituted all there was of Andersonville.

The land around is broken and undulating, and at the time of the occupation was covered with forests, mostly of the long-leafed pine common to the uplands of the South. The bases of the hills are lined with oozy springs, which unite to form little rivulets, one of which winds sluggishly through each of the intervening valleys.

The original enclosure of nineteen acres was made in the unbroken woods, and the timber was only removed as it was wanted for the necessity of the prison. The enclosure was made in January, 1864, and enlarged during the summer to twenty-five and three-fourths acres, being a quadrangle of 1295 by 865 feet. The greatest length is from north to south, the ground rising from the middle towards each end in rather a steep, rounded hill, the northern one being at once the highest and of the greatest extent. A small stream, rising from springs a little to the westward, flows across it through a narrow valley filled with a compost washed down by the rains. The enclosing stockade is formed of pine logs, twenty feet in length, and about eight inches in diameter. This is again surrounded by two successive and precisely similar palisades—a portion of the last of which is gone. It seems never to have been completed. The two inner walls remain entire. Within the interior space, at a distance of about seventeen feet from the stockade, runs the famous dead-line, marked by small posts set in the ground, and a slight strip of pine boards set on the top of them. The gates, of which there are two, situated on the west side, were continuations of the stockade, inclosing spaces of thirty feet square, more or less, with massive doors et either end. They were arranged and worked on the principle of canal locks. Upon the inner stockade were fifty-two sentry boxes, raised above the tops of the palisades and accessible by ladders. In these stood fifty-two guards with loaded arms, so near that they could converse with each other. In addition to these, seven forts mounted with field artillery commanded the fatal space and its masses of perishing men.

Under the most favorable circumstances, and best possible management, the supply of water would have been insufficient for half the number of men who had to use it. The existing arrangements must have aggravated the evil to the utmost extent. The sole establishments for cooking and baking were placed on the bank

(Inscription.)

This tablet is erected in commemoration of the patriotic work of the Woman's Relief Corps, auxiliary to the Grand Army of the Republic, in the preservation and improvement of this historic site comprising 87 acres, of which 72.5 acres were acquired in 1896 by deed of gift from the Grand Army of the Republic of Georgia and 14.5 acres were acquired by the Woman's Relief Corps by purchase to complete the tract. The Woman's Relief Corps was incorporated under the laws of Ohio for charitable and patriotic purposes on February 3, 1904, by the following named women: Sarah D. Winans. Jennie F. Wright, Kate B. Sherwood, Cora Day Young, Mary C. Wentzel, Mary M. North, Sarah E. Phillips, Lizabeth A. Turner, Clara Barton and Allaseba M. Bliss. During the convention held in 1908 the Woman's Relief Corps having improved and cared for those grounds at its own expense formally tendered the land to the United States Government as a gift free of all indebtedness, and in pursuance of an Act of Congress approved March 2, 1910, the Secretary of War was authorized and directed to accept the land so tendered with all improvements thereon.

Board of Trustees.
1909-1910.

Sarah D. Winans, Chairman
Abbie A. Adams
Allaseba M. Bliss
Sarah E. Fuller
Carrie R. Read

Committee on Transfer.
1909-1910.

Kate E. Jones, Chairman
Kate B. Sherwood
Mary L. Gilman
Mary M. North

of the stream immediately above, and between the two inner lines of palisades. The grease and refuse from them were found adhering to the banks at the time of our visit. The guards to the number of about 3,600, were, principally, encamped on the upper part of the stream, and when the heavy rains washed down the hillsides, covered with 30,000 (at one time 35,000) human beings, and the outlet below failed to discharge the flood which backed and filled the valley, the water must have become so foul and loathsome that every statement I have seen of its offensiveness must be considered as falling short of the reality. And yet within rifle-shot of the prison flowed a stream fifteen feet wide and three deep of pure delicious water. Had the prison been so placed as to include a section of the "Sweet Water" (Sweetwater), the inmates might have drank and bathed to their hearts' content.

During the occupation a beautiful spring broke out, like the waters of Meribah, from the solid ground near the foot of the northern slope, just under the western dead-line. It is still there, cool and clear, the only pleasing object in this horrid place.[1]

The scarcity of water, the want of occupation, and perhaps the desire to escape by tunneling, impelled the prisoners to dig wells. Forty of these, finished and unfinished, remain, those on the highest ground being sunk in the hard soil to the depth of eighty feet. The work was done with knives, spoons, sticks, and other tools but little better. The diggers brought up the earth in their pockets and blouses and sprinkled it about the ground to conceal the quantity. In some wells excellent water was reached, and in others horizontal galleries were attempted for escape. In at least one instance a tunnel was carried through the hill and a few prisoners are said to have got through.

The steep face of the northern hill is burrowed throughout its whole extent. The little caves are scooped out and arched in the form of ovens, floored, ceiled and strengthened so far as the owners had means, with sticks and pieces of boards, and some of them are provided with fireplaces and chimneys. It would seem that there were cases during the long rains where the house would become the grave of its owner by falling in upon him during the night. In these burrows are still found remnants of wretched food and rude utensils of the occupants—drinking cups made of sections of horns, platters and spoons wrought from parts of old canteens, kettles and pans made without solder from stray pieces of old tin or sheet iron. I brought away a considerable number of these articles, which may some day be of interest to the curious.

Five sheds stand on the top of the northern hill, erected in the early part of the occupation, and five more on the opposite height, built a short time before the evacuation.

Like nearly all Southern land, the land is liable to be washed away by the rains, and on the slopes of the hills ravines are now formed, gullied to the depth of twelve feet. It seems impossible that men could have kept their footing on these hillsides when slippery with rain.

Outside the enclosure ond nearly parallel with its south end is the hospital stockade, 800 by 350 feet. It contains twenty-two sheds, for the most part without sides, erected about three months before the place was abandoned. The old hos-

---

[1] This is now known as "Providence Spring." See photograph.

PROVIDENCE SPRING.
Many prisoners believed that it gushed forth in answer to their prayers.

pital, occupied up to that time in which so many brave men died, consisted only of tents enclosed by a board fence and surrounded by a guard. Confused heaps of rubbish alone mark the place it occupied.

About half a mile from the main prison, and near Anderson station is the officers' stockade, a small enclosure, in which were never imprisoned more than 250 officers, and it was chiefly used for the confinement of rebel offenders.

The cemetery, around which the chief interest must gather, is distant about 300 yards from the stockade in a northwesterly direction. The graves placed side by side in close continuous rows cover nine acres, divided into three unequal lots by two roads which intersect each other nearly at right angles. The fourth space is still unoccupied, except by a few graves of Confederate soldiers. No human bodies were found exposed, and none were removed. The place was found in much better condition than had been anticipated, owing to the excellent measures taken by Major-General Wilson, commanding at Macon, and a humane, public-spirited citizen of Fort Valley, Georgia, a Mr. Griffin, who, in passing on the railroad, was informed by one of the ever faithful negroes that the bodies were being rooted up by animals. Having verified this statement he collected a few negroes, sunk the exposed bodies and covered them to a proper depth. He then reported the facts to General Wilson, and requested authority to take steps for protecting the grounds. That patriotic officer visited Andersonville in person, appointed Mr. Griffin temporary superintendent and gave him such limited facilities as could be furnished in that destitute country. It was determined to enclose a square of fifty acres; and at the time of our arrival the fence was nearly one-third built from old lumber found about the place. He had also erected a brick kiln, and was manufacturing brick for drains to conduct the water away from the graves and protect and strengthen the soil against the action of heavy rains. We found Mr. Griffin with a force of about twenty negroes and a few mules at work upon the ground. I have understood that that gentleman furnished the labor at his own cost, while General Wilson issued the necessary rations.

The part performed by our party was to take up and carry forward the work so well begun. Additional force was obtained from the military commandant at Macon for completing the enclosure and erecting the headboards. It seems that the dead had been buried by Union prisoners, paroled from the hospital and stockade for the purpose. Successive trenches capable of containing from 100 to 150 bodies each, thickly set with little posts or boards with numbers in regular order carved upon them, told to the astonished and tear-dimmed eye the sad story of buried treasures. It was only necessary to compare the number on each post or board with that which stands opposite the name on the register and replace the whole with a more substantial, uniform and comely tablet, bearing not only the original number, but the name, company and regiment and date of death of soldier who slept beneath.

I have been repeatedly assured by prisoners that great care was taken at the time by the men to whom fell the sad task of originally marking this astonishing number of graves to perform the work with faithfulness and accuracy. If it shall prove that the work performed by those who followed under circumstances so much more favorable, was executed with less faithfulness and accuracy than the former, it will be a matter of much regret, but fortunately not yet beyond the possibility of correction. The number of graves marked is 12,920. The original records, captured by General Wilson, furnished about 10,500; but as one book of the record had not been secured, over 2,000 names were supplied from a copy (of his own record) made by Atwater in the Andersonville Prison and brought by him to Annapolis on his return with the paroled prisoners.

Interspersed throughout this death register were 400 numbers against which stood the dark word "unknown." So, scattered among the thickly designated graves stand 400 tablets, bearing only the number and the touching inscription "Unknown Union Soldier."

Substantially nothing was attempted beyond enclosing the grounds, identifying and marking the graves, placing some appropriate mottoes at the gates and along the spaces designed for walks and erecting a flagstaff in the center of the cemetery. The work was completed on the 17th of August, and the party took the route homeward by the way of Chattanooga, Nashville and Cincinnati, arriving at Washington on the morning of August 24th.

The health of the party during the expedition was remarkably good, when the season of the year, the fatigue and want of customary accommodations are taken into consideration. Cases of slight chills and fever were not infrequent; but during the entire time we had only one case of severe illness, and that, to our grief, terminated fatally. Edward Watts, of Georgetown, D. C., a clerk in the quarter master's department, in this city, sickened of typhoid fever during the passage up the Savannah River, and died on the 10th day of August. His remains were taken home to his friends. Mr. Watts was a young man of education and refinement, and of the highest type of moral and religious character; he suffered patiently, and died nobly and well. I have thought that he might be regarded as the last martyr of Andersonville.

The future of this historic spot cannot fail to constitute a subject of deep and abiding interest to the people of this entire country, and it would seem fitting that it should be preserved as one of the sanctuaries of the nation, and in due time dedicated with appropriate honors. Its susceptibility of internal improvement was very great. Water can be had for irrigation, and the climate will produce nearly all the flora of the temperate zones. Both national gratitude and personal affection will suggest the erection of a suitable monument within the cemetery, where, if desirable, may be preserved in durable form the names of the martyrs who sleep around. And as the land on which these interesting associations are clustered is still the property of private individuals, never having passed from the hands of the original owners, it would seem desirable that the cemetery, at least, and its immediate surroundings become the property of the nation. A mile square will embrace all points of general and historic interest.

There are numerous smaller burial places in the state of Georgia, which from their seeming lesser importance, will scarcely be kept up as national cemeteries, and in reference to which, without venturing to suggest, I would merely remark that the fifty acres enclosed at Andersonville would afford ample space for all whom it might ever be deemed advisable to remove to that point.

During the occupation of Andersonville as a prison it was a punishable offense for a colored man or woman to feed, shelter, aid, or even converse with the prisoners on parole. To others they had no access. I have been informed that they were not allowed about the prison grounds; and so great was their superstitious horror of the cruelties perpetrated upon the prisoners that only a comparatively small number had ever found the courage to visit the cemetery up to the time of our arrival. But the presence of so many Northern people on such an errand, and especially a lady, entirely overcame their fears, and they visited the cemetery and myself by scores, men, women and children, sometimes a hundred in a day. It was no uncommon occurrence, upon opening my tent in the morning to find a group standing in front of it who had walked fifteen or twenty miles to see the "Yankee lady" and ask her "If it were true that Abraham Lincoln was dead, and they were free," and "How Massa Lincoln's paper read," and "What they ought to do," and tell her how the "poor Yankee prisoners" ran before the dogs "like us" and they could not save them—starved, and they could not feed them—died—and they could not see them.

Remember, mothers, that the pitying tear of the old-time slave, whom your son helped to freedom, is the only tear that falls upon his distant grave to-day.

I have endeavored to point out to you, as faithfully as I am able, the various objects of interest, painful or otherwise, which presented themselves to my observation during the time occupied in the work of the expedition; and while I could not dwell upon the terribleness of the sufferings imposed upon our prisoners, nor stir the hearts already sunk in grief to deeper woe, still we owe it alike to the living and the dead that a proper knowledge and a realization of the miseries which they endured be entertained by all. We are wont to attribute their chief sufferings to the insufficiency of the food, and while this is probably just, still to the mind of one who has looked over the scanty, shelterless, pitiless spot of earth to which they were confined, and taken into consideration the numberless trials which must have grown out of the deprivation of space and necessary conveniences of life, the conviction will force itself that these latter woes fell but little short of the former. It is to be remembered that during thirteen months they knew neither shelter nor protection from the changeable skies above or the pitiless, unfeeling earth beneath.

The treacherous nature of the soil, parching to seams in the sun, and gullying and sliding under their feet with every shower, must have augmented their ills almost beyond conception. I watched the effect of a heavy fall of rain upon the enclosed grounds, and in thirty minutes the entire hillsides, which had constituted their sole abiding place, were one rolling mass of slippery mud, and this the effect of a mere summer shower. What of the continued rains of autumn? Think of thirty thousand men penned in by a close stockade of twenty-six acres of ground, from which every tree and shrub had been uprooted for fuel to cook their scanty food, huddled like cattle, without shelter or blanket, half clad and hungry, with the dreary night setting in after a day of autumn rain. The hill-tops would not hold them all, the valley was filled with the swollen brook; seventeen feet from the stockade ran the fatal dead-line, beyond which no man might step and live. What did they do? I need not ask you where did they go, for, on the face of the whole green earth there was no place but this for them, but where did they place themselves? How did they live? Ay! how did they die? But this is only one feature of their suffering, and perhaps the lightest. Of the long dazzling months when gaunt famine stalked at noonday, and pestilence walked by night, and upon the seamed and parching earth the cooling rain fell not, I will not trust me to speak, I scarce dare to think. If my heart were strong enough to draw the picture, there are thousands upon thousands all through our land too crushed and sore to look upon it. But after this whenever any man who has laid a prisoner within the stockade at Andersonville would tell you of his sufferings, how he fainted, scorched, drenched, hungered, sickened, was scoffed at, scourged, hunted and persecuted, though the tale be long and twice told, as you would have your own wrongs appreciated, your own woes pitied, your own cries for mercy heard, I charge you listen and believe him. However definitely he may have spoken, know that he has not told you all. However strongly he may have outlined, or however deeply he may have colored his picture, know that the reality calls for a better light and a nearer view than your clouded distant gaze will ever get. And you need not confine your sympathies to Andersonville, while similar horrors glared in the sunny light and spotted the flower-girt garden fields of that whole desperate, misguided people. Wherever stretched the form of a Union prisoner, there rose the signal for cruelty and the cry of agony, and there, day by day, grew the skeleton graves of the nameless dead.

But braving and enduring all this, some thousands have returned to you. And you will bear with me, and these noble men will pardon me, while in conclusion I speak one word of them.

The unparalleled severities of four years' campaigns have told upon the constitutional strength even of the fortunate soldier, who alone marched to the music of the Union, and slept only beneath the folds of the flag for which he fought. But they whom fickle fortune left to crouch at the foot of the shadowless palmetto, and listen to the hissing of the serpent, drank still deeper of the unhealthful draught. These men bear with them the seeds of disease and death, sown in that fatal clime, and ripening for an early harvest. With occasional exceptions, they will prove to be short-lived and enfeebled men, and whether they ask it or not, will deserve at your hands no ordinary share of kindly consideration. The survivor of a rebel prison has endured and suffered what you never can, and what I pray God your children may never. With loss of strength, and more of sad and bitter memories, he is with you now, to earn the food so long denied him. If he ask "Leave to toil" give it him before it is too late; if he need kindness and encouragement, bestow them freely while you may; if he ask charity at your hands, remember that "The poor you have always with you," but him you have not always and withhold it not. If hereafter you find them making organized effort to provide for the widow and orphan of the Union soldier, remember that it grows out of the heart sympathy which clusters around the memories of the comrades who perished at their side; and a well grounded apprehension for the future of their own, and aid them.

In conclusion, tremulously, lest I assume too much, let me hasten to commend to the grateful consideration of this noble, generous people alike the soldier who has given his strength, the prisoner who has sacrificed his health, the widow who has offered up her husband, the orphan who knows only that its father went out to battle and comes no more forever, and the lonely distant grave of the martyr, who sleeps alone in the stranger soil, that freedom and peace come to ours.

One word of explanation, in conclusion, and I have done. You have long and justly felt that some report of this expedition, embracing a record of the graves identified was your due, and three thousand letters addressed to me upon the subject have revealed only too plainly and painfully the bitter anxiety with which you have watched and waited.

A mere report, unaccompanied by the "record," seemed but a hollow mockery, which I would not impose upon you, and this is my first opportunity for such accompaniment. For the record of your dead you are indebted to the forethought, courage and preserverance of Dorence Atwater, a young man not yet twenty-one years of age; an orphan, four years a soldier, one-tenth part of his whole life a prisoner, with broken health and ruined hopes, he seeks to present to your acceptance the sad gift he has in store for you, and, grateful for the opportunity, I hasten to place beside it this humble report, whose only merit is its truthfulness, and beg you to accept it in the spirit of kindness in which it is offered.

[Signed] CLARA BARTON.[1]

THE DEAD AT ANDERSONVILLE—REPORT BY DORENCE ATWATER.

To the Surviving Relatives and Friends of the Martyred Dead at Aadersonville, Georgia:

This record was originally copied for you because I feared that neither you nor the government of the United States would ever otherwise learn the fate of your loved ones whom I saw daily dying before me. I could do nothing for them, but I resolved that I would at least try to let you sometime know when and how they died. This, at last, I am able now to do.

So many conflicting rumors have been in circulation in regard to these rolls— the list of the dead—and myself, that I deem it prudent to give a brief statement of my entire connection with this death register, and to show how and why it has been so long withheld from you.

On the 7th day of July, 1863, I was taken prisoner near Hagerstown, Maryland, and taken to Belle Isle, Richmond, Virginia, via Staunton, where I remained five months. I then went to Smith's tobacco factory, Richmond, where I kept the account of supplies received from our government, and issued to Federal prisoners of war. In the latter part of February, 1864, I was sent to Andersonville with a squad of four hundred other prisoners from Belle Isle, arriving there on the first day of March. I remained inside the stockade until the middle of May, when I was sent to the hospital. On the 15th of June I was paroled and detailed as clerk in Surgeon J. H. White's office to keep the daily record of deaths of all Federal prisoners of war. I also made monthly and quarterly abstracts of the deaths. The latter one was said to be for the Federal government, which I have since learned was never received.

The appalling mortality was such that I suspected that it was the design of the rebel government to kill and maim our prisoners by exposure and starvation so that they would forever be totally unfit for military service and that they withheld these facts. Accordingly, in the latter part of August, 1864, I began to secretly

---

[1] I am indebted to Mr. J. M. Bryant, superintendent of the cemetery, for copies of this and other reports referred to in this chapter and also for the copies of inscriptions on the monuments there erected.

copy the entire list of our dead, which I succeeded in doing and brought safely through the lines with me in 1865. Arriving at Camp Parole, at Annapolis, Maryland, I learned that I could not get a furlough on account of my term of service having expired some seven months before. I immediately wrote to the secretary of war, asking for a furlough for thirty days, for the purpose of having my death register published for the relief of the many thousands anxious in regard to the fate of their dead. Before an answer could have returned I received a furlough from the commandant of the camp. I then went to my home in Terryville, Connecticut, where I was taken sick the next day after my arrival, which confined me three weeks. On the 12th of April I received a telegram from the war department requesting me to come immediately to Washington and bring my rolls, and if they were found acceptable I should be suitably rewarded. I started the next day for Washington. Arriving there I went to the war department and learned that the person (Colonel Breck) with whom I was to make arrangements was absent at the Fort Sumter celebration. I left my rolls with the chief clerk for safe keeping. In a day or two Colonel Breck returned, and he informed me that the secretary of war had authorized him to pay me three hundred dollars ($300) for the rolls. I told him I did not wish to sell the rolls, that they ought to be published for the benefit of the friends of the dead for whom chiefly they had been copied. He told me that if I meant to publish them the government would confiscate them; that I could have until 9 o'clock the next morning to decide whether I would take the three hundred dollars or not. The rolls were then in his possession. I told him if I could have a clerkship in the department which he had described to me, three hundred dollars and the rolls back again as soon as copied, I should consider it satisfactory. To this he agreed. He then informed me that it would be necessary for me to enlist in the general service in order to get the clerkship. To this I objected, but in no other way was it available, and I accepted. I was then mustered out of my original enlistment, and given permission to visit home, and return for duty by the first of June. While in New York the latter part of May I telegraphed Colonel Breck, asking if my rolls were copied, to which I received a reply, "Not yet."

Soon after my arrival in Washington in June I called upon Colonel Breck, and asked the privilege of taking sheets of my rolls out after business hours, to copy and return them the next morning. He said he would have to ask General Townsend's consent. I again met him in a few days. He told me that he had been unable to see General Townsend. I then wrote to Colonel Breck asking if he did not intend to return my rolls; that I had promised that the rolls should be published for the benefit of the friends of the deceased. He returned my letter, indorsed as follows: "I have fully explained the matter to General Townsend, and he says the rolls shall not be copied for any traffic whatever." I had never spoken of trafficking in them; I only wished to give them to the people for whom I had copied them at some personal risk. Nothing more was said about the rolls until after my return from Andersonville in August.

Miss Clara Barton, of Washington, D. C., upon learning the condition of the cemetery at Andersonville, and that the graves could be identified, had reported the facts to the secretary of war, who ordered the necessary arrangements to be made for marking the graves. A party charged with this duty left Washington on the 8th of July, consisting of Miss Clara Barton, Captain James M. Moore, myself and forty-two letterers, painters and clerks, arriving at Andersonville on the 25th of July.

Before leaving Washington it was found that the original register captured by General Wilson, was deficient in one book containing about twenty-four hundred names, and my rolls were sent to supply this deficiency. The original was also found blurred and imperfect, through want of care, and my rolls were frequently needed to aid this defect. They were, therefore, publicly and constantly in the hands of all who had occasion to consult them and so came into my hands in the course of duty. They had been copied in Washington, according to my agreement with Colonel Breck, and were mine, and lawfully in my possession. I proposed to retain them and give them to you as soon as I could. I did not propose to injure anyone, to do anything unlawful or improper with them, much less to traffic or speculate on the information they contained, but I did retain them. When the originals were needed in the Wirz trial at Washington, they and my copy were in my tent when the messenger arrived at Andersonville. He took the original and left my copy.

When we started home I placed these rolls with my other property, in my trunk, and brought them to Washington. Upon my arrival I reported to Colonel Breck, at the war department. He asked if I knew where my rolls were. I said, "I have them; will you allow me to keep them, now you have them copied here?" He told me, "We might as well come to an understanding about these rolls. This is the last conversation we shall have about them; if you will pay back the three hundred dollars you can keep the rolls, otherwise you must return them." I asked him "if he did not agree to give them back when copied." He said "Yes, but you are going to set yourself up in business by publishing them, and we do not consider ourselves held to our agreement." I told him "I had a right to publish them (if he called that setting myself up in business), and it was my duty to do so." I then turned to leave, intending to see Secretary Stanton. He said, "I infer that you do not intend to give up the rolls." I said, "Not yet; I must go further to see about them." He said, "You will go to the Old Capitol if you do not give them up" and then sent for a guard and had me arrested. My trunk and room were searched, but the rolls could not be found. I was then put in the guard-house for two days and then transferred to the Old Capitol prison and in a few days I was arraigned and tried by court-marshal on the following charges and specifications:

Charge 1. Conduct prejudicial to good military discipline.

Charge 2. Larceny.

Specifications: In this that said private Dorence Atwater, of the general service of the United States army, did seize and unlawfully take from the tent or quarters of J. M. Moore, assistant quartermaster, U. S. army, certain property of the United States then and there in the proper charge and custody of the said Captain J. M. Moore, to wit: A certain document, consisting of a list written on about twenty-four sheets of paper, of Federal prisoners of war who had died at Andersonville, Georgia, the same having been prepared by the said Atwater, while a prisoner of war at Andersonville and sold and disposed of by him to the United States for the sum of three hundred dollars, and did appropriate and retain the said property to his own use. This at Andersonville, Georgia, on or about the 16th day of August, 1865.

I was convicted and sentenced as follows: To be dishonorably discharged from the United States service, with loss of all pay and allowances now due; to pay a fine of three hundred dollars; to be confined at hard labor for the period of eighteen months, at such place as the secretary of war may direct; to furnish to the war department the property specified in the second specification as the property stolen from Captain J. M. Moore, and stand committed at hard labor until said fine is paid, and the said stolen property is furnished to the war department.

On the 26th of September I arrived at Auburn state prison, New York, where I remained over two months at hard labor, when I was released under a general pardon of the president of the United States.

I reached New Haven, Connecticut, the following day, and learned that the record had not yet been furnished you. I immediately set about preparing it for publication, and have arranged to have it printed and placed within your reach at a cost of the labor of printing and material, having no means by which to defray these expenses myself.

I regret you have waited so long for information of so much interest to you.

[Signed] DORENCE ATWATER.

There is no doubt but that we are indebted to Dorence Atwater for the preservation of the names of a large number of the dead at Andersonville, and that he performed the labor of copying the death register at great personal risk and when he was scarcely physically able to use the pen. Of his career after having been pardoned by President Johnson I find the following in the San Francisco *Chronicle* of May 28, 1911, written by Mr. A. V. H. Hoffman:

In 1867, under date of July 4th, the state of Connecticut presented Dorence Atwater with a testimonial signed by John T. Waite, speaker of the House of Representatives; James E. English, governor, and Eph. E. Hyde, lieutenant-governor, "in grateful remembrance of the courage and patriotism by him displayed in the late war for the suppression of rebellion and the preservation of constitutional liberty."

In 1868 President Andrew Johnson appointed Dorence Atwater consul at the Seychelles islands in the Indian ocean.

In 1870 he was appointed by President Grant to the consulship at Tahiti in the Pacific ocean.

In 1898, during President McKinley's administration, Congress removed all remaining disabilities.

On July 18, 1872, while serving as consul at Tahiti, Dorence Atwater was married to Princess Arii Noore Moetra Salmon of the royal family of Tahiti, and nearly forty years of happiness followed this union. Desiring to visit his old home again, he returned to the United States last summer, was taken ill in this city, where he passed away on November 28, 1910, in his sixty-fifth year.[1]

---

[1] On January 10, 1912, his remains were, by members of his family and surviving widow placed aboard ship for final interment at Tahiti. A large number of his comrades of the Grand Army of the Republic participated in the impressive burial ceremonies of the Order, placing the American flag on the casket as a final tribute to his memory.

It should be explained that Atwater's story was written in explanation of his original purpose to relieve the anxiety of thousands of widows and orphans, the fate of whose dear ones was shrouded in mystery. I believe his motive was upright and honorable, and that he was most unjustly accused and convicted. And yet the war department was not without some justification, though less severity might have been equally effective of its object. It was thought to be undesirable that the list of the dead should be published at that time, and before all doubt had been removed as to its accuracy, and this view has since to some extent been confirmed. The Atwater list has been published in at least two books which I have read, and I had thought of including in this volume the true and corrected list, but as it would occupy not less than one hundred pages it seemed better to use the space with other matter, especially as the war department has not yet given out the finally corrected roster of the dead. The doubt has not been as to the number, but as to the identification of the graves and their occupants.

When we consider the evidence, the method of keeping the records, the manner of handling and burying the dead, the great number dying daily in hospital and in the stockade, many of them so disfigured by disease and the unclean surroundings as to be unrecognizable, I cannot myself feel any assurance that the markings of the graves can be implicitly relied on as correct in all cases. The dead are there and the identity of the dead reasonably assured, but the identity of the place where the remains of a particular soldier lie I cannot regard as certain in every instance. And we know that several hundred graves are marked "unknown soldier."

Mr. James M. Bryant, the superintendent of the cemetery, to whom I wish to acknowledge my indebtedness for many courtesies in the preparation of this volume, has written some facts relating to the subject which will be read with interest. In his letter he states the reasons for his belief that the markings may be relied on as "fairly correct." His letter follows:

ANDERSONVILLE, GEORGIA, NATIONAL CEMETERY, June, 10, 1910.

HONORABLE N. P. CHIPMAN, *Sacramento, Cal.*

DEAR SIR: Your letter of 2d instant reached me yesterday, and was read with much pleasure, and I trust with profit also.

I regret having kept you waiting so long for the photographs, but it was not as easy to find the Wirz photograph as I supposed it would be. The photographer who made that picture moved to Birmingham some little time ago, but I supposed

Center: J. M. Bryant, Superintendent of Andersonville Cemetery.
Upper left hand: Entrance to Cemetery. Upper right hand: Entrance to Prison Park.

he continued to have the picture for sale, but receiving no response to a letter sent him relative to it I went on a hunt for what was wanted, and the one sent you was taken out of a show case, none others being on hand. This either indicates an unusual demand for the view of the mounment, or else that they want to have them disappear from the market, and to that extent, reduce the talk about the monument, and I am inclined to think the latter is the explanation of the matter.

As I wrote you the Wirz photograph costs fifty cents, the others twenty-five cents, including postage. I sent more views of the cemetery and prison grounds than you will want, but you can select such as you desire and return the others.

You write you would like to use a portion of my letter of May 20th in your book. I did not keep a copy and cannot recall just what I wrote, therefore will take the liberty of writing a rather lengthy letter, and if you are able to cull from it anything that will be of use to you there is no objection on my part.

I thank you very much for your remarks relative to the Wirz trial. It seems quite plain to me, after reading your explanation, that one might very easily see one kill another, identifying the murdered, but being a perfect stranger to the one killed he could not name him, though perfectly able of swearing to the act itself.

I am glad I referred to that part of the trial as your remarks have removed a doubt from my mind regarding the matter.

ANDERSONVILLE CEMETERY, AND CONCLUSION. 495

The report of Miss Clara Barton will doubtless give you a better idea of the conditions prevailing at Andersonville in the summer of 1864 than anything I can produce. Yet there are two or three facts connected with the matter she fails to refer to, and are not mentioned in the other papers I am sending you, and which are necessary to a clear and full understanding of the question.

When a man died there was an effort made to identify him, and I am informed by ex-prisoners that usually there were members of the same regiment near by, who furnished the facts needed. Where identified a small card or piece of paper was secured to whatever the deceased might have on in the way of clothing, and that card bore merely a number, which corresponded with the same number in the burial register, where the name and record were written out as full as circumstances permitted. When a man's body was placed in the trench, a small post or board was put at the head bearing the number found secured to the remains when received from the prison. By looking up any number found on one of these posts, in the register, all the known facts in the case would be found. Where the dead man could not be identified he was buried as "Unknown." I have talked with two or three ex-prisoners who were on duty at the cemetery, and they assure me that every possible care was exercised in performing their tasks with accuracy. You will notice Miss Barton refers to the same matter. Since I first came to Andersonville (1883) we have disinterred three or four bodies for shipment to friends and re-burial in family lots. In two of those cases the bodies were identified through a peculiarity of the teeth, which last, perhaps, longer than any other part of the body. From what I have learned by reading articles written by eye-witnesses, and in conversation with those who took part in the sad duty of burying the dead at Andersonville, I am quite confident the records are, with exceptions mentioned later, fairly correct, and that when a grave is pointed out to anyone as containing the remains of a certain soldier, the probability is that it does.

Miss Barton is a clear-minded woman, one of varied experience, and I imagine it would be somewhat difficult to mislead her in a question of this nature, and you will see from her report that she has entire faith in the accuracy of the method used.

And the government would hardly have spent thousands upon thousands of dollars for headstones unless it was satisfied the stone would mark the grave of one of its soldiers, and would stand just above where he slept.

That there were errors made, a great many of them, is only what might reasonably be expected from the conditions and circumstances surrounding the prison and everything connected with it.

When all the facts are considered, the large number of deaths, the rush and turmoil that is never absent under such environments, the hardened, calloused condition of the men in constant contact with the dead, it appears wonderful that we have as correct a record as we now possess.

We commenced, three years ago, an effort to eliminate as many of the mistakes known to exist in the records as possible. New York having the largest number of any state buried here (over 2200), we commenced with that state. I first made an alphabetical list and sent it to the adjutant-general of that state for comparison with his records and such corrections as might be found necessary. As a result we learned of quite a number of men supposed to be resting beneath the sod here but who the adjutant-general's records show were mustered out with their regiments, or died elsewhere than at Andersonville. I made a separate list of these cases and sent them to the commissioner of pensions. Through him we learned that several were yet alive and on the pension roll, others had died during recent years (since the close of the war). We have got into communication with some of those still living, and know just how the error was made. In one case a soldier had a blanket, on one corner of which appeared his name and record. He was on the list for exchange, and on leaving gave his blanket to a cousin who was very sick. This man subsequently died and the record found on the blanket was supposed to be his record. In another case two men, both named "Smith," were in the hospital, one a patient, the other a nurse. The patient died, and in some way the nurse's name was recorded as the one who died.

Two men belonging to the 16th Connecticut infantry, supposed to be buried here, were reported by the adjutant-general of that state as having been killed at Antietam, Maryland, and buried on the battlefield. The commissioner of pensions reported that a widow was drawing a pension in one of the cases, and that claim was filed on account of children in the other case, and that both men were certainly killed at Antietam in 1863. We then got into communication with sergeant-major Kellogg of the 16th Connecticut infantry, and the explanation in these cases is very interesting indeed. I enclose a newspaper clipping giving all the particulars. Please return it.

These are samples of the causes leading to some of the errors, and doubtless the others are of a similar nature. The percentage of real mistakes is very small, and will approach the vanishing point when we get through with the list. Every available source of information has been followed out, and within a year we will be in a position to commence writing up the new register, and while there are some errors that can never be corrected, yet in comparison with the whole are not a drop in the bucket.

You stated that it might be advisable, or rather would add interest to it (the book) if it contained a list of the dead. Any list that could be supplied at the present time would necessarily be inaccurate, for reasons given above, for in addition to the errors mentioned are those of spelling of names, errors in rank, company and regiment, etc. These are simply innumerable. Then we have found several duplicates. The greater portion of these will disappear in the new register. If you will not need the names before another year rolls around it would afford me pleasure to prepare the list for you.

But as stated, a correct, approximately correct list, cannot be supplied at the present time. I am through with the preliminary work, and the list of discrepancies, which number thousands, is now in the hands of the quartermaster-general for the purpose of being verified. As soon as returned I can make a commencement on the new register, and when once under way it can soon be completed. . . .

One who had viewed the cemetery as the Washington expedition left it in 1865, in its crude and unimproved state, would hardly recognize it at the present day. It has been improved from year to year by the government, trees and shrubs in large numbers have been planted, and every effort put forth to give the grounds the appearance of a park. Pennsylvania, Maine, Indiana, Iowa, Connecticut and

New Jersey have erected handsome monuments within the cemetery. Wisconsin, Massachusetts, Rhode Island, Michigan and Ohio placed their mounments within the old prison grounds, now known as "Prison Park." That property is now owned by the Woman's Relief Corps; but an act has passed Congress and been approved by the president, authorizing the government to accept it as a gift.[1] The details of the transfer are now being worked out by Colonel Hopkins, of Washington, and probably within a year the title will pass to Uncle Sam. . . .

It will give me real pleasure to aid you in any way within my power. Any time I can serve you please command me.   Very truly yours,

J. M. BRYANT, *Superintendent.*

ANDERSONVILLE, GEORGIA, NATIONAL CEMETERY, July 6, 1910.
HONORABLE N. P. CHIPMAN, *Sacramento, Cal.*

MY DEAR SIR: Referring to my last letter I append the inscriptions on the state monuments within the cemetery, namely,

IOWA.

On the west side of the die the seal of Iowa is engraved, beneath which are the words "Iowa honors the turf that wraps their clay. The Unknown. Their names are recorded in the archives of their country." On the base: "Act Thirtieth General Assembly."

On the south side of the die is engraved a water scene with overhanging willows and a mountain rising in the background, under which is engraved the following quotation from the seventh chapter of Revelations, sixteenth and seventeenth verses: "They shall hunger no more, neither thirst any more; neither shall the sun light on them, nor any heat. For the Lamb which is in the midst of the throne shall feed them and shall lead them unto living fountains of water; and God shall wipe away all tears from their eyes." On the base: "God smote the side hill and gave them drink: August 16, 1864."

On the east side of the die are the words "Death before Dishonor." Beneath that legend are the names, with company and regiment, of one hundred and seven Iowa soldiers who died while confined in prison. On the base: "Erected A. D. 1905."

On the north side of the die are the words "Death before Dishonor" and the names, with company and regiment, of one hundred and seven more Iowa soldiers who died while confined in the prison. On the base: "Commissioners: Sergeant D. C. Bishard, Co. M, Eighth Iowa cavalry, prisoner nine months; Corporal M. V. B. Evans, Co. I, Eighth Iowa cavalry, prisoner eight months; Captain J. A. Brewer, Co. C, Twenty-third Missouri infantry, prisoner seven months; Captain M. T. Russell, Co. A, Fifty-first Indiana infantry, prisoner eighteen months; Corporal W. C. Tompkins, Co. D, Twelfth U. S. infantry, prisoner eight months."

INDIANA.

South side: "Under authority of an act of the Sixty-fifth General Assembly of the State of Indiana. Indiana mourns for her fallen heroes, the 702 brave sons, who for the cause they loved, gave up their lives in Andersonville Prison from February, 1864, to April, 1865. Death did not affright them, nor fear subdue them nor could famine break their incorruptible spirit."

---

[1] Since conveyed to the United States by the Woman's Relief Corps.

498   THE TRAGEDY OF ANDERSONVILLE.

East side: "With great pity for their sufferings, but a greater admiration for their unfaltering fidelity."

West side: "Not theirs the matchless death by sword or shot; instead the agony of martyrdom."

North side: "Till the mountains are worn out, and the rivers cease to flow, shall their names be kept fresh with reverent honors, which are inscribed upon the book of national remembrance."

PENNSYLVANIA.

This monument is built with an enclosed arched passageway through it, and the inscriptions are upon bronze tablets secured to the walls within the arch. On the east side is a bronze engraving illustrative of the stockade, showing the palisades, dead-line, guards in their guard-boxes, and the prisoners procuring water from the spring by using long poles with cups on the ends of them. Above cut in the marble wall are the words "Death before Dishonor."

West side: This monument has been erected by the State of Pennsylvania in pursuance of an act entitled an act to commemorate the heroism, sacrifices and patriotism of the Pennsylvania soldiers who died in Andersonville Prison, Georgia, while confined there as prisoners of war: by the erection of a suitable monument in the cemetery at that place; creating a commission for such purpose, and appropriating the necessary money therefor. Approved July 18, 1901, by His Excellency,

WILLIAM A. STONE, *Governor.*

Commissioners: James Atwell, president; Ezra H. Ripple, secretary; William T. Ziegler, Harry White, James D. Walker, superintendent.

On another bronze tablet adjacent to the above appears:

In Memoriam Pennsylvania's Sons at Andersonville.

To the 1849 of her devoted sons who died at Andersonville Prison, where they were held as prisoners of war, in the years 1864 and 1865, and who are buried here, Pennsylvania dedicates this memorial of her undying love. The faithful men whose names adorn this monument and the pages of their country's history, were loyal unto death, to the flag of the Republic, their lives are woven into the precious fabric of American freedom. Through their sufferings they have left a legacy of strong, patient endurance to the coming generations. With gratitude to Almighty God, who gave this nation such heroic spirits in the time of trial, Pennsylvania cherishes their memory, their loyalty, their sacrifices and their graves, a priceless heritage for evermore.

This monument to their soldiers, is here built by a people ever fretted, blazoned and decked with the hearts they built it of; and let it here securely stand, in form, in stone, in cap, in gate, till every shrine in every land will their lives commemorate.

MAINE.

North side: First are the words "Death before Dishonor." Then comes a bronze shield with the coat of arms engraved on it, "In grateful memory of those heroic soldiers of Maine who gave their lives that the Republic might live, and of those who daring to die, yet survived the tortures and horrors of Andersonville Military Prison. 1864 and 1865. The word "Maine" is cut in large letters on each side of the monument.

NEW JERSEY.

West side: First there is a scroll cut from the solid stone with the words "Death before Dishonor."

"Go stranger, to New Jersey, tell her that we lie here in fulfillment of her mandate and our pledge to maintain the proud name of our state unsullied, and place it high on the scroll of honor among the states of this great nation."

North side: "Number of dead, 255."

East side: "Erected by the state of New Jersey in commemoration of the fidelity and heroism of her soldiers, who died at the Andersonville Confederate military prison, Georgia, in faithful adherence to their pledge of patriotism."

CONNECTICUT.

West side: First a bronze shield containing the coat of arms of the state. "In memory of the men of Connecticut who suffered in Southern military prisons, 1861-1865."

These are all the monuments that are completed within the cemetery. New York and Illinois have monuments under way. The inscriptions to be placed on the former are not yet known. Those on the Illinois monument will be as follows:

ILLINOIS.

In the center: "Erected by the state of Illinois in grateful remembrance of the patriotic devotion of her sons who suffered and died in the military prison at Andersonville, Georgia, 1864-1865."

Left side: "We here highly resolve that these dead shall not have died in vain that this nation, under God, shall have a new birth of freedom and that government of the people, by the people, for the people, shall not perish from the earth." —*Abraham Lincoln* (Gettysburg address).

Right side: "The mystic chords of memory, stretching from every battlefield and patriotic grave to every living heart and hearthstone all over this broad land, will yet swell the chorus of the Union, when again touched, as surely they will be, by the better angels of our nature."—*Abraham Lincoln* (first inaugural address).

The following are the inscriptions on the monuments erected within the old prison grounds:

WISCONSIN.

West side: Near top is cut the coat of arms of Wisconsin. "This monument erected by the state of Wisconsin, in grateful remembrance to her sons who suffered and died in Andersonville Prison, March, 1864, April, 1865." On the base, in large letters, "Let us have Peace." On one of the projections is inscribed: "Commissioners appointed in 1904 by R. M. La Follette, Governor." On another projection appears: "D. G. James, president, Richland Center, Wisconsin, 16th Wisconsin Infantry."

East side: First is cut the coat of arms of Wisconsin. "Known dead, 378. To live in hearts we leave behind us is not to die." On one of the projections is inscribed: "L. Williams, treasurer, Columbus, Wisconsin, 1st Wisconsin Cavalry." On another projection appears: "C. H. Russell, secretary, Berlin, Wisconsin, 1st Wisconsin Cavalry." On north and south sides appears "W" within a wreath.

The Illinois monument has since been erected; see page 437, and the inscriptions are as above given.

COMMITTEE ON TRANSFER OF ANDERSONVILLE PRISON PROPERTY.

ANDERSONVILLE CEMETERY, AND CONCLUSION.

RHODE ISLAND.

West side, coat of arms and names of the dead; east side, names of the dead; north side, names of the dead; south side, names of the dead.

MASSACHUSETTS.

Near the top is cut the words "Death before Dishonor," and underneath that the coat of arms. "Erected by the commonwealth in memory of her sons who died at Andersonville, 1864-1865." At the bottom in large letters, "Massachusetts."

East side: Cut with a keystone, "Known dead 765." Beneath "Resolves 1900, chapter 77, approved May 28th. WILLIAM MURRAY CRANE, *Governor*.

"Commissioners: Charles G. Davis, Thaddeus H. Newcomb, Francis C. Curtis, Levi G. McKnight, Everett S. Horton."

OHIO.

North side: Coat of arms.

West side: "To her 1055 loyal sons who died here in camp Sumter from March, 1864, to April, 1865, this monument is dedicated."

South side: Seal of the United States.

East side: "Death before Dishonor."

MICHIGAN.

West side: "In memoriam. Erected by the state of Michigan to her soldiers and sailors who were imprisoned on these grounds, 1861-1865."

INSCRIPTIONS ON MONUMENT TO MRS. LIZABETH A. TURNER.

Badge of Woman's Relief Corps at top. "Lizabeth A. Turner, Past National President, Woman's Relief Corps, Auxiliary to the Grand Army of the Republic. Life Chairman Andersonville Prison Board, died at Andersonville, April 27, 1907. Erected by the Woman's Relief Corps to memorialize her work in hallowing these grounds."

INSCRIPTIONS WITHIN THE PAVILION OVER PROVIDENCE SPRING.

In center over the fountain: "With charity to all and malice towards none."

Marble tablet at left of fountain: "This pavilion was erected by the Woman's Relief Corps, Auxiliary to the Grand Army of the Republic, in grateful memory of the men who suffered and died in the Confederate prison at Andersonville, Georgia, from February, 1864, to April, 1865.

"The prisoners cry of thirst rose up to heaven, God heard, and with his thunder cleft the earth, and poured his sweetest waters gushing here."

"Erected in 1901."

ENTRANCE GATE.

A large arch spans the entrance, on which appears in large letters the words, "Andersonville Prison Park." Suspended under the arch is a tablet with following inscription: "This arch was erected by the Woman's Relief Corps, No. 9, Department of Kansas, and Woman's Relief Corps, No. 172, Department of Massachusetts, in memory of the unknown in Andersonville, Georgia."

The above comprises all the inscriptions you asked for, possibly more.

Very truly yours,

J. M. BRYANT, *Superintendent*.

PROVIDENCE SPRING.

"Providence Spring" has been the source of much speculation, and by many its appearance was attributed to the direct interposition of God in answer to the prayers of the prisoners. Mr. Hiram Buckingham, who was quartermaster's sergeant, Sixteenth Connecticut Infantry, and a prisoner at Andersonville, now residing at Washington City, wrote me of date October 18, 1910, the following account of the appearance of this spring. I think it will be accepted as the true explanation at least of the physical fact:

You asked me about Providence Spring. The majority got their water by reaching under the dead-line, as it came in through the rebel camp above. The prisoners went from north to south of the prison by following the dead-line; by so doing they had packed a hard path. One afternoon in August, an awful thunderstorm came up, flooded the stream through the prison, undermined the stockade and swept it away and the next morning a spring broke out on the sidehill just under the dead-line. It was a natural spring; our tramping up the hill near the dead-line had so packed the earth that the spring was forced to empty in the stream out of sight, but this heavy rain forced it to resume its old opening up on the hill. It now opens into a handsome marble house.

There have been some unexpected and disappointing delays in getting out this volume, but they are not without their compensations.

The published proceedings of the Woman's Relief Corps have just been placed in my hands, in which I find some very interesting matter relating to Andersonville Prison which should in addition to what has already appeared, have place among these pages.

Enhanced value is given to the book in the half-tone likenesses I am able now to present of the noble women who have done so much to glorify and perpetuate the memory of the martyred dead at Andersonville.

The committee having charge of the transfer of this property reported to the national secretary of the Woman's Relief Corps the progress of its efforts, culminating in the formal transfer of which we have just read. This report should appear in this volume and is as follows:

ILION, N. Y., August 4, 1910.

GEORGIA WADE MCCLELLAN,
National Secretary Woman's Relief Corps.

MADAM: The Committee on Transfer of Andersonville Prison Property respectfully submit the following report:

The failure to pass the bill by the Sixtieth Congress was reported; also that it had been put on the calendar of the Sixty-first Congress in special session, both House and Senate.

With renewed courage and a prayer for success. your chairman began making a list of new Representatives in the House where our bill 6971 was resting. Booklets and letters sent to them brought favorable replies.

Representatives General Isaac Sherwood, Ohio; and Major Thomas W. Bradley, New York, who from the beginning had been deeply interested in our bill, had it taken up in the House at an early period, and on December 10, 1909, our Bill H. R. 10,106 was "committed to the committee of the whole House on the state of the Union, and ordered to be printed."

January 17, 1910, the bill passed the House of Representatives unanimously, and victory was assured.

Senator William Warner had charge of the bill in the Senate, but business called him out of the city and its passage was delayed some weeks, when it passed the Senate without opposition. Vice-President Sherman was favorable.

On March 2nd, William H. Taft, President of the United States, signed our bill and it became a law.

The last clause of the law, "the details incident to the transfer of said land to be arranged and perfected by the secretary of war," made it necessary for the Woman's Relief Corps to employ an attorney-at-law. Colonel Thomas S. Hopkins, of Washington, D. C., a comrade and able lawyer, by advice of Mrs. Sherwood and national president was consulted, and he has given undivided attention to the land survey, and all legal lines of the deed of transfer.

Much research has been necessary to unravel the tangle of deeds of conveyance and disputed land survey; but Chief Clerk Lewis W. Call, of Judge Advocate-General Davis's department, has promised Attorney Hopkins that he will submit to him the deed of transfer approved by the judge advocate-general in time for presentation at the G. A. R. encampment greetings in Atlantic City, September 20, 1910.

Our national president requested me to extend an invitation to General Davis to be present to receive the final deed of Andersonville Prison property to the United States government.

The Woman's Relief Corps is greatly indebted to Honorable Joseph B. Foraker, who introduced Bill 6971 to the Senate, May 5, 1908, and safely piloted it to the House; also to Representative John A. T. Hull, chairman of the House military committee, and Senator William Warner, of the Senate committee.

Your transfer committee, Kate B. Sherwood, Mary L. Gilman and Mary M. North, have rendered valuable assistance, also Carrie Sparklin Read, while it was pending in the Senate. Your chairman has tried to do her duty in superintending detail work to its final completion. Looking back to March 27, 1908, when as national president, with the consent of my executive council, in the name of the Woman's Relief Corps, I formulated and proffered the free gift of Andersonville Prison property to the United States government, my heart is full of thankfulness and gratitude to our national convention and national president that I was continued to the end of the work, and thus permitted in my declining years to see the glorious fruition of the cherished hope of years.

It was the harvest time of the work while the veterans of the Civil War held high places in legislation, while many women of the war yet lived and remembered the suffering of Andersonville Prison, the greatest battlefield of mental and physical suffering known in the annals of war, and we are proud of our government to-day, that has accepted the gift, and will perpetually guard Andersonville Prison grounds in honor of our Nation's defenders.

The Woman's Relief Corps has been faithful to a sacred trust. Lizabeth A. Turner, as our national president, sixteen years ago received the gift of the Andersonville Prison pen from the G. A. R., department of Georgia. She devoted the remaining years of her life in hallowing the grounds as a sacred spot. It was a beautiful devotion of the Woman's Relief Corps to care for and beautify these grounds, and in surrendering them to the higher care of our government, we will not forget. It will ever be a sacred memory, and our offerings of love will continue in gifts to the beautiful rose garden that is consecrated to Memorial Day in Andersonville Cemetery.

Respectfully submitted in F., C. and L.,

KATE E. JONES, *Chairman,*
KATE B. SHERWOOD,
MARY M. NORTH,
MARY L. GILMAN,
Committee.

I find in the proceedings referred to the report of Mrs. Sarah D. Winans, chairman of the prison board, to the national secretary of the Woman's Relief Corps, which will fittingly round out the account of the work of this valuable and patriotic auxiliary to the Grand Army of the Republic. I quote:

TOLEDO, OHIO, August 1, 1910.

GEORGIA WADE MCCLELLAN,
National Secretary, Woman's Relief Corps.

MADAM: I have the honor herewith to transmit to you, and through you to the Twenty-eighth National Convention, the report of the Andersonville Prison Board for the past year.

On account of the great distance, it has never been possible to hold a meeting of the board at Prison Park. On that account the responsibility of the care and improvements has rested chiefly upon the chairman of the board. I have endeavored to keep in close touch with its members by writing, and am proud to say that I have had their most loyal support in all that seemed necessary to be done.

Early in April I was directed by the national president to go and make all necessary repairs and put everything in good order before making the transfer to the government. Upon my arrival there I found work which detained me over three weeks. Both wells were in bad condition; the quicksand had to be drawn out and a new curbing put in; their depth now is ninety feet, with fifteen feet of water. Much to our surprise, the pump at the windmill during the winter froze and burst, necessitating the purchase of a new pump. The tank was also newly painted, and now there is an abundance of good water for use at the house and at the rose garden.

Providence Spring was never in such fine condition as now. I had the floor of the pavilion newly cemented. The water is running through the fountain furnished by the Ex-Prisoners of War Association into a basin, and into a pool in the floor, and out through the pavilion, clear and sparkling as when it first burst forth to quench the thirst of the starving prisoners. The ground around is beautified by growing ferns.

The pecan orchard is well cared for, and in a few years will be bearing nuts for profit. The grounds are well kept, and the Woman's Relief Corps can well be proud of what has been accomplished by the indomitable will and perseverance of her whose monument stands under the folds of the flag near by the rose garden she loved so well, Lizabeth A. Turner.

During the past year four hundred and eleven visitors have registered, thirty-eight ex-soldiers and eight ex-prisoners.

The caretaker, Comrade Bickell, and his wife have proven themselves the right people in the right place. Having been a prisoner there, he is interested in preserving all the landmarks, and the wells where the boys dug in vain for water. These wells, some seventy and eighty feet deep, are well preserved and will stand forever in memory of those who made the great sacrifice loyal and true to their country and died for the cause of freedom, and whose bones are washing out of the ground on the hillside at every heavy rainstorm.

Mrs. Bickell, a typical Southern woman, proves herself an agreeable hostess; she is loyal and fully in sympathy with the oft-repeated story of starvation and suffering, as told by the ex-prisoners while visiting there, and repeats the truth of the same to those who would fain believe that such inhuman cruelties never could have existed in a civilized country.

The Wirz monument, standing in the village, is its own condemnation. It need only stand there; a time will come when the South will be glad to bury it from sight.

Our gifts this year are not numerous, but much appreciated. Through Kate G. Raynor, national patriotic instructor, the Sons of Veterans Auxiliary gave cocoa matting for the main hall in the cottage.

The Department of Ohio, through its president, Mary C. Wentzel, gave a large wool bunting flag for the flagpole which was dedicated on Memorial Day.

Mr. William Easterlin has promised to give land for a boulevard to connect Prison Park with the cemetery, making a deed to the government when the transfer is made.

To make and keep our country great and strong, education must go hand in hand with patriotism; and as the Woman's Relief Corps transfers to the United States government her sacred trust of preserving the hallowed spot where thousands suffered martyrdom because of their patriotism, what more fitting use could be made of a part of the fund, set aside for Andersonville Prison Park, than to use it to encourage this grand moral sentiment? . . . The Memorial University, located in the geographical center of the United States and dedicated to the veterans and loyal women of 1861-65, is only in its infancy and needs our patriotic and loving support. We now have the opportunity of helping to build this living monument to a size as big as the biggest. . . .

And now as this sacred place is about to pass into other hands, and I think of laying down the work so near to my heart, and in which I have labored for fourteen long years, I must confess a feeling of loneliness comes over me, and I shall long to journey to that Mecca once more and see it made more beautiful as the years go by.

ANDERSONVILLE PRISON BOARD.

Woman's Relief Corps Committee, Andersonville Prison Board, who have had the care and keeping of the prison pen grounds for years; and who have restored this sacred spot from a withering waste to a place beautiful in memory of nearly 14,000 soldier boys who suffered "Death Before Dishonor."

ANDERSONVILLE CEMETERY, AND CONCLUSION. 507

To the members of the board and members of the advisory board, who with kind words and advice have rendered valued assistance, I return sincere thanks.

I wish to express to the national president my thanks for the trust, confidence and counsel throughout the entire year; and to all who have placed a flower in my pathway I express heartfelt thanks.

Respectfully submitted in F., C. and L.,

SARAH D. WINANS, *Chairman*

At the National Encampment of the Grand Army of the Republic, convened at Atlantic City in September, 1910, there was a semi-official meeting of welcome held on the evening of September 20th. Among other interesting proceedings, all of which were of the most inspiring and patriotic character, was the formal transfer of the title to the prison grounds. I quote as follows:

COMMANDER-IN-CHIEF VAN SANT: The next number on the programme is of great interest to every member of the Grand Army of the Republic, the presentation to the United States government, by the national president of the Woman's Relief Corps, of Andersonville Prison grounds.

JENNIE IOWA BERRY, national president of the Woman's Relief Corps: Commander-in-chief and friends: One of the great spots of American history, hallowed by sufferings known to America and to the world, the sight of Andersonville Prison pen, is about to pass from the keeping of the Woman's Relief Corps to that of the United States government, and I have requested the woman who has been instrumental in bringing about the acceptance by the government of this historic and sacred spot to make the presentation, Kate E. Jones, past national president of the Woman's Relief Corps.

KATE E. JONES: Commander-in-chief, veterans of the Grand Army and citizens assembled: Sixteen years ago the department of Georgia, Grand Army of the Republic, presented to the Woman's Relief Corps a tract of land known as the Andersonville Prison pen, famous in the history of the Civil War.

The Woman's Relief Corps accepted the gift as a sacred trust, and year after year improved, cultivated and beautified the grounds till the barren desert waste became a garden of beauty. Five states erected beautiful monuments thereon to the memory of their heroic dead, and far above the highest ground in the old stockade the stars and stripes floated in the breeze, seen for miles around.

As the years went on the feeling grew apace among comrades and members of the Woman's Relief Corps that these hallowed grounds should be under the care of and belong to the United States government. March 27, 1908, I, as national president, in the name of the Woman's Relief Corps, proffered, as a free gift, the Andersonville Prison property to the United States government. Finally, after some delay, the bill passed the Senate and House of Representatives unanimously, and March 2, 1910, President William H. Taft signed the bill, and it became a law.

To-night I have the honor to present to the representative, Lewis W. Call, chief clerk of Judge Advocate-General George B. Davis of the war department, the transfer deed of Andersonville Prison property from the Woman's Relief Corps to the United States government. It is a deed of a battlefield, the battlefield of the greatest mental and physical suffering known in the annals of war, where nearly 14,000 men imprisoned, suffered, starved and died in defense of their country, preferring death to dishonor.

> It is land blessed by God in Providence Spring when
> The prisoners' cry of thirst rang up to Heaven;
> God heard and with his thunder cleft the earth
> And poured His sweetest water gushing there.
> a crystal spring to-day.

We are proud of our government that it accepts our gift, and will perpetually guard and care for this hallowed spot in honor of our nation's defenders.

As I surrender to you this deed to the Andersonville Prison property the heart of the Woman's Relief Corps goes with it. Many of us are old, gray-haired women of the war, that knew of the sufferings of Andersonville. We shall never forget, but continue our gifts to the beautiful rose garden with its wealth of blossoms consecrated to Memorial Day and the graves in Andersonville National Cemetery.

LEWIS W. CALL: Ladies of the Woman's Relief Corps: In accepting from you this gift to the government of the hallowed spot which has been your care for sixteen years I feel that it is fitting that it should pass into the hands of the government for whom 14,000 men suffered martyrdom, and especially fitting that it should be placed under the care of the war department, whose judge advocate-general has authorized me to accept your donation.

I feel sure that your trust will be faithfully executed, that the grounds will ever be held as a memorial of the heroism of the men who there proved themselves the highest type of patriots, that future generations may journey there, and reading the inscriptions upon the monuments you have caused to be erected, honor their memory, and realizing, in a measure, the individual sacrifice and patriotism that were necessary to preserve this nation, be inspired to do their part to keep this a government of the people, for the people and by the people. I thank you in the name of the United States government for this gift.

Some of the defenders of Andersonville Prison have alluded in contemptuous phrase to the fact that many prisoners believed that Providence Spring burst forth as a direct answer to their prayers for relief from the thirst which was consuming them. Inscriptions on some of the monuments erected at the cemetery have crystalized this belief. Are we at liberty to treat the matter as pure superstition—the idle conjuring of disordered minds? This spring figures throughout the testimony; several lives were sacrificed at this spot in cases where the cry of suffering nature overcame the dictates of prudence and the fatal dead-line was unintentionally infringed upon. But these life-giving waters saved many souls from perishing, and can we wonder that Providence Spring was worshipped with unreasoning superstition—a sort of fetishism! What right have we dogmatically now to say that God's hand was not made manifest in this unexpected source of relief?

While these pages were being passed through the press the bronze tablet to the Woman's Relief Corps was on Memorial Day, 1911, dedicated at Andersonville. Mrs. Sarah D. Winans, chairman of the Andersonville Prison Board, has sent me a report of the dedicatory proceedings as published in the Atlanta *Constitution* June 4th, which will be read with interest by all who are in sympathy with the noble work of this patriotic organization. Among the illustrations in this volume I have been able to secure two of especial value—namely, the monument to Lizabeth Turner and the tablet commemorating the work of the Woman's Relief Corps. The report of the proceedings on the latter occasion follows:

At the dedication on Tuesday, May 30, of the bronze tablet to the Woman's Relief Corps, recently erected in Andersonville Park, interesting addresses were made by a number of prominent men and women, and many visitors were present to witness the exercises which commemorate the work of the Relief Corps, auxiliary to the Grand Army of the Republic, in presenting the park to the United States government.

The opening number on the programme was the raising of "Old Glory," which was presented by past department presidents of the Vermont Woman's Relief Corps. After the ceremony, Mrs. Harris, national president of the corps, sang the "Star Spangled Banner."

Mrs. Crane, national chaplain of the ladies of the G. A. R., gave the invocation. The history of the purchase of Andersonville by the department of the Georgia G. A. R. was read by Past Department Commander W. M. Scott, of Atlanta.

A poem, written for the occasion by T. C. Harbaugh, was read by Mrs. Emmogene Marshall, whose brother was among the first to enter Andersonville, and lies buried there.

The history of the work of the Woman's Relief Corps at Andersonville since 1896, was given by Mrs. Sarah D. Winans, chairman of the Andersonville prison board.

The monument was turned over to the national president of Women's Relief Corps, she in turn presenting it to the United States government, through Captain Bryant, superintendent of Andersonville cemetery, who responded briefly for the government.

The address of the afternoon was delivered by Mrs. Lue Stuart Wadsworth, of Boston, national patriotic instructor of the Woman's Relief Corps, and was a finely worded and inspiring tribute.

Preceding her address Mrs. Wadsworth recited her original poem, "A Tribute to the Heroes of Andersonville," among whom was her uncle.

Mrs. Dr. Bliss, of Saginaw, Mich., paid a tribute to the women of the war, and an original poem by Past National President Mrs. Kate Brownlee Sherwood, of Toledo, Ohio, was read, and also a letter from Miss Barton, an honored member of the order, after which there was a song by National President Mrs. Harris, "The Flag Without a Stain."

The exercises closed with singing of "America" and the benediction.

The monument was unveiled by Master J. Corey Winans, Jr., of Ohio, and three hearty cheers were given by the veterans for the completed work of the noble women.

Members of the two G. A. R. posts in Fitzgerald and their auxiliaries of Woman's Relief Corps and Ladies of the G. A. R. were present in large numbers. Many members of the order were present, among whom were National President Mrs. Belle C. Harris, of Emporia, Kansas; National Patriotic Instructor Mrs. Lue Stuart Wadsworth, of Boston, Massachusetts; Chairman of the Executive Board Mrs. Alice C. Dillworth, of Omaha, Nebraska; Past National President Mrs. Sarah D. Winans, of Toledo, Ohio; Mrs. Allaseba M. Bliss, of Saginaw, Michigan; Assistant National Press Correspondent Mrs. Isabel Worrell Ball, of Washington, D. C.; Mrs. Elenora Marshall, of Sandusky, Ohio; Past Department President of Idaho, Mrs. Emma C. Grinnell, of Beloit, Wisconsin; National Chaplain of the Ladies of the G. A. R. Mrs. M. C. Crane; Mrs. T. C. Wainman, of Bainbridge, Georgia.

Comrade J. T. Bicknell and Mrs. Bicknell entertained those who remained overnight at the park.

In reply to inquiries made relative to the work of the Woman's Relief Corps at the Andersonville Cemetery, Mrs. Winans has written me some facts which should find a place in this volume. I quote:

You refer to the work of the Woman's Relief Corps in beautifying the cemetery grounds. In this you are under a misapprehension. The cemetery has always been cared for by the general government. It is the prison pen, the ground where the boys suffered and starved that we thought should be held as sacred ground. It lies about one-fourth of a mile from the cemetery and contains eighty-seven acres, which include all the earthworks and forts surrounding the stockade; also Wirz's headquarters. The Grand Army of the Republic organization of Georgia first purchased the grounds but were not able to improve them and asked the Woman's Relief Corps to accept them as a gift, which we did, pledging ourselves to improve and keep them in order. We found it necessary to purchase fourteen acres additional to include all the forts. We took possession of the property in 1896. We put a woven wire fence around the entire eighty-seven acres, built a nine-room house and placed a care-taker on the ground. Later we built a granite pavilion over Providence Spring and made improvements from year to year. Five states have erected monuments in the stockade, believing they should stand on the ground where the men whose memory they commemorate suffered and died. The monuments erected by Ohio, Michigan, Massachusetts, Rhode Island and Wisconsin are within the grounds. . . . I presume you are aware that the government has accepted a deed of this property from the Woman's Relief Corps. I am yet in charge, but they promise to take possession very soon. We have planted 400 pecan trees that are now coming into bearing. I think the government will make a boulevard joining the stockade and the cemetery. . . . I do feel that as the English government guards with reverent care the "Black Hole of Calcutta," so

THE EMPTY SLEEVE.

John S. Koster, a Union soldier now residing at Port Leyden, N. Y., and his little grandson "Bob." This picture has no direct relevancy to Andersonville, but it represents a phase of the sacrifices caused by the rebellion which should lead us to pause before bestowing honors and rewards upon the participants in that rebellion. The touching story told by this graphic picture will appeal to the surviving veterans of the Union Army and, it is hoped, may not be without its lesson to the youth of our country.

we should with more reverent care guard the sacred ground on which so many suffered and died for our flag.

Then the miracle of Providence Spring should be recorded in history. The wells dug there are in perfect preservation—some seventy to eighty feet deep.... After a heavy rain you can pick up human bones in the stockade grounds. When they dug to set up the flag-pole they came upon the remains of a body; also when the Michigan monument was erected; and also when the pecan trees were being set out, which proves that many lie buried there in addition to those buried in the cemetery. We gathered and placed some of these bones in our monument."[1]

After the first edition of this volume had come from the press I received from Comrade John O'Breiter, a copy of a letter written to him by Lizabeth A. Turner, who gave her life to the restoration and preservation of the Andersonville prison-pen. The story of the labors and sacrifices of the noble women who stood by this pathetic work should have permanent place in the history I have tried to give of that prison.

"THE BIGGEST BATTLE FIELD OF THE CIVIL WAR."

NEW BRITAIN, CONN., Dec. 5, 1903.

JOHN O'BREITER, ESQ.,
    Lancaster, Pa.

Dear Comrade: I was much pleased to receive your letter of November 26th. Yes, there is much to be done to make Andersonville all we hope to do for the place. Could you have seen the place seven years ago when the Relief Corps began work there, you would wonder how it was possible for them to accomplish so much as they have done. It was then wild land, no fences, and covered with scrub oaks and poisonous vines. The swamp was entirely impassable, and what is now a good road from outside our grounds and through the entrance gate to the main road was a washout and a gully. You can have no idea of the place and its desolation when the women took hold of it, and no one but women would have had the courage to try to improve the place in that country unless they had a mint of money at their disposal. Our caretaker slept for three years with a pistol under his pillow and an axe under his bed; his life was threatened, and I was looked upon as a woman interloper; but we plodded on quietly, but determined to keep the ground and improve it in memory of the men who gave life and health for the Union.

We have become respected, and Andersonville is now the show-place of the two counties. We own the roadway (100 feet inside) from the entrance to the county road. So you see there was no other suitable place for the gate but at the entrance to our property, as we must fence in the land to keep out cattle and hogs, as they would ruin our grounds. Our fences and gates cost us over seven hundred dollars, the house nineteen hundred, barn three hundred, planting the

---

[1] Witnesses testified that bodies were buried in the prison pen because their condition made their removal to the cemetery impossible. Thus is confirmed the horrors which surrounded those unhappy prisoners.

prison-pen to Bermuda grass roots two hundred, the pavilion over the spring fourteen hundred, and so on, with items such as salary of caretaker, mule and farming implements, has brought the cost of the place at the present time up to over $20,000. Much more, I suppose, could have been done, only I refused to go one cent into debt for anything. Gate and other markers will be added as time goes on. Improvements are added each year and will be continued so as to make the grounds worthy of the men in whose memory it is held sacred.

When the G. A. R. of the Department of Georgia bargained for the prison-pen they hoped and expected that the Northern posts would raise a fund for its improvement and support. This was not and could not be accomplished. They then offered it free of expense to the National Government (the W. R. C. had paid off the mortgage of $700). The United States would not take it because it was not a battlefield, when in reality it was the very biggest battlefield of the Civil War. It was offered to the government at two different times and twice offered to the National G. A. R. at encampments. Then the women woke up and took the grounds, buying 14 acres more, so as to have all that has ever been used for prison purposes. Every well, fort, earthworks and rifle pit stands just as it did when the prisoners of the Union marched out of the stockade.

The original owners of the land came into possession of it after a four years' lawsuit. They burnt up or carried away most of the stockade, so that eight years after the war only that part under the ground remained. Some few logs are still owned by the colored people there.

I have been very careful not to have one tree cut from any of the (these trees sprung up since the place was used as a prison) entrenchments or forts, as their roots held the soil in place; otherwise they would soon be obliterated. No roads or streets of any kind were on the survey or defined on the ground when it came into our possession. That was over thirty years after the war; it was wild land. The place where the house stands and the forts behind and back of the house, with the parts of the pen where the flagpole stands, were bought by the W. R. C. after it came into their hands.

We are planting pecan trees to help make the place self-sustaining and shall establish a fund for the perpetual care of the grounds. We should have accomplished more ere this, but we care for a home for army nurses and soldiers' wives that cost us from $12,000 to $14,000 a year. We must look after the living and then perpetuate the memory of those that suffered and those that died in Andersonville prison-pen.

Thanking you for your kind words in appreciation of what is being done and for suggestions for marking of localities, I am respectfully yours,

LIZABETH A. TURNER.

A PARTING WORD WITH THE READER.

My purpose in publishing this volume is to rescue the salient facts: relating to one of the most startling and dramatic, as well as the most-melancholy and deplorable chapters in the history of the War of the Rebellion, and to refute the grossly inaccurate, not to say false, statements to be found engraved upon the Wirz monument and being widely disseminated as the truth concerning the Andersonville Rebel Prison.

Having been, in some measure, personally responsible for the conduct of the trial of Wirz, I will be pardoned if, in this review, I have shown more the spirit of the advocate than of the judge. A society, respectable in numbers and in its personnel, has declared that Captain Wirz was innocent of the charges of which he was found guilty, and was judicially murdered, and it seeks to fix the ultimate responsibility for the Tragedy of Andersonville upon the Federal government.

It can hardly be expected that under such circumstances I would publish a record which would impeach the verdict of the court or would justify the very grave charges now being promulgated in relation to the trial. I submit, with confidence, to the unprejudiced reader, whether I have shown unwarranted feeling and whether the court drew unsupported conclusions from the evidence adduced before it.

I have endeavored to fairly state the evidence on both sides, and, while, necessarily, much had to be omitted to bring the book within reasonable compass, I am not conscious of having suppressed any fact which would have tended to strengthen the defense of the accused, nor am I conscious of having in any wise attempted to exaggerate or obscure any of the important issues. I think it will be found that nearly all of the incriminating evidence is found in the testimony and official reports of rebel witnesses, and upon that alone, under settled rules of criminal law, the prisoner was proven guilty of conduct and acts sufficient to justify the sentence imposed and the findings of a conspiracy to destroy Union soldiers, helpless prisoners of war.

It has been said to me, by persons for whose opinion I have high regard, that it was unwise to re-open the question of the Andersonville horror. It is quite likely others will share this opinion, and they may censure me for unveiling the ghastly scenes of suffering and death through which our unhappy prisoners of war were forced to pass. Be it so. I still think complete justification is shown in the earlier pages of this record for placing the facts before the world.

That differences of opinion should exist as to the wisdom of reviving the facts herein narrated, is in keeping with a disposition manifested by the thoughtless to break down the distinction which, for many years has been recognized between the services rendered in defense of the Union and the services given in the effort to destroy the Union.

Step by step the youth are being led to regard the Rebellion as but a venial political misadventure, reflecting no great discredit upon those who were engaged in it, since it failed of its purpose and since we are again a united people.

Gradually the public mind is being taught to accord equal honors, which may be followed by equal rewards to those who fought to dissolve the Union of States and those who fought to perpetuate the Union handed down to us by the Fathers of the Republic. In a flux of good feeling we are putting out of sight the underlying issues of the great conflict of arms and forgetting the stupendous sacrifices which were made and the precious lives which were lost in the settlement of those issues. Can we with safety do this? Can we as a nation overlook the motive of the Rebellion and all its awful consequences and enter upon a policy of bestowing honors and rewards upon those who were engaged in that rebellion and for no other reason than that they were so engaged? That they were admitted to full participation in the affairs of government naturally followed the restoration of the Union. But this concession came not as a reward for their military prowess in their resistance to the constituted authorities of the Union; it came to them as citizens of a common Union who had laid down their arms and renewed their allegiance to the Union. As citizens they were welcomed but as military heroes the government can never with consistency or with justice bestow upon them the honors and rewards which rightfully belong to those who staked their lives to preserve the nation. Any other view is to place a premium on disloyalty and must result in destroying all motive for supporting the government against the perils of rebellion.

I have been led to make these observations in view of the fact that a bill is now before the Senate of the United States, recommended by the Committee on Military Affairs, appropriating $125,000 "for the erection of a Confederate naval monument at the Vicksburg National Military Park to commemorate the services of the Confederate navy."

The Congressional Record of July 18th, 1911, contains this bill as amended and reported to the Senate by the Committee on Military Affairs. Section 1 reads:

That for the construction of a memorial to cost not to exceed $125,000 commemorative of the services of the Confederate Navy on the Mississippi River and its tributaries during the Civil War at the site and in accordance with the design approved by the Secretary of War, the sum of $50,000 is hereby appropriated out of any money in the treasury not otherwise apportioned.

516   THE TRAGEDY OF ANDERSONVILLE.

Senator Williams of Mississippi, having charge of the bill, stated that it had the approval of the Vicksburg National Military Park Commission and the recommendation of the Secretary of War. Senator Cummins of Iowa, representing a State that sacrificed hundreds of lives to save the Union, and Senator Works of California, who was himself a Union soldier, spoke in favor of the bill on sentimental grounds, apparently neither of them being conscious of the principle involved nor mindful of where such a precedent may lead. Senator Taylor of Tennessee advocated its passage from the standpoint of one who sees no great difference in the motive which actuated the contending forces during the war. He argued that as the South had contributed its share towards the erection of monuments "to commemorate the deeds of the brave men who followed the Federal flag, it was not asking too much to build a monument to the brave men who met them face to face on the battle field and upon the water." He said: "Why not build it? The Southern people were not guilty of treason. They fought for what they believed was right."

But two Senators raised their voices in opposition—Senator Heyburn of Idaho and Senator Dixon of Montana. Senator Heyburn spoke with much force. He showed how the so-called Confederacy was regarded in the eye of the law as decided by the United States Supreme Court, citing the case.[1]

It is well for us to remember that the Confederacy, as an association of States, never had any recognition by our government. If the Confederacy as such could not receive recognition by the Federal Government, how can that government now extend recognition in the highest and most honorable form it can be bestowed, to those who fought to establish the Confederacy? In the case cited by Senator Heyburn the Supreme Court said:

The rebellion out of which the war grew was without any legal sanction. In the eye of the law it had the same properties as if it had been the insurrection of a county or smaller municipal territory against the State to which it belonged. The proportion and duration of the struggle did not affect its character. Nor was there a rebel government *de facto* in such a sense as to give any legal efficiency to its acts. . . . The Union of the States, for all the purposes of the constitution, is as perfect and indissoluble as the union of the integral parts of the States themselves; and nothing but revolutionary violence can in either case destroy the ties which hold the parts together. For the sake of humanity certain belligerent

[1] Hickman vs. Jones, 9 Wall, 197.

rights were conceded to the insurgents in arms. But the recognition did not extend to the pretended government of the Confederacy. . . . The Rebellion was simply an armed resistance to the rightful authority of the sovereign. Such was its character, its rise, progress and downfall.

The view taken by Senator Dixon cannot fail to deeply impress one who will give a moment's thoughtful consideration to the question. I quote:

Mr. President, it is much easier at times to vote in accordance with your feelings of sentiment than it is in accordance with a strict sense of public duty, and I confess that this bill raises a question in my mind which makes me somewhat halt between two opinions. I am a member of the Committee on Military Affairs, and this is the first time I knew that this bill had ever been reported to the Senate. That probably is on account of my dereliction of duty in not attending at all times every meeting of the committee. It is a little difficult for me personally to express my real feelings regarding a matter of this kind. I am a Southerner born, Mr. President. My mother's people served in the Confederate Army, while my father's kinsmen, some of them, served in the Army for the preservation of the Union. I think, without a feeling of egotism, that I can therefore look on the period of the Civil War with as broad and catholic a spirit as any patriotic American citizen can do.

Personally, I have only the greatest feeling of admiration for the heroic men who laid down their lives for the cause of the Confederacy. I doubt whether in all history there is any more superb example of devotion to what they believed to be a principle than that which inspired the people of the South from 1861 to 1865.

At the same time the principle for which they contended was eternally wrong. It was one of the questions which rise from a great disturbance of men's minds, not questioning any man's feeling of right or wrong. But looking back 45 years to that period, we know that the principle for which the South contended was wrong, that it would have been fatal to the very existence of republican institutions.

After paying a tribute to the bravery of the men who were connected with the Confederate Navy on the Mississippi River and its tributaries and expressing a willingness to personally contribute to the cost of a monument to their memory, he said:

But, Mr. President, is this the proper time for us to appropriate money from the Federal Treasury to perpetuate by Federal law the acts of those who sought to destroy the very Government from which this appropriation is sought? . . . There are probably half a million Federal soldiers still living. I doubt, Mr. President, the wisdom that would take money from the Federal Treasury at this time to perpetuate by official act of this Government during the life time of the half million men who wore the blue and who by their own heroic sacrifice perpetuated this Republic, to build a monument—I read—"commemorative of the service of the Confederate Navy on the Mississippi River and its tributaries during the civil war." I do not believe the time has come for this Government to do these things officially. . . . I do not believe at this time the Government should entertain this plan, which is merely the entering wedge. A monument at Vicksburg to the Confederate Navy is merely a prelude to a hundred other appropriations for a hundred other battlefields. . . . By the same rule of action and applying the same yard stick, if it is right to appropriate $150,000 for this monument at Vicksburg, then we ought also to dot the battle fields of the Civil War with bronze monuments to the men who died in the cause that they believed to be right. With this feeling, Mr. President, and with a feeling of regret that my judgment and my conscience do not allow me to vote for this measure, and wishing only to make my own sentiment plain, I am compelled by what I conceive to be my duty to all the country at this time to cast my vote in opposition to the appropriation.

Upon what just consideration of principle, policy, or even of sentiment, can any other view than that expressed by Senator Dixon be taken? The dangerous precedent condemned, the opening wedge warned against, means more than the money outlay involved. If the comparatively insignificant services of the Confederate Navy on the Mississippi River call for such recognition, what must be done to adequately signalize the appreciation of the Federal Government for the valiant services of the Confederate Navy on the high seas to destroy American shipping?

But the greater services of the insurgents, in their effort to divide and destroy the Union, were on the hundreds of battlefields and these, as Senator Dixon said, must if the Government be consistent be dotted with monuments erected by that government to honor those who fell while fighting to destroy it. Nor can this spirit of forgiveness, this blotting out of all memory of stupendous sacrifices made to preserve the Union, halt with these memorials.

The two contending forces had each a commander-in-chief. The day will come, if the policy of the pending Senate bill be adopted, when the Nation must commemorate the services of Jefferson Davis as the leader of the Rebellion with the same evidences of gratitude and appreciation as has been done by the Nation to commemorate the services of Abraham Lincoln. It is impossible to differentiate a "National Monument to Commemorate the Services of the Confederate Navy of the Mississippi River and its tributaries," from like monuments to the greater naval force of the Confederacy, to the armies it assembled and indeed, to its chosen civil and military leader. To the memory of all alike are we now asked to do homage.

I repeat, this policy places a premium on disloyalty and is destructive of the sentiment of patriotism—the highest motive to which the Nation can appeal in times of threatened danger to the integrity of the Republic.

The Senate did not reach a vote upon the measure. Let us hope that the wiser and better thought of its friends may realize its impropriety and withhold it.

Singularly, the newspapers have not discovered this insidious piece of legislation. In but one have I seen it commented upon, and I give it as stating the question in a nutshell. I quote from the *Sacramento Bee* (California) of July 25, 1911:

Senator Heyburn's remarks in opposing an appropriation for the erection of a monument in honor of Confederate soldiers were intemperate.

Yet the justice of his opposition cannot successfully be attacked. It is not right for Congress in any wise to honor men who fought through four bloody years in an endeavor to destroy the Union.

There is a principle involved here that no false sentiment should be allowed to make us forget. The Confederate dead and living have been honored in many ways since the Civil War, particularly by their former enemies, whose magnanimity has been very great, but to ask the Government itself to commemorate their assaults upon it, however brave, is carrying sentiment to an absurd extreme.

If the Southern States should raise the money for a monument by private subscription, it would be more appropriate and representative.

Fortunately, since these pages were written and came from the press the senate has adjourned without action on this bill. It appears that this proposed measure did not pass unnoticed by the newspaper press of the country, nor did it escape the condemnation of some of the leading journals, which doubtless had influence, as well as the lateness of the session, in bringing about a postponement of further consideration of the bill.

Many posts of the Grand Army of the Republic hastened to make known their unalterable opposition and denouncing a policy which would impliedly extend governmental recognition and tacit approval of facts which the government once characterized as rebellious and treasonable, and which had for their object the overthrow of the government itself.

Nor is the principle involved in the least changed by the proposal to strike out the word "service" and insert the words "courage and constancy." Why should our government reward the "courage and constancy" of Confederate soldiers and sailors in view of the admitted fact that they exhibited those attributes in an uncompromising effort to destroy the government? It is impossible to distinguish in its ultimate meaning and effect the commemoration of the "courage and constancy" with which the rebel soldiers and sailors fought, from like tribute to the "service" in which they were engaged and to which they solemnly pledged their lives.

"Such journals as the New York *Times, Tribune, Sun* and *Evening Post*, and the Detroit *Journal*, declare that there is no possible justification or excuse for the proposed appropriation. That it should be 'seriously urged,' observes the Boston *Herald*, advertises Uncle Sam as an 'easy mark.' The Roanoke (Va.) *Times* asserts that 'no such appropriation should be made, and no such monument should be built by the government,' because, 'if we Southern people want a monument to the Confederate navy, we should go down in our own pockets and build it ourselves.' "[1]

Let the Blue and the Gray fraternize, as they have ever since the war. Let them rejoice that we are a united people. But do not let the government be called upon to give its official sanction to the rebellion.

While the arrangements for this Vicksburg re-union were being made, the following message, presumably sent by the Associated Press agent, appeared in the newspapers of the country:

MEMPHIS, Tenn., Sept. 4.—The stars and stripes and stars and bars will be displayed on an equal plane, neither above the other, in the coming first national Blue and the Gray reunion to be held in Memphis, beginning September 27th. The Grand Army of the Republic and local Republicans, decided that throughout the decorations on all floats the colors should be entwined and equal prominence given to both.

In the light of the proposed appropriation by Congress such an arrangement was perfectly logical and every way consistent. But does it not emphasize the significance of the pending bill? What is a flag but the representative of an idea or principle or cause? In itself it has no meaning, but when used to represent a principle or a just cause men will face certain death in its defense. All that is precious in our history clusters around the American flag as the symbol of our country's greatness and glory. Let it not be dishonored by being entwined with a flag which typified rebellion and treason; which stood for an abortive effort to destroy the Union; and which, if it means anything now, must mean what it ever has signified. The Confederate flag can serve no other or higher office at this time than to inspire in the minds of the youth of the South a belief that the cause for which it stood was grounded in justice and righteousness, whose memory must not be permitted to fade. This blending of the "Stars and Bars" with

[1] Literary Digest, Aug. 5, 1911.

the "Stars and Stripes," this display "on an equal plane," is but another step towards the obliteration, not only of all distinction between those who fought to preserve the Union and those who fought to destroy the Union, but it is a concession that there was nothing in the rebellion which posterity may condemn.

Secretary of State John Hay, in his eulogy upon the life and services of President McKinley, delivered at the joint session of the senate and house of representatives, said:

It is easy for partisanship to say that the one side was right and that the other was wrong. It is still easier for an indolent magnanimity to say that both were right. Perhaps in the wider view of ethics one is always right to follow his conscience, though it lead him to disaster or death. But history is inexorable. She takes no account of sentiment and intention, and in her cold and luminous eyes that side is right which fights in harmony with the stars in their courses. The men are right through whose efforts and struggles the world is helped onward and humanity is moved to a higher level and a brighter day.

If, notwithstanding the opinion of those who would throw the cloak of oblivion over the scenes in this volume depicted, and would obliterate all distinction between the loyal defenders of the flag and those who fought to dishonor it, I shall have quickened a sense of gratitude towards the armies of the Union and particularly those who suffered and died in Southern prisons, it will compensate me for all the labor involved and will sustain me under adverse criticism.

In my belief the loftiest heroism and the most self-sacrificing patriotism exhibited throughout the Civil War are to be found in the annals of rebel prisons among the suffering and dying Union soldiers. Impelled by a sense of the crime of which they were the innocent victims, and in the discharge of a small part of the obligation under which, as an American citizen and a fellow soldier, they have placed me, this brief epitome of their heroic sacrifices is now submitted by

THE AUTHOR.

INDEX

A

Adams, Abbie A., 506.
Allcock, Brevet Colonel, member of Military Court, 31.
Andersonville, Ga., location healthy; provisions abundant in region; yet prisoners starved to death by thousands, 20.
Andersonville Cemetery, 474.
Andersonville, condition of; its horrors well known by Richmond authorities, 65.
Andersonville, why chosen, 219.
Andersonville Prison Board; Woman's Relief Corps; work of, 502-513.
Area of the prison; Col. Chandler estimated at one time six square feet to man; actual space at best 27 square feet or 3 by 9 feet for each man, 66, 140.
Argument on special pleas of accused, 37.
Armstrong, James—Ohio Reg.—Robbed by James Duncan of picture of mother, 288.
Atlanta *Constitution,* Report by, 509.
Atwater, Dorence, kept death register; report to relatives of dead—Died in San Francisco and body taken to Island of Tahiti, 489-493.
Augur, Major-General C. C., executed sentence of death and buried Wirz, 436.

Baker, O. S., one of Wirz's attorneys, 36.
Bakery, the, slow in completing it; wholly inadequate, 60, 67.
Ball, Isabel Worrell, 510.
Ball and chain, many witnesses testified to use of for trivial offenses, 262, 276.
Ballier, Brevet Brigadier-General John F., member of military court, 31.
Barton, Miss Clara, report on cemetery; marking of graves; condition of prison grounds; evidences of gross cruelty and mismanagement, 480-489.
Baxter, Alice, monument erected to Wirz's memory; why erected, 15, 17.
Bed-sacks and sheets on hand and undistributed, 208.
Belford Magazine, article by Jefferson Davis, defends management; declares Wirz died a martyr; illegally convicted; Davis's article answered, 19, 25, 356.
Berry, Jennie Iowa, 507.
Bliss, Allaseba M., 505, 510.
Bicknell, J. T., 510.
Bloodhounds, the; court found that ferocious dogs were used and caused death, 25, 35, 64, 119, 124, 242, 244, 249, 250, 251, 260, 262, 275.
Bodies of our dead were frequently used "in the interest of science" and identity destroyed, 100.
Bradley, Major Thomas W. (New York Rep.), promoted bill for improvement of prison grounds, 503.

Bragg, Brigadier-General E. S., member of court; relieved on account of illness before verdict, 31.
Bread, made of unsifted cornmeal ground with husks on, underdone and shortened with flies, 217.
Brooklyn *Eagle,* anti-administration paper, 324-325.
Brown, D. Wolfe, reporter at the trial for court, 32.
Bryant, James M., superintendent cemetery, says markings fairly correct; letters of interest on several subjects, 493.
Bucked: Gagged: Whipped: for small provocation; inhuman punishment, 250, 256, 261, 276.
Buckingham, Hiram, origin of Providence Spring, 502.
Burying the dead in trenches; many bodies stark naked; no coffins used; no boards to protect bodies; laid on ground and covered with earth, 215, 256, 265, 281, 282.
Burt, Brigadier-General, U. S. A., commanded colored troops; gives interesting account of their services, 448.
Butler, General Benj. F., on exchange of prisoners, 388, 441, 458-463.

C

Call, Lewis W., 508.
Cameron, Simon, Secretary of War, refused to return negroes to slavery; policy of government pointed out regarding negroes and slaves, 442, 445.
Campbell, J. A., rebel Secretary of War; action on Col. Chandler's report; endorsement, 70, 412.
Cartel, suspension of, violated by confederacy; subject thoroughly discussed in chapter XV, 438-473.
Causes of death, chief; every form of cruel treatment; starvation most potent, 94, 120, 121, 125-132.
Chandler, Col. D. T., Rebel Inspector-General, reports condition of prison and prisoners; six square feet to man; Gen. Winder's inhuman suggestion for relief of; important document, 66, 388.
Chain gang, in constant use in cruelest form, 244, 251, 253, 258, 266, 272, 279.
Charge of murder, evidence chapter XII, 333; comments on, chapter XIII, 354.
Charges and specifications on trial, 32.
"Chickamauga" ordered shot by Wirz, 260, 270, 320.
Chilton, Colonel R. W., endorsement Chandler's, Report, 70, 412.
Chipman, N. P., frontispiece, 31, 35, 36, 354, 387, 429, 464.
Civil War, biggest battle in, 512.
Clay, Cal. H. L., Rebel Assistant Adjutant-General, endorsement on Chandler report, 61.

INDEX—CONTINUED.

Clothing from friends appropriated by officers within the stockade, 162.
Clothing and provisions from friends, 161.
Clothing, received from fellow prisoners by poisoning them, 85.
Clothing of the dead was immediately appropriated by the other prisoners, 181.
Clavereul, Father (diary), reveals climax of horrors, 198.
Cobb, General Howell, communication, 54; letter of, suggests necessary improvement of prison, 58.
Commission for trial of Wirz, members of, 31
Comparision of rebel prisons with federal prisons; important statistics; photos compared, 371-375.
Compilation of deaths, 181-182.
Conditions known at Richmond, 360.
"Confederate Veteran" defends Wirz monument as memorial of noble life, 16.
Confederate authorities had full knowledge of facts, 65.
Connecticut monument in cemetery, 450.
Congressional Record, July 18, 1911, bill for confederate monument defeated, 519.
Conspiracy, the, to destroy prisoners far-reaching and involved high officials, 363.
Conspiracy charge, the, 400.
Cook-house very filthy, 217.
Corn bread unfit for use, 106.
Corn meal: corn and cob ground together: often wet and mouldy: 279.
Crane, Mrs. M. C., National Chairman Ladies of G. A. R. dedication of Womans' Relief Corps tablet, 498, 510.
Cruelties practiced towards prisoners, 420.
Cummins, Albert B., U. S. Senator, Iowa, favored monument to confederate dead by the government, 516.
Cutler, A. D., conditions at Fort Delaware prison, 380.

D

Daily record of deaths, 375.
"Damned Yankees—let them die," said General Winder; refused them donated provisions, 152.
Davis, Jefferson, 11, 17, 19, 22, 23, 25, 28, 35, 43, 71, 100, 193, 219, 356, 363, 414, 451-2; defends prison management; says Wirz victim of suppressed testimony; only foxhounds to track prisoners; Wirz verdict an indictment of Davis; Prison condition known to him; portrait of; Andersonville chosen in region of plenty.
Daughters of Confederacy, 12, 13, 15.
Davis, Gen. Gee. B., Judge Advocate-General, 503.
Dead the, 67; "cords of them," 169; "piled up like hogs," 265.
Dead, the one man died and lay so long that he had to be buried where he died, 177.
"Dead house," the, 200.
Dead house (Dr. Jones), 362; corpses lay on bare ground covered with filth and vermin.
Dead-line, the, how originated; built also around hospital; man shot at dead line without warning; insufficiently constructed; to touch it meant death; furloughs given for shooting prisoners on; random shots killed innocent men not near, 57, 137, 140, 141, 165, 248, 258, 261, 268, 274, 283, 286, 347.

Death and disease, consolidated report, 93.
Deaths at Andersonville Prison, 13, 171, 369; Wirz monument insult to dead; dead sought for dissection; caused in innumerable ways as shown by witnesses.
Deaths, record of, 88.
Debris: all from 30,000 human beings passed within few yards of the so-called hospital, 110.
Deleware Fort, prison conditions at, 380.
Detachments, 166; prisoners divided in three squads of 90 each, 270 one detachment.
Diarrhœa the general complaint, 202, 253.
Diet more important than medicine; medicine useless without proper food, 114.
Diseases; diarrhea, fevers, ulcers, 88, 114, 172; scurvy in variety of dreadful forms; ulcers slowly eating away flesh and tissues down to bones.
Diseases; mosquito bites and smallest abrasion of skin caused gangrene and death, 89.
Diseases, report concerning, 88, 108.
Disposition of the dead, 91; left exposed for hours covered with filth and vermin, 171; dead in midst of dying; many post morterms; Dr. Jones's report, 81.99.
Dividing squad rations by numbers, 167.
Dix, General John A., 442.
Dixon, Joseph M., U. S. Senator, Montana; "The principle for which the South contended was wrong and would have been fatal to the very existence of republican institutions," 516.
Doane, Scott, conditions at Johnson's Island prison fully described, 379.
Doctors and surgeons insufficient, 103.
Duncan, James, acts of extreme cruelty by.

E

Eldridge, Chief Surgeon E. T., report, 60; recommends prison improvement.
Emaciation, starvation, wasting away, none among the confederate soldiers, 207; they had food and fuel in plenty and shelter.
Exchange of prisoners, 448; refused to white officers and negro troops, see chapter on Exchange, XV.
Excrements of sick and well, 91; handled in disgusting and unsanitary way.
Execution and burial of Wirz, 436.

F

Facts and results of trial, 30; sources as shown in this volume.
Fairclough, Richard, "I die from sheer staryation," 339; last request that his wife might not know how he suffered.
Fessenden, Brigadier-General Francis, member of military court, 31.
Findings and sentence, 428.
Findings of Commission, 35.
Findings of the court could rest upon rebel testimony, 298.
Filth six inches deep, 262.
Fitzgerald Post, G. A. R. and Auxiliaries, Georgia, 510.
Food unfit for human beings, 230.
Food, undigested, that had passed through men's bodies, 258, 263.
Food, clothing, shelter and soap, 66.
"Had to buy food or we would have starved," 180.

Food that had passed through men's bodies, undigested, eaten, 263.
Food not fit to eat, 232.
Food and clothing contributed by Methodist ladies refused by General Winder, 152.
Food; "I frequently saw men hunting around the sinks for food that had once passed through men's bodies undigested," 177.
Fort Deleware Prison, conditions at, 380.
Foraker, Hon. Joseph B., 503; aided in passing bill for acquiring prison grounds.
Fremont, General John C., 439; issued order, revoked by President Lincoln, that armsbearing citizens be shot.
"Frenchy (Frado), escaped seven times and brought back by dogs, 328.
Frightful conditions; a starving ration induced endless catalogue of diseases; incurable gangrene readily induced by; hospital reeking with miasmatic and gangrenous effluvia, 108, 109, 110, 130.
Fuller, Sarah E., 506.

G

Gangrene, frequent cause of death, 244, 361.
Gary, Brevet Major-General J. W., member of military court, 31.
Gangrenous sores filled with maggots and flies, which men were too weak to fight off, 168.
General orders, about number of prisoners and other regulations, came from Richmond, 211.
"General summary"; sick and dead by Dr. Jones, March, 1864, to August, inclusive,
Georgia good country for corn and wheat, 157; provisions available and in abundance.
Gilman, Mary L., 504.
Grinnell, Emma C., 510.
Grant, General U. S., 440; on exchange of prisoners, 461, 462; rebels put paroled prisoners in field; refused to exchange colored soldiers and their white officers.
Grave of Wirz, 50; body now in Olivet Cemetery, Washington, D. C.
Graveyard, no care of by the rebel government, 294; bodies exposed; dead buried in long trenches side by side like sardines and unprotected, and covered with earth.
Guard of the prison, 173.
Guards, the, were ordered to shoot any man attempting to speak to them, 278.
Guards rewarded for killing persons at deadline, 356.

H

Hall, Major W. Carvel, letter from Confederate records, 79; denies that he ever said that rebel prisoners were on a par with Federal prisoners.
Halleck, General H. W., on exchange of prisoners, 458; excluding negroes from Union camps, 439.
Handcuffing Wirz to prevent his suicide, 334.
Hanging of the six raiders, 194.
Hanging of six prisoners for theft and murder, 85
Harris, Belle C., National President Womans' Relief Corps, dedication of tablet, 510.
Harris, Martin S., and *New York News*, 22.

Hayes, Henry G. (reporter for the court), 32.
Hay, Hon. John, eulogy of President McKinley, 521.
Heyburn, Welden B., U. S. Senator, Idaho: "The rebellion was an armed resistance to rightful authorities," 516.
Heads of departments at Richmond warned, 78.
Hinks, William (reporter for the court), 32.
Hitchcock, General A. E., report of to Secretary of War giving full history of controversy concerning exchange of prisoners, 449; also number of deaths in prison on both sides, 370.
Hoffman, A. V. H., in *San Francisco Chronicle,* May 28, 1911; 492; vindication of Dorence Atwater; his death.
Holt, J., Judge Advocate-General, 27; argument of, 37; review of trial and verdict of court, 429.
Hosmer, Major A. A., Assistant Judge Advocate, 32; photo of, 36; assignment to duty.
Hospital, 2,000 patients crowded together in small and almost useless tents on less than three acres of ground, 110.
Men were not taken to the hospital until it was quite certain they would not live more than a week, 174.
Hopkins, Col. Thos. S., 503.
Hospital, the general, was outside the stockade, so planned as aided death of patients, 171, 361.
Hospital a rough enclosure of plank fences, 207.
Hospital, men in had ball and chain to their ankles, though in dying condition and unable to escape, 182.
Hospital, the, Dr. Jones, let him speak, 361.
Hospital outside of stockade, 62.
Hospital condition, 90; see Dr. Jones's report; violative of decency; shockingly inhuman, 90.
Hughes, Denver and Peck, Wirz attorneys who withdrew from case, 36.
Hull, John A. T., chairman of House Committee, gave support to Women's Relief Corps in matter of cemetery improvement, 503.
Hunt, Samuel F., through him the Robert Ould letter obtained; very important document, 388.
Hunter, Major-General D., letter to Stanton, explains why he mustered negroes into military service, 446.
Hunting for fuel in swamp saturated with human excrement, 80.

I

Idiotic, prisoners became, 173.
Illinois monument, 437.
Illustrations, list of, 5.
Imboden, General, disingenuous use of statement by Davis, 22.
Indiana, monument in cemetery, 337.
Initial movement for the Wirz monument, Daughters of the Confederacy seek to vindicate Wirz, 12.
Injunction to abate the prison nuisance, 54.
Inscriptions on the Wirz monument shown to be falsification of history, 11 et seq.
Inscriptions on the state monuments within the cemetery and prison grounds; many noble and patriotic sentiments; eloquent tributes to dead, 486.

526 INDEX—CONTINUED.

Inscriptions on Wirz monument, 18.
Inspecting officer, "there was nothing of the sort," 171.
Inspectors came and went, but no improvement, conditions grew worse, 217.
Iowa, monument in cemetery, 373.
Ironed, cruel and inhuman, 262.

J

Jones, Dr. Joseph, important report on prison; causes of death; horrible conditions existing, 83.
Jones, Kate E., 504.
Johnson's Island, Federal prison compared with Andersonville, 372; photos of the two prisons compared, 377; deaths at Johnson's Island 1.5 per cent per month; at Andersonville, 8.3 per month, 372.
Johnston, General Joseph E., Wirz not included in his surrender, 36.
Jurisdiction of the military commission fully discussed, 389; same as military commission that tried assassins of President Lincoln.

K

Kean, R. T. H., chief of Confederate War Bureau, recommendation for improvement of prison ignored, 76.
Ketcham, General Wm. A., Wirz monument, a monument not to honor but to infamy; reasons why erection of should be prohibited, 13, 15, 16, 78, 149.
Koster, John S., picture, the Empty Sleeve, 511.

L

Lashed, cruelly whipped on bare back, 266.
Law, the, of Nations, as applicable to case, 416.
Lee, General R. E., omitted from list of conspirators, 35; refused to have negro soldiers treated as prisoners of war, 458, 464.
Lee, General Stephen D., 16.
Letters: written to Wirz received no answer, ignored all complaints, 273.
Lincoln, President A., modified General Fremont's order, 429.
"Little Frenchy," pursued and bitten by dogs, 253, 255.
Lord Wolseley, criticised President Davis, 19.
Losing our standards, The Nation, New York, 6.
Lumber, how it was disposed of, 408.
Lumber in great abundance, 156.
Lumber, disappearance of fifty carloads and none used for prisoners, 212.
Lumber, no trouble to get for confederate use, 217.

M

Marshall, Elenora, at dedication of tablet, 510.
Marshall, Mrs. Emogene, dedication of Woman's Relief Corps tablet, 509.
"Maggots 15 to 20 inches deep," covering surface of swamp, 182.

McClure's Magazine, September, 1910, Goldwin Smith condemns Andersonville, 190.
McElroy, Colonel John, statement of facts, 464.
Maine, monument in cemetery, 466.
Massachusetts, monument in cemetery, 303.
McClellan, Georgia Wade, 504.
Mechanics in stockade, 2,500 and sufficient lumber, 207.
Medical attendance and medicine, wholly inadequate, 66.
Medical officer, one to 2,000 sick in stockade; at least twenty needed, 87.
Military Commission, photographs of, 29.
Mitigating circumstances, no, nor extenuating facts, 219.
Money, about one-third of prisoners had money, 228.
Monument to Lizabeth A. Turner in prison park; chief worker in restoring prison grounds, 476.
Monuments erected by: Connecticut, 450; Illinois, 437; Indiana, 337; Iowa, 373; Maine, 466; Massachusetts, 303; Michigan, 329; New Jersey, 367; Ohio, 394; Pennsylvania, 418; Rhode Island, 357; Wisconsin, 345. Noble in design and bearing appropriate inscriptions.
Moore, Captain Jas. M., report on condition of prison and cemetery; also indication of cruel treatment of prisoners, 475.
Moore, Confederate Surgeon-General S. P., assigning Dr. Jones, 82, 413.
Mortality great, causes of, 94, 101.
Mortality, its extent not suspected, 27.
Mortuary statistics, 369-372.
Motive for writing this history, 7, 11.
Mott, Brevet Major-General G., member of military court, 31.
Movement in the U. S. Senate for an appropriation for a confederate naval monument, 515.
Mud at times foot deep, 150.
Murder in violation of the laws of war, 193.
Murders among prisoners frequent, 116.

N

Naked, many in the stockade, 147.
National cemeteries, 84 in United States in which are buried 350,000 soldiers, 474.
National encampment G. A. R., the 44th, letter from officers urging publication of this volume, 8.
Negative testimony cannot neutralize testimony of eye witnesses, 365.
New York News, letter to, 234, 322.
New Jersey, monument in cemetery, 367.
New York Evening Post, colored troops took important part in war, 448.
North American Review, Davis's Belford article first referred to, was found by editor and withdrawn by Davis, 19.
North, Mary M., 504.
Number of prisoners, 84; 35,000 at times, 140.

O

Objections by the prisoner, exposed and refuted, 397.
Obrieter, John, letter to by Lizabeth Turner, 512.
Ohio, monument in cemetery, 394.
Order convening the trial court, 31.

INDEX—CONTINUED. 527

Order of the President, approves findings of the court, 436.
Organization of the court, 30.
Ould, Ro., on exchange of prisoners, 23, 388, 457; discharged as witness at request of Wirz attorneys; said got rid of a lot of miserable wretches in exchange for men in fine condition and refused exchange on equal terms.
Ovens were too small; never enlarged to meet necessities, 217.

P

Parting word with the reader; motive of the volume, 513.
Pathological investigation, 80, 82, 414.
Pelot, J. Crews, surgeon, report of; hospital deficient in every essential, 106.
Pennsylvania, monument in cemetery, 418.
Percentage of deaths; mortality ratio progressive, 63.
Personnel of the court, given by General Stibbs, one of the members of the court, 386.
Petition for exchange, 314.
Plan of stockade, 56.
Pleas interposed, 36.
Post mortems, conducted for benefit of Confederate medical department, 415.
Preface, 7.
Prendiville, Morris, 7th Indiana Reg., Co. H, shot in his tent while asleep, 287.
Prescriptions by numbered formulas, contents unknown, 123.
Prison conditions described by confederates, testimony of many witnesses; Col. Chandler and other rebel officers, 65, 70.
Prison, description of, Jones, 83.
Prisoners, number of, Jones, 84.
Prison pen, its terrors, converted good men into degenerates, 358.
Prison and surroundings sketched by a prisoner, 245.
Prisoner allowed himself to be put into the dead-wagon for purpose of escaping, 254.
Prisoner blacked himself, tried to escape as a negro, 266.
Prisoners, sick and well, murdered at night for scant supplies of food and money, 85.
Prisoners paid money to be the first taken out for exchange, 265.
Prisoners, many wore nothing but a shirt and pair of drawers, 267.
Prisoners in utter destitution, lying in their own filth, 168.
Prisoners, 33,000 to 36,000, covered the whole space when they lay down, 246.
Prisoners, number of 33,000, 228.
Prisoners wandered about the stockade, dazed and idiotic, and often committed suicide, 174.
Prisoners, 35,000 within an area of 27 acres, 231.
Prisoners crying for food and water, 170.
Providence Spring, believed by prisoners to have burst forth as act of God for their relief, 484, 502, 508.
Provisions abundant in Georgia, 191.
Provisions: corn, wheat, and potatoes raised in abundance, 156.
Punishment of theft and murder abandoned to prisoners, 85.

R

Raiders, the, an organized band of about 500, committed all forms of crime; six of them hung by outraged prisoners, 264.
Rain, twenty days in succession; prisoners without shelter; many with scant clothing; some naked, 267.
Rations frequently stopped, 222, 226.
Rations, none on July 4 within the stockade, 234.
Rations carried in same wagons in which the dead had been carried, 258.
Rations, articles and quantity, 277.
"Rations not sufficient to sustain life," 180.
Ration, daily; two oz. boiled beef and one-half pint rice soup; compared with English dietary and U. S. ration, 107.
Rations, distributing, picture, 142.
Rations stopped for the entire squad when a man was missing, 161.
Rations very poor, scant, some days nothing, issued very irregularly, 166.
Rations stopped for a day for not falling into ranks properly, 274.
Rations; rain, no fuel nor utensils, 67.
Read, Carrie R., 506.
Rebel witnesses, none denied the awful sufferings and the needless mortality, 218.
Record of the sick previous to September 14, 1864, 87.
Relics gathered by Miss Clara Barton at the prison grounds; picture of, 203.
Return of prisoners for July, 1864, 69.
Return of prisoners for August, 1864, 28 taken up by the dogs, 63.
Report on sanitary condition of prison by R. R. Stevenson, surgeon in charge, 105; 41 per cent died in October in hospital.
Report on prison conditions, 72; increasing death rate.
Report of Surgeon R. R. Stevenson, September 14-20, 1864, 88.
Report of Dr. Amos Thornburg, 108.
Report of Assistant Surgeon F. J. Wells, September 14-20, 1864, 87.
Responsibility for overcrowding, 55, 65.
Rhode Island, monument in cemetery, 357.
Reports sent to Richmond suggesting relief slumbered in pigeon holes, 103.
Rules for government of proceedings, 42.
Rules governing prisoners in time of war, 384.
Russell, B. F., of 17th Penn. Cavalry, Co. A, in stocks for 48 hours without food or water, 297.

S

Sacramento Bee (California): "Let the money for monument to confederate navy be raised in the South," 519.
Salt, traffic in; thrown over stockade to purchasers, 228.
Salt sold to the prisoners by cooks and traders, 227.
Salt sold to the prisoners by the guards, 221.
San Francisco Chronicle, story of Dorence Atwater and his death, 481.
Sanitary conditions but a mockery, 67.
Saw-mills, "Four or five in the vicinity of Andersonville," railroads hauling lumber to and fro, 155.
Scott, W. M., Past Department Commander, G. A. R., Georgia, 509.

528   INDEX-CONTINUED.

Scurvy was general; many had to crawl on the ground, 169.
Schade & Baker, attorneys for Wirz, 36.
Seddon, J. A., rebel Secretary of War; reports to pigeonholed, 61, 63.
Sentinels, 30 days' furlough to every man who would shoot a Yankee, 338.
Sentries, said they got 30 days' furlough for shooting prisoners, 273.
Sherwood, General Isaac (Ohio Rep.), great help to Women's Relief Corps in restoring prison grounds, 503.
Shelter for prisoners impossible, lumber used for other purposes, 54.
Shelter, lack of, from sun and rain, 128.
Shelter largely obtained by digging holes in the ground, 170.
Sherman, General W. T., surrender of Johnston, 36; early in war ordered slaves returned to masters, 440, 443.
Sherman, General, letters to General Grant, supplies in Georgia abundant, 191.
Sherman's march to the sea, 191.
Sherwood, Kate B., 503.
Sick and wounded, morning reports, 87.
"Six square feet to the man," 66.
Sifters for bolting meal "not to be had in the Confederacy," but could have been easily made. 212.
Sick call, etc.; "Many would crawl on hands and knees pleading for medicine," 182.
Sick, the; "Take him back to the stockade - not hospital - he will live until to-morrow," 182.
Sick, the, majority in hospital had to lie on bare ground; much rain, and food unfit, 175.
Sick men, many, with no friends to carry them to the gate, either in their blankets or upon their backs, failed to get prescriptions. 116.
Slaves as "contraband of war," when captured should have been declared free, 441
Slaves as United States soldiers, 446.
Smallpox, patient with put in tent with men not affected, 172.
Smith, Goldwin, visited prisons; condemned Andersonville, 190.
Soap, no, nor change of clothing, 147.
Specific acts of cruelty, 163.
Stanton, Edwin M., 27; on exchange of prisoners, always willing to on equal footing, 458.
Starvation, many died from, record abounds in evidence of, 181.
Statement regarding number of prisoners, deaths, etc., 61.
Stevenson, Surgeon R. R., reports of, 88, 105. See Index, reports of.
Stewart William, 9th Minn. Inf., murdered by Wirz, 351.
Stibbs, Lieutenant-Colonel J. H., 31, 386; now in Chicago; member of court, gives interesting account of trial, 354.
Showing incredible malice and criminality, 407.
Stockade, 51.
Stockade, view of from south gate, 167.
Stockade, the, concentrated all iniquities of perdition, 355.
Stockade, conditions indescribable, 355.
Stockade, one huge latrine, 356.
Stockade, "Indescribable suffering in," 357, 358.
Stockade, overcrowded, with difficulty one could elbow his way in any part of the camp, 170.
Stockade, "the a perfect hell upon earth," men fight for room to lie down, 177.
Stockade of, 51, 56, 57, 353.
Swamp, "offensive enough to kill," 166
Swamp, the unspeakable, 103.
Swamp, filled with untold impurities, 230.
Supreme Court, the "The rebellion out of which the war grew was without any legal sanction," had no status as recognized government, 516.
Stores sent to prisoners, no evidence that they were ever received at Andersonville, 159.
Storehouses, large quantities of sugar, rice, molasses, corn, wheat and flour stored in Macon, 156.
Stocks and lashes, men stood in "like the image of Christ crucified," 282.
Stocks, two kinds described; exposed to sun and rain in; man died form exposure in, 242, 243, 249, 262, 272, 275, 276, 297.
Stone, Governor Wm. A., 498.

T

Tablet of Woman's Relief Corps, 471.
Taft, William H., President of United States, 503.
Tanner on Wirz monument, address of 1906, 12; reply to Torrence 15.
Taylor, Robert L., United States Senator, Tennessee, motives of Confederate and Union soldiers same, 516.
Thomas, Brevet Major-General L., member of court, 31.
Thompson, General Jeff, order in retaliation of General Freemont's order, 439.
Thunderstorm and hurricane, a most dramatic moment, broke down stockade; guns trained on prisoners, 201.
Timber; it was a timber country-enough to supply the camp and more, and within easy hauling distance, 173.
Timber, plenty of it, 131.
Total deaths at Andersonville over 13,000, 373.
Torrence, Ell, remarks on Wirz monument at G. A. R. National Encampment, 15.
Traders, every man traded who had means, 231.
Transfer of prison grounds, 508.
Trench for the dead, dug two or three feet deep; no covering of dead except earth; buried naked often, 256.
Trenches, the, for burial, 281.
Trial of Henry Wirz, brought to light inner motives of rebellion, 27.
Tribute to Union prisoners, 517.
Turner, Limbeth, 76, 512.
Turner, Major Thos. P., recommended Wirz' promotion 61.
Turner, Wesley W., in charge of the bloodhound under Wirz' direction, 25
Typical soldier of the Union, half-tone picture, 269.

U

Unidentified dead, 486, marked as unknown; 229 without known resting place-not even marked "unknown," 376.
United Daughters of the Confederacy, 12.

INDEX—CONTINUED.

V

Vaccination and smallpox, 109, 243, 260, 290, 297, 326.
Van Sant, Governor Samuel R., Commander-in-Chief G. A. R., 507.
Vegetables in abundance, 119.
Vegetables in abundance in surrounding country, 171.
Vermin and lice, 126.
Views in Andersonville Cemetery, 315.

W

Wainman, Mrs. T. C., dedication of Woman's Relief Corps tablet, 510.
Wadsworth, Mrs. Lue Stuart, National Patriotic Instructor, Woman's Relief Corps, 509.
Wallace, Major-General Lew, president of Commission, 31, 429.
Warner, Senator William, promoted acceptance of grounds by Government, 503.
Washington *National Tribune, Colonel* McElroy, editor of, 464.
Water, inadequate and exceedingly filthy, covered with floating grease and offal, 166.
Whelan, Rev. Father Peter, testified at great length of conditions at Andersonville; Davis said not allowed to testify; see his testimony, 22, 193.
Wells, Surgeon F. J., reports, 87.
White, Surgeon Isaiah H., reports of, 72, 102, 397.
Whipped and put in stocks for being unable to work, 270.
Willett, Major J. M., 38.
Williams, John Sharp, U. S. Senator Mississippi, in charge of the Confederate Naval Monument Bill, 516.
Wilson, Major-General J. H., U. S. A., important testimony as to prison location; indicated design to kill, 47.
Wilson, Governor Woodrow, 370.

Winans, Mrs. Sarah D., report of Woman's Relief Corps; took important part in restoring prison pen and inducing the Government to purchase, 504-507.
Winans, J. Corey, Jr., 510.
Winder, W. S., assigning Surgeon Jones, 414.
Winder, W. S., 32, 53.
Winder, W. S.: "We will kill more damned Yankees than can be destroyed at the front," 153.
Winder, Richard B., 32.
Winder, Captain R. B., his duty to furnish fuel and shelter, 212.
Winder, General J. H., 61.
Winder, General John H., 32; letter of, 61, 63.
Winder, General J. H., recommends the atrocious policy of starving the prisoners to death or killing them by exposure, 74; the moving spirit of evil, 76.
Winder, General J. H., in face of unspeakable conditions, promoted, 78.
Wisconsin, monument in cemetery, 488.
Wirz monument, inscriptions on, 8, 18, 24, 25; reason for erection, 12, 13, 15.
Wirz, Captain Henry, assumed command of prison March 27, 1864, 393.
Wirz, Captain H., brutality, profanity and vulgarity, specific acts of shown by testimony culminating in deliberate murder, 119, 163, 175, 223, 241, 247, 249, 250, 251, 259, 260, 263, 264, 265, 266, 268, 270, 272, 273, 275, 277, 278, 280, 282, 283, 284, 286, 296, 332, 337, 345.
Wirz, Captain H., 17, 27, 32, 36; pictures of, 43, 44, 49.
Wirz, Captain H., report of, 60; return for July, 1864, 69; return for August, 64; return for October, 101.
Woman's Relief Corps, work at cemetery, 499.
Wood, "no man allowed outside for wood unless three dollars were paid guard," 180.
Works, John D., U. S. Senator California, favors appropriation, to erect monument to Confederate Navy, 516.

INDEX OF NAMES OF WITNESSES

It has not been thought of special value to the reader to give a synopsis of the testimony of each witness. In the general index attempt has been made to note the subjects sufficiently to give a clue to the principal salient facts and where to find them in the book. To give the testimony of each witness would not aid in this search. The testimony of witnesses covers a wide range and relates to many facts and should be carefully read. A perfectly satisfactory index is rarely met with. It is hoped that the one here given may be found to be reasonably satisfactory.

A

Achuff, Joseph R., testimony of, 261.
Adler, Joseph (nurse), testimony of, 174, 267.
Alden, J. Everett, testimony of, 181, 295.
Allen, Nazareth, testimony of, 252.
Andrews, Samuel J. M., testimony of, 182, 297.

B

Balser, Dr. William, testimony of, 139.
Bates, Dr. John C., testimony of, 125.
Belcher, O. S., testimony of, 258, 338.
Blair, A. G., testimony of, 284.
Boyle, Major Archibald, testimony of, 177.
Brown, J. D., testimony of, 335.
Brown, Samuel D., testimony of, 334.
Bull, William, testimony of, 282.
Burns, James H., testimony of, 283.
Bussinger, Daniel W., testimony of, 263.

C

Cain, John A., testimony of, 182.
Cashmyer, Philip, detective, testimony of, 77.
Castlen, Dr. F. G., testimony of, 119, 250.
Chandler, Col. D. T., testimony of, 52, 66, 68, 73.
Clancy, James, testimony of, 174.
Clark, J. Nelson, testimony of, 174.
Conway, George, testimony of, 347.
Corbett, Boston, testimony of, 166.
Crandall, W. W., testimony of, 275, 288.
Crouse, William, testimony of, 273.
Culver, Jasper, testimony of, 278.

D

Davidson, James K., testimony of, 258.
De La Baume, Felix, testimony of, 342.
Dillard, William, testimony of, 254.

F

Fairclough, Oliver B., testimony of, 339.
Fisher, John, testimony of, 276.
French, Captain Wilson, testimony of, 180.

G

Gibbs, Colonel T., testimony of, 241.
Goldsmith, John H., testimony of, 277.
Gray, George W., testimony of, 351.
Griffin, J. R., testimony of, 294.
Griffin, W. A., testimony of, 155.

H

Hall, Major W. Carvel, testimony of, 79.
Halley, P. Vincent, testimony of, 259.
Hamilton, Rev. W. J., testimony of, 143.
Head, Dr. B. J., testimony of, 137.
Heath, Captain John F., testimony of, 253.
Henman, Ambrose, testimony of, 353.
Hogan, Martin E., testimony of, 170, 249, 333.
Hopkins, Dr. G. S., testimony of, 119.
Horne, Thomas H., testimony of, 176.
Huneycutt, Calvin, testimony of, 255.

J

Jennings, William Henry, testimony of, 270.
Jones, Dr. Joseph, testimony of, 81, 83, 99, 359.
Jones, J. B., testimony of, 77.

K

Kean, R. T. H., testimony of, 75.
Kellogg, Edward S., testimony of, 260.
Kellogg, Robert H., testimony of, 164, 222.
Kennel, Alexander, testimony of, 271.
Keyser, Joseph D., testimony of, 172, 249.

M

Maddox, Frank, testimony of, 265.
Marsh, Dr. M. M., testimony of, 158.
Marshall, James E., testimony of, 274.
Moesner, Augustus, testimony of, 159, 327.
Mohan, James, testimony of, 256.

N

Noyes, Captain Henry E., testimony of, 45.

O

Orcutt, D. S., testimony of, 348.

P

Peebles, William M., testimony of, 275.
Persons, Colonel A. W., testimony of, 52.
Pond, L. S., testimony of, 272.

R

Rice, Dr. G. L. B., testimony of, 122.
Riker, Samuel M., testimony of, 289.
Robinson, Mark D., testimony of, 44.
Roy, Dr. G. G., testimony of, 135.
Russell, Charles H., testimony of, 287, 348.

WITNESSES—CONTINUED.

S

Scott, William Willis, testimony of, 340.
Selph, Captain C. M., testimony of, 58, 65.
Smith, Charles E., testimony of, 290.
Smith, Goldwin, testimony of, 190.
Smith, Sidney, testimony of, 272.
Snee, Hugh R., testimony of, 349.
Spencer, Ambrose, testimony of, 150.
Spring, Andrew J., testimony of, 173, 251.
Stearns, D. H., testimony of, 175, 270.

T

Tate, Robert, 52nd Penn. Vol., testimony of, 296.
Terrell, Horatio B., testimony of, 264.
Thornburg, Dr. Amos, testimony of, 108, 111.
Tibbles, Charles E., testimony of, 344.
Tracy, Prescott, testimony of, 341.

V

Van Buren, Willis, testimony of, 177.
Van Valkenburg, James, testimony of, 156.

W

Walker, John Burns, testimony of, 179, 286.
Walsh, Thomas, testimony of, 179, (diary) 292.
Welling, Colonel George, testimony of, 189.
Williams, Charles T., testimony of, 291.
Wilson, Major-General J. H., testimony of, 47, 184.
Wright, Lieutenant J. H., testimony of, 157.

Y

Younker, John L., testimony of, 280.

WITNESSES FOR DEFENSE

A

Allen, Nazareth, testimony of, 202.
Armstrong, Captain J. W., testimony of, 202-301.

B

Bardo, Vincenzo, testimony of, 219.
Bates, Dr. John C., testimony of, 205, 302.
Boate, Edward Wellington, testimony of, 229, 314.

C

Castlen, Dr. F. G., testimony of, 206-302.
Clavereul, Father (diary), 198.
Crandall, W. W., testimony of, 315.

D

Dilly, Benjamin F., testimony of, 321, 316.
Duncan, Rev. E. B., testimony of, 208.

F

Fannin, Col. James H., testimony of, 209, 306.
Fechtner, George W., testimony of, 235.
Flewellen, Dr. E. A., testimony of, 207-302.
French, Major S. B., testimony of, 209.

G

Gleich, August, testimony of, 232, 316.
Guscetti, Frederick, testimony of, 233, 319.

H

Hall, Samuel, testimony of, 201, 308.
Hamilton, Rev. W. J., testimony of, 305.
Hammack, W. D., testimony of, 210, 309.
Harris, Martin S., testimony of, 226, 323.
Heath, Lieutenant John F., testimony of, 204.

K

Kellogg, Robert H., testimony of, 222.

M

Moesner, Augustus, testimony of, 224, 327.

P

Persons, Colonel A. W., testimony of, 211, 310.
Proctor, Major Geo. L., testimony of, 213-311.

R

Roth, Fredreick, testimony of, 220, 324, 330.
Roy, Dr. G. G., testimony of, 302.
Ruffin, Lieutenant-Colonel F. G., testimony of, 213.

W

Whelan, Rev. Peter, testimony of, 193.
Wright, Captain J. H. testimony of, 216, 311.

www.ingramcontent.com/pod-product-compliance
Lightning Source LLC
Chambersburg PA
CBHW020938230426
43666CB00005B/69